SHAKESPEARE, FILM STUDIES, AND THE VISUAL CULTURES OF MODERNITY

SHAKESPEARE, FILM STUDIES, AND THE VISUAL CULTURES OF MODERNITY

ANTHONY R. GUNERATNE

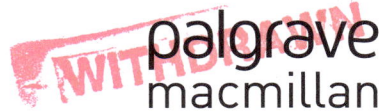

SHAKESPEARE, FILM STUDIES, AND THE VISUAL CULTURES OF MODERNITY
Copyright © Anthony R. Guneratne, 2008.

All rights reserved.

First published in 2008 by
PALGRAVE MACMILLAN®
in the US—a division of St. Martin's Press LLC,
175 Fifth Avenue, New York, NY 10010.

Where this book is distributed in the UK, Europe and the rest of the world, this is by Palgrave Macmillan, a division of Macmillan Publishers Limited, registered in England, company number 785998, of Houndmills, Basingstoke, Hampshire RG21 6XS.

Palgrave Macmillan is the global academic imprint of the above companies and has companies and representatives throughout the world.

Palgrave® and Macmillan® are registered trademarks in the United States, the United Kingdom, Europe and other countries.

ISBN-13: 978–1–4039–6788–6
ISBN-10: 1–4039–6788–1

Library of Congress Cataloging-in-Publication Data

Guneratne, Anthony R.
  Shakespeare, film studies, and the visual cultures of modernity / by Anthony R. Guneratne.
    p. cm.
  ISBN 1–4039–6788–1
  1. Shakespeare, William, 1564–1616—Film and video adaptations. 2. Film adaptations—History and criticism. 3. Motion pictures—History. I. Title.

PR3093.G86 2008
791.43'6—dc22   2007036160

A catalogue record of the book is available from the British Library.

Design by Newgen Imaging Systems (P) Ltd., Chennai, India.

First edition: August 2008

10 9 8 7 6 5 4 3 2 1

Printed in the United States of America.

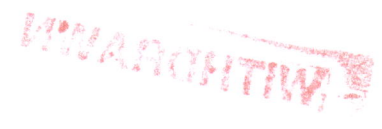

For my dear mother, Bernadette, who kept all her promises but the last, and failed in that only because Death could not await this book's birth.

> When wasteful war shall statues overturn,
> And broils root out the work of masonry,
> Nor Mars his sword nor war's quick fire shall burn
> The living record of your memory.

We can say that neither Shakespeare nor his contemporaries knew that "great Shakespeare" whom we know now. There is no possibility of squeezing our Shakespeare into the Elizabethan epoch...He has grown because of that which actually has been and continues to be found in his work, but which neither he himself nor his contemporaries could consciously perceive and evaluate in the context of the culture of their epoch.

M.M. Bakhtin (1970)

CONTENTS

List of Illustrations		xi
Acknowledgments		xiii
Preface		xix
What's in a Name? Or, Something like an Introduction		1
One	Reconstituting *King John*: Victorian Theatrical Photorealism and the Protocinema of Adaptation	75
Two	Featuring the Bard: Frederick Warde's Shakespeare and the Transformation of American Cinema	95
Three	The Exfoliating Folio, or Transnational and International Avant-Gardes from Bernhardt's *Hamlets* to Hollywood's Europeans	115
Four	Genre, Style, and the *Politique des Auteurs*: Orson Welles versus "William Shakespeare"	173
Five	Six Authors in Search of a Text: The Shakespeares of Van Sant, Branagh, Godard, Pasolini, Greenaway, and Luhrmann	211
Notes		251
Works Cited		293
Index		311

LIST OF ILLUSTRATIONS

Cover: Detail (toned blue, as in some contemporary reproductions) of Alphonse Mucha's poster for Sarah Bernhardt's production of *Hamlet* (1900)

Introduction: The reprint in the fine arts journal *Verve* accessible to the makers of *Henry V* (1944) of the calendar illustration of May from the *Très Riches Heures du Duc de Berry* — xxii

One: Caricature of a scene from Herbert Beerbohm Tree's 1899 stage production of *King John* — 74

Two: Poster for *Richard III* (1912) by Frederick Warde and James Keane — 94

Three: Asta Nielsen as the young Prince of Denmark in *Hamlet* (1920) — 114

Four: *The Arnolfini Portrait*. Oil on panel by Jan van Eyck, used as iconographic inspiration by Orson Welles in *Othello* (1952–1954) — 172

Five: *The Rokeby Venus*. Oil on canvas by Diego Velázquez, pictured in Pier Paolo Pasolini's *Che cosa sono le nuvole?* (1968) — 210

Poster to Fred McLeod Wilcox's *Forbidden Planet* (1956) — 250

ACKNOWLEDGMENTS

This work is not intended to be an inventory of film adaptations of Shakespeare's plays, much less an enforcement of artificial chronologies that facilitate speculations about what is good or bad about them. Those are tasks that have been achieved elsewhere, often and sometimes well. Indeed, with the exception of the still-challenging films of Orson Welles, I have devoted a greater proportion of my attention to films that have either not attracted sufficient discussion or, as in the case of more recent examples, have yet to receive adequate contextualization. Yet this book does attempt to tell a different kind of film history and propose a new approach to adaptation as cultural history, and so it encompasses a very wide variety of films seen at times at large, glowing public occasions (as with an early Lubitsch comedy at the National Gallery in Washington, D.C.), and at others in the dim light of basement archives. I have avoided received critical opinion whenever the films themselves have been available to me, and so it also represents a fifteen-year labor forged in those archives, at special film showings, at conferences, in the pages of books and journals, and in the course of dozens of conversations—a task that neither was, nor could have been, achieved alone.

My greatest debt, of course, is to my mother. As a university student, she played the Shrew (a role she reputedly never quite stopped playing), and when I was still a child took the parts of different Shakespeare characters, giving them different voices as she read the plays to me, editing out the naughty bits—as I discovered later—as she went along. I can only hope that the words on these pages reflect the joy she took from life even in the most trying circumstances, rather than the prolonged, terrible tragedy of her death. My father Rex, too, subsidized me when I took leave from work when both my health and this book seemed threatened during and after my mother's decline, and I am grateful to the chair of my department, Susan Reilly, for granting me leave at a moment of personal and family crisis.

Nor could I have achieved what I have without a fellowship granted by the Folger Shakespeare Library for the summer of 2003 that initially made it possible for me to undertake serious research toward a book, and two key awards by my university, the 2005 Arts and Letters Fellowship of the Dorothy F. Schmidt College and a Research and Creative Accomplishment Grant by the University's Division of Sponsored Research administered by Gerald Goldberger. Had it not been for his support and that of members of both committees I could never have persevered in what has been a labor of half a lifetime, and more. I am also grateful for an invitation to work at the archives of Harvard's W.E.B. DuBois Institute, where I completed the preliminary work for the chapter on Orson Welles.

In quoting from the plays or searching for their sources I have relied primarily on *The Riverside Shakespeare* edited by G. Blakemore Evans, for which a concordance is available. In more specialized cases that are acknowledged in the text, I have drawn from *The Norton Shakespeare* compiled by Stephen Greenblatt, Walter Cohen, Jean Howard, and Katharine Maus. The first of this last group of editors has also been an heroic and patient teacher, occasional disputant (although it is only because we look in the same directions that we do not always see eye-to-eye), and unfailing friend of many years. It is at his invitation that I spent a year at Harvard where a substantial portion of Chapter 2 happened to be written. Among other influences whose presence can be felt in these pages are a number of teachers from Bloomington, Bologna, Berkeley, and the University of Southern California. Prominent among them are Carlo Ginzburg (to whom I owe a microhistorian's approach to texts and a Renaissance approach to food and wine), Kristin Thompson (to whom I owe a rational skepticism toward most historical conjecture and an introduction to French Impressionist and German Expressionist cinema), and, most of all, Harry Geduld, whose innumerable interventions have transcended the years and saved me from many an error (for which he combed the text with inexhaustible vigilance during a pleasant stay with him and his wife Carolyn in Bloomington). It is to him that I owe the structure of the book, for in making some consequential editorial suggestions he fundamentally influenced the arrangement of the contents. Those who know his manner of describing a film in such a way as to accomplish a number of tasks at once will not fail to see his influence in its pages.

The thoughts of other teachers, too, have borne fruit over the years, and all of them have found their way into this work in one way or another. David Shepard truly shepherded my immersion in early cinema, and I must thank him in addition for the restoration of a number of the films I have discussed here: along with the work of Martin Scorsese, his has been one of the most important contributions to preserving the legacy of film. It was Guido Fink at the university of Bologna who kick-started the project, first by allowing me to sit in on his seminar on Shakespeare and Film where he introduced me to Pasolini, then through his generous invitation to me to participate in a festival devoted to Ingmar Bergman (in which he discussed Bergman's *Hamlets*), and finally through an invitation to speak on Welles and Shakespeare at the Biennale in Venice. With Douglas Hofstadter, another formative influence, I seem to share a certain way of making connections (and owe the observation to another friend, Paul Wilson, who pointed out that connection some twenty years ago; it is he, two decades later, who has brought a true professional's eye to proofreading these pages and who chose the multi-talented indexer, Timothy Wright, as his collaborator). During the years when I was first a student, and then an experimental researcher in evolutionary genetics, my lab professor George Hudock (with some assistance from Milton Taylor and Craig Nelson) taught me how to think straight, to avoid the conjectural in favor of the logical, and to recognize science and scientific thought as approaches consonant with those of comparative studies. I am deeply indebted, also, to Michael Holquist, who gave me a respect for Bakhtin and for otherness, and to Bruce Cole and to Thomas Sebeok, one an eminent and overwhelmingly busy Renaissance art historian and the other an eminent and overwhelmingly busy semiotician, but each willing to indulge my interests in their fields and devote time to take me on as an independent student. I owe just as much to James Naremore, Peter Bondanella, Mark Musa, Giancarlo Maiorino, Claudia Gorbman, Barbara Klinger,

Acknowledgments

David Hertz, Kenneth Gros-Louis, Claus Clüver, Clifford Flannigan, Breon Mitchell, Willis Barnstone, Charles Forker, Matei Calinescu, Marsha Kinder, and Michael Renov, whose classes in film studies, in the interrelationships of the arts, in Renaissance literature, culture, and the visual arts, and in Modernism have found their way in forms, probably unrecognizable to them, into this work. Professor Walter Cassell was my voice teacher of many years when I was a student at Indiana University's School of Music: he first heard my renditions of baritone arias written for Hamlet, Macbeth, Iago, Falstaff, and Ford, and guided me through songs written for Shakespeare's lovers, shepherds, and clowns; and I have been grateful to audiences at Indiana University, the University of California at Berkeley, and the National University of Singapore for being (willing) auditors when even my mother, at times, was not. I have benefited from the generous collaborations and interventions of colleagues in Singapore, England, and Italy, especially those of Arthur Lindley, as well as those of a remarkable diversity of students first at Indiana University, then at UC Berkeley, then at USC, then at the National University of Singapore, and latterly at Florida Atlantic. One of them, Steve Volan, now a city councilor and an owner of a DVD rental establishment, even helped me locate some of the films I discuss. Likewise, alert conference participants at meetings devoted to film, literature, and, most of all, popular culture, among them James Welsh, Winston Thompson, and Emily Stockard, have been sources of insightful comments and queries that have yielded fruit in the chapters that follow. On occasion I have incorporated comments and suggestions made to me by those who have participated in the films I discuss, and in this regard I am grateful to Ismail Merchant, Molly Ringwald, Paul Mazursky, Leslie Nielsen and Katia Ricciarelli. A variety of Shakespearean debts impossible to repay are owed to Joseph Moyles, Gordon Ewen, Harriet van Deusen, Father Theo Matthias, Jay Mendel, and Dr. B.V. Rao, friends and mentors all.

Colleagues stateside have been especially helpful and perceptive. Richard and Judy Vela, co-conspirators in various Shakespeare plots, have enlivened ideas contained in these pages, and stepped in to help whenever help was needed. Fernando Cioni assisted with the difficult puns and dialect of Pasolini's Shakespeare film when we resaw it at the Folger, and he posted a pristine Italian DVD version to me. The most eminent of Shakespeare scholars, some even scholars of Shakespeare on film, have been no less generous with their time and thoughts. Michael Anderegg received a copy of the manuscript and treated my foibles leniently. Peter Donaldson squeezed in time for suggestions, gentle proddings, and Vitagraph reanimations as they could only be accomplished at the Massachusetts Institute of Technology, where, too, Diana Henderson's clear thinking and demands for clarity proved fortuitous (I should add that I have also tried to live up to Elfie Raymond's high standards of prose). In the true spirit of Shakespearean fellowship, Stephen Buhler helped me locate a copy of Yutkevich's film at the Folger, and Jolene Felkner sent me information on Branagh's film *Love's Labour's Lost*. Patricia Parker invited me to give a talk on Rushdie's *Othello* adaptations at a "Shakespeare in Asia" conference at Stanford University and made many a helpful comment about shared ideas, as did other participants. José Ramón Díaz Fernández invited me to a memorable conference hosted by the University of Málaga celebrating the centenary of Shakespeare on film, and I have to thank him and his dear friend (and Orson Welles's), Pilar Lezcano, for two eventful and memorable visits to the city of Ronda, where I also had the chance to converse with Welles's collaborator Juan Cobos. Tom Gunning set some key ideas in motion with suggestions and encouragement. I have no adequate way, I think, to thank Clare Carroll for advice, friendship, and generosity of spirit, all freely given at crucial moments in the gestation of this work.

I would also add that but for the untiring efforts of one reference librarian, David Frasier, I would not have much of a career, let alone this book. For many years, he has found seemingly inaccessible materials for me, and played the role of film professor manqué with editorial suggestions, encouragement, articles, and, in the case of the present work, secret service work. This book belongs to my mother, of course, but another soon will be his. The staffs of other libraries have revealed their secrets to me: Erin Blake has helped with costumes and illustrations, Fred Burchsted at Harvard's Widener, with finding a crucial promptbook, and Ken Wlashin and Kim Tomadjoglu of the American Film Institute loaned me copies of recently restored films and located colleagues working in related areas. Librarians at the Library of Congress and the New York Public Library researched details of theatrical history and costume design for me, as well as copying a number of rare illustrations (one of which introduces the first chapter). At the film archives of the Library of Congress, Madeline Matz offered solace when solace was needed, and even researched answers to telephoned questions. In an extraordinary gesture, Patrick Laughney, the former LOC head, made the hitherto folded, flattened Vitagraph paper prints accessible to me, and I cannot fail to add thanks to the many members of the staff (including Zoran and Rosemary) who undertook partial restorations and researched books and films on my behalf. Helen Adair at the Harry Ransom Center at the University of Texas found exhibition catalogues for me and photographed the poster from which the cover illustration derives, while Wayne Woodward of moviegoods.com sent me some illustrations with instant alacrity. Margaret Daly at the National Gallery in London rushed the last needed illustrations across the seas.

A book such as this could not have been written had not the curators and staff of a number of archives made their treasured prints available to me. Eric Le Roy, Michelle Aubert, and Gilles Langlais introduced me to new films at the French national archive (CNC) at Bois D'Arcy. Laure Marchaut, Monique Faulhaber, and Claudine Kaufmann made it possible for me to see films at the archives of the Cinémateque Française. At the British Film Institute archives Kathleen Dixon, Nina Harding, and Steve Tollervy worked with amazing efficiency to allow me to see an astonishing amount of footage and obtain illustrations. Mario Musumeci arranged for screenings at the national film archives in Rome, while the indefatigable Marianna De Sanctis arranged for screenings of films at the archives of the Cineteca of Bologna. Mike Mashon and Jennifer Ormson helped with screening Vitagraph paper prints at the Library of Congress. Most of all, Paolo Cherchi Usai and Jan-Christopher Horak gave me access to the George Eastman House collections on more than one occasion, and I must thank Paolo for the unfailing invitations to the Giornate del Cinema Muto, an annual festival of silent cinema, where, for instance, I first saw Asta Nielsen's films.

I read Italian well enough not to have required translations for cited articles and books: but Antonella Borghi, Marianna De Sanctis, and even some of their friends took turns to translate my own work into an Italian so refined as to challenge me even as a reader. After that talk at the University of Bologna, Professor Michele Canosa pointed out Georges Didi-Huberman's debt to Aby Warburg, whose work I knew previously only in other contexts. I am grateful to young Dr. Marianna's own researches, some of which have found their way into these pages, and for her help when arcane references defeated me. I have struggled with works in French and Spanish, having forgotten years of study. I also studied

German and was the despair of my teachers, and an occasionally faulty translation of an intertitle might be mine. The avoidance of gratuitous error necessitated an array of skilled translators. To Laura Besses I owe the biggest debt: she sat through Raoul Ruiz's *Richard III* having already studied Victor Hugo's translation of Shakespeare, so Ruiz's elisions (and use of an updated translation) became apparent from the occasional chuckle or whispered suggestion. Marion de Graaff spent the better part of a day at the Nederlands Filmmuseum translating the Dutch intertitles to *The Adventures of Lieutenant Petrosino*, which, to my knowledge, enabled me to provide the first confirmation that this was the complete American print. Marina Gundareva translated passages of Yutkevich's book for me. Stephanie Hamels translated Balázs from German and, in deep rebellion, gave me literal renditions of the original German intertitles in Asta Nielsen's *Hamlet*, while Renate Mesmer gave me the English versions of Vitagraph intertitles. Ron Bogdan interrupted his work on a Folger exhibition to translate passages of Latin for me. Renate and Ron are two members of my extended family at the Folger, and I cannot fail to mention without special affection Betsy Walsh who, year after year, guided me through the Folger collections, even when my overly-recondite researches were not making much sense to anyone, even the most tolerant.

Friends too numerous to name have helped with advice, although I would be remiss not to mention Bernhardt and Masha Trout and Ari and Bonnie Juels, who have contributed materially to my research. Chris and Jennifer Jaffe, friends with whom I have stayed for weeks while writing the last part of this work, have been especially kind, as have Stuart Diamond and Nevena Silic, who gave me a chance to write while succumbing to Manhattan's limitless distractions. Pages were also written in Ann Arbor in the company of Elizabeth Shadigian and her delightful family, and in Washington where I had to earn Suzanne Etcheverry's tolerance. I owe a huge debt of thanks to the Cerovseks, Sophia, Helmut, and Katja, who became close friends as the result of a review that I wrote (and who have stayed so ever afterward), and to Corey's multitalented Franco-Italo-English friend Lucy Boccadoro who took me to Shakespeare and Co. during an eventful visit to Paris. When Shakespeare had brought me to a low ebb in Berkeley, Anna Chodakiewicz kept me afloat and added sails to the first stirrings of this project, while Michelle Brown played the zephyr's role in Bloomington, Indiana. I am also grateful to my friends at Palm Valley Cemetery, Jacqueline, Patricia and Brent, who set out a table for me when I needed to write and in whose lush gardens I strolled as I thought through and reworked a number of these chapters in my mother's shadow. I think kindly of helpful employees of the public libraries of Ponte Vedra and Fort Lauderdale, and of Shelby's, Walkabout's, and a number of Starbucks coffee shops in Jacksonville, as well as similar locations in Bloomington, London, and Manhattan, where my blood could be thinned with caffeine and my writing proceed uninterrupted.

I have reserved until last, partly to preserve a sense of sequence, my grateful thanks to my editor Farideh Koohi-Kamali, who from the start believed in this book and fought many a battle for it, and to her principal assistants Julia Cohen and Brigitte Shull, to whom I must extend the most grateful thanks for standing by the project even as their charge tried to write as he bore the whips and scorns of time. Farideh offered me the first convincing explanation of why most academics live on other planets and only visit Earth occasionally when they want to cause publishers difficulties. Without the alert Erin Ivy's production team, and the unfailingly courteous and keen-eyed efforts at copyediting and typesetting of Maran Elancheran and his team at Newgen, it could never have achieved its present, pleasing aspect. To them I owe the fruition of a lifetime of intellectual gestation.

It is customary, of course, to end one's acknowledgments by acknowledging possible errors and absolving those here named from them. In this instance, the opposite is true. I am fed up of being assumed for what I am not or being blamed for things I have not done, and so would like to take the opportunity to alert you to the fact that whatever may be amiss is probably all their fault, but that the task of discovering their whereabouts to inveigh against them is yours, dear reader.

PREFACE

Can one write a history of cinema based on adaptations of Shakespeare's works? The simple answer that the pages that follow suggest is "yes," but it is a kind of film history that has not been attempted previously. It is this feature, I think, that constitutes this work's most significant contribution to Film Studies and Shakespeare scholarship. It also contains much that has been insufficiently addressed, or not even been attempted, in previous books about Shakespeare and the cinema, and it is in order to allow readers to be aware of what it tries to accomplish that I adopt the expedient of cataloguing some of its innovations at the outset.

In a disciplinary context, it is the first book of its kind to map out relationships between various practices (film studies, Shakespeare studies, theories of translation, theatre history, archival scholarship, historiography, postcolonial theory, media theory, art history, visual culture, and cultural history), with the explicit intention of laying a substantial groundwork for future studies of Shakespeare films, a term I use as inclusively as legitimately possible. I have used concrete film examples in my Introduction to illuminate the intersection of four now largely separate terrains of inquiry, primarily in order to map out the key issues that pertain to the cultural history of film adaptation. In terms of film history, this is the first work to provide a thematic survey of the relationship of film and other media, from the photorealism of the 1860s that transformed theatrical practices and the visual arts (which in turn had a formative influence on early cinema) to the impact of televisual and digital media. A study of early Shakespeare films inevitably contributes to formal film history not only in terms of its aesthetic, technological, economic, and social dimensions, but also to discussions of the medium's role in the process of globalization, one that actually begins at the start of the twentieth century with cinema at its vanguard: films designed to "elevate" American audiences were also designed for export; early Danish cinema had a profound influence on world cinema, but foundered after a brief ascendancy, only to survive abroad; American capital financed the Italian epic films (some devoted to Shakespeare) and promoted a proliferation of French Shakespeare films, while imports of European films permanently altered the film-going and filmmaking experience for American film audiences and producers alike; one of the most striking instances of transnational filmmaking, that of European directors in Hollywood, finds intriguing reflection in films (often loosely) based on Shakespeare; modernity and postmodernity are even more difficult to define in cinema than in the other arts, but from Orson Welles onward filmmakers have employed the challenge of Shakespeare's early modernity to try to shake up established aesthetic, social, and political categories.

I have resisted the temptation to discuss all the Shakespeare films I have watched. D.W. Griffith's hustling and bustling *Shrew* of 1908 and his sentimental depiction of an out-of-work Shakespearean actor in *The Old Actor* are, despite the presence of Mary Pickford in the latter, cloyingly patriarchal—perhaps the least of his vices—and feeble representatives of what he could achieve at Biograph. The words I devoted to them disappeared during the initial drafts of these pages not so much because they are wretched, but because they were subordinated to the lager flow of my argument. Nor have I spent pages lamenting the loss of representative films from the first Shakespeare cycles produced by Vitagraph, Film d'Arte Italiana, and Thanhouser: more than enough remains of their efforts and those of later filmmakers to obviate the need for such academic indulgences.

Theorists of media and of visual culture might be intrigued by the extent to which Shakespeare scholars and theatre directors such as Edward Vining, Georg Brandes, Jan Kott, Peter Brook, Grigori Kozintsev, Laurence Olivier, and Orson Welles drew on varied media in proposing interpretations of Shakespeare or in giving visual dimensions to textual readings. Intimations of their activities can be found in numerous other studies, but, to my knowledge, they have never been treated as systematically in this context. Shakespeare has, in a sense, allowed me to wallow in theory at times, but I have tried to avoid being splashy: I suspect that I am the first to claim that, paradoxically, Freud's fondness for theatre reveals psychoanalysis to be an expression of his repressed desire for cinema; that early theories of film performance suggest that acting in the cinema hewed more closely to classical ballet as art form and approximated that of theatre only after synchronized sound and spoken dialogue attained ubiquity; that Antonio Gramsci's social theories reconfigured Pier Paolo Pasolini's readings of both Shakespeare and Foucault; that postcolonial discourses have influenced directors as avant-garde as Peter Greenaway and Baz Luhrmann. I have touched on numerous aspects of film theory, but never gratuitously, because, in negotiating the complexities of taking a widely known and circulated message in one medium to another, makers of Shakespeare films have either shown a preexisting sensitivity to key theoretical issues or cultivated them in the process of reconfiguration. Indeed, the entire content of this volume can be taken to be an extended celebration of Shakespeare's unsurpassed contribution to the art of adaptation, and of the medium in which it has witnessed the greatest efflorescence.

Notes about Usage and Conventions

The release dates and directors of films appear on the first occasion the title of a film occurs in the text. Curly brackets have been used to indicate intertitles in order to distinguish between descriptive and dialogue intertitles. Film genres, as well as nouns and adjectives designating artistic movements or periods, begin consistently with a capital letter. In distinction to *Merriam-Webster's Collegiate Dictionary*, the text retains the original French term *auteur* to distinguish it from its later use among American critics. Consistency in indexing titles has been maintained by disregarding first words that are definite or indefinite articles.

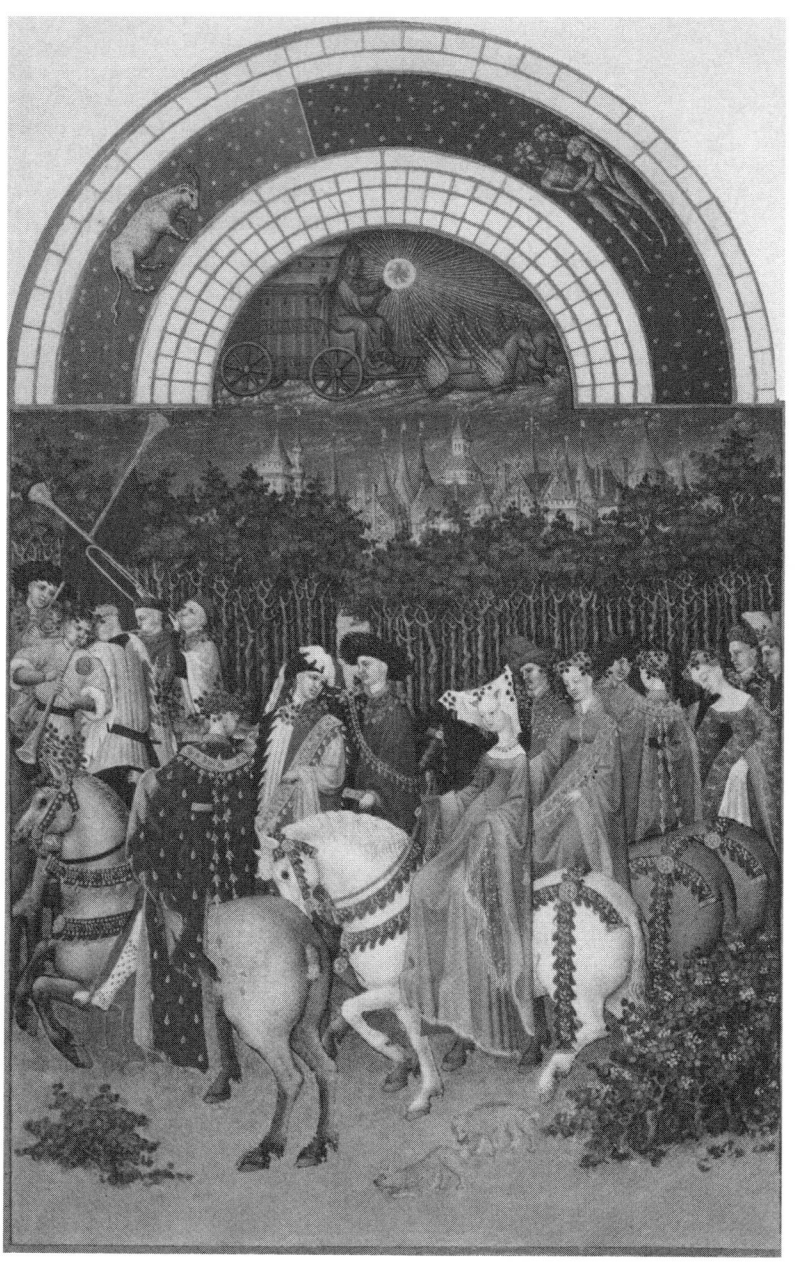

The reprint in the fine arts journal *Verve* accessible to the makers of *Henry V* (1944) of the calendar illustration of May from the *Très Riches Heures du Duc de Berry*.

What's in a Name? Or, Something like an Introduction

In which the author contrives to explain his title and propose a theory of adaptation ★ *A fantastical operation in which Shakespeare gives birth to Julius Caesar* ★ *Belated stardom for the onetime small-part player* ★ *The Bard is discovered to be Sri Lankan, German, and Italian* ★ *National traditions and cold war Shakespeares* ★ *Kozintsev and Yutkevich, or Pasternak's post-Pushkin Shakespeare* ★ *No Shakespeare without a Hitch* ★ *Genre Shakespeare as an antidote to network television* ★ *The triumphs of coexistence* ★ *The medium that once was cinema* ★ *On the three registers and the five tendencies of adaptation, and Rohmer* ★*A genre based on dialogue?* ★ *Two Shakespearean takes on established genres* ★ *Quotation, misquotation, and disquotation* ★*A new machine for an Old Vic, and the play's the thing* ★*The Eugene O'Neill effect and the horrors of disquotation* ★ *The Vincent Price effect and the mirthless minstrel* ★*Intermediation and a trip to the Greek isles for a Tempest* ★*Bergman's three* Hamlets ★ *Visual culture(s)?* ★ *Rise of the Shakespeare cult* ★ *Cervantes, Shakespeare, and animating life* ★ *Botticelli in L.A. and* Romeo and Juliet *in Verona (?)* ★ *Hours with Olivier* ★ *Kurosawa's true colors* ★ *Fighting words from early modernity to postmodernity, and from colonialism to globalization* ★ *The dragon's wrath, a Tiv tiff, and bashful Baabu* ★ *Global displacements, or exporting Scandinavian Shakespeare* ★ *Voluntary modernity and the Japanese return to tradition* ★ *Replying to imposed modernity, or India's postcolonial and global syncretism*

The best titles, one is warned, usually consist of a word or two, the subtitle being unnecessary or safely tucked away from the marquee offered by a cover, and fitted in small type at the foot of an interior page. Yet if one is to propose an adequate theory of film adaptation, as I propose to do, these are unavoidable terms, and their darker import, as much as the light they shed, should be clear from the outset. My method has been to introduce a topic by addressing a series of questions. What meaning does Shakespeare have in different linguistic, national, and cultural contexts? What benefits might Film Studies derive by applying a wealth of Shakespeare adaptations to its own historical and theoretical assumptions? How can the foregoing discussion contribute to the emergent discourse of visual culture? And what bearing does a cinema derived from Shakespeare's plays have on the heated debates concerning the nature of modernity? In the majority of instances, I have extracted examples from films only as needed; in others, paused to discuss entire films or parts of them at greater length when such discussions contribute materially to my argument. The novelistic headings to the chapters and to this introduction provide a narrative summary of these contents in an internal dialogue of sorts with the section breaks and captions. They are best read *sempre leggiero*, but with care.

Shakespeare?

One of the definitive comments on a successful young entrant to the lists of playwrights in the latter part of the Elizabethan Age is that of an older rival, Robert Greene, to whom is attributed a famous posthumously published attack on a certain "Shake-scene," an "upstart crow" who appeared to have some image or, more precisely, plumage, problems. Shake-scene is almost certainly Shakespeare, who was to plunder the Falstaffian Greene for more than just his plots, according to Stephen Greenblatt.[1]

Less certain is the view (supported, for instance, by Michael Wood), that, after completing his schooling in Stratford, Shakespeare might have been a schoolmaster who found refuge in Lancashire, where the old religion still prevailed: Frank Kermode dismisses the possibility that the common regional name "Shakeshafte" would have been an adequate disguise.[2] As part of his shake-up of the old order in Stratford, Shakespeare, who had seen his father disgraced and denied a gentlemanly title despite his service as town bailiff, must have had to delve into the intricacies of one aspect of Elizabethan visual culture: heraldic emblems. When, eventually, he helped his father obtain his longed-for coat of arms, perhaps in consolation for the recent loss of John Shakespeare's grandson, the design incorporated an insouciant falcon fluffing out its feathers ("shaking") while brandishing the heraldic equivalent of the spear, a lance, that also figures prominently on the escutcheon.

★ ★ ★

If we translate those bright, borrowed Aesopian plumes into the resplendent flags of many nations, we have a suitably mixed visual metaphor for the ways in which some three hundred years of cultural interactions can transform upstart crows into the best of Avon's swans. Georges Méliès's *Shakespeare Writing Julius Caesar* (*La Rêve de Shakespeare* or *La Mort de Jules César*, 1907), a film of 344 feet or about four minutes—every foot counted in the age of hand-coloring prints—is not among the spate of recent Méliès rediscoveries in archives in France, Austria, and Russia, although we know that complete prints ended with a flag-waving apotheosis of the "Bard of Avon."[3] Méliès was the first filmmaker to attempt to adapt a complete Shakespeare play (albeit as a series of vignettes as in the case of his *Hamlet*, earlier that year), the first to use multishot compositions within scenes, and the first to use all the technical resources then available to cinema in adapting literary classics. He was also the first creator of a fully equipped studio, the glass-walled Star Films, whose physical structure resembled the Crystal Palace and whose solvency relied on an international clientele: even some of his earliest efforts have corresponding English-language versions, a spectacular example being that of a dancing, musical Méliès character who cavorts beneath what appears to be a gigantic musical staff and who at regular intervals pulls off his head and tosses it upward. The heads, coming to rest neatly on the musical staves, continue to babble in confusion despite their function as musical notes, a visual feat accomplished through the use of numerous invisible splices and at least seven multiple exposures. In the French version of the film, *Le Mélomane* (1903), the notes spell the first phrase of the "Marseillaise"; in the British one, "God Save the King."

Méliès's downfall, however, came not as a result of losing his head or an inordinate admiration for things foreign, but rather through a gradual process of attrition. He persisted in selling his often laboriously hand-stenciled and colored prints outright, even while his entrepreneurial competitor Charles Pathé made more money by renting prints and having his directors, such as the unscrupulously talented Ferdinand Zecca,[4] copy Méliès's special effects. For the filmmaker who is credited with pioneering cinematic storytelling and who mastered dissolves, cheat cuts, multiple superimpositions, stop-motion photography, and a host of special effects, not to mention the generic innovation of the first Biopics including a fictionalized one involving Shakespeare, it must have been something of an irony that the last successful Méliès films were workaday Westerns made by Wallace McCutcheon—the man D.W. Griffith replaced momentously at Biograph in 1908—in an unauthorized outfit set up by his brother Gaston in 1909 as the G. Méliès Company.

It is not only to the profligate Gaston, who appears to have contributed to his brother's ruin, but also to the researches of the indefatigable Robert Hamilton Ball, that we owe an enchanting description of Méliès's flights of fancy that might otherwise have vanished in the equivalent of a cinematic puff of smoke.[5] Knowledge of the kinds of special effects Georges used greatly facilitates the process of mental reconstruction, and in the catalogues of the films prepared for U.S. distributors and exhibitors when Star Films entered into an agreement with the Motion Picture Patents Company (MPPC) in 1908, Gaston describes the film in such a way as to make the scenes palpable. "The idea of the film is a novel one," he begins quite correctly, and goes on to describe Shakespeare at wits' end, pacing his study, trying to devise the assassination scene. Eventually he collapses into an armchair where, while still struggling with his thoughts, the Forum gradually takes shape before him. At this point "classical female figures" appear for the express purpose of burning incense, clearly more on Shakespeare's behalf than Caesar's. As Shakespeare-Méliès stands watching, Brutus, Cassius, Casca, and the other conspirators enter to debate the dictator's fate, eventually drawing swords and pointing them to the ground in joint resolve, a visual iconography presumably derived from Jacques-Louis David's celebrated canvas, now in the Louvre, of *The Oath of the Horatii*. Caesar enters, flanked by consuls. Two of the conspirators approach, in turn, to voice their grievances, but the third raises his "dirk," only to hesitate when Caesar covers his face; but a fourth intervenes to do the deed. As Caesar falls, we return to Shakespeare in his study. On recognizing that his scene has taken shape, he begins to "stalk" excitedly, even stabbing a loaf of bread brought in by a servant. When the latter leaves the study, Shakespeare steps back and folds his arms, and "the scene dissolves into a bust of William Shakespeare, around which all the nations wave flags and garlands."[6]

While one might imagine this reverential conclusion to be a convenient and plainly ahistorical reification of an international genius, even a sop to Méliès's English-speaking distributors, to do so is to disregard the cultural context of the film. As Stephen Buhler remarks, since the time of Voltaire's indictment of the playwright's alleged "savagery" (i.e., his violations of the principles of civilized stagecraft "rediscovered" by the Neoclassicists), to which, for instance, the great eighteenth-century English actor David Garrick took heated exception during his campaign to enshrine Shakespeare's reputation, the Renaissance dramatist has served as a site of territorial contestation. He is an index to "centuries of imperial rivalry between England and France, through alliances almost as bitter as their conflicts, and through ongoing French concern with the preservation of [the country's] language and culture."⁷

Méliès was in some respects daringly politically progressive, although obviously not to the standards we might and should expect of him today. What he sought in Shakespeare was not—despite the appearance of Shakespeare's butler—an appeal to British class sensibility but rather to the Romantic sublimation of the aesthetic as a transnational (if often nationalist) realm. Shakespeare thus assumes the Méliès-like guise of shared cultural property, in itself a form of national appropriation.⁸ The described action of the film might, to a dream-disentangling Freud, signify antipathy toward a phallocentric imperial order (not as immoderate a turn of phrase as might be imagined, since the mighty Caesar did ornament his triumphal chariots with phalluses). The ideal of empire is invoked only to be transcended by its opposite, a nascent postnationalist (Eurovisual?) ideal in which the imagination is privileged and in which Caesar, equated with a loaf of bread, can be subject to the unkindest cut of all and thus edited out of Shakespeare's subsequent glory. The flags, then, are a recognition that the good burgher who once chose to return to Stratfordian domesticity had, at least as early as a century ago, achieved a different and more lasting conquest of worlds both old and new.

Méliès's *Rêve* did not help him stave off *La Mort*. Even so, the demise of Star Films and the eventual penury of the filmmaker who starred in so many of his films had no appreciable impact on the star system. Unlike its inspired hero, Méliès's Biopic did have lineal descendants, the most recent and most outstandingly popular being John Madden's 1998 *Shakespeare in Love*. The critical reception of the latter has been largely at odds with the popular one, since not only did it showcase sexy stars with lots of teen appeal, but also contrived to make rather good-natured fun of contemporary Shakespeare scholarship: psychoanalysis, cultural materialism, and gender studies, not to mention New Historicism, are all subjected to carnivalesque mirth. Since I am profoundly sympathetic to a number of the ideas (if not the occasional rhetorical profligacy) associated with these critical approaches, I cannot help but agree that the film indulges in an array of unauthorized fantasies; but it is also difficult not to be amused by its self-parody and devilishly clever construction, some of which may be attributable to Tom Stoppard's participation. Near the start, it appropriates the finest lines of a very early play, *The Two Gentleman of Verona*, just in order, one imagines, to make Christopher Marlowe its true genius and WS the journeyman toiler and minor plagiarist. As with all such tormented intellectuals, CM's reward for his benevolence in rectifying his junior colleague's defective plotting is to be Oedipally overthrown (just as his own lines from *Doctor Faustus* are supplanted in importance by Shakespeare's during drama rehearsals, as its astrologer-psychoanalyst character might observe). Eventually the film, having alluded to a number of plays, contrives to end with a vision based on *The Tempest*, an autumnal work controversially posited as Shakespeare's valedictory address to the King's Men, so confirming that the action of the film, like that of Méliès's fable, is a result of imaginative extension.⁹

★ ★ ★

Among those who might have taken offense at its ahistoricism most justly is Stephen Greenblatt, who received a screen credit for consultation with one of the screenwriters, Marc Norman; instead, at a talk given on October 24, 2004 at New York's 92nd Street Y, he expressed surprise at receiving any credit at all since he had suggested Marlowe as a more exciting subject for biography! No one, of course, knows better than Greenblatt some of the more "serious," highbrow uses to which Shakespeare has been put, no less than seemingly trivial popularizing ones, and hence perhaps his circumspect disavowal of his screen credit.[10] The probably unintended but entirely predictable consequence of the film's overt fictionalization, however, was to create a discursive space for speculation about the historical Shakespeare. Inevitably, *Shakespeare in Love* made room for *Shakespeare in London*.

This is not to suggest that biographical genres connected with Shakespeare are new, but rather that they are reflective of contemporary concerns and preoccupations. Indeed, the very paucity of information that survives contributes to the interpretive strategies—some of great ingenuity—to which Shakespeare seekers have recourse. That there is no one Shakespeare but a whole series of them, each appropriate to a particular cultural climate, rather than a transcendent but inaccessible one who, as Ben Jonson declared in his endorsement of the First Folio, was "not of an age, but for all time," emerges as the central thesis of Gary Taylor's *Reinventing Shakespeare*. One might even go further and argue that there is no guarantee that any one age or any society has achieved anything akin to consensus about "its" Shakespeare. Even at the height of the British Empire in the nineteenth century, a fascinating minigenre of mutually exclusive texts (almost unique to Shakespeare) emerged. Members of various professions in Britain began to claim him as one of their own: he was obviously a tricky lawyer, a physician conversant with the latest surgical techniques of his time, a navy man of at least middling rank, an angler, and, for the more venturesome, either the leading natural philosopher of his age or the Earl of Oxford.

The post-*Shakespeare in Love* biographical turn, however, has available to it a much more formidable array of historical instruments and a larger corpus of materials relating to the poet's life than any previous period since his time and ours. Thus, most biographers can today agree on the generalized portrait of a hardworking, somewhat litigious individual who made good in the metropolis, retired early to properties inherited and acquired, maintained business interests in London and Stratford, and died prematurely without a male heir. More, though, is known about many whose lives straddled the Tudor and Stuart reigns. Knowledge that might be fundamental to reading his extant oeuvre, such as his religious background and sentiments, continues to provoke contrasting opinions (as well it might, for a presumed onetime or secret Catholic who could have had associations with French Huguenots and who made his Puritan son-in-law his principal heir). For instance, not only does Stanley Wells aver that Shakespeare had little sympathy for his Catholic inheritance but also that he was a true Stratfordian: this Shakespeare found the hustle and bustle of London so intolerable that Wells decides that "our [sic] first great literary commuter" sought refuge in Stratford when he needed to write.[11] Peter Ackroyd traces variants of "Shakespeare's name" as far back as Normandy, ferreting out two sixteenth-century prioresses of the nearby nunnery at Wroxall who bore a name that suggested debasement, the Warwickshire equivalent of Durbeville.[12] Frank Kermode provides a seemingly sympathetic account of William's recusant background, only to suffer a sudden *peripatesis*, expressing skepticism about such "Catholic" appropriations of Shakespeare's biography.[13] While the Shakespeare of Greenblatt's *Hamlet in Purgatory* might be mistaken for a Catholic in crisis, the Shakespeare of *Will in the World* reveals him to be a skeptic: his is a fictive world where "powerful prelates" are "disagreeable," one in which "the only sainthood in which [he] seems passionately to have believed throughout his life... [was] erotic sainthood."[14] Wood opts for a cautious Catholic capable of brilliant disguise, and Richard Wilson for one who disdained the suicidal tendencies of the more militant recusants.[15]

Of the textual traces, perhaps more is known, but even less is certain. Indeed, if the issue of Shakespeare's belief system seems far from settled, then one that has similarly perplexed textual editors and critics is that literary dukedom that contributed to his wide reading. Was it a single trove such as a library in one of the posited Lancashire households where the recusant sought refuge, or was it one possessed by a cantankerous classmate, Richard Field, who worked in London as a printer? Did his noble patrons lend him favorite volumes? Or could those arcane and often complex layers of reference have come packaged with the plots that were handed to him from above (or below) for reworking?

This insistence on uncertainty is not by any means an excuse for failures to try to understand what we can establish as best we can, as Geenblatt, Wilson, Andrew Gurr, and numerous textual commentators have proved, but rather a caution against the perils that some discourses of authenticity present. Unadulterated Shakespeare was early put to the test by the competing demands of stage and page, as evidenced by what many believe to be his own revisions and those made by others even in his lifetime. Early readings and criticism were far from uniform. Gurr has catalogued a series of responses to contemporary plays, not only those of visiting foreigners but also of such colorful Londoners as Simon Forman, whose readings of Shakespeare as a moralist would strike many today as unusual (but perhaps to contemporaries less so).[16] Even as the playwright was still hard at work, versions of his plays left British shores, at least in one instance in the dubious company of the British East India Company. As played aboard ship, they were intelligible to at least to one West African translator who had been educated by Portuguese missionaries, although he may have been no more aware of "Shakespeare" than Dutch, Spanish, and Italian visitors to the original Globe, or present-day schoolchildren who throng the reconstructed edifice.[17]

★ ★ ★

Clever burlesques of Shakespeare as national property have emerged, as might be expected, from the lands in which the East India Company gained political ascendancy and which formed the nucleus of the British Empire. In the postcolonial calamity that befell Sri Lanka (then Ceylon), political satirist Tarzie Vittachi expressed his objection to a British touring company acting arbitrarily arranged snippets of Shakespeare by seizing the occasion for some self-directed antinationalist humor. "I mean to say," writes Vittachi of "Herr Marius Göring" and his "strolling players," "these boys carry on as though Shakespeare was an Englishman." On the contrary, asserts Vittachi, he can furnish incontrovertible proof that Shakespeare was not Marlowe buried in Earl Walsingham's grave, but a Sinhalese named Villiong Shakesperera. Referring to the bitter ethnic conflicts fanned by the early nationalists, Vittachi adds, "Of course the minorities tried to claim him for their own: our brothers in the North said that his name was actually Shakesperiyanayagam and the Muslims swore that William Shakespeare was in fact Vilcassim Sheik Sufeer."[18] What is important is not his particular ethnic affiliation, but that Shakespeare is Ceylonese and shows an understanding of contemporary politics that only a native could possess, and to prove his point Vittachi includes a slightly modified passage of *Macbeth* and lengthy extracts of *Julius Caesar*, both bearing an unmistakable relevance to the local goings-on.[19]

More important, perhaps, than Vittachi's parody of nationalist biomania is his sense that one of the flags waved on Shakespeare's behalf should be as multicultural as it is Ceylonese. Or, to put it another way, even if Shakespeare is not all things to all people, the *fons et origo* of modern psychology as Harold Bloom asserts in *Shakespeare: The Invention of the Human*, he has come to mean many different things to many different constituencies, and it is these later accretions of meaning that are of true importance to the study of cultural history. However, such a view does not subscribe to the notion that there is any recoverable historical character or perfectible textual residue, any "authentic Shakespeare," as Stephen Orgel phrases it, on the first page of his book of that title wherein he declares that "at the heart of our texts lies a hard core of uncertainty." Indeed, that "Old Historicist" fiction of certainty might turn out to be uninteresting, or worse, as unpalatable as any another fundamentalism. So a Renaissance Studies fundamentalist well versed in Castiglione or Firenzuola might insist on the humanist and Neoplatonist associations of physical characteristics with inner spiritual states, and thus may reject any but an unwittingly funny and monstrously hump-backed Richard III; but she would have to disregard often-repeated contemporary counterexamples such as Lorenzo de Medici and Emperor Charles V whose deformities contributed to the aura of divinely ordained greatness that attached to them. The casual scholar of medieval drama, unaware that both Shakespeare and his father made a practice of lending money for interest, might insist on seeing a red-wigged and carrot-nosed Shylock as he may possibly have been played on stage. But is this recognition of anti-Semitic calumny, or the gallows humor in the play's references to the execution of the queen's *converso* physician, Roderigo Lopez, sure proof in the Elizabethan playwright of the overwhelming human tragedy that resulted from later anti-Semitism, and thus a fitting excuse to disregard that long exculpatory performance tradition that culminated with Olivier's BBC portrayal of Shylock as a fragile old man driven to sputtering irrationality by the loss of his only child to his conniving enemies? If Shakespeare did not see himself as Shylock, he certainly did not see himself as Antonio either, since his own use of venture capital did not encompass the most risky and lucrative of the investments of his time, the speculative sea trade involving both Old World and New, but was limited to colonizing bits of his hometown and his adopted city. And if actors might be credited with an instinct for scene stealing, the enduring attraction of Richard, Shylock, and Caliban for the best of them certainly attests to a complexity of characterization.

★ ★ ★

Far more interesting to us than pinning the crimson vices of his age onto Shakespeare's present-day lapels is the fate that befell him posthumously, for neither biographical nor historical uncertainty has prevented accretions of textual matter, performance traditions, and even a specialized visual culture surrounding the cult of Shakespeare, not merely in Britain (as a matter of national and local pride), but in nations as far flung as India and Japan. Indeed, it is the meaning with which those of later generations have invested Shakespeare that makes a greatness that was obvious even to his contemporaries a transcendent one. For the philosopher Benedetto Croce, Shakespeare epitomizes the universal function of literature by communicating the thought of one individual to another at the highest level.[20] And yet, there is a certain territoriality that carries over from literary and theatrical tradition into national cinemas, and further, even to the criticism generated by those cinemas. At its basest level this takes the form of Shakespeare as excuse (he is assumed to be racist, xenophobic, sexist, given to cultural stereotypes, all of which legitimates our being so); but even in the realms of "high culture" it appropriates Shakespeare as paragon (see what English culture can achieve in contrast to the barbarous Whatchamacallits). Then there is the issue of his nationality. "Goethe," writes Jorge Luis Borges, "is Germany's official religion," while the worship of Shakespeare is more "private." He adds the parenthetical remark, "In England the official religion is Shakespeare, who is so unlike the English; England's sacred book, however, is the Bible.[21]

Goethe, however, is by no means an exclusive deity, and even in Germany he has, in a sense, always had to yield pride of place on the literary Olympus to Shakespeare's Jovian eminence. In one manifestation, the Bard of Avon was a German Romantic deity, effecting the establishment of German verse drama (anteceding Goethe) through the translations of A.W. Schlegel.[22] In another, he is the progenitor of an Italian divinity. Long before Giuseppe Verdi's series of Shakespeare operas, the Italian Shakespeare had been wedded to the tradition of *music lirica*: indeed, Gioacchino Rossini's earlier *Otello*, compounded of Shakespeare and his source, Giraldi Cinzio, showcased the talents of the great, tragically short-lived mezzo-soprano Maria Malibran, while later baritones of the stature of Mattia Battistini and Titta Ruffo proved celebrated interpreters of the bibulous Amleto in the Italian version of Ambroise Thomas's *Hamlet*. It stands to reason, then, that the international success of stage actor Tommaso Salvini in the role of Othello and the comparatively subdued Shakespearean heroines of Eleanora Duse—two actors Konstantin Stanislavsky credited with convincing him to take to the stage—were filtered through a musical-dramatic tradition. Indeed, Duse was not only Verdi's admirer but also Arrigo Boito's lover during the time he wrote the libretti for *Otello* and *Falstaff*. So intimate is the connection between Verdi and Shakespeare within Italian cultural tradition that in Bernardo Bertolucci's film adaptation of Jorge-Luis Borges's short story, "The Theme of the Traitor and the Hero," to which we return in due course in discussing the "Irish" origins of Orson Welles's conception of filmed Shakespeare, he substitutes one for the other.

Verdi, of course, is not the only innovative composer to be smitten by Shakespeare. Beethoven, Gounod, and Tchaikovsky claimed him as an influence, as did innumerable others. In 1827 his most ardent musical fan, Hector Berlioz, attended a performance of *Hamlet* at the Odeon in Paris and fell simultaneously under the spell of the poet and of the Ophelia, Harriet Smithson. The former remained unbroken, for while the *Symphonie Fantastique* (the result of her initial coldness to his passionate advances) was the high point of their relationship, at least musically, Shakespeare remained an idée fixe throughout Berlioz's career and played a larger role in his highly literary imagination than any other writer (*Roméo et Juliette* and *Béatrice et Bénédict* remain in the regularly performed repertoire of specialists). Even so, it is to Verdi that Kenneth Rothwell and other commentators refer when they note the influence of operatic staging on Franco Zeffirelli's Shakespeare films:[23] the musical set pieces commissioned from opera composer Nino Rota (Fellini's longtime collaborator) are elaborately choreographed in *Romeo and Juliet* (1968). Indeed, Mel Gibson's virile Hamlet in Zeffirelli's 1990 film followed fast on the heels of an equally virile Plácido Domingo, albeit in the latter case in the director's film of Verdi's *Otello* rather than of Shakespeare's play. A protégé of Luchino Visconti as both director of opera and film, Zeffirelli is also conversant with the history of Shakespeare in the cinema: thus the nettings and other visual metaphors of entrapment that Sergei Yutkevich adapts from Orson Welles's *Othello* (1952–1954) for his own (1955) find their way into Zeffirelli's *Otello*, as does the borrowing of a flashback sequence of Othello's youth (albeit transposed from the perspective of Yutkevich's Desdemona, Irina Skobtseva, to that of Otello, and motivated by the lyrics Boito gave him). Zeffirelli also filmed a *La Traviata* (1982) with Domingo as Alfredo, and in Michael Hoffman's similarly lush, Edwardian cinematic setting of *A Midsummer Night's Dream* (1999), the drinking song Verdi imagines as a coded duet of erotic invitation serves as an evolving commentary on the diegesis. It functions as a musical elixir that brings Alfredo and Violetta together, reminding us of the intoxicating power of love juices, just as Hoffman's use of Pietro Mascagni's intermezzo from *Cavalleria Rusticana* (1890) hints at the darker consequences of illicit love, which may, as critics and stage directors have often noted, underlie Shakespeare's apparent nonchalance.

★ ★ ★

In cinematic terms, two of the more intriguing instances of the divine Shakespeare, a divinity deeply inscribed into national traditions, are perhaps those of the superpowers whose contending aspirations defined the cold war that loomed ominously over most of the last half of the twentieth century. Since many of the films treated in this book originate in the United States, I concentrate here on three Russian adaptations that have as their unifying feature the intermediary texts of a famous, but far from faithful translator.[24] That their infidelities are seldom infelicities, but more often manifestations of cultural heritage and social circumstance, might also be observed of some of the American films I subsequently treat as examples of a Shakespearean "rivalry" that briefly "heated up" as a result of the cold war.[25]

Russia's Shakespeare takes root at the very inception of a modern Russian literature. The earliest known reference to Shakespeare in Russian literature occurs in Alexander Sumarokov's *Epistle on Poetry* (1748).[26] In the 1820s Shakespeare became a "national" issue that coalesced around the iconic poet Alexander Pushkin, when the Decembrists, reacting to Napoleon's invasion of 1812, sought to define a national literature. "It was as a clearly original, national writer, a genius whose imagination was unhampered by imposed precepts and rules," argues Yury Levin, that Shakespeare inspired them, and Pushkin himself confessed that his 1825 play *Boris Godunov*—later transformed by Modest Mussorgsky into the most often performed of Russian operas—was "arranged...according to the system of our Father Shakespeare."[27] Pushkin wrote commentaries on Falstaff and Shylock, but made especial note of the character of Angelo, just as Feodor Dostoyevsky similarly found Othello more compelling than Hamlet and Falstaff. Dostoyevsky's insistence that Othello is a great and pure soul who is not jealous by nature, but trusting and destroyed by the betrayal of that trust (as expounded in *The Brothers Karamazov*),[28] inevitably marked Boris Pasternak's reading of Shakespeare's controversial protagonist.

Shakespeare was staged in Russia long before Dostoyevsky was born. According to Joyce Vining Morgan, even Peter the Great might have seen adapted versions of Shakespeare's plays, but it was only in the 1830s that significant translations from the originals began to appear in print. Before a decade had passed, the longstanding debate as to whether Shakespeare's blank verse should be rendered as poetry or colloquial prose began, and from Vissarion Belinsky onward the tendency to create native characters based on ones detached from Shakespeare's plays established itself as a quasi genre.[29] Having written a short story, *The Hamlet of Shchigiri District* in 1849, Ivan Turgenev, in a lecture of contrasts entitled "Hamlet and Don Quixote" (1860), excoriated what he regarded as Hamletism, which, in contrast to late nineteenth-century French *Hamletisme* (which ascribed the prince's tragedy to a lack of resolve), set forth the idea that "analysis and egotism" had led to Hamlet's exaggerated concern with his "situation" and "never with his responsibilities."[30] Levin argues that in time Turgenev's critical view of Hamlet became enshrined in literature as a form of national self-criticism, typifying self-serving despondency (vide Boris Eifman's extraordinary 2002 ballet, *Russian Hamlet*, based on the life of Paul III), a characterization only to be contradicted in the early twentieth-century ferment of experimental theatre.[31]

Of the domestications of Shakespeare's characters, perhaps the one to enjoy the most celebrated and, eventually, disastrous future was Nikolai Leskov's "Lady Macbeth of Mtsensk District" (1865),[32] transformed memorably to film as *Sibirska Ledi Magbet* (1961) by the celebrated Polish director Andrzej Wajda (one of the films resulting from the brief period of a "thaw" during Soviet domination that led to a resurgence of the national cinemas of Eastern Europe). As with many a Shakespeare film, it alludes to plays other than the one being adapted (a dead mouse, for instance, reminds us of *Hamlet*, which may in turn allude to Akira Kurosawa's interpolated reference to the Mousetrap in his well-known version of *Macbeth*). *Sibirska Ledi Magbet* is also clearly a film celebrating the liberalization of the Khrushchev years, for, a quarter of a century earlier, an opera of Leskov's title resulted in various official censures, including the loss of Dmitri Shostakovich's university post as a professor of music. The disaster that befell a musical composition destined to become the best-known Russian Modernist opera is rendered even more ironic by the fact that its principal inspiration was drawn not so much from Leskov himself but from the painter Boris Kustodiev, whose illustrations of Leskov's tale, according Shostakovich, prompted him to write the opera.[33] It is to Shostakovich too that we are indebted for a vivid account of a number of stage *Hamlet*s for which he provided music, as well as some envisioned by stage director Vsevolod Meyerhold (who in one projected staging apparently wanted a comic Hamlet to irritate the tragic Hamlet during the monologues) and actor-director Mikhail Chekhov who, in a sort of anthroposophist anticipation of Stephen Greenblatt, set all the action in purgatory.[34]

On January 28, 1936 Shostakovich stopped at a railway station to buy a copy of *Pravda* and discovered a review of his popular and long-running opera, which in fact moderated and motivated the bloodthirstiness of the heroine, Katerina Ismailova. The editorial had been "promoted" to the third page, but without acknowledgment of authorship. Its title was "Muddle Instead of Music." A few days later Stalin attended a performance of Shostakovich's ballet *Bright Stream* at the Bolshoi Theatre and there followed a second scathing attack, confirming the authorship of the first one. Soon, numerous commentators began describing the composer as an "enemy of the people," and he relates that he felt lucky to survive.³⁵ As in literature and the other arts, the accusations of Formalism and Modernism that had destroyed the literary avant-garde and those of the plastic arts were leveled with similar consequence against composers, the most serious purge occurring in 1948 and involving Shostakovich, Sergei Prokofiev, Aram Khachaturian, and even lesser figures such as Vano Muradeli and Nikolai Myaskovsky. Muradeli, the proximate cause of the fracas, was reduced to groveling for what was probably—but in those days it was hard to tell—his life.

With the knowledge of what was at stake, few more chilling accounts of the composition of a piece of music could possibly exist than that extracted by Solomon Volkov from his conversation with Shostakovich about the genesis of the Soviet national anthem. It was common at the time, when state occasions demanded a constant supply of music, for composers to resort to the use of orchestrators as a time-saving remedy for pressing deadlines. Even Prokofiev, whose *Romeo and Juliet* (1938) is one of the greatest and most often performed ballet scores, used an orchestrator for film director Sergei Eisenstein's *Alexander Nevsky* (1938) and for the two surviving parts of *Ivan the Terrible* (1945–1948); only a scene and a few test fragments (and no music) remain of the third part whose destruction Stalin ordered. During the anthem "auditions," Stalin, who fancied himself an expert critic of all the arts, decided that the orchestration of the tune composed by Alexander Alexandrov was inadequate. Shostakovich then adds, "I saw that things could end badly; Stalin was interested in Alexandrov's pathetic justifications. It was an unhealthy interest, the interest of a wolf in a lamb. Noticing the interest, Alexandrov began laying it on thicker. The poor arranger was being turned into a saboteur, who had purposely done a bad arrangement..." Stalin so enjoyed the anthems of Shostakovich and Khachaturian that he ordered them to compose one in collaboration—which they proceeded to do with comically poor results. An unlikely Alexandrov emerged the victor.³⁶

If Shostakovich and Khachaturian were not immune to official displeasure, then even more expendable artists such as writers had still greater terrors to face. One who had originally studied musical composition but who changed course, only to be placed under "observation" after his conversation (in 1936) with a fellow Shakespeare translator, André Gide, was the poet and linguist Boris Pasternak. According to Tony Howard, Meyerhold intended his wife Zinaida Raikh (an outspoken critic of Stalin) to play one of his Hamlets. On receiving news of her murder and his arrest, Pasternak set aside the translation of *Hamlet* they had commissioned.³⁷ Official scrutiny of Pasternak only intensified after his novel *Doctor Zhivago* was condemned upon publication in 1957, and he was forbidden to accept the 1958 Nobel Prize in Literature.³⁸ It is his bold translations of Shakespeare and, to some extent his opinions of the plays, that form a unifying link between Yutkevich's *Othello* and two other "great" tragedies directed by Kozintsev, *Hamlet* (*Gamlet* 1964) and *King Lear* (*Korol Lir* 1970). Indeed, in a profound sense, the Shakespearean collaboration between the giants of Soviet music, literature, and filmmaking celebrated the post-Stalin era, and the films and the descriptions by Yutkevich and Kozintsev of their genesis can be appreciated only in this context. In his closely observed account of Yutkevich's *Othello*, for instance, Stephen Buhler notes that for over seven minutes at the start, as Othello relates his stories to Brabantio and Desdemona and then departs, Desdemona lingers at a window to observe his departure and then approaches the gigantic armillary sphere Othello had just contemplated, after which a dissolve from a close-up of her face to Othello's past exploits announces them as her projection of him. Even during the scene that follows of the solemnization of their vows, Khachaturian's music plays triumphantly, uninterrupted by dialogue.[39] The entire montage, in fact, is assembled according to the rhythms of Khachaturian's score, synchronized with the tempo of the action and the editing. This dependence on the musical score even necessitates near pauses in the action, as when Desdemona sings a Verdiesque Willow Song. The effect is reminiscent of a somewhat undisciplined version of Sergei Eisenstein's conception of tonal montage, the citation of technique quite notable when, for instance, the first statement of the love theme (played rhythmically by the strings) gives way to martial music during Desdemona's imaginative flashback: the sword-blows are caught in the music's downbeats, as is the firing of cannons in a montage that evokes the culmination of the Siege of Kazan in the first part of Eisenstein's *Ivan the Terrible* trilogy.

It would, of course, be quite pointless to emphasize the traditions accruing to such plays as *Hamlet* in Russia or to ponder the fate of musicians such as Shostakovich and Khachaturian if such histories were irrelevant to a film director trying to find a decent script or mood music. However, Yutkevich was the author of a wide-ranging book, *Shakespeare and Cinema* (1973), and Kozintsev of a number that illustrate an intimate familiarity with Shakespearean theatrical traditions as well as cinema history. Both had participated in the film-making avant-garde of the 1920s and witnessed its destruction in the 1930s. And both, perhaps without even conceiving of them as such, made Shakespeare films that reference Alexander Pushkin, the founding figure of modern Russian literature.

Perhaps Kozintsev spoke for both of them in pointing to the interplay of word, image, and music in their films: "I would not be able to make a Shakespearean film without [Shostakovich's music] just as I would not be able to do so without Pasternak's translations."[40] Much of the opening section of *Shakespeare: Time and Conscience* is devoted to the visual culture pertaining to illustrations of Shakespeare's plays and interpretive performing traditions. He praises Akira Kurosawa's use of Noh masks and acting conventions, commenting that "Shakespeare and naturalism are as incompatible on the screen as they are on the stage";[41] and he regards Peter Brook as "the most interesting [theatre] director in Europe," finding that his stylized sets and costumes present not the usual weak copy of real life but its "algebraic formula."[42] Yet, once again when he contrasts Paul Scofield's Lear with that of Solomon Mikhoels, and when he argues that Hamletism has a specific character in relation to each theatrical epoch, Kozintsev returns to the distinctively Russian "reading" of Shakespeare.[43] Kozintsev, in fact, felt the Russian Shakespeare to be culturally unique, and dilated at length on its character in discussing the centrality of Shostakovich's music to his *King Lear*: "[T]he main point about it...[is that it embodies] not just tragedy...but a special kind of goodness...In Russian art goodness does not exist without a fierce hatred of everything which destroys a man. In Shostakovich's music I can hear a ferocious hatred of cruelty, the cult of power and the oppression of justice. This is a special goodness: a fearless goodness which has a threatening quality."[44]

Kozintsev, moreover, did not regard Russia's Shakespeare as a static tradition. He insists that one of his reasons for his attachment to Pasternak's translation was its eschewal of the Romantic accretions that inhered to Shakespeare: Pasternak, he observes, felt that when Shakespeare's rhythms were properly captured, they revealed "the Shakespeare that is greater than Tolstoy."[45] Paradoxically, according to Anna Kay France, Pasternak's rejection of later Romanticism brought him closer to Pushkin who has been variously claimed for both Classicism and Romanticism. She maintains that Pasternak's translations of eight of Shakespeare's plays attempt to achieve a "Pushkin style" and quotes Henry Gifford to the effect that "the Shakespeare of Pasternak has inevitably become the fellow countryman of Pushkin."[46] France suggests that Pasternak's obvious liberties with Shakespeare, in modernizing the language to some degree, simplifying the Baroque imagery in favor of a classical simplicity and economy of means, and concentrating on visual details in rendering space and time palpable—notably a preoccupation of such Russian theorists of literature as Mikhail Bakhtin, and reflected in Kozintsev's titles for his books on Shakespeare—all owe a considerable debt to the Pushkin style.[47] In keeping with Pushkin's sense of Shakespeare's clarity, Pasternak rejected the indecisive *Hamlet* of Russian Hamletism, insisting that "Hamlet is a tragedy of will...Lack of will-power wasn't a known theme in Shakespeare's time...On the contrary, it [feebleness] is excluded, and the audience is asked, instead, to judge how great Hamlet's sacrifice must be, when he commits himself and all his great expectations to a loftier duty."[48] France notes that while embarking on his prior stage production of *Hamlet* using Pasternak's version, Kozintsev requested a translation of Sonnet 74 (which underlines the Oresteian reading of Hamlet, the sonnet obliquely suggesting the hero's knowledge that his body will soon be food for worms—a word used in both play and sonnet—indicative of his acceptance of his duty, only his uncorrupted spirit remaining immortal).[49] Bernice Kliman sees the fruits of the collaboration as an anti-Stalinist allegory, in which Claudius plays the role of the sanguinary usurper.[50] If such an allegorical reading was inspired by the translator, then Yutkevich's *Othello*, with its mustachioed, self-possessed Iago, also lends itself to a similar interpretation, although the film predates Nikita Khrushchev's 1956 denunciation of Stalin. Even in *King Lear*, which does not lend itself so easily to allegorical readings, Pasternak's ghost is present. Anthony Davies mentions that Kozintsev chose the Estonian actor Yuri Yarvet (Jüri Järvet) for the role of Lear because of his penetrating gaze, short stature, and physical dynamism;[51] for Kozintsev the moment of transformation, when the entire cast was galvanized by the certainty their Lear was physically present, was when Yarvet insisted on overcoming his halting Russian to speak Pasternak's lines.[52]

The polyphony of Kozintsev's oeuvre is not reliant on his collaborators alone. His books are replete with memories of the betrayed golden efflorescence of Modernist art in the 1920s, and the occasional melancholy of his reveries is offset by his enthusiastic relation of the influence his colleagues had on him, in particular that of Eisenstein's theatrical mentor–and to some extent his own–Vsevolod Meyerhold. Meyerhold, Kozintsev relates, taught him how to seek out the inner substance of a text, such as the matter of Ophelia's pregnancy in *Hamlet*, an idea that still retains interesting resonances for the *Hamlet*s directed by Branagh and Zeffirelli.[53] It is this search for the visual essence of *King Lear* in Kozintsev's film that necessitates a cumulative illustration of the chaotic forces that Lear unleashes with his ill-advised abdication. In casting off ethical responsibility, Lear's dereliction of his duty to his family and subjects fast reduces friend and foe to indistinguishable clots of metal-encased men, distancing him from the camera and showing the once vigorous monarch increasingly dwarfed by the mise en scène as he undergoes his purgation,[54] a mortal torment culminating in his off-screen howls that forewarn us that Kozintsev requires Cordelia not merely to be dead but to dangle in an arch-like break in the castle's stone walls with the terrifying grace of a medieval martyr.

Among those to comment on Kozintsev's *King Lear,* perhaps the most authoritative was Yutkevich.[55] He had proposed filming his own *Othello* in 1937 to the unreceptive, state-centralized studios, and according to A. Lipkov, revived his plan to film that version upon seeing Welles's *Othello* (1952–54) in which he felt he could not recognize his favorite Shakespeare heroes.[56] Although not uniformly well received among Soviet critics, especially in its portrayal of Desdemona,[57] the film won Yutkevich the 1956 award for direction at Cannes. Recent critics such as Buhler see much more in the film's opulence and its Desdemona, who, he points out, displays the undaunted optimism of one of Shakespeare's comic heroines.[58] Anna France finds that Pasternak's attempt to render Iago more psychologically convincing robs him of some of the subtlety of Shakespeare's character; but in his film Yutkevich puts Olivier's strategy in *Hamlet* (1948) of using voice-overs for some soliloquies representing thought processes to good use, rendering Pasternak's emphasis on Iago's ability to disguise his villainy from the other characters more credible.[59] That Stalinesque duplicity is nowhere more evident than in a series of memorable shots of a soliloquizing Iago stalking his "prey" on the battlements of the Cypriot fortress, a sequence that depicts him observing Cassio and Desdemona through a distorting optical device, his face in extreme close-up and rendered larger than the figures below him, an extension of depth-of-field cinematography first noted by critics such as André Bazin in Welles's *Citizen Kane* (1941).

Welles's *Othello* also seems the inspiration for a number of shot compositions.[60] For instance, upon Othello's arrival in Cyprus he bounds up a series of staircases to the ramparts of the fortress, an ascent Yutkevich visualizes with a Soviet wide-screen technology that rivaled CinemaScope, and effected through complex crane shots (a Welles trademark) that move from close-ups of Othello and Desdemona to panoramic views of fluttering flags. Once Iago has convinced Cassio to ply Desdemona with his suit for reinstatement, he approaches a well in the center of a courtyard and gazes at his own reflection. As the camera tilts down to catch the glassy, self-satisfied smirk, a visual effect reminiscent of the cistern in Welles's film, it becomes apparent that Iago's voice-over monologue has been prerecorded, timed to his changing expressions, his face dissolving in a triumph of synchronicity as he swirls the water on "make the net that shall enmesh them all." The metaphor acquires a further Wellesian dimension in the sequence that follows. Adopting the long tracking shot that Welles took on the ramparts of the fortress of Mogador (during which Iago finally "seduces" Othello), Yutkevich finds himself having to piece together four shots in place of Welles's single long take. In compensation, Yutkevich turns Iago's metaphor into a visual metonymy: as Othello leads and Iago follows him, they walk past rows of fishing nets hanging out to dry, so that by the time Othello declares that he is bound to Iago forever, and Iago catalogues the deficiencies that Desdemona might see in him, Othello has to hold up the net in which both are enmeshed.

Just as Welles's film had Verdi's opera in its background, so did that of Yutkevich and Khachaturian. Perhaps that influence is even more obvious in Yutkevich's film because of the conscious theatricality of the acting and the long, held moments (in service to the score) that pay tribute to its musical predecessor. An obvious instance is Khachaturian's *vocalise* for Desdemona, which can be reheard at crucial moments when they seem to have an ameliorative effect on Othello's state of mind: at one moment she even floats by on a sailboat, singing, as Othello writhes in anguish on a docked galleon. When Iago and Othello swear their pact (the famous "Sì, pel ciel" duet from the opera), Yutkevich follows the stage convention of having the protagonists kneel. The action also slows to near complete stasis to accommodate Khachaturian's version of Desdemona's most famous aria, his version of Verdi's setting of the "Willow Song," which so protracts the action that Zeffirelli infamously omitted it from his film of Verdi's opera.[61]

While acknowledging his association with the Soviet avant-garde of the 1920s, setting himself up in competition with Welles, and illustrating the "superiorities" of Soviet technology (the Sovcolor process he used, for instance, emphasized the reds of costumes and flags against muted palette of earth tones, especially bringing out Othello's deep brown makeup and Desdemona's traditionally pale "fair warrior" tones, highlighted by the dominant creams or browns of their attire), his film's discursive address again bends Russian tradition to contemporary issues. It was a matter of national pride that Pushkin's grandfather was a black Ethiopian general in the service of Peter the Great, who was also (and as tragically) married to a celebrated court beauty at the express wish of the monarch. Then, there was also the further dimension of the socialist concern about the mistreatment of African Americans that assumed the status of national propaganda in Stalin's period (with a series of depictions of lynchings by celebrated poster artists such as Victor Deni), a legitimate socialist critique that only intensified during the first stirrings of the U.S. civil rights movement and the rising temperature of the cold war (even Kozintsev, in his book on *King Lear*, likened Cornwall's followers to the Ku Klux Klan).[62] Paul Robeson, a good friend of Eisenstein's, had visited him in 1934 and had contemplated making a film with him on his next visit in 1937 (when Robeson also met with Stanislavsky). Robeson had campaigned for a second front (as did Welles) during World War II to relieve the pressure on the Nazi-besieged Soviet capitals; he had played a particularly famous Othello (as betrayed hero) in 1943 opposite Uta Hagen at New York's Schubert Theater; and he was awarded a Stalin Peace Prize in 1952. Despite being less politically astute than he was forthright and courageous in defense of African American rights, he was certainly the most visible black American on the Soviet cultural scene, and at the time Yutkevich's film appeared, he could not travel to Canada, let alone the Soviet Union, as he had been deprived of his passport in 1950 for his Soviet associations. The heroic warrior Othello, as portrayed by one of the most esteemed Russian actor-directors of the next generation, Sergei Bondarchuk, robs Iago of victory through his unhesitating suicide when he recognizes his error, according to Yutkevich (who also makes the point that Iago wishes to restrain him, an event that occurs more in Iago's eyes than his limbs, which are held fast).[63] Othello's potential heroism and his complexion are issues to which we have occasion to return in our discussion of Welles's *Othello*. Like Yutkevich's, it has Robeson in its background, which in a convenient way allows us to return from some of Europe's Shakespeares to that—or, perhaps more precisely, those—of the United States.

★ ★ ★

America's Shakespeare is no less grand than Russia's, and no less fought over. As Thomas Cartelli points out, the nineteenth century witnessed a relationship between Britain and the United States that was as fraught as those of many nations gaining independence from a colonial power in the twentieth century, and initially indicative of an equivalent stage of "postcolonial ambivalence."[64] As in Russia, Shakespeare had to be given a native cast, albeit in this instance one somewhat "sicklied o'er" by the problem of cultural and linguistic inheritance. It is an inheritance that influenced the nation's Founding Fathers and thus precedes Shakespeare's elevation into a figure of national importance in Britain, and perhaps it is the very ability of one cultural formation to run parallel with and to speak to another in its own vernacular (and thus be argued against) that led to one of the more celebrated recorded instances of a clash of competing "Shakespeares" on the night of May 7, 1849 at the Astor Place Opera house in New York. (In the previous year, the rivalry between leading American Shakespearean actor Edwin Forrest and his British counterpart William Charles Macready culminated in the sabotage of the latter's performance of the role of Macbeth.) After noisy interruption by his rival's supporters, Macready attempted to stare them down, demonstrating a singular lack of perspicacity in light of social tensions that had no doubt been exacerbated by the ill-feeling English profiteering had occasioned during the Great Potato Famine that had just decimated Ireland's population. Wrote one chronicler of the ensuing riot, which resulted in more than twenty deaths, "Had he [Macready] adopted a different course—one more suited to our National feelings, and the well-known good nature of the American people—we question if the scenes which followed would have occurred." "It was," concludes John Reese, "John Bull defying brother Jonathan."[65]

Reese's conclusion is indicative of the nature of the clash: a sense of betrayed fraternal affinity rather than purely an expression of sibling rivalry, as much a mitigation as it is an assertion of Yankee independence. And it is perhaps illustrative of this sense of national distinctiveness coupled with ancestral longings of various kinds that defines the critical distance between Cartelli and a writer such as Michael Bristol who, to the same extent that Cartelli emphasizes native autonomy, weights his argument toward Shakespeare as fraternal "appropriation" (to use a term consistent with Cartelli's argument). Neither Cartelli's appeal to theories of postcoloniality nor Bristol's to cultural studies is medium-specific, an issue to which I will return in treating Baz Luhrmann's Zeffirelliesque cinematic trajectory in the concluding chapter. However, the felt contradictions are already in evidence in America's earlier cultural products. A purely cinematic portmanteau of this ambivalence can be found, for example, in the intertitles of D.W. Griffith's film *America* (1924), which while celebrating the revolutionary spirit attempts to emphasize a fraternal international bond (comparable, in this regard, to the intertitles to the 1915 *The Birth of a Nation*, when he sought to emphasize an equivalent intranational bond in the United States between the warring North and South).

It should be noted, however, that Griffith's 1924 film proved almost as significant a box-office failure as did his earlier and more innovative *Intolerance* (1916). In fact, during the course of a decade in which Griffith found himself increasingly out of touch with developments in cinema, any colonial relation that existed between the nations had been decisively reversed. Films, in fact, were the New World's gift to the Old, although the extent of that gift initially passed unnoticed. Invented at behest of one of the icons of American technological innovation, Thomas Edison, motion pictures had from the start been considered an enhancement to an auditory experience. Sensing their potential as a peep-show amusement, Edison modeled his Kinetoscope parlor apparatus on the methods he had already established for the exploitation of other inventions, and thus the first films were marketed as mass entertainment (ranging from cockfights to prize fights) mobilizing a business strategy that long predated the maturation of the medium in the 1890s. Studio filmmaking, as became the accepted practice in most industries that developed commercially viable cinemas, originated within the orbit of Edison's other corporate enterprises in the United States. Curiously, Edison's policies may even have stymied the development of the film industry in the United States because of his determination to maintain monopolies on his technological innovations: almost until the advent of the multireel "feature" film, the cartel of ten production and distribution companies he and a few associates organized in 1908 into the MPPC sought to dominate the American film industry through technological standardization and by controlling access to the mechanisms of film production. It remained to the French entrepreneur Charles Pathé, one of the original signatories, to introduce cinema to the system that is now known as vertical integration, whereby studios engaged in the practice of acquiring theatres thus guaranteeing exhibition for films produced and distributed by stock companies and personnel placed under contract, all rendered feasible and maximally efficient by renting prints rather than selling them outright. Even before venturing on full-scale vertical integration, a number of the early film studios in the United States, such as the New Jersey-based Vitagraph company, recognized (in distinction to Edison) that audiences were less interested in the novelty of the apparatus than in the product screened for them, a fact crucial to the cycles of Shakespeare films ventured by Vitagaph and the family-run Thanhouser company. Pathé was still the world's leading production company until the advent of World War I, and American production remained rather haphazard, if lucrative. Until 1916 most films were made in New Jersey and New York, with Jacksonville, Florida, serving as the winter capital for the roving companies (including Thanhouser). However, the onset of World War I affected industrial production in the Northeast, the lull in European filmmaking created an unprecedented demand for American films, and Jacksonville's mayoral election of 1916 brought in an administration less predisposed to promote filmmaking, with the result that in short order relatively unlegislated Los Angeles became the epicenter of American film production. Kristin Thompson notes that "from 1916 onwards the United States became the number one supplier of movies in the world market, a position it has held ever since."[66] The synecdoche we term "Hollywood" designates more than a locale colonized by the most successful studios, for by the close of World War I it already stood for a certain corporate enterprise and system of industrial production that increasingly dominated European screens. By 1924, the majority of "British" films were Anglo-German coproductions and the majority of films shown in British theatres were America's English-language product, a process of "linguistic imperialism" compounded by the advent of films with synchronized dialogue in the late 1920s. In fact, it is the failure of the quota system by which the British government sought to limit imported films in the 1930s that led to a British screenwriter, Alfred Hitchcock, who had begun his directing career in Germany, rising to sufficient prominence with his "quota quickies" to be lured away by the sirens' song of Hollywood's production values.

To Hitchcock may be credited one of the more energetic parodies of America's Shakespeare, a short and supremely noisy send-up of the earliest full-length "talkie" Shakespeare made by the husband and wife team who were founders (with Griffith and Charlie Chaplin) of Hollywood's first actor-director-controlled studio, United Artists. The nominal director of their 1929 *Taming of the Shrew* had the effrontery to announce in an opening credit: "Written by William Shakespeare, with additional dialogue by Sam Taylor," a claim that has attracted derision. The changes in linguistic register heard on the film's soundtrack, however, are intended to be funny and, indeed, Pickford's famous entrance contains no dialogue at all except for the yelps of those fleeing the objects that an off-screen figure—who eventually reveals herself to be our Kate—hurls at them with practiced accuracy. Interestingly, it was a reviewer for the London *Observer* who warned: "Before we make superior noises of disgust, let us remember that the business of 'pepping up' Shakespeare is an old English industry...and that the talkie public is not a Shakespeare Association." Indeed, after the gala premier in London at the Bijou, James Agate pointed out that the film was "not a travesty of Shakespeare" but essentially a reworking of David Garrick's 1754 stage adaptation, *Catherine and Petruchio*—a plausible argument in light of the republication in 1924 of the 1878 promptbook of this version prepared by William Winter for Edwin Booth.[67]

Hitchcock was unconvinced. In 1930 Britain's Elstree Studio announced its acquisition of sound technology with a review film consisting of musical numbers and vaudeville-like routines (in competitive emulation of such films released by the major U.S. studios to showcase their rival sound systems). Adrian Brunel was made supervising director for *Elstree Calling* and was possibly responsible for the framing device of a continually thwarted attempt to stage Shakespeare. Hitchcock, who had already made a film that had sequences reshot for release as a talkie, the 1929 *Blackmail*, was entrusted with the direction of the comic sketches and "other interpolated items," most of the film, in other words, although on the title card his name appears in smaller type than Brunel's. Along with a regrettable minstrel act (a practice that remained popular on British television into the 1970s), and some vividly colored scenes of the Adelphi Girl Ballet, made on soundstages for live broadcast on "the marvelous invention of television," the film boasts comic Tommy Handley as the MC determined to present "Shakespeare, in a manner befitting his great genius." The organizers attempt to thwart him ("You see, they don't want me to do my Shakespeare, even though I have told them that you can make Shakespeare just as entertaining as Lily Morris, who is on next.") Handley offers a reading of "To be, or not to be," pulling a rabbit out of a hat, and assures the audience of romance, pathos, mother love, sex appeal, youth drama and, above all, patriotism (after which a Union Jack unfurls to resonant lines from *Henry V*). Finally, "Mr. Calthorp" is announced as "the greatest Shakespearean actor in captivity," and his chosen subject as "his marvelous impersonation of Douglas Fairbanks" in *The Taming of the Shrew*. Handley ascribes "good taste" to Calthorp's selection of Anna Mae Wong, already a famous international star, as his leading lady. It is clearly another jibe: Wong starred in the first two-strip Technicolor feature, *The Toll of the Sea* (dir. Chester Franklin, 1922), and achieved prominence as the villainous Asiatic betrayer in Fairbanks's most popular film, *The Thief of Bagdad* (dir. Raoul Walsh, 1924) by casting many a furtive glance while adorned with attire that revealed a former dancer's grace (etc.). Following that, she played one of the two preferred roles then available to Asian actors (paralleling the male equivalents of Sessue Hayakawa, who came to fame slightly earlier as a sexual "collector" in

Cecil B. DeMille's *The Cheat* of 1915), that of the ineradicably Asiatic villainess or the demure Chinese American sophisticate.

In Hitchcock's burlesque, the leather-clad Donald Calthorp rides onto a soundstage on a large motorbike with an even larger sidecar, demanding "[H]ast thou a daughter Mary...I mean Katherine?" Unable to stop the bike circling, even after he leaps out, he cracks his whip in its direction, announcing "Gaze on me then, and go tell her that Doug has come to woo her." A rain of tires, basins, and other improbably large missiles precedes the emergence atop the stairway of a bikini-clad Wong, screaming what sounds like Chinese obscenities. The first pie she hurls misses him, but the second hits him squarely in the face. William Shakespeare enters, guffawing, to Doug's annoyance. One of the Shrew's pies levels Shakespeare. Amidst the chaos, the screen fades ominously to black. Hitchcock vacillated, but eventually made Wong's homeland his own adopted country, as did a considerable number of European émigré directors, a subject treated at greater length in due course.[68] He continued, on occasion, to steal lines and routines from Shakespeare, as the titles of his films confess.

It will suffice for the present to note that a particularly important element of the genius of Hollywood's system was its syncretism and capacity to assimilate, and in so doing transform, varied sources of influence. Hitchcock, who carried both the British genres in which he specialized and his early German Expressionist training to the United States, might be one of the proofs that the fraternal bond proved more durable than the sense of sibling rivalry. It was, as Michael Bristol contends, evident from an early period in Ralph Waldo Emerson's description of Shakespeare as the individualist "who wrote the text of modern life" and who was "the father of the man in America."[69] The bond is further affirmed in the cultural geography of public monuments, as revealed, for instance, by the Folger Shakespeare Library, the most extensive archive of materials that specializes in the works of a single author. Its conscious placement near the U.S. Capitol and the memorials to Washington and Lincoln, he suggests, cemented the notion that "Shakespeare constitutes a crucial link or point of mediation within what is now conceived as a historically unified Anglo-American culture."[70] While this notion of cultural continuity is certainly a crucial component of the "Shakespeare industry" on which Bristol focuses, its particular manifestations are far from uncomplicated, as we will have cause to observe in greater detail in this book's second chapter, which is devoted to the first surviving feature film based on Shakespeare that happened not only to be American, but also to be one that could not have been made elsewhere.

Moreover, by the time Hitchcock began to make his most important feature films in the United States in the 1950s, the focus of industrial competition had shifted from rival film industries to that of network television, a phenomenon that, together with postwar suburbanization, rapidly depleted the audiences at movie theatres. America's cinematic Shakespeare of the period reflects a concern with winning back its audience through technological innovation and an appeal to quintessentially "cinematic" genres that the colorless small screen, with its then paltry sound system, could only emulate feebly. Hence, as recently as 1988, one finds the following observation by the same Samuel Marx who had a hand in the MGM *Romeo and Juliet*: "[C]oncerning Shakespeare on film, which may be of interest to students of adaptation, it strikes me that in the Musicals of Shakespeare, the writers take the greatest liberties, yet make the best movies. *Kiss Me Kate* had music by Cole Porter and was adapted by Sam and Bella Spewack from *The Taming of the Shrew*. When that same play was done straight, or fairly straight, with Elizabeth Taylor and Richard Burton, it wasn't as good. Then, of course, there was that marvelous picture *West Side Story*, which is generally known to be a modern version of *Romeo and Juliet*."[71]

★ ★ ★

Even before the emergence of the Musical as a technological counterblast both to network television and scary Reds in the 1950s, the studios occasionally ventured into Shakespearean territory in search of prestige productions and star vehicles. That the genius of the system, as French theorist André Bazin dubbed Hollywood's production-line system of film manufacture, was not an entirely constraining phenomenon that suppressed individual creativity (as such deliberate appropriations of Shakespeare suggest), finds ample illustration in two divergent adaptations that came at the beginning and end of the efflorescence of the studio era, both made by one of the quintessential studio directors, George Cukor. The better known of them, even if for its negative influence on Laurence Olivier, Renato Castellani, and Franco Zeffirelli, was his first. In 1935, following the introduction of Hollywood's most drastic self-censorship up to that period (the Production Code of 1934, known as the Hays Convention after its principal author), Warner Bros. had filmed a version of *A Midsummer Night's Dream* based on a stage production by noted German stage director Max Reinhardt. The latter, despite heavy publicity, was only a moderate success at the box office, but, as we have occasion to note subsequently, it did win Will Hays's personal approbation. Although the film hardly sparked a Shakespeare cycle, MGM, in many respects the most successful studio of the "Golden Age" of the 1930s and 1940s, which boasted of having "more stars than there are in the heavens," promptly announced an even more stellar *Romeo and Juliet* (1936) that it claimed had been in production for more than two years. It had been assigned to Cukor, who had already gained something of a reputation for his skill with actors, a skill perhaps necessary to lend credence to a group of supposed teenagers played by a less than youthful Norma Shearer, Leslie Howard, and Basil Rathbone, and to a permanently intoxicated, fifty-four-year old John Barrymore, once the great American Hamlet of his generation and America's first Shakespeare specialist among actors to try his hand at the talkies, but now requiring maintenance in a nearby sanatorium during the shooting.

It's mismatched stars notwithstanding, *Romeo and Juliet* received intense publicity. Two tie-in books by such leading publishers as Random House and Batsford, the first containing the stars' interpretations of their roles and the second the shooting script, came out in the year of its release, as did an early example of a film advertising a prestigious feature, *Master Will Shakespeare* (1936), a short directed by one of the future masters of the B-Horror film, Jacques Tourneur.[72] The intricacy of such advertising, detailing even costume designer Oliver Messel's use of Renaissance paintings as inspiration, was no doubt due to the interest taken in the project by the most influential head of production then working in Hollywood (and Shearer's doting husband), Irving Thalberg. Selecting it as the studio's "prestige project" of that year, Thalberg commandeered his most important personnel and imported Cornell Shakespeare scholar William Strunk, ostensibly to preserve the authenticity of text and ambience (the professor obtained a credit title to himself, as "literary consultant," in lettering second in size only to that of the stars). The art director was to be Cedric Gibbons who, like Messel, reportedly spent months researching Renaissance art for the project. Like the neo-Expressionist Anton Grot at Warners (who designed *A Midsummer Night's Dream* simultaneously), and William Cameron Menzies, who had come to fame with his monumental sets for Douglas Fairbanks's 1924 *Thief of Bagdad* and who also designed Sam Taylor's production of *The Taming of the Shrew*, Gibbons belonged to a rarified elite among art directors who gave each of the studios its signature visual style. By the late 1920s the notion of going to Italy to shoot on location (which had proved a near disaster in the case of MGM's 1924 epic *Ben Hur*) would have been thought preposterous, and so Gibbons fashioned an ideal, camera-friendly Verona of the mind, based on preserved locales and paintings of Renaissance Italy, but nevertheless redolent of his own style. James Welsh, Richard Vela, and John Tibbets note the film's shimmering black-and-white contrasts (due in part to high key lighting), a pervasive characteristic of Gibbons's Art Deco-inspired style and that today register as charming artifice.[73] A contemporary critic praised the production as having "the most expensive sets ever used ... by far the most realistic and hence the most satisfactory."[74]

Thalberg's extraordinary interventions on behalf of this film (he even watched all the takes of the monumental balcony scene) no doubt contributed to his premature demise not long after its release, but even his own comments suggest that this notion of Realism is highly relative: "The minute fidelity with which the screen can produce every detail of background and setting has led to the belief that the special province of the screen is Realism. This is undoubtedly true when the period of the play is our own mechanistic age. But the screen is equally able to portray the setting appropriate for *Romeo and Juliet*... This is the new province which the art of the motion picture has now captured."[75]

Such a conception of a "period Realism" became, in effect, a cornerstone of spectacle films not only in Hollywood but also in the Italy of the 1930s and the post–World War II French "Films of Quality" sponsored by the government, and later reviled by François Truffaut and the critics of the avant-garde journal *Cahiers du cinéma* who provided the impetus for the French New Wave of the 1960s. Indeed, when the Italian Neorealist movement that seemingly arose from the ashes of World War II revitalized European filmmaking in the late 1940s, its cause was taken up by the journal's founder and the most important of the phenomenological critics of film, André Bazin, who proclaimed that the works of such directors as Vittorio De Sica were quintessential examples of Realism in the cinema, the fulfillment of the ontological veracity promised by the medium. Yet Kristin Thompson has famously pointed to a number of assumptions that Bazin makes about the Realism of De Sica's *Bicycle Thieves* (1948), and that its version of Realism defines itself against the Hollywood narrative model which it continually cites (most obviously in the form of celebrated Hollywood movie posters such as the one of Rita Hayworth as Gilda that the hero is smoothing onto a hoarding when his bicycle is stolen).[76] Symptomatic of this stress on Realism is Renato Castellani's version of *Romeo and Juliet*; indeed, the director went so far as to claim that he entered filmmaking as a result of his disgust with MGM's *Romeo and Juliet*, underlining his disavowal of his studio antecedent by employing a number of trademark Neorealist techniques such as the use of what Bazin called an "amalgam of players," a mix of professional and nonprofessional actors, "authentic" locations in preference to studio sets, and semidocumentary elements in cinematography (as well as a postsynchronized dialogue track that

Anderegg describes as "perhaps the signal curse of postwar Italian cinema").[77] It is Anderegg, also, who points out that Castellani's Neorealism departed significantly from Bazin's Realist doctrines, despite his apparent rejection of Hollywood's codes.[78] Castellani "recreated pictorial works for the camera," quotes Rothwell, who adds slyly, "before the idea was discovered by Jonathan Miller and made into a house style for the BBC Shakespeare plays."[79] Nor was Castellani able to locate an ideal Verona in Italy, for he found himself having to blend locations in a number of Italian cities to conjure one of his own.

At first Cukor's second Shakespeare-based film, the 1947 *A Double Life*, for which MGM engaged in another insufficiently studied studio practice in "lending" him to Universal, might seem a particularly egregious star vehicle, designed solely for the bravura performance of its lead. Even here, however, a more in-depth consideration of the nature of what appears to a be a Ruth Gordon-Garson Kanin riff on *Othello* (in which there is no Iago as such but an Othello who is his own worst enemy, played by an actor who has trouble making distinctions between his day-to-day existence, the lives of the characters he inhabits, and even the objects of his fatal attentions)[80] reveals an entire theatrical history as its inspiration. It also reveals that far from cultural autonomy, American cinema could still borrow from that Russian strain of Modernism that had not survived Stalin, even though to describe the plot is to suggest a sense of comedy entirely absent in the film itself: for instance, the great showstopping innovation by Anthony John, well known to his fans for his ability to transform himself into the characters he plays on stage, is the coup de théâtre he administers fatally to his Desdemona. Runaway success and an interminably extended theatrical run proving unendurable, John's suffocating osculations grow in intensity, with predictable consequences (albeit to the "wrong" victim who has more in common with Bianca than Desdemona).

Although Method Acting had not yet achieved a suitable name for itself, let alone the eminence it was to occupy in post-Marlon Brando Hollywood, Kanin, who was both dramatist and stage director, was obviously familiar with its precepts, and rather archly points to its inherent dangers. The trepidation that Method Acting provoked was probably not due to Red Scares alone (which is not to deny that Hollywood proved an easy target for politicians attempting to make the most of such scares, as Elia Kazan and Brando were soon to discover), but due rather to the painful lessons of history. The most celebrated instance of Shakespearean Method Acting-gone-wrong had occurred nearly a century earlier. In 1864, in the hope of raising funds to build a statue to Shakespeare in Central Park, America's most famous family of Shakespearean actors undertook a production of *Julius Caesar*, with Edwin Booth as Brutus and his brother John Wilkes as Antony. Michael Kauffman notes that even early in his career John Wilkes acted in a succession of plays involving tyrannicide, and that he was, by a curious irony, an admirer of John Brown, whom he called "the grandest character of the century."[81] He missed his own chance to be the grandest character of the stage when he accidentally shot himself on the night he was to open as Hamlet, that role becoming the virtual property of his brother Edwin, who played it to triumphant acclaim when a year after Abraham Lincoln's assassination he reversed his decision to give up the theatre.[82] Lincoln, whose prose was immeasurably more eloquent than John Wilkes's turgid effusions, and which owes much to Shakespeare (even to the extent of inviting the ridicule of the *New York Herald*), sought to avert civil strife when in his first inaugural address he called upon the "better angels of our nature" to allow the reconciliation of North with South.[83] Yet the role John Wilkes assigned to him was not Hamlet but Caesar, and in seizing Brutus for himself he finally upstaged his brother, usurping his role in casting himself as Michelangelo's and Milton's self-sacrificing Republican (rather than Dante's traitor): uttering Virginia's revolutionary state motto, "Sic semper tyrannis," he leapt onto the stage upon fatally wounding Lincoln at Ford's Theater, bringing the curtain down on the Good Friday performance of the comedy *Our American Cousin*.

Kanin, however, probably had more recent developments in mind than the younger Booth's objections to rival Shakespeareans. The Actors Studio, from which the Method soon emerged, was founded in November 1947, only months after the release of the film. But the Stanislavskian inheritance of Method Acting could not have been unknown to Kanin, who was already established as Broadway's insouciant answer to Noël Coward: indeed, it is difficult to resist the temptation to think that Kanin was probably spoofing Stanislavsky's predilection for *Othello* as a play, a role for which the latter studied costume and gesture (just as Olivier was to do later) before performing it as a Moor, and which he staged both at the start and toward the end of his illustrious career.[84] A number of Stanislavsky's protégés, including Olga Baclanova, Mikhail Chekhov, Maria Ouspenskaya, and Richard Boleslavsky, chose to immigrate and pursue careers in the United States, and Boleslavsky (presently joined by Ouspenskaya) founded the American Laboratory Theatre in 1923. Among their students were Lee Strasberg, Stella Adler, Elia Kazan, and Robert Lewis. It is with the intention of re-creating an American version of Stanislavsky's Moscow Art Theatre that in 1931 Strasberg cofounded the Group Theatre, stressing ensemble acting in the contemporary plays written by such playwrights as Clifford Odets. A widening rift between Adler and Strasberg led to the demise of the Group Theatre in 1939 (with Adler complaining to Stanislavsky, working with him in Paris to perfect her approach, and subsequently with Erwin Piscator at the New School in New York). Lewis and Kazan attended the courses she then offered, and revived the idea of Group Theatre by founding the Actors Studio (together with Cheryl Crawford).[85] Although Lewis left soon thereafter, Strasberg joined them and by 1951 was appointed artistic director. It was he who dubbed the approach to the acting technique being developed in New York "the Method." The parallel history of the Method on screen began almost simultaneously, when Kazan introduced it to Hollywood in spectacular fashion with his 1951 adaptation of Tennessee Williams's *A Streetcar Named Desire*, in which Adler's pupil Brando played Stanley Kowalski with an animalistic brutality designed to contrast with Vivien Leigh's gossamer Blanche DuBois.[86]

In this instructive sense, Shakespeare presided over yet another cinematic milestone, for here the soon triumphant Method found itself parodied even before it debuted on screen. While Cukor may have been aware of the long theatrical history to which Kanin and Gordon alluded in their comically dour screenplay, he was probably more concerned with its critical and box-office reception. Although the bravura lead role was initially written with Olivier, Vivien Leigh's partner and already a Shakespeare superstar, in mind, in the end it was tailored to the needs of a reluctant Ronald Colman, another British import and one of Hollywood's great matinee idols of 1930s and 1940s: Cukor supposedly enticed him with the promise that it would win him the Oscar that had twice eluded him. It did.

Shakespeare, then, was certainly good to his actors and to Hollywood studios seeking prestige or legitimacy of one kind or another; but at the box office he was what Anthony John might have referred to as the kiss of death. This situation prevailed even after the critical and box-office successes of later versions of *Romeo and Juliet*. According to Douglas Brode, the immense success of Franco Zeffirelli's 1968 *Romeo and Juliet* resulted from his absorption of criticisms of his earlier (1966) *Taming of the Shrew* and a conscious avoidance of the mistakes of his predecessor, Renato Castellani: with his collaborators Zeffirelli found what for Brode is an ideal balance between Shakespeare's words and the cinema's ability to translate description into visual fact, a balance that "remained the norm ever since."[87] One of Castellani's infelicities, according to Brode, had been an unfortunate reliance on Hollywood's then waning studio system. In the wake of the dismantling of theatre chains and the block-booking system mandated by the 1948 antitrust legislation enacted against Hollywood's studios, as well as an emergent post–World War II youth culture, the 1950s saw the emergence of drive-in theatres and exploitation genres on the one hand, and a restricted number of megabudget spectaculars that took advantage of technologies of which the television of the time was incapable, on the other. Among the latter were Technicolor and wide-screen epics such as the Elizabeth Taylor vehicles (in which as Cleopatra, for instance, she seemed burnished with all the wealth of Egypt), and the features that starred the youthful James Dean in the rebel-without-a-cause type of role. Brode observes that Laurence Harvey was at that time being sought as a replacement for the ill-fated Dean, and that in casting him as Romeo, Castellani might have wanted to import a teenaged rebel.[88] In the event, Harvey fell back on his theatrical experience and fell in love with his lines rather than with his winsome and sincere Juliet; the experience, or at least the critical reaction, must have worked wonders on Harvey as he was soon to turn into the perfectly disagreeable angry young man for his later performances in the British Free Cinema movement. It was Zeffirelli, most critics agree, who found the right formula for emphasizing the generation gap at a time when Hollywood had given up on Shakespeare, and whom Fortune favored with a propitious historical moment at the height of the youth protests against the Vietnam War, so discovering a ready audience locked in its own civil strife and with complaints far more specific than those Dean (or indeed Harvey) could articulate in the 1950s.

★ ★ ★

Paradoxically, the 1950s also witnessed a second high point in the history of the Musical, and its mixed ancestry and stylistic revamping in the post–network television era recapitulate the synthesizing genius of Hollywood's system. (Arthur Freed, for instance, was assigned a specialist unit that produced MGM's most glittering examples of the genre.) Its revival might best be explained by Rick Altman's well-known formulation of genre as a particular constellation of cinematic characteristics that he defines as semantic and syntactic in nature, so that "genre history is ... the story of the stabilization of a particular semantic field and its progressive association with a specific syntax."[89] The semantic and syntactic elements of Musicals had prior origins: the type of Musical to reach "maturity" earliest was the fairytale Musical, which borrowed from a tradition of European and American operetta spawned, above all, by the phenomenal success of Franz Lehar's celebration of Viennese frivolity, *The Merry Widow*.[90] The first director to specialize in the Musical, Ernst Lubitsch, adapted Viennese and French operetta even in the silent period, before his famous collaboration with Jeannette MacDonald and Maurice Chevalier, the latter a French import during the early talkie craze when "romantic" accents were at a premium.[91] Like most successful film genres, the Musical adapted easily to industrial and social change. By 1933 Busby Berkeley's elaborate choreography of chorus numbers had transformed it into a "New Deal" genre in which we repeatedly encounter the notion that one could entertain one's way out of the Great Depression.[92] Of course, World War II did more to hasten the end of the depression than the Musical, and Hollywood's audiences grew to unprecedented numbers in those years; it was the postwar economic boom that brought on the crisis, first of the 1948 Supreme Court decision to end studio monopolies of theatre chains, followed in short order by the advent of network television. Hollywood's response was to assert its superior technologies—and nowhere more so than in the Musicals produced by Arthur Freed's specialist unit at MGM. Another outstanding example of technological innovation and lavish production values typifying the big-budget films of the 1950s was *Kiss Me Kate* (dir. George Sidney, 1953) that in narrative terms adhered to the formulas for a fairly traditional Backstage Musical while employing technologies of which television was then incapable: vivid, highly saturated Technicolor images, a wide-screen aspect ratio requiring anamorphic lenses for projection, and stereophonic sound. It also incorporated the flights of fancy of Hollywood's great choreographer of the period, Hermes Pan, who had Sidney's actors practically leaping out of the screen by means of a short-lived 3-D technology that required audiences to wear stereoscopic spectacles. In contrast, the most talked about innovation of *West Side Story* (1961) was not its dynamic use of Super Panavision 70 technology, but its incorporation of naturalistic violence into what had hitherto been regarded as a genre more attuned to fantasy. Despite initial critical discomfort with its generic experimentation, its references to contemporary ethnic conflicts and street gangs, and its troubled genesis (Jerome Robbins, director of the musical numbers, was fired midway), the film went on to win more Academy Awards (10) than *Shakespeare in Love*.

Characteristically "American" genres (i.e., those dependent on their physical geographies and associated with Americana) were also pressed into service. Actors trying to recite Shakespeare in the Wild West could be found in Jean Yarborough's *Under Western Skies* (1945) and one of John Ford's most acclaimed Westerns, *My Darling Clementine* (1948); indeed, in Ford's early classic, *Stagecoach* (1939), both Shakespeare and Marlowe contribute to the repartee. But the 1950s, finessing of the "problem" of Renaissance idiom led to Shakespeare's resurrection as one of Hollywood's leading scenarists, one that eclipsed his former incarnation as a significant Hollywood screenwriter—or rather, he was to become so after one last grand, financially profligate gesture with Joseph Mankiewicz's big-budget *Julius Caesar* of 1953 for MGM, in which he not only preserved most of Shakespeare's lines but also contrived to have the reputedly inarticulate Marlon Brando (Antony) speak many of them. Brando's presence was in part due to producer John Houseman's insistence on the use of a mixed cast that included American actors (John Gielgud was Cassius and James Mason Brutus): it is possibly Houseman's earlier collaboration with Orson Welles on the anti-Fascist contemporary dress production of the play in 1937 that has led to considerable speculation as to the film's allegorical (anti-Red Scare) intent. It is thus worth observing that one of the first successful examples of the genre Shakespeare cycle of the 1950s that exploited him as scenarist was a film by Edward Dmytryk, one of the original "Hollywood Ten" impeached by the House Un-American Activities Committee. His *Broken Lance* (1954), one of the first Westerns made in CinemaScope, was based on *King Lear*, albeit rather loosely so, with the patriarch's sons disputing the use to which their premature patrimony could be put. Its parallels with Akira Kurosawa's 1985 *Ran* and only slightly more distant ones with the made-for-television *King of Texas* (dir. Merlin Miller, 2002) should not pass unnoticed. The film won Philip Yordan an Academy Award for Best Screenplay, and he went on to adapt another "Great Tragedy" into *Joe MacBeth* (1955), directed by the British B-movie specialist Ken Hughes. Set in New York, it was shot on London soundstages (*pace* Hitchcock), but was coded as a Hollywood Gangster film (in which the cast gamely attempts to translate some of Shakespeare's big speeches into the appropriate patois); the film proved the fountainhead for the Gangsta' *Macbeth*, which found its way into later stage and film adaptations, notably William Reilly's ironic New York Mafioso version of 1991, *Men of Respect*, that contains similarly witty translations of Shakespeare's lines into underworld argot. Appearing just months after the release of Martin Scorsese's *Goodfellas* (1990) and Francis Ford Coppola's *Godfather III* (1990), *Men of Respect* borrows from the past only to mimic and parody Hollywood's present-day gods. Another genre with a language of its own, the Western, thrived through the 1950s and still continues to reappear as an occasional *auteur* excursion. An example that came late in the Western's heyday was directed by one of its specialists, Delmer Davies, who succeeds in making the Cassio character (Jubal Troop) the hero of *Jubal*, the 1956 version of *Othello* in which Desdemona (Mae Horgan), trapped on a ranch owned by an ill-suited husband, turns seductress.

Without question the most fascinating and most discussed of the upscaled B-genre films attributed to Shakespeare's influence happens to be MGM's first big-budget Sci-fi film, *Forbidden Planet* (dir. Fred M. Wilcox 1956), shot in special-effects-enhancing CinemaScope and a vivid palette of colors made possible by recent improvements to the Technicolor process. It was initially conceived as a low-budget B film by Allen Adler (shortly to join a minor army of black-listed writers) and special-effects expert Irvin Block (a Shakespeare enthusiast). To Allen's and Block's surprise, MGM's executives were sufficiently persuaded by their enactment of the various roles in the film to budget it at a million dollars (a figure that nearly doubled during the course of shooting, so equaling that of the studio's preceding ancient Roman *Julius Caesar*).[93] *Forbidden Planet*'s many parallels with *The Tempest* did not prevent an initial rejection of such ex post facto attributions by Judith Buchanan, whose views have moderated over time to include it among "*Tempest*-evocative" narratives.[94] On the other hand, Chantal Zabus devotes a substantial portion of a chapter to the film in *Tempests after Shakespeare* and uncovers a source of influence that makes the debt to Shakespeare more evident (actually an instantaneous novelization of the film by Philip MacDonald under the pseudonym of W.J. Stuart). She adduces a range of characteristics to suggest that *Forbidden Planet* belongs to a venerable tradition of adapting the play to contemporary concerns, most notably those of the poets and playwrights of the "postcolonial" moment.[95] The film incorporated the use of a "robot" character (Robbie, the weightiest and most terrestrial of cinematic Ariels) and inaugurated the use of electronic music in film soundtracks. It also allegorized the cold war fear of intellectualism through its association of Freudian pop psychology with the dangerous use of the mind to unleash physical forces beyond (rational) human control. The planet on which the action takes place was once the domain of a super race of Krel, whose extinction is explained as the result of their abandonment of embodied corporeality for a state of pure consciousness unfettered by material desires and the social institutions that regulate them. For his part Morbius, the Prospero character, appropriates the technologies of mental projection not as the result of superior scientific training, but through his study of philology and his powers of decipherment: like scientists toying with translations of matter into energy, creating technologies and weapons whose science they do not fully comprehend, he, too, is the architect of visions he cannot contain or repress. Zabus holds that his name suggests *morbidus* (disease) and *morbus* (death);[96] but it also suggests Morpheus, and it is in the quasi-dreamlike state that Freud attempted to induce through hypnosis that Morbius proves his most controlling and, therefore, most dangerous. When the Ferdinand character, Commander Adams of Starship C57-D, and his crew are forced into an emergency landing on the Planet Altair IV despite Morbius's attempts to dissuade them, the crewmen begin to meet violent deaths. One of their number ventures unprepared to sample the Krel mind-enhancing technologies recuperated by Morbius, with fatal consequences: as he lies dying Dr. Ostrow explains that the Krel, unaware of what lurked in the recesses of their brains, had unleashed "monsters of the Id." The phrase is an apt description for a Caliban figure that is neither fish nor flesh, pure matter nor pure energy, but one eventually revealed to be Morbius's own psychic projection. The conscious Morbius's attempt to manipulate the thought processes of others has also suggested the predominance of the Superego in his mental constitution,[97] an explanation of sorts for his overdetermined paternal possessiveness, or his suspiciously Edenic explanation for the attire sported by his evidently nubile daughter (designed by Robbie, the paragon of the age of mechanical reproduction, but whose tastes are obviously of a minimalist variety). Of course, possessed of such mental powers, Morbius might have been secretly aware that back on terra firma the 1950s saw both a relaxation in film censorship and a new trend in advertising that Vance Packard described in 1957 as mobilizing "built-in sexual overtones," with psychological consultants in league with ad men when submitting that the scandalously revealing ads that appeared on giant billboards (captioned "I Dreamed I Stopped Traffic in My Maidenform Bra") were harmless since they represented a common dream-state wish fulfillment.[98] It was also in the 1950s, of course, that Hogarth Press began its publications of an authorized complete edition of Freud, containing James Strachey's translations of "das Es" (as "Id"), "Ich" (as "Ego"), and "Überich" (as "Superego"). In addition to its technological innovations and exemplary illustration of 1950s genre upscaling, *Forbidden Planet*'s recourse to Shakespeare also honed the cutting edges of Hollywood's pop science and mass marketing.

What is lacking on Altair IV and enters with Adams, the brave New World man (from the Old World, as is Ferdinand), is a properly developed Ego, equated in the film with normal human drives. His survival and eventual union with the Miranda character (Altaira or Alta, as in "alta/ego"), however, can be ensured only when the Superego relinquishes control over both material "possession" (daughter) and secret knowledge (of the quasi-nuclear technology that eventually consumes the planet). While it toys with its own Shakespeareanness, *Forbidden Planet* proves a more revealing commentary on popular cold war sentiments than that of Yutkevich's technologically competitive, cinematically more refined, and textually more literal version of Shakespeare. While Yutkevich's *Othello* affirms the Soviet vision of technology as an expression of collective enhancement, Wilcox's film takes advantage of the most sophisticated technologies then available to the medium to express its skepticism of technocracy.

This cycle of films bears comparison with the later one of the 1990s in that the latter came in the wake of the abatement of the cold war once Soviet hegemony over its Eastern European satellites imploded in the 1980s. The period witnessed the first American teen generation with sufficient disposable income to influence advertising, product marketing, and the prevalent themes and genres of both film and television. The "youth drama" Tommy Handley refers to in *Elstree Calling* may not have succeeded in harnessing the Bard's celebrity to British talkies with any notable success, but similar motives spurred a cluster of examples coinciding with the (1999) Best Picture Oscar—one of seven—for *Shakespeare in Love*. As with the 1950s cycle, the approach to Shakespeare's plays varies widely. The later films do, however, have distinctive elements in common. One is that they celebrate teen-queen stars of yore (Drew Barrymore, mitigating the caricatures in Raja Gosnell's 1999 *Never Been Kissed* with self-caricature) or now (Julia Stiles stealing the subplot in Gil Junger's 1999 *10 Things I Hate about You*, speaking Shakespeare and losing it very naturally as Ophelia in Michael Almereyda's *Hamlet* of 2000, and playing a pert, vulnerable version of the trophy girl, Dessie, in Tim Blake Nelson's 2001 *O*). What is more, while the earlier cycle sought to efface debts to Shakespeare, Almereyda goes so far as to present an abridged original text in a setting as contemporary as Kurosawa's and Kaurismaki's. In the other cases, Shakespeare is imposed on those who have crept unwillingly (or at times all too willingly) to school. Reporter Josie Carter gets to relive her adolescence and read passages of *As You Like It* in the classroom, and even to quote *The Merchant of Venice* while dancing; the militantly African American English teacher of *10 Things*, Mr. Morgan, gets to rap the first quatrain of Sonnet 141, while sidekick Michael borrows Macbeth's explanation of the events following Duncan's murder as a pickup line, as well as the first line of Sonnet 56 which he offers as social commentary about the simultaneous hunts for Kat and Bianca; in *O* a pregnant teacher discusses maternal instincts of a sort by scanning Lady Macbeth's hendecasyllabic, trochaic line about the "babe that milks me." Arguably the most intriguing instance of summoning the Bard, his cultural capital now redeemed with interest at the box office, occurs in the made-for-TV version of *The Tempest* (1998), in which the creole-affecting and voodoo affected Peter Fonda's Prosper, dispossessed of his plantation and exiled to Civil War Louisiana's swamplands, suddenly forgets himself and all sense of time and place, unleashing the first line of Prospero's abjuration of his occult power as if he were Shakespeare preparing to return to Stratford.

Yet in an age before the prevalence of teen sitcoms and *Home Alone* (or With Company) film series, network television more threatened than influenced cinema's magic. Television initially showed little promise of promoting a new audience for cinematic Shakespeare. On the contrary, suggest the notes included with the Criterion DVD reissue of Olivier's 1955 *Richard III*, the simultaneous NBC broadcast on the night the film opened in theatres brought a viewership in excess of sixty-two million. However, the cropped, edited, black-and-white version promoting General Motors might have led to the innovative film's rapid loss of distribution, a widely held misimpression of the film's production values no doubt compounded by the poor sound reproduction of Olivier's rapid-fire delivery. Inevitably, it was not long before the Bard began to appear as an object of fun on television, although his stock rose, according to Michael Bristol, as his commercial potential became increasingly apparent. His dual role as the snobbish representative of Europeanate highbrow culture and as the benign paternal New Englander envisioned by Ralph Waldo Emerson serves the often contradictory needs of consumer culture: he is a badge of academic respectability while at the same time being subject to the anti-intellectual parody on such TV shows as *Gilligan's Island* and *Happy Days*; he is accorded a high seriousness on *Star Trek*, but that seriousness may result from his success as a salesman of real estate and not merely as an entertainer.[99]

★ ★ ★

A recent revelation by the Lear-Picard of *King of Texas* might bring this discussion of the long-settled border dispute between television and film, now locked in symbiotic commercial embrace, to a fitting close. Patrick Stewart, best known for the role he plays as captain of the Starship Enterprise, is fond of relating the story of his reaction to critics accusing him of betraying his training as a Shakespearean actor by accepting a sinecure on on a television series. Yes, he is at times chagrinned by his automatic association with Jean-Luc Picard, he admitted to the BBC actor-turned-talk-show-host Sanjeev Bhaskar (in an episode aired in March 2005 on U.S. cable television), but then, as he once informed a snooty detractor, all those Shakespearean kings he played for the Royal Shakespeare Company were merely a preparation for taking the helm of a starship.[100] Besides being an outstanding actor fully cognizant of the demands of the different media, Stewart is also a figure of cultural negotiation whose activities encompass terrains that exploit a form of friendly (and lucrative) rivalry rather than renewing the atmosphere of the riotous spectatorial clashes of yesteryear. Born in the north of England and required to shed his regional accent for the purpose of achieving the correct standards of "received pronunciation" (a matter that also caused Branagh difficulties in his student days at the Royal College of Dramatic Arts), Stewart's once and future role consists of playing an adopted Frenchman endowed with Royal Shakespearean tones, condemned to wander space for eternity like a futuristic Flying Dutchman who, but for his commonplace reasonableness, could be at the helm of one of Herman Melville's allegorically multicultural vessels.

Even before the advent of Stewart, however, Shakespeare played an indirect, if by no means insignificant, role in mediating the success of British film personnel in Hollywood: the actor who has received the largest number of nominations for Best Actor (9) happens to be Laurence Olivier, and the Hollywood director who has by far the largest volume of critical literature devoted to him happens to be Hitchcock, who turned his Britishness into something of a trademark in his later television appearances. Branagh's use of Hollywood stars in extravagant cameos or as posterized versions of themselves parallels Zeffirelli's use of Hollywood's glitterati. In his *Hamlet* Zeffirelli amplifies the role of Gertrude, for instance, to allow Glenn Close to reprieve, albeit with well-observed cunning, her customary Hollywood role of sexual predator/prey, while leaving smaller roles to seasoned British Shakespearean actors; indeed, in this instance Zeffirelli may avail himself of a marketable amplification of divergences of performance styles and traditions. So, for instance, the controversy over a remark once attributed to Trevor Nunn, proves according to the researches of Maria Magro and Mark Douglas to have originated not with Nunn himself but with the (American) organizers of the Telluride Film Festival whom they quote as saying "The film

[*Twelfth Night*] succeeds in part due to Nunn's decision to ignore the box-office lure of Hollywood stars, and to cast all the parts with outstanding British actors who can actually speak Shakespeare's lines with proper cadence and clarity."[101] It suggests a typical commercial strategy for independent filmmaking, turning a deficit (the dearth of "bankable" Hollywood stars who would bring in the film's revenue over a weekend) into a virtue, and, in the process, feigning the resurrection of a rivalry long laid to rest as a means of boosting its spectatorship.

Even the New York theatre scene seems to have come full circle. Writing of the prevalence of British stage directors on Broadway (in the 2004–2005 season), Charles Isherwood pens a *New York Times* article that has a Union Jack flying above an original cast photograph of *A Streetcar Named Desire*. "A Strong British presence on Broadway," he claims, "is hardly new." And he continues: "The Great White Way has long suffered from a mild case of Anglophilia, and is, without a doubt, much healthier for it. But this striking confluence of British directors teamed with American classics suggests that American directors may not be equally esteemed by producers, at least when it comes to the classics—even the most American of classics."[102] In the end, even cultural anxiety yields to common cause.

If productive distinctions are to be made between national Shakespeares, the effort should not be in the cause of the increasingly outworn concept of nation: like the aesthetic objects they catalogue, studies of alternative traditions of Shakespeare should at once celebrate cultural distinctiveness and cultural diversity. In this context it might serve us to return once more to the contrast I drew between the Russian and American Shakespeares who are products of a complex and much-debated nexus of traditions, foreign and local, high and low. The Russian Shakespeare, who like the characters of *King Lear* has lived long and seen much, is a diachronic one whose present has been shaped profoundly by his past, while the American one (if we can call this multifarious Shakespeare "one") is more of the moment, living in the kind of passionate present of the lovers in *Romeo and Juliet*, transcending the limits of spatial separation from a "homeland" to participate in the mosaic resulting from the confluence of differing but constantly renewed traditions. Kozintsev's Lear can only shed the torments of existence by proceeding backward through the pages of Russian history and learning through experience to feel what wretches feel; the Puerto Rican Juliet of *West Side Story*, Maria, lives on in the knowledge that while everything is not free in America, the transcendence of cultural difference remains the foundation of its promise of individual freedom.

Film Studies??

While the "category" of Shakespeare, which underlies the discussion of adaptation as a cultural process, justly takes up a substantial portion of this chapter, the other similarly invoked titular categories, Film Studies, Visual Culture, and Modernity, merit the same kinds of consideration. To take the first of these terms, few today would question the ascendancy of Film Studies as an academic discipline, but the struggle to achieve such standing remains evident in a persistent, if fictive, claim to autonomy that relegates discussions of cinema's many borrowings to a primitivist discourse; and this is no doubt the result of a Cinderella complex wherein the more established areas of study to which it was once invariably annexed, English and various language departments, serve as the wicked, burly stepsisters. Thus, without ever having been modish, adaptation, particularly after the polemics of the New Wave *auteurs*, began to seem outmoded. This is not to argue that a theorist such as Eisenstein was not better aware than anyone else of Dickens's or Pushkin's contributions to film form, of the possibilities painters such as El Greco could offer the medium, or that adaptation (whether of fiction or history) was culturally determined.[103] Rather, it is to emphasize that from the time of such early intuitions as that of George Bluestone's pioneering *Novels into Film* (1957) up to the recent appearance of comprehensive works of the order of Robert Stam's and Linda Hutcheon's, the study of adaptation in cinema has been patchy, unsystematic, and unrepresentative of the attention merited by the proportion of films that are, in fact, recognizable reworkings of drama, literature, the visual arts, and even music.[104] In his book on François Truffaut, Stam observes that even a militant *auteur* could, in time, come to elaborate an increasingly sophisticated idea of engagement with prior texts, even to the extent of providing an early intuition of the distinction that Hutcheon makes between adaptation as [textual] product and [cultural] process, for audiences are often as aware as authors of a "'palimpsestuous' intertextuality."[105] In an impressive act of accommodating the various sorts of textual slippages between media and the rapid emergence of digital film technologies, increasingly common phenomena in what Hutcheon describes as an environment in which adaptation has "run amuck," a recent (2004) plebiscite added a term to what used to be the SCS, now the SCMS (Society for Cinema and Media Studies). At the organization's conference, the following year, Thomas Elsaesser joked that we were now engaged in the study of the Medium-Formerly-Known-As-Cinema.

★ ★ ★

While space does not permit a discussion of all the implications of cinema's increasingly blurry boundaries, its properties as a medium suggest some of the potential paths that discussions of film adaptations may yet profitably traverse. Following the general adoption of synchronized soundtracks after 1927, films began to consist of four simultaneous aspects or dimensions: editing, cinematography, mise en scène, and sound. I have made particular note of these features in the individual films I discuss since they are fundamental to understanding one of the three simultaneous registers of adaptation, the movement from medium to medium.[106] Of the two other registers the most commonly discussed happens to be that of text to text; the least that of culture to culture, although no one doubts that by their nature texts are culturally embedded.[107] Those who undertake film adaptations are thus compelled to make a series of interpretive decisions at the outset, and these decisions in turn suggest a typology of tendencies that may be expressed in a convenient, tabular form:

Tendencies in Film Adaptations

To preserve the printed text, score or choreography (A+)	To alter the printed text, score or choreography (A−)
To preserve the setting (B+)	To alter the setting (B−)
To preserve the time period (C+)	To alter the time period (C−)
To preserve the performance tradition (D+)	Not to preserve the performance tradition (D−)
To preserve the sociopolitical context of the original (E+)	To amend the sociopolitical context of the original (E−)

So, for instance, we may encounter a film such as Kenneth Branagh's *Hamlet* that pieces together a "complete" version of Shakespeare's *Hamlet*s with added explanatory narration; but the meaning of those lines undergoes a subtle transformation because, as Sarah Cardwell inquires of those critics who have seen the film as an intense expression of fidelity, "how can a filmic presentation, set in [the Regency period] long after Shakespeare's death, possibly be seen as approximating most accurately the play that Shakespeare envisioned?"[108] Even if one grants that it is a moot point whether temporal authenticity would require a medieval Danish setting or a Renaissance English version of it (on the grounds of liberality I would grant either a C+), Branagh's admixture of acting styles ranging from the Hollywood cameo to the broadly Royal Shakespearean stage delivery of old makes his film A+, B−, C−, D−, E− according to the scheme given above. In contrast Branagh not only trims the majority of the lines from his version of *Love's Labour's Lost* but adulterates them with interpolations dragged in (sometimes with the flimsiest of verbal cues and musical pretexts) from the lyricists who composed the more celebrated classical Hollywood Musicals, a translation that is only occasionally, and sometimes goofily, evocative of one of the medium's technical high points. Surprisingly, this approach is more consonant with the practices of Renaissance theatre than the *Hamlet* approach, as amply attested by Shakespeare's treatment of his sources and as evidenced by what we know of stagecraft at the Globe, which accommodated but two hours' worth of actors' traffic with time set aside for singing, dancing, and brawling. A−, B−, C−, then, but yet resolutely D+ and, with a World War looming instead of a Spanish threat, perhaps even E+.

Many of the more intriguing adaptations are those by directors who contrive to turn − into +, or to play with the possibilities of doing so. Laurence Olivier and his text editor Alan Dent, vigorous pruners of text, struggled to maintain the balances of characterization even at the expense of reassigning lines. In *Henry V* (1944) Olivier also finds ingenious correspondences to achieve B+, C+, and D+ in representing both theatrical conventions and cinematic ones; even so, like Kozintsev, he did not shirk from reformulating the sociopolitical determinants to serve an ideological purpose, in his case the explicit one of war propaganda. Alone among adapters of Shakespeare, Orson Welles strived to straddle the tendencies in all of the categories, and his films are of such interest in this regard that I devote a separate chapter to them. Likewise, Akira Kurosawa (to persist with the anglicized name under which his films were released outside Japan) is among the more surprising directors in terms of this schema, as he went to great lengths to seek dramatic as well as historical equivalents for his *jidai-geki* (or period film) versions of Shakespeare. To this end, he uses the filter of "national" culture to achieve B+, C+, and D+ at the necessary compromise of A, which is nevertheless reflected in paraphrased dialogue and borrowed imagery. Furthermore, like some of Shakespeare's Renaissance contemporaries, he attempts to provide moral commentaries on the action through narrative amplifications, thus attaining a form of E++. That in many ways this final E category is the one most important to him might be seen in his willingness to abandon all the other + tendencies in his version of *Hamlet*, so subtly contemporary that it escaped detection as a Shakespeare film for more than a generation despite a title, *The Bad Sleep Well* (1960), that even in Japanese alludes to *Macbeth*. Another interesting "E" devotee, and one clearly less concerned with matters of narrative fidelity, is Eric Rohmer who was one of the group of filmmakers who were critics working for Bazin's journal *Cahiers du Cinéma*. A little older than fellow Shakespeareans Chabrol and Godard, he remained closer to Bazin's theories and hewed to the literary tastes of such Left Bank filmmakers as Alain Resnais and Agnès Varda, avant-garde companions to the Parisian New Wave directors but given to rather more "elite" artistic tastes (his films repeat Pascal's Wager in various forms, and even his assumed name comes from the notorious realist Erich von Stroheim and the novelist Sax Rohmer, the latter a homonymous pun in English).[109] Best known for conversational, Balzac-like cycles of films that evolve over the years, his adaptation of Chrétien de Troyes's medieval romance *Perceval* (1978) creates an extreme, audacious version of the flattened perspectives that Olivier borrowed from illuminated medieval manuscripts for his *Henry V*. The second of his Four Seasons tetralogy, *Conte d'hiver* (*A Winter's Tale* 1992), although played in a very un-Olivieresque palette of drab browns, blues, and grays—each film having its own color scheme—makes even more insistent claims on Shakespeare and seems to pay tribute to Truffaut's idea of an engagement between the adapted work and the adaptation, and to his not-long-deceased colleague's love of incorporating theatrical scenes into his films. The film, like the play, revolves around the fate of its female protagonist, and for those who see this late work of Shakespeare's as a Christian allegory, the film has unmistakable thematic parallels to the original in its almost anti-Pascal-like embrace of faith, celebrating the triumph of divine providence and the redemptive power of art.[110]

★ ★ ★

While a number of such films and even entire episodes of the long-running TV series *Star Trek* similarly rework Shakespeare's themes in an attempt to draw social or political parallels, even more common are those in which the dramatist makes a guest appearance and to which the schema I have suggested above does not apply. These are obviously not Shakespeare films as such. Nevertheless, a number of them cannot fail to be of interest to those concerned with the subject. Even a cursory survey yields some nuggets: Cecil B. DeMille's *Triumph* (1924) parodies the balcony scene from *Romeo and Juliet*, while Alan Parker's *Fame* (1980) does not; Charlie Chaplin's *A King in New York* (1954) enables him to demonstrate possible readings of "To be, or not to be," while Penny Marshall's *Renaissance Man* (1994) permits Danny DeVito his shot at Hamlet; Jocelyn Moorhouse's *A Thousand Acres* (1997) works with *King Lear*; Peter Weir's *Dead Poets Society* (1989) incorporates scenes from *A Midsummer Night's Dream*, while Miss Piggy was known to regale Kermit the Frog with lines both from this play and *Romeo and Juliet*; and, naturally, when Shakespeare hit the Big Time in the 1990s, a riot of Bardic cameos and bardoclastic spoof sequences ensued both on film and television, if only to amplify what had been happening for the better part of a century.[111]

For those who continue to share an interest in the Medium-Formerly-Known-As-Cinema perhaps the Shakespeare films that have the most immediate interest are those that contribute to discussions that have been enduring scholarly preoccupations. Of crucial interest in this regard is the fact that in addition to its four simultaneous dimensions, film is a compound medium consisting of five tracks, each assembled separately through entirely different technologies and channeled through diverse media: the acoustic tracks consist of recorded dialogue, music, and sound effects, and the visual ones of images and written text. Perhaps more than any other adaptations, those of Shakespeare are deeply connected with the functioning of these tracks and, being so, address much-debated issues of genre, performance, and the relationship between media. One of the few sustainable arguments that Shakespeare films constitute a genre, for instance, as advanced by Michael Anderegg, is that, as in documentary films (but certainly not fictional ones), the acoustic tracks take precedence. Whereas in documentary the narrator's voice determines all meanings, in the Shakespeare genre it is the dialogue that has come down to us that enjoys preeminence. The rigor of this argument is unassailable. Two recent (2001) films such as Billy Morrissette's *Scotland, PA* and Tim Blake Nelson's *O* (2001) are close paraphrases of *Macbeth* and *Othello* respectively, modernizing the language but presenting abridged and slightly modified scenes in the approximate order found in the Folio versions. However, they require no prior knowledge of Shakespeare to stand on their own as coherent texts: they may be paraphrases, derivatives, spin-offs, or offshoots (all terms used by critics), but by this rigorous measure they are films of Shakespearean inspiration or derivation rather than Shakespeare films. The only alternative argument for such a genre might be one based on media specificity, namely that film is predominantly a visual medium and that therefore a Shakespeare film should be judged only by the excellence of its translation of words into images.

I will return to this argument, already made in 1927, in another context, but pause here to articulate a paradox. Morrissette's film offers surreptitious parodies of a number of previous Shakespeare films, and effects its spoofing not through overt physical comedy but through a sophisticated use of different film tracks. The principal target is Roman Polanski's *Macbeth* (1971), whose youthful protagonists' sexual attraction to each other (conceivably influenced by Playboy organization funding) becomes the subject of satire. Restauranteur Joe McBeth (James LeGros), who supplants "Duncan's" with a name-logo that bears an unmistakable resemblance to that of a well-known fast food chain promoting carnivory, possesses an uncanny resemblance to his predecessor, Jon Finch, even if his name suggests a *reductio ad absurdum* of the Gangsta' *Macbeth*. Polanski's Horror-film metaphysics, including the cyclic opening and closing (attributable to Jan Kott and critic-scriptwriter Kenneth Tynan), yields to a theory of history-as-accident in the face of divine indifference and the incompetence of evil, here represented by a flamboyantly weird flower-child-gone-wrong triumvirate (two of whom even get into a stag costume to send up Michael Cimino). So it is that Duncan gets his head deep-fried by accident, that the postcarnivorous police lieutenant (a deadpan Christopher Walken) kills McBeth unintentionally, and that rural America gets a vegetarian fast food restaurant. A musical reference to the MC's voice in *Cabaret* (dir. Bob Fosse 1972) refers to a Christopher Isherwood story that serves as a snapshot of Weimar Germany, an intriguing possibility for Scotland, PA. In another scene, Lieutenant McDuff, having been misled by Mrs. Pat McBeth, plays an inspirational New Age recording as he drives back from a distant hunting ground. At this point the dialogue track parodies Almereyda's Zen-like reworking of "To be, or not to be" ("To be, is to inter-be," and so on), and a pacifying voice intones on the car stereo: "Tomorrow is tomorrow. Tomorrow is not today. Today is who I am." Meanwhile, the image track treats Julie Taymor's *Titus* (2000) ruthlessly, for Pat McBeth imagines that she cannot rid herself of the damned burn mark left by the oil spattered by the frying Duncan, and ends up by hacking off her left hand. Unlike Titus (and indeed Lavinia), she succumbs to the injury leaving not a spot of blood, damned or otherwise.

Bloodlessness was certainly not a characteristic of Polanski's richly conceived film. Consummate in its use of reds, blacks, and browns to heighten the gore, and in its selective sound amplification (of hacked flesh, the clash of steel, the cries of birds, the patter of water drops, and the flutter of feathers), it certainly raises another question about genre. Not only is it one of the most consistent examples of re-creating a period complete with bearbaitings and casual executions (adopting Shakespeare's Renaissance setting rather than an early medieval Scotland), but it is also one that borrows its conventions of treating the acoustic and visual tracks from the Horror film. Indeed, Banquo's floating ghost, the Charles Mansonesque-slaughter of the Macduff family heightened by offscreen diegetic screaming, monstrous point-of-view shots such as those from the perspective of Macbeth's decapitated head, all confirm the film as belonging firmly to the aesthetic established by the highly successful, visually lavish midbudget Hammer Films cycle that in the capable hands of actors Christopher Lee and Peter Cushing contributed significant revenues to the coffers of a near-moribund 1960s British film industry. These characteristics so embarrassed Jack Jorgens, an early and sensitive commentator on Shakespeare films, that he all but apologizes for them at the start of his discussion of Polanski's work. It is Jorgens, however, who notes that for Polanksi the true epitome of evil does not reside in the bewitched protagonists or even the Weird Sisters themselves, but in the perfectly "ordinary" Ross, for he alone and without conscience manages to commit acts of treachery and ruthlessness that at every turn win him social advantage.[112] With the possible exception of *West Side Story*, perhaps no generic transformation has been as subtle, faute de mieux, in its invocation of the history of the "receiving" medium, and if Welles attempts to create films that might be categorized as A, B, C, D, E, then Polanski enlists genre and the terrors of his own life to obtain the effect of A+, B+, C+, D+, E+. Since I can find no comparable example and because the schema's applicability to cinematic versions of stage drama is reasonably obvious, I allow it to remain implicit in the discussions that follow. Before leaving Polanski's film for the present, however, I would point out that it foregrounds an intriguing commonality among Shakespeare adaptations, namely, that certain plays like *Macbeth* seem to invite generically centripetal adaptations, creating microgenres of a sort: the Horror or Gangster *Macbeth*, the *gendai-geki* (contemporary film) Big Business *Hamlet*, the apocalyptic *Lear*. Others, particularly the troublesome Comedies, seem to invite a centrifugal diversity of approaches.

Perhaps another type of film that complicates the idea of genre by toying with it is Al Pacino's *Looking for Richard* (1996), ostensibly a documentary *cinéma vérité* about his intended stage version of *Richard III*. Here the very idea of what should be an A+ or C+ or even an E+ becomes the focus of attention: with Pacino explaining the action and motivations of the characters, debating readings with actors, chatting to partygoers about their Shakespearean experiences, and taking a handheld camera to the streets to waylay passersby for comments, the acoustic tracks can legitimately prevail in the manufacture of meaning as a matter of generic expectation.[113] The discourse of authenticity is finessed to the point of dismissal: a seemingly inebriated British visitor to Stratford grants an interview by leaning into the handheld camera and denigrating foreign versions of Shakespeare; a gimmicky search for Shakespeare's birthplace culminates in the setting off of an alarm and the arrival of the fire department. Sir Derek Jacobi and Sir John Gielgud, reigning Stratfordians, pronounce on the possibilities of American actors doing Shakespeare, with Jacobi suggesting that English Shakespeare might have inhibitory qualities, and Gielgud pointing out Americans' lack of a sense of period owing to a dearth of reading and insufficient visits to art galleries; Peter Brook and Kenneth Branagh are roped in, to give it a film-savvy smart-theatre edge; and Kevin Kline offers anecdotes about the erotic potential of stage performances (for bored teenagers) in apology, one imagines, for not playing a more formal role. Pacino acts out the part of the inhibited American, but he certainly researches his role and admires the pictures in Shakespeare editions while doing so: he appears at the start on stage in a small theatre, costumed in period attire à la Olivier, but chickens out and retreats muttering a backstage "fuck" when the sole member of the audience, a William Shakespeare brought to life from Droeshout's Folio portrait, looks at him quizzically (an identical camera setup is used when at the end of the film the self-same Shakespeare looks away in dismay). Actors recite snatches of *Twelfth Night* and *Henry V*, and an Italian tourist mumbles "To be, or not to be" to prove that he is not totally unaware of the Bard. The film, in effect, cultivates its sense of documentary hodgepodgery, but in this instance an intentional and artful one, a disguise for some of its sophistications.[114]

Despite the pretense of filming a stage version, the actors are clearly always arranged for a film camera: this is most evident in the costumed set pieces, as in the placement of a bowl of strawberries on a table (allowing for the right kind of cut-in) before the soon-to-be-condemned Hastings, a table at which he is abandoned by the intimidated lords of the land, a conference described in the previous scene by a Shakespeare "expert" as a gathering of mafia dons. A flashback to Jane Shore, the mistress he shared with the dead king, envisions a comely character with no other function in the film but to magnify Richard's malevolence. Some shooting locations are simply too vast for theatrical enclosure, so it is clearly impossible that this is a film about a theatrical *Richard III*. It is, instead, a discourse on the choices facing film directors (and by extension actors) in both film and theatre. The narrative pretext thus exists to enable Pacino to explore more variations on processes of acting (at one point he even invokes "the Method") than perhaps found in any other Shakespeare film: actors debating and rehearsing readings in joint rehearsal, a director and his sidekick (Frederic Kimball) making interpretive decisions for them, actors playing theatrically as if on stage, actors playing theatrically for the purpose of filmmaking, actors playing as if being filmed (always true, for instance, of Winona Ryder during her "theatrical" rehearsals), actors playing to an invisible camera for close-ups, Richard adopting a cinematic declamatory style for addresses to large audiences, onlookers improvising for a camera, and others acting out *verité* in the full knowledge of the filmmakers' intent. The conceit of the film notwithstanding, Pacino is not really looking for Richard: he is trying to discover his inner Richard, revealing covertly throughout that he intends to reprise his best-known role. If his delivery is, on rare occasions, too insistently syllabic, his remains among the most provocative and well articulated Richards, particularly since the idea of playing his character as a Mafia don repeats not only by his sitting in funerary attire and dark glasses deciding the fate of the cast while in a limousine, but also through explicit verbal references in the film. The equation of Mafia don to dynastic politician seems complete, in fact, when the first part of *The Godfather*, in which Pacino's Michael ridicules the idea that politicians do not hire assassins, makes an appearance: Kevin Spacey's importunate

Buckingham is introduced with the suggestion that he plays a familiar pointman role as in the "Iran-Contra stuff."

What emerges is that Pacino's line readings, in particular, are deeply thought out, and his rehearsal scenes (not being rehearsals at all) are among the most intriguing in Shakespeare films of the kind. Kimball suggests, in introducing the great seduction sequence in *Godfatherly* tones, that Ryder, a spitfire Anne of frightened vulnerability, "needs protection." Yet, in Marlovian fashion, she seems to forget the social-climbing Nevilles' aspirations and her dangerous Lancastrian sympathies in succumbing to the idea that her dastardly Mafioso beau is indeed offering her the love token of her dead relatives. Not so Richard, for in a brief, startling insert of Pacino in his backward-turned baseball cap, he utters a cry of triumph that reveals his own lack of illusion: from this point we know that the character knows what the director is thinking. The generic borrowing, the transformation of high-class Gangster film to *verité* via Shakespeare seems complete when Richard begins to ail, imagining himself running a temperature and collapsing on a stairway in a public rehearsal of Richard's impending demise. The scene turns out in the end to be a tribute to Olivier and Kurosawa, but in rehearsal sans armor, it is a memorial reenactment parading as Method Acting, for the stairway business, done in the blackest of suits and matching glasses, inevitably invokes the ghost of Michael Corleone at his most Lear-like moment when he witnesses his daughter's assassination on a staircase (with a token nod, too, to the diabetic seizure that spells the end of Michael's reign as the *capo di tutti capi*). It is a role he cannot cease to inhabit, as he recognizes when the self-same *cinéma vérité* effect reappears when, as Shylock, he backs away from a prowling, Christian camera, reminding us inevitably of his little *Richard*.

★ ★ ★

Still another objection to the rigorist generic argument might stem from the way dialogue is used in Shakespeare films, for even before the advent of the medium one could discern quotation (either in the original or in translation), misquotation (as when Sigmund Freud misremembers the phrases he sprinkles throughout his work, when the Duke in *Huckleberry Finn* mangles what he can remember of them, when Orson Welles or Branagh substitute modern equivalents for words whose usage has changed), or dis(s)quotation (when the words are taken entirely out of context). Dis(s)quotation might be a genre in and of itself: the few moments of mirth in Eugene O'Neill's *A Long Day's Journey into Night*, for example, arise from a family love of Shakespeare that leads to witty remarks consisting of lines wrenched from their contexts. It is entirely possible that the exquisitely apposite cento in Robert Redford's *Quiz Show* (1994), in which a family meal is delayed as father and son dispute an ethical point entirely with Shakespeare's lines (a joust terminated by the mother's quote from *King Lear*), pays tribute to the play. A particularly famous example of this Eugene O'Neill effect occurs in Tom Stoppard's inventive film adaptation of his stage play *Rosenkrantz and Guildenstern Are Dead* (1990). Charged with spying on and betraying Hamlet, the hapless duo soon become his targets for verbal massacres that, save for occasional interruption by eructions, the clucking of Hamlet's pet rooster, or the like, proceed exactly as Shakespeare wrote them. Yet precisely because the befuddled courtiers obsessively analyze the rhetorical skullduggeries by which they are initially outwitted and eventually undone, and because their own provincially inflected "private" language is markedly different from the courtly jargon affected by characters speaking "Shakespeare," the net effect of the Renaissance playwright's words could not possibly differ more from those of the original play. There is something of Galileo and Newton in Rozenkrantz, who nevertheless keeps forgetting who he is. "What are you playing at?" he asks at one moment. "Words, words, they are all we have to go on," responds the more pragmatic Guildenstern, assessing what Gertrude meant by the reward of a "king's remembrance" for their labors. With words thus defined as razor-edged things, Richard Dreyfuss, otherwise notorious for his "flaming queen" rendition of a few lines of Gloucester, the future *Richard III*, emerges as quite the most natural character in the role of Shakespeare's grandiloquent Player King and ubiquitous agent of the strumpet Fortune. It is he who presides over the only "complete" version of Hamlet that we get to see, a melodramatic pantomime played before an audience of lunatics; it is he who narrates a similarly wordless Mousetrap played by masked actors who suddenly turn into the witnesses of the same tale enacted in a musical Marionette theatre, with a second reverse transformation revealing the players to be the courtiers, thus confirming the play of illusions and putting the spectator in her place.[115]

★ ★ ★

These games of language notwithstanding, the utility of Anderegg's generic argument reveals itself most clearly in a consideration of the technological history of film. Historians Robert Allen and Douglas Gomery advance the theory that the history of cinema consists of a number of at-times-discordant separate histories, aesthetic, technological, economic, and social. Significant moments of transition occur when, for instance, an emerging technology coincides with an economic boom that facilitates the rapid acceptance and adoption of the technology as happened with the 1927 transition to films with synchronized dialogue.[116] Almost as if it were an idée fixe, filmmakers attracted to Shakespeare felt the need to reproduce the voices of actors, and even if there is no evidence that Sarah Bernhardt actually spoke when she committed an episode of her theatrical *Hamlet* to film in 1900, there are suggestive historical hints that films of 1907 (Oskar Messter's *Othello*, taken from Verdi), 1913 (Edison's *Julius Caesar*), 1915 (a British and Colonial *Taming of the Shrew*), and 1917 (Beckfilm's *Merry Wives of Windsor*, adapted from Otto Nicolai's opera) may all have constituted attempts to synchronize dialogue recordings with the images. However, the first adequately amplified system, a great improvement over the ephemeral (1913) Edison Kinetophone device, resulted from Lee De Forest's co-invention of the Audion Tube in 1923, after which he made short films with Méliès-like regularity to demonstrate his Phonofilms apparatus. His competitor, Western Electric, a branch of the telephone conglomerate American Telephone & Telegraph, was already at work on two rival systems destined, eventually, to win the attention of the Wall Street investment bankers Goldman Sachs (then at the height of their financial power), with whose financial backing they entered into partnership first with Warner Bros. and then, independently, with Fox. The rest, as they say in Hollywood, is history, as Vitaphone's sound-on-disc and then Movietone's sound-on-film technologies inaugurated the age of the talkie. Hampered by lack of funding and constrained to mortgage his patents, De Forest slowly sank into a mire of litigation.[117] Some Phonofilms experiments survive, most being brief and obvious demonstrations of amplification and synchronization, but one of the later ones (probably from 1925 or 1926) exists as a series of rushes in the British Film Institute (BFI). One of the earliest successful recordings of dialogue, De Forest's *The Merchant of Venice*, captures the Old Vic company restaging one of its repertory pieces. The survival is especially fortunate because it has long been thought that John Barrymore's in-costume vignette of battle-ready Richard III (from *3 Henry VI*) for Warner's 1929 review, *The Show of Shows*, represents Shakespeare's grand entrance into the world of the talkies. In fact, the Phonofilm anticipation of Vitaphone clearly attempted to redact an entire play rather than a scene, albeit a more impressively staged scene than any of the restrained Old Vic efforts. Together with very precisely redone alternate takes (twenty in all), some without cuts as is common in modern television production, and boasting a singing and dancing number suggestive of modest revelry (and nicely synchronized music), the film remained unfinished or is incomplete. Yet what survives confirms Anderegg's idea that from the beginnings of the synchronized sound film dialogue was all-important, the mise en scène subordinate, the camera so tethered to the word as to often be reduced to immobility. Facing the recording apparatus the bearded Shylock stands at the base of a scaled-down Rialto and, with the added conflation of earlier lines, delivers his great speech as his interlocutors (here Antonio and Bassanio) withdraw a little to let him spread his arms and occupy center screen. His voice rises to a crescendo, the final word of "And if you wrong us, shall we not revenge?" filled with anger and agony. In his exchange with Tubal, he takes his coreligionist by his sleeve, and on hearing news of Antonio and Jessica, undergoes violent alternations of emotion, rather well rendered as the actors have to contrive to turn slightly toward the camera as each speaks his lines. We are all set for the courtroom scenes, but at least at the BFI Antonio is spared that indignity.

Not so in another unusual film made half a century later, one that again slyly incorporates the Eugene O'Neill effect even as its stresses the possibilities offered by dialogue to the Shakespeare film. Douglas Hickox's *Theater of Blood* (1973) is also a masterpiece of performance by its leads, Vincent Price and Diana Rigg, and perhaps the first unabashed example of "postmodern" Shakespeare if a mockery of Modernist aesthetics (rather than a mere abandonment of them) might be attributable to postmodernity. To the tune of a lascivious lute (imitating, of all things, the flute arabesques of the "Dance of the Blessed Spirits" from C.W. Glück's opera *Orfeo*, later supplemented by a fantasy based on the tender slow movement of Beethoven's Emperor Concerto heard during a decapitation), the film begins by denouncing the melodrama of early modernist Shakespeare films in the form of vigorous, twenty-four frames-per-second murders culled from available prints of silents. I have used the term "early modernist" not only to refer to the period of filmmaking but also to Shakespeare's period, for the film makes the discrepancy obvious by intercutting these snippets into a credit sequence in which an oval medallion containing the portrait of a nobleman by Nicholas Hilliard—the most famous work of the miniature painter and author of a celebrated posthumously-published theoretical treatise *The Art of Limning* (1624)—displaces the credits to the left of the frame. Like much else in the film, it is by no means a casual reference, since the painting turns out to be the model for a coveted statuette, awarded annually by members of the Critics Circle to the best actor of London's West End season. Their failure to award it to Edward Lionheart, the most persistent Shakespearean in England, and their scornful jibes, in fact, lead to the perennial lead actor disrupting their final meeting, set in a plush apartment overlooking the Thames. Seizing the statuette that is about to be awarded to a novice ("a twitching, mumbling boy who can barely grunt his way through an incomprehensible performance," a.k.a. Stanley-Antony-Marlon Brando), he wanders onto the balcony and recites the better part of Hamlet's "To be, or not to be" before choosing differently from the prince and, to their delight and his daughter's dismay, plunging to his death below. Only, it turns out that he does not die but is rescued by a band of derelicts, with whom he restores the burned-out Burbage Theatre and embarks upon a series of well-deserved and apt murders based on what we eventually discover from a playbill is the repertory of his last season.

The film could be a farrago of melodramatic nonsense, since its raisón d'être is Shakespearean pastiche, but limns instead an exquisite series of Hilliardesque miniatures. It is undoubtedly a vehicle for Price, citing *in extenso* his film career, but it also assimilates the career of Diana Rigg, television secret agent and mistress of disguise (from 1966 to 1968 the female half of the long-running TV series *The Avengers*), a well-known Shakespearean, and Peter Hall's scene-stealing Helena in his film of *A Midsummer Night's Dream* (1968). Indeed, since her role as dutiful daughter does not oblige her to overplay, she is permitted a greater range: the fuzzy-haired, mustachioed London street tough of the period (broad), slinky, white-booted seductress (slightly heightened, in the manner of *The Avengers*), Shakespearean stage partner to her father in *The Merchant of Venice* and *Cymbeline* (suitably theatrical), and finally a Cordelia who abandons her identity to her role (subtly underplayed). Thus she too proves to be a beneficiary of the Vincent Price effect. Partly because of his extraordinary voice and diction, combined with his physical stature, from early on Price found himself playing larger-than-life characters, soon becoming a staple Horror-film lead (indeed, he entitled a talk he gave at Indiana University in the 1980s "The Villains Still Pursue Me"). One of his early performances was as Clarence in Rowland V. Lee's *The Tower of London* (1939) that relied heavily on the same effect. Boris Karloff, fresh from his performance in Lee's *Son of Frankenstein* (1939), similarly a Universal Studios project, took the role of the gleeful, shaven-headed, limping torturer and executioner, Mord. Like many a Universal Horror film, it was vigorously self-parodic, despite being only marginally of the Horror genre, and that endorsed entirely by Karloff's presence. At one point Mord, hiding behind a bush, intercepts one of the Tower's princes, delightedly tossing the flowers the little boy carried into the frame to the accompaniment of an offscreen shriek (an arch send-up of the famous scene in the 1932 *Frankenstein* in which the Monster, having run out of detachable flower petals, throws the little girl who is watching him into a pond). The decisive Richard (Basil Rathbone) and the Machiavellian Edward (Ian Hunter) are rather more interesting than the more pleasant characters such as Elizabeth and Anne, while Clarence is a simpering, effete weakling who succumbs easily to Richard in a malmsey drinking contest, enabling the waiting Mord to substitute the barrel immersion trick for pond immersion. In 1962 Roger Corman, king of the 1950s and 1960s "B" films (due in no small part to his star, Price), made another *Tower of London* replete with his familiar grotesquerie: ghostly apparitions, dangerous corpses, lethal rackings, man-eating rats, and the like, stealing from the earlier film but also borrowing from *Richard III, Macbeth,* and the Henriad. Price plays an ironic, sullen Richard-Macbeth, with a pathological desire for violence and a palpable terror of divine retribution. In 1971 Price played the revenger in *The Abominable Dr. Phibes* (dir. Robert Fuest), in which in the finest Hammer Films' tradition he finds ingenious and gruesome ways to dispatch the nine members of the medical team he holds responsible for his wife's death.[118] In *Theater of Blood* Price bags, in turn, actors Michael Hordern, Dennis Price, Arthur Lowe, Harry Andrews, Robert Coote, Jack Hawkins, Coral Browne, and Robert Morley, the elite of British theatre and film performers of the time, and has his most vituperative critic, Ian Hendry (in the devilish role of Peregrine Devlin) at his mercy. Enslaved by theatrical convention (i.e., his last official season), however, Lionheart spares him for the more fitting fate of Gloucester in *King Lear*, heedless of the play's other implications.

The virtuosity of Anthony Greville-Smith's script allows for careful introductions of unfamiliar plays (in which Price can offer comparatively low-key and remarkably convincing readings of Shakespeare's lines), and also allows for each of the actor-victims to reprise his or her previous Shakespeare characterizations. There is really no quotation, only dis(s)quotation (practically every quoted line is shorn of its context) and some heroic mis(s)quotation. While assuming Brutus's role, Price delivers the most famous of Antony's lines; he tosses coins to his minions with one of Iago's offhand remarks; he interpolates Hamlet's rhyming quatrain introducing Ophelia's cortege into a restrained, even dignified reading of Achilles's frenzied incitements in *Troilus and Cressida*; with the help of his daughter he gives a Philip Sidneyesque line alternation of the famous lament in *Cymbeline*, dramatically altering its meaning; he plays a stern Shylock to his daughter's stage prompter Portia, prompting her concession of the inadequacy of the "pettifogging" legal trickery that could formerly reprieve Antonio; he recites Hamlet's most famous soliloquy before his critics, dangerously reversing the meaning of his last line; he outdoes Olivier in reminding Clarence of past injuries and his own past roles; he plays the vengeful swordsman Romeo on a trampoline and even borrows a line from Miranda in explaining his post-Hamlet survival to Devlin; he takes only two words from *Othello* for himself, "die strumpet," but donates some to his victim; he baits his Joan of Arc with both York's and Warrick's sarcasms; he borrows Cassio's, Titus's, and even Romeo's dis(s)quoted lines during the force-feeding of his Tamora, gourmet Morley; he snatches lines from the beginning and the end of *Lear* as he and Edwina prepare to compel Devlin to present the Critics Circle Award belatedly.

In this abundance of dis(s)quotation one can easily overlook the mis(s)quotations that are far from accidental. In his rereading of *Hamlet* Lionheart divides his last line into three phrases: "There's the respect" (spitting it at his disrespectful critics)..."that makes calamity" (said to himself bitterly)..."of so long life" (with a very American "so long" before he dives off the balustrade). "Clarence" gives way to "Larding" in "Be subtle in the execution. Do not hear him plead. For Larding is well spoken, and may move your hearts to pity." Romeo's despondent "Alive, in triumph, and Mercutio slain," yields to an ebullient "Alive, in triumph, and you thought me slain." Only a mis(s)reading of Warrick's "And hark ye, sirs; because she is a maid, Spare for no faggots, let there be enow" could prompt Lionheart to assume the role of a flamboyantly gay hairdresser. In other words, except for the profligate waste of some Chambertin '64 (à la the Beatles's song), a "vintage that comes on very well," and a weak *Othello* sequence, it is, in its gaudy, slummy way, a near-perfect spoof.

The comic-macabre effect Price creates is entirely due to his earlier roles attaching to him, not just the screen persona with which he was indelibly associated. Moreover, the presence of a silent version of *Richard III* in the prologue, as well as vocal mannerisms borrowed from Olivier's screen Richard (high-pitched, nasal, and emphatic in the pronunciation of "r"s and labored vowels, at once unctuous and raspy) in his more declamatory moments who, despite Devlin's parting jibe offers a creditable "theatrical" Lear, make clear that Price's parody is not self-parody alone. Although I offer the film as a paradigmatic instance because of its obviousness, the Vincent Price effect can carry over into Shakespeare films in less extreme, if still intense, forms: from the stage (Olivier, Gielgud, Welles, and Branagh are notable examples), from the screen (action heroes such as Mel Gibson and Arnold Schwarzenegger), and perhaps most commonly—as Richard Vela has pointed out to me in conversation—from Shakespeare film or television performance to performance (Molly Ringwald, Al Pacino, or Charlton Heston, the last of whom played the lead in his own 1971 *Antony and Cleopatra* and a younger Antony in both David Bradley's 16 mm *Julius Caesar* [1950] and Stuart Burge's 1970 version alongside John Gielgud and Jason Robards).[119] Likewise, actors' vignettes or cameos, such as those in Branagh's films, might not necessitate their demise, but they play roles akin to Price's readily familiar victims.

I treat the intricacies of the evolution of film acting and of film stardom as they pertain to Shakespeare films in the central, third chapter of this work. Yet I would be remiss not to discuss an instance when the Vincent Price effect could have unexpected repercussions; namely, when an actor does not intend it to take place, but may suffer from "star" readings by constituencies of fans and critics whose reflexes associate that star with a particular role or character. Sean Connery, for instance, could never escape James Bond, and resented him. In Shakespearean terms the most prominent sufferer from such an unintended Vincent Price effect has probably been Ben Kingsley, son of a (part Jewish) European mother and Kenyan father of Indian descent, who despite playing Shakespeare on stage and a series of curmudgeons and psychotic gangsters on film, is better known as a "goodie," having taken the Academy Award-nominated part of Itzak Stern, the Jewish factory manager and secret assistant to Oscar Schindler, in Steven Spielberg's *Schindler's List* (1993), and the role of Mahatma Gandhi in Richard Attenborough's eponymous 1982 epic for which he won the Best Actor award. The latter film has left such an indelible impression on Catherine Eggert, for instance, that on seeing his Feste in Trevor Nunn's *Twelfth Night* (1996) she offers two possible instances when (as "something of a shock") Kingsley may, according to her, lapse into postsatyagrahist "mimicry of a colonial-Indian native soldier." One such instance occurs when he declares, with a lost pun on Shakespeare's favorite tavern, that "Malvolio's nose is no whipstock, my lady has a white hand, and the Myrmidons are no bottle-ale houses," here given with a military salute and the assumption of a parodied Indian accent, the second of five such subcontinentalisms. She reads his later riposte that "ginger shall be hot i' the mouth" (again prompting a salute and overdone accent) as an invocation of such senses as scent and taste associated with native soldiers ("spicy, gingery food," for example, having an "Indian" connection). Having previously explained that British actors in American films are often relegated to "minstrel" positions, caricaturing their own national origins, she argues that Branagh (at least in *Love's Labour's Lost*) fails to achieve a "post-postcolonial" minstrelsy that adequately references "the history of race and colonialism in the British Empire," at least in contrast to Trevor Nunn whose use of Kingsley granted the actor a lead role that addressed the issue. This said, even Nunn according to her, fails to make adequate use of Nigel Hawthorne (who won an Academy Award for the character of the title role in *The Madness of King George* [dir. Nicholas Hytner, 2004], and who plays the hypersensitive, object-fetishist Malvolio), or that other persistent Shakespearean,

Helena Bonham-Carter (who, like the Caesario/Viola of Imogen Stubbs, seems to me quite fetching in her impatience and abandonment).[120] Eggert's article takes to task the idea (common in European theatre, if not film) of race-blind casting, but it is not a position held with any academic unanimity: Peter Donaldson, for instance, reads Liz White's *Othello* (1966) as an interesting attempt to adopt race-blind casting that actively rejects the racial stereotypes commonly associated with the play, and in his survey of national and racial dynamics in Shakespeare films Neil Taylor excludes Kingsley's cerebral performance altogether.[121] It seems to me that only in moments of frustration in dealing with upper-class twittery does Kingsley's fierce, brooding, troubadour Feste (originally written for the musical Robert Armin), resort to such tactics, well ridiculed as such in light of Margaret Thatcher's use of impoverished Nepalese soldiers as expendable cannon fodder in the Falkland Islands War. More to the point, the Vincent Price effect may in this instance obscure a distant homage to a director who has a tendency to win many an affectionate homage, Ingmar Bergman. Despite Nunn's rather non-Bergmanesque propensity for montage with deft cuts to matching words or lines in the different plots (accomplished with the preservation of much of Shakespeare's text),[122] this connection seems more evident in the full-length version of *Fanny and Alexander* (*Fanny och Alexander* 1982). Here Bergman has one of his veteran players, Gunnar Björnstrand, dust pink makeup on his face, carry an artificially wet umbrella (with no less artificial rain in the foreground of a theatrical proscenium), place a lighted candle on his balding crown, and sing Feste's "with a hey and a ho" in apparent dismay. We see only this brief interlude from the play, and even that is cut from the theatrical film release, but it may nevertheless survive in Kingsley's interpretation, for his Bergmanesque rendition of this song (a bit more lively than Feste's other existential ditties) plays over the credit sequence at the start and serves as epilogue. This is not to say that the film might not have offered a still more sophisticated (E+) reading of the play, less grave and truer to Shakespeare's imagining, had Malvolio been made up as Churchill, with a more insistent Feste in a homespun dhoti and the rest of the cast in imperial togs or Nehru jackets. For, as Richard Wilson contends, *Twelfth Night* may well have ridiculed the idea of violent rebellion in favor of nonviolent Catholic resistance.[123]

★ ★ ★

Fanny and Alexander, to which I return presently, brings up another feature of Shakespeare films that I refer to as intermediation. I use this term to signify the increasing symbiosis between different media, particularly digital media and older technologies such as nitrocellulose film stock. In *Shakespeare on Film* Judith Buchanan refers to John Dryden's tripartite idea that adaptation could be metaphrase (literal translation), paraphrase (a sense of the text with the author kept in mind), and imitation (wherein some aspect of the original finds reflection), as well as to Dudley Andrew's definition of transmediation as "the systematic replacement of verbal signifiers by cinematic signifiers."[124] Adhering to the frameworks Buchanan and Andrew invoke, one might observe that critics of filmed Shakespeare have either chosen to favor the idea that the best adaptations best preserve Shakespeare's dialogue metaphrastically, or gravitate to the other extreme of valuing those that depart as much as possible from the original transmedially. Yet the key idea that a Restoration dramatist and a film theorist share, in this instance, is that words such as those of Shakespeare can be rendered recognizably in another medium, although neither definition is conclusive: Dryden might have further refined his categories and Andrew, as Yuri Lotman and other semioticians might observe, discusses two separate semiotic transactions (the translation of printed texts into verbal signifiers, and the translation of verbal signifiers into equivalent images), which is not to say that cinema has not been the beneficiary of translatability. When the Vitagraph studio was engaged in a cycle of Shakespeare films, for instance, it appears to have relied on narrators in the nickelodeon theatres to explain the action, and journals such as the *Motion Picture Story Magazine* carried occasional criticism of the films by readers in addition to devoting the majority of their pages to furnishing elaborate plot digests of such films as *Cardinal Wolsey* (1912) and *As You Like It* (1912).[125] Describing an even more complex process of interaction between media in *A World History of Film*, Robert Sklar has pointed out the intriguing instance of Teinosuke Kinugasa's 1926 film *A Page of Madness* (*Kurutta ippeiji*), among the most complex of all surviving examples of montage in cinema, which was made not as a result of seeing Soviet films such as Eisenstein's instantly famous 1925 *The Battleship Potemkin* but from reading translations into Japanese from German journals that featured accounts of Soviet montage theories.[126]

An analogous formulation has been that of media theorists Jay David Bolter and Richard Grusin who propose a new concept to account for Marshall McLuhan's idea that the content of a medium is always another medium, a process that they regard as increasingly evident in the digital age (post-1990), which leads them to define "remediation" as "the representation of one medium in another." In contrast to earlier theories, in which the "consumed" medium is simply incorporated into another, Bolter and Grusin offer the possibility that older "source" media might survive because they are merely alluded to or slightly improved upon; or else they may survive as the result of adjusting to "aggressive" challenges offered by new media, or even simply by making attempts at complete assimilation.[127] Such a theory of competitive media absorption or assimilation is especially interesting in the case of films such as those of Peter Greenaway, Baz Luhrmann, or Michael Almereyda, which I discuss in due course. but, in fact, the emerging mediascape of our time appears to be less one of remediation and increasingly one of intermediation, the symbiotic interaction of different media. Whereas at one time (in the 1950s and 1960s, especially), cinema and television seemed locked in a life-and-death struggle, TV networks today happily produce 35 mm film (those based on Shakespeare being quite "hot") to be broadcast integrally, at times even without commercial interruption. Films reissued in DVD format not only allow for illuminating commentary—with Olivier and Kurosawa being particular beneficiaries—and the opportunity for frame-by-frame studies of films by researchers, but also contribute to the restorations such as those undertaken for Olivier's *Richard III* (1955) using Spirit Datacine and Cintel machines for the transfers, as well as the MTI Digital Restoration process. As digital technology improves, films are being preserved both in their (often fragile) original state and as more durable digital copies, and by a transcendent irony very early films can only be restored through the digital manipulation of the various tracks, a process used, for instance, by the peerless Hollywood sound engineer and editor Walter Murch to distend and compress the soundtrack of the first Edison film to be shot with synchronized sound (so that it would align once more with the surviving images).[128] In the last decade celluloid film restoration involves going digital, adopting processes that either clean individual frames of 35 mm film once digitized (such as the Ultra Restoration technology used to restore some of the acknowledged Hollywood classics of the 1930s and 1940s), or technologies that use information from flanking frames to restore damage, so allowing for the movement back and forth from 35 mm film.[129] *The Shakespeare Web*, created by Peter Donaldson at the Massachusetts Institute of Technology, not only archives text and images associated with Shakespeare on the Internet, but is also engaged in putting the decaying Vitagraph paper prints held at the Library of Congress onto a Web format where they can be reanimated to the correct speeds and supplemented by shot-by-shot annotations. Far from declining into oblivion, celluloid film may be rescued for generations to come through such synergistic intermediation.

The evolving mediascape, particularly in relation to television, can perhaps best be exemplified by two divergent Shakespeare films, one arguably the great Manhattan Shakespeare film (directed by Paul Mazursky), and the other, without question, the quintessential *auteur* "re-vision" of a Shakespeare play by Ingmar Bergman. In Mazursky's *Tempest* (1982), the great independent actor-director and New York cultural icon John Cassavetes, who made of film improvisation an art form, plays Phillip Demetrios as both Prospero and Demetrius. Phillip is a star architect undergoing a debilitating midlife crisis, as a remedy to which he sets off for a mirror version of unbuilt Manhattan, a desolate, starkly beautiful Greek island. For company he has his urban(e) daughter Miranda who brings along an imposing boom box and a scant wardrobe, as well as a sexy nightclub singer and her terrier (Susan Sarandon's Aretha and Nino, but both together Ariel). On arriving they discover the resentfully servile island inhabitant Kalibanos, a Pan-like goatherd, factotum, and clarinetist extraordinaire as played with gruff good humor by Raul Julia, whose pride, joy, and engine of seduction turns out to be a TV set installed in his cave. Phillip's estranged Broadway actor-wife Antonia (Gena Rowlands) and her new lover, the Mafioso boss (played by the distinguished Italian veteran actor Vittorio Gassman) of his architectural firm, twice interrupt his idyll. Their final visit to the island, accompanied by a seductive, Gurdjieff-quoting companion, Dolores (Gonzalo), precipitates a pleasant denouement and the return to Manhattan (Civilization). As it proceeds, the film provides narrative excuses for improvisation, the planned and the rehearsed increasingly giving way to a series of aleatory star turns.

Tempest is decidedly of its period, one in which emerging media conglomerates were commodifying popular entertainment and eviscerating the Broadway Musical through restringent copyright laws and mass-produced entertainment. It was also a period in which television still competed with film for audience revenues (the home video was booming, adding further confusion to the mix). Naturally, in such an atmosphere, Mazursky's nonaesthetic technologies become instruments of surveillance, while subaesthetic media (rock and roll, television) turn into dangerous distractions. As Phillip's narcissism intensifies and he undertakes the rebuilding of an ancient Greek auditorium, causing dissent among his "assistants," the New York stage itself must come to the tension-diffusing rescue, posing as a Broadway Musical *Milan* where even goats can take imaginative leaps. Indeed the film, which features musical numbers including a "New York, New York" played and danced by Kalibanos to amuse his goat companions, who find Greek folk songs less of a turn-on, is defiantly constructed as a "talking" Broadway Musical (with occasional intrusions of set-piece numbers and the cast taking a final collective bow), a structural feature that either escaped critical notice or that prompted intense hostility emanating—as the dismayed Walter Coppedge notes—even from those as distinguished as Vincent Canby, John Simon, and the very paragon who imported *auteur* criticism into the United States, Andrew Sarris, one of the few instances when he was in complete agreement with his nemesis, Pauline Kael.[130] Perhaps noting Mazursky's fondness for Shakespearean themes in his films, they heaped contempt on what they imagined to be feeble references to the Bard in this one.

For a would-be patriarch and control freak, one given to spying on Antonia, Miranda, and even Aretha through various devices even as he is outmaneuvered by his bosses and loses control of his pet project, Phillip sees his faraway island more as a temporary refuge and playground than a place of exile ("it's all here, dog," he says at one point to furry Nino, "beauty, magic, inspiration, and serenity, not to mention silence, amazement, intimacy, enchantment"). When Miranda first emerges for breakfast he turns down the noisy ruckus emerging from her boom box, and so wins the retort to his announcement of the recurrence of a dream that she too had a dream–that she was having pot at a GoGos' concert. She plays a zippy piece as she dives unclothed into the sapphire-blue waters of a cove, only to be observed (in a glimpsed reference to *Macbeth*) from behind a detached bush by Kalibanos with anything but detachment. As he launches into the TV jingle from a chewing gum advertisement, "the son-of-bitch" Nino attacks him. She is outraged, and Phillip, who has obviously been observing the goings-on, threatens to kill Kalibanos if he touches her. A flashback takes us back to the technology- and media-saturated world of Manhattan: Woody Allen, at work on his own Shakespeare film, is spotted atop a spiral staircase at a New Year's Eve party, reminding us of Demetrios's/Demetrius's connection to *A Midsummer Night's Dream*. We travel to the rusting steel framework of Alonso's unfinished grand casino where the burned-out Phillip imagines throwing himself off it, and is threatened with mayhem by a lawyer when he asks to quit; he uses a portable telescope for observation, flies in his boss's private jet and chartered helicopter, has electrodes hooked to a heart monitor after a bitter quarrel with Antonia (they storm past a *Romeo and Juliet* production poster that hangs in their apartment, where later Miranda complains about *Macbeth* and Harold Pinter, and guests join in to reprise numbers from film and Broadway Musicals); he succumbs to the notion that he can summon lighting with the mere incantation "show me the magic"; and eventually he heeds his widowed father's advice to him to take a vacation on the Greek islands. The escape from technology can never be total, for the film is also about the increasing ubiquity of media. Kalibanos almost succeeds in having his way with Miranda by enticing her into his cave with a twelve-inch Sony Trintron TV set where she watches the "B"est of Western series, *Gunsmoke*, dubbed into Spanish, as he attempts to discuss "agape" and proceeds up her arm with a John Barrymore-esque series of kisses to the accompaniment of the jealous goats lounging on his bed; at another moment Miranda wears a purple toga and dances a slinky solo tango to strains emerging from her boom box, and she is soon joined by her father (practicing "celibacy" on a tower of his own) who tries to force her to dance with him, provoking an equally vehement rejection. Phillip, unaware of his hypocrisy, then provokes a close paraphrase of *The Tempest* dialogue when Kalibanos responds angrily upon being beaten by the outraged patriarch with an oar. The concluding sequence again begins when Phillip peers through his cyclopean telescope on being informed by a delighted Kalibanos of the arrival of tourists, at which point he again summons "the magic," creating the storm that leaves Alonso and company at his rather feeble mercy. However, the downpour also brings with it a good soaking and a Lear-like dawning of self-recognition. The buffoonish comics, one of whom finds Kalibanos "attractive in a Third World sort of way," never get as far as plotting. Reconciliation comes in the form of a goat sacrifice and a communal dance to an old-fashioned tango emerging miraculously from the same trusty boom box, all culminating with a high-powered boat and copter (the triumphs of human technology) returning the protagonists safely to the first among island worlds.

Entirely different in texture and purpose, Bergman's last cinematic masterpiece, *Fanny and Alexander*, is profoundly nostalgic in tone and affectionately languorous in presentation. Had it been made in another age, it might have suffered a fate similar to that of Erich von Stroheim's 1923 *Greed*, reduced progressively from over nine hours to well under two with something akin to a chainsaw. Yet knowing that an alternative television version was available to him, Bergman was unafraid to curtail some of the film's most revealing moments in the interests of reducing it from four acts (lasting 312 minutes) to a continuous 188-minute theatrical-release version, edited more briskly at its start and conclusion, but lacking some of the information that makes the characters' motivations and its deeper connection to *Hamlet* clearer. In fact, the "complete" film, whose making was also filmed and transformed into a separate document, did not appear until the Criterion DVD release of 2004, which includes all three versions.

Despite its title, *Fanny and Alexander* concerns Bergman's surrogate, the sensitive, artistically inclined Alexander, to a greater extent than his younger sister. A Magical Realist autobiography, it contains both a remarkable miracle wrought by the *Kabbala* (harking back to the Christian one that concludes *The Virgin Spring* [*Jungfrukallan*] of 1960) and an extraordinarily rendered "confession" at the end that culminates in the imaginative extermination of his father's usurper and nothing less than a twilight exorcism of all the ghosts of Bergman's past. The story begins on Christmas Eve in 1907 and concerns the family of a famous actress, Helena Ekdahl (who like her Shakespearean counterpart was paired with the wrong man), that of her longtime lover Isak Jacobi, and that of the oppressive, Puritanical Bishop who rather too soon takes the place of his beloved father. The web of relationships can be discerned more readily in the TV version, as the theatrical film omits sequences that explain the special connection Alexander shared with his father Oscar, scales down some dimensions of the particular fascination the theatre itself held for the adolescent, and elides the centrality of *The Twelfth Night* to the flight of imagination that leads to the children's rescue and Alexander's rebirth into the world of imaginative creation. The longer version contains Oscar's mesmerizing story about the miraculous nature of an ordinary chair to the children of the household, a fiction whose fictionality Alexander alone can share with his father. Likewise, it is only in this version that Alexander is witness to his father's frailty (Oscar forgets his cues and lines and has a heart attack while rehearsing the part of the Ghost in *Hamlet*), to the dramatic power of his recitation of verse (that makes the scene all the more painful to watch), to his eventual recollection of the lamp that his father strikes and sets away with his oversized, plumed helmet, and to the import of his white-suited ghost. In the DVD supplement that tells the story of the film's making, we see Bergman bullying the ideal performance out of Gunnar Björnstrand, insisting on repeated takes during which the actor naturally grows progressively more forlorn as he sings one of Feste's mirthless songs. And when he finishes, and Alexander's despairing mother, Emilie, calls all the cast together, her son surreptitiously remains on stage in his red velvet costume to approach the lamp, make it sway as his father once had by accident, and, before she discovers him and drags him away, declaim Orsino's "If music be the food of love, play on; / Give me excess of it." *Twelfth Night* explains the occult power that Renaissance humanists associated with the hermaphrodite: the concluding half hour that Alexander spends with the androgynous Ismael Jacobi, locked away to protect the world from his/her magical siren song, proves to be his initiation into the realms of adult imagination.

Bergman was seldom as revealing. His affable nod to *A Midsummer Night's Dream*, *Smiles of a Summer Night* (*Sommarnattens leende* 1955), became generally admired as such only after one of his great cinematic fans, Woody Allen, adopted the theme of mismatched lovers (limiting himself to three pairs for his sex-tangle) in his *A Midsummer Night's Sex Comedy* (1982). Allen made the sequence of references more evident by reusing the incidental music inspired by Felix Mendelssohn that Warner Bros. had once imposed on Erich Wolfgang Korngold for their version of Shakespeare's play. As Bergman did, so Allen, for his characters are drawn from varied sources, his pompous Professor also nodding to that of Bergman's *Wild Strawberries* (1957). Allen's own character in the film seems a little reminiscent of Dick Van Dyke's Caractacus Potts, the eccentric inventor in Ken Hughes's *Chitty Chitty Bang Bang* (1968), but this last observation may be supposition, for I saw it once as a child, in Sri Lanka, when Tarzie Vittachi was yet alive and discovering new Shakespeare plays, and I have not seen it on DVD.

Visual Cultures???

How (k/c)ultur(e) made its way via Franz Boas into "culture," a term that even in Germany designates an American usage to signify a distinct and separate way of life, serves as the basis of the inquiry Michael Elliott undertakes in *The Culture Concept*. At its heart is the problem of what "culture" designates, for by the end of the nineteenth-century social thinkers were beginning to worry about whether the demarcation of difference that the term allocated to isolated groups of people also had the effect of homogenizing them.[131] Elliott concludes his introductory remarks by revealing that he shares Jim Clifford's cultural agnosticism, but concedes that by the multiplicity of its uses it has become a term we cannot do without.

★ ★ ★

In the waning years of the twentieth century, a new discipline announced its arrival with the near- simultaneous publication of a series of theoretical articles, a spate of books attempting to define and delimit the field, and the appearance of a journal devoted to its promulgation, the *Journal of Visual Culture*. Since the majority of opinions regarding "visual culture" align it with cultural studies (where the secondary category "popular culture" serves a transnational, postethnic, and subtribal function), the broad implication of the term is not that it designates the way a particular constituency sees or looks, but instead denotes an emergent critical practice. Jessica Evans and Stuart Hall relate it centrally to cultural studies.[132] Asking the same question, "what is visual culture?," Nicholas Mirzoeff speaks of a "need for visual culture as a field of study" not so much because of a perceived disciplinary insufficiency (as Evans and Hall maintain), but rather because of the unprecedented proliferation of visual media in everyday life.[133] It is exactly the same question that had also preoccupied Malcolm Bernard, who begins with W.J.T. Mitchell's contention that "one cannot simply graft a received notion of visual experience to a received notion of culture" to arrive at a satisfactory conception of visual culture. Taking the distinction between "dominant masculine mass culture" and "multilinear popular (sub)culture" to be the key problematic, Barnard argues that the discipline of visual culture should by its nature accommodate and negotiate between such differences.[134] In contrast to these definitions, Marita Sturken and Lisa Cartwright resist applying the term "visual culture" to a disciplinary framework, but grant it instead to various forms of perception in fields such as medicine, to aesthetic objects such as films, and to cognitive processes, such as the relationship between sight and hearing.[135]

The central issue that has provoked considerable debate about visual culture, one of the few disciplines or fields to be claimed as such by numerous constituencies of scholars and announced with a remarkable synchronicity in a supernova of introductory texts, is the fact that besides the persistent problem of "culture" most definitions treat it as an activity undertaken by academics. The majority of these definitions failed to distinguish between constituencies of perceivers, or to allow the term to designate transitions in perception that can lead from one sense of the world to another: one could not effectively speak of a medieval visual culture that informed painting and illustration, to take a pertinent example, and a contrasting one emerging in the Renaissance during which the rediscovery of vanishing points and the representation of perspective in depth led to myriad innovations. It stands to reason, therefore, that as photorealistic media proliferated in the period we associate with aesthetic Modernism, the ways in which Virginia Woolf and Vanessa Bell created, collected, and organized photographs, and thought about literary form and cinema, would suggest to Maggie Humm a book by the title of *Modernist Women and Visual Cultures*. One can even return to Shakespeare's period and draw a similar distinction between the ways of seeing shared by learned humanists and theologians and those of rebellious peasants, a disparity that led to a crisis of representation and the emergence of new genres according to Stephen Greenblatt in a well-known analysis of Shakespeare's history plays and Albrecht Dürer's design of a monument to celebrate the defeat of a rural insurrection.[136]

Without any particular desire to contribute to the polemics surrounding "visual culture," I have adopted the plural fully aware of its disciplinary connotations but also in an effort to underscore some of the distinctions between the kinds of spectatorship elicited by visual texts (woodcuts, paintings, engravings, lithographs, typographic illustrations, posters, photographs, films, and film posters) produced in a plethora of "cultural" contexts. It is a matter of particular significance because "Shakespeare" has in a sense generated a visual culture indelibly associated with nationalism and cultural imperialism (which like many such "-isms" proves on close inspection commercially motivated), yet one that despite its unwholesome origins generated an artistic efflorescence that has continued to influence theatrical productions, photography, and film. Moreover, no "period" Shakespeare film can escape the art of Shakespeare's time or the epochs in which he set his work. The Period Film, moreover, is subject to residual influences as it is not simply an evocation of a particular time and place but of layers of representational traditions. The visual culture associated with Shakespeare has its own history, and painters of the Romantic period such as Henry Fuseli or a Pre-Raphaelite painter such as John Everett Millais can exert unseen influences (Kozintsev having pondered whether to represent the death of Ophelia as Millais did; Zeffirelli deliberately inverting that iconography, physically turning her face downward, in showing a pregnant, drowned girl in a womb-like estuary).

★ ★ ★

The William Shakespeare visual cult(ure) is also a cult, and a little unusual among cults in having a precisely traceable point of origin. M. Moelwyn Merchant offers a prefatory account of the startling ascent of Shakespeare's reputation due to the promotional activities of leading actor David Garrick as a curtain raiser for a description of the consequences of a dinner party discussion held at the home of Josiah Boydell on November 4, 1786. It was a well-planned event, for present were some of the leading artists of the age including George Romney and Joshua Reynolds.[137] Winifred Friedman writes that he finds it fitting to give the first word on the project to the latter as his "exhortations about [a British School] of history painting in his Royal Academy Discourses" were in part "responsible for the inception of the enterprise." In an 1787 letter composed in his own manner Reynolds writes: "[T]he greatest news relating to virtu is Alderman Boydel's scheme of having pictures and prints taken from those pictures of the most interesting scenes of Shakespeare, by which all the painters and engravers find engagements for eight or ten years."[138] The celebratory note was premature. Despite the virtual establishment of the school Reynolds had hoped for (167 major canvases eventually hung on display in a purpose-built gallery for paying patrons), Boydell's print edition foundered due, ironically, to a generally low standard of engraving resulting from an unsuitable mixture of processes: William Blake contributed only one engraving, and when Boydell rejected the talented James Gilray's offer to create an engraving from a painting by James Northcote, Gilray published a scathing caricature depicting him in his Alderman's robes burning editions of Shakespeare's plays before a personified Avarice.[139] Competitors such as John Bell, the publisher of illustrated editions of Shakespeare's plays (from 1773 onward), including portraits of individual actors, succeeded in attracting and holding subscribers, although he too came to eventual grief in the tempestuous seas of the book trade.[140] In 1803 parliament granted the Boydell family permission to hold a lottery that included as a prize the gallery and its contents, which were auctioned off shortly thereafter.[141] The once retiring Shakespeare, however, was now engraved into the annals of national history and, indeed, those of art history.

Shakespeare scholars are by no means alone in their appreciation of the extent of his influence. Even leaving aside a host of articles, and accounting only for books devoted to illustrations of Shakespeare's works, I have to date encountered one work that treats Shakespeare's influence on art (Merchant) and another in which such an influence plays a substantial role (Altick), one based on the proceedings of a conference devoted to the subject of "Images of Shakespeare" (Habicht et al.), another anthology devoted to *Shakespeare and the Visual Arts* (Klein and Harner), an analytical catalogue based on an exhibition of paintings and illustrations based on the plays (Anderson) and another devoted to major paintings (Martineau and Desmond Shawe-Taylor), one concentrating on *Hamlet* illustrations alone (Young), and even a sumptuous, uncredited catalogue of the Korein Shakespeare Collection of paintings (that includes Reynolds's dramatic study of Lear's storm-blown head), *The Art of Shakespeare*.

★ ★ ★

There are two moments in Shakespeare's oeuvre that have attracted the especial attention of scholars of art history. Both come from the later part of his career. Perhaps the best known is his citation of the Mannerist painter Giulio Romano in *A Winter's Tale*, whom he appears to mistake for a sculptor.[142] Another is his extended, cheeky parody—in the rivalries of the parasitic Painter and Poet in *Timon of Athens*—of the Italian literary debate on the representational truth of the different arts, the *paragone* (named as such by an editor of Leonardo's manuscripts). It is a discourse to which I have cause to return in my discussion of Peter Greenaway's film *Prospero's Books* (1991).[143] Philip Sidney had resorted to it in his *Defense of Poesie*, allowing the poet to demolish his rival, while *The Art of Limning* allows the painter to triumph. More pertinent, perhaps, is the example of Cervantes, whom Shakespeare and John Fletcher probably adapted in a now lost play, since the novelist parodies the *paragone* in the *Quijote*. Cervantes had elaborated on one aspect of the *paragone* with the conceit of bringing a painting to life in inscribing the contradiction of Titian's three most famous portraits of Holy Roman Emperor Charles V into the texture of his work: one as the standing gentleman grasping a fine hunting hound, another the equestrian portrait as the armed and mounted warrior king, victorious at the Battle of Mühlberg against the legions of heresy, and a third as the retiring scholar seated in his study in black cap and gown, book in hand. Elements of Cervantine satire pervade not only the physical portrait of the Don (accomplished at the very opening), but also the events of both parts of the novel: as recipient of his brilliant father's ceaseless stream of advice and as a failed defender of Christian orthodoxy, Philip II is Sancho, the spinning crosses of the windmills are indeed the giants of Protestantism in Spain's rebellious provinces, lions, as in Falstaff's discourse, recognize the true king, and so on. The technique Shakespeare borrows in his extant plays is, in fact, the idea of using words to animate a fixed image, as for instance when he brings the equivalent of a historical painting to life in Enobarbus's description of Cleopatra's barge, and most famously when he restores a statue to life—complete with the signs of its subject's sixteen years of aging (perhaps two actors played the part)—in *A Winter's Tale*. The latter play's sensitivity to motion and stillness finds interesting expression in Baldassare Negroni's vigorous 1913 film version of it (with some references to Greene's *Pandosto*), *Una tragedia alla corte di Sicilia*, which features volcanoes, midnight escapes on horseback, and even a medal bearing the inscription "LEONATUS REX SIGILLAE" and the profile of the king's daughter, which leads to Paulina's recognition. Dependent on intertitles, "silent" cinema displayed a sensitivity to the relationship of words and images seldom found after the watershed of 1927.

Just as the *paragone* obsessed Leonardo and his generation, the use of painting to capture the immanence of motion or to suggest it, particularly in rendering the movement of hair or garments, was "prevalent among Northern Italian artists from the first third of the fifteenth century onwards, [and] finds its most telling expression in [Leon Battista] Alberti's *Libro della pittura* [1435],"claims Aby Warburg, in a famous study of Sandro Botticelli's monumental canvases, *The Birth of Venus* and *Primavera*. Warburg prefaces his confirmation (based on duplicated errors) of Botticelli's apparent illustration of a poem in these paintings with the remark that just as painters of the order of Agostino di Duccio and Luca Signorelli appear to have been aware of Alberti's theoretical writings, the poet Angelo Poliziano turned to Ovid and "the poets of antiquity for accounts of motifs of movement," which he then reproduces "faithfully" in his own poems. In turn Botticelli, working for the same Medici patrons as Poliziano, appears to have an intimate knowledge of Poliziano's *La giostra* modeled on [an apocryphal] *Homeric Hymn* to Aphrodite and his other verses. Illustrating the points at which Poliziano departs from the *Homeric Hymn*, Warburg shows that Botticelli diverges from the original at exactly the same points. Thus the wind gods wafting Venus to the shore, the "Hora of Spring" who holds a robe for her, her own garments aflutter, the similarity of the poses of the three [Albertian] Graces in the *Primavera* to a contemporary medallion, the awkward pose of the figure of Hermes on the left of the *Primavera*, once again adopted from Poliziano, the central figure of the now robed Venus who steps forth from the previous canvas, the two figures on the right who conform to Poliziano's borrowings from Ovid's description of the pursuit of the nymph Chloris by Zephyrus, her precursor being the resplendent figure of Flora, and the Goddess of Spring, who strides before her—indeed all the accessory forms of motion in the two paintings—translate verbal descriptions.[144]

I have dwelt on this iconographic analysis in part to illustrate the intimacies of word and image that Shakespeare and his contemporaries inherited from the dawn of the Renaissance, but also for the extraordinary reason that of all painters Botticelli is perhaps the one who appears to have exerted the most profound single influence on Shakespeare films. Greenaway's Ariel figures derive from Botticelli's wind gods and treat air as the life-giving spirit, as does an unusual mural on an apartment wall in Mick Jackson's *L.A. Story* (1991). The latter film is, in fact, best known for its comparison of Los Angeles to a particularly fetid version of Hamlet's Denmark. A ribald satire on Angelenos' adoptive mimicry of Europeans' class structures in the creation of their own, it includes some memorable performances including that of the tyrannical maître d' of the new restaurant, L'Idiot, played by that notable Englishman-turned-Frenchman Patrick (Jean-Luc) Stewart, a master practitioner of the "new cruelty."[145] As with one of Shakespeare's later fools, or the figures Mikhail Bakhtin associates with carnival, the hero (a Steve Martin consciously summoning the Vincent Price effect) remains a liminal figure throughout: a failed Prospero (he makes fun of the weather, but a freak storm ruins his career) who becomes both object of derision (Yorick/Blunderman) and wayward hero (Hamlet), his visit to a graveyard allows him, literally, to contemplate the comi-tragic-historical fate that awaits him. The film has its subtle touches, perhaps being the only one of its kind to distinguish between the paraphrase of Shakespeare and quotation. When TV weatherman Harris Telemacher's judgment is at its most feeble, when he participates most actively in the Angeleno rat race, he paraphrases Shakespeare: he even confesses that he steals from *Macbeth*, early on, and mangles lines from *As You Like It*. Only when he learns to trust his purer instincts and starts to quote Shakespeare "properly" does he redeem himself. Harris's doubleness plays out in a number of ways. He skates casually through the L.A. County Museum and the gaudy masterpieces acknowledge his presence, but when he wishes to impress Brits with their own quasi-aristocratic pretensions, he stands in front of a large red splash on a canvas pretending to discern figurative patterns and narrative trajectories. He succumbs to the charms of a New Age youngster, played winningly by Sarah Jessica Parker, with a strange name and equally weird proclivities, but who turns out (like the allegorical figures of Botticelli's paintings) to have a rejuvenating effect on him. At one point SanDeE★ invites him to her apartment; he resists, but cannot help noticing the mural that adorns her complex. A closer framing depicts the wind gods puffing over green waves. She stands in the doorway enticingly, in the approximate pose (and relative position in terms of the canvas) of Venus. SanDeE★ (Sandro translated into LAese) proves the catalyst for true love, which has come already to the confused Greco-Shakespearean hero Telemacher/Telemachos in the form of British journalist Sara when, on a jaunt with her to visit mummified remains of European musical High Culture (a museum containing Verdi's baton, Mozart's quill, and Beethoven's balls, among other treasures), she takes over the role of Hamlet at the end of an initially satirical exchange with a smart Cockney gravedigger. It is *Romeo and Juliet*, naturally, that in the end saves the day.

A Shakespeare film that makes a more elaborate use of Botticelli happens to be Italian. Renato Castellani's *Romeo and Juliet* is set in Verona, but John Gielgud makes an appearance as the Chorus-Shakespeare at the start to give it the right pedigree, pronouncing dire, if expected, warnings. The film, charmingly amateurish in its use of untrained extras and its halfhearted evocation of Neorealism (Anderegg attributes it to *neorealismo rosa*),[146] turns out to be something of a cultural inventory, necessitating an explanatory broadsheet supplied with the film prints (and intended for the use of educators) that catalogues the visual references, some rather obscure and some simply inaccurate. The crew that spent a year scouting locations and sources obviously spent quite a bit of time in Florence, where many of the cited paintings and frescoes originated. Castellani's Verona includes famous landmarks from Venice, such as the Ca' d'oro, and the candy-striped duomo of Siena. In discussing the film Meredith Lillich usefully distinguishes between the use of paintings as visual influences for props and costuming, and the more complex use of mise en scène to recreate paintings and frescoes (as in the tableaux vivants popular in the early years of cinema), but for the most part she makes the references no clearer.[147] I have not located the "Veneziano" work mentioned. Raphael painted two papal portraits, although here the reference is probably to that of Leo X and his nephews (although Capulet's resemblance to him is marginal); Antonello da Messina painted two St. Jeromes, but it is not to the one set in the desert that it refers. On the other hand, Juliet's ball gown does resemble that of Botticelli's Flora if not as closely as that worn by Juliet at the start of George Cukor's 1936 version of the film (the latter also derives costumes and props from the works of Benozzo Gozzoli and Vittore Carpaccio, and takes Juliet's hairstyle at one point from the angel in Fra Angelico's fresco of the Annunciation in a cell of the convent of San Marco, in Florence, also glimpsed in Jean-Luc Godard's 1980 version of *King Lear*). Rosaline actually appears in Castellani's version, wearing an elaborate period headdress (a *balzo*) modeled on Pisanello's fresco of *St. George and the Princess of Trebizond* in Verona's church of St. Anastasia; Juliet's bath scene before the ball reenacts the central figure grouping from Domenico Ghirlandaio's fresco of *The Birth of the Virgin* in Santa Maria Novella; her funeral procession borrows another set of costumes and groupings from Vittore Carpaccio's *Funeral of St. Ursula* (now at the Accademia in Venice); a group of singing boys re-creates a glazed terracotta work by Luca della Robbia in Florence; and Friar Laurence's desk resembles that given to St. Jerome in his study by Antonello. Some of the panels of Botticelli's illustration of Boccaccio's story of Nastagio degli Onesti (a *concetto* suggested to him by Lorenzo de Medici) are now housed in the Prado, in Madrid, but one that remained in Florence of the wedding banquet inspired the setting of a celebratory table in the film.

Despite the intensity of the desire to create a certain visual look, or perhaps because of it, the acting remained somewhat subdued, its postsynchronized Shakespearean dialogue both sounding and seeming dubbed. The disparity in critical reactions—it won the Golden Lion at the Venice Film Festival that year, but has found little favor with anglophone critics—might be explained by the comparative inattention to details of dialogue. Unlike Franco Zeffirelli's *Romeo and Juliet* (1968), in which a more substantial Verona still proves subordinate to the actions and in which a simple gauze curtain reveals the tenderness of first love, Castellani's exquisite and memorable mise en scène imprisons his actors.

★ ★ ★

The grace of its pastel-hued visuals, however, probably stemmed from the presence of Robert Krasker, the award-winning cinematographer who filmed Laurence Olivier's *Henry V* (1944). Before joining Olivier on location in Ireland to shoot this epic of wartime propaganda, Krasker had not worked with the Technicolor process, hitherto believed to yield rich color only in bright light. Through experiment he and the director discovered new techniques such as the wintry look of dawn shooting. Perhaps because of their success, Olivier proved to be one of the most technologically innovative makers of Shakespeare films: in *Hamlet* (1948) the prince alternates easily between declamation and whispered dialogue, between voiced thought and interior monologue, between theatrical leaps and all but imperceptible gestures, all with the aid of a "gliding, stalking" camera Dale Silviria recognizes as the presence of his father's restless spirit.[148] In the later *Richard III* (1955) the camera takes the place of a member of the audience to whom Gloucester gestures conspiratorially as if she were a tame lapdog or acquiescent courtier, so rendering his trademark slow forward and reverse tracking shots all the more ominous in their enforcement of spectatorial collusion. This intimacy is lost precisely at the moment Gloucester becomes Richard III, and the former duke's need for confederates abates.

Olivier also adopted the new VistaVision technology (using a 1.67:1 screen aspect ratio), and of all Shakespeare films, with the possible exception of *Prospero's Books*, *Richard III* may be the one most deeply marked by technological innovation. His emblematic approach to the Middle Ages, rendering the ethos as a series of symbolic motifs (complete with anthem-like musical figures supplied by Sir William Walton), his interpretations of characters as essentialized and largely invariant types such as the medieval Vice, and even the physical appearance of the film and his use of actors, owe their origins to the 1950s fascination with wide-screen technologies. The process also had its limitations: in another autobiographical extract included as a supplement to the Criterion Special Edition DVD, Olivier attributes the rapidity of his delivery to his aversion to having a major speech truncated by the frequent reel changes, although he claimed to regard this imposed necessity as a fortunate addition to his characterization, emphasizing Richard's nimbleness. The advantages VistaVision offered are still more apparent. In addition to facilitating panoramic compositions (amply featured in the long climactic battle sequence), it took advantage of a film stock that permitted beautiful color separations. One consequence was a particularly bright–hued medieval world in which courtly attire attained an opulence that would have been the envy of Pieter Brueghel the Elder (whose presence can be felt in figure groupings and massed battle scenes), and such other contributors to the physical appearance of Olivier's courtiers as Hans Holbein and the Flemish artists of the fourteenth and fifteenth centuries. Another was that, perhaps because the least optical distortion occurred in close-ups, Olivier reserves these for revelations of true character: the emblems dangling from chains, such as Gloucester's boar, undermine his pleasantries; a zoom-in captures the evaporation of his affability when one of his doomed nephews refers to his deformed back; the delicacies for which the decadent Buckingham gropes with mock(ing) nonchalance contribute to Gloucester's increasing anxiety and impatience as he awaits news; and when Richard's dead body lies strapped to the horse, a final irony reveals the malediction of the Order of the Garter, "Honi soit qui mal y pense," still adorning his boot.

The prevalence of Gloucester's boar emblem can be explained by the interpretive necessities of the play's highly referential dialogue, some of which his surgically precise long-term redactor, Alan Dent, could not trim away (even though scarcely half of the words remain). Margaret and her predictive curses disappear altogether, but Elizabeth's tirade, in which her dialogue paraphrases the first lines of the papal bull excommunicating Martin Luther (demanding the extermination of the wild boar ravaging the Lord's vineyard), persists. The two dominant visual motifs, however, owe less to Shakespeare and more to Olivier's use of VistaVision technology to provide objective correlatives for Shakespeare's themes. The vertical image compression scales down the oversized crown that remains suspended over the throne of England at the start of the film, symbolic not only of royal prerogative but also of the lust for power, for after introductory scenes borrowed from *3 Henry VI* (here and elsewhere Olivier resorts to the self-contained version of the play by Colley Cibber that had been popular from 1700 onward), we see three crowns adorn the heads of the victorious Yorkists. As the scene ends the king's crown rolls off the cushion borne by an inept page. Anne, played as a wronged innocent by Claire Bloom, all but refuses one before Gloucester's coronation. Eventually his own coronet, struck off his head in the heat of battle, rolls along the full width of the frame and beyond to rest beneath a hazel bush to await its retrieval by Stanley. Another such motif is the shadow, a stygian gloom that spreads over the bright colors. It frequently precedes Gloucester (as it does the vampire, Nosferatu, in G.F. Murnau's 1921 film of that name), and attests to Olivier's Richard-like rivalry with the greatest of his fellow Shakespearean actors. Having smilingly "overlooked" Gloucester's interception of the letter of reprieve for yet another rival he subdues, the saintly, attenuated Clarence of John Gielgud (granted much lamentation but not the moving speech with which he almost dissuades his murderers), Buckingham makes the mistake of treating Gloucester as his client during a meal deceptively rendered as a luminous Dutch still life painting. He should have known better, for not long previously Gloucester's shadow had engulfed his as they entered into conspiracy. Taking the form of the shadow (garbed entirely in black), Richard's first act on accepting the crown is to compel

Buckingham's submission. This is the moment, as historian Bruce Eder points out in the DVD commentary, when the shocked audience loses any residual sympathy for the once engaging Machiavel.

The vivid, painterly quality of the images in *Richard III* notwithstanding, Olivier's most profound contribution to the cinematic visualization of paradigms of seeing, no less indeed than to the pictorial transition from the medieval to the early modern, was the first Shakespeare film he directed. With the help of Art Director Paul Sheriff and inventive costume designer Roger Furse, Olivier contrived to combine pictorial beauty with comedy, grandiose action, and rousing oratory in such a way as to eradicate the memory of his out-of-place Orlando in Paul Czinner's static *As You Like It* (1936). One of Walton's most acclaimed film scores, of a stature comparable to his incidental music for Gielgud's 1941 stage production of *Macbeth*, it blends the Agincourt Hymn and other medieval music with Tudor songs, French folksongs from the Auvergne, and his own inspirations, granting contrasting instrumental groupings to the English and French and even to individual characters, while suggesting the martial music that could inspire Allied troops preparing to retake Europe from the Nazis. With the government's support and that of understanding producer Filippo Del Giudice, but sorely pressed for time and hampered by the inclemencies of the weather, Olivier produced a film that proved, despite its vicissitudes, to be a meticulously wrought essay in the representation of the movement from the theatrical to the cinematic, and from the flattened perspectives of medieval illumination to the spatial illusionism of Renaissance painting.

Henry V is not a film that has inspired critical unanimity. Commentators have warned against the simplistic critical binarism it seems to inspire (did Shakespeare whitewash a national hero or paint a more complex portrait traduced by Olivier's simplifying propagandistic cause?).[149] Yet from the start Olivier's film had vocal proponents, among them André Bazin and Jean Mitry, who thought the stylized setting and mise en scène "exceptional solutions to the dilemma of a play adaptation for the cinema."[150] Bazin, as Silviria notes, argued that in Olivier's hands both Shakespeare and the theatre "become the cinema's prisoners" as they are envisioned through its lenses. Mitry at once recognizes the subtlety of the shifts in spatio-temporal organization that allow for a cinematic representation of a world view of the Middle ages, one different from our own but which Henry has to negotiate when he moves from the battlefield to the French court.[151] Its very opening, in which a camera seems to swoop into the Globe (accomplished using a model of London), establishes the use of the moving camera as an instrument of (cinematic) imagination. It at once places us in the theatrical world (where we begin and end) and introduces the idea of a heightened cinematic verisimilitude by exposing political expediency for what it is (the deriding of the archbishop's interpretation of the Law Salique by the groundlings), while illustrating a series of gaffes, artificial conventions (such as the use of boy actors), and histrionics (the bombast of the Chorus). Olivier thus underlines the limitations of the Renaissance theatre as an epic medium and prepares spectators for the eventual abandonment of the theatre's "wooden O" for the cinematic one of the "vasty fields of France."[152] Anthony Davies has commented that in this respect the film is a "treatise on the differences between cinema and theatre as media for the expression of drama."[153]

Olivier achieves this effect partly through giving the camera a language of its own, as the tracking shot (moving either forward into a space or backward revealing more of that space) becomes a figure for the distinction between the fixed spectatorial position of the theatre and that of cinema's "transportable" spectator. The moving camera hovers over London and moves back in time to the Renaissance; when the Chorus strides forward and begs of the audience "On your imaginary forces work" the camera, on cue, moves backward, and so again when Henry rises in anger to answer the Dauphin's mock, declaring his intention to set forth for France. We are thus prepared for the camera to track backward to reveal multitudes of his eager, expectant soldiers when Olivier delivers what would otherwise be the "theatrical" set-piece declamations of the "Harfleur" and "St. Crispin's Day" speeches, although as Harry Geduld observes this literally reversed the standard filmmaking practice of the time.[154] The Chorus, initially the most "stagey" of the characters, invites the audience to Southampton beckoning the camera through a translucent stage drop (by means of a rapid dissolve), past a compressed, blue-towered castle. Even as he concludes his lines, the camera pans left past a fluttering sail to a setting that, despite its "fairy-tale" character, contains living figures. The English become progressively more cinematic (the Chorus is himself increasingly integrated into the action), while the French remain trapped in the flattened perspectives of medieval art until disaster befalls them, at which point it is Henry who adopts French manners in asserting his sovereignty. Davies perceives that by using such transitional devices Olivier also creates three layers of time. Renaissance time occurs in London at the Globe, medieval time remains associated with the French and later, ephemerally, with the English who imitate their customs to effect reconciliation, and "universal time" that is at once connected to the mythic (Agincourt) and congruent with that experienced by the spectator in subsuming the other layers.[155] The layers merge with the return to the theatrical setting and its time-space upon the espousal of Henry and Catherine.

Although the film borrows from a number of painters (Uccello's massed cavalry and infantry at *The Rout of San Romano,* for instance, and Hilliard and other painters for details of costuming), the dominant visual influence is that of the twelve calendar illustrations from *Les très Riches Heures du Duc de Berry* which, as Geduld points out, Olivier and Sheriff must have seen as high-quality reproductions in the seventh (April to July 1940) edition of the art magazine *Verve*, since the original lay in occupied France.[156] The colors of the costumes, vibrant greens, azures, reds, blacks, and pinks, pay homage to Pol Malouel (called Limbourg after his birthplace), who with his brothers as assistants began work on the illuminations in 1409, only to leave it in an unfinished state when Jean de France, Duc de Berry, died on June 15, 1416, less than a year after the Battle of Agincourt (in the film the Duke appears and examines a bound folio that may well be his still-to-be-finished Book of Hours). When in 1485 it passed by marriage to the Duke of Savoie and Blanche de Montferrat, they decided to have it completed, which Jean Colombe accomplished within two years with the additions of parts of September and all of November. It is precisely because of Pol de Limbourg's extraordinary technique (which owed much to Netherlandish and Flemish painting and to such Italian masters as Taddeo Gaddi) in its anticipation of innovations in linear perspective that Olivier and Sheriff found so contemporary a model to provide the inspiration for a number of scenes from the film. Among them are the gold-patterned blue robe worn by the Duke himself in his portrait in January (modified into the frail Charles VI's decorative robe), the scene of Pistol's thievery drawn from wintry February, the castle inhabited by the French king and his court modeled on that found atop the ploughed fields of March, the richly caparisoned horses (observing a French predisposition for horses in the play) derived from May, and the castle from October that inspires the one seen during the camera's miraculous journey to Southampton. Curiously, Sheriff and Furse make a mistake about the costuming, perhaps an intentional one. In the month of May, one of the figures wears the red and white royal colors, although the male nobles for the most part are dressed in vivid blues. In the film it is the English king and his nobles who wear red, while the French colors are predominantly blues and pinks, suitable for a conceit of the English as bright-hued harbingers of the Renaissance, for as Raymond Durgnat reminds us, France as much as Germany needed to be won over on the eve of D-Day.[157] Others certainly were. Writing for the American publication the *Nation*, James Agee claimed not to be a Tory, a monarchist, a Catholic, a medievalist, or a supporter of war, but conceded that the film inspired him to be them all. "I was persuaded, and in part still am, that every time and place has since been in decline, save one, in which one Englishman used language better than anyone has before or since, or ever shall; and that nearly the best that our time can say for itself is that some of us are still capable of paying homage to the fact."[158]

★ ★ ★

Not everyone found Olivier as persuasive. Few directors could have appreciated the visual values of *Henry V* as well as Kurosawa, who had been trained as a painter and who became one of cinema's most admired pictorialists. Nevertheless, he broke off his correspondence about *Macbeth* with Olivier on receiving the advice that his Lady Macbeth, Asaji, should give birth to a deformed child (she announces her pregnancy at the moment her husband mentions that he may formally make the Banquo character, Miki, his heir, converting thoughts of adoption to assassination). Nevertheless, in some respects, Kurosawa's approach to re-creating a period, as he does in this film and in the later *Ran* (1985), is notably similar. Just as Olivier first translated Shakespeare into the conventions of Elizabethan theatre and then into cinema, Kurosawa and his writers translated Shakespeare into Noh drama and then into the conventions of *jidai-geki*. They differ in that Olivier drew very specifically from visual sources of the period, while Kurosawa's borrowings appears to have been a more general, "aesthetic period," approach. By the same token Olivier's references to specific historical events (a trademark Kurosawa characteristic) do not define a stylistic trait but coincide with Shakespeare's historical inclinations, and in *Hamlet* he largely sets aside the antiquarian approach; in contrast, even in contemporary reworking of the same play, *The Bad Sleep Well* (1960), only the watchful eyes of the censors prevented Kurosawa from being even more explicit about contemporary business and political corruption.[159] In a famous interview that Japanese film historian Tadao Sato conducted on behalf of Roger Manvell (for the latter's book on Shakespeare films), Kurosawa points out to Sato that he had the idea of adapting *Macbeth*, a favorite play, because the events portrayed resemble those that occurred during the period of the civil wars, a historical genre in its own right (*ge-koku-jo*). He added that he used not only the movements of Noh and its set designs for his interiors, but also four of the masks, Heida (heroic warrior), Shakumi (mature woman on the verge of madness), Chujo (apparition of a fallen warrior), and

Yamauba (witch), whose characters the actors assume, with the leads Toshiro Mifune and Isuzu Yamada actually transforming their facial expressions into the appropriate masks in certain instances. Sato himself adds that Asaji shuffles along the floor (in a dance-like movement) with her kimono rustling to the appropriate Noh instrumentation, that on returning after the murder Wahizu stamps on the floorboards (the warrior's sign of anxiety), that the characters face away from each other as often happens in Noh drama, and that the use of fog and rain symbolizes mystery in Japanese aesthetic theory.[160]

It is in this interview that Kurosawa mentions a style of Japanese painting (*sumi-e*), in which figures and elements of landscape occupy largely empty, unpainted space, a characteristic of Japanese art that emerges spontaneously in his compositions.[161] Ana Laura Zambrano also mentions that Kuroswa drew from the painted scrolls of the Kamakura period (1185–1333), especially in his depictions of battle, even going to the lengths of hiring Kohei Esaki, an expert in Kamakura scroll painting, as the film's art consultant.[162] Even so, and despite the studio's active policy of promoting the revival of lavish *jidai-geki* for foreign festivals (Toho's policy had been vindicated when Kurosawa had won the Golden Lion at the Venice Film Festival in 1951 for *Rashomon*, which paved the way for his rival Kenji Mizoguchi to win twice in the following years), the visual influences that inform his work are not exclusively Japanese. Some of Kurosawa's images, such as the invasion of Washizu's castle by ravens, derive explicitly from Shakespeare's text (which, like the film, is replete with avian metaphors), while others are attributable to his admiration for Vincent van Gogh.[163] I treat Kurosawa's syncretism in the next section of this introduction; however, in concluding the discussion of his visual aesthetic, I should point out that the most celebrated example of *sumi-e* to be found in his work, and one of his most striking uses of color, occurs in *Ran*. This film, an adaptation of *King Lear*, eschews the tightly woven, circular, and deterministic construction of *Kumonosu-jô* (1957)—a cause célèbre for those disputing whether the most successful adaptations depart from Shakespeare in the service of the medium or serve the medium best by remaining faithful to his intent[164]—but it furnishes an even more elaborate backstory. Whereas Lady Asaji manipulates the past to her own purposes by persuading Washizu that killing Tsuzuki (Duncan), who had gained power by murdering his own lord, is a matter of self-protection, Lady Kaede, the catalyst for much of the action in *Ran*, has legitimate motives for inciting a series of revenges as her own kinsmen were put to death by the Lear figure, Hidetora, who with his three sons Taro, Jiro, and Saburo, leads the Ichimanji clan. Initially Taro's wife (he is shot by Jiro's loyal samurai retainer Kurogane when civil war breaks out), she meets with Jiro and overpowers him with lightning speed, using his own sword to draw blood from his neck, after which she licks it clean in the manner of a vengeful warrior (she and Hidetora are the most clearly Noh-derived characters, while Kyoami, the Fool, refers to the Kabuki tradition of the *onnegata*, or female impersonator). Having crushed a moth that settles on her kimono, she promptly seduces Jiro. Lady Sué, Jiro's Buddhist wife, flees with her blind brother Tsurumaru, and when Kaede demands her head Kurogane presents instead the ceramic head of a vixen (a duplicitous animal credited in folklore with assuming human guises).[165] After a sniper's bullet kills Saburo, who has returned to rescue his father and battle for the kingdom, the broken-hearted Hidetora expires and the soldiers do indeed kill Sué and deliver her head to Kaede. It is at this point that Kurosawa includes an internal self-reference. The wall of the chamber in which Asaji and Washizu confer bears the indelible bloodstain of a traitor forced to commit *seppuku*, but on black-and-white stock it registers as a characteristic dark gray. After the death of Hidetora, Saburo, and Sué, whose bundled head he intercepts, Kurogane revenges the clan by seizing Kaede over Jiro's feeble protests, and decapitating her, producing a fountain of red that splashes against a gray-lacquered wood surface.

In an interview for the journal *Positif*, included as printed extracts in the sleeve-notes to the Criterion DVD reissue, Kurosawa explained his concerns with the proper reproduction of color. The green of the opening shot, for instance, varies with the intensity of light falling on near-emerald mountain-tops, against which three tiny horsemen appear on the slope at the lower right corner of the frame (Kurosawa's credit line eventually appears over this, the letters as large as a horse—his favorite symbol of pure instinct). The flattening of space, which has the effect of transforming it into a pattern of irregular quadrilaterals, is indicative of a technique Kurosawa adopted early in his career of using telephoto lenses to achieve the same effects as the school of Japanese Modernist painting that deliberately evoked traditional styles (*nihonga*). It is probably also because of the demands he made on his actors to move within the confines of such painterly compositions that he almost always used two or more cameras on each take. The effect is consciously evocative of *sumi-e*, in which a black ink derived from burned pine needles or bamboo was combined with pine resin or fish-bone glue to create a black, water-soluble pigment traditionally applied with a brush onto cream, yellow, gold, or orange backgrounds. In time, the vertical hanging scroll, for which the technique was popular, gave way to more elaborate gatefold screens as the dominant vehicle for the art form, and Kurosawa's use of wide-screen compositions (divided into vertical planes, sometimes effected with wipes) is often reminiscent of such screens.[166] As in the case of this credit sequence, Kurosawa varied the colors of his backgrounds. Moreover, he coordinated the foreground color schemes with great precision. The ancient imperial color (a deep purple) is seldom found in his films. The colors of the court, however, dominate many scenes, particularly those of massed troops: the highest-ranking colors (orange-yellow) suggest the bright yellow worn by Hidetora's heir, Taro, and his followers, Jiro and his wear red (the color of both sacred and secular authority), and Saburo's men wear blue (the dominant color that was prevalent in daily use and a favorite of such nineteenth-century ukiyo-e landscape painters as Hokusai and Hiroshige).[167]

Ran is the last of Kurosawa's epic films, and his much-discussed concluding sequence—that makes dramatic use of the orange-brown background of later *sumi-e* painting—depicts the funeral cortege winding past a vast, bleak volcanic landscape. Using a series of cuts in and out, a favorite technique, he reveals the blind Tsurumaru standing on the escarpment of a cliff, an obvious allusion to Shakespeare's Gloucester subplot. The Lear-Hidetora character is dead and so is the character closest to Edgar, Sué. There is a brief cut to a scroll painting that, as he almost stumbles over the edge, Tsurumaru drops into the abyss, a depiction of the Buddha of Compassion in the *yamato-e* style adopted by painters of the Zen Buddhist sects.[168] Even as it alludes to the flute theme with which Kozintsev concludes his version of *King Lear*, *Ran* ends with a final vision of Tsurumaru, a lone figure hovering on the edge of a precipice against a misty background, the tragic flute of Noh drama announcing the end of an epoch.

Modernity????

Few terms in aesthetics or social studies have invited as much controversy and as many varied definitions as "modern," and its implied aftermath, "postmodern." Although the architect Mies van der Rohe had used the term "postmodern" to describe his own work in the late 1920s, aesthetic modernity usually defines literature or painting from the late 1880s almost to the advent of World War II;[169] a second modernity, social modernity, generally refers to the rapid urbanization of rural and agrarian populations following the industrial revolution;[170] and perhaps a third modernity partakes of a long history of ideas that extends back to the clergy of the Middle Ages and that intensified into a "philosophical discourse" in the nineteenth century.[171] Matei Calinescu thus refers to "two distinct and bitterly conflicting modernities." Placing the point of bifurcation in the first half of the nineteenth century, he distinguishes between the concept as a stage in Western civilization and as an aesthetic concept that had its origins at least as early as 1888 when Rubén Darío described *el modernismo*. Modernity, for Calinescu, subtends the categories of Modernism, avant-garde, Decadence, kitsch, and postmodernism, where "Kitsch," the title of an unfinished 1917 play by Frank Wedekind, is the art of "vicarious experience and faked sensation" as defined, albeit at the distance of a generation, by Clement Greenberg.[172] When categorized by its constituencies of consumers, modernity appears to encompass six artistic cultures, "High art," "Modernist art," "Avant-garde art," "Folk art," "Popular art," and "Mass art"; but its four maxims (as distilled by Fredric Jameson) appear to make it indefinable: "we cannot periodize,"; we have to accept modernity as a "narrative category" rather than as a concept; modernity "resists conceptualization and representation,"; and modernity makes sense only in the light of a break with the "postmodern."[173]

As for Shakespeare, his frequent inclusion in an already embattled discursive terrain makes for the further complication that he is often taken as a paradigmatic exemplar of a moment of transition from the medieval world of the early Tudor monarchs to the "early modern" one of the Elizabethans. Thus, postmodern Shakespeare has a fraught relationship with Modernist Shakespeare (Halpern), an even more complex one with early modern Shakespeare (as envisioned collectively by New Historicists), and "Shakespeare" himself has the most complicated relationship of all with the "postmodern" which, although initially advanced as a state of being (Lyotard), rapidly came to be seen as a pathology (Jameson) or "condition" (Harvey).[174] And then we have the case of cinema, that unlike the other arts claims two distinct periods of Modernism, the first consisting of the experimental cinemas of the 1920s, the second of the American underground of the 1950s augmented by the French and other European new waves of the 1960s.[175] The latter coincided with the crises stemming from decolonization movements and struggles for national self-determination, with the result that scholars who concerned themselves with the less wholesome aspects of modernity and thought of it in terms of the consequences of postcoloniality (rather than a transition to postmodernity) contributed an alternative set of historical explanations that have coincided with recent concerns about the phenomenon of globalization. Critiques of the exclusionary nature of Western historiography by scholars such as Ranajit Guha and Dipesh Chakrabarty, and theorists of the diasporas resulting from colonialism (an alternative Modernism in exile, perhaps), have augmented the range of methodologies that such scholars as Ania Loomba and Martin Orkin, for instance, have brought to bear on Shakespeare Studies.[176]

Some scholars of the phenomenon have taken pains to emphasize the unequal exchanges that globalization implies. Arjun Appadurai argues that existing power structures are preserved in emerging cultural landscapes through the dispersal of hegemonies. Anthony Giddens has warned that the speed of change may actually have inhibitory effects on the spread of democracy. Others, such as some contributors to a well-known anthology by Frank Lechner and John Boli, have taken the hopeful view that as demands for labor increase a more equitable distribution of the world's resources may result, or (as in the case of John Tomlinson) have expressed a guarded optimism that deterritorialization will lead to cultural pluralism.[177] A central tenet of all these discussions appears to be that the problems of modernity are yet to be resolved, or even (as Mike Featherstone, Scott Lash, and Roland Robertson contend) that globalization is the unfolding resolution to which we are witnesses and in which we are participants.[178] What is more, the early modern inheritance through colonialism and, in some instances, neocolonialism, documents a historical trauma whose impact extends to the present day, whether as the result of supplanting eradicated local technologies and cultural forms with new languages and religions (as Walter Mignolo argues of the Renaissance colonization of the Americas), or as a modern-day ambivalence to modernity itself, as Néstor García Canclini observes.[179] One of the lasting consequences to cinema has, indeed, been the result of the inequalities of modernity as it shaped continents, inhabitants, and, eventually, technologies of representation, and much of the present discussion of Shakespeare films turns on the distinction between the kind of voluntary modernity adopted by Japan after the 1867 Meiji Restoration, and the imposed modernity that overtook Africa, Latin America, and the Indian subcontinent in the wake of colonial domination.

★ ★ ★

By an unusual coincidence, Shakespeare offers the historical record an early modern mo(ve)ment that is at once a curious and transcendent singularity that spans all these discourses. Whether in this instance he was read as an antihegemonic "Chicaspeare" (which if true would no doubt delight García Canclini), is a moot point, for we have only the barest of inklings as to the first—if we discount the literal truth of the preliminary formula common to the quartos, "lately acted by"—recorded rendition of *Hamlet*, assumed to be Shakespeare's since the only quarto editions then in print were his. It took place on September 5, 1607, on board the *Dragon*, one of two merchant ships bound on a successful "trial" voyage to India. Of the four separate extant journals, two for that day recount an elephant hunt that would have shocked George Orwell; but the journal of the captain, William Keeling, emphasized that Shakespeare was also to be had that morning: "I sent the Portuguese interpreter [Lucas Fernandez, a Christianized Temne native who had lived in Portugal's Cape Verde colony], according to his desire aboard the Hector, where he broke fast, and after came aboard of me, where we had the Tragedy of Hamlet; and in the afternoon we went altogether ashore, to see if we could shoot an elephant."[180] To this account Gary Taylor adds parts of the entries for September 29, 1607, when Keeling's "company" acts *King Richard II* for the benefit of Captain Hawkins of the *Hector*, and another for March 31, 1608, when *Hamlet* was done again over a "fish dinner" shared with

Hawkins, the digestive processes no doubt enhanced by the eccentric belief that acting was (in an astonishing reversal of the Puritan proclamations of the time) a preventative against "idleness, unlawful games, or sleep."[181] It is unclear (and rather doubtful) whether Farim Buré, the Temne king of the land, attended the first *Hamlet*, or indeed who did, although for a variety of reasons the Catholic Fernandez might have understood the play rather differently from Hawkins.

In contrast to this account, in which the diarists keep expressing surprise that the black inhabitants seem so capable and cognizant of European mores, anthropologist Laura Bohanan recounts her amusing version of *Hamlet* as recited to a gathering of the Tiv people of West Africa. Master storytellers, they find fault with the details, but rescue the narrative through proper interpretation: since ghosts do not exist, Hamlet merely imagines that an omen sent by a witch happens to be his dead father; Claudius takes the only acceptable course in marrying his brother's widow promptly; Laertes kills Ophelia so that he can sell her body to the witches and pay off his gambling debts, and so on. Paradoxically, it is Bohanan who is here in the position of Fernandez. Just as his English was probably imperfect, she had limitations as a translator, and so kept adjusting the details to avoid complexities, thus necessitating a very thorough hermeneutics of consensus on the part of her audience. The prologue leaves us with the idea that Americans can, despite British notions to the contrary, understand Shakespeare, or at least rather better than the Tiv.[182] It is a nice yarn, and intended to give the lie to notions about the universality of literary comprehension, but it is also a measure of cultural distance. *Hamlet* on board the *Dragon* was entertainment and perhaps display; the Tiv *Hamlet* is the literary reworking of a social experiment conducted on a vanishing group of inhabitants of a shattered continent. When the Nobel Prize-winning Nigerian dramatist Wole Soyinka created a satire on the legacy of the European presence in Africa, whose chief result was the retardation of democratic processes and the enthronement of postcolonial dictators, his *King Baabu* bore the subtitle "a play in the manner—*roughly*—of Alfred Jarry." The reference was to Jarry's Ubu plays, one of which became a founding text of French Modernist theatre, a Dada *Macbeth* called *Ubu Roi*. "Sheige!" swears the title character at the start, in honor of Jarry's "Merdre." Early on, the future king General Basha Bash refers to "this summer of our contentment," and he dies poisoned in the manner of Gertrude.[183] As Edward Said remarked of Aimé Césaire's *Une Tempête*, *King Baabu* is "not *ressentiment* but an affectionate contention with Shakespeare."[184] It is much further from the narrative trajectory of *Macbeth* than the Tiv version of *Hamlet*; but then so was Jarry's, and it is to that refraction of the play through the prism of history that Soyinka alerts us.

★ ★ ★

It is not the colonial crisis and postcolonial rupture felt in Africa, but the first crisis that befell twentieth century Europe, World War I, that forever disrupted modernity and irrevocably changed the hitherto successful cinemas of Denmark and Sweden. Here, as elsewhere in the world, Hollywood has played the role of a postcolonial dictator, dominating the film box office in most countries, and in many instances stifling local production through aggressive marketing strategies. Ingmar Bergman's unprecedented international success in the 1950s was due only to the post–World War II emergence of film festival circuits, with the consequence that for many filmgoers he alone represents the Swedish film industry.[185] This lopsidedness was, until recently, felt even more acutely in Finland. By cultivating an underplayed, ironic out-of-placeness in his films, of which several were road movies set abroad, Aki Kaurismäki claimed a much larger international movie audience than a Finnish one, but, with his brother and collaborator Mika, he was for many years the international face of Finnish cinema. His *Hamlet Goes Business* (*Hamlet Liikemansaa* 1987) might owe its conceit to Kurosawa, but it is a much closer paraphrase of the play, and it actually incorporates quotes that accord with its business setting. A hound's-eye-view shot of a barking, tethered dog indicates the ironic use of genre conventions from the outset, as subsequently confirmed by both plot and music (Shostakovich at his most portentous mixed with Tchaikovsky and the blues, a send-up of Kozintsev).[186] Hamlet initially fails to notice that his father, who heads a conglomerate, is dead, and the major business deal that underpins the machinations of the murderous Klaus (Claudius) consists of divesting from sawmills and shipping lines and taking over a rubber duck factory. The film's address to a transnational audience reveals itself in an opening pun that would be most obvious to English speakers: in an otherwise unmotivated sequence, Hamlet walks into a basement kitchen, takes the knife from a woman in an apron, and carves himself a slice of the ham on her cutting board.

The Scandinavian Shakespeare film that has most often been associated with globalism in critical discourse, however, is the fourth film to be certified as belonging to the Dogme 95 movement. The movement came into being (as did the New German Cinema and Third Cinema) with a manifesto, a much-derided Vow of Chastity whereby filmmakers from any country who voluntarily abstained from a list of ten indulgences—associated primarily with big-budget Hollywood films and their imitations—could request inclusion. Lars von Trier, who with Thomas Vinterberg drafted the manifesto, has acknowledged his indebtedness to Cassavetes for the idea behind the insistence on a handheld camera and improvised acting, although other constraints, such as shooting in unmodified locations,[187] simultaneously recorded unmixed sound, avoidance of familiar genres, melodrama, or indulgence in any stylistic idiosyncrasies or expressions of personal taste, partake of the Third Cinema critique of Hollywood's First Cinema and *auteurist* Second Cinema. The first three Dogme films already deviated from the "code," albeit subtly, and by the time Kristian Levring's *The King Is Alive* appeared in 2000, calamitous events, certainly, had become commonplace. Mette Hjort, however, describes Dogme 95 as a "small nation's response to globalization," and points out that if the Vow of Chastity was something of a publicity stunt then it brought about the right publicity, its "metacultural" address gleaning an international audience that shared certain normative values with the filmmakers.[188]

Just as Jean-Marie Straub and Danielle Huillet experimented with stylized acting in their films, and Peter Brook did in the spare, Robert Bresson-like approach of his 1971 version of *King Lear*, *The King Is Alive* elicits a certain kind of theatrical performance (i.e., theatrical rehearsals as a desperate diversion) but treats it as the natural consequence of a situation and integrates it with a consciously nonshowy cinematic performance style. Improbably, this style is imposed on reputed actors from England, France, South Africa, Zimbabwe, Namibia, and even America (true to form, the Hollywood star Jennifer Jason Leigh delivers a scene-stealing performance). Brook seems to cast an ominous shadow, for along with story elements that could be out of Herman Melville and Guy de Maupassant, an adult version of *The Lord of the Flies* (1963) seems to hover over the plot.[189] An ill-assorted group of tourists, trapped in a deserted Namibian mining village with only rusting cans of food for sustenance, soon falls prey to the individuals' intense rivalries and personal demons. A man of action leaves to locate a rescue party, his later discovery in the desert and burial permitting a natural visual tribute to the last sequence of Ingmar Bergman's *The Seventh Seal* (1957), with its procession of linked shadows. Henry, the intellectual of the group, a former theatre man, suggests a performance of *King Lear* that he proposes to reconstruct from memory (a possible reference to a similar device in Jean-Luc Godard's 1980 version of *King Lear*). Treating Cordelia as a plum role, he initiates a rivalry between his partner Catherine, a French woman, and Gina, an American whose thespian aspirations seem connected to her former employment as showgirl. Liz, playing Goneril to the Edmund of the driver, Kanana, pretends to want to have sex with him, but provokes a humiliating response on admitting, "I brought you here to piss my husband off." Still, in rehearsal she insists on repeating a scene so that she kisses him three times. Paul, a racist, later confronts Kanana and beats him to the ground, and Paul's wife, Amanda, who seems otherwise a conscientious Fool capable of remembering her lines, gets to play Susan (from *Citizen Kane*) when she walks out on him. Catherine taints Gina's food and she suffers from food poisoning, but when Charles attempts to help her she derides both his motives and his much-prized virility, with the consequence that when the others leave to inter Henry's corpse, he suffocates her, urinates on her face, and hangs himself, oblivious to some of the Dogme strictures. By the time some African workers arrive by truck and find the stunned survivors seated in the flickering glow of a funeral pyre, Henry has fallen into Lear's role (delivering five lines of the "Howl, howl, howl!" speech as epitaph), to which Ron, hitherto uncomfortable as Kent, responds in all sincerity: "Is this the promised end?"

Critics at once praised the film's visual qualities (in particular the astonishing burnt orange provided by the light of the Namibian desert), and noted its narrative complexity: there is nothing accidental or aleatory about its structure, while the acting improvisations fall within a minutely prescribed choreography. The citations of Shakespeare are also far more involved than critics have allowed, for while the idea that the play rehearsal progressively becomes the characters' reality does belong to the Dogme critique of fantasy,[190] some of the roles allude to the Renaissance convention of doubling parts (Gina is Reagan and Cordelia), others mix characters (Liz, Kanana, and Paul take on various aspects of Othello, Iago, and Desdemona, without speaking any of the lines), and Levring and his cowriter Anders Thomas Jensen create in Charles a grim fantasy on what might have happened had Angelo's sexual blackmail succeeded. Nor is the setting, despite its similarity to Brook's, merely a convenient choice. We discover at the end of the film that the entire train of events is a flashback told by a *griot* character, Moses, the Old Man of the abandoned village, who intervenes from time to time to provide narrative commentaries in the past tense: the character alludes to the storyteller who similarly narrates *Ceddo* (1976), the most widely distributed film of one of the towering figures of Third Cinema, Ousmane Sembène, whose oeuvre is a relentless critique of colonialism and postcolonial corruption and atavism. For many years Namibia was a satellite of an apartheid South African government, used as a source of minerals and tourism. The parallel to the self-positioning of the Dogme 95 filmmakers vis-à-vis Hollywood's First Cinema should not pass unnoticed.

★ ★ ★

Japan's entry into modernity could not have been more different from Namibia's, and Kurosawa again provides an exemplary model of a filmmaker whose work represents the cultural history of that process. A coup in 1866 toppled the long, de facto rule of the Japanese Shoguns (or great warlords), and by 1868 the process of imperial reinstatement was complete. The first edict issued by the restored emperor contained as Article 5 "knowledge shall be sought throughout the world so as to strengthen the foundations of imperial rule."[191] Thus Japan's voluntary entry into modernity permitted a selective approach to its various guises. In 1871 a mission sent to study the arts and technology of the West accumulated some 2,000 pages of notes about what might be best emulated in the national interest, and this sparked debates about modes of dress, hairstyles, diet, Western building materials, even the possibility of intermarriage as the fastest route to modernization. In the 1870s the translation of Western literature became a major genre, and its first great exponent, Tsubouchi Shoyo, published widely on the modernization of prose and poetry as well as translating all of Shakespeare, regarding the latter as the major dramatist whose techniques most resembled those of Japanese dramatic forms.[192] Already during the shogunate, painters such as Shiba Kokan had adopted the style of Dutch realist painting, but newer styles entered Japan only when the Meiji government invited the Italian Antonio Fontanesi to teach at the new Industrial Art School. Despite his early departure he left a generation of devoted students. Almost simultaneously, the American philosopher Ernest Fenellosa arrived to become a passionate advocate of the preservation of traditional styles, as did his student Okakura Tenshin, even as a simultaneous school of Westernized painting came into being (indeed, some painters sent to France for study recognized the indebtedness of French Modernism to Japanese art and remained to make careers there). The lifting of Tokugawa restrictions on drama also resulted in a resurgence of Kabuki as well as a new genre with political overtones, modern drama or *shimpa*. Shoyo produced theatrical performances, and sometimes mixed scenes from Shakespeare with those from Kabuki plays, whereas director Osanai Kauro adopted Western naturalistic styles of playing, producing the works of Ibsen, Chekhov, and Gorky. The first Shakespeare production was Genzo Katsu's Kabuki version of *The Merchant of Venice* at Osaka's Ebisu Theatre in 1885, and Otojiro Kawakami began a series of contemporary versions using translations beginning with *Othello* in 1903. In 1911 Shoyo helped produce the first full-scale translated play in an original setting, *Hamlet*, at Tokyo's new Imperial Theatre. Moviemaking began in Japan in 1896, although for nearly twenty years reproductions of Kabuki and *shimpa* dominated cinema, lending it a deeply ingrained narrative tradition. Kurosawa's revered elder brother was, for instance, one of the more admired among the ubiquitous *benshi*, whose function was not only to impersonate voices and relate a story, but also to provide didactic commentary as events unwound on the screens.[193] Kurosawa's films, all made with synchronized sound, nevertheless hark back to this cinematic convention of the 1920s by underlining the humanistic, message-laden meanings of his narratives.[194]

In his prefatory chapter to Kurosawa's Shakespeare films, John Collick notes that the extreme nationalism (resulting from a military cooptation of the government) of the 1930s and 1940s led to a climate of suspicion against Western literature and to its proscription. Thus, in his *jidai-geki* films, especially, Kurosawa's appeal to traditions aligned him with the previous generation of Meiji-era intellectuals.[195] It is for this reason that Collick finds his more consistent use of Noh in *Kumonosu-jô* preferable to that of the less challenging *Ran*: for him it is Kurosawa at his most authentically Japanese. Mitsuhiro Yoshimoto, on the other hand, warns against a romanticization of pre–World War II Japan as excessively idealistic (while not colonized there was then an ingrained sense of cultural underdevelopment), and instead stresses both the cultural continuity and the challenge each of Kurosawa's films offered to the society of his time. In the Meiji period, Western-influenced painting (*yoga*) and music (*yogaku*) acquired a generic status, distinct from traditional woodblock prints (*nihonga*) and traditional music (*hogaku*). However, argues Yoshimoto, unless there was a Western demand for *nihonga* (as promoted by Fenellosa and Okakura), it could not have existed in a climate of intense modernization. Rather than rigorously conforming to Japanese aesthetics, Kurosawa challenges cultural assumptions by infusing the *jidai-geki*, which was deeply influenced by Kabuki, with the conventions of Noh. Likewise, Kurosawa's appeals to tradition in his use of painting happens to be refracted through the Modernist debates on aesthetics, a point Yoshimoto underlines with the argument that the idea of a visual translation of verbal poetry has nothing to do with "Japaneseness" per se.[196] We can, however, reconcile both arguments by allowing that Kurosawa simultaneously challenges both Japanese and Occidental spectators. This kind of dialogical synthesis of two cultural traditions that inform each other because of the friction that results from their incorporation into a well-characterized genre is perhaps most evident in *Ran*. Here Kurosawa urged the use of Gustav Mahler's *Das Lied von der Erde* to the most renowned of Japan's avant-garde composers, Toru Takemitsu, who was also a prolific and greatly respected film composer who had composed the music for his *Dodeskaden* (1970). One of Takemitsu's principles was that film scores should accord so well with the images that they remain entirely unobtrusive, and so, in addition to such striking effects as the piercing sound of the Noh flute at such moments as when Hidetaro discharges an arrow with fatal effect, and the melancholy symphonic solemnities associated with battle and calamity, his music is suffused by *ma*, sudden, concentrated silences.[197] Of all Shakespeare films its vision of history's retributive forces, perhaps derived from Buddhist theology, is paradoxically the one that most nearly approximates Kott's vision of calamitous history. As with most of Kurosawa's films, *Ran* was an international coproduction funded in part by the French producer Serge Silberman: by this time the exacting director was considered too great a box-office risk in Japan, which had become one of the world's technological giants.

★ ★ ★

Unlike Japan's, India's entry into modernity was neither voluntary nor accompanied by a social revolution with universal education and modernizations as its aims. Colonialism also entailed the creation of an English-speaking elite that facilitated the governance of multitudes by a privileged minority, Lord Macaulay's stated aim in enacting the Indian Education Act of 1835. Shakespeare was part of this civilizing mission, even if at first social conventions served as a bulwark against infiltration by natives (even the ushers in the theatres constructed in the mid-eighteenth century were British), something of a compound irony because many of India's flourishing theatrical traditions had outlived England's Renaissance theatre by many centuries.[198] In time wealthy Indians owned and operated the same establishments where once they could not set foot, and Shakespeare, however conservative he may have seemed to his fellow Stratfordians, rapidly underwent a conversion. After various experiments at indigenization that began with a Bengali actor playing Othello (which provoked the hostility of the authorities), followed by performances of translations of the plays in the mid-nineteenth century, his theatrical oeuvre attained lasting popularity as adaptations that became hybrid theatrical presentations, particularly those absorbed into Parsi theatre. Such was his popularity (at least among the literate upper classes) that only in the 1920s, with the intensification of the nationalist movement, was there a corresponding decline in translations and performances.[199]

Almost from the showing of the first Lumière films in Bombay in 1896, however, cinema established itself as a popular medium in India. It was also a highly syncretic form that adapted the structure of the 1930s Hollywood Musical into a huge array of indigenous genres. As Rajiva Verma points out, a popular film of 1961 might contain a song that quotes Wordsworth's lyrics and Mozart's music, and the films based on Shakespeare were often seized willy-nilly from Parsi theatre. He goes on to catalogue a series of identifiable adaptations, beginning in 1927, that derived from *The Merchant of Venice*, *The Taming of the Shrew*, *Measure for Measure*, *Antony and Cleopatra*, *Cymbeline*, *Pericles*, *Twelfth Night*, *A Comedy of Errors*, a conflation of *Richard III* and *King John* (by the same Sohrab Modi who directed the second film version of *Hamlet* in 1935), even ones based on *Macbeth* and the same scenes of Arthur pleading with Hubert not to blind him.[200] This is only a partial list of films produced in India's film capital, Bombay (Mumbai), popularly called Bollywood: there are probably many more in the other popular cinemas of Madras (Chennai) and Calcutta. There are also at least two versions of *Othello* involving classical dance forms, Govindan Aravindan's *Marattam* (1988) and Jayaraaj's *Kaliyattam* (1998), the first made by one of the canonical filmmakers of the New Indian Cinema (whose films have the austere look and poetry of Antonioni and Ozu), the second by a star director of a vibrant, popular Malayali cinema based in the state of Kerala. Two of the most interesting adaptations must be direct imitations of previous films: the great female star of her generation, Nargis, ran her own production company, and made a *Romeo and Juliet* based on the MGM film of 1936 without changing the setting; and Kishore Sahu's *Hamlet* (1954) might be a "shot by shot reproduction of Laurence Olivier's 1948 adaptation" (omitting even the customary Hindi musical interludes), although its dialogue is not Olivier's, as it appears to have been "taken over verbatim from Ahsan's *Khoon-e-Nahak*" (one of a significant number of *Hamlet* adaptations to cinema).[201] The production of an imitation as an index of cultural value, as Homi Bhabha points out, is a function of colonizing discourse, and thus the mimicry encouraged of colonials is ambivalent, producing at once resemblance and deformation. Within the shadow of mimicry is a penumbral region of mockery and menace.[202] Sahu's intriguing synthesis shows that cinema has made Olivier available in more than one sense to Indians, even to the extent of facilitating a deformation of the dialogue track through a process of doubled mimicry (i.e., passing off the indigenous as Royally Shakespearean, while attempting to render the

Royally Shakespearean open to indigenous appropriation). One is not surprised, therefore, to encounter a critic determining in a moment of intense enthusiasm that it was time to get rid of an "inferiority complex" since "Nargis proves equal to Norma Shearer!"[203]

A work that unlike Nargis's survives and is, indeed, well known, is *Shakespeare Wallah* (1965), the breakthrough film of the James Ivory-Ismail Merchant team. Shot in luminescent textures by Satyajit Ray's cinematographer, Subrata Mitra, and given a wistful musical score by Ray himself, it tells the story of a British theatrical troupe wandering from palace to prep school in an effort to keep a vanishing tradition alive. Merchant's affable account of its genesis makes its production values—it is set in recently independent India—seem all the more remarkable. The authenticity of the details underscores the poignancy of the narrative, that of the daughter of the troupe leader losing her heart to a dashing, errant Indian playboy, who is presently reclaimed with feline panache by a Bollywood star played by Madhur Jaffrey. The basic conceit derived from the diaries of Geoffrey Kendal whose itinerant theatre company, Shakespeareana, served as the model for the traveling company, and it was his daughter, Felicity, who played the beguiled young woman opposite one of the rising matinee idols of Indian cinema, Shashi Kapoor.[204] One of the most dramatic scenes of the film, one that probably won Jaffrey a Silver Bear at the Berlin Film Festival, was Manjula's deliberate sabotage of a performance of *Othello* given by the troupe in an elegant theatre. She begins to complain loudly enough to distract the entire filmstar-besotted audience, among them her embarrassed beau who happens to be enamored of Desdemona. Poor Othello has to beat the stage floor and command silence before continuing with "It is the cause, it is the cause, my soul" and the concluding suffocation of his victim. Yet from its outset, when we see a group of actors costumed for a Restoration drama performed on a riverfront lawn, the film establishes a tone that is less melodramatic than elegiac, a feature that has led, in some instances, for its import to be mistaken for Raj nostalgia (in fact, the actors conclude this performance with a jocose rendition of "Rule Brittania" in their very proper English, a scene that has resonances for the final scene when the heartbroken Lizzie Buckingham boards an ocean liner taking her back to school in Britain). In most instances, the players inhabit humbler venues, at one point being haughtily dismissed by the Indian principal of a school on the grounds that that other British introduction, cricket, was now of greater interest to the boys.

One grouping of scenes reveals the catastrophe that has befallen the actors, cast adrift on the tides of history, with understated clarity. When they arrive at the palace of a maharaja, a butler announces that "the Players have arrived," thus commenting on the actors' situation by transforming troupe leader, Tony, and his Buckingham Players into the Player King and the motley entourage who have to be coached by Hamlet to act with greater subtlety. Although charged with performing an abridged *Antony and Cleopatra*, the proceedings begin with a sumptuous dinner where the potentate, in studied English, recalls being spellbound by an actress in his tender youth. Then, by way of illustration, he launches into Portia's "The quality of mercy is not strained." He smiles and looks about for approval as he continues in high seriousness, "it droppeth as a gentle rain..." until garbling a line and apologizing with a smile, "you flatter me." He continues to munch while explaining that Indians also appreciate Shakespeare for his "wisdom," for no one better understood the turbulence of the heart or the heavy burdens of kingship. "Uneasy lies the head that wears a crown." He then bewails having to turn rooms of his palace into offices and the passing of the days of yore when his father would process through throngs on a royal elephant offering the grateful populace his blessings. "Let us sit upon the ground and tell stories about the death of kings," consoles Lear-Buckingham. "How some have been depos'd, some slain in war, some haunted by [those] they have deposed," adds his wife and costar. The Maharaja cuts them off in some alarm, before the plays grow even more obscure than *2 Henry IV* and more kings come to grief. When the aptly named Buckinghams point out that they are used to modifying their plays to suit the occasion, he offers: "You know, we are all forced to make cuts in the texts offered by Destiny." They laugh. *Antony and Cleopatra* begins with the camera zooming in on the redoubtable Tony Buckingham who is here Enobarbus, and who with his crisp, nasal diction recites the famed description of Cleopatra's barge. As he proceeds we hear the gentle strumming of a lute and then the arabesques of an Oriental melody as a slow zoom out reveals more and more of the Moghul-inspired arcade beneath which he stands. A billowing fan in the foreground gradually creeps into the widening frame to reveal the servant (wallah) who stands ventilating a seated figure. When the speech ends and another actor enters, there is a reverse cut to reveal the smoking figure, with his retainers seated behind him in rapt attention. After another balcony scene, a cut takes us backstage where one actor tries to cadge a little money from another while they listen to recordings of Bollywood music. We return to Cleopatra cradling the dying Antony.[205] When the performance ends, the maharaja leads his retainers in the applause, and with florid praises places garlands on the Buckinghams' necks. We cut abruptly to a roadway where a monkey trainer walks toward a rickety, broken-down vehicle, part of the actors' caravan. The tinny sound of his drum serves as accompaniment. The monkeys cavort as the actors attempt roadside repairs. Lizzie and an older actor, Bobby, set off in his car to get help. The monkey trainer insists on making those who remain his audience, claiming that he is not doing too well nowadays, as people no longer care for his art. "Our story exactly," comments Bobby. The trainer, beating his drum, convinces one monkey to start playing the cymbals, and elevates the stick to which both are chained so they can circle around him. Shown no encouragement, he wanders off on the roadway that stretches into the distance. The layers of reference—to Macaulayism, to the consequences of industrial modernity, to the craft of acting itself—are unmistakable. The zoom out at the maharaja's command performance embeds the actors in the decaying splendors of his palace, an edifice that recounts the history of India's occupations and cultural syntheses, and as this happens, the music acquires a more native hue. Taken out of the protective palatial cocoon and returned once more to their mundane milieu, the actors prove not to be cast in the role of the monkey trainer, as Bobby thinks, but—like the rest of us—that of the monkeys. Gently relegated to the shadows of the film's other texts, here Destiny appears in the flesh.

Few films could offer a greater contrast than one also made in India some forty years later, perhaps the most interesting of all the Gangster *Macbeth*s, Vishal Bhardwaj's *Maqbool* (2004). The symphonic complexity of the music score, composed by the director, might explain the unusually sophisticated rhythms of its editing: in the scene in which Nimmi (the Lady Macbeth character played by Bollywood star Tabu) forces Miyan Maqbool to confess his love to her at gunpoint, for instance, contains a montage of medium close-up low-angle shots taken from different positions and intercut phrase by phrase, as if to a musical beat. For the first half hour there are no musical interludes (indeed, up to this point the film could well be taken to be one of the "art films" of the 1980s), and when thereafter they do occur they are integrated into the narrative as festive interludes. Jahangir Khan, whose name alludes to the Moghul emperor imprisoned by his son, Shah Jahan, is far more developed as a character than Shakespeare's snide Duncan. Miyan, both beloved "son" Brutus and treacherous Macbeth, seems to acquire motivation through the logical, if extraordinary, plot device of making the seductive, masochistic Nimmi, for whom sexual conquest is revenge and who is turned on by such things as having pistols pointed at her, Jahangir's youthful and rather dangerous wife. It is Jahangir's cultivation of an even younger mistress, in fact, that leads to Nimmi's determination to set Miyan on the path to murder.

There are numerous references in the film to India's Islamic history, and it is predominantly set in a courtly, feudal milieu associated with the Moghul inheritance: at one point when he is arrested by a zealous new assistant chief of police, Devsare, Jahangir quotes the emperor's poetic lament: "I, Jahangir, had to bear the humiliation." Yet it is not this social history alone that contributes to the film's celebration of polymorphous hybridities. The language spoken by the gangsters and policemen who are in their pay is up-to-date Bombaytalk, a mixture of Hindi with numerous borrowed words and anglicisms (one of the policemen, Puroshit, hands a cell phone over to the other, Panditji, since he speaks English, but the English that results is broad Indian English). Part of the humorous irony involved is that the theme of the corrupt policeman was a particular favorite of India's "art film" movement, the New Indian Cinema of the 1970s and 1980s that its government sponsors regarded as an antidote to the supposed banalities of popular Hindi and Tamil cinema. The two leading male actors of the New Indian Cinema also happen to be Naseeruddin Shah (Puroshit) and Om Puri (Panditji), who have spoken Standard English with facility when acting on stage in Peter Brook's *Hamlet* or when taking part in British films. For the first half hour, until the change in the police administration temporarily curtails their activities, the film seems to follow their story. The opening sequence, in fact, shows Panditji casting a horoscope on a fogged windowpane while Puroshit loads a revolver and demands information from a captive gang member who recognizes too late that the policemen are in Jahangir's employ. When Puroshit eventually shoots his squealing victim, the blood spatters onto the horoscope (of Mumbai itself, confirms Panditji), and the stain it leaves resembles that left by Lady Kaede's severed arteries. Like the Greek gods or Hindu minor deities, and quite unlike the Weird Sisters, they intervene in the course of human affairs to ensure the efficacy of Panditji's predictions, and it is Panditji who makes the case that leaving the gangs to their own rules maintains a balance of power, like the equilibrium of such elemental forces as fire and water. In a later scene of revenge, the director deliberately manipulates our knowledge of the massacre of Macduff's family in Polanski's film when the plaintive cries of a child actually move the executioners to pity (as Arthur's pleas once moved Hubert, in a scene obviously effective with Indian audiences). The baited bear of Polanski's film finds an equivalent of a goat whose slashed throat releases a river of blood. Other references are more obscure in the manner of the cinéphile creators of the New Indian Cinema: making a prophecy Panditji raises an arm in his best Charlton Heston manner and informs Miyan that he will be the "king of kings."

Perhaps the most intriguing allusions are to Coppola's first *Godfather* film, but even here, the events are modified as custom and India's cinematic conventions demand. When we first meet him, Jahangir's hoarse voice and stooped carriage are unmistakably modeled on Marlon Brando's aging Don Vito Corleone. Like the don, whom we first meet granting a favor to a client, Jahangir adopts similar inflections in forgiving a kneeling supplicant. Even so, it is not Coppola's Don Vito alone who informs the characterization. When arraigned and taken to a police station, Jahangir demands and receives proper treatment, and at this moment the character he most resembles is the eponymous Naayakan from Mani Ratnam's (1987) film, in which actor Kamal Hassan played both Robert De Niro (as the young Corleone) and Marlon Brando as his character ages. At one moment in *Maqbool* the Banquo character, Kaka, modeled on Scorsese's short, rotund, ultraviolent enforcers, suggests putting Nimmi into a movie directed by one of Bollywood's leading lights, mentioning some names. When she stalks off, he adds in apologetic bewilderment, "perhaps even Mani Ratnam" (Ratnam being India's most popular director of the 1990s). The territory that Jahangir grants his favorite Miyan happens to be a "den of thieves," Bollywood. Far from being an appropriation of Shakespeare or a rip-off of a multitude of cinematic traditions, *Maqbool* flaunts its referential layering. Its unapologetic and self-conscious synthesis of a once distant culture with the native art of the New Indian Cinema, and of Hollywood storytelling with the growing sophistication of Bollywood melodrama, suggests that for all its apparent one-sidedness, globalization may also allow even its less geographically privileged participants a choice between a range of modernities engrafted selectively onto the shifting cultural dynamics of a postcolonial present.

Bhardwaj has also gone on to make an adaptation of *Othello*, *Omkara* (2006), set in rural India and again featuring Naseeruddin Shah as a very active Duke. Beginning as Welles's *Othello* does with the Iago character taking the moronic equivalent of Roderigo into his confidence (the first of a number of such homages), the film translates the discourse of race into one of caste and the play's setting for a contemporary Indian one in a mountainous region rife with bandits. For the most part *Omkara* retains the essential motivations of the characters, although, for once, it is a machete-wielding Emilia who deals with Iago's perfidy. It was Bhardwaj's earlier version of *Macbeth*, however, that coincided with Indian cinema's entry into a global marketplace (by July 2002 Sanjay Bansali's *Devdas* had become the leading box-office hit in Britain), and in so doing reinvigorated India's long Shakespearean tradition. An allusion in the film to one of the major writers to have concerned himself with the impacts of globalization may be coincidental, but is surely worthy of note. In *Maqbool*, Jahangir Khan is known, respectfully, as Abbaji or Big Daddy, and even the two devilish policemen are caught lapsing into the honorific. The turning point in Salman Rushdie's novel, *The Moor's Last Sigh*, occurs when the hero, Moraes Zoigby (the Moor), scion of an ancient spice-trading family, overhears the old blind detective (a figure as formidable as the Grand Inquisitor in Verdi's *Don Carlo*) refer to his father Abraham with that very appellation and recognizes that Bombay's vast underworld, its film industry, and its political empires, all fall under the control of his own secretive and monstrous father. The reference in Rushdie's title to Luis Buñuel's quasi-Surrealist autobiography, rendered literally into English as *My Last Sigh*, is not coincidental. Aurora, Moraes's mother, paints canvases whose successive layers cohere into something akin to an archaeological exploration of time, their underdrawings or *sinopie* ever shifting under an avalanche of *pentimenti*, reconsiderations that rediscover the past and foretell the future. So her last and greatest work, *The Moor's Last Sigh*, remains not only unfinished, but unfinishable. The Moor and all the other characters are lost amidst the iterations of each successive layer. In a sense, when Moraes searches for his origins following the trail of a myth left by the Jews who fled Spain, he also retraces the path that leads from Magic Realism to Surrrealism, from Buñuel's Mexico to his home in Calanda. Other than Magic Realism, the most pervasive sources of influence on Rushdie's literary techniques are Shakespeare and the cinema, and they lie close beneath the surfaces of his texts. As for the latter, the moment at which Dorothy in *The Wizard of Oz* (1939) opens her front door and finds herself transported from the drab sepia tones of Kansas to the glowing Technicolor world of Oz has had an indelible impact on him. He tells us that as a child of ten he saw the film at the Metro Cinema in Bombay and was moved to write his first short story, an event that decided his future profession. When established as one of the great innovators in that profession he added the volume devoted to *The Wizard* in the British Film Institute's series on individual films, in whose pages he includes this primal scene. In the novel that first brought him international acclaim, *Midnight's Children*, India's second decisive postcolonial rupture is announced in a movie theatre when its manager interrupts a screening of a laughable potboiler, *The Lovers of Kashmir*, to reveal that Mahatma Gandhi, the father figure of the nation, has just been assassinated.

Shakespeare is a frequent point of reference, and *Othello*, in particular, seems to recur in Rushdie's work with the unexpected regularity of an involuntary reflex. Consumed by jealousy, one of the two survivors of terrorist bombing of an airplane with which *The Satanic Verses* begins, Saladin Chamcha, uses his mastery of voices to play a relentless Iago to the hapless Othello of the other, Gibreel Farishta. Rushdie appears not to intend to write a fantasy on *Othello* in his collection of short fiction, *East-West Stories*, but having begun a rambling shaggy dog story about the Court Jester's claim to Hamlet's paternity in "Yorick," and with many a nod to Shakespeare's sources, he veers toward the end into Emilia's version of *Othello*. And when Rushdie feels confident enough to journey as far as the United States (via India, Europe, and Mexico) in a retelling of the Orpheus myth in *The Ground Beneath Her Feet*, his mythic imagination once again melds Shakespeare and the cinema into a riot of "pop culture" references. Mr. Hulot (borrowed from Jacques Tati's films) cites the work of Kenji Mizoguchi and Jean-Luc Godard, Cyrus Cama confesses to being the notorious "pillow murderer," who like Othello suffocates his victims, Sukumar Sen (bearing traits of directors Satyajit Ray and Mrinal Sen) makes a guest appearance as the greatest of Indian filmmakers, and even his exuberant photographer-narrator, Umeed Merchant, pays oblique tribute to producer-director Ismail Merchant.

Yet it is in *The Moor's Last Sigh* that Rushdie invents a myth that provides his most enduring image of the forward pull of globalization and the restraining shackles of history, an image that may serve to sum up the legacies of Shakespeare, of film, and of the visual cultures that through, from, into, and out of languages, inform adaptations. According to a Moraes family tradition, the crown of Boabdil, the last Moorish king of Granada, found its way to India when spirited away by an ancestor. How it found its way to Granada from Stratford can only be told by the hand that shaped its bejeweled contours.

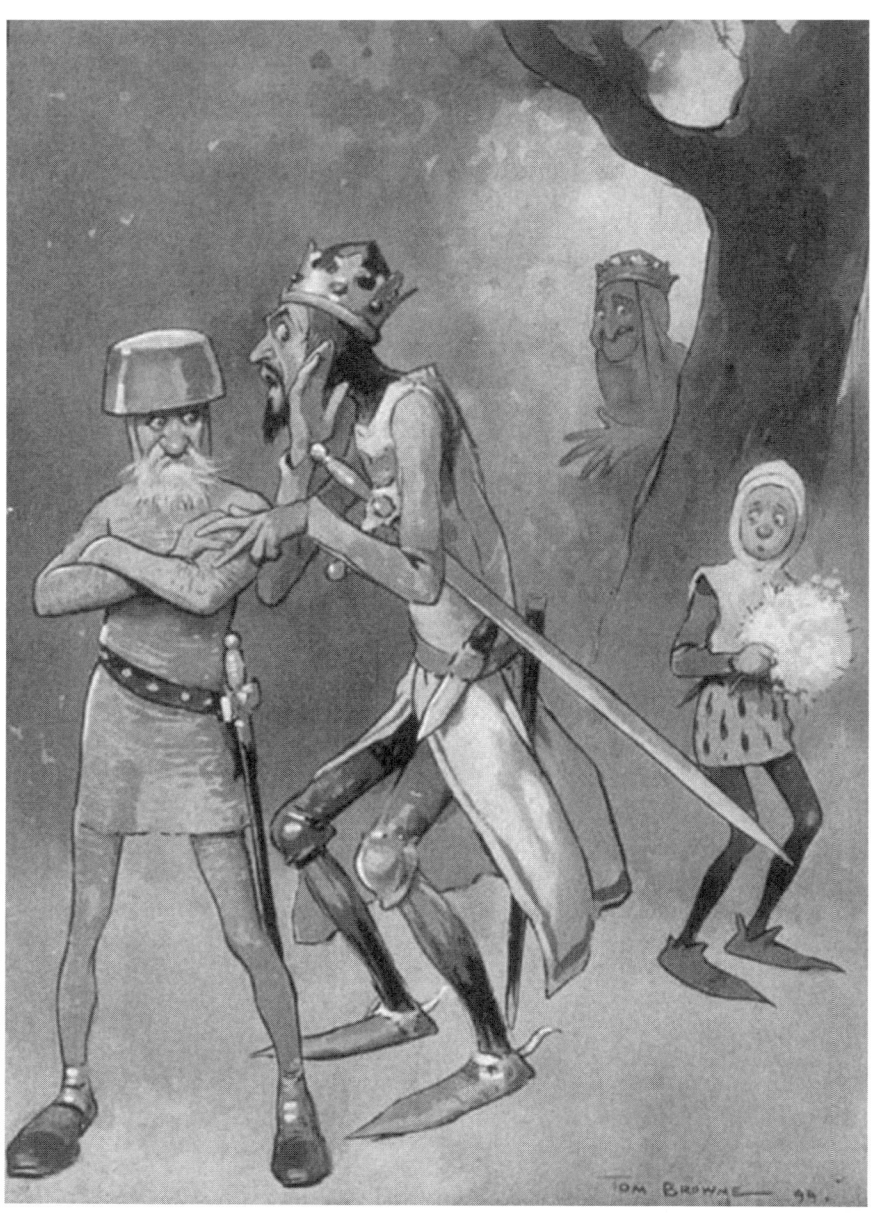

Caricature of a scene from Herbert Beerbohm Tree's 1899 stage production of *King John*. Courtesy of the Library of Congress.

CHAPTER ONE

Reconstituting King John:
*Victorian Theatrical Photorealism
and the Protocinema of Adaptation*

In which the medium of cinema and its social and aesthetic uses are (re)considered ★ Playing with history ★ A Shakespeare film that should exist ★ The "despair of authors" ★ From antiquarian Shakespeare to photorealism ★ The truth of beauty ★ Rediscovered fragments ★ Vertov's legitimacies and Eisenstein's attractions ★ "Better to be seen than heard" ★ Disciplinary perspectives and historical reconstruction ★ Regarding the nightly granting of the Magna Carta

McLuhan's Fallacy and the Origins of Film Adaptation

There is a moment of cinematic magic in Woody Allen's early film *Annie Hall* (1977) when the protagonist he plays, Alvy Singer, frustrated by a pompous professorial critic declaiming his opinions while standing in line to buy tickets to an Ingmar Bergman film, refutes the latter's version of a "hot medium" by pulling out Marshall McLuhan from behind a billboard. Despite the professor's expertise (he teaches a course on "TV, Media, and Culture" at Columbia University), McLuhan assures him in the plummy tones of authority for which he was noted: "You know nothing of my work. You mean my whole fallacy is wrong. How you got to teach a course in anything is amazing."

McLuhan's lighthearted debunking of his cult is doubly intriguing in that by this time he was not alone in describing his theoretical perspective as a fallacy. His most famous antagonist in this regard was Raymond Williams, whose riposte consisted of a critique of the "technological determinism" that he regarded as having attained its zenith in McLuhan's theories. As his cameo on Allen's film attests, McLuhan's celebrity was then at its apogee, and Williams took issue with some of the more consequential theses of his influential *Understanding Media* in pointing out that most media only gradually assume their final form through interaction with social phenomena and that, moreover, most do not have the unique properties ascribed to them by the determinists. Williams suggests that the point at which communication theory began to abstract a medium from its social context had its inception even earlier with Harold Laswell's celebrated formula for the methodological principle governing communication studies: "[W]ho says what, how, to whom, and with what effect?" With any such question, reasons Williams, we must be wary of "intention," and thus he adds a parenthetical interrogative, "with what purpose?" Williams's "why?" has become, in various permutations, a cornerstone of the discipline of cultural studies as it evolved both in British universities such as Birmingham, and in various locales in North America.[1]

The study of early cinematic adaptation, whether of the peep-show attractions in which Edison specialized, or those of publicly screened high drama that soon followed, amply illustrates Williams's contentions. Therefore, it is not surprising that one of the best-surviving examples of a film on the threshold of "true" cinema is the earliest-known attempt to record an actor in a fully staged performance, in this instance Sir Herbert Beerbohm Tree in the role of Shakespeare's King John. The film, at first believed lost, and now known only from brief, temporally sequential fragments, has been the subject of no fewer than five carefully reasoned attempts at reconstruction or, more properly, imaginative reconstitution. Part of my purpose in this chapter is to indicate why these efforts have yet to provide a sufficiently thoroughgoing historical contextualization of that recently rediscovered "relic" whose status as progenitor of a long and growing tradition has led to a clash of two perspectives (one assertively of the "film studies" mould, the other emanating from literary studies and theatre history). An instructive instance of the mobilization of star power for a medium still in its infancy, Tree's brief but vivid reenactment of the poisoned monarch's agonizing demise is also an outstanding example of the challenges faced by cultural historians attempting to answer fundamental questions about the nature of early cinema, and about Renaissance politics restaged in that medium in such a way as to address contemporary concerns. The fragmented minute we have of *King John* allows us to make connections between forms of political power (e.g., the contrast between Renaissance autocracy and appeals to public opinion in the age of mass media), forms of textual authority (what makes a text's author the author?; what is the "text" that confers authority?), the interactions of communicative media (how does intermediation, particularly in effecting the interaction of images and words, work?), and the relation between film criticism and the material facts of film history. An intermediate form in a still embryonic medium, a bold intervention in contemporary political discourse, and a striking instance of the Victorian appropriation of Shakespeare as national propaganda, Tree's innovative film is a paradigmatic refutation of one of the commonly encountered pseudo-evolutionary mythologies embedded in what we regard as film history.

★ ★ ★

King John's Problem

Even a child presented one of the old synopses of Shakespeare's plays (perhaps in an edition made safe for children by Charles and Mary Lamb or their fellows) might be able to appreciate that at the heart of Shakespeare's *Life and Death of King John* there is a telling absence. In the minds of generations of youngsters brought up on Walt Disney's cartoons, the historical John serves as an effete obstacle to a foxy Robin Hood's courtship of Maid Marion. John, voiced by a lush-toned Peter

Ustinov at his cringing and cowardly best, is the representative of social "evil" necessary to all Disney films such as the *Robin Hood* (dir. Wolfgang Reitherman) of 1973. The enterprising teenager browsing through some of the restored reissues of classic films on DVD may also encounter Warner Bros.' *The Adventures of Robin Hood* (dir. Michael Curtiz, 1938), and thus snarl her own defiance of Claude Rains as the foppish usurper who is less authoritative monarch than acquiescent collaborator in the oppression of the dashing Errol Flynn and his Merry Men in Technicolor green. But even for fully adult historians, John comes to mind primarily for a single enforced deed, the signature he placed on the equivalent of the first legislative constitution, the Magna Carta, as granted to Simon de Montfort and his rebellious barons on a spit of land adjacent to a river that would have flowed into oblivion were it not for John's unwilling presence there in the summer of 1215. Somehow the Magna Carta, no less than the already thriving early modern folklore of Sherwood Forest, seems to have escaped Shakespeare's attention.

Perhaps it is because the play is so conscious of its own rewriting of history, and so detached from the larger concerns of Shakespeare's cyclical Histories, that it served throughout the nineteenth century as the historical play par excellence of the poet's oeuvre. Richard Schoch observes that "the first comprehensively historicist production of Shakespeare in the British theatre" was one mounted by actor-impresario Charles Kemble and antiquarian J.R. Planché in 1823.[2] While Kemble's older brother and predecessor at the playhouse in Covent Garden, John Philip Kemble, had been content to banish the more egregious among the then prevalent theatrical anachronisms (even as he continued to model his scenery on the historical paintings of Nicolas Poussin), Charles took to heart Planché's complaint that makeshift productions of Shakespeare did him an injustice.[3] Four months before the November 28 première of their *King John*, Planché published a book of designs based on historically accurate reconstructions of the costumes of the Plantagenet period, indicating to Schoch that in being "divorced from any dispositive [Shakespearean] textual referent...the strength of the intended performance would lie in its historical reality."[4] Schoch's surmise appears to be confirmed by Planché's account of the opening night, when the spectators, on discovering "King John dressed as his effigy appears in Worcester Cathedral, surrounded by his barons sheathed in mail, with correct helmets and correct armorial shields, and his courtiers in long tunics and mantles of the thirteenth century," let out "a roar of approbation, accompanied by four distinct rounds of applause."[5] In matters of costuming, Planché has remained a historical touchstone almost to the present: the mise-en-scène of the fragmentary film of Tree's *King John* preserves the details he describes. So it is not surprising that when the most prominent Shakespearean actor-manager to follow Kemble, Charles Kean, produced the play at the Park Theatre in New York in 1846, he imitated the staging practices of the 1823 production.[6] Kean's even more explicitly antiquarian staging of the play at London's Princess Theatre early in 1852 won the approbation of the young Queen Victoria, who commissioned history painter E.H. Corbould to make drawings of the production.[7]

Despite Planché's spirited defense of Shakespeare's historicism, we cannot readily deduce whether the latter regarded himself as writing history, or whether he was even concerned with what history he wrote. We do not, for example, know whether an earlier version of the events Shakespeare recounts, *The Troublesome Reigne of King John*, was among the plays performed by a traveling theatrical troupe styling itself the Queen's Men when they visited Stratford in 1587.[8] By then Elizabeth's spymaster, Francis Walsingham, had transformed the company into an instrument of royalist propaganda and the dissemination of the new religious orthodoxy;[9] but when the company had visited the Stratford of five-year old William in 1560, it was his probably recusant father John, then town mayor (or bailiff), who had ordered their payment.[10] Even the company of 1587 numbered many of Shakespeare's future long-term collaborators, and his rewriting of a number of the "hits" enjoyed by the Queen's Men has suggested some form of association with them. In the case of *King John*, however, that rewriting—at least according to the editors of *The Norton Shakespeare*—mutes the earlier work's "conventional Protestant and English chauvinism."[11] Indeed, *King John* challenges the very notion of a "fundamental meaning" to history, replacing the providential with the accidental, so contradicting the "moralizing strategy of the Renaissance humanist historians."[12]

In terms of performance tradition, *King John*, the earliest of Shakespeare's Histories by chronology though not by date of composition, appears to have enjoyed a greater popularity with impresarios and critics than with audiences (even Kean's 1852 production played one night a week, while the company's concurrent performances of Dion Boucicault's new adaptation of the elder Dumas's *The Corsican Brothers* played to "capacity houses five times a week").[13] In contrast *Richard III*, widely regarded as having been composed earlier and Shakespeare's first big "hit," held the stage consistently through Colley Cibber's reconfiguration of it a century later as a freestanding play detached from the *Henry VI* cycle. *King John*'s revival—in some cases even its survival—seems to occasion surprise. Frank Kermode, writing of a Second Folio that fell into the clutches of a papal Inquisitor, remarks that the latter "bafflingly cut the whole of *Measure for Measure*," while he "spared *King John*, a frankly anti-papistical play."[14] Robert Hamilton Ball, the first of our breed to approach early cinema with objective thoroughness, seemed to think that it was Tree's additions to Shakespeare in the form of grandiose tableaux (arranged by Walter Hamm) that might have been regarded as material suitable for a motion picture.[15] Perhaps it was this sense of surprise that contributed to an enduring fantasy on his part to which this chapter, in a certain sense, pays tribute.

The Ramifications of Tree's Shakespeare

Ball has a recent tenant of No. 10 in the Adelphi Terrace, overlooking the Thames Embankment, witness an unusual spectacle:

> If Shaw stood at his window contemplating Cleopatra's Needle and glanced obliquely elsewhere, he saw...groups of people in elaborate and antiquated costumes who walked and gestured in a strangely theatrical manner...Two individuals were in charge...The name of the first man has vanished, but what he was operating was a motion picture camera. The second man Shaw might have recognized—he had indeed known him for some years. It was Herbert Beerbohm Tree, and he wore the crown of King John. This was the first Shakespearean film...It is improbable that much of the film was photographed. Perhaps the site on the embankment gives a clue. Here was greenery and the Thames, an approximation to Runnymede. The tableau of the granting of the Magna Charta needed no words, only pantomime for its effect. This may have been all. If so, it is ironic that the first film of a performance of a Shakespeare play was of a scene which Shakespeare did not include.[16]

The "bright day in London" on which these events transpired was not to linger long in the imagination, although the man who was behind the camera (at least figuratively, if not literally) has been tentatively identified. Before taking leave of the scene, however, we might note that that finestral figure observing the proceedings happened to be none other than George Bernard Shaw, and that the eye that he cast on them would no doubt have been severely critical. Shaw is rather unlikely to have cultivated an instant distaste for the new medium (indeed nearly three decades later he was to perform an amusing caricature of Mussolini for a test sequence of early newsreel footage using synchronized sound),[17] but was seldom moved to kindness by performers. While he portrayed the singers and actors of his day as textual libertines (he was no less critical of Tree's rival actor-manager, Sir Henry Irving, who had founded the Lyceum Theatre), his experience of working with the equally disputatious Tree on a staging of his *Pygmalion* left a lasting impression.

"Tree," writes Shaw in a commemorative anthology compiled shortly after the former's death by his half-brother, Max Beerbohm, "was the despair of authors. His attitude towards a play was one of wholehearted anxiety to solve the problem of how to make it please and interest the audience...[he] felt that he needed nothing from an author but a literary scaffold on which to exhibit his own creations. He too turned to Shakespear (*sic!*?) as to a forest out of which such scaffolding could be hewn without remonstrance from the landlord... As far as I could discover, the notion that a play could succeed without any further help from the actor than a simple impersonation of his part never occurred to Tree. The author, whether Shakespear or Shaw, was a lame dog to be helped over the stile by the ingenuity and inventiveness of the actor-producer."[18] Continuing in the same vein, Shaw attributes his success in the role of Richard II to the talents of a rather more sprightly beast. When Richard's pet hound "turned to Bolingbroke and licked his hand, Richard's heart broke; and he left the stage with a sob." The dog, adds Shaw, was not one of Shakespeare's dramatis personae.[19]

It is no doubt because of critics as ascerbic as Shaw that there has been a tendency to treat Herbert as the bumptious, social-climbing foil to his ultrarefined, caricaturist-novelist sibling. With Shaw's blessing Max succeeded him in May of 1898 as chief theatrical critic for the influential the *Saturday Review*, and was thus in the position of having to evaluate his brother's productions, although his reticence to comment on his sibling's acting is painfully evident. There is perhaps also a further connection between the half brothers that deserves note. In biographies written some five decades apart, Hesketh Pearson and N. John Hall go to some lengths to defend the rights of Herbert and Max to be as Jewish as they pleased. Having received a note from Max denying that the family had a Jewish background, Pearson writes of Herbert that "it was generally believed by his contemporaries that he was Jewish, but there is no trace of such descent in his paternal pedigree... But as the peculiar charm, courtliness, sensitivity and intelligence of a cultured Jew were united in Herbert Tree, it is possible that he inherited these racial characteristics from the distaff side of his father's or mother's ancestry."[20] Shaw was characteristically direct in asking the younger Beerbohm about his forebears, and was teased about his Irishness after a denial (containing misinformation), a denial as elaborate as that which Max sent Pearson fifty years later. Nevertheless, in 1965 Malcolm Muggeridge claimed that for most of his life Max was in "panic flight" from his "his Jewishness and his homosexuality." Hall, who elaborates on these claims and the brothers' casual connection to the

Oscar Wilde circle, points out that Max's wives were of Jewish extraction, and dismisses Max's "putatitive Jewishness" as a "non-question."[21]

It would be a nonquestion for Herbert, also, were it not for the ambivalence he seems to have demonstrated about his origins and for the popular acclaim that greeted his assumptions of "Jewish" stage roles. Rather than subtracting the "Beerbohm" from his stage name, Herbert only drew attention to it through a punning doubled signification, "tree" being the near equivalent of "baum," "bohm" or, as Max was wont to insist, "boom." The adopted name was incorporated as one of his scenic trademarks: hardly a production passed at Her Majesty's without foliage, even forests, covering sizeable tracts of the stage. A number of critics (Max among them) remarked on a particular felicity in the staging of *King John* when the equivocating monarch, pacing beneath a "glade of slim beeches," insinuates to Hubert that the young serpent Arthur might imperil his rule: as he speaks, he absentmindedly lops the heads off the daisies underfoot with the tip of his sword.[22] While, in fact, no film sequence of the scene has come to light, an amusing caricature—in which it is almost impossible not to discern elements of Max's already famous style—does exist (see illustration, "A scene from Herbert Beerbohm Tree's 1899 stage production of *King John*"). Tree's vision of moral degeneracy under the beeches is by no means that of the desolate plain of Miklós Jancsó's adaptation of Euripides in *Electra, My Love* (1974), let alone that of Eugene O'Neill's borrowings from Greek drama, but the cartoonist (Tom Browne) deftly captures the expressions of the scheming protagonists even as he lampoons the costumes and props.

Another Tree trademark stemmed from his acting rather than his stagecraft, in that he could summon a particularly wide-eyed and baleful expression perfectly suited to the gallery of dynamic ruffians who provided him with his favored type of role (as they did Orson Welles in the latter part of his career). Tree fared better as a deviously sentimental Richard II or naively self-absorbed Malvolio than as the better-known tragic heroes, although his popular triumphs took place not in his beloved Shakespeare but in melodramatic adaptations of novels. According to the captions to the photographic illustrations in Frances Donaldson's book *The Actor-Managers*, Tree met with his greatest successes when sporting wild beards and long tassels of unruly black hair for the Fagin of J. Comyns Carr's 1905 adaptation of Dickens's *Oliver Twist* ("one of Tree's greatest roles") and the Svengali of Paul Potter's 1895 stage version of George du Maurier's *Trilby* ("this play made a fortune and enabled Tree to build Her Majesty's Theatre").[23] Shortly after he died his wife Maud described his Shylock (denounced by some critics as being melodramatic) as "picturesque, passionate, long-suffering; by turns majestic and debased—he breathed the very spirit of the Jew of the Middle Ages. Alternately he provoked great pity and great scorn...(One need not say how he *looked*—he *was* Shylock)...Yet, on the whole, I preferred Irving's Shylock."[24] Surprisingly, it was Irving's reputedly definitive performance that to some extent restored the perception of "bloody-minded" intent that Edmund Kean had sought to suppress. For Irving the deep sense of injury that governs Shylock's actions, and that must perforce elicit the audience's sympathy, served as a veneer. Thus, there were times even during the recitation of seemingly innocent lines when by means of the staging he conveyed "a viperous impartment of the *Jew's* inherent treachery and deep-seated malice—the duplicity which is characteristically false in circumstances in which it would be much easier to be true." So reads the account furnished by Edwin Booth's friend and collaborator, the critic William Winter, who noted also that Irving's first London production of *The Merchant of Venice* (using a heavily abridged text) ran for an unequalled two hundred and fifty consecutive performances.[25] That the role could be played in this way and that Winter could write of it in the way he did seems to us in the far remove of history all the more surprising as Irving's triumph took place in the Age of Disraeli, whose concurrent second ministry brought the British Empire to its apogee, and at whose persuasion Queen Victoria was to assume the title of Empress of India.

Throughout his career Tree was criticized for his poor "voice" or "diction" (i.e., his manner of speaking, not his volume, as he seemed to choose his words carefully and labored over their correct pronunciation: surviving audio recordings reveal an operatic voice given to building climaxes by chanting the lines in ascending cadences). Having in his youth traveled to Germany to study (at his father's behest), he may well have continued to suffer a certain immigrant anxiety, plausible motivation for the curious evasiveness of his *nom de théâtre* and for his theatrical modus operandi, part of which consisted of a show of ultranationalism then thought necessary for the public demonstration of social assimilation. Although hardly akin to Woody Allen's perfect assimilationist, Lou Zelig, Tree, a corn merchant's son, played the social role of the *grand seigneur* to the hilt once circumstance had surrounded him with pomp. Indeed, David Schulz invokes Thorstein Veblen's contemporary (1899) *Theory of the Leisure Class* and its author's formulation of "conspicuous consumption" (i.e., that which defines the "gentleman of leisure") to describe the refurbishing undertaken during the process of transforming an older building into Her Majesty's in 1897. Decorated in the Louis XIV style favored by Maud Tree, festooned with over ninety paintings, drawings, and watercolors, and with its more expensive seats richly upholstered in red velvet, the palatial edifice must have seemed worthy of the royal livery sported by attendants (a practice soon discontinued after an expression of governmental disapproval). The "royal" connection, however, was not severed, and in 1904 Tree founded the Royal Academy of Dramatic Arts—where a number of today's prominent Shakespearean film actors have honed their skills—under the auspices of the newly rechristened His Majesty's, the Victorian era having come to an end in the interim. Sir Herbert's knighthood was conferred in 1907, more than a decade after Sir Henry Irving's.

Theatrical Photorealism and Shakespeare

A casual remark Tree made on December 6, 1891 to the Playgoer's Club at St. James's Hall (in the course of decrying what he regarded as the baneful influence of Maeterlinck and the Symbolists on modern theatre) allows us to appreciate his understanding of what his public expected of him. It also illustrates his sensitivity to innovation in media other than those requiring live performance. "The approved attitude of the dying century is one of post-prandial cynicism," he observes, and illustrates his claim with the story of his encounter with a photographer. "Monsieur," says the latter (for most respectable photographers at the time pretended to be French), "your regard is too menacing, too serious,—the expression a little more *fin de siècle*, if you please; that's better."[26] Artifice, Tree knew, even in the matter of the feelings of the moment could, through the new medium, pass for realism, even if that feigned realism consisted of making light of a century with a smile.

That he begins an address on the state of the theatre with a photographic anecdote is equally revealing. Elsewhere I have discussed some of the ways in which photography had a profound effect on related artistic media following

Louis Daguerre's improvement of the process in the 1840s. By the 1860s, as commercial photography began to assume something akin to its later ubiquity, Nadar, Degas, Mucha, Thomas Eakins, and a number of other artists were conducting experiments in photography and making aesthetic claims for photography as an autonomous art form.[27] In the theatre, the result was most noticeable in the effect it had on scenic design. According to A. Nicholas Vardac, P.M. Roget's 1824 paper "The Persistence of Vision" and Joseph Plateau's invention of the Phenakistoscope revived interest in the photographic reproduction of motion, and coincided with the pictorial realism of Planché, Edwin Forrest, and Edmund Kean. A second phase of midcentury theatrical realism (for Vardac exemplified by Charles Kean and Edwin Booth) occurred concurrently with the second surge in the development of photorealism as a means of representing motion (Baron Uchatius's projection of the Phenakistoscope's sequential pictures, Coleman Sellars's Kinematoscope, and so on). The final phase of theatrical realism took the form of photorealistic mise-en-scène, rapid scene changes, and dramatic effects such as fires and explosions in the theatrical practice of Dion Boucicault, Augustin Daly, Steele McKaye, André Antoine, the Saxe-Meiningen Group, David Belasco, Henry Irving, the Moscow Art Theatre, and a series of novelists equally susceptible to "the pictorial bias in the arts of staging, the drama, and the novel," a phenomenon that according to Vardac corresponded with the 1895 advent of projected cinema.[28]

While Vardac's broader comparisons are not always easy to substantiate, Tree's efforts to obtain photorealistic and protocinematic effects in the theatre can be discerned quite readily. Indeed, he was not the first to rely on the authenticating potential of photography for scenic effect, his efforts having been preceded by those of Irving. Vardac quotes contemporary reviews to argue that the *Romeo and Juliet* mounted at the Lyceum on May 8, 1882, notable for its complex illusionistic sets (given added depth and dimension through heightened effects of light and shadow) "sought to create a photographic reproduction of the time, the place, and the very events of the play."[29] For both Irving and Tree, the most influential artist-proponent of theatrical realism (in terms of architectural illusionism in set design) was Sir Laurence Alma-Tadema. Alma-Tadema's reputation as one of the leading Pre-Raphaelite painters and his impact on the visual culture of the artistic avant-garde were already widespread. In Italy, for instance, his influence was disseminated through the agency of the poet (and future scenarist of such films as Giovanni Pastrone's 1913 epic *Cabiria*) Gabriele D'Annunzio. Having seen an exhibition of his paintings at the Espozione Nazionale in Rome in 1883, D'Annunzio wrote a series of articles on Alma-Tadema, and incorporated the painter's floral symbolism and female figures (and later those of his fellow Pre-Raphaelite Dante Gabriele Rossetti) into the recurrent "feminine icon" of his own poetry.[30] Alma-Tadema was equally noted for his meticulous research into classical architecture for his paintings depicting antique settings and for his theatrical designs, for which he used photographs of Roman monuments, his own scale models, and the "terra cotta cornices, slabs, and figures which have been preserved in Florence, Rome and...the British Museum."[31] Observing that Alma-Tadema filled 164 volumes with the photographs he took while visiting Herculaneum and Pompeii soon after a comprehensive program of excavation began in 1861, Caroline Dunant notes that they became the "basis of his work in reconstructing the daily life of antiquity."[32]

Having been commissioned to create the sets for a classical *Julius Caesar* during the Lyceum's 1895 season, he withdrew from the elaborate commission (a rift occurring when Irving suggested that the painter imitate some of the effects of the

Orientalist Jean-Léon Gérôme), consoling himself with designing a production of *Cymbeline* placed in a pastoral English setting of indeterminate period. Instead, it was Tree who mounted the authentically "Roman" *Julius Caesar* in January of the 1898 season, and although he was roundly criticized for making his Antony the hero of the production, it was a great popular success, running for five months and eliciting from Bernard Shaw the characteristic remark that it was Alma-Tadema who was the hero of the occasion.[33] It was perhaps the high watermark of the artist's contributions to the theatre: the *Coriolanus* he did for Irving's 1901 season finessed the difficulties of photorealistic set constructions (as in Tree's expensive experiment) and relied on elaborate backdrops for its trompe l'oeil effects, as Phené Spiers notes in a published tract (illustrated with Alma-Tadema's designs) sent to Tree as a presentation copy and now preserved in the Folger Shakespeare Library.

Another of Tree's predilections suggests his penchant for imitating the effects of emerging visual media. Despite using abbreviated theatrical performance texts, many of his productions lasted the better part of four hours because of the massed tableaux vivants he interpolated into the action. Conducted without spoken dialogue, these "dumb shows" appeared to freeze the action photographically at the decisive moment (a technique also encountered in early cinema and already practiced by Georges Méliès) and were calculated to please the eye. In her reminiscences Maud Tree is particularly fond of the adjective "beautiful" when recounting her husband's productions, a descriptive term characteristic of late Romantic aestheticism (as manifested in John Keats's equation of truth and beauty). In noting that "his setting of *The Merchant of Venice* was a dream of loveliness," she adds that Herbert's great innovation in the production might have been a musical one when a "beautiful Jewish hymn...was lifted up, sonorously and religiously, against the light music of the revelers."[34] *The Tempest*, as can be imagined, "was immeasurably beautiful." She comments on the seemingly ethereal use of music and offstage voices, but omits to mention an innovation in staging that was repeated twenty years later with more direct consequence on our prevailing conception of the history of cinema. However, her comments on Tree's picturesque conclusion suggest a visual anticipation of Caliban's subsequent heroic emergence in the literature of postcoloniality. "Caliban, too (though I wanted Herbert to be Prospero), was strangely wistful and pathetic: his eyes were those of a beseeching dumb thing—and a picture never to be forgotten was his long, lone gaze across the water as, Ariel released, the full-sailed ship and its happy mortals faded out of sight, leaving him and his island desolate."[35]

Maud refers to the tableaux vivants as "stage-pictures" and has this to say about *King John*: "In the autumn (of 1899) Herbert produced his splendid, his beautiful *King John*. It was superbly given, superbly acted...And the exquisite stage-pictures—who should describe their utter beauty? The play of *King John* is less human, less appealing to a public than *Julius Caesar*; but Herbert's courage, perception of beauty and genius of stage-management were manifest no less in one than in the other; one was no less a tribute of love and reverence to Shakespeare than the other."[36]

The Place of the Motion Picture on Tree's Stage

I have thus far devoted considerable attention to Tree's attitudes to photorealism partly in anticipation of an objection that film scholars might raise with regard to attribution. Crediting Tree with the first attempt to adapt a fully staged theatrical performance to the new medium of cinema could potentially be a source of dispute. Contrary to the early literature on the film, the surviving scene is not a re-creation of its stage equivalent;[37] it flattened the mise en scène, bringing the backdrop suggestive of Swinstead Abbey into focus, and it required the actors to be grouped tightly around a throne placed just before it and, with some textual assistance from Shakespeare on this occasion, a blossoming tree. The surviving fragments of film (which have been transferred to 16 mm film and divided into two reels available as archival prints at the British Film Institute) place the poisoned monarch, already seated on a large chair just right of frame center, with three members of his retinue carefully grouped on the margins (two on the left, including the prince, and one on the right, to balance the composition). John clutches his breast in agony as the prince steps towards him, while the knight standing beside the prince moves slightly forward in apparent concern. Before the prince makes contact, John clutches his head and turns, in agonized torsion, in the opposite direction. Once more he extends his right hand toward the prince, clutches his stomach with his left, and throws his head back as the prince kneels, still positioned far enough away not to interfere with the full range of John's contortions. The prince attempts to take his hand, but John snatches it back and appears to hallucinate once more. The prince draws back slightly as he rises, again taking care not to interpose his figure between the camera and John, and turns his head toward the courtier at his side. The shot appears to end with the king in extremis, his right leg pointing directly back to screen left. In the second fragment, the still-seated king tries to rise from his chair, and the figures on the edges of the frame begin to move toward him again, but he slumps back onto the throne.

In visual terms, the larger-than-life image of the king remains the center of attention—the centripetal movements of the prince and knights occupying the peripheries of the frame are tentative, and never "complete" motions. The camera is fixed and stage-bound, but fixed at a proximity that no spectator of the theatrical production could have achieved. On film, Tree's *King John* was literally larger than life, and none of the other scenes proposed as part of the film could have "centered" the composition as effectively. In other words, the stage business has been reduced and modified for the camera in such a way that the high point of the drama takes place with very little progressive action, and is recorded from the point of view of a spectator who might have been standing on the stage close to the action. It is not necessarily even the most dramatic scene of the play, as Jonathan, the young actor chosen to play Arthur in Penelope Fitzgerald's novel, *At Freddie's*, discovers in a conclusion too poignant for me to spoil by further description. Instead, the scene's cinematic drama was in its transposition from center-stage to center-frame.

One is tempted to imagine that such a rearrangement was probably suggested by the seasoned camera operator, who is very likely to have been William Laurie Dickson, or by his assistants. It had been Dickson who realized Thomas Edison's dream of inventing a device that could record images that would synchronize with his sound recordings, the first operational movie camera; but upon falling out with Edison over claims to the paternity of this Kinetograph, he cofounded the rival American Mutoscope and Biograph Company, and then returned to his native Britain to help establish a branch there. There is another reason to suppose that Dickson may have had a hand in the filming of *King John*. In 1896, Dickson and the man who was later D.W. Griffith's cameraman, Billy Bitzer, filmed the vaudeville star Joseph Jefferson (on location) in eight 20-second scenes of Dion Boucicault's stage adaptation of Washington Irving's *Rip van Winkle*, an adaptation considered worthy of being copyrighted as a single film by Biograph on December 29, 1902.

It may thus have been Dickson's idea to use another experimental technology pioneered by the British division of Biograph to create publicity materials for one of Tree's spectacular offerings at Her Majesty's. Recording images at forty frames per second on large-format (68 mm) stock, the technology could serve equally well to capture short scenes in "real" time on celluloid or as a considerable number of still photographs on Mutoscope flip-cards. As the eminent film historian Luke McKernan (who has taken an especial interest in this *King John*) points out, the film premiered on the same night as the theatrical production at London's Palace Theatre, a variety theatre that was Biograph's main exhibition venue, where the gigantic screen size drew enthusiastic audiences.[38] Indeed, the similarity of the methods used to create the short films, the Mutoscope cards (the September 27, 1899 issue of the *Sketch* that appears to reproduce Mutoscope-card images from four different scenes), and the illustrations for the theatrical program souvenir (lavishly supplied with still photographs) resulted in a misleading statement (as reported by an unnamed correspondent of the *Westminster Gazette*) by G.W. Smedley, chairman of the British Mutoscope and Biograph Company. Smedley was either less technologically sophisticated than Dickson, or was misquoted to the effect that "10,000 series of King John pictures were posted from London last night, and were now 'unreeling' before the public gaze at their destinations."[39] McKernan notes that, were the "pictures" instead "frames" (as seems clearer later in the interview), the boast would not indicate 10,000 separate prints but something that at forty frames a second lasted a little over four minutes.[40]

Despite his probable participation and pedigree, no one has described the rediscovered fragment as W.K.L. Dickson's *King John*; and those who have offered ascriptions are correct, if not entirely fair, to grant Tree the lion's share of the film's authorship. One imagines that if the Biograph executives could have exerted the power of choice in selecting subject matter, they would have opted for a play more familiar to potential audiences, or they would have chosen to film an "attraction" (a term borrowed from Eisenstein and given by Tom Gunning and other historians of early cinema to a visually striking and self-explanatory event), as indeed Dickson had done when working for Edison.[41] And we know that a far more flamboyant production of *A Midsummer Night's Dream*—also designed by Percy Anderson, and by common consent his visual masterpiece—went into rehearsal at Her Majesty's not long after the same actors who were to don the ethereal costumes of Shakespeare's "fairy" play trudged to Dickson's studio by the Thames, garbed in stage armor and heavy cloaks to commit scenes of *King John* to film.[42]

The choice of *King John* was thus unlikely to have been casual, and was almost certainly determined by Tree, who was in sole charge of all aspects of production at the sumptuous theatre Charles Phipps had completed barely two years earlier at his behest. An advertisement for *King John's* stage opening reveals the extent to which Tree had rearranged Shakespeare for Her Majesty's dramatic requirements: not only had he condensed its highlights into his customary three acts, but also added his much-remarked panoramic tableaux of the French and English armies confronting each other at Angiers and of the signing of the Magna Carta, the latter redressing Shakespeare's omission in conformity with the prevailing dictates of a historicist theatre.[43] Biograph's photographs of these tableaux of massed, costumed extras, as well as the more intimate ones of the principal actors, figure prominently in contemporary reviews and trade advertisements. In a long, thoughtful review of Tree's production for *Le Théâtre*, P. Villars praises Tree's earlier use of Alma-Tadema and the latter's lingering visual influence, evident in the depth of the sets illustrated by the photographs (each with a prominent credit to Biograph printed below). Although the photograph of the Magna Carta tableau is not among them, Villars suggests a motive for Tree's inclusion of it: "Entre le second et le troisième acte, M. Tree a intercalé une scène qui n'est pas dans Shakespeare. C'est un sacrilege, dira-t-on. Pas le moins du monde. M. Tree a trop le respect du genie pour se permettre une license reprehensible. La scène qu'il intercalée est une scène muette, un tableau vivant, qui représente le roi Jean octroyant aux barons anglais la Grande charte qui est aujourd'hui encore le palladium des libertés du peuple anglais."[44]

To presume that Tree merely borrowed Biograph's photorealist technologies as a form of advertisement for his populist parades is, however, to see no more than half the picture. Such a view hinges on the assumption that the film is a record of the scene as it transpired on stage. Yet in the rigorous definition Dziga Vertov offers, the *King John* film would not belong to the category of true cinema at all as it is not a documentary of a stage performance but one arranged and acted for the camera: true cinema was either taken with a hidden camera (which worked best for such intimacies as a kiss) or else one in which the cameraman remains visible but apart from the action, and observes "life caught-unawares," thus ensuring a kind of ontological authenticity for every shot.[45]

Then again, the production of *The Tempest* that Maud Tree describes might suggest that the lone figure surveying his isle might have been well aware that Victoria's passing signaled the end of an age—an age in which technology had given rise to cinema as narrative spectacle and where the theatre itself, in the form familiar for three hundred years, was soon also to pass. It seems unlikely that Tree was at that point the lumbering dinosaur that later critics have assumed. The opening scene of the production of *The Tempest* that ends so wistfully had begun with a storm-tossed vessel occupying the entire stage, its crew darting frantically from side to side as the mast cracked and crashed onto the deck amid peals of thunder and flashes of lighting. Ball gives an intriguing account of the lost film made of this sequence for the company run by Charles Urban, the Anglo-American documentarian, producer, international distributor, and technological innovator. According to one reviewer, it was intended to replace the complicated stage machinery that effected this illusion while the production was on tour. "Modern science has enabled Mr. Tree to fairly stagger us by some wonderful storm effects," wrote another. Tinted to suggest moonlight, the two-minute film is recorded as having been offered for sale independently in 1905 by Urban's American distributor, George Kleine, for $13.00.[46] Lest the idea that incorporating a film into a stage production was simply a scenic innovation (even an unrealized one, as Ball could find no evidence of such a production), it might be well to recall that in 1923 Eisenstein, then a student of Meyerhold's, produced a version of Alexander Ostrovsky's newly completed play *Enough Simplicity in Every Wise Man* that ran concurrently with one staged by Meyerhold. Both interpolated numerous circus routines into the performances, but Eisenstein also rewrote the play with Sergei Tretyakov and included as one of the attractions a short film version of the "Glumov's Diary" episode. Indeed, it was this very production that led to his article on the montage of attractions and his subsequent 1924 essay on "The Montage of Film Attractions."[47] The walls of Angiers and the events at Runnymede, no less than the filmed shipwreck, were among the competing attractions Tree offered his expectant public.

In adherence to his maxim that Shakespeare must be seen and heard with the eyes and ears "of our generation," by the time Tree next acted in a film version of one of his stagings, he was grappling with an Edwardian "mind-set" that was even more at odds with "the seventeenth-century *Zeitgeist*" than the Victorian one.[48] B.A. Kachur illustrates Tree's adjustment to the Edwardian ethos with his arrangement of *Othello*, a play that had by this time been reduced to "a tragedy of...unions forbidden by Nature." To create the requisite sympathy for the hero, he not only muted his complexion but also reshaped the play "into a readily recognizable genre still much in vogue...the romantic tragedy."[49] By this time, the cinema was also making a determined effort to claim the "middle class" audiences that had hitherto been monopolized by Tree's brand of theatre. There is considerable evidence for the careful preparation of Tree's 1911 hit production of *Henry VIII*, a modification of still earlier modifications of *All Is True*, foregrounding the dispute between Wolsey (in which, of course, he played a prelate both powerful and unpleasant) and Queen Katharine. Among the durable artifacts resulting from the production was his quasi-historical account of the mores of the time published as *Henry VIII and His Court* (1910). Thus, it appears that it was not the view that celluloid was ephemeral or trivial, but rather his reluctance to allow a competing product to reduce his theatrical audience, that prompted a curious clause in Tree's agreement with the London filmmaker William Barker to commit five of the eleven scenes of his adaptation to film. Barker had set up his own film company in Ealing, and he came fresh from the exploit of shooting a *Hamlet* over two days, complete with a re-creation of John Everett Millais's flower-bedecked Ophelia floating downriver, one of the quintessential Pre-Raphaelite paintings. It is thus rather unlikely that he found the terms congenial: a thousand pounds for the star's services and an exclusive deal whereby all twenty circulating prints were to be destroyed within six weeks. It was Barker's *Henry VIII* rather than Tree's, for once, if only from February 27 to April 3, 1911, when the prints were burned publicly. What we know of it derives from R.H. Ball's conscientious research, and we would perhaps have known even more, except that Barker died just as he was about to communicate with Ball.[50]

While the critics Ball cites regarding *Henry VIII* were unanimous in their praise, the reception of Tree's final Shakespeare project for the screen, filmed nominally under the auspices of D.W. Griffith, provoked a markedly divergent response and may well have contributed to the rapid failure of a production company. Possibly influenced by the impending 1916 tercentenary of Shakespeare's death, the Triangle Film Corporation (founded by Harry and Roy Aitken with the explicit intention of supplying films for a theatre chain that would attract a "better" class of clientele), in collaboration with Griffith's Reliance, offered Tree a multifilm contract for a reputed $100,000. In the wake of the commercial triumph of *The Birth of a Nation*, Griffith was too busy with the gargantuan *Intolerance* to do more than rehearse the actors from time to time, and the scenario and direction were left to John Emerson. To Tree's apparent surprise, Emerson selected *Macbeth* and reported enthusiastically that, since Shakespeare's dramatic structure approximated a modern film more closely than contemporary plays or novels, most of the play would find its way into the nine-reel film, which in addition would contain scenes such as Macbeth's coronation that Shakespeare only suggests.[51] Despite the enthusiasm of many reviewers, the film proved a commercial disaster: even the anticipated ten-week run at His Majesty's had to be curtailed after a week.[52] Rob King has suggested that the entire Triangle venture was doomed at the outset, and Ball adds that when Tree refused to rescind his contract they dropped Shakespeare and had him play a gentleman farmer from rural America, after which he did "tear up his contract."[53] By then the eminently Scottish J.M. Barrie, who had come to fame with his own 1904 dramatization of his *Peter Pan* stories, had written a (filmed) parody of *Macbeth*, *The Real Thing at Last* (1916), and so, having made some patriotic speeches in support of the war effort, Tree returned to England.

William Uricchio and Roberta Pearson suggest that the change in the reception of Tree's Shakespeare began in the theatre with the "the Bloomsbury crowd and the Greenwich Village aesthetes" deserting spectacular Victorian stagings in favor of Spartan Modernist experiments by the likes of Gordan Craig and Harley Granville-Barker, and the seemingly Elizabethan austerities of William Poel.[54] They note the paradox that even while Griffith developed a more restrained, camera-specific acting style, Tree felt it necessary (at least in 1916) to overplay for the camera and was praised by film critics for his elevated style: theatre critics complained of his productions at His Majesty's, but the productions proved profitable; film critics lavished praise on him, but with no remedial consequence on his box office.[55] What appears to have contributed most to the film's failure is that the medium did have a newly minted audience with decidedly different views from those in charge of Triangle, popular consumers with increasing financial clout who determined the course the feature film took and who preferred homegrown stars (a burly Francis X. Bushman as Romeo, or a vampish Theda Bara as Juliet) to the likes of imported knight errantry. At long last, Tree did find himself a dinosaur in more than one camp, a verdict with which he smilingly concurred when shortly before his death a year after his American adventure he excused his participation in such a silent *Macbeth* on the grounds that he had reached an age at which it was better to be seen than heard.[56]

Proofs of History: Contemporary Politics and Constitutional Rights

Considering the wealth of detail uncovered about his later Shakespearean films whose loss Tree would have been the last person to lament, it might seem strange that the early *King John* has occasioned such intense speculation and critical dispute. Its primordial position in the annals of Shakespeare films,[57] no less than its documentary value, has undoubtedly contributed to the eagerness of critics to identify what it actually represented. However, the waters of Runnymede were muddied very early on when, shortly after his book appeared in print, Ball received a letter from one of the actors, Lt. Col. C.C.S. O'Mahony (who played Arthur under the stage name Charles Sefton). The upshot was Ball's publication of an immediate correction of his previous attempt to restore the film to life. In his correction Ball once more laments the film's loss, suggesting that if it did exist, the scene we would witness would in fact be "that in which King John incites Hubert into agreeing to kill Prince Arthur," the only one described by O'Mahony.[58]

There the matter rested for two decades until theatre historian Kachur resolved to revisit this primal Shakespearean scene. Sifting through a wider spectrum of evidence than Ball, including six heavily notated prompt books detailing ground plans, blocking, and maps of the action, she pointed out that the filming need not have occurred outdoors and that at least part of it would have taken place in the Biograph studio located by the Adelphi embankment of the Thames (where Ball had correctly dispatched the actors in his initial reconstitutive effort). Taking Tree's claim that the film was a photographic "transcript" of the stage play to mean that it was a digest of Tree's three-act version, she surmises that the film might well have been a compilation of five or more scenes, each some three to four minutes in duration which, when assembled, might have made a film of approximately twenty minutes.[59] The following year Kachur argued convincingly that many elements of Tree's stage revival derived from its topicality, in particular with regard to the impending declaration of war in South Africa (although not gifted with prophecy, Tree was likely to have been aware of the gradual buildup of British military forces since June, and war did break out in the Transvaal twenty days after the premiere).[60] Indeed, Tree was neither unduly apologetic for his cavalier treatment of Shakespeare nor reticent about the political valences of his rearrangement. In the handsome souvenir program published by Biograph, featuring its photographs prominently, Tree suggests that Shakespeare's Chorus in *Henry V* was chagrined by the limitations of his stage. He implies that his own revival of a three hundred-year-old play has run for sixty consecutive performances because of his employment of "those accessories which, although denied to the stage of Shakespeare's time, are happily within the reach of the theatre to-day." He concludes his description of the scenes he stages with the citation of the closing lines given to Faulconbridge, which he describes as the "most beautifully patriotic speech to be found in Shakespeare's works."[61]

In ascribing political motivations to Tree's *King John* Kachur is by no means imposing a modern critical viewpoint on Shakespearean theatrical history. Gary Williams advances the same argument for Tree's production of *A Midsummer Night's Dream* later in the season.[62] And it should be of more than passing interest to cultural historians that even with the earliest documented performances, the political dimensions of Elizabethan theatre, and of Shakespeare's plays in particular, provoked powerful responses. His works engaged issues that preoccupied Renaissance political thinkers from Guicciardini and Machiavelli to Montaigne and Grotius, although it was as part owner and manager of a theatrical troupe rather than as political theorist that the dramatist played an oblique, if for him no doubt alarming, role in Tudor intrigue. Almost three hundred years before Tree staged his version of *King John*, a suitably modified version of what many historians believe to be Shakespeare's *Richard II* was enacted at the Globe. The following day, on February 8, 1601, the Earl of Essex on whose behalf the performance had been commissioned led his abortive rebellion, and amidst the arrests and impending executions, the players were sought for questioning. The queen's personal objection to the entire episode was recorded some months later by William Lambarde, Keeper of the Rolls: "I am Richard, know ye not that," she is supposed to have said, adding, rather curiously, that "this tragedie was 40^{tie} times played in open streets and houses."[63]

The sulfurous fumes of insurrection were unlikely to have emanated from the plush seats of Her Majesty's, but the press of contemporary events weighed no less heavily on the stage. Just as the editors of *The Norton Shakespeare* attributed the cinematic interpretations of *Henry V* to shifts in contemporary politics, Tree's decision to film *King John* (rather than the more optically opulent *A Midsummer Night's Dream*) was almost certainly designed to play to the news of the moment. The night on which *King John* opened should have coincided with the close of the most celebrated fin-de-siècle legal scandal of the nineteenth century. The latter had provoked the most famous of published open letters (novelist Emile Zola's "J'Accuse") and incited riots in the streets of Paris. In their bourgeois way Zola and Tree thus contributed to a phenomenon accelerated by the proliferation of mass media in the nineteenth century, one characterized by philosophers of social change such as Oskar Negt and Alexander Kluge as the revitalization of a dynamic popular public sphere, a countervailing force that continuously reshaped and redefined the bourgeois public sphere.[64] When Zola published "J'Accuse" in the January 13, 1898 issue of *L'Aurore*, intensifying his attacks on the government and quadrupling sales of the newspaper that day, he was forced to flee Paris for London to evade charges of defamation brought by authorities he named as complicit in the wrongful, ethnically motivated conviction of Alfred Dreyfus. However, the heat of popular opinion he generated (and not necessarily emanating from those who read newspapers) compelled their reopening the case; had his words not had a social effect beyond his own control, he would have remained in exile. *King John* opened on the night scheduled for the announcement of the release of the pardoned prisoner, and news concerning him briefly displaced the imminent Boer War from the headlines even in England (the *Times* grants very little space to the advertisement for Tree's premiére, its pages filled with editorials on Dreyfus). The events of the case continued to resonate for some time as the disgraced army captain fought to clear his name: the same Georges Méliès who had made the earliest multiscene adaptation of a Shakespeare play (*Hamlet*, 1907) had already turned the Dreyfus controversy into the screen's first multiscene Biopic, *L'Affaire Dreyfus* (1899).

War talk too was ubiquitous, and if by any chance the political implications of Tree's staging of *King John* were initially obscure to the public, they could not have been after the demonstrations of one of the spectators. Colonial Secretary Joseph Chamberlain, the most active proponent of the war holding high office, stepped forward to bow to the audience from the royal box at Her Majesty's, and proceeded to applaud passages about English military prowess.[65] As Kachur observes, Tree played up the patriotic angle by commending the closing speech (lit by a glowing sunset and accompanied by the orchestra) in which Waller's Faulconbridge uttered a "resounding cry of British victory."[66]

Despite Kachur's insight into the nationalistic impulses of Tree's adaptation, a correction of her attempt to reconstitute the film from the available traces was not very long in coming, albeit in a circuitous way. It began with McKernan's sensational confirmation in the *Shakespeare Bulletin* (Winter 1993) that *King John* had been rediscovered. "One can never say with finality that a film is lost," wrote McKernan, who assumed that the minute of *King John* found during an inventory at the Nederlands Filmmuseum represented Tree's entire film.[67] He may have based his assumption on a statement in the Palace Theatre's program of November 6 that announced "A Scene 'King John'—now playing at Her Majesty's Theatre."[68] McKernan soon offered a correction based on Kachur's observation that four frames reproduced in the London news magazine the *Sketch* were extracted from scenes that had been filmed, although McKernan preferred to think of them as representing three scenes rather than four.[69] Moreover, he demonstrated that the 5,000-foot film that Kachur's twenty-minute version would indicate was technically impossible, and that films of 1899 were not constructed sequentially from shots in an integrated form as we presently understand film narrative. "*King John* was a news event, and the Biograph film a report on that event."[70]

McKernan now concurred that only a fragment of the film was represented by the known extant material, but the three scenes he describes are not those he settles on in his next attempt at reconstituting the film. In the book *Walking Shadows* he repeats his assertion that the film was not a good "record" of either the stage production or Shakespeare's play, and that it was adapted to the screen to "provide what amounted to an advertisement for Tree's production, or better still a news report, for the Biograph company were making their reputation with actuality coverage."[71] He also identifies the four scenes suggested by *The Sketch* stills: "The Battlefield near Angiers" (where John attempts to persuade Hubert to do away with the captive Arthur), "The French King's Tent" (where Constance laments Arthur's fate), and John's final agony and Prince Henry's coronation in "The Orchard of Swinstead Abbey."[72] Of these, only the third has been rediscovered. We can probably guess (but only with a modicum of safety) that the additional surviving fragment, showing the king attempting to rise and the prince and the courtiers beginning to move toward him, extends the previous scene slightly rather than offering part of the last scene. In this regard, it is our good fortune that for once Max Beerbohm appears to be tongue-tied when writing about a stage performance in his September 30, 1899 contribution to the *Saturday Review*, which he devotes to his brother's production. Rather than his usual analytical approach, Max adopts a form of presentational (rather than evaluative) plot summary. One section of the summary suggests that John was crowned again before he expired, and that some further action intervened before the crown was placed on the prince's head:

> The dying king is borne out on a chair. He is murmuring snatches of a song. The chair is set down, and with weak hands he motions away his bearers. "Ay, marry," he gasps, "now my soul hath elbow-room; it would not out at windows nor at doors. There is so hot a summer in my bosom, that all my bowels crumble up to dust... And none of you will bid the winter come, to thrust his icy fingers in my maw." The bastard comes in hot haste, and the king, to receive his tidings, sits upright, and is crowned for the last time. He makes no answer to the tidings. One of the courtiers touches him, ever so lightly, on the shoulder, and he falls back. The crown is taken from his head and laid on the head of the child who is now king.[73]

Max's effort to be ethical fortuitously makes it clear that the fourth image in the review in the September 27 issue of the *Sketch* (i.e., a frame-blow up probably taken from a Mutoscope card or the 68 mm print) follows the stage action closely. Having arrived in "hot haste," Faulconbridge kneels before the king, whose lifeless head is tilted backwards, while the standing Prince Henry is about to be crowned. Therefore, we can surmise that the second fragment of the surviving film extends the first but shows neither John's recoronation nor the dramatic conclusion Max describes (and that clearly did exist at some point). Indeed, the second film fragment makes it even more difficult to reject a modified version of Kachur's hypothesis that a number of sequential–if not necessarily consecutive–takes might have been devoted to each of the filmed episodes, for by this time the Brighton filmmakers George Albert Smith and James Williamson were on the threshold of breaking scenes down into shots, and Dickson's own experiment with Jeffords's *Rip van Winkle* had, after all, consisted of eight individual takes of sequential scenes.

While the matter of the actual *King John* film seen by the audiences in September 1899 remains far from resolved, what is striking about this series of amendments and self-corrections (each couched in a tone of confidence, at times even certainty) is the recurrent desire to recover a lost object, the same passion for getting to the truth of that lost object, that in *The Authentic Shakespeare* Orgel ascribes to the theatre criticism and literary scholarship associated with Shakespeare. This is not to contend that such a search is fruitless: despite being couched in combative terms, McKernan's emphasis on the technology of filmmaking and the film's generic context (i.e., the publicity news bulletin), as well as his ability to examine a rediscovered text from an archival standpoint, permit him a series of insights that are at variance with Kachur's, but no less significant in mapping the cultural history of a Victorian performance ethos than is the latter's emphasis on the sociopolitical dimensions of both the theatrical and cinematic versions of Tree's *King John*. In fact, this particular phase of intermediation may—as more and more tangible evidence resurfaces—prove an ideal testing ground for the nature of historical hypotheses that, as Carlo Ginzburg has demonstrated in a number of contexts, may be derived from sources that are not explicitly historical in intent.[74]

The Ends of *King John*

Among the first entertainment media to exploit the leisure capital of non-elites, the English Renaissance Theater was nevertheless of greatest political consequence for aspiring gentlemen (such as theatre managers) and aristocratic patrons. That at the midpoint of his successful career Shakespeare's company ran into trouble over an unauthorized production at the Globe should come as little surprise: there never was a definitive text left inviolate by the erosions and accretions of the social world. *King John* had something missing from the start, but it was an omission even the original audiences must have felt and one that the nineteenth century felt ready to redress. Jonathan Bate contended that in historicizing the play in 1823, Kemble and Planché "put Shakespeare safely back in the past" (i.e., diminished the force of the reference to a mad king and a reprobate regent); but Richard Schoch disagrees and points out that just five years earlier the influential Whig historian Henry Hallam had declared the Magna Carta to be "the most important event in our history." For the nineteenth century, adds Schoch, "John served as a woeful example of unchecked royal authority," and audiences would have "memorialized the event" and so were capable of "filling in the historical blank...just as Beerbohm Tree materialized his audience's pre-existing mental picture."[75]

That Shakespeare's audiences too could shape the spectacles presented to them on stage is a natural outgrowth of transplantation and cultural recontextualization. Precisely by being transculturally and transtemporally significant texts, Shakespeare's plays offer the cultural historian valuable insights into the changing role of media in society, about questions of authority vis-à-vis technologies of communication and performance practices, and about the process of symbiotic intermediation. Whether what is adapted of Shakespeare consists of his words, his appeal to a common cultural foundation, or his prestige, what survives as source material is, as Orgel observes, vivified only in the process of cultural inflection. No less revealing than the socially specific reshaping of discourse is the study of the movement of "Shakespeare" from one medium to another, and in this regard, the fragmentary *King John* remains of exceptional significance. Although McKernan is correct to argue that the spectacle granted the audience at the Palace Theatre on September 20, 1899 was a news bulletin, it was both more (having a wider range of significance than imparting news) and less (in that it was not quite a film in the way we conceive of cinema). Its closest modern generic analogue, in fact, might be a movie trailer, although in this case, the trailer advertised a live performance in the theatre. To at least one of its contemporaries, it remained 10,000 still photographs strung together to simulate a moving picture. To another, a reporter contributing to the September 20, 1899 issue of the *Sketch*, who noted the actors heading off to be "biographed," those who performed the deed were "shrewd" suppliers of "Animated Photographs."[76] Then yet another reporter, perhaps with fatal consequence to that moving picture if Tree read the news, wrote, "Why pay half a guinea for a stall at Her Majesty's when you can see the play round the corner for a penny?"[77] Could this be why the only rediscovered scene depicts Tree occupying the center of the frame, deadly serious in his regal suffering and writhing, while those around him look amused at the outset and then all but inert (i.e., impressive as spectacle but a poor substitute for theatrical action)? To imagine that performance in the theatre and performance before cameras were conceived of as generically different, or that a clear sense of separation existed between still photography and moving photography, is to run the risk of being charged with anachronistic media chauvinism.

Who, then, is not to say that what the anarchic philosopher Jacques Derrida calls the "trace" still survives of the film Ball imagined, an absence invoked by what is there? The review of the opening night in the *Times* suggested that, far from being presented as allegories for the overthrow of the monarchy, Shakespeare's history plays might well be made to move a little faster in a new age: "Mr. Tree's aim has been so to regroup and recast the scenes as to accelerate the action of the play without impairing anything of its truth and spirit. This is a proper aim, for rapidity is of the very essence of a 'chronicle play'—which should have something of the kaleidoscope, or rather of the kinematograph."[78] And of the scene that Shakespeare forgot to include, a certain E.F.S., writing for the *Sketch* has this to say: "At present the Dreyfus case is really quite a King Charles's head with most of us, and I could not keep it out of my mind when glancing at a copy of the famous charter which Mr. Beerbohm Tree will be granting nightly, for many days to come, I hope at Her Majesty's Theatre. 'None shall be condemned on rumors or suspicions, but only on evidence of witnesses.' It does seem quaint that even by now France is not sufficiently civilized to have a law of justice deemed fundamental on July 15, 1215."[79] This is a sentiment to which Dreyfus might have been especially attuned, for a substantial number of the books his wife sent him during his four-year incarceration on Devil's Island consisted of volumes of Shakespeare.

Even as Tree's play was going into production, Zola was leading a quiet, industrious life in Upper Norwood (he returned on June 5, 1899, two days after the verdict against Dreyfus was annulled). It was his Naturalism that revolutionized the European novel and, through Jack London and Frank Norris, American letters and cinema. Although Paul Cézanne's closest friend for much of their lives (before Zola's portrait of him as a failed genius in his 1885 *L'oeuvre* led to a permanent estrangement), Zola's passion for photography owed little to Modernist aesthetics and much to the landscape and portrait photography of such early pioneers as Nadar, Étienne Carjat, and Pierre Petit.[80] The contentious journalist and prosperous novelist arrived in London without luggage, but one of his first acquisitions in England was a camera (in France he kept ten different cameras and had three separate darkrooms in his homes).[81] His diary, a new novel, and his photographic activities apparently kept him fully occupied as he remained incognito as Monsieur Beauchamp, although he did follow the news from across the channel. What he may have though of Tree's attitudes to photography or of King John's nightly granting of a charter that affirmed his own deeply held convictions seems no more in evidence than Ball's bountiful Shakespeare film.

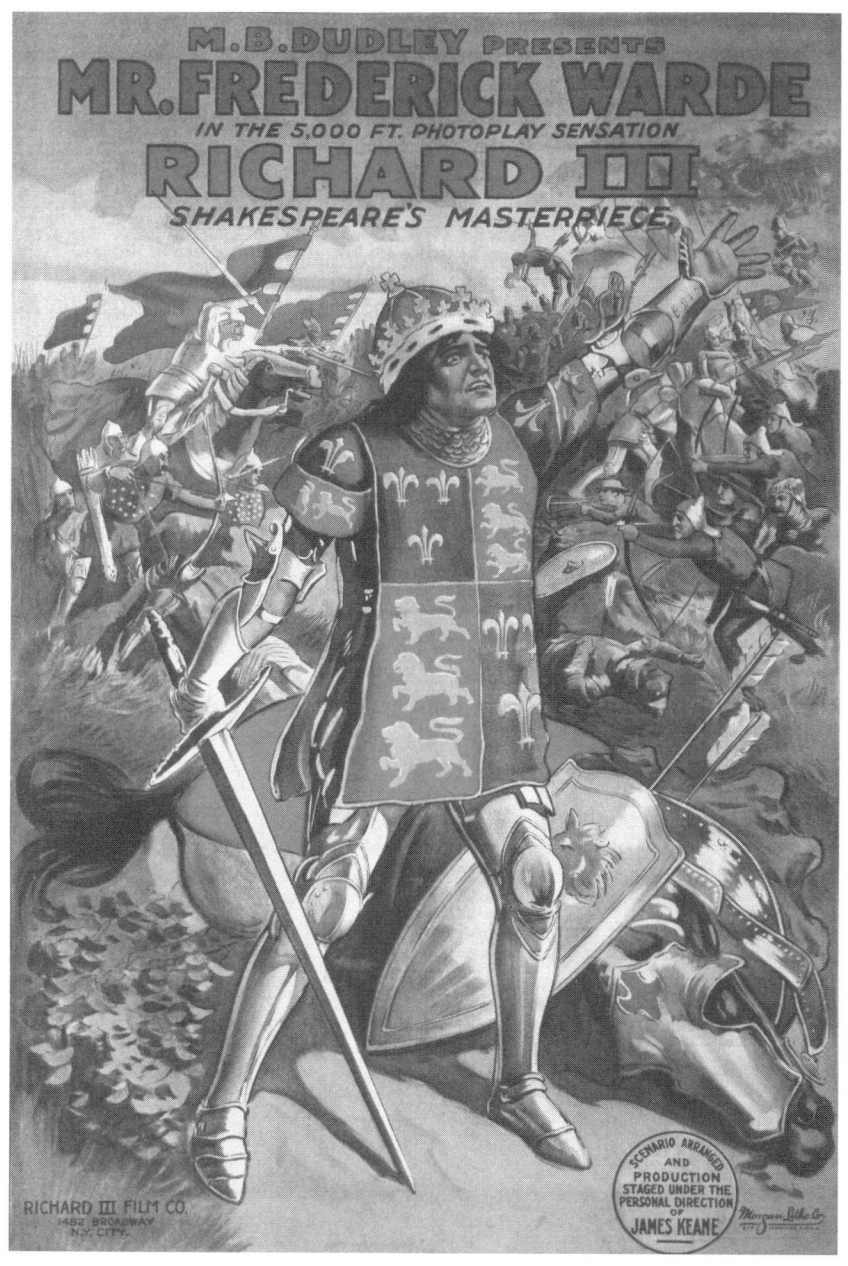

Poster for *Richard III* (1912) by Frederick Warde and James Keane. Courtesy of www.moviegoods.com.

CHAPTER TWO

Featuring the Bard: Frederick Warde's Shakespeare and the Transformation of American Cinema

In which it is revealed that Shakespeare had a hand in establishing the American feature film ★ The Eco cult and the early feature film as live theatre ★ Critics and audiences old and new ★ An English actor abroad ★ Raoul Ruiz and the poetics of (non)abridgement ★ Rival performance traditions in Worlds Old and New ★ King Lear and the last of the artisan-producers of American Shakespeare films

Of Film Screens and Audiences

At the Ritz in the London suburb of Swindon, some time in the late 1980s, the Friday performance of *Richard III* is about to take place. So familiar is the audience with the weekly Shakespeare special that the performers are usually announced half an hour before the curtain and plucked from a public that is also called upon to interact with the actors and to swarm onto the stage to create a suitable melée for the climactic battle scene. "When is the winter of our discontent?" demand the spectators in unison, as their Richard enters. Ralph Swanavon replies with Shakespeare's opening line and a cruel smile.[1]

★ ★ ★

In 1912 the audiences for film in rural America may not have been quite as demonstrative, nor would they have had the faintest conception of what a *Rocky Horror Shakespeare Show* would look like, but they loomed just as large as in Jasper Fforde's "pre-futuristic" fantasy. One might argue that such a sphere of interactivity remains part of television's staging of the "live" event, but in film, where the texts are "fixed," such direct engagement must be incorporated into the textual form of the work, as is evident in Pacino's *cinéma vérité* version of *Richard III*. Indeed, today the notion of an audience's collective interaction with a screened spectacle, or even a staged one, has come to seem aberrant, and the anticipatory recitation of favorite lines from *Casablanca* or *Gone With the Wind*, the déclassé province of what cultural critics of the stamp of Umberto Eco term a cult audience.[2] But at the moment when the feature film was establishing itself as the dominant part of the program of films shown at movie theatres in the United States, the presence of a narrator or even of the star in the flesh was considered a near-compulsory ratification of the charismatic authenticity of the image.[3] It was Sarah Bernhardt acting for the movie camera who could command an audience commensurate with her $350.00 a night appearance fee, not the actions she performed on screen (which, even in 1912, some reviewers found unconvincing).[4] Almost from the moment of their inception in 1912, the makers of full-length feature films began to proclaim their works as autonomous, requiring no ancillary lecture or commentary. Chief among them was Helen Gardner, who formed her own company when embarking on a *Cleopatra* distantly related to Shakespeare through another of Bernhardt's favored playwrights, Victorien Sardou (although in Gardner's case it was an appropriation intended primarily to showcase her own voluptuary powers in the role of the eponymous heroine, rather than a tribute to the recently deceased playwright Bernard Shaw accused of "Sardoodledom"; her rival "vamp" Theda Bara was to play Cleopatra in 1917).[5] Yet in the period preceding Griffith's assertively freestanding *The Birth of a Nation* (1915), there were regular complaints among film reviewers of the trade papers about the confusion resulting from assailing spectators' eyes for the better part of an hour without pause to elucidate what they beheld.

I do not mention Bernhardt casually or without forethought. In his early history of the motion picture, *A Million and One Nights*, Terry Ramsaye attempts to explain the extremely rapid adoption of the feature-length film in the United States in the 1910–1913 period and begins with Bernhardt's three-reel *Camille* (*La Dame aux Camélias*, dir. André Calmettes, 1912), which he argues "failed utterly of theatre attention."[6] He then steps back in time to mention Vitagraph's earlier multireelers, *The Life of Moses* (1909) and *Uncle Tom's Cabin* (1910), both of which were initially released one reel at a time. However, after some description of further efforts at multireel film production, he settles on the triumph of an independent producer-director, Adolph Zukor, as the turning point. Forming a partnership with Edwin S. Porter and Joseph Engel, Zukor secured the American rights to Bernhardt's next feature, *Queen Elizabeth* (also 1912, directed by Henri Desfontaines and Louis Mercanton). As in *Camille*, her leading man was the future Hollywood matinee idol Lou Tellegen, and so the filmmakers no doubt already envisaged an American market for the film. Zukor's partnership was reorganized and under the banner of Famous Players in Famous Plays Company "road-showed" *Queen Elizabeth* (i.e., showed the film as gala performances in venues he had acquired or rented in different cities). Eventually, it was sold very profitably to buyers for individual states' rights.[7] Zukor's success with Bernhardt's film "started the rise of the feature picture and the re-formation of the entire industry," claims Ramsaye, who is not always accurate in his assessments, but his view gains renewed support in the work of film historian Lewis Jacobs writing more than a decade later.[8] Douglas Gomery points out that by 1921 the company over which Zukor gained control in 1916, eventually Paramount Pictures, had become "the most powerful and profitable film making and distribution company in the world."[9] Both Calmettes and Desfontaines, interestingly enough, were directors of Shakespeare adaptations, the former of a *Macbeth* of 1908 for the Films d'Art and the latter of *Hamlet* (1910), *La Mergere approvoisée* (a version of *The Taming of the Shrew*, 1911), and *Shylock, ou le Marchand de Venice* (1912) for Urban-Eclipse.

The school of early cinema historiographers that emerged in the 1980s also concerned itself with the emergence of the feature film as a signal transformation of the American filmgoing experience. Writing of the experiments in programming longer films from 1910 onward, Eileen Bowser and others have noted the importance of literary adaptations in spurring the establishment of feature filmmaking in the United States. She also makes mention of the frequent presence of narrators to accompany these films.[10] Thus, while Vitagraph's multireelers from the 1909 *Les Miserables* (sic) onward were promoted as being amenable to being exhibited singly or sequentially (as full-length features), the first features marketed as such were travel-adventure films released in April and May of 1912, *Paul J. Rainey's African Hunt* and *The Alaska-Siberian Expedition*, each an accompaniment to a lecture given by expedition leaders Rainey and Captain Frank Kleinschmidt (or at times an associate). Some contemporary comments about the latter production suggest that the emergent multireel feature film might have taken any of a number of directions, including those found cultlike by Eco and hyperinteractive by Fforde, or it may perhaps have even retained a multilayered mode of address reflective of the epistemic shift that the French historian of forms of knowledge, Michel Foucault, would have discerned in the audiences' insistent "desire for knowledge":

> The pictures in New York at the Maxine-Elliott Theater are being lectured by Captain F.E. Kleinschmidt, who conducted the expedition through Alaskan and Siberian waters, and who took the pictures that are now on exhibition. In Philadelphia [at the Garrick Theater] the pictures are being lectured by Mr. Clark, who was with Captain Kleinschmidt on the expedition, and who has an equally good understanding of Alaska in general, and of these pictures in particular...so interested were the spectators, that in both Philadelphia and New York there came from the darkness of the auditorium numerous questions from persons in the audience who evidently wished to know all they could about different phases of Alaskan life. These questions were in all cases answered promptly and intelligently by the speaker; all of which lent an added interest to the entertainment and indicated a desire for knowledge on the part of those who came to see the pictures.[11]

The narrator, then, was considered an integral part of the entertainment, and a feature without one offered a lesser level of entertainment. By November 4, 1911, W. Stephen Bush, noted critic for the *Moving Picture World*, could insist that "what the feature film...demands absolutely is proper presentation...Music, effects and lecture are indispensable adjuncts...A lecture will relieve that natural tension and impatience, which a long, dumb show is bound to cause, and will make the story plainer and the enjoyment of the patrons keener."[12] Not surprisingly, the following week *The Moving Picture World* ran the following quarter-page advertisement: "W. STEPHEN BUSH Has prepared and may be engaged to deliver lectures on all the great FEATURE FILMS—SUCH AS—DANTE'S INFERNO...—AND—ALL OTHER FEATURE FILMS...*INCREASE YOUR BOX OFFICE RECEIPTS*."[13]

Even a cursory survey of these early features complicates many of the assumptions made by historians of that period of American cinema, such as the prevailing view that the eventual collapse of the Motion Picture Patents Company cartel consisting, by then, of ten firms that had hitherto dominated the U.S. film business, resulted from a failure to appreciate the potential offered by full-length features of four or more ten-minute reels. To cocoon themselves in so stubborn a state of dinosaurian petrification would have necessitated their having been deaf to the entreaties of all the trade journals of the time and innocent of the innovations of their competitors. Besides, Vitagraph, the MPPC member with the largest European distribution, which by 1908 already shot films with foreign markets in mind—its Pathé affiliate released a version of *Romeo and Juliet* (1908) in which Romeo purchases poison in a locale identified by the macaronic shop-sign APOTHECA—was the first American production company to experiment with sequential multireel formats. Another MPPC company, Kalem, also specialized in multireelers shot on location in Ireland and what was then Palestine, and the major distributor for the MPPC, the General Film Company, was quick off the mark in advertising a new line of feature films.[14]

Also common is the presumption that the coming of the feature accelerated the process whereby the old audience was gradually shed for a new, "upscaled" one that could afford higher ticket prices. Treating a slightly earlier period, William Uricchio and Roberta Pearson devote their book *Reframing Culture* to the tone of gentrification that dominates much of the criticism of the first decade of the professionalization of American film reviewing, treating it in terms of what sociologist Pierre Bourdieu labels cultural capital (here the marketing of a better "class" of films as a form of moral and social "uplift") and what the Italian leftist cultural critic, Antonio Gramsci, regards as hegemony (in this instance the instrumental use of media to win the consent of the populace by those in power). Their reticence to make overcommittal assertions, however, seems fully justified in the light of a double suspicion shared by the more sophisticated reviewers of the period that the "old" spectator could not be cast off and, indeed, that there probably never was such a "down-market" consumer who needed to be exorcized from the movie theatre. Stephen Bush, for instance, spoke of the demise of the nickelodeon with mixed feelings in 1912:

> THE MOVING PICTURE WORLD, in its issue of August 29, 1908, had this to say about the price of admission: "The most crying need of the moving picture business at this moment is an absolute divorce from the nickel"...The horrible words 'nickolet' and 'nickelodeon' have [in the intervening four years] become obsolete, and have long since been regarded as badges of cheapness by intelligent exhibitors...To be sure there will always be the five-cent show with us. There are in every city a large number of people to whom the difference of five cents is a matter of importance. This is the very class to which the motion picture wants to be useful and instructive. The cinematograph will never be ashamed of its friendship with the poorer classes...It should, however, be the task of the organized exhibitors to regulate and limit the number of cheaper theaters...The best basis for a proper solution, it seems to us, will be the basis of population. The question of neighborhood will enter into the problem, and likewise the grade of service...The subject has many angles

to it, and its treatment will largely depend on local conditions. We only desire to point out the general possibilities of an intelligent and harmonious action among exhibitors.[15]

Such remarks were, of course, made very much in the sprit of the passing of an age. In the context of the Gardner *Cleopatra*, for instance, an anticipatory blurb on the back cover of the June 5 edition of the *New York Dramatic Mirror* announced her new company and featured a large frontal photo-portrait of the star, assuring exhibitors that "[n]othing yet undertaken in the motion picture art has been greater than the work undertaken by Miss Gardner and her company... Motion pictures have passed the swaddling clothes period. The big winners to-day are the big productions. The 'low brow' picture patron has gone. It is doubtful if he ever was. A new sun is rising. All of the old-fashioned producing companies are stumbling over each other's big feet to get out of the way of each other in the production of big stories... If those old-fashioned people can't give you what your patrons want, cut 'em out."[16]

While harmony among exhibitors to raise prices appeared to be a common enough goal advocated in trade papers, no such harmony can be seen among the latter-day writers on the first decades of American film. For instance, while Robert Allen hypothesized a mixed "blue-" and "white-collar" audience for the nickelodeons, Ben Singer unearthed evidence to show that recent immigrants of a decidedly "blue-collar" stripe dominated the moviegoing demographic in populous Manhattan. Allen's response in "Manhattan Myopia" was to point out that audiences are highly socially mobile and that Manhattan was not necessarily a good model for the rest of the nickelodeon audience.[17] Despite these differences of interpretation, there is little to dispute about their mode of address to their spectators: many of them undoubtedly sought to cleanse the unwashed immigrant masses still thronging to the heavily populated coastal metropolises no less fervently than the similarly culturally displaced rural migrants pouring into such cities as Chicago, introducing them to urban civilization. Miriam Hansen, in fact, asserts that "if the suppression of class and ethnic diversity was in keeping with the cinema's pretension to a bourgeois public sphere, the effort to co-opt such diversity into a generalized aesthetic appeal was more in touch with large-scale transformations in the capitalist economy. The film industry's aim was not, as [Lewis] Jacobs implies, to exclude the working class, but to integrate them, allegedly into the melting pot, yet more effectively into a consumer society of which mass culture was to become both agent and object."[18]

As I presently (and cautiously) suggest when looking at the direction successful features took after 1912, Bakhtin's view that undercultures and cultural elites always engage in complex social negotiations might prove an even more apt model than the Frankfurt School one of a top-down determination of social forms. Yet it should not escape our attention that, if the coming of the feature coincided with the advent of luxurious movie palaces and the end of the nickelodeon era, there remains little substantial evidence that the audience composition underwent a drastic change or that there was a marked fall in attendance, as such a strategy (the equivalent today, of raising ticket prices from about $8.00 to $80.00 in three years) would necessitate. The business sense of film entrepreneurs was developed enough to suggest that the rhetoric was a ruse to harness a greater proportion of the leisure capital of an upwardly mobile clientele; the posturing of the trade papers probably had less to do with the actual "elevation" of the medium (except in countering moral censorship) and everything to do with exploiting a craze for moving images. Had the audience being courted already belonged to the genteel classes, they were very likely to have enjoyed the cultural capital that would have obviated any explanatory narration for adapted literary classics, and the text between the lines of the trade paper reviews seems to suggest that the feature film was not so much a mechanism to casting off the old audience or even winning a new one, but rather a way of selling a more expensive product as one that conferred status. Hence, the "new" patrons of the feature film are less likely to have been a ready-made bourgeois clientele won over by such upscaling than members of an emergent bourgeoisie drawn from the ranks of the urban migrants and immigrants who, as Lauren Rabinovitz illustrates in the case of women migrant workers in Chicago, constituted an early phase of a new status-based consumer culture that wielded considerable economic power in determining its preferred forms of entertainment.[19] Even in this instance, however, large-scale social phenomena such as the change in spectatorial patterns in the 1910–1913 period remain difficult to determine, the explanatory frameworks often varying according to the particular data selected to buttress preferred hypotheses. And these hypotheses are further complicated by the paucity of surviving early features and their reliance on trade literature and local statistical tabulations.

Shakespeare Survives!

Most of the films of this crucial historical moment of American cinema have been lost. Thus, when in 1996 the American Film Institute announced the rediscovery of the first complete fiction feature released in the United States, the story of its near-miraculous survival contributed to the feeling among historians of early cinema that if it were not quite the Holy Grail or Ark of the Covenant, it was at least the equivalent of the Veil of Veronica. Around 1960, William Buffam, a part-time movie projectionist, had swapped a few later silent features for an old, beautifully tinted and toned color print from the dawn of feature filmmaking, the 55-minute *Richard III*. Knowing that nitrate and acid decomposition of images and film base had already claimed most of the films from the early years of American cinema, he had preserved it by storing it in cool temperatures and rewinding it annually to prevent the stiffening and disintegration of the fragile stock. In an Aristotelian moment of anagnorisis, Buffam was startled to learn that he was entrusting the American Film Institute with one of the most sought after of all "missing" films, one believed to have been lost for some eighty years.[20]

In fact Dickens, whose impassioned readings from his novels were well within living memory for some American metropolitan dwellers, had an approaching centenary and might even have beaten Shakespeare to the mark since General Film released a feature-length *Oliver Twist* (May 1912) adapted from the concurrent stage version and featuring the star of that production, Nat Goodwin. Another film that heralded the direction American feature films were soon to take, *The Life and Adventures of Lieutenant Petrosino* (1912), also achieved general release earlier than this *Richard III*. And Edison's first prominent director, Edwin Porter, who had by then joined Zukor, adapted another dramatized novel, *The Prisoner of Zenda* (February 1913), showcasing its star, Charles Hackett. In this period too, a large number of French and Italian multireelers were also being imported and exhibited in the United States. Thus, temporal precedence was hardly the distinguishing feature of *Richard III*, and its true importance may well have been overlooked in the general rejoicing. As an almost pristine artifact from the very moment in which the conventions of classical cinematic narrative were crystallizing in the United States, it retains a greater importance to film and cultural historians than many a later cinematic masterpiece. It documents one of the most profound transformations of the American filmgoing experience perhaps better than any other surviving film of the period, serving in its textual form as both evidence for and an allegory of social change. The medieval story it attempts to relate, in fact, chronicles the astonishingly short space of time in which film spectatorship developed from furtive entries into shopfronts and small theatres where a nickel secured a viewing space for one-reel shorts (run continuously to the accompaniment of improvised music and sound effects) to pilgrimages to extravagant movie palaces in which patrons could pay a dollar or more for the privilege of watching an edifying feature accompanied by an orchestra (which if it were at the 1920s New York palace, the Roxy, for instance, would outnumber the venerable New York Philharmonic).[21]

Even as film historians began to saddle their hobbyhorses, others began to take an interest in the new discovery. Shakespeare scholars, for example, were soon exchanging knowing winks, for here once again was their man proving his unfailing ability to insert himself into nearly every post-Renaissance watershed in Western culture. In short, once the film's rediscovery was announced, it became the subject of intense speculation and, with its accessibility limited while it was undergoing restoration, scholars had recourse to some rather unreliable secondary sources. In his first attempt to describe the film, for instance, one critic claimed that the actor who played Richard, Frederick Warde, had already completed a brief *King Lear* (he was to play Lear in an ambitious film for the adventurous Thanhouser company in 1916), that Richard's succession of murders begins with that of Henry VI (he plunges his sword into Prince Edward in an opening scene interpolated from the post-Tewkesbury events in Shakespeare's *3 Henry VI*), that having run Henry through and wiped his blade with his hand Richard—perhaps in anticipation of the Vampire films soon to infest Germany and Denmark—licks off the blood (he merely tosses it aside contemptuously), that Clarence "drowns in ale" (he is stabbed fatally), and that the film "hardly rates as a masterpiece on any aesthetic level."[22] In defense of this latter assessment, he repeats an insistent prejudice of film historians, namely, that in comparison with D.W. Griffith, the "solitary genius" who was the progenitor of the narrator system that gave rise to the language of classical cinema, James Keane's editing and cinematography were primitive. In fact, when we consider the conditions of its production and its particular audience, its superficially retrograde aspects emerge as a far from primitive attempt at complex niche marketing and product differentiation.[23] Certainly, the contemporary reviews quoted by the first indisputable authority on Shakespeare on film, Robert Hamilton Ball, suggest that what audiences saw (and heard) in 1912 was at the cutting edge of innovation.[24]

Ball, who by his own admission relied heavily on far from disinterested journalism and trade papers, declared more cautiously than his sources that "since the film is not extant and there are no detailed reviews, it is impossible to know what success was achieved...Whether it could have stood on its own feet without Warde's explanatory intercessions is highly questionable."[25] We now know that the film, which omits Shakespearean dialogue from its intertitles, was probably designed to benefit from Warde's interventions in supplying narrative bridges and individual voices—probably Shakespearean ones—in the manner of the ubiquitous Japanese *benshi* or *katsuben*, a tradition of living narration that took such a powerful hold on its spectators that it persisted into the 1930s. But the filmmakers also inserted a prologue and epilogue in which a formally attired Warde can be seen bowing to the audience, sequences quite likely to have been omitted if he were actually present as a narrator. They had probably calculated that if the film were successful with Warde, then his bows and reputation would continue to carry it without him, provided that the action was rendered sufficiently self-explanatory to finesse the historical complexities of the Plantagenet-Tudor transition that Shakespeare allows to unfold over a cycle of plays.

A more recent historian of Shakespeare on screen, Kenneth Rothwell, writes with the benefit of having seen the rediscovered film; and he has been among the first to appreciate its obvious departure from the proscenium style of staging in a British *Richard* produced hardly a year previously by F.R. Benson's theatre company, a film that amazingly does succeed in incorporating a few touches of cinematic dramaturgy while cramming nuggets of Shakespeare's dialogue into verbose intertitles within its comparatively short length of fewer than 1400 feet.[26] What is most interesting in Rothwell's analysis of the Warde-Keane *Richard*, however, is that he, like Ball, attributes aspects of the staging and some departures from Shakespeare's play to the influence of Colley Cibber, whose 1700 version of *Richard III* effectively displaced the Bard's and held the stage (despite some efforts at "restoration") until Henry Irving's polemical rejection of it in the 1870s.

Or Is It Cibber?

The question of how a *Richard* made for a twentieth-century American audience could employ the by-then "outmoded" Cibber while clearly elaborating on scenes suggested by Shakespeare (and omitted by Cibber) is something of a detective story and one that richly illustrates the mutual illumination of textual hermeneutics, performance tradition, and cultural history. A potential answer, although in this instance a deceptive one, might also involve a seldom-studied aspect of the visual culture that pertains to film exhibition: the movie poster. The handsome and vividly colored poster for *Richard III* is doubly informative in that it credits James Keane with the scenario in a small roundel inset into the scene chosen by the illustrator, an oft-quoted moment in the climactic battle not to be found in the extant version of the film. Since this print appears not to have shots missing, the desperate Richard's readiness to exchange his kingdom for a horse (his own lying wounded behind him in the poster) had not been discarded at the outset. It suggests a conscious omission, for there is no equivalent in the film. Admittedly, the lines are not entirely easy to film in the absence of an acquiescent horse: they create a notable semiotic disjuncture in Richard Loncraine's exuberant "Fascist" 1930s *Richard III* (1995), in which Ian

McKellen-Oswald Mosley-Gloucester seems to reject the technology of modern warfare altogether when his military jeep gets bogged down while escaping an oncoming tank, and he demands a horse rather hoarsely. But horselessness was certainly not a problem in the earlier film. Indeed, Warde rides one at a fair canter in the second scene of the film, and one can only surmise that, if filmed, the footage was spoiled irredeemably. Or perhaps Warde, feeling his age, demurred, fallen horses being none too safe and Hollywood and its stuntmen being things of a not-too-distant future.

As for the attribution to Keane, this, too, is somewhat suspect. Despite possessing a name homonymous with thespian greatness, he remains a rather obscure figure. A partially surviving later film whose scenario is indisputably his, *Spreading Evil* (1918), has its reels out of sequence, but the story they tell is clear enough. In contrast to the economy of the intertitling in *Richard III*, Keane's film is oversupplied with them, with underlining and boldfaced lettering being favorite methods of emphasis. A further stylistic difference is that the plot has only the faintest of echoes of those of Shakespeare. An American doctor, John Carey, convinced that the blight of syphilis must be cured before it "destroys the human race," locates a German scientist, Emil Hartsell, who breaks his "word of honor" to provide his cure "to the world free, irrespective of nationality and creed." The intrigues of World War I place his son in the United States, while Emil remains loyal to Germany. It is only when Carey informs him that Karl is "stricken with the very disease for which you invented a cure," that Emil decides to hitch a ride on a marauding U-Boat to the shores of the United States, his secret formula in hand. An alert captain of the Coast Guard not only spots the submarine but also takes command of his own and blows the intruding vessel up spectacularly. A self-reflexive intertitle informs us of the fate of Emil's son, now writhing on the shore having observed his salvation disintegrate before his eyes: {"Although too late to save / Karl of this photodrama / and the millions who / have gone before, Carey's / work is being carried / on with the entire strength / of the United States Government. / A brighter day has dawned."} Another intertitle consists solely of large letters suggesting abstinence as the best cure for such plot devices: {MORALITY}. Nevertheless, the film also prints a congratulatory letter from the Secretary of the Navy, Joseph Daniels, who expresses the conviction that "any young man who has seen your photodrama will be strengthened in his resolve to live a clean life." A brief sequence of Daniels in vivo shaking Keane's hand concludes the film.

We can thus surmise that Keane's commitment to Shakespeare was less acute than his perception of pressing social needs, and that his screenwriting credit is perhaps not to be taken any more seriously than those of present-day directors whose names appear alongside the originators of the scripts. The clues leading to the more likely author of the redaction of the "modernized" Cibber point to Warde (who by all accounts was the inspiration for the film), his knowledge of the play and its performance history, and his quite complex relationship with his audiences. As we have observed, the makers of early features shared the fear that longer narratives would perplex audiences; but the revival of the antiquated practice of incorporating a narrator also suggests a secondary entertainment that would justify a higher ticket price, not a regression to "primitive" filmmaking. Thus *Richard III* made a virtue of a necessity, and thanks to Ball's industrious researches, we have at least one description of how Warde was himself the principal attraction at a showing. According to the January 12, 1913 edition of the *Charleston News and Courier*:

> While the eyes rest in the intermissions between the showings of the reels, Mr. Warde entertains the audience with a dramatic recital of the famous passages in the play, elucidating them at the same time. During the showing of the pictures he explains the situations. The result is amazingly good.

As Ball suggests, this manner of exhibition is confirmed by the copyright file on the film that describes a "Recital by Mr. Warde" during the screening and further commentaries after each reel. The film was not placed under copyright until Warde had completed touring the provinces with it, at which point (in September of 1913) it was offered for sale for general distribution.[27] The film we possess today is almost certainly this recension starring an entirely silent Warde who—if the framing sequences were inserted as one could conjecture—is reduced to bowing (if not scraping) to his now imaginary audience.

Rothwell, among the more generous of commentators on early filmed Shakespeare, initially did Warde an injustice in paraphrasing Alan Woods to the effect that he was "an old-fashioned, ranting performer...who toured the hinterlands of the United States as an itinerant Shakespearean, never quite making it on the New York Stage, until he 'drifted' into a film career. In his regal appearance Warde embodied every nineteenth-century Bardolator's ideal of an authentic Shakespearean actor."[28] In his subsequent commentary, Rothwell has made handsome amends for this early dismissal, but perhaps Warde is worth considering in greater detail not only in a redemptive context but also as a rather surprising key to a textual mystery. Certainly, the Warde who emerges from his 1920 autobiography does not seem quite as stiff and formal as his first cinematic prologues suggest (in his 1916 film of *King Lear* he begins as an affable gentleman puffing on a cigar who dissolves into the title character, such framing devices being common in early feature films). According to his report, in coming to the United States, Warde increased his income fourfold and had the chance to play leading roles, motives that no doubt impelled a number of his fellow British actors to follow suit. He was not a journeyman when he arrived on the American stage, nor a barnstormer when he chose to leave it: indeed, in the midst of the wry anecdotes of his autobiography, *Fifty Years of Make Believe*, we discover an actor who as a young man was chosen to play alongside Britain's most renowned Shakespearean, Sir Henry Irving, and who even after he left the great Booth's Theatre in New York following a dispute over star billing was still counted worthy of touring the South in Edwin Booth's company in the latter's first southern tour after Lincoln's assassination, even alternating the roles of Iago and Othello with him.[29]

While disputes over American or British Shakespearean acting styles could ignite bloody riots a few generations earlier, Warde's career extended into a period when competing entertainments compelled even the greatest actors to seek culture-starved audiences in America's hinterlands to supplement their incomes from ever-shorter metropolitan seasons. He continued to receive good notices, but as he grew older and the theatre he knew best gave way to the illusionistic, protocinematic spectacles of David Belasco and his former mentor Dion Boucicault, he elected to join the prestigious American Chautaqua

Association lecture circuit, traveling to the provinces with a secure income and audience (an audience whose genuine desire for knowledge elicited his respect and concern).

Before turning to screen acting in his sixties, Warde both edited and wrote critical commentaries about Shakespeare's plays and, at first, he found the experience of acting for the screen risible. As direction, the method Keane preferred (in anticipation of Fellini) was that his actors, left ignorant of their parts, had to rely on the instructions he shouted to them; Warde, meanwhile, regaled them with Shakespeare's modified lines.[30] Camera movement had been used extensively ever since Alexandre Promio placed a Lumière Cinématographe on a Venetian Gondola in 1896 and tracked laterally past the Doge's palace. Keane could be forgiven for his failure to master the tracking shot: attempts to show troops in movement evidence an unsteady hand, but then it was not until the famous introduction to the Babylonian excesses of *Intolerance* (1916) that such a shot, taken on an epic scale (possibly from a tethered balloon) arrived on the American movie set as a result of Griffith's competitive emulation of Giovanni Pastrone's lavish use of a dolly mounted on tracks in *Cabiria* (1913). He was no Griffith, however, and appears not to have mastered one of the oldest tricks in the book, since he retains a poorly executed panning shot of the ship on which he (playing Richmond in the manner of Nick Bottom) returns to establish a Tudor monarchy. Griffith would have discarded the spoiled portion of the footage instantly; Keane's only excuse might have been that he was denied the choice by the prepublicity in the trade papers that followed a practice endemic to early features, that of assuring exhibitors and audiences that they received their money's worth by emphasizing production values: prints dyed in expensive and mood-creating colors, a cast (and cost) of thousands, real locations, and even a ship large enough to ferry an army and capable of outdistancing a cameraman's eye.

Since Warde's performance can at times seem superbly expressive, as in the flick of the hand ridding itself of Henry's spent blood (in his autobiography he emphasizes the need to know both the lines and the stage "business" associated with a role), it is tempting to think that the occasional clumsiness derives from the director's suggestions as much as the novelty of the new medium. Some of these suggestions seem, in fact, to have been improvised, for Warde occasionally finds himself having to pause in mid-motion in order not to exit the frame prematurely. It would seem, then, that his contribution to the film should not be sought in his acting but in the task of textual adaptation, for which he was admirably qualified having adapted Shakespeare earlier for a range of audiences. It is perhaps with an eye to his varied audiences that Warde selected his first screen vehicle, for although Cibber's Richard provided the two most celebrated actors of the English stage, David Garrick and Edmund Kean, with their most popular "Shakespeare" role, Warde's only lengthy recollections of the play are those of his early days on British and American stages.[31] He and his associates may have been inspired by the Vitagraph *Richard* of 1908 that adopts a scene order suggestive of an abridgement of Cibber whose simplification rescued later playgoers from a ready familiarity with the arcana of Tudor history. Yet even this version was not wholly Cibber's, for according to Vitagraph's publicity material, Gloster enters after the Tower scene reciting "Now is the winter of our discontent,"[32] lines that Cibber famously dispensed with—possibly because they contained an obscure punning reference to the heraldic "sun" in the Yorkist banner—as he transposed the opening to a more suitable spot.

Cibber's cinematic persistence (evident as late as Olivier's screen adaptation two and a half centuries later where he and Alan Dent borrow the prologue and some lines from the 1700 adaptation, and present even in the opening intertitles and also part of the prologue to Loncraine's, still another fifty years on), can well be explained by the secondary fact of the eccentricity of Shakespeare's opening. Perhaps as the result of being part of a sequence of plays, *Richard III* grants its antihero a protracted and all but unfilmable soliloquy that in the theatre invites the audience into an immediate complicity with his Machiavellianism. (In comparison, Marlowe's Machivel who introduces the action of *The Jew of Malta* in person, asks much less of the audience in inviting their laughter and not their collusion.)[33] Even a journeyman screenwriter is advised to avoid lengthy speeches, however, and the intimacies of cinematic dramaturgy favor brief exchanges and visual storytelling. Olivier's solution to the problem of this dilatory, if necessary, creation of intimacy is to trim the speech and allow his character a gleefully conspiratorial direct address to the camera; Pacino's is to filch the same lines Jarman merely transposed into the opening of his version of *The Tempest*, and to give them to an unseen dreamer; Loncraine has us follow Richard into what one might even posit as a privileged and socially licensed site of homosocial intimacy, a toilet, a cunningly apt spot for verse more excreted than delivered by a surly Ian McKellen who in effect sneers during the first, "public" part of his declamatory address, and concludes by rounding on the camera and even gesturing to it to follow him. But the cleverest of all avoidances of Cibber's unkindest cut might be that of Raoul Ruiz, who prefers a Richard getting pissed to one pissing (the impairment of the senses, especially that of vision, functions as a major trope in the film). Ruiz contrives to film the entire soliloquy in two parts by first showing a Richard drunk on the blood of his enemies and, later, with celebratory mugs of malmsey at the contemplation of Clarence's fate. The film opens with the camera appearing to point to a sky with dark clouds scurrying across it. A caption informs us that the place is "Mildendo, 203 avant Gulliver." As the caption disappears, brassy trumpets (in a score that appears to anticipate Ennio Morricone's for the Warde-Keane film as well as Zeffirelli's *Hamlet*) announce an armored fist holding aloft a broadsword, its hilt suggesting an inverted cross. The camera continues to draw back and rise, as a voice speaks a modern French translation, by Jean-Marie Déprats, of "Now is the winter." At the emphasized word "déplaisir" (discontent), the camera tilts down to reveal the speaker, a black, metal-clad figure lying on the field of battle, who turns his cynical eyes toward the camera. Then, in a shot reminiscent of the studio release of Orson Welles's *Touch of Evil* (1957), the camera rises on its crane and tracks with Richard as he continues the opening soliloquy during which captions give us the credits. Eventually, he mounts the caparisoned steed held by his groom and rides away, concluding the first part of the soliloquy with "lascivious lute." It is only after he has promised deliverance to Clarence, being ferried away in a boat to his imprisonment, and after Lady Anne has laid a curse on him as she accompanies Edward's funeral procession, that we find him entering a cave-like seaside cellar. As Richard sits with a mug of malmsey, chortling, a henchman tips a fish freshly plucked from the receding tide head first into a mug of the brew, and Richard's mirth at the frantic thrashings of its inverted form are all we get to see of Clarence's proposed fate beyond the stylized preliminary stabbing soon shown in painful detail. It is at this point that the monologue resumes, spoken over a sequence of thirteen sharply angled and carefully composed shots that in their emphasis on foregrounded beakers of sanguinary cyclamen blossoms and meticulously arrayed glassware evoke seventeenth-century Dutch still life painting; indeed, the "lascivious" lute of which Richard speaks can be found in just such a painting that hangs behind the heads of the hooded murderers with whom he communes. The cave-like lair seems an extension of his character, a milieu even more revealing than the stalactite- and stalagmite-encrusted caverns where the ailing king holds court, as it allows for heightened shadows that are more deformed than a protagonist whose physical appearance and mannerisms closely resemble those of the power-hungry, delusional conquistador Lope de Aguirre (as played by Klaus Kinski in Werner Herzog's 1972 film, *Aguirre, the Wrath of God*). The effect of thus emphasizing the later, often truncated lines, is to have Richard relish his deformity as the enabling excuse for his defiance of divine providence.[34] Why Ruiz, heir to the Third Cinema tradition of being a filmmaker-theorist and the author of an anthology called (even in its original French) a *Poetics of Cinema*, would choose to circumvent Cibberian abridgement, and instead insist on a much more drastic one of his own by omitting most of the last two acts, will be discussed in the context of Orson Welles's transnationalism. For the present it must suffice to note that Cibber, rude mechanical though he may be in taking a handsaw to the play rather than a scalpel, hardly deserves the excoriation to which he is subjected with such regularity.

Quite early in the century following his 1700 adaptation, however, the growing Shakespeare-as-national-treasure cult had even spread as far afield as *Mansfield Park*,[35] so that by midcentury the Popish manner of attacking Cibber in print had become something of a bicontinental obligation for editors of the Bard's "Complete and Unadulterated Works." F.A. Marshall, the principal editor of *The Henry Irving Shakespeare*, no doubt felt an urge to continue the polemic with which Irving had restored Shakespeare to the British stage on January 29, 1877, commenting that Cibber's version, "to the eternal discredit of the national intelligence and taste, held the stage for over one hundred and fifty years."[36] Nevertheless, he probably recognized that Irving's suggested cuts and nearly all his stage directions were heavily indebted to Cibber, possibly a contributory factor in his eventual decision to eschew his promised commentary on Cibber's adaptation. Not to be outdone, on December 25, 1877 Edwin Booth produced a prompt-book version that he hoped would one day lead to the complete abandonment of Cibber's edition with its invented soliloquies and the "ugly and low scene in which the king is made to berate his wife and advise her to kill herself."[37]

Astonishingly, it is this very scene that provides one of the high points of the Warde-Keane adaptation. The 1913 film visualizes a variety of scenes inspired by Shakespeare's dialogue and these elaborations, as in the translation of Clarence's report of the prophecy that condemns him into a scroll strategically flung through a casement into the throne room, serve to enhance the visual storytelling while rendering the plot even more temporally linear than Cibber's. This linearity in fact enhances the mirror effects that enable the film's audience to appreciate the symmetrical nature of divine justice. In the wooing scene, Gloster bares his breast and offers Anne the very sword that he thrust into Prince Edward and King Henry, at which point she follows Cibber's directions and raises it thrice only to let it fall.[38] In the "ugly and low scene" that occurs shortly before the final battle, Richard hands her his dagger, this time goading her to take her own life. As he surmises, her courage again fails her, and her physician has to administer a fatal draft at Richard's shadowy instigation. She shortly returns as a ghost (through the power of double exposure), along with the usurper's other victims, leading to the inevitable closure of the circular narrative when we finally see the last of the Plantagenets lying dead on the field of battle, run through just as Prince Edward was by Gloster at the start of the film.

Where, then, could the filmmakers have encountered such varied source material? The numerous illustrated editions of Shakespeare's plays available to them tell us nothing about the borrowing of specific iconographies as most provide a visual introduction to Gloster (Cibber's version of Gloucester) at the close of *3 Henry VI*. Moreover, in the play that follows, they illustrate the same scenes down to details of attire, again owing much (most notably Richard's heraldic insignia) to Planché. In the film, Richard's iconographically "authentic" shield, for instance, keeps changing position from shot to shot, surely an inauspicious sign on the eve of battle.[39] Nor could an edition of "Shakespeare" be the answer, for as Rothwell points out (and other features such as the reduction of the parts bear witness), at least one piece of staging seems to be suggested by Cibber's reworking of Henry's murder.[40] Could there have been a version known to them that was neither entirely Cibber nor entirely Shakespeare?

Paradoxically, one such version was published under the aegis of none other than Edwin Booth, who in 1872 produced and starred in the play at Booth's Theatre. For twenty-five cents a prospective member of the audience could have bought a printed copy of *The Tragedy of King Richard III*. In minuscule print below the title is the parenthetical observation: (Colley Cibber's Version). In this edition some lost lines are restored, a few Cibberian theatrical directions and invented lines omitted (though not the lines necessitating the wiping of the sword), and the cast reduced to the same extent as in Cibber.[41] Even if the youthful Warde played Lord Hastings in a Manchester version using "the full text of the poet" rather than the still popular but often "melodramatic" Cibber, his second American season at Booth's Theatre granted him the opportunity to adjudge the British actor Barry Sullivan superior to Booth in the role,[42] thus implying a familiarity with a Booth performance that at that time could only have been of the older version. Booth, incidentally, began his career in 1849 playing Cibber's Tressel to the Richard of his father, Junius Brutus; his younger brother, John Wilkes, first trod the boards at the Charles Street Theatre in Baltimore as Richmond, the part appropriated by Keane. Warde's familiarity with Edwin Booth's repertoire gives us at least one connection with the American performance tradition accruing to the play. The sight of Warde urging his steed toward the camera in his anxiety to commit his second murder thus attests not only to an extraordinary conflation of the original, Shakespeare, and its derivative, Cibber, but also to a well-developed sense of a narrative form that demanded visual rather than verbal cues.

Good Lieutenants and Tyrant Kings

The audiences who had once gone to hear Warde lecture must have been delighted to see something of his skill as a performer; the critics imply as much. Even so, such an elaborate mode of exhibition and multipurpose filmmaking could not continue for long. The early feature film no doubt represents a unique moment in the gradual emergence of consumer culture in the United States, when film producers learned to market high-class fare to an emerging bourgeoisie by carefully training audiences to sit still for unprecedented periods of time and to pay handsomely for the privilege. But spectators, then as now, have always preferred narcissistic identification with characters to education and edification. Even before the Warde-Keane *Richard III* achieved a general release, the low-budget feature *The Life and Adventures of Lieutenant Petrosino* (November 1912), a contemporary crime film based on a true story of the Sicilian underworld in New York, was establishing yet another market niche that was soon to achieve spectacular success. And it is this film celebrating a contemporary Italian American detective from New York rather than the less edifying tale of the last of the Plantagenets that was to set the agenda for the prevalent form of feature filmmaking to follow. The flamboyant Petrosino was an exemplary illustration of the triumph of assimilation, an Italian immigrant who identified more closely with the predominantly Anglo-Saxon arbiters of culture and the upwardly mobile members of his own social group than with the unassimilated villains (not merely violators of the law, but also those such as his wife's stereotypically abusive father). In the complete print that survives at the Nederlands Filmmuseum, the mobsters Petrosino pursues are identified as the Camorra, and in the titles (and American reviews) as the Black Hand. It is the *New York Times* that a few years later would give secret organizations with both Neopolitan and Sicilian connections the generic appellation of "Mafia," but even at this early stage the "newspaper of record" took an avid interest in the activities of the historical Petrosino. When, for the first time, months passed with no mention of his exploits in its pages, it was because it withheld news known to European readers such as those of the *Times* of London. Petrosino had been assassinated while on undercover duty in Sicily. It is for the newly assimilated audience of the feature that the role of Petrosino is played in an effectively understated manner and that he is mourned elaborately as a martyr at the conclusion of the film. This is in sharp distinction to the atavism of monarchical absolutism left behind in the Old World as allegorized by Warde's crumpled, unmourned figure in the last shot of the Shakespearean film adaptation. From 1912 onward the early feature turned increasingly toward contemporary melodramas and such current legislative issues as "white slavery," while another European import—the one-reel serial melodramas, quite often with endangered heroines as protagonists—vied with them for popularity. Yet if history was once again not on Richard's side, the 1912/1913 film remains a fascinating document not only of daring experimental cinema but also of a two hundred-year-old tradition of Shakespearean performance practice that endured on American stages even after it had expired in Britain.

★ ★ ★

Warde had not finished with Shakespeare films, of course, and in many ways his next endeavor proved more characteristic of the style of acting with which he was most familiar. Indeed, to compare Warde's Gloster with his King Lear is to see the distance that the feature film had traversed in the space of three years. The most compelling similarity between the films consists of a plot that reiterates the perils of absolutism. Moreover, as if to satisfy the audiences' increasing demands for redemptive endings, the film's sponsors, Edwin Thanhouser and his company, had begun to experiment with filming the later Shakespearean Romances. By 1610 Shakespeare appears to have spent increasing amounts of time in Stratford, and perhaps with the newly leased indoor theatre the Blackfriars in mind, had begun to compose more episodic plays incorporating music furnished by court composers, as well as the pageants and masques beloved of his royal patrons. Elizabethan tragedy was never far from comedy, and such plays as *King Lear* evidence Shakespeare's deliberate rewriting of his sources to heighten the tragedy. But in his late Romances, comitragedy changed to tragicomedy, with these sometimes melancholy and often melodramatic fantasies invariably concluding with scenes of forgiveness, redemption, and reconciliation. Whether the Thanhousers were sensitive to the extraordinary transformation that had taken place in his style is not evident in their films, but it might explain some of their inventions. Their first-known effort to survive, the *Winter Tale* (a.k.a. *The Winter's Tale*) of 1910, begins with a title card that reveals their approach to Shakespeare if the treatment of his title is anything to go by. Even so, subtraction was not their only intent. Judith Buchanan, who describes the Thanhouser Shakespeare films in greater detail than any other commentator, suggests that, in incorporating an unwritten part for a rather intrusive Fool, the studio continued a tradition of ironic treatment of Shakespeare's high-cultural associations initiated by Vitagraph: it was their *Julius Caesar*, which came very early in their 1908–1912 Shakespeare adaptations and takeoffs, that set the tone for the rest of the series, in that it boasts a somnolent senator who manages to doze through Caesar's assassination, his fellow senators' panic, and even Marc Antony's forceful entrance.[43] At the time of its Shakespeare cycle, which even included a *Richard III* (1908), Vitagraph enjoyed the biggest European distribution of any American studio (Buchanan attributes "imperial ambitions" to the delight they took in emblazoning their trademark of an American eagle with wings outstretched forming a "V" on many of their props);[44] but the studio was to fall on hard times during World War I and was eventually bought out by Warner Bros.

The Thanhouser Film Corporation of New Rochelle, New York, on the other hand, was quite literally a family business, and in this last period in which artisan filmmaking still flourished in the United States, it labored to remain solvent from film to film. By 1917 the studio system had already consolidated in Hollywood, and an industry accommodating hundreds of small-scale film producers at the start of World War I in short order contracted to few more than a dozen large entities.[45] Perhaps mindful of pointed criticism about the leisurely, Europeanate pacing of *Winter Tale*, the 1911 Thanhouser *Romeo and Juliet* reorders the scenes and goes much further in its radical abridgement of the play, most notably of the early scenes. The entire drama, in fact, is condensed into fewer than thirty shots, of which more than a third consists of intertitles. While the Thanhousers seemed as fond of religious symbols as Vitagraph of its eagles, there is much less sense of an active engagement with Shakespeare's text than in their preceding film. Hardly has it begun before Romeo finds himself avenging Mercutio and facing exile, without even having enjoyed Capulet's ball. Some of the most familiar scenes are given short shrift, at least in one instance to preserve Shakespeare's moral fiber. A title of doubtful literary merit {"Farewell, my love / one kiss, and I'll be gone"} announces a scene of Juliet in her chamber, a kiss the lovers exchange in a doorway, and Romeo's rapid descent from a balcony that we must assume he had ascended not too much earlier. While in *Winter Tale* the Thanhousers gave the function of the interpretive lecturer to a frolicsome Fool (as Jean-Luc Godard was to three score and ten years later in his reading of *Lear*), here that function is taken over by a forthright friar. Friar Laurence has as large a part as either of the lovers, his exaggerated reactions (like those of the Fool in

Winter Tale) cuing the appropriate responses for the audience. His potion places Juliet in her tomb before the half-way point of the film, which consists mostly of the tragedy in the latter part of the play, and it ends not with Escalus's epitaph but with the Friar's horrified discovery of three corpses.

That these devices represent experimentation to test audiences' responses to varied approaches rather than a craven retreat into stylistic anachronism is evident in Thanhouser's next surviving Shakespeare project, a *Cymbeline* of 1913.[46] In some ways it harks back to the approach first ventured in *Winter Tale*, but perhaps it would be more correct to argue that it veers in the opposite direction from *Romeo and Juliet*. In addition to granting its Imogen, Florence LaBadie, the chance to rival Warde's Richard in a deft display of cloak-swirling and equestrian agility, the film seems to grant a graver tone to the play and seems ever-anxious about its own elisions of such things as headless corpses (which it tries to mitigate with a profusion of intertitles ranging from summaries of lost portions of plot and quotations of modified Shakespeare to temporal markers and handwritten documents). The improbabilities of Shakespeare's intricate plot (derided by his editor, Samuel Johnson, and given an ironic alternative ending by G.B. Shaw) are treated lightly, and from the end of the battle between the Romans and the Britains no more than eleven shots, five of them intertitles, encompass a multiplicity of moments of joyous anagnoresis: the king rediscovers his rustic sons, a defeated Roman general offers proof of Imogen's survival, Leonatus makes amends, and all is forgiven.

The *King Lear* of 1916 proceeds still further in this direction. Buchanan notes that the felicitous intercutting of point-of-view shots of battle scenes and reaction shots seems to be borrowed from *Cymbeline*, and it well may be so (although Griffith and other directors had already established this convention in advance of the Thanhousers' arrival on the scene).[47] Certainly, in matters of camera movement and montage, the film is a distinct advance over the Vitagraph *King Lear* of 1909 whose brief thirty-one shots are nevertheless replete with visual delights fit to quicken Thomas Hardy's heart. Vitagraph's storm scene does not occur on the usual desolate heath but against a backdrop suggestive of Stonehenge, itself set against a livid, painted sky. All the laws of nature, in fact, are subordinate to dramatic necessity. When upbraided by Goneril for his mistreatment of her insolent servant, Lear falls to his knees and throws his crown almost vertically out of the frame, and the gravitas of the situation requires it not to fall back down again. In contrast, the Thanhouser *Lear* does not strive for effect, but from the beginning announces its learned approach to Shakespeare's original with its lengthy, calligraphically handwritten intertitles. The first of these informs us that "King Lear was written in 1607, during the time when the immortal dramatist was at the height of his creative Power." In addition to the modern framing device, the titles introducing actors (with cuts to them affecting looks expressive of their characters) suggest a familiarity with the most recent narrative conventions of feature filmmaking.

On the other hand, the occasional eccentricities of the analytical editing suggest an observant but inexperienced filmmaker, which indeed was the case with the young Ernest Warde, Frederick's son and Fool, who was entrusted with direction. His father must have been proud of him, just as Thanhouser must have been pleased to have nabbed an actor of Warde's stature and experience: two production stills from the film make their way into *Fifty Years of Make-Believe*, one representing the very beginning of the film with the Fool sprawled before Lear's throne and another showing Ernest alone, emphasizing the similarity of his attire and props to that of the earlier Fool of *Winter Tale*.[48] While the still photograph of the opening might suggest a spacious throne room, in the surviving prints of the film the scene is both protracted and extremely crowded. Considering the number of exchanges between characters, one might assume that the scene would require numerous point-of-view shots (as indeed might have been the case if Griffith, then in the flush of the success of *The Birth of a Nation*, would have employed). However, Ernest Warde minimizes the number of camera setups through strictly choreographed figure movements and tight groupings of characters (Goneril and Regan with their husbands behind them, Lear seated on a raised throne directly in front of the camera toward the background, with the Fool enjoying a certain degree of mobility poised beneath him, Kent to the right of the throne amidst suitors and courtiers, and Cordelia closer to the foreground than her sisters). Thus, by placing Lear at the center of his introductory establishing shot and merely rotating his camera slightly (and invisibly, through the use of cuts) to the other groupings when reaction shots or remonstrances were called for, Ernest Warde contrived to keep his Lear (and of necessity his Fool) at the center of the action rather than yielding the scene to Cordelia, as most stagings do. The spectators are kept spatially oriented by repeated cuts back to the original master shot, the shots of other groupings being at times taken from different angles or closer framings, thus suggesting a favorite device of Akira Kurosawa's, the cut-in. The spectators are thus unlikely to notice that many of the cuts occur in violation of what gradually became codified in the system of classical continuity editing as the thirty-degree rule, which insists that a camera be moved at least thirty degrees from its initial position for each consecutive cut to prevent imparting the sensation of an accidental jump cut.

Although Lear's world is not yet the "chaos" of Kurosawa's *Ran*, its formality and hieratic performance style are strangely reminiscent of those of Brook's later film version of the play. While Kozintsev's Yuri Yarvet begins as a vigorous monarch and descends into maddened self-realization, Paul Scofield plays Brook's Lear much as Frederick Warde does, as a stricken old man of enfeebled reason and the plaything of a cruel destiny. And it is Warde, battling not only Fate's implacability but also the silence of his medium, who most completely visualizes (and even sentimentalizes) the king's fall. Warde's Lear trembles in his rage and is never the dragon Shakespeare allows him to imagine, as one of the modifications of dialogue in an intertitle reveals: {"Peace Kent! Come / not between me and / my wrath—I loved / her most."} Although the film is evidently not shot in continuity, Lear's stiff feebleness gradually gives way to a growing tremor that the elder Warde would have had to calibrate from shot to shot. The most poignant of these is the moment at which he advances toward and then past the camera, his outstretched staff aquiver.

★ ★ ★

The Thanhouser *Lear* may seem worlds away from Warde's protofeature of 1912. But Fforde's literary detective Thursday Next would require no portal to transport her or her literary heroes back and forth in time to detect a reminder of Warde's first attempt to communicate Shakespeare to a filmgoing audience. In Loncraine's film much is made of the imagery Shakespeare developed from Gloucester's crest, a rampant boar. In a secondary tribute to one of Pier Paolo Pasolini's metaphors for a Fascist state, *Porcile* (1969), for instance, Loncraine's Gloucester and Tyrrell meet opposite a pigsty (the pig being, appropriately, a boar, Gloucester's heraldic emblem, at which he tosses half an apple and elicits a Pasoliniesque squeal). Seated on Lear's throne the already fragile Warde seems a generation older than his earlier incarnation as Gloster just three years earlier. Above his head, however, at the apex of his throne, is affixed an emblematic boar's head.

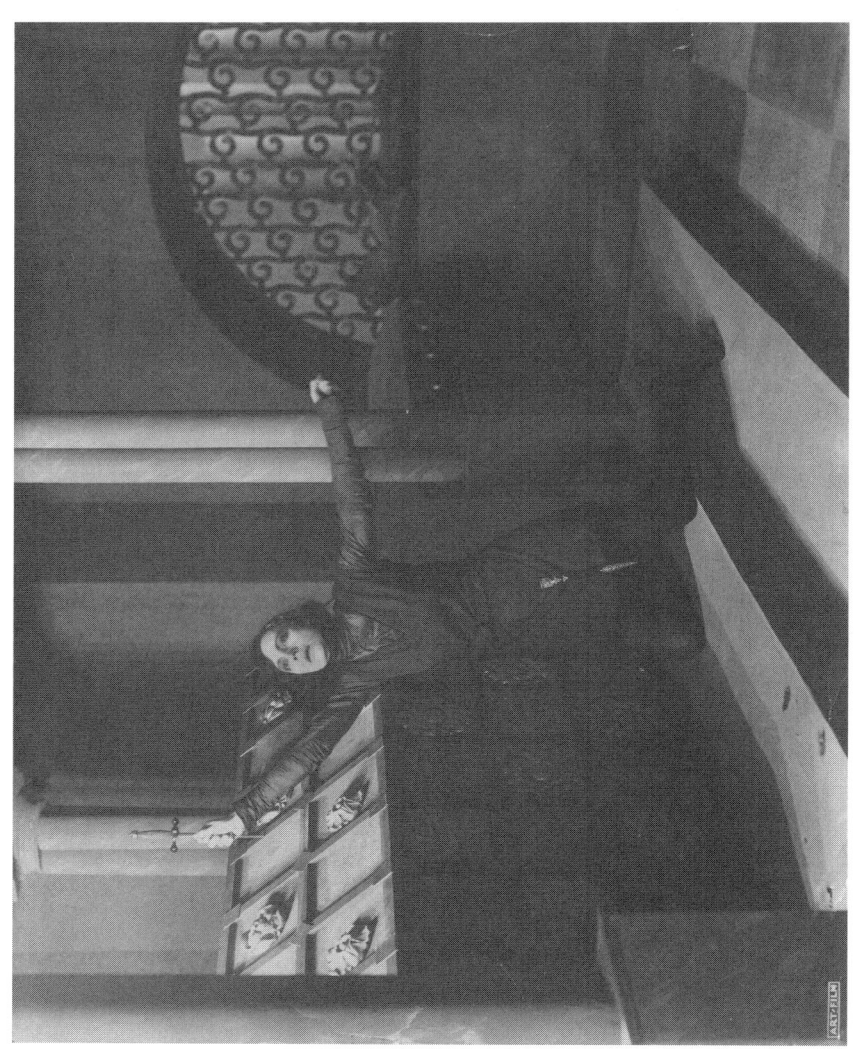

Asta Nielsen as the young Prince of Denmark in *Hamlet* (1920). Courtesy of the British Film Institute.

CHAPTER THREE

The Exfoliating Folio, or Transnational and International Avant-Gardes from Bernhardt's Hamlets *to Hollywood's Europeans*

In which the author attempts to relate cinema's international success to Shakespeare's ★ From Hamlet in Paris to Oedipus in Vienna, or How Alfons became Alphonse, Sigismund became Sigmund, and Henriette-Rosine became divine ★ Mrs. Siddons, Mr. Reynolds, Mr. Shakespeare, and the visual economies of stardom ★ Francesca Bertini and the rise of the film diva ★ Eine Kleine Filmmusik, or how American capital underwrote French contemporary Shakespeare and Italian historical spectacle ★ On Béla Balázs's astral inclinations, or how Asta Nielsen and film theory came to Berlin ★ Ufa's Ur-Shakespeare ★ Sausages, sauerkraut, and the Ham(let) in Hollywood high culture.

Although it occupies only a modest place in the posthumous First Folio of 1623, five plays from the end, *Hamlet* was a signal moment in Shakespeare's development. For Stephen Greenblatt, it marks the dramatist's transformation from a successful writer to a self-conscious artist, containing irresolvable ambiguities of character for the first time in his known oeuvre, a decisive phase-shift that seems indicated by a larger proportion of invented words than in any play before or since.[1] Aptly, then, it is the most adapted of Shakespeare plays, if one discounts the possibility that *Romeo and Juliet* (whether borrowed literally or ironically) may be the distant origin of countless plots in popular cinemas the world over.[2] Regarded from a very early date as a touchstone of great acting, *Hamlet* is also the play that when translated into cinema has attracted the widest range of performance styles, from the seeming replication of a theatrical performance on celluloid to a commentary on the incipient rottenness of the business world so verisimilar as to have escaped detection as a Shakespeare film for more than a generation. It has inspired directors to try to capture the flavor of a decidedly French prose translation (Bernhardt) and an equally Gallic tour de force of special effects (Méliès); it has functioned as something of a rebuke in an Italian cinematization (Rodolfi) that owes fragments of inspiration to a quasi documentary of a British stage performance (Plumb-Hepworth), and it has served the finest of its interpreters as both a bravura extension of her star persona and a learned essay on Shakespeare's sources and critics (Nielsen). Considering only the most distinctive of later versions, one is still struck by the range of interpretations: *Hamlet* has lent itself to metatheatrical psychodrama (Olivier), contemporary Naturalism

(Kurosawa), New Wave send-up (Chabrol), political allegory (Kozintsev), arch parody (Kaurismaki), ensemble star performance (Zeffirelli), didactic opulence (Branagh), paracinematic New Age grunge (Almereyda), actorly seriousness (Scott), and even historical trauma (Cavanagh). Bernice Kliman and Marianna De Sanctis provide intriguing commentaries on the surviving fragments of the *Hamlets* directed by Mario Caserini (Cines 1908) and Gérard Bourgeois (Lux 1910), De Sanctis observing of the former that it followed the general pattern of Italian Shakespeare films of that moment in condensing the film's story into "pictorial scenes [in this case seven of them] summarizing the key narrative events," although as Kliman notes these are not static tableaux; a brief summary of the effects to be found in them would include parallel inset compositions and repeated cuts in and out for the Ghost's narration and for Hamlet's "staging" of Gonzago's murder, camera movements when the players arrive, the insertion of imagined scenes of Ophelia's madness, and a split-screen effect accomplished with an arras viewed sideways-on in order to pan from Hamlet and Gertrude to a scene of Claudius urging Polonius to attempt his fatal evesdropping.[3] Even some of the unrediscovered films have left a tantalizing trail of traces: we have descriptions of a 1908 *Hamlet* now attributed securely to Luca Comerio that may have been the inaugural film released by Milano Films,[4] the Urban-Eclipse *Hamlet* of Henri Desfontaines (1910) that was very likely to have been intended for British as well as French distribution, a *Hamlet* variously dated to 1910 and 1912 that was part of a (sometimes parodic) cycle of English Shakespeare films essayed by Will Barker, and even a 1910 *Hamlet* featuring actors from Copenhagen's Royal Theatre shot in Kronborg Castle (Shakespeare's Elsinore) for Nordisk by August Blom, soon to gain international recognition with his epic feature *Atlantis* (1913). Among them at least one missing *Hamlet* film probably existed only on paper, for as De Sanctis hypothesizes, the occasional references to a 1914 Ambrosio film of that title ascribe its direction to Arrigo Frusta, a prolific scriptwriter, while the only known Ambrosio Shakespeare film of that year was the resplendent *Otello* directed by veteran Luigi Maggi.[5] This list of highlights is fragmentary and in a constant state of revision as a result of archival discoveries and rediscoveries; and new film interpretations show no signs of abating.

Such proliferations are too numerous to be contained in these pages, but some of these reincarnations of the melancholy prince serve as a fitting point of entry to the issues central to this chapter in that *Hamlet* happens to be the play whose film versions have been most influenced by disparate performance traditions and by scholarly interpretations. In cinema, as in theatre, the playwright's most influential work has very much been an actors' vehicle, so that, as filmmaker Amy Heckerling would have it, we are witness not just to Shakespeare's *Hamlet*, or Zeffirelli's, but also Mel Gibson's. While among writers on Shakespeare on film, Jack Jorgens made the early and useful distinction between "theatrical," "realistic," and "filmic" modes of adapting the plays to the screen, it was not until Anthony Davies's *Filming Shakespeare's Plays* that any sustained attempt was made to survey the kinds of acting that such movements from one medium to another necessitated; filmmakers have not shown such reticence, for Branagh cleverly makes a reverse allusion to Hollywood's star system and to *Clueless* when he borrows Alicia Silverstone as his own spoiled princess.[6] The critical literature has remained scant, particularly with regard to the early films: the surviving *Hamlet* films alone show a marked complexity in their mixture of Jorgens's modes, in the national and supranational traditions to which they appeal, and hence of their performative styles. Moreover, they encapsulate a range of issues central to any consideration of the idea of film as a medium that readily transcends the confines of nation. It seems hardly a coincidence that, in addition to a sea of troubles at home, Hamlet has a German education, an almost English exile, a French-trained bête noir, and an implacable Norwegian foe whose forces appear at the end to be supplemented by Poles: by the time Hamlet falls into Shakespeare's hands he is Danish only in so far as Denmark stands for a corrupting rottenness like the Caravaggioesque fruit of a *natura morta*, possibly a teasing reference to the drama-addicted wife of England's soon-to-be king and probably not unconnected with the fact that since the 1570s Helsingor and its toll-taking castle had risen to maritime prominence. As I have pointed out in considering its translation into an acceptable story by the Tiv and the early recognition of its exportability, *Hamlet* is surprisingly universal in its appeal and adaptable to the taste of a wide variety of audiences. It is curious indeed that *Hamlet* also happens to be a play to which Shakespeare, usually the busiest of adapters, probably added little by way of plot. According to James Shapiro, the twelfth-century story about the Danish revenger Amleth, recorded by Saxo Grammaticus and reprinted in Latin in 1514, revealed that the prince's uncle had openly murdered his father and taken the queen as his wife, and that her son undertook a single-minded and socially sanctioned revenge.[7] François de Belleforest had already greatly embellished this tale, as when he assumes Queen Geruth's foregoing adultery and her initial collusion with her brother-in-law; eventually, Hamblet's wife betrays him in like fashion, and Belleforest, who cannot resist moralizing commentaries, confirms the conviction in his source that women are the principal cause of discord. "The Ghost, the play within the play, the feigned madness, and the hero's death—familiar features of the revenge drama of the late 1580s—are all likely to have been introduced by the anonymous author of the lost Elizabethan *Hamlet*" (i.e., the *ur-Hamlet* some scholars conjecturally ascribe to Thomas Kyd) adds Shapiro, who credits Shakespeare solely with the innovations of an imminent military threat in the form of Fortinbras and an unprecedented grammatical complexity, particularly in the play's use of paired words. Perhaps Shapiro does not give the clownish First Gravedigger, the only character with a verbal dexterity on a par with Hamlet's, his due, and perhaps he assumes a trifle too much in apparently granting to the putative *ur-Hamlet* the elevation of Polonius (or Corambis, as the First Quarto calls him) as well as the apparent invention of his son Laertes (who has no parallel in Belleforest, but who is vital to Shakespeare's conclusion). But he wisely observes that the changes were of a sort that were then in the air. Even Hamlet's acute introspection is, according to him, Shakespeare's first engagement with the fashion for Montaignism that overtook contemporary writing: John Florio was not alone in having embarked on translating the *Essais* into English; and Ben Jonson was soon to deride theatrical imitations of Montaigne in *Volpone*.[8] Shapiro goes on to note, as had Greenblatt in discussing the play's eschatology in *Hamlet in Purgatory*, that its "updating" made it unmistakably contemporary, addressing a constellation of socially charged issues.

It is by now almost a truism that Shakespeare had a way not merely of borrowing from, but also burying his sources. So their persistence in cinematic adaptations is, in itself, quite extraordinary. The prose stage version commissioned by Sarah Bernhardt from the antiquarianist Marcel Schwob and Eugène Morand might well have taken its brusque moral Hamlet and its pageantry from a residual influence of Belleforest,[9] although the event chosen to be filmed,

Hamlet's duel with Laertes, has no precedent in Shakespeare's French source. One finds an apparent survival of Belleforest, or of Belleforest via Cines, in the 1917 Italian *Amleto* of Eleuterio Rodolfi that was possibly made with French distribution in mind: the adulterous queen casts a sly glance at the approaching poisoner, her future husband, and by engaging in festive frivolities provokes an antifemale outburst from her son at the outset of the film. And in the 1920 *Hamlet* created for Asta Nielsen, the film's intellectual reach not only extends backward to Saxo for its elaborate prologue containing the backstory of the elder Hamlet's slaying of the elder Fortinbras and at least the idea behind the younger Hamlet's gory revenge on his uncle, but also forward to then recent criticism, including a group of title cards that credit the American Shakespearean Edward Payson Vining with its principal plot device. (It is by no means trivial to note that, among the well-known screen Hamlets, Nielsen is the only Dane to play the Dane.) Recent films have emphasized Ophelia's role as bait, and Branagh, whose interpolated flashbacks make her unambiguously Hamlet's lover, regards her as an acquiescent spy, the very font of the betrayed prince's inability to prevent feigned madness being compromised by outbreaks of the real thing. Perhaps a flavoring of Belleforest remains even in Franco Zeffirelli's *Hamlet* in which Glenn Close plays a rapacious, competitive Gertrude, attracted equally to new husband and erstwhile heir, and secretly delighted by Ophelia's fate (a perfectly acceptable reading of her recollection of the incident, which with Enobarbus's recollection of Cleopatra's barge, is the most celebrated actual flashback in any of the plays).[10]

Shakespeare's rewriting of *The Merchant of Venice* (derived from an Italian tale from the compilation *Il Pecorone*, with some significant changes treated later in this chapter) and of *King Lear* (taken from recent English sources that he deliberately contradicted in giving the play its remorselessly sadistic ending) also remain at issue in a wide variety of films that deserve to be placed in their historical context.[11] One of the most imaginative of recent Shakespeare films, a *King Lear* set in Africa, records a desperate attempt to stage a play, if in a darker key than Branagh's backstage *Hamlet* drama *A Midwinter's Tale* (itself something of an extended tribute to the 1964 Broadway version played as a dress rehearsal, which John Gielgud directed and in which Richard Burton was the Hamlet). A key moment in the life of a film movement, Kristian Levring's 2001 Dogme '95 commentary on the play *The King Is Alive* is, like Asta Nielsen's oeuvre, indicative of a conscious transcendence of nationality, albeit in this instance representative of a film movement's trans-Danishness rather than a star's. Indeed, Shakespeare's universality was such that from its beginnings to the present film exhibitors have capitalized on audiences' desire to witness foreign film versions of these familiar texts. The most prominent American film distributor of his time, George Kleine, contributed to the proliferation of Italian Shakespeare films just before World War I, and it is partly the inability of Italian producers to meet his contractual demands that resulted in an industrial decline apparent even before the catastrophic advent of hostilities. In the period of hyperinflation following the war, the German film industry thrived on cheap labor and sales in foreign currencies, with the consequence that the spate of German Shakespeare films of the 1920s, beginning with Nielsen's successful venture, cannily marketed their uncanniness as a form of product differentiation in the face of Hollywood's increasingly dominant product. With the decline of the Weimar government, many of the Ufa directors further internationalized adaptations of Shakespeare by carrying their distinctive styles to Hollywood, an issue touched on in an earlier portion of this book, but which deserves renewed attention in this context.

★ ★ ★

Hamlet Nouveau

A woman, who like Beerbohm Tree was also widely rumored to be Jewish, Sarah Bernhardt, defined a rich theatrical tradition at one of its apogees in late nineteenth-century France. In the wake of Zola's open letter to President Félix Faure in *L'Aurore*, Bernhardt addressed her own to the writer, ending "merci, Émile Zola, maître aimé, merci au nom de l'éternelle justice."[12] Of course, her origins would be an issue but for the fact that critics such as William Dean Howells, in his case writing two seasons after the London staging of her slightly abbreviated *Hamlet* (scenes had been shed since the fiasco of the fifteen-scene five-hour opening night), seemed much given to adverse biological criticism: "She had three things overwhelmingly against her," he recalls, "her sex, her race, and her speech [for] you never ceased to feel for a moment that it was a woman who was doing that melancholy Dane, and that the woman was a Jewess, and the Jewess was a French Jewess."[13]

More important to us, perhaps, was that Bernhardt was also an accomplished sculptor and draftswoman and, in a curious way, the greatest artistic patron of her age, for it was she who "discovered" Alfons Mucha, signed him to a multiyear contract, and in doing so became the godmother of Art Nouveau, the ephemeral but consequential Modernist movement that once and for all erased the distinction between the fine and the decorative arts. Mucha was not the first practitioner of the style: indeed, he was not even among the once better-known coterie of artists who formed the nucleus of the Galerie de l'Art Nouveau opened in Paris in 1895 by the erstwhile dealer in Japanese art, Siegfried Bing.[14] And even Bing had his precursors. In his emphasis on functional art, the influential mid-nineteenth-century critic John Ruskin promoted new approaches to painting, a call taken up and transformed into wrought iron and furniture design as well as the plastic arts by the Glasgow-based Arts and Crafts movement led by Rennie Macintosh, a call apparently heeded in the United States by Louis Comfort Tiffany and also in England by William Morris and his followers such as book illustrator Walter Crane. Jugendstil and the Vienna Secession, similarly aligned to functional art, might also have drawn their inspiration from such theorists as Aloïs Riegl. As Benjamin Binstock notes, the Viennese professor's compendious publications in the 1870s and 1880s not only set the stage for the later responses to him by Irwin Panofsky and Ernst Gombrich, but also formulated a systematic approach to art history that transcended distinctions between "high" and "low" in such a way as to anticipate "what would now be called visual culture."[15] Yet it was Mucha, the beneficiary of Bernhardt's mastery of the available apparatus of publicity, whose name and style were to become synonymous with Art Nouveau. He was to design her theatrical posters, sets, costumes, and personal adornments, but was also to create widely circulated designs for her commercial endorsements. Even as he corrects some of the legendary accretions surrounding Bernhardt's discovery of Mucha, Victor Arwas observes that no other Art Nouveau artist achieved such contemporary acclaim, and that the entire movement was "referred to by Goncourt as the 'Mucha style.'"[16]

While there is little evidence that Bernhardt dictated a particular style to Mucha, there is nothing to dispute that before their association he seemed under the sway of an altogether different aesthetic. His son, Jiri Mucha, himself an art critic, points out that prior to Bernhardt's belated, Christmas eve commission for a poster for her production of Victorien Sardou's *Gismonda*, the academically trained Mucha gravitated to the style of such large-scale historical painters as Hans Makart and Puvis de Chavanne, and far less to those of his radical friends such as Paul Gaugin or the innovative poster designers Jules Chéret and Toulouse Lautrec.[17] By the time the poster began to appear on hoardings on the first day of 1895, the year that began with the establishment of Art Nouveau and concluded with the establishment of cinema as public spectacle, Mucha, with only a trace of debt to the iconography of Eugène Grasset's *Joan of Arc* poster for the same patron, appears to have arrived at a complete style, a synthesis of Japanese, Catholic, Byzantine, and Mozarabic influences with the recent ideas of Morris and the Symbolists.[18] Renate Ulmer observes that its "sumptuous, priestly-vestment-like costume, the symbolic palm frond [that Gismonda holds aloft], the mosaic-like background that hints of a halo, all suggest a sacred atmosphere, not least the veneration of the actress as a cult figure, the muse of the *belle époque*."[19] Although elements of this iconography were recurrent in all of Mucha's posters for her, this first example caused a "sensation," claims Ulmer, adding, "it is adduced time and time again as a prime example of the modern conception of the poster."[20] Bernhardt promptly ordered 4,000 copies from the publisher Lemercier and, being able to sell them at considerable profit, sued the publisher when the firm failed to deliver the stipulated number.[21]

This is not by any means to suggest that Bernhardt's involvement with Mucha was parasitic. Mucha was little known, his style unformed, while Bernhardt's reputation as actor-manager had already spread far beyond the boundaries of France. Even Jiri Mucha, who inherited a considerable portion of his father's preparatory drawings and later work, could find no explanation for his father's conversion to Art Nouveau but her guiding presence and the "emotional force of the scene" of her Gismonda poised to enter the church on Palm Sunday. She occupied a "unique position" in his life he asserts, "her patronage had been the instrument of his success, her plays provided a showcase for his designs, and it was the force of her personality more than anything else which led to the famous transformation of his style in 1895."[22] It was she who translated Alfons to Alphonse, by which name he is still better known as his attempts to reclaim his Czech heritage and eventual reversion to grandiose subjects and large-scale works in the national cause proved less memorable. Mucha's and Bernhardt's characteristic styles were made for each other, not least because the painter was keenly aware of what was expected of him as the actor-impresario's chosen artist, just as he certainly was instrumental in her rapid transformation in the 1890s into a one-woman international culture industry.

One of Mucha's felicities is to capture a reasonable likeness of Bernhardt while transforming her features into those of a younger woman and, at times, those of a younger man. The latter is unmistakably the case with his 1896 poster of Bernhardt as Alfred de Musset's eponymous revenger in *Lorenzaccio*, but less so in the *Hamlet* poster that emphasizes her noted profile.[23] Bernhardt won early recognition in a male role and continued to play men with success: the French tradition of *travesti* as canonized by Pierre Beaumarchais had a long history traceable to the Baroque fascination with artifice and gender impersonation (while gradually losing supremacy to the female mezzosoprano, the heroic operatic castrato persisted long enough for Crescentini to draw the admiration of Schopenhauer and the singer-susceptible Napoleon; he was mentioned by Balzac in *Massimilla Doni*, and even as late as 1830 might have inspired his *Sarrasine*).[24] But she impressed her stamp on a multitude of roles as actor and, subsequently, as manager of the most famous international touring company of the period. Playwrights, it proved, did more than fall over each other to write leading roles for her. Such was the devotion she could command that when, still slender after three decades on stage, she commissioned a new prose translation of *Hamlet* and took on the role of the prince, the inaugural event of the 1899 season in her newly constituted Théâtre Sarah Bernhardt, two men (one a onetime member of her entourage of lovers in whose play, *Médée*, she had appeared in the previous season) fought a duel over the issue of her suitability to play a part probably intended for the corpulent Richard Burbage.[25] It is perhaps in commemoration of this extratheatrical textual intervention, but perhaps also with a nod to Shakespeare's established international stardom, that Bernhardt chose to immortalize her performance by filming her duel with Laertes for the purpose of exhibition at the 1900 Exposition Universelle held in Paris. Yet the choice of the scene demands explanation, for amongst other things, other than the prince's fanciful, swirling cloak,[26] what survives on film seems little infused with the spirit of Mucha.

The scene was not by any means the most obvious choice. If parody is tribute, then it is the graveyard scene from *Hamlet* that after the balcony scene from *Romeo and Juliet* invites the most frequent spoof versions, as evident in the very different Steve Martin vehicle *L.A. Story* (dir. Mick Jackson 1991), in which it is the most readily apparent of a number of borrowings from the plays, and the Arnold Schwarzenegger vehicle *Last Action Hero* (dir. John McTiernan, 1993), in which the jester's remains are put to rather unexpected uses. In the iconography of French visual representation, Hamlet seldom seems an action hero—at least not until Bernhardt—and the most arresting moment of the play remains the prince's contemplation of Yorick's skull: the scene is repeated in numerous variations in Eugène Delacroix's engravings, for instance, and also provides the only known visual trace of the earliest attempt to film a multiscene adaptation of a Shakespeare play (in the form of a production still in the Museum of Modern Art film archives of Georges Méliès's 1907 *Hamlet*). It is Delacroix, too, according to Gerda Taranow, who provided the iconographic backdrop to Baudelaire's interpretation of *Hamlet*.[27] In his accelerated version of the play David Garrick once jettisoned the graveyard scene altogether as a possible response to a French critical tradition that abhorred the interludes of base humor,[28] and it is a good measure of the jester's restoration to French favor that in turn some anglophone critics took grave exception to the length of time the Divine Sarah toyed with the malodorous prop by which we know him. Taranow astutely suggests that this behavior was not unconnected with the fact that Victor Hugo had presented Bernhardt her very own cranial memento mori bearing a few of his octosyllabic couplets; but since Bernhardt then observes the traditional French reluctance to leap into graves (both Laertes and Hamlet refrain from doing so), this could hardly be attributed to necrophilia.[29] It might occasion humor that critics even carped about the color of Yorick's mortal remains, but physical appearance and its connection to actions and states of mind were no less important to the late nineteenth century than they had been to early modern sensibilities, and according to avant-garde eyes both Bernhardt and Nielsen *looked* like Hamlet, a resemblance that in Nielsen's case coincided with the issue of physical appropriateness that preoccupied such early film theorists as Béla Balázs. Delacroix's Hamlet was drawn from life, as was Baudelaire's, although the former's living model happened to be a young woman by the astoundingly apt name Marguerite Pierret, who, pregnant by one of the painter's friends, was abandoned.[30] This is perhaps why so many of Delacroix's engravings and an unusually pensive Méliès appear to contemplate not mortality, but their own situations, when they hold Yorick's skull aloft.

There was, however, at least one compelling reason for Bernhardt to choose a scene that—sans its lengthy and sanguinary termination with four dead principals crowding the stage, and another awaiting burial—could best be described as representative of an abridgement of particularly intricate stage business. Bernhardt was probably easily persuaded that were the attempt made to capture elaborate stage business, such as Hamlet's exchanges with unseen interlocutors that took place across the length of the stage, her inimitable voice would register poorly for the technological marvel of the Phono-Cinéma-Théâtre, whose principal attraction was a promised synchronized sound recording to accompany the projected image. The cylinder that probably contained the soundtrack of swords clashing synchronously with the action is presumed lost, but the image track that survives attests to an awareness of the principles of containing the complex choreography of a duel within a fixed-frame composition, and it certainly does illustrate Bernhardt's famed quickness of movement (Bernhardt was fifty-four when she played her first Hamlet; when in 1913 an even older Johnston Forbes-Robertson decided to commit his famous stage Hamlet to film, he too seemed to favor a similarly youthful and frenetic prince). Unlike Forbes-Robertson, however, Bernhardt does not stray unawares beyond the boundaries of the frame, even in the process of displaying some prodigious swordsmanship.

By all accounts it is the irrepressible showman Clément-Maurice Gratioulet (who called himself Clément Maurice) who must have been instrumental in rearranging the theatrical choreography to suit the screen's aspect ratio. A noted photographer who by some accounts introduced Louis Lumière to the Kinetoscope, who was among the first to operate the Cinématographe, and who arranged for the public showing of the Lumière films at the Salon Indien on December 26, 1895, Maurice apparently approached theatrical stars with the idea of immortalizing them on film and wax cylinders of the Phono-Cinéma-Théâtre, whose synchronized phonograph soundtrack was amplified by a "morning glory" bell.[31] Georges Sadoul reproduces the Rue de Paris poster for the Exposition, a program that also featured variety acts and singers (Footit and Chocolat, Cossira, Little Tich, Polin), and Harry Geduld observes that the earliest successful synchronized sound experiment designed for theatrical audiences probably occurred at the Exposition where in competition with this apparatus was also the Phonorama devised by L.A. Berthon, C.F. Dussaud, and G.F. Jaubert.[32] Maurice might even have lured his stars with the promise of international exposure, for subsequently the Phono-Cinéma-Théâtre enjoyed a European tour, featuring among other attractions yet another theatre star, Réjane, reprising her most famous role, the celebrated courtesan Cléo de Merode doing a "Javanese Dance," and the great baritone Victor Maurel, creator of Verdi's Iago, as Falstaff, another part Verdi wrote for him.³³ Geduld notes that voices sounded nasal and that the imperfect sound contributed to the brevity of the Phono-Cinéma-Théatre's ascendancy. In addition to the difficulties of capturing dialogue, matters of amplification and synchronization probably contributed to Coquelin (also on the program with Bernhardt) electing to record the duel scene from *Cyrano de Bergerac*, and necessitated her own abridgement of the scene with Laertes. It is perhaps a good measure of the incestuousness of the theatre world of the time that, when Bernhardt took her *Hamlet* to New York, the First Gravedigger was none other than the creator of Cyrano.³⁴ Maurice, Coquelin, and Bernhardt may also have opted for moments of vigorous action because of the spectacular nature of the "competition," for in some respects these films were intended to be part of an industrial exposition, the Phono-Cinéma-Théâtre being but one example of a new technology: according to Tom Gunning, in addition to the spectacular cinematic attractions at the Exposition—the Cinématographe géant Lumière (with a screen that dwarfed all later experiments until those of Abel Gance in the late 1920s) and the promised panoramic aerial photography of the ill-fated Cinéorama of R. Grimoin-Sanson—there was a Mareorama that used a continuously scrolling kilometer-long canvas that simulated a Mediterranean sea voyage.³⁵ In comparison, the scale of the duel scenes must have seemed modest to spectators presented with a phantasmagoria of modern technologies of vision. Even so, enough survives of Bernhardt's efforts to convince us that the theatrical version, at least, was the first—and perhaps definitive—Art Nouveau *Hamlet*.

Perhaps the most intriguing visual commemoration of the complete performance is a slim volume, containing rhapsodic prose-poetry (in Spanish) and elegant Art Nouveau illustrations of Bernhardt's various poses in key moments of the play. Fittingly, the work is entitled *Hamlet y el cuerpo de Sarah Bernhardt*, evidently yet another male duel over Bernhardt's body, although this time joined in pen and ink. The text is by the prolific G. Martínez Sierra, but Ricardo Marín's drawings (*dibujos*), a valuable visual record of Bernhardt's held moments, get first billing on the title page. Martínez Sierra not only provides translations of appropriate snatches of Shakespeare for the drawings, but also addresses Bernhardt herself in impassioned tones: "Señora: en cuantas líneas está aquí prisionera la remembranza de vuestros bellos ademanes, de la noble actitud romántica con que generosamente prestásteis vuestra carne al alma del príncipe Hamlet. Yo, con otras pocas palabras, quisiera aprisionar también la memoria de vuestro espíritu, el crystal claro de vuestra voz, el sortilegio de feminidad triunfante, merced al cual habéis logrado infundir tan amable dejo sentimental en las negruras de aquel atormentado corazón." (And he is just beginning.)³⁶ The most valuable feature of the drawings is their emphasis on Bernhardt's characteristic poses (with arms held aloft or in studied gestures, for instance), and also for what they reveal of Bernhardt's treatment of mise en scène. In one, for example, Hamlet holds Yorick's skull high above his head, as Bernhardt did before lowering it and punctuating the lines by tapping on its teeth (a moment caught on a famous posed photograph).

Marín's drawings of the duel reveal that, unlike Beerbohm Tree's *King John*, Bernhardt's film version all but abandons the mise en scène of the theatrical production. They also intimate that while Bernhardt may well have been the regal actor-impresario, Maurice handled the direction. The film in turn provides confirmation that, contrary to almost every description of them (including Taranow's in justification of a "back" translation into theatrical action),³⁷ these early snippets of "filmed theatre" did almost the opposite of registering theatrical performances on celluloid: the limited light-sensitivity of film stock and the low depth of field of lenses required the apparatus to be much closer to the performers than any theatrical spectator could be, and the mise en scène was invariably restructured accordingly. Two of Marín's drawings pertaining to the Hamlet-Laertes encounter offer proof of the modifications. In the first, one rather unusual in the extent of its background detail, the contest is just beginning. The combatants occupy the foreground, while Claudius and a gallery of seated courtiers appear to lurk in a raised area directly behind them. Gertrude sits on an elevated platform projecting into the scene from the left with Hamlet's back to her and Laertes on the right. In the film Hamlet always begins his combats on screen right in avoidance of any confusion of screen direction. Instead of the depth of field Marín's design suggests, the film's background is foreshortened and reduced to a painted theatrical backdrop, with plumed soldiers and a page standing against the colonnade it represents. A second Marín drawing illustrates the moment in which Hamlet, having disarmed Laertes, offers him his own weapon: here the background detail has been lost, but Hamlet holds the épée above his head, dangling from the hilt, while Leartes's, lying neatly on the ground, transforms the composition into a skewed triangle.

In a fraction of its stage duration, the film shows the entirety of the action that transpires between these two events and more. Thus, quite unlike Tree's *King John*, whose surviving scene fragment attempts a temporal approximation of the same event as it transpires on stage, Bernhardt's *Hamlet* film has thus lost even more to time than to space. Taranow, who supplements careful observation of the film with newspaper reports and stage directions, remarks that the film conflates the three episodes into which Bernhardt eventually divided the fencing scene and the final duel, eliding the intervening dialogue. The rather elaborate bowing (to an unseen court) and sword-kissing follows the prescribed practice for ritualized combat with the weapon Taranow identifies as the épée. Having approached each other and parted twice, Hamlet and Laertes (played by Pierre Magnier) walk to the far corners of the frame, she to the right and he to the left, and then engage. In a trice the first two bouts have ended with Hamlet's successful parrying and lunging. In the third encounter Hamlet receives his fatal scratch and tucks his sword under his arm to examine his wounded hand. Removing his glove, he glances disdainfully at Laertes and, showing the effects of the poison, assumes a deathly expression before flinging the glove offscreen and resuming combat. Raising the point of his sword to eye level, Hamlet stares at Laertes again with renewed resolve, then seizes the offensive drawing close enough to engage daggers and, with a deft motion of the épée, disarms him. With a haughty nod he presses his own épée, held aloft by the hilt, on the deceiver, and with another commands the hitherto motionless page—in real life Bernhardt's secretary undertaking an even more Beaumarchaisesque gender traversal—to retrieve the fatal weapon for his own use. Schwob and Morand had suggested a *corps à corps*, a technique of bodily contact permissible in the etiquette of épée, for the disarmament, but instead in the film Hamlet uses the technique at this climactic point to force his opponent, quite literally, to the left edge of the frame, only withdrawing far enough to wound Laertes, who staggers offscreen. As the standing courtiers in plumed helmets move forward to support him, Hamlet's cloak slides off and he dies in their arms, whereupon they raise him above their heads and carry the body offscreen to the left (as with many films of the period, there is a resolutely right-left axis of action and the frame boundaries are charged with meaning, here nothing less than mortality).[38] The concluding sartorial reference to Mucha notwithstanding, it is Marín who truly serves as witness for the defense of early cinema: the near certainty that intervening dialogues for Gertrude, Claudius, Hamlet, Laertes, and Osric were cut has probably more to do with the extreme compression of action than with the limitations of the recording apparatus (as Taranow and others have suggested).[39]

Intriguing and valuable though they are, neither Marín's drawings nor even the film itself constitutes the definitive visual record of Bernhardt's performances: indeed, for us the most significant, revealing, and characteristic images of her from the period remain the series of posters executed by Mucha at her behest. In all of them she is the central figure and dominates the compositions to an extent no other human figure does in his early work; they also happen to be the quintessential exemplars of that visual style, and it is entirely appropriate that the same technique used to create the full-sized poster was also employed by Mucha to create folio versions of the posters, restaurant menus, and the ubiquitous postcards of her. Chromolithography was one of the triumphs of what the first major philosopher of modernity, Walter Benjamin, termed "mechanical reproduction" or "mechanical reproducibility." Unlike Jules Chéret, the first great master of the lithographic poster, Mucha abandoned broad fields of color for a hitherto unprecedented subtlety of shading. While compartmentalization into units of color and tonality was facilitated by his use of quattrocento, Pre-Raphaelite outlines, and bold, bordered lettering of unique design, he achieved an unerring sense of volume in his figures (despite their integration into complex organic forms and motifs) by means of another controversial and characteristic medium of the late nineteenth century, photography.[40] In Bernhardt's case, he at times posed models in the positions required for the poster design, but used his sketches of Bernhardt to modify the features accordingly.[41] As with Aby Warburg's famous demonstration of immanent motion in early Renaissance painting, in which he shows that Botticelli's extraordinary concentration of the effect of breezes on hair derived from the poetry of Poliziano, Mucha was particularly famous for the delicacy of his treatment of hair, and his series of posters of Bernhardt is notable both for thematic aptness and the careful integration of decorative and iconographic elements (so that she is blonde, red-headed, or dark-haired, as necessary). So too is the typography, since "during this period Mucha made an effort to express the theme of the play he was advertising in his lettering... for *Hamlet* we get a narrow, nervous looking style, while the lettering for *Gismonda* has a medieval look, the lettering for *The Samaritan* has a Middle Eastern look and *Medea* features a Greek style."[42]

If by these means Mucha achieved a degree of integration of technique and iconography unprecedented in lithography, perhaps even in all of Modernist art, there was still little question as to the authority that underwrote the production of those images. In the poster for *Gismonda*, for example, the title of the production appears to surmount the design, and Mucha's large custom-drawn letters are a vivid dark blue recessed on a gold mosaic background. Bernhardt's own name, rendered in the purest white, forms a halo around her head in letters almost as large, the "Sarah" artfully obscured by her upraised palm frond. Gismonda stands on a ledge, beneath which an anxious imp holds a scroll announcing the "théâter de la Renaissance." His head is partly displaced by Gismonda's trailing gown, as is the text, and it is in the small space beneath the fold of that gown, framed by the ends of the imp's scroll that we see the fragile, if still distinct signature of the artist: only the publisher's name is rendered in a smaller (if bolder) typeface. And so it continues through the series: in the *La Dame aux camellias* color, even more than size, sets apart the star's name and incorporates Mucha's into the surrounding design; in *La Samaritaine* "Sarah Bernhardt" gives rise to the most perfect of haloes. In the last major example of the series, the *Hamlet* poster, the change of venue obliges Mucha to create vignettes above and below the design, spelling Bernhardt's name with redoubled effect, his own, as in the rest of series, recessed modestly into a space near her feet. Yet his control over the materials and the sense of collaboration they impart are undeniable, and even as early as the April of 1895 Mucha was credited with coproducing the Théâtre de la Renaissance's version of Edmond Rostand's *La Princesse Lontaine*, for which he designed the sets, costumes, and even the printed programs.[43] So it is not surprising that, even after the move to the larger Théâtre Sarah Bernhardt, an entire scene of *Hamlet* showcased his art: neither he nor his patron could have been unaware that they furthered the cause of a particular aesthetic, for one of the most commended glories of Bernhardt's production was the flower-bedecked funeral procession for Ophelia, a scene for which Mucha gave Bernhardt a particularly detailed drawing and which occasioned much comment among reviewers (who expressed astonishment at seeing a "lifeless" actress borne off the stage in Art Nouveau efflorescence).[44] In Mucha's *Hamlet* poster it is no longer the profane imp that is underfoot: the pointed toe of Hamlet's boot touches a second vignette, a flower-strewn Ophelia suffused in blue, resting on her bier.

Mucha was not the only admired collaborator to be put in his place as Bernhardt fostered an individualistic, quasi-religious cult. I have in my possession an exquisitely autographed cabinet photograph of her as Sardou's Tosca, taken by Gaspard Félix de Tournachon, the redoubtable Nadar, a renowned photo-portraitist. The frozen moment has her still holding the knife with which she has dispatched the treacherous, licentious, and now quite dead Baron Scarpia, an event that was to gain even greater recognition in musical form. For her Sardou created a succession of leading roles in *Fédora*, *Théodora*, and *Tosca*, consciously permitting her to improvise the stage business for the crucial moments of the plays.[45] The first and last of these works were to be transformed into two of the most often performed masterpieces of *verismo* opera, the latter provoking English music critic Henry Chorley's remark that Tosca was a "shabby little shocker," largely because Giacomo Puccini and his librettists "borrowed" Bernhardt's choreography of Tosca's stabbing of Baron Scarpia and the betrayed protagonist's subsequent leap from fortress battlements to her death. That like Mucha Nadar happened to be the most famous contemporary innovator in his favorite medium mattered less to a star of her magnitude than her determination to orchestrate all the elements of the theatrical spectacle, as if this characteristic were insufficiently evident when she renamed her theatrical company after herself.

Her justified killing of her antagonist was, however, by no means unique to this play (which in 1908 was to be made into a film in which, to her subsequent regret, she starred). Mucha's posters amply document her propensity for extremes of stage violence. Indeed, in a significant number of her roles, acts of male and female vengeance take a particular form; and Mucha's posters for these, her most popular and, in terms of box-office receipts, lucrative roles, have an almost reckless Freudian emphasis on daggers and swords. In *Lorenzaccio* the pensive, bookish Bernhardt's hair is cropped and the hilt of her dagger placed on a suggestive diagonal. In *Medée* the bloody dagger points downward toward a lifeless boy who was once her son. In *Hamlet* the elongated épée hangs pendulously, but intersects precisely with a dagger pointing upward with greater phallic assurance. James Naremore observes that any object (or "accessory") an actor touches turns into an extension of the character's personality, and in his posters of Bernhardt Mucha suggests a cumulative personality, *avant* Chaplin, accessorized accordingly.[46] In one of Mucha's surviving preparatory sketches for the *Hamlet* poster, the dagger is even more prominently placed against the prince's long legs. This is not to say that once in a while decapitation might not suffice: Oscar Wilde wrote the part of Salomé for her, and as Elizabeth I she reluctantly sends her lover Essex to the headman. Yet there can be little doubt as to Bernhardt's favored stage prop, for which some explanation might be sought in the uncertainties of a traumatizing childhood (about which biographers have speculated endlessly). Little wonder, then, that when Henriette-Rosine grew up to be the Divine Sarah, her favored plot consisted of a victimized protagonist who either transcended the cruelties visited on her or exacted revenge for them. Nor did the medium modify the message. If the 1908 *La Tosca* film proved a disappointment, it did not prevent a triumphant reprise of her stage archetypes in her best-known films, *Camille* (1911) and *Queen Elizabeth* (1912), in the first of which she sacrifices herself for her lover (played on-screen and offscreen by the much younger actor and soon-to-be American matinée idol Lou Tellegen), and in the next sacrifices him for reasons of state.[47]

Apart from Salomé, the Symbolist woman par excellence (as depicted obsessively by the painter Gustave Moreau), the role closest to Bernhardt's own famously complicated, mercurial real-life persona was the Modernist woman par excellence, Hamlet.[48] And there is little question that Bernhardt intended to play Hamlet as Sarah Bernhardt. For all its discreet, fraternal venom, Max Beerbohm's "Hamlet, Princess of Denmark" might well be the most perceptive review she received. Max's loyalty to an already old-fashioned British Shakespeare, notwithstanding his aversion to the local custom of treating Hamlet as "a hoop through which every eminent actor must, sooner or later, jump," takes the form of defending the prince's manhood: although Hamlet is not always manly, he is no less a man than Lady Macbeth is a woman. Villonism is villainism, for the manufactured archaism of Schwob and Morand can only sound risible to those who know both Shakespeare and French. The customs officials at Charing Cross should have restrained her and confiscated her Hamlet habiliments. Max squeezes out some faint praise and a damning compliment at the end. In delivering herself of Hamlet with her characteristic poise and self-assurance, says Max, she was from first to last "très grande dame."[49]

Maddened Max aside, some measure of explanation as to why a woman would want to play a woman playing a man might best be left to one of Mucha's similarly Moravian-born, Viennese-trained contemporaries, Sigismund Schlomo (better known as Sigmund) Freud. It is, of course, unlikely that Bernhardt had any profound familiarity with Freud, or even with his influential mentor at the Salpêtrière, Jean-Martin Charcot; but it is even less likely that Freud could have remained unaware of her *Hamlet* production that she took to Vienna in October 1899. Showman that he was, Charcot's studies of hysteria might possibly have had some general influence on acting, but of Freud's knowledge of her as performer we can be certain. During the initially lonely five months he passed in Paris in 1885, he began to frequent the theatre and could have seen her in a number of roles (including that of Ophelia); he did see her as Sardou's Théodora and wrote home to rhapsodize about her enthralling voice.[50] Intriguingly, although Freud corresponded about Hamlet's problems and those of Oedipus with his friend and confidant, Wilhelm Fliess, the observations remained in utero until the publication of *The Interpretation of Dreams*, which appeared (in German) months *after* the first performance of the Bernhardt *Hamlet*. Nevertheless, as Peter Gay points out, from the start Freud acknowledged that in their depictions of characters' thought processes artists, particularly sculptors and writers, had anticipated him: he ascribed considerable psychological insight to Michelangelo and Leonardo, to the writers of the Old Testament, to Shakespeare, to Goethe, and to a handful of more recent writers (mostly of prose) including Kipling, Zola, Twain, and Dostoyevsky. In one instance, having psychoanalyzed the characters in Wilhelm Jensen's novella *Gradiva*, concentrating on an episode of repression that contains a curious parallel to Vladimir Nabokov's *Lolita*, Freud wrote to the author for confirmation of his analysis. Jensen's disarming reply was that, having no acquaintance with psychoanalysis, his insights could only have been unconscious.[51]

Freud's ready familiarity with Shakespeare was such that he did not feel the need to refer to books when quoting, with the consequence that on occasion he misquotes, a type of failure of memory that obsessed him. He found his addiction to cigars and an overflowing collection of antiquities puzzling. He vacillated for years about what to call his "discovery" of boys' incestuous drives, as is clear in his correspondence and in *The Interpretation of Dreams*, which contains his first ruminations on *Hamlet*, a play to which he returned considerably later in his consideration of melancholy. Originally a footnote, perhaps in reluctance to accord either the playwright or his interpreters too much credit for the form taken by his central argument, the *Hamlet* section only made its way into the full text in the 1914 edition of *Dreams*. Here, having just discussed Sophocles he claims that, unlike Oedipus, Hamlet is unable to realize his "wishful phantasy"; its repression leads to the form of neurosis that has baffled critics who have succumbed either to Goethe's view that Hamlet represents the type of man whose excessively developed intellect paralyzes his power of action, or to the belief that he is a "neurasthenic character" of pathological irresolution. His rebuttal of these notions consists of the very incidents that Bernhardt developed into her most Arnold Schwarzenegger-like hypermasculine action hero sequences. Freud reminds us of the "sudden outburst of temper" in which Hamlet slays the evesdropping Polonius, and the contrasting cold "callousness of the Renaissance prince" when he condemns Rosenkrantz and Guildenstern to his own intended fate.[52] Critics noted Bernhardt's expressions of grim satisfaction at these moments: Hamlet treats Polonius and the courtiers as if they were jesters. In mistaking Polonius for Claudius, Hamlet assumes an expression of "jeering rage" and strikes through the arras, holding the sword in place to savor the moment.[53] His treatment of his old schoolmates occasioned from a Viennese theatre critic the complaint that he was overly fond of knocking their heads together.[54] Why then, asks Freud, does the prince hesitate to fulfill the task set for him by his father's ghost? It must be the peculiar nature of the task, he concludes: Hamlet is able to do anything except take vengeance on the man who by killing his father and taking his father's place illuminates his own repressed childhood fantasies. His sudden aversion to Ophelia is precisely the result of neurosis resulting from the consequent self-reproach. Citing Georg Brandes's 1896 commentary on the plays, Freud concludes that Shakespeare too was writing shortly after the death of his father, and as the result of the repression of the memory of his dead son Hamnet.[55] We cannot now agree with the historical sequence, perhaps, but surely an overactive superego is at least as good an explanation for Hamlet's affliction as the lack of an "objective correlative," as T.S. Eliot was presently to insist.[56]

Nearly a decade elapsed before Freud made a definitive choice between Oedipus and Hamlet. If Bernhardt, who for most of this period kept Hamlet in her repertoire, was still on his mind, then it would be indicated by a remark in the fourth of his five lectures at a symposium on psychoanalysis convened at Clark University in Worcester, Massachusetts, in September 1909, an event that was to prove the decisive breakthrough for the international acceptance of the clinical practice. In this talk he observed that "the myth of King Oedipus, who killed his father and took his mother to wife, reveals, with little modification, the infantile wish, which is later opposed and repudiated by the *barrier against incest*. Shakespeare's Hamlet is equally rooted in the soil of the incest-complex, but under a better disguise."[57] He does not elaborate on the precise nature of the disguise. According to James Strachey's note to this statement, Freud named the incest complex the Oedipal complex the following year, no doubt confirmed in his opinion that the Hamlet complex was too complex.[58] Considering the attention he devotes to issues of gender, in particular to homosexuality and bisexuality in these years (arguably culminating in his celebrated analysis of a patient he calls "Dora," published in 1908), Freud obviously continued to wrestle with Hamlet's problems, keeping before him an image much akin to Bernhardt's vigorous revenger.[59]

Since it is Mucha who most clearly links Freud's approach to art with Bernhardt's interpretation, we need not linger on the extraordinary temporal coincidence of the footnote in *Dreams* and Freud's renewed acquaintance with Bernhardt. We would be remiss, however, to evade the inevitable conclusion that Art Nouveau, Jugendstil, and psychoanalysis arise out of the same cultural moment. For Mucha, as for those who worked in his style, the human body and the forest of symbols that inevitably surrounded it were outgrowths of thoughts, feelings, and sensations. In Vienna Riegl's refusal to distinguish between the applied and fine arts blossoms into the idea of an organic connection between body and mind that reversed a strain of thought that had dominated Western philosophical inquiry from Descartes onward. The neuroses of Freud's clients seldom failed to manifest themselves as various physical symptoms for he regarded these as direct emanations of states of mind, and saw the mind as conditioned in specific ways by the action of the world upon it. Freud's Hamlet, like Bernhardt's, is an organic Hamlet, at one with his violent world, who instead of breaking out in sniffles or sneezes, succumbs to outbursts of punitive corporeality. And if it is, indeed, Bernhardt's influence that we can trace in Freud, who better to give us the Oedipal complex?

Screening Hamlet's Aura: Star Power from Sarah Siddons to Mickey Mouse

Few proponents of the young medium could possibly have possessed an understanding of it comparable to that of Clément Maurice. Even so there is little indication that his Hamlet, Bernhardt, felt any need to modify the style of performance she gave before a camera. As with Herbert Beerbohm Tree, the star embodied a particular theatrical style, and the films made were displays of the capacity of the medium to record a suitably tailored performance given by a famous actor, as well as an internationally accessible form of dissemination of a particular stage production. What we see on screen is Bernhardt as grande dame of the French theatre, and for audiences waiting to see her on her European and American tours of 1900, in particular her new *Hamlet*, it might (like *King John*) have been conceived as a form of advertisement, a filmic preview of a theatrical event. Today film previews consist of episodes of films, often edited together with greater sophistication than the film itself. They were once the exclusive province of cinemas projecting prefeature fare; but their eventual appearance on television, video releases, and DVD suggests synergies of intermediation Tree and Bernhardt recognized.

By the time Freud was lecturing in America, however, considerable change had taken place in the medium; indeed, his arrival in Massachusetts coincided with a paradigm shift in film acting later attributed to the new director at the Biograph Studio, D.W. Griffith, but probably only better appreciated by him than by any of his immediate contemporaries and more evident to us because a greater proportion of his films have survived than those of almost any other figure of the period.[60] In all probability Tree and Bernhardt probably do not represent a beginning (i.e., of Shakespeare as "filmed theatre") but instead the end of the road for a certain kind of performance, for by 1907, when Méliès came to film scenes from *Hamlet*, he was already something of a star of motion pictures, and that had probably more to do with the ubiquity of his screen presence than with his thespian skills. When in the following year the New Jersey-based Vitagraph Studio initiated a highly successful series of Shakespeare films, it intended to capitalize not only on the movement to "improve" American film audiences but also on Shakespeare's international currency: the latter had already been affirmed in the Méliès film that depicted the artist in the throes of creation, whose conclusion is Shakespeare's triumph over the materials of history (the flags of nations appear in celebration of the world's great dramatist, not Rome's first Caesar). Many of the Vitagraph films survive only in fragmentary form as successive bits of scenes printed on photographic paper and deposited in duplicate for copyright at the Library of Congress. Regrettably, most of the duplicates contain no more than a minute's worth of footage and a few differing frames, yet the fragments are invaluable in giving us a clear picture of the fewest number of possible shots in the undiscovered films, and samplings of two to five seconds of some of the most dramatic moments of those shots.[61] It should be kept in mind, however, that one of the most highly regarded of the Vitagraphs, *A Midsummer Night's Dream* (thought to be from 1909) in which the lessons of Méliès are put to good use, made its way into Britain's National Film and Television Archive, and no evidence survives to indicate that any attempt was made to submit the customary copyright deposits. Even more secure evidence that Vitagraph's Shakespeare series was intended for foreign distribution, perhaps even made in alternate prints for different countries as Méliès had done, comes from the films themselves. In one Library of Congress fragment, for example, the 1908 *Romeo and Juliet*, the Apothecary proves to be neither true to Shakespeare's idiom, nor to modern American English, nor even to the language of fair Verona. When Romeo visits his shop in the fourteenth of the fifteen-scene fragments, the shield-shaped shop sign bears the diagonal inscription "APOTHECA." The full

German print of *King Lear* at the Folger begins with a German title card "KOENIG LEAR SHAKESPEARES TRAGÖDIE" beneath two Vitagraph logos; a subscript in smaller letters within a cartouche announces "THE VITAGRAPH CO. PARIS" (by the MPPC agreements of the previous year, Pathé helped distribute Vitagraph's films using their established outlets in many of Europe's major cities). The intertitles sometimes even affect an archaic German, but this Folger print also offers the disappointing confirmation that only a limited number of scenes were preserved in the paper prints (sixteen in this instance, whereas the existing celluloid print contains thirty shots in addition to the title).

Despite the internationalist intent, there is no sense that the actors are aware that conventions borrowed from American stages might have been less than suitable for foreign audiences; indeed, it is likely that the cycle represents only part of Vitagraph's upscale marketing of adaptations of literary classics.[62] Tragedy brings out the worst of the Vitagraph company's stage-bound acting; in comedy, which could occur in unexpected spots, there seems to be a greater sense of freedom and the improvisatory quality suggested by actors doubling as costumiers and carpenters (as has been claimed of a number of early studio concerns).[63] This is not to contend that film actors at this date were any less conscious than their theatrical antecedents of differing modes of performance: it is, of course, entirely a critical fiction, albeit a persistent one, that in the early years of cinema little distinction was made between what James Naremore refers to as "ostensive" acting and performance that seems (and seemed) more verisimilar.[64] There was, in fact, a clearer separation than today between naturalistic acting and the heightened style used for what was regarded as drama based on a photoplay: this is nowhere more evident than in the thriving genre of faked "newsreel" footage such as Edwin Porter's cinematic reenactment of the execution of Leon Czolgosz, President McKinley's assassin (1901), or Méliès's about King Edward VII's coronation (1902), where the acting technique carries greater conviction as direct cinema or as *cinéma vérité* than the reality television or filmmaking of today.[65] It is abundantly clear that the Vitagraph actors are having a wonderful time, and just as obvious that they fully comprehend the needs of the camera. The latter registers most clearly in the films that make complex use of props and special effects, where the actors must observe certain positionings in frames to allow for superimpositions, dissolves, and other filmic "tricks" (Puck flying over a rotating earth is complex but ineffective, yet Bottom holds his position admirably for his transformations using Méliès technique of combining dissolves with stop-motion substitution). Even the isolated fragments that survive of the very early *Macbeth* of 1908, to take the best of paper print examples, indicate that it might have been among the most visually impressive of the series. When Macbeth imagines that he sees a dagger before him, we have a substantial one in the foreground (the effects of time permit us to see that it was shot suspended by a wire over a black background, and then superimposed over the scene with the actor). He faces the camera, but looks toward the dagger. This is not Méliès directly addressing the camera, but rather an actor addressing the camera eye as if it were that of an unseen spectator, and as if he were actually Macbeth.

The actor does not, however, see himself as a star as his contemporaries imported from the theatre for the most part did. Indeed, it was not really until 1910 that an incipient star system began to assert itself, and that form of recognition came entirely as a studio-regulated mechanism of publicity: after the unexpected disappearance of the Biograph Studio's lead actress, the trade press carried reports of the fatal streetcar accident that had befallen this Biograph girl, identified as Florence Lawrence, only to declare her alive and announce her defection to Carl Laemmle's Imp studio (the publicity from first to last being a characteristically incendiary Imp defiance of the Motion Picture Patents Corporation cartel).[66] Despite local critics already deploring the excesses of her style, Bernhardt's *Queen Elizabeth* of 1912 proved of seminal importance to the industry. Unlike the only recently acknowledged American film actors who were recognized for the most part by the kind of role in which they starred, she was unquestionably the star around whom the production revolved. This is not to say that a discourse of stardom did not exist in critical discourse: Pathé had in a sense necessitated it with their Films d'Art cycle initiated in 1908, and they were emulated by other studios that saw in the theatre both a model and a supply of big-name actors.[67] Certainly, by 1914 stars whose names could carry films constituted a major focus of interest in Robert Grau's early industrial history, *The Theatre of Science*. Concurrently, film was beginning to attract its first theorists, among them Hugo Münsterberg and Vachel Lindsay in the United States, Jean Epstein, Germaine Dulac, and their fellow French Impressionists, and a significant coterie with an anthropological bent writing in Germany. Just as the industry began to require films it could bill as features, the discourses surrounding stardom and its relation to film as a vehicle of modernity were beginning to mature.

It was, however, a modernity viewed with ambivalence. Assenka Oksiloff observes that the myth of the "primitive spectator" disarmed by technology seemed to dominate theorists' meditations on the medium. Even in 1916 Münsterberg, she notes, warned that the intensity with which film takes hold of audiences, particularly rural ones unable to refrain from applause, "cannot remain without strong social effects."[68] Although he was later to denounce cinema's pretensions, György Lukács initially celebrated the medium for what he saw as its unassuming claim only to be entertainment, removed as it was from the theatre's intimacy of physical presence.[69] While he agreed with Lukács that the basis for cinema's power was the depiction of motion, Hugo von Hofmannsthal, Richard Strauss's playwright-librettist (and with Max Reinhardt cofounder in 1920 of the Salzburg Festival) did not agree that this consisted of depicting realistic events but saw cinema's art instead as residing in its capacity to stylize human movement, to which end he crafted a number of ballet film scenarios. No less a lover of precivilized dance as his contemporaries in Paris in the Ballets Russes, he defended film's technological capacity to create alternative "dream" states.[70] A few years later, just after World War I, Béla Balázs, also a writer of controversial libretti (for the avant-garde composer Béla Bartók), a future filmmaker, and scenarist of distinction, took a view friendlier to modern technology and wrote polemically to defend the cinema against the German critics who in this period emphasized its naïve qualities: Otto Lindt, Otto Foulon, and Rudolf Harms.[71] In the process he was to become the first major theorist of film acting as acting (in postrevolutionary Russia Dziga Vertov and Sergei Eisenstein had already begun to debate the legitimacy of actually "acting" for the camera). Although some of his more enthusiastic publications just after World War I make heady reading today, Balázs's apparent adulation of "star" actors actually served to emphasize the affective power of their performances and the range of styles they could command: exemplary in this regard were Asta Nielsen, Lillian Gish, Emil Jannings, and a few other mostly German and American notables; Chaplin, another favorite, was the exception in that after his early films he spent two decades experimenting with an established character.[72]

Balázs notwithstanding, the most influential postwar philosopher of modernity in all its manifestations, and the most profoundly ambivalent about the role of emerging technologies of representation, was Walter Benjamin. In extolling the "optical unconscious" captured in a photograph, for instance, he celebrates what lies beyond the knowing determination of its maker.[73] Moving images move him in the opposite direction to Grau, who applauds the consolidation of an entertainment industry. For Benjamin film expresses something akin to a collective consciousness representative of its audiences rather than its manufacturers. His theories of photography and cinema, influenced by Riegl's more systematic study of the relationship of art and society,[74] are of especial importance to us, in that his writing, like Balázs's, was contemporary with the films of the first three decades of the twentieth century, and thus free of the anachronisms to which much of film criticism of later vintage subjects these early films and their performers.

Benjamin's most frequently cited essay, which as Miriam Hansen shows entered English-speaking consciousness through a translation of a much-amended and deficient version, is his meditation on "The Work of Art in the Age of Mechanical Reproducibility."[75] In this work Benjamin suggests that man's first pictorial depictions of nature sought to effect a unique relationship of object and representation: the Neolithic hunter's symbolic invocation of his intended prey, for instance, possessed an aura that charismatically connected them. To a lesser degree, a work of art such as a painting still partook of this singular, auratic relationship by virtue of its unique connection to its object. With the advent of printing, and later lithography, this aura began to erode.[76] As Hansen argues, Benjamin initially reacted to the shock of World War I by welcoming technological media such as photography, film, and the gramophone "because they promote a 'liquidation' of cultural heritage, of bourgeois-humanist notions of art, personality, and experience that have proved bankrupt in, if not complicit with, the military catastrophe and the economic one that followed." Benjamin at this time remained optimistic about the potentialities of what his older contemporary and teacher Georg Simmel regarded as an alienating culture of glass and steel in which the victims of urban "massification" desperately preserve their individuality by erecting a defensive shield against an unceasing plethora of sensory stimuli. The decay of aura would, in Benjamin's thought, lead to a healthy proletarian "culture of barbarism."[77]

But with the onset of Fascism and the impending new world war (which Hansen claims Benjamin saw coming as early as 1933), he became increasingly concerned by the capacity of technological media to disturb the balance between voluntary memory (recollection) and involuntary memory (remembrance) by vastly expanding the archive of the former.[78] Thus what Marshall McLuhan as yet viewed with optimism in the 1950s in North America—the extension of the sensorium through the agency of media—Benjamin saw (in anticipation of Jean Baudrillard's "simulacra") as "phantasmagoria." Alone among media of mass communication, cinema offered the possibility of redemption. In ideal form cinema could overcome man's increasing disconnection from nature through a form of somatic-psychological feedback loop that Hansen translates as "innervation."[79] Benjamin's analysis of the processes that generated innervation shares a kinship with Balázs's notions of "physignomism" and star power (to which we presently return), but at its center was his conception of film performance. According to Hansen, in fact, Benjamin "discerned specifically cinematic forms of innervation in two highly popular figures of American provenance: Chaplin and Mickey Mouse."[80]

A comparison of Bernhardt to Mickey Mouse (less so to Chaplin) might seem unduly provocative, but Benjamin's exemplum for the medium's capacity to effect innervation depended on the very technology that eluded Bernhardt (i.e., a means of transcending the limits of the medium through the spell of her voice). Sonic synchronicity was Mickey's defining characteristic, whose actions, however contrary to the laws of nature, attained a suprareal technological plausibility: to this day we refer to the technique of sonic mimesis of action in the cinema as "mickey-mousing." When the Soviet theorist and filmmaker Sergei Eisenstein began to write about Mickey in the 1940s, he was, as Michael O'Pray observes, struck by the same "magical" quality of Mickey's image, an almost frightening synchronicity of sound and motion that appealed to the primordial, precinematic sensorium of the spectator: Mickey was the perfect visual deception and hence capable of projecting his viewers into a state of childlike wonder.[81] Or one could modify that perspective to suggest that Mickey's comical ability to disregard normal physical forces could (as Benjamin contends) provoke in audiences a collective, "barbarous" release of energy.[82] Benjamin's correspondent at the time, Theodor Adorno, rejected his positive reading of the potentialities of the medium, and expressed a characteristic distrust of collective phenomena: "the laughter of the cinema audience," he asserted, "is anything but good and revolutionary; instead, it is full of the worst bourgeois sadism."[83] But a still younger contemporary, Mikhail Bakhtin, shared Benjamin's views on the potentiality of what he referred to as carnivalesque laughter, a collective derision of the forces of authority.[84]

Benjamin's choice of Mickey is certainly not casual. Many of the debates about the potentialities of cinema as a medium, particularly those of the 1920s in Germany, centered on the issue of stardom. "Let us have none but stars," proclaimed Béla Balázs, in one of an incessant flow of articles, defending his theory of physiognomism by pointing to the heightened intimacy that such devices as the close-up effected between a spectator and the inner essence of the actor as revealed on the screen.[85] Mickey is Benjamin's escape from technological reality no less than the spectator's, as he is at once both actor and character (to an even greater degree than Chaplin was Charlie), and thus Benjamin can use him to bypass the chief conundrum of his difficult concept of aura. For, if film stardom depends on the "recognition" by the spectator of the actor from behind the mask of character, then the reproducibility and the proliferation of images of a star can only diminish the disauratic and barbarous potentialities of the medium.

As Richard Dyer argues in *Heavenly Bodies*, the management of a star's image is, in fact, a complex process of negotiation, ranging from the artifices of the studio to self-invention, from selective role choices to willful readings of a star persona by varied constituencies of fans. The "star" is a construct whose image depends on "promotion through pin-ups, public appearances, studio hand-outs, and so on, as well as interviews, biographies and coverage in the press of the stars 'doings' and 'private' life. Further, a star's image is also what people say or write about him or her as critics or commentators, the way that image is used in other contexts such as advertisements, novels, pop songs, and finally the way the star can become part of the coinage of everyday speech."[86] Benjamin, for his part, begins by pointing out in his "Work of Art" essay that, unlike a stage star, a film star's physical presence is a construct of the camera. Pirandello, he points out, was one of the first to consider the consequences of a film actor having to play himself (unlike the stage actor, who has to transform himself ad hoc into a multitude of different characters). Benjamin continues: "The aura which, on the stage, emanates from Macbeth, cannot be separated for the spectators from that of the actor. However, the singularity of the shot in the studio is that the camera is substituted for the public. Consequently, the aura that envelops the actor vanishes, and with it the aura of the figure he portrays."[87] Benjamin agrees with Dyer about the constitution of film stars' images, but regards the "aura" generated by promotion as fakery. "The cult of the movie star, fostered by the money of the film industry, preserves not the unique aura of the person but the 'spell of the personality,' the phony spell of a commodity."[88]

Despite Benjamin's dismissal of promotional techniques, the emergence of a consumerist ethos, with its ubiquitous proliferation of images, assured film stars a tangible connection with audiences. Few stage stars of the 1920s could have died to such scenes of public hysteria as Rudolph Valentino. What might be considered a form of synthetic aura radiating from a "personality" was already, by Benjamin's time, beginning to assume a supracorporeal reality. Here again, however, one must treat the attribution of the invention of this kind of stardom to cinema with some caution because the process by which images are "connected" to stars was one well understood long before the advent of the medium, and depended not on the proliferation of imagery due to technological reproducibility per se, but rather on the careful management of image circulation. To put it another way, Bernhardt was not the first actor to create a fan base sight unseen; but she was indisputably the greatest star of her age because she could regulate and micromanage the dissemination of her image more adeptly than any of her contemporaries.

No better example of the phenomenon exists, in all probability, than the first female Hamlet to make something of a trademark of the role.[89] It also seems a curious coincidence that at a comparable stage of her career Sarah Siddons, like Bernhardt after her, chose to portray an athletic Hamlet. By then, having been transformed into the "living embodiment of Melpomene, the Muse of Tragedy" by painter Joshua Reynolds, all her stage assumptions were received rapturously, as was this Dublin revival, but her most innovative piece of stage business led to the solitary scandal (almost on a par with the Catulle Mendès-Vanour duel) that tarnished an otherwise immaculately crafted image.[90] Siddons has a good claim, in fact, to be the greatest beneficiary among stage actors of an emergent visual culture, and of a growing demand for reproducible star images. Hamlet was something of a comeback role for her, a tour de force designed to eradicate the memory of her disastrous season with Garrick's theatrical enterprise at Drury Lane in the 1775–76 season.[91] It was during her involuntary exile from London, in fact, that she engaged in the practice—hitherto associated with prominent courtesans and the mistresses of the nobility—of posing for self-celebratory portraits assuming the guise of historical or mythological figures.[92] Based in Bath, she sat for Thomas Beach, and had already regained something of her reputation when William Hamilton painted the first widely acclaimed portrait of her, submitting *Mrs. Siddons in the Character of the Grecian Daughter* to the 1780 showing of the Royal Academy of Art. By the time he painted her again in 1783, after her rehabilitation at Drury Lane, he sold the painting to an admirer but retained it for some weeks and advertised in three leading newspapers that the public could "inspect" it at his studio.[93] The exploitation of her star persona was already well under way: Robyn Asleson comments that on October 11, 1782, the day after her triumphant return to Drury Lane, mezzotints after the manner of Beach began to appear on the London market.[94]

Her enduring claim to fame was secured when Reynolds, no stranger himself to the arts of crafting a public image, exhibited *Sarah Siddons as the Tragic Muse* in the 1784 showing at the Royal Academy; and, fittingly, when she returned to London from a tour of Scotland and Ireland in 1785 to a triumphant Lady Macbeth, one of the gowns she wore was reputedly of his design. As Michael Wilson shows, Reynolds, in pursuit of his own ideology (to grant a national school of painting the requisite "dignity"), transformed the genre into a respectable one that elevated its subject matter through an explicit evocation of the sculptural style believed (at least until the Pre-Raphaelite rebellion) to epitomize the High Renaissance: in fact, Siddons's pose is that of Michelangelo's Prophet Isaiah from the Sistine Chapel.[95] Thus if Siddons's extraordinary patience in sitting for one artist after another derived from the calculation that it would contribute to her star appeal, then the fact that artists vied with each other for famous subjects might explain why her stubborn features contributed to some of the finest portraits by a gallery of celebrated artists, among them Thomas Lawrence, George Romney, and Thomas Gainsborough.[96]

Reynolds's *Tragic Muse*, as well as winning plaudits from fellow artists and connoisseurs, also proved to be a masterpiece of publicity.[97] In her own account of the painting's genesis, one contradicted by an eyewitness in the studio who claimed that she arrived exhausted and slumped into a chair, she plays something of the role of a cocreator. Reynolds, according to her, began by offering her more encomiums than she "dare repeat," and upon her ascending the throne of the Tragic Muse and seating herself suitably, decided not to alter the pose she adopted. (In fact, he calculated even the upward tilt of her head to present the most flattering profile.)[98] Nor is there any indication that the sepia tonalities of the painting derived from her insistence that he subdue his instinct to enliven the flesh tones with "rich and glowing colors."[99] Even if little of what she reported of her self-fashioning as Melpomene seems historically credible, the gravitas of her own self-portrait in her autobiography was essential both to her public image and to questions of decorum; it was, after all, notions of taste and sensibility that in such portraiture established a distinction between the heroine and the harlot.

Of the fact that she very carefully selected the manner of the painting's reproduction and thus the spread of its fame, on the other hand, there can be little doubt. Reynolds intended to keep the painting, setting the unprecedented sum of 10,000 guineas on it (about ten times the price of a large Rubens at the time, according to his own estimate).[100] His general practice, to augment their reception, was to commission Valentine Green to reproduce his paintings as mezzotints, but Siddons, even while the painting was under way, recommended instead an accepted exponent of the newly fashionable stipple process of engraving. She enjoyed distributing the autographed results among friends and admirers, further fanning what one of the latter referred to as "Siddonimania."[101] For a once derided actress, it must have been the sweetest of revenge for her to participate in Garrick's Jubilee of 1785 by staging a tableau vivant of the painting.[102]

Asleson, who devotes considerable attention to the reception of the painting, at one point makes a remarkable statement about the reciprocity between the needs of Georgian painters entering the age of mechanical reproducibility and stage actors experiencing an entirely new kind of audience reception. She writes of an "aura of glamour" that made theatrical stars the most effective lure employed by artists seeking publicity.[103] In so doing she corroborates the argument I have set forth that Benjamin's conception of aura had been problematic for much longer than he cared (and dared) to admit. What I have termed a synthetic aura does, indeed, consist of glamour, a fan-based image culture that has not merely persisted but even thrived with the rise of film stardom. While the aura that connects the Neolithic hunter's effigy and his prey was culturally specific, glamour has to be cross-culturally transmissible and readily decoded in a variety of cultural settings. The naughty postcard, the enticing fashion magazine, the larger-than-life film, must all travel. Depending on the critic, stardom may traverse the yellow brick road or the primrose path, but none denies that films are vehicles of glamour that are increasingly juggernauts of publicity. So much so, in fact, that today no teenager would confuse stardom with skilled acting: that a Michelle Pfeiffer, Nicole Kidman, Charlize Theron, Glenn Close, Richard Gere, Harrison Ford, or Mel Gibson could be a consummate actor while exuding glamour simply reflects an industrial demand and can no longer be held for or against them. Moreover, a synthetic aura readily rubs off on the star's accessories. In a deliciously Benjaminian fantasy, the novelist Salman Rushdie paints a lurid picture of the triumph of commodification: at an auction featuring the ruby slippers that have transported Dorothy back to Kansas from Oz, a band of minor devils waits to bid on human souls. Here again, the extension of commodity fetishism to footwear indicates only that cinema has merely amplified a process that was long under way. The Folger Library, for instance, guards what may be the very cloak that Charlotte Cushman, a celebrated Romeo who played masculine roles with conviction (and maintained a female entourage), borrowed from Edwin Booth when she played Hamlet. What is significantly different, and probably began to emerge a little before 1910 (with international marketing and purpose-made stars), is that when Cushman wore Booth's cloak she partook of his charisma. She was playing Booth playing Hamlet, at least in terms of a theatrical tradition to which she could allude. When a film actor dons Batman's cloak, he does not put on the aura of the previous actor, but of the character.

A Diva and a Distributor

That movies groped their way to the establishment of stardom and its appurtenances, and that this process was more than merely coincident to the internationalization of the industry in these very years can be discerned not only in spurts of French and Italian Shakespeare films in this very period, but also in the meteoric career of America's best- known film distributor of the early silent period, George Kleine. A considerable portion of Kleine's archive survives in the Library of Congress, and reveals a great deal about the particular strategies adopted by French and Italian filmmakers in pursuit of wider audiences and more stable profits. That these films have not survived in significant numbers in their original state is disheartening, but once in a while "displaced" survivors can actually tell us how films of the period traveled. There are as-yet-unsubstantiated rumors of Russian Shakespeare films made in the Romanov period, for example, but we can be reasonably certain that Russian audiences did get to view the efforts of their French and Italian contemporaries. The Library of Congress holds an incomplete Pathé *Othello* (probably made as early as 1908) that contains Russian intertitles and that even begins with a title card bearing two of the studio cockerels, the traditional symbol of France and hence a sure sign that the titling was done by or on behalf of Pathé's recently established Russian affiliate anxious to fly the banner of the studio logo. So too is Mario Caserini's 1909 *Macbeth*, a complete version that incorporates fourteen Russian intertitles as well as an illustrated introductory card with "MACBETH" in Cyrillic surmounting the she-wolf logo of the Rome-based Cines company. As with most films of the period, the titles are proleptic, at times unnecessarily so in explaining the action that is to come. Even so, the technical finesse (including a split-screen effect using front projection to depict Macbeth either recalling or imagining one of the Weird Sisters handing him a crown), the extensive location shooting, and the handsome production values, explain the rapid rise to international prominence of Italian films from 1910 onward when, led by Cines and the Ambrosio and Itala companies of Turin, rival producers vied with each other to export national culture in the form of spectacle films based on epic poets and the historians of classical Rome.[104] This was hardly a coincidence since Italy was the only country in Europe with the requisite edifices (not to mention costumes and extras) capable of accommodating such a gargantuan revival of the Roman Empire.

The partiality to scenic grandeur is evident even in the early Shakespeare films. In these films the actors are very much part of the ambience, as is true even of Francesca Bertini (born Elena Vitiello), whose eventual emergence as the nation's most acclaimed film diva derived from the cultivation of a personal style that took the affective device of a retardation of motion to the grandest of extremes. Curiously, her part in *Assunta spina* (1914), which she codirected, and which was markedly more veristic than many of her later roles, was something of a tribute to the paradigmatic stage naturalism of Bernhardt's Italian counterpart Eleanora Duse, who did take part in a film and was a favorite of Shaw and Ibsen. By the time it had blossomed fully, as in the near complete *Il nodo* of 1920 directed by Gaston Ravel, Bertini's style—entirely dissimilar to those of such contemporary Italian film divas as Lyda Borelli—had attained a singular intensity. Poised before a mirror, in which we see reflected the full weight of her philandering husband's betrayal, she raises a hand to her stricken face, loosens a cascade of hair, and then resumes reading a letter in a take of a greater duration than Beerbohm Tree's *King John* and even approaching Bernhardt's near five-minute *Hamlet*. Designed for the camera rather than the stage, hers is the quintessence of the gestural language that Pearson describes in *Eloquent Gestures*, a style whose eloquence consists primarily of the ability to extend physical action into an expressive form of temporal dilation.[105] Attenuated both in appearance and manner, she was Art Deco incarnate to Bernhardt's personification of Art Nouveau.

She was yet a novice when she starred under the direction of the prolific Girolamo Lo Savio in her surviving Shakespeare films produced by Film d'Arte Italiana, a Roman affiliate set up by Pathé and modeled on the Films d'Art venture. The films made much of the cachet of using historical locations the dramatist specified, and Lo Savio's first Shakespeare film took him in 1909 to Venice for a visually attractive *Otello* that may survive in fragmentary form at the Library of Congress. The fearsome rages for which Bertini was later famous are fairly conventional tantrums in the 1910 *Taming of the Shrew*, and in *The Merchant of Venice* of the same year she takes the choice role of the attractive, feminine Jessica (another of those parts that, like Ophelia's, had its stock rise in the age of Romanticism). Other than the rebarbative caricature of Shylock (hook-nosed, all smiles until the Christians' backs are turned, weighed down with immense keys hinting at immense secret hoards, and armed with a dagger of still more shocking proportions that he whets from the very start of the trial), the film invites favorable comparison with the near contemporary Vitagraph *Merchant*. With almost casual ease, Film d'Arte Italiana substitutes a glimpse of the actual Rialto for the prominent backdrop used by their counterparts, gondolas bobbing on the Grand Canal as Antonio and Bassanio walk past. Yet unlike Michael Radford's recent and still more opulent *Merchant*, there is no attempt at psychological justification (the film even ends with the seated Doge pronouncing sentence on Shylock as Portia assumes a smug expression). This is also true of the British Film Institute print of the *Shrew* that incorporates fragments of Shakespeare into illustrated intertitles but turns acting into incessant action: Petruchio gets to behave unreasonably and assaults the servants, and his once unreasonable wife gets to mope a great deal and to be grateful for the smallest of mercies at the end. The three-reel *Giulietta e Romeo* (1911), shot in medieval Verona's cloistered gardens and porticoed piazze, has won her generous acknowledgment from Kenneth Rothwell, while Judith Buchanan, who notes that the Christian iconography grants sanctity to thwarted love, pays her the compliment ("gently beguiling") best applied to this characterization.[106]

Technically, figure behavior is part of the mise en scène, and these films ensure their ready translatability by condensing Shakespeare's plots into a series of coherent events that subsume characterization. Even so, Bertini's expressive powers are already evident, and no more so than in the distinct premonition we obtain of her eventual finesse in the opening of the 1910 *King Lear*. The Lear is Ermete Novelli, a seasoned actor with a powerful presence (hence the offensiveness of his Shylock; he is none too pleasant a Lear either, lavishing more affection on a splendid hound than on the Fool who takes its place at his feet). The redaction is clearly tailored to suit his facility for stage business (so much so that one scene requires a series of stones, one of appropriate size to permit him to raise it in his fist when comparing it to the ossified hearts of his elder daughters, thus converting the "men of stone" who execute Cordelia to stony-hearted women). Nevertheless, it is Bertini's facility for facial and gestural expression that carries the scene. The first character to have a solo turn is the Fool, who precedes the other characters as they issue from a staircase leading from a porticoed palace. He clambers onto the elevated throne set on the left of the screen, playing a grinning Lear until the king arrives and he has to scamper off. Lear's daughters follow him and occupy the right of the screen, with Cordelia occupying the foreground. Consequently, as her sisters kneel at the enthroned king's feet to compliment him, Cordelia remains close enough to the camera for her expression to change visibly from shock to embarrassed resistance. Then, with hands clasped in mortification, she bites her lip and lowers her head in resignation. When her turn arrives and she refuses to join in the flattery, she spreads her arms out, hands raised in denial, as she tilts her head heavenward, a gesture she repeats when her father rises and rages. In the same take, Kent protests and is banished, upon which the Fool attempts to distract Lear but to no avail, for the monarch grasps his recalcitrant daughter's right arm and throws her across the screen toward France at whose feet she falls. Briefly, she holds her position on one knee in a very precise framing, and we see the future in her inimitable expression of patient suffering.

One might contend that, in this extended take, Bertini reveals no more than an accomplished version of what was then generic, and that she might even have profited from some of studio cameraman Billy Bitzer's revealing Biograph close-ups. Or, perhaps, even some Vitagraph medium shots as in *Twelfth Night* (1910) in which Charles Kent, an animated Malvolio, benefits from a cut-in to a closer framing in which his expression changes from astonishment to supercilious preening as he reads the letter that deceives him (as well the hodgepodge of lines might). Even though the Italians do acquire the American style of montage in short order, as evident, for instance, in the open-air two-reel *A Midsummer Night's Dream* of 1913 credited to Paolo Azzuri, the mise-en-scène-driven Italian films travel farther, faster, and with greater consequence than American ones of the same date. Paradoxically, the figure most associated with their success, and at least in part with their downfall, George Kleine, was the only founding member of the Motion Picture Patents Corporation who did not run a studio but relied on film distribution. Having initially sided with Biograph in their patent disputes with Edison, he soon acquired recognition as a skilled negotiator and was a key player in the cartel's formation. Not coincidentally, he became the only licensed importer of films (at the initial rate of 5,000 feet a week) exhibited at MPPC-sanctioned venues. He was not the first international distributor to enter into contractual agreements with foreign studios—years earlier another American, Charles Urban, had founded a British studio and entered into a partnership with the French Eclipse company (for which Kleine in turn became the American distributor)—but he was, without question, the first to negotiate contracts so favorable that he pressed his collaborators to the limits of their productive capacity as he (not they) made fortunes from the exhibitions of their films.

Also a major distributor of American films, Kleine did not depend exclusively on foreign imports and could afford to court or drop partners as he pleased. That they were rather more reliant on him might well be seen in the kinds of films they offered him; it is far from coincidental that in France and Italy production of Shakespeare films peaked in the period of his greatest interest in their respective national industries. The contract records in the Library of Congress leave little doubt as to the extremely specific demands he made. For instance, in one 1913 memorandum (whose precise date I have not established) Kleine demands of Ambrosio that "the quality of the negative is equal to the best work of the day, and specifically, is to be as good in quality as the Cines production, 'QUO VADIS,' and when the scenes permit there is to be the most liberal use of performers, and in one or more scenes there are to be used no less than two thousand (2000) people. The staging in all the scenes is to be as elaborate as possible." This film, *The Last Days of Pompeii*, was to be delivered on September 1, 1913 and be in excess of 2,000 meters exclusive of intertitles, a recurrent stipulation. Other correspondence attests to his incessant demands for the requisite quantities of new film of high-toned subject matter, and Giuliana Bruno has argued that film history has sided with Kleine's choice of exploitable films as being representative of the period as a persistent myth of Italian cinema that "by force of its circulation has assumed the value of truth."[107] Kleine paid modest sums for these visions of immoderate living: for instance, he paid Ambrosio 32,000 lire a month by the exclusive contract of June 14, 1913. By June 20, 1913 he was in a position to demand four new pictures from Ambrosio with "liberal use of performers" and "one or more scenes" of a "spectacular" nature, the first, *Othello*, being deliverable by December 1, 1913. If high-class fare partook of emerging consumerist demands for lavish filmmaking, Kleine's advocacy of what now seems to represent an extreme of commodity fetishism exceeded the mere fetish for footage. Italian films might have led the world in production values, but Kleine's correspondence and marketing strategy make it abundantly clear that the great age of the Italian national epic was sustained by American capital. By the same token at least two of the films imported and distributed by American distributors contributed to the consolidation of the American studio system in California and the drive toward intensive vertical integration by which means studios could guarantee a steady supply of films to their own theatre chains: one was *Queen Elizabeth*, roadshowed by Zukor for unprecedented profits; the other was *Quo Vadis?* (1912), directed by Enrico Guazzoni for Cines (although one can barely discern its origins from Kleine's publicity posters and lobby cards in which "GEORGE KLEINE PRESENTS" occupies a lot more space than "A CINES PHOTO PLAY"). Kleine made an immense fortune when he rented New York's legitimate Astor Theatre during Holy Week, charging upward of a dollar per seat. The extent to which a contract that gave him exclusive rights for a monthly stipend worked in favor of his company, General Film, might be seen in his actual pro forma payment for licensing *Quo Vadis?* which amounted to a dollar—less than the price of a ticket—by the terms of the contract of June 12, 1912.[108] The first full-length fiction feature to be shown in the United States was the hour-long *L'inferno di Dante* (1911) made for Milano films by Giuseppe de Liguoro, which despite its money-spinning grandeur was still outdone by the Ambrosio-Kleine version of *Gli ultimi giorni di Pompeii* (dir. Mario Caserini, 1913) and Giovanni Pastrone's 1914 *Cabiria* for Itala, the latter supplied with a scenario and intertitles by Gabriele D'Annunzio, as well as strongmen, pet leopards, proficient cinematographers, and richer scenic effects than any previous film.[109]

Unable, and perhaps unwilling, to crucify saints, immolate children, and sacrifice extras by the thousand, French producers relied on the double strategy of borrowing from theatrical productions and the old Russian approach of "contemporary localism." The circumstantial evidence suggests that Kleine's interest in French films waned as the less commercially entrenched Italian industry, with whose representatives he could negotiate favorable contracts, waxed. More precisely, Kleine's involvement in French cinema dates to the October 16, 1908 agreement with Urban-Eclipse, and passes its high watermark when Gaumont's frustrated executives rescind their licensing contract on December 8, 1911. The MPPC agreement permitted its signatory, Pathé, to import film into the United States, and it is possible that André Calmettes's 1908 *Macbeth*, with its handsomely illustrated intertitles and a busy cast moving with great collective precision (within a frame used as a theatrical proscenium), made its way stateside just as the Vitagraph cycle got under way. Eclipse, like the rival Film d'Arte Italiana, takes to Shakespeare a little later, at the tail end of Vitagraph's cycle. Its principal Shakespeare director, Henri Desfontaines, achieved a certain degree of local color, no doubt, if he lived up to a reputed extravagance of taking his actors to Hamlet's Elsinore in 1910. In his *Taming of a Shrew* in 1911, he purloined the cast of the Odéon Theatre, each of his thefts being acknowledged as such on the introductory title card. Kleine brought this film over as he did Desfontaines's 1912 *Shylock*, whose elision of the Jessica plot conforms to a conceit that surpasses mere hubris. Four successive intertitles take us from the acknowledgment of

Shakespeare as source to a contemporary experience of crafty moneylenders. Even without the intervention of Kleine's associates, who may have contributed to the English intertitles, the dominant theme is obvious: Bassanio needs to prove his net worth (*pace* Freud) before having a shot at the caskets, and apparently the grasping usurers target Antonio for being a more risk-taking venture capitalist than they happen to be. Harry Baur, the Shylock, brandishes his moneybags gleefully, transforming the knife he employs to cut their fastenings into a potential meat cleaver that he strops on the sole of a shoe in anticipation of his pound of flesh. Yet the most shocking moment of the film is not its courtroom denouement but its start, when a man appareled in bourgeois—presumably a banker's—attire dissolves into the bearded, mincing, toothy Shylock.[110] The allusion to the Rothschild and the Warburg families is clear enough: the effect was to be redone, notoriously, in Veidt Harlan's Nazi propaganda film *Jud Süss* (1943), when it exposes the superficially civilized Jew for what he truly is. Baur played alongside Bernhardt in Léon Abrams's 1923 *La Voyante*, and his fruity voice and dour presence made him one of France's leading actors of the 1930s; yet in an irony scarcely to be believed, his death in 1943 followed his arrest and torture by the Gestapo.

Despite its incomplete state, a film that seems a more sustained attempt to grant Shakespeare contemporary relevance is Gaumont's *A Village King Lear* (1911), directed by one of the giants of French cinema, Louis Feuillade. (We owe Michelle Pfeiffer and Charlize Theron in skintight black outfits to him, and no director of action films is not in his debt.) In 1911 Feuillade was yet to develop the suspenseful cliff-hanger; being set in rural France, the film lacks even the cliffs of Dover. However, its character substitutions are especially clever, for Gloucester's absence contributes to Lear's blindness and attempted suicide. A faithful servant, dismissed by the faithless eldest daughter to whom Lear's village equivalent has legally transferred his own home, takes on aspects of Kent's and Edgar's characters when she reappears to prevent the old man from throwing himself into a stream. At this point, however, just as his children are informed, what we have of the film ends.

Some of the Italian films of the period evidenced even more pronounced divergences from Shakespeare. The Cines *Bruto* of 1910 borrows from *Julius Caesar*, but owes more to Plutarch and would have intrigued those given to Republican readings of the play. Marc Antony secures the imperial title for Caesar—who in one intertitle is referred to as a "tyrant"—over Brutus's objections. The footage of the assassination is missing, but during the climactic battle, Caesar's ghost uses the full powers of superimposition to appear and accuse his assassin, who promptly stabs himself. Another Cines superproduction, announced in an enthusiastic letter of August 23, 1913 to Kleine as "Cleopatra," emerged as *Marcantonio e Cleopatra* (1913). Kleine now created his own Shakespeare film from Plutarch, and his publicity included a printed score of the music that refers to the KLEINE-CINES production of *Antony and Cleopatra*, albeit in lettering dwarfed by the subscript announcing a "GEORGE KLEINE ATTRACTION." As war approached, Italian production suffered. A memorandum to Kleine of April 29, 1914 addresses a copyright dispute with Cines citing three new films, two based on Plutarch-Shakespeare subjects; and from the acrimonious correspondence of July 29, 1914 it is apparent that the agreement with General Film was drawing to a close.

Within the year, an accelerated conscription and the recycling of machinery for armaments further depleted the Italian studios. So it is something of a surprise that one of the most subtly developed of the Italian Shakespeare films of the period emerged at the height of the war, made by veteran actor-director Eleuterio Rodolfi, who had worked for Ambrosio until 1916 and then attempted to establish his own production company. *Amleto* (1917) was the inaugural effort of Rodolfi Film, and starred notable stage and film actor Ruggero Ruggeri. Robert Hamilton Ball managed to track down two reels, somehow, and there was enough in the film to give him a generally favorable impression (although he thought that a Gertrude who seemed younger than Hamlet an anomaly). He observes such cinematic felicities as the intertitles being incorporated into the action rather than serving as scene descriptions, and he notes the skilled use of close-ups as reaction shots. But he concludes that in the end the protagonist was too "theatrical," with a face too lined and a belly too protuberant to capture the sensitivity and poetry of the Forbes-Robertson version, from which Rodolfi appears to have borrowed the association of the Ghost with the sea and the prince's posthumous coronation.[111]

Those who have had a chance to see the complete French version of the print (which exists in the archives of Toulouse and Bologna) have cause to reevaluate its merits. Ball justly complains of the staging of the Mousetrap and decries the acting, but Judith Buchanan (who also notes its emulation of Forbes-Robertson) excuses Hamlet's maniacal laughter and gestural excesses on the grounds of its filmic wealth of detail. Ruggeri cannot simply be Italianate (i.e., Salviniesque) as Ball suggests, since having overacted himself in the presence of his Ofelia, Elena Makowska, he promptly instructs the First Player in the correct manner of toning down his performance. In every instance we have encountered, in fact, actors appeal to national formations of various kinds to market their product abroad. The existence of a French print reveals, moreover, that the film's Italianness by no means implies untranslatability. Even so, Buchanan's suggestion that Rodolfi's successful persuasion of Ruggeri, a renowned stage Hamlet, to renounce the temptations of the spoken word for a gestural language that at times necessitated a compensatory effusiveness, and that the latter is a byproduct of Rodolfi's use of the medium to generate meaning through montage and special effects (such as one Branagh would later resurrect in giving Yorick a living face), also merits elaboration.[112] Certainly, a comparison of the sequence in which the Ghost appears suggests that Rodolfi was attempting something other than emulation of the most famous British Hamlet of his generation. It seems, in fact, something on the order of correction or revision. But this was perhaps inevitable because the Forbes-Robertson version, frequently and inaccurately discussed as something of a transposition of his stage Hamlet to film, is nevertheless notable for being the last Shakespeare film of its kind, an enduring relic that remarkably illustrates the tension sometimes felt between the demands of the stage and needs of the camera.

It might be good to begin comparison of the two Hamlets' supernatural encounters by consulting the impressions of the codirector of *Hamlet*, Cecil Hepworth, one of the pioneering giants of the Brighton School. (Hepworth, incidentally, is often denied credit on this film because as a producer he was rather cavalier about depriving his associates of it, but in this instance his autobiography reveals that Hay Plumb, an actor and occasional director for the company, filmed the interiors.) He notes that his Hamlet was recently knighted (as Laurence Olivier was to be after his film *Hamlet*), but then adds an anecdote in which he makes fun of the peerage. The sequence that he discusses in greatest detail does not involve Forbes-Robertson at all, but is the film's only example of cross-cutting (that also features one of his famed camera movements, a reverse tracking shot) of a passage—Gertrude's description of Ophelia's demise—that he rather cannily observes was otherwise "useless for the purpose of the silent pictorial version." Most subsequent directors, with the notable exception of Branagh (who makes liberal use of explanatory flashbacks), have followed his example. Thus intercut with the queen's holding court in a garden, we see the distracted girl wandering the banks of a sunlit stream and then the customary tribute to John Everett Millais's "inescapable" Pre-Raphaelite painting of the flower-framed, waterborne waif.[113] Although on occasion technically flawed, these exterior sequences are examples of playing for the camera and were shot in various private country estates in the Southeast of England; Ophelia is indeed buried in one of Gray's country churchyards, as Yorick had been. The interiors, on the other hand, strived to re-create the sets of the stage production and were filmed in the studio at Walton as a documentary reenactment of the stage performance, although one marred at times by Sir Johnston's tendency to enliven his lines by darting about with youthful nimbleness, now and then extending a fluttering hand (or more) beyond the frame.

Once in a while Sir Johnston even loses his head, but it is only in his first encounter with his father's ghost that he succeeds in losing himself altogether. This scene begins on the ramparts of a castle that Hepworth informs us was constructed with Gaumont's money on a suitably flat promontory on hospitable Lulworth Cove.[114] A handsome castle might have been the price of persuasion, for Hepworth had by then convinced Sir Johnston that they could not merely record a valedictory postretirement performance; and for his part Forbes-Robertson strives gamely to be cinematic. It must have been sheer chaos. Since the Ghost was shot separately against a dark background and the two negatives superimposed, Hepworth or an associate would have stood somewhere behind the camera yelling instructions as to correct positions. Hamlet and his companions turn to face the Ghost but cannot quite react in time as it glides over and past them to the left of the frame. Hamlet turns to face the apparition of his father and kneels, and the Ghost raises his royal scepter before beginning to move to screen right. As Hamlet overhastily attempts to follow him off frame, Forbes-Robertson's companions must have been instructed to restrain him, which they struggle to do as the camera, at first attempting to pan with the ghost, swings back in an effort to keep them centrally framed, an exercise rendered futile once the prince breaks free and runs off screen right. A title beginning, {I am thy father's spirit.} and ending, {Of life, of crown, and queen at once dispatched}," comes to the rescue. A kindly cut transports Hamlet to the boulder-strewn shores of Lulworth-Elsinore, and in a marvelous piece of naturalism the prince steps gingerly from rock to rock, glancing down occasionally to establish his footing.[115] Taking cognizance of the white profile on the left of the frame, he raises a hand to his head, then falls to his knees and collapses sideways right out of the frame. A desperate camera operator tries to pan and simultaneously tilt downward to center the prone figure, but cannot reach far enough. Presently, a hand rises back into the frame from below, no doubt to silence the hollering from beyond. Another saving cut reveals the prone prince, and a further intertitle permits another repositioning. As noted contemporary theatre critic Clement Scott remarks, Forbes-Robertson epitomized the nineteenth-century idea of the prince, a role he was "born to play": when, in an interesting departure from the play, the Ghost enjoins him to silence and he kisses its spectral sword, he first consults his little black book, for Forbes-Roberson's Hamlet was, above all, an intellectual, deprived of a throne but regal in bearing.[116]

In the equivalent scene in *Amleto* the prince abides by the entreaties of his companions and pays a midnight visit to the ramparts, but Rodolfi, rather than throwing the figures together with an elaborate special effect, isolates them in shot/reverse shot compositions that allow Amleto to be seen in medium-long shot and the Ghost's armor to glint as he stands against a dark background. Amleto, his arms outstretched, falls to his knees and raises his left hand to his heart (as Bernhardt did at this point), while a companion supports him from behind. A title, {L'évocation de crime} leads into a flashback of Old Hamlet leading his smiling wife to a throne and seating her on it. He leaves. As her smile begins to fade, two hands throw open the curtains at the rear to reveal Claudio, who approaches. An intertitle then has the shade of Hamlet's father revealing his uncle's role in his death, and after a cut back to a medium shot of the armored Ghost, we have another flashback depicting the king asleep upright on a park bench in the foreground. The women are gathered in the distance, and as Claudio sidles up to the king from behind and pours the contents of a viol into his ear, he keeps glancing backward toward the women (presumably one is Gertrude). The next cut takes us to the equivalent of Lulworth Cove, where the still-armored Ghost stands before a huge boulder on the right of the screen as a crumpled Hamlet occupies the opposite corner of the screen, poised on a flat rocky ledge extending from screen left. When the Ghost vanishes, the prince collapses neatly into the frame and comes to rest in a supine position along the bottom edge.

Despite some deteriorated and missing footage, the more self-conscious playing for the camera in the later Hamlet is obvious. Leaving aside the nuances of staging, the proximity of the actors to the camera allow for facial expression to play a greater role than in the Hepworth-Plumb film. The special effects are more integrated. And as interpretation, Ruggeri's Amleto is anything but Bernhardt's or Forbes-Robertson's. He has to twice restrain himself from losing his actors' mask and embracing Ofelia (who nevertheless throws herself feet first into a stream after creating elaborate bouquets from what appears to be a flower garden, those wreathed in her hair mostly washed away before we see her in the condition of Millais's Ophelia). As in this scene, Amleto engages in hyperbolic acting when he wants to share his feigned madness with the audience, hence his overdone gesticulation just before the Mousetrap is sprung, at the moment when he recognizes that his conversation with Ofelia is not a private one. As Ball notes of the filming of *The Murder of Gonazgo*, Claudio and Gertrude face into the theatrical space and so we see no more than Amleto's reactions to their reactions. When Claudio enters his own chamber and falls to his knees beneath a standing crucifix, Amleto steals in, draws the parting curtain aside, and unsheathes his sword. The tricky issue of whether he would dispatch Claudio heavenward restrains him, as in Shakespeare's play, but for Catholic audiences unfamiliar with the idea that private confession without a priest's intercession might suffice for absolution, the presence of the imposing crucifix alone might, no doubt, have sufficed to explain his hesitation. Later, after practically chasing the mourners away, Amleto strews large quantities of flowers at Ofelia's grave and falls down alongside it weeping. Before the combat with Laertes, a title warns us: {La trahison}. True enough, we presently have cuts in to illustrate Claudio's anointing of Laertes's epée with a pot of poison, and before the two engage, he empties the contents of a ring into one of the chalices. The latter scenes are intercut nicely with the return of the soldiers from the Polish campaign, illustrating the imminent consequences of Denmark's rottenness. There is a shocked pause when Gertrude, enthroned at Claudio's side, offers Hamlet a toast and inadvertently takes a sip from the poisoned chalice. The fencing is less elaborate than Bernhardt's, but on recognizing the treachery, Amleto disarms Laertes with an equivalent flourish and forces his own sword on him in like manner. The scene ends with the poisoned prince possessing barely enough strength to stab Claudio who is so intent on flight that he leaves his regalia behind. Supported by two companions, Amleto is practically carried to the throne, and when he gestures toward the crown, it is placed on his head while the scepter is placed in his limp right hand. With the complex maneuverings of Italy's monarchs during the peninsula's reunification still in living memory, and the government's duplicity and inglorious militarism increasingly evident, the scene could not have failed to evoke symbolic resonances. Amleto dies enthroned: Orazio raises his still-crowned head, only to see it sag, and the courtiers kneel just as Fortebraccio and his army enter. The Italian Amleto is an ordinary man, a reluctant avenger, a hero only by force of circumstance, an inversion of Bernhardt's.

To find Forbes-Robertson's opposite, we more or less have to return to the present. If the film made by Hepworth and Plumb encapsulates the tension between theatricality and the cinematic, then Michael Almereyda's *Hamlet* (2000) is replete with myriad such tensions, not only in quoting other films rather elaborately, but in emphasizing the role of cinema as a parasitic and parasitized medium, one whose endless borrowings effect a form of predatory remediation. If Hepworth's aim was to simulate the immediacy of the stage, to capture Forbes-Robertson's actual aura, then Almereyda's is to present events that have already taken place as media constructions. Whereas Baz Luhrmann's *Romeo + Juliet* is news, and presented as such as the action unfolds, the presence of Robert MacNeil (from the respected PBS MacNeil-Lehrer News Hour) to deliver an epilogue confirms Almereyda's film to be a commentary about corporate responsibility, perhaps a report commissioned by Fortinbras following his successful hostile takeover of Denmark Corporation. Indeed, the entire film is suffused with the sense of disillusionment that beset the Watergate years, as apt an historical parallel as one could imagine for a film from 2000 in the light of the scandals that were shortly to contribute to the fall of a government. That Hamlet prefers handguns to swords seems natural to the contemporary Manhattan setting; certainly, Almereyda's conceit is more consistent than Branagh's or Campbell Scott's made-for-TV *Hamlet* (2000), whose bare rapiers and bodkins belong neither to the late Romanov period nor to nineteenth-century New England gentility. Yet the ubiquity of spying and recording gadgetry (even the Ghost is first spotted on a surveillance tape) reveals Almereyda's suspicion of the very technologies that can bring Shakespeare's *Hamlet* into the twenty-first century. Nor do all the narrative elements merely sustain that conceit. A toy duck, for example, alerts us to one of Almereyda's antecedents (Kaurismaki, who finds power struggles over such stakes as dominance of a toy-manufacturing conglomerate risible) and a Buddhist monk to another (Kurosawa, the moralist-humanist whose version of *Hamlet* was a critique of post–World War II Japan's wholehearted embrace of consumer culture).[117] What the tape recorder and telephone are to Kurosawa, the bugging device, answering machine, personal computer, and video camera are to Almereyda. While Kaurismaki pays tribute to Kozintsev by using sinister passages of Shostakovich rather than through explicit visual reference, Almereyda relies on Brahms and, like Kaurismaki, on the blues. His bookish protagonists fill the shelves in their apartments with works such as those of suicidal Modernist poet and film enthusiast Vladimir Mayakovsky. As in many of the recent Generation X cycle of Shakespeare films, the older generation is irredeemable (the obverse of Kurosawa's point about corrupt elders leading a new generation astray). The fathers, especially, are a sorry lot: Bill Murray's Polonius, not quite the Walsinghamesque spymaster of Branagh's film but here again Claudius's willing flunky, hides raw cunning and an unsavory interest in his own daughter behind the mask of bumbling affability; Sam Shepard plays Almereyda's elder Hamlet as a wistful, overpresent agent provocateur; and Claudius is a Mafia boss-Wall Street tycoon hybrid who beats Hamlet up in a not very beautiful launderette, with henchmen Rosenkrantz and Guildenstern in attendance. Gertrude's redemption comes too late when she sacrifices herself to save Hamlet. Youth is fragile. Ophelia is a photographer who brings still images to life by immersing them in liquids, and whose final immersion in a fountain is redolent of Dustin Hoffman's similarly shot, though far from fatal "release" in a swimming pool in *The Graduate* (dir. Mike Nichols, 1967). In a Dantesque contrapasso, Ophelia's private betrayal of Hamlet culminates in a very public scene of madness at the Guggenheim Museum, one of New York's capitals of Modernism. The *Mousetrap* is not a silent film as in Claude Chabrol, to whom we will return, but a student video evoking 1950s melodrama and more recent pronography, complete with a cover derived from the poster to Hitchcock's *Vertigo* (1958). The film contains room even for silent cinema, for when Hamlet needs to contemplate the frailty of flesh (as well this Hamlet might), the memento mori is the one Forbes-Robertson holds up, albeit a Forbes-Robertson cropped away from his theatrical roots and brought much closer to the camera than he would have wished; and even here Forbes-Robertson serves as a low-budget evocation (in reverse orientation) of Arnold Schwarzenegger's momentary contemplation of Yorick's skull in the spoof trailer imagined by a youngster forced to endure Olivier's *Hamlet* by schoolteacher Joan Plowright, the actor's wife, paying an affectionate tribute to her recently deceased husband in John McTiernan's *Last Action Hero*. Here then is one of those rare films for which no critical somersaults are necessary to sustain the claim that its insistent citations of the crises of Modernism serve as an overt gesture of postmodernity. No wonder "To be, or not to be" is recited twice, first as a video pondering the efficacy of handguns as suicide weapons and then, in more extended form, as a "talking-to-oneself" monologue at a Blockbuster's video outlet. A millennial film whose citational excess draws attention to *Hamlet*'s successive cinematic reinscriptions, Almereyda's *USA Today's* take on its predecessors seems to ponder the question of cinema's continued existence even as digital straight-to-video films (the weapons of youth) launch their own corporatist revolution against the entrenched interests of the big screen.

From a Transnational Star to a Transplanted Aesthetic: Danes in Berlin and Germans in Hollywood

The very different crisis of 1920, one that contributed to the period that Peter Wollen has described as the first phase of cinematic Modernism, was the result of the catastrophic armed conflict that had recently engulfed Europe. World War I had a decisive impact on all the world's film industries. It led to the consolidation of American cinema whose huge domestic market necessitated a steadier supply of films than the beleaguered European national industries could supply; imminent U.S. war involvement, in fact, precipitated the reorganization of the studio-centered system in then untrammeled Hollywood, and with it a dominance of world film markets never thereafter relinquished. In contrast, the war took a particularly heavy toll on smaller national industries that relied on export for an audience base: one of the world's major studios, Denmark's Nordisk Film, for example, relied on German and American distribution, and never recovered in its aftermath.[118]

The proximity of the German film industry to that based in Copenhagen, in particular, meant that a phenomenon we associate principally with Hollywood beginning at a slightly later date, the "assimilation" of personnel who had achieved success elsewhere (in France, Denmark, Sweden, Germany, England, Australia, Hong Kong, and now Mexico), was already under way in Berlin by 1910. The German government's actions as the war began and during the hyperinflationary postwar economic collapse attest to the close ties between the Danish and German industries in that an embargo effectively put an end to all film imports save those from Denmark. Unhindered in its exploitation of a large domestic market with the elimination of competition from foreign films and profiting by earning export revenue in more stable foreign currencies, the Berlin-based film industry was second only to Hollywood in size and production capacity by the time the five-year ban ended on December 31, 1920.[119] Denmark's nascent export-based industry, on the other hand, declined irrevocably during the war, having in its brief heyday influenced not only its German counterpart, but also a host of other national industries large and small. Denmark's liberal censorship laws gave it at least one major advantage over national cinemas that were concurrently being legislated to an increasing degree, and genres concerning evil women, sexual libertinage, even sorcery, thrived. In 1907, for instance, Nordisk made one of the nation's earliest surviving fictional films, an eight-minute potboiler, *Den Svide Slavinde* (*The White Slave*, dir. Viggo Larsen), about the sexual enslavement of women. On April 11, 1910, Fotorama released an expanded three-reel version of this film as *Den Hvide Slavehandel* (*The White Slave Trade*, dir. Alfred Cohn), which was distributed by Nordisk's U.S. branch the Great Northern Company. In turn, Nordisk released its own extremely successful two-part film of the same title (on September 2, 1910 and January 23, 1911) that seemingly copied the scenes of the earlier film of 1910, both having derived from a popular novel (with obvious parallels to *Pericles*) about the deception and sexual enslavement of a Danish woman in a succession of other countries. The director of both parts of the Nordisk film was August Blom, whose lead actress in the second, Clara Wieth, was fast establishing an international following that she consolidated in 1912 with Blom's *Vampyrdanserinden*, in which she played the seductive vampire dancer of the title. As Maren Prust points out, the first contemporary fiction feature to be a blockbuster in the United States, *Traffic in Souls* (dir. George Loane Tucker, 1913), and the cycle of Vamp films in which Theodosia Goodman (a.k.a. Theda Bara) starred, were strongly influenced by these Nordisk films.[120] For his part, Blom went on from his *Pericles*-like saga to the Elsinore *Hamlet* of 1910 (of which only stills appear to survive in the Danske Filmmuseum).

It is difficult to tell to what extent Blom carried on a rivalry with Viggo Larsen, who also directed a yet unrediscovered *Othello* in 1908, but his *For Abent Taeppe* (1912), released in the United States as *Desdemona*, is Blom's contemporary resetting of *Othello* in which the jealous Iago is an actor whose advances are spurned by lead actress Marie Lowe who is rehearsing Shakespeare's play with her husband, Einar, slated to play Othello. Save for some missing frames at crucial moments (as when the suspicious Einar disguises himself as Marie's lover and may receive a kiss), the film is available on DVD as a supplement to the American release version of the 1922 Ufa *Othello*. I summarize a few details only to emphasize the adaptation's cinematic sophistication (if admittedly in presenting a story that would have made Ibsen spin in his grave). Despite evidencing a less complex editing system than that developed by Griffith at Biograph, the restraint of the acting seems all the more remarkable because of the melodramatic conclusion, while the repeated use of the mirror (itself a figure of narrative duplication, as Branagh realizes elegantly in the sequences flanking his whispered "To be, or not to be") would delight the likes of film theorist Gilles Deleuze. In a noteworthy departure from Shakespeare, Desdemona's "real life" counterpart has little patience for her husband; indeed, she kisses her lover after each meeting and shows her husband the same tenderness only when he is in disguise (which prompts him to rip it off and order her out). Nor is her lover any more circumspect, for he arrives at the theatre and takes the royal box, cradling a large bunch of flowers. This causes Othello to throttle his Desdemona with such force that he tears her from the bed, which accomplished he advances to the footlights and accuses her seducer. The jeering audience turns to the box and the miscreant slinks away. Although the film ends as Verdi's opera does, Iago escapes both notice and justice. For its date the film seems extraordinary and, despite bearing a clever title that emphasized its reworking of Shakespeare, it showcased the talents of its Othello, the emerging matinee idol Valdemar Psilander.

In contrast, the remarkably similar British film *Carnival* (dir. Harley Knoles, 1921) uses lengthy intertitles to emphasize Shakespearean parallels and makes a lyrical use of Shakespeare's Venetian setting. However, Matheson Lang's stage play, from which it derives, sets the action during the *Carnevale*, and the *Commedia dell'arte* aspects of the plot (not unexpectedly those adapted by Ruggiero Leoncavallo in his opera *I Pagliacci*) dominate the dramaturgy. Silvio, an actor who is about to play Othello on stage, misses his train and returns home just in time to catch his best friend, Andrea, and wife, Simonetta, return from what he believes to be a tryst. Having already had his suspicions provoked by her blackmailer brother, Lelio, he restrains the murderous impulses that he regards as barbarous, only to mistake his Desdemona for Simonetta and come close to strangling her in the emotion of the moment. The film ends on a note of reconciliation, suggesting perhaps that Desdemona's best course might have been a more knowing mixture of confession and denial. While most Othello performances are dominated by Iago, this may be the only one to make Cassio a leading figure; it was indeed the first such role for another future matinee idol, Ivor Novello. Knoles (also known as Knowles) appears to have had a considerable career in the United States (including an association with Helen Gardner on *Cleopatra*) before returning to make this film, but his opportunities faded after the sound watershed of 1927. To add insult to injury, Herbert Wilcox directed a sound remake of *Carnival* in 1931. Knoles's predecessor, Blom, elected to stay in Denmark after World War I and his directing career ended in 1925, having peaked with the 1913 megafeature *Atlantis*, whose Titanic-like ship disaster and a panoply of special effects rivaling those of the Italian superproductions established him as one of the most innovative of all prewar film directors.

Yet if any Danish film made an instant international splash in the prewar years, it was the 1910 *Afgrunden*, and that not because of its talented writer-director, Peter Urban Gad, but because of his lead actress and partner, Asta Nielsen. While Lillian Gish was becoming well known in the United States and Francesca Bertini was consolidating her reputation in Italy, Nielsen, who performed a widely censored erotic dance and played the role of a fallen woman fallen so far that she stabs her lover to save the reputation of a virtuous man, became an international sensation. So sensational, indeed, that she even invited spurious criticism according to an anecdote embedded in an account of the origins of the Hungarian film industry: "In the Spring of 1911, when Mor Ungerleider saw the first Asta Nielsen film of Nordisk, *Avgrunden*, he quickly published a scathing review, lest somebody else should conceive the idea of purchasing this treasure, but he quickly bought his railway ticket to Copenhagen, where in a few days he secured an option on all Nordisk films for years to come."[121] In a sense, Nielsen influenced cinema even before her first film was in the can. *Afgrunden* was shot outdoors for a paltry 8,000 Krøner, and attracted fascinated onlookers, one of whom happened to be Benjamin Christensen, the most important director Denmark exported other than fellow occult enthusiast Carl Theodor Dreyer; indeed, Christensen went on to make films specializing in the macabre in Germany and, briefly, the United States. Having watched her complete a scene, he declared: "Now I know that film can be an art."[122] Immediately after *Afgrunden*, Nielsen (and her director) received an invitation from Paul Davidson, a onetime door-to-door curtain salesman who had established a studio called the Projektions Union based in Frankfurt. In 1912 Union moved operations to a new studio in Berlin that was to rival Nordisk's operations there, and so formed the nucleus of what in 1917 became Europe's largest studio complex, Ufa.[123] Although she did return on occasion (as when she acted in Blom's 1911 *Balletdanserinden*), Nielsen maintained her affiliation with Union and Deutsche-Bioscop before their merger into Ufa, and together with Gad made some twenty-nine films before she returned to Denmark in 1916 (she had been denied permission to leave until troops were mobilized), remaining there for the course of the war under the banner of her own company Neutral Films.[124] Gad stayed on, directed intermittently, and wrote books and articles on the cinema.

When, after her return to Germany Nielson formed another company, Art-Film, her first project followed the well-established tradition of Shakespearean inaugurations. Nothing else about the project, however, smacked of tradition. Siddons, Cushman, Bernhardt, even her contemporary Zinaida Raikh (Meyerhold's wife, who was to be stabbed to death by Stalin's NKVD after his arrest, by which time an alarmed Pasternak had set aside his translation of the play for them), each played Hamlet as a man, with their audiences fully aware of the virtuosity of the very different artifices behind the illusion. Alone among them Nielsen played Hamlet as a woman, and not just any woman but one constrained to play the role of a man. As comments by the peripatetic director, Svend Gade (sometimes also credited by the Swedish variant of his name, Sven Gade), make clear in his justification for jettisoning a filmed prologue that had both Georg Brandes and Vining appear on screen, the concept originated with her. It might even have been her confident challenge to a noted model: as a poor orphan working at a bakery and inspired by Henryk Ibsen's plays to try the stage (and who did play Hedda Gabler in a film of 1925), she must have known of Bernhardt whose Mucha-designed ending, with the prince borne out on a shield, makes its way into the film.[125] Whatever the motives, it was a propitious moment for such a film. Having entered prewar theatre above all through the experiments of the director of Berlin's Deutsches Theater, Max Reinhardt, Expressionist art was producing a reaction and undergoing a renewal as the *Neue Sachlichkeit* (or New Objectivity, Gustav Hartlaub's term), and was poised to reinvigorate itself in the service of a postwar cinema in which even such Realist genres as the intimate drawing-room film, the *Kammerspiel*, or the social commentary of the dour Street Film, developed in relation to Expressionism's challenge to representational art.[126] The transgressive and even macabre elements of Danish films no longer seemed supernatural after the continuing horrors of World War I, and as such found visible embodiment in the travails of the leading star of the period. Nielsen, moreover, played up the aspect of postwar border dissolution through the simultaneous repudiation of the boundaries of both nation and gender; when she returned to filmmaking in Germany, even some of the sets were fabricated from the material remains of war's aftermath.[127]

Despite the volume of conscientious commentary the film has attracted, Nielsen's portrayal of Hamlet remains a subject of continuing debate and critics, even those who like Lisa Starks and Judith Buchanan have offered acute insights into the film, have taken almost opposing views on whether Nielsen augmented the ambiguities of Shakespeare's play or attempted to clarify them.[128] A frequently encountered critical commonplace, that the film is "Expressionist," is in fact misleading.[129] The only reason many films of the period are so designated is the canonical status later assumed by a midbudget film directed by Robert Wiene for Decla-Bioscop, *The Cabinet of Dr. Caligari* (*Das Kabinett des Doktor Caligari*), partly as a result of a brilliant advertising campaign in which the January 1920 release was preceded by a rash of posters all over Berlin declaring in the words of an animated intertitle from the film: "You must become Caligari." Although not nearly as successful at the box office as the costume dramas of Lubitsch or some later epics of Lang, it was about as close as cinema ever got to a paradigmatic exemplar of a style. The historian most responsible for according *Caligari* this unique position in world cinema, Siegfried Kracauer, saw in its perspectival distortions, overwrought *schrei* acting, and abject narrative (in which the original scenario was muted to depict the inevitable triumph of authority) nothing less than a foretaste of the mental climate that gave rise to Nazism. It was very much a case in this instance of history conforming to the historian's selective presentation of evidence. The first German film to receive popular acclaim in the United States was one assigned to Lubitsch by Davidson who, following the success of the director's comedies and exotic adventure films, had determined to start making big-budget historical films at Ufa: the result, *Madame Dubarry* (1919), established an eager American market for German films (more than two years before *Caligari*'s arrival), with the ironic consequence that it took both its winsome star Pola Negri and its director to Hollywood.[130] *Hamlet, Ein Rachedrama* (*Hamlet, A Revenge Drama*) was under way while *Caligari* was yet showing in theatres. When released in February 1921, it proved the most successful German film of the year but merited only a footnote in Kracauer's *From Caligari to Hitler*, and that too only to assimilate it into the grand project of "Expressionism."[131] Regarding all departures from Realist representation and Ufa's tendency to monumentality as being of ill portent, Kracauer insisted that Lang's vast sets for his 1924 films based on the Niebelungen sagas "reduced human beings to accessories of primeval landscapes or vast buildings," adding in his footnote that "a similar ornamental style had already asserted itself in *Hamlet* (1920)."[132] If anything, the only overtly Expressionist moment occurs when Hamlet, who enjoys baiting Claudius and had watched him recoil on showing him his rediscovered dagger in a Mousetrap moment, toasts his impending death in an underground chamber decorated in abstract zigzag patterns. She then sets the hall ablaze, overpowers her drunken uncle, and, in a distinctly post–World War I image, seals the door, leaving the revelers to suffocate in the fumes: if this is a figure of the Neue Sachlichkeit overpowering classical Expressionism then it chronicles yet another Nielsen anticipation, for the former term does not come into general use until 1923.

Writing in part as a corrective to Kracauer, Lotte Eisner attempted to distinguish between Expressionism and other styles of the period. Even when the principal film actors associated with Reinhardt's varied experimental theatrical productions, Paul Wegener, Werner Kraus, Emil Jannings, and Peter Lorre, had come to seem exemplars of an outmoded aesthetic, Nielsen's hold on memory remained undiminished according to Eisner. Decades later, when the important film theorist Rudolf Arnheim recollects the period, he speaks of a time when "Lubitsch was working in Germany, when Emil Jannings played Henry VIII and Asta Nielsen Hamlet."[133] "People nowadays cannot understand what that pale mask, with its immense blazing eyes, meant for the nineteen-tens and twenties," Eisner reminisces, in continued astonishment at Nielsen's ability to change personae, even her gender, from role to role.[134] Of Arthur von Gerlach's 1922 *Vanina*, for instance, Eisner states: "If this film is more astonishing to us today than many others, the reason is that Nielsen's acting is intensely modern—her eyes, her hands, the sweep of her figure betraying an immense sorrow, give a violent intensity and resonance to this Kammerspiele of souls."[135] In her chapter on Street Films, Eisner, trying to describe Nielsen's performance alongside that of the young Greta Garbo in Georg Wilhelm Pabst's much-admired *The Joyless Street* (1923), argues that scenes that would otherwise be commonplaces of human suffering "come alive" because of her. And she prefaces her own appreciation of Nielsen with Balázs's admiring remark on seeing her Hamlet: "Dip the flags before her, for she is unique." Recognizing the impossibility of pinning a label on her, she continues,

> she was neither "modernistic" [meaning influenced by Neue Sachlichkeit] nor "Expressionistic." Her warm humanity, full of the breath of life and presence, refuted both abstraction and the abruptness of Expressionist art. Never did she stoop to mawkishness, never did her travesty shock. She could play in trousers without ambiguity. For Asta Nielsen's eroticism was without equivocation; her passion was always authentic... In every film this woman who seems the quintessence, the epitome of her era, renews herself. In *Hamlet* she is as vibrant as a Damascus sabre, the Danish Joan of Arc."[136]

Much has been irrevocably lost to time, but what such an assessment amounts to in terms of technique, and what Eisner meant when she contrasted Nielsen's intellectualism to Pola Negri's spontaneous sensuality, can still be discerned.[137] Hers was a style based on the economy and efficiency of gesture, with medium close-ups and close-ups often used to comment on the shot that follows or to cue point-of-view compositions. To a greater degree than Gish, and at an opposite extreme from Bertini, her movements were quick and lithe, her formal poses held very briefly and in such a way as to minimize their ostentation. When she added innovations to the standard gestural repertoire, she paused longer or repeated the gesture, as in the memorable instance when Hamlet reveals Claudius's treachery to Horatio and then has to keep tapping his lips until he is silent. Her tapered fingers were often used to expressive effect, with her hands frequently being brought to her face (or, in the case of *Hamlet*, to a dagger): having waved Horatio away on her first visit to her father's tomb, for instance, she sinks to her knees, her face against the marble, as her hands glide down to frame her face in a striking, intensely private composition. The noted experimental director Hans Richter thought she revolutionized acting because of her exact command of emotional effect, and Balázs claimed that it would only be possible to catalogue the range of her gestures after the completion of a cinematographic encyclopedia of them.[138] The complete production still that heads the present chapter provides a more ample framing than the corresponding shot in the film and recreates Hamlet's final visit to her father's tomb, when, wielding the incriminating dagger found beside the castle's snake pit, she steels herself for vengeance. The lines of the columns illustrate the absolute verticality of the dagger held, as it most often is, by its blade. Having regained their strength, her legs, still folded in a near seated posture, extend dramatically outward as her clenched left hand reaches back toward the effigy of her father, while her whole body is at a slight angle mirrored precisely by that of a Muchaesque sheath. It is the same dagger she holds downward by the hilt, waist-high, when she lurks outside Claudius's door only to discover a situation even more discouraging than finding him fallen on his knees in prayer—he is hosting an orgy surrounded by drunken revelers.

    The virtuosity contemporaries attributed to great virtues, and to which they had a greater sensitivity than we enjoy, may be discerned in a description Balázs gives in his *Theory of the Film* of the "polyphonic play of features" in the well-known chapter "The Face of Man." It is of a film in which Nielsen seduces an innocent youngster, while the man who has hired her to do so stands behind a curtain watching. When she feigns love "the whole gamut of appropriate emotion is displayed in her face." But there's the rub, for during the course of the scene she really falls in love with her victim. Her change of expression is "scarcely perceptible," but yet "immediately obvious," and the sham of one moment turns to deep emotion the next. Then she remembers the curtain, and realizes that she cannot allow her feelings to be known. "So Asta now pretends to be pretending," and there is another slight change of expression. Drawing a metaphor from Chinese theatre, Balázs describes Asta, whose "lying is now a lie," as having put one mask on top of another. His next section concerns the "microphysiognomy" permitted by the close-up. Asta appears again in a new role, facing a cracked mirror in a film of 1927. For ten years her imprisoned lover has avoided the consequences of economic deprivation while she has weathered the world. On the day of his release, she tries to apply layer upon layer of makeup on a face ravaged by poverty, misery, disease, and prostitution. "She tries to save her life with a little rouge! No good! She wipes it off with a dirty rag. She tries again. Then she shrugs her shoulders and wipes it all off... a close-up shows the rag falling on the floor, and after it has fallen, sinking down a little more."[139]

Such contemporary commentaries may give us enough of a window into the past to appreciate the extraordinary integration of multiple registers of performance Nielsen brought to her Hamlet, ones grasped instantly even by contemporaries as far afield as New York. Not coincidentally, Franz Boas, whose theories of ethnography had won wide acceptance, was then teaching in the city at Columbia University, and Nielsen's film adopts a quasi-anthropological approach to Shakespeare's play, taking the precaution at the outset of claiming only to adapt the legend on which the playwright based his story. Purportedly grafting Vining's thesis onto Saxo's account of interminable strife among Scandinavian tribes, *Hamlet* has hardly begun when an illustrated intertitle depicting single combat alerts us to the war between Norway and Denmark, and to England's vassal state (obviously so dominated by Denmark that it vanishes thereafter leaving Hamlet's good friend, Fortinbras, the task of polishing off Rosenkrantz and Guildenstern in situ). In foretelling the fate of the courtiers, I have consciously violated the principles of an art then only recently acquired by film editors; namely, splicing dialogue intertitles into the speeches and otherwise not anticipating actions actors could communicate without their aid. So it is only on witnessing the results of the combat that we discover that the elder Hamlet, himself mortally wounded, has slain the elder Fortinbras. It is thus that the newborn daughter of the Danish queen is proclaimed heir to the throne, a deception that for reasons of state must be maintained even after her injured father's return. Nearly twenty years have elapsed when we first encounter Hamlet, with her back to us, seated alone on the balustrade of the grand staircase of Elsinore. When she turns, it is with a smile on hearing and then seeing her father, in whose embrace she can be the girl playing the boy, even as her unyielding mother's attentions have already turned unambiguously to Claudius who fast approaches. Her father's death traps her in a single role, and she discovers it while a (male) scamp at the university, and the news effects an extraordinary transformation from faux boy to faux man. Wittenberg, which apparently serves the northern nobility as a finishing school and where she befriends Fortinbras, involves Hamlet in yet a third kind of performance. She has just arrived when a handsome stranger, one Horatio, accidentally bumps his head against hers, at which point she must make an effort to stay in character as he, obviously attracted, makes conversation with the new boy. Horatio is a man who can obviously look both ways, for while facing one direction walking arm in arm with Hamlet he turns almost a hundred and eighty degrees following the passing Ophelia (who resembles the young Henny Porten, Nielsen's less talented rival); Hamlet's jealousy aroused, when they sit she has to make a determined effort not to stroke his head when he casually places it in her lap.[140] Ophelia is not Hamlet's foster sister as she is in Saxo, but is once again offered as "bait" to test him, and in the "seduction" scenes, in which Hamlet cleverly translates a climactic kiss to a kiss on the hand, she plays the swooning (male) adolescent. In contrast, when feigning madness, Hamlet pretends to be a female adolescent (to Bernhardt's male one), batting her eyelids, walking with an affected gait, carving childish trinkets with her uncle's dagger, and being quite as nasty to the clownish Polonius as her predecessor. She is revealed (literally) in her full femininity only after Ophelia's suicide when she walks through a graveyard with Horatio who is too preoccupied to notice the long bare legs or an errant breast visible through her ragged penitential shift. Yet even this anatomical concession does not reveal her full character. Monika Seidl notes how often the camera isolates the prince in the frame,[141] and it is at those moments when she is alone that Nielsen reveals her sixth and most revealing register of performance. Gazing in secret longing at Horatio from her dormitory window, foregoing both womanhood and lover with a single gesture at her father's tomb, exulting at her "defeat" of Ophelia with arms outstretched and a shadow looming behind her (both crucified and crucifier), regaining her lost resolve once more at the feet of her dead father, and closing the door with cold contempt on Claudius and his ilk, the most characteristic of the six Hamlets is no Tootsie.

This, of course, brings us back to Vining's supposed thesis, another source of much critical confusion. Having lost the guest appearances of Brandes, Vining, and the like, Gepard had to content himself with intertitles that diminish Shakespeare's contribution and augment Saxo's and Vining's. Despite the disclaimer, most of the plot situations, many of the characters, and a number of near quotations display an unmistakable indebtedness to their disavowed author. Saxo is ushered away after the prologue, only to reappear occasionally to preside over Ophelia's introduction, Claudius's death, and the queen's eventual display of her true colors. The latter, something even more out of the monster-mother canon of Jakob Grimm's retold folk tales than Saxo's chronicle, is far more formidable than the sybaritic Claudius and is a precursor of Fritz Lang's Kriemhild (perhaps provoking Kracauer's antipathetic reflex). Having denied Hamlet's accusation that the gender swap was the result of her lust for power, Gertrude turns into a virago just as Hamlet's femininity asserts itself, and after the fumigation of Claudius and his vermin, the revenge drama is the queen's. The outcome of her attempt to pour a liquid as white as mother's milk into a chalice that is accidentally displaced by a pasty-faced butler is grim indeed, and the tip of Laertes's epée, envenomed by her own hand, finds its mark at the instant Hamlet is distracted by her stricken cries. As in a mythic folktale the no less liminal Horatio remains blind to the obvious: he fails to see Hamlet's bared anatomy, and so she has to die to set things straight and alert him by touch to the true nature of his desire.

Of course, all of this has little to do with Vining. According to Guntner when his book appeared in German in 1883, the "modest amateur from Omaha, Nebraska," became "Professor Vining."[142] Vining, a railway executive, was an ardent bibliophile and enthusiastic amateur philologist, and his various *Hamlet* arguments—although exhaustive and the subject of a number of lectures and two books—contain curious anomalies. Critics of Nielsen's film have generally accepted Gepard's claim that Vining makes Hamlet a woman, when in fact Her(r) Professor begins modestly by drawing a parallel with the masculine Lady Macbeth and suggesting that some men (like our prince) are perfectly female in temperament and therefore irresolute, impulsive, sharp-tongued, and as averse to women as they are attracted to men. He proceeds in subsequent chapters to make the case that, in the course of composing the play, Shakespeare recognized Hamlet's essential femininity and modified the text in conformity with his insight.[143] Edwin Booth recommended *The Mystery of Hamlet* as interesting oddity to his scandalized biographer and collaborator William Winter,[144] and in the year after Nielsen's film won accolades in every European metropolis, Sylvia Beach published the full text of James Joyce's beleaguered *Ulysses* (in whose ninth episode he ponders Goethe, *Hamlet,* and *Wilhelm Meister,* wondering why if Vining could make Hamlet a woman he could not be an Irishman) under the imprimatur of her own Parisian bookstore, Shakespeare and Co. Nielsen had no need of Vining's assistance to make love to women as she did in Urban Gad's *Jugend und Tollheit* (*Youth and Folly*, 1913), or to cross-dress in order to illustrate the art of seduction to a man, the principal plot device of Magnus Stofter's *Das Liebes-ABC* (*Love's ABC*, 1916) made for Neutral Film: no one understood the constituent elements of her stardom as well as she did, and in *Hamlet* she is true to what was expected of Danish cinema and to her own androgynous fascination.[145] In any case, Gepard disregards Vining when it comes to most narrative details, and he invents characters as the plot changes demand. Thus while the Nebraskan professor attributes Gertrude's actions to feminine weakness, in the film a midwife presses that possibility on the queen in the aftermath of childbirth and the news of her husband's fatal wounding. A gardener conveniently appears when Hamlet needs to discover that the serpent who stung his father was not quite his uncle, but close cousin to the brood of vipers lurking in the royal snake pit. The Wittenberg scenes, the arrival of a physician, and a dazzling constellation of plot devices are of the filmmakers' invention.

Rather than paying homage to intellectual antecedents, *Hamlet* satirizes them. Unlike Forbes-Robertson's prince, Nielsen's has no patience with books. "Words, words, words," she exclaims while flipping through scatterings of heavy, bound volumes, and she ridicules her professors with antic imitations of their pedagogy. We get twisted Vining and mangled Freud, and neither scapes whipping. The two cheeky intertitles that introduce Vining actually claim to confirm ("bestätigt") his thesis. If Polonius wears a clown's motley, then the persistent physician he ushers in to examine Hamlet has the appearance of a mountebank professor of medicine. In the preceding years Franz Boas had already thrown doubt on the efficacy of cranial measurement as an index of human intelligence, but the harlequin professor begins by attempting to locate the source of Hamlet's problems in "his" head, declaring it too small for such an intellect. Perhaps recalling with alarm that Freud tended to find physical correlatives for neuroses in various extremities, Hamlet attempts distraction by pointing first to one side of her neck and then the other. Undiscouraged, the professor now heads for the heart and places an ear over what Vining might have declared the solution to the conundrum, Hamlet's left breast. Nothing! There is no couch at hand, but she indicates a bench where she can show them the toys she has carved with her uncle's dagger, contriving to get rid of the intruders by forcing Polonius to sit on a suggestively sharp spike.

Her appropriation of her uncle's dagger is equally interesting in that its symbolism is significantly more developed than Mucha's and Bernhardt's. Indeed, part of *Hamlet*'s satire of intellectualism consists of a "snakes and daggers" game. The film leaves open the possibility that Claudius acts at Gertrude's instigation when making his way into Denmark's rotten underbelly, announced as the royal snake pit by an intertitle composed of distended serpents for letters. When Claudius drops his erect dagger in extracting a particularly limp example from the seething mass, it proves his undoing. Hamlet has her own dagger and one more formidable than, for instance, the dainty utensil Olivier contemplates while disporting himself on Elsinore's parapets. She holds it to her heart when she first hears her father's voice upon observing the revelries at the castle. Then, stirred to vengeance, she seeks out the Gardner, discoverer of his body, and on hearing of the snake descends to the pit where, in trying to pry its lid open, she chances on Claudius's dagger. This she retrieves and apparently substitutes for her own. Associated with a masculine imperative to vengeance, the stylized dagger appears on two illustrated intertitles, and becomes a talismanic prop. Saxo's mad Hamlet whittles wood into fishhooks, but Nielsen's carves a delicate miniature crown and shows it to her uncle, pointing the ornate handle to him as she clutches the blade. When he recognizes it and draws back in alarm, she slithers along the ground after him (as she does toward the royal couple during the perfunctory, literal Mousetrap). Throughout, Hamlet baits Claudius, even proposing a toast to his impending death, and yet on two occasions when she contemplates taking her own life, she raises her father's brother's weapon to her own wrist. She carries it past guffawing guards to her uncle's chambers, and, unable to use it, retreats to her father's vault over which she raises it, again grasping it by the blade, like a crucifix, when she resolves finally to take arms against a sea of troubles. Yet her inability to use it anticipates the compensation associated with a Lacanian lack, the proof of which might be that, when in a position to smite Claudius with a sword, she desists (if ostensibly to reserve a more fitting punishment for him).

The fifth edition of *The Interpretation of Dreams*, to which Freud had added a discussion of one of his recent nightmares, appeared in 1919, the year before the film's production. Just as Freud's dream logic mixes up the sequence of events, the order of the lines in the defining "To be, or not to be" soliloquy are fragmented and reordered. Hamlet is asleep when an intertitle printed over a swirling spiral and incorporating the word "traum" announces: {"To sleep ≈ perchance to dream."} She awakes with a frightened start and addresses her father. Then, throwing a swirling cape over her shoulder, she first resolves to stab Claudius and, thwarted, descends into the tomb where she completes the soliloquy putting the blade to her wrist and then, by resolving to use it on her uncle, transforming it into a raison d'être. Transference, condensation, displacement, inverted Oedipal complexes, all are to be had for a price in Denmark.

Remarkably, Franco Zeffirelli's "To be, or not to be," rendered integrally in a single extended sequence of eighteen shots, occurs precisely in the same subterranean setting. Mel Gibson's Hamlet is given to similar outbursts of violence. If Stoppard had stopped the show at the Venice Film Festival by teasing Olivier (who had done away with Rosenkrantz and Guildenstern even before his film began and won the Grand Prize there, as Stoppard would do), then Zeffirelli gives the treacherous courtiers an increased prominence largely to have them kicked around, not verbally but physically. Gibson gets to manhandle his erstwhile companions, toss things at fuddy-duddy Polonius, and exasperate his initially conciliatory uncle, portraying anything but gender ambiguity. Yet, clearly, he has his own sexual problems. Gertrude, who seems to be "turned on" by witnessing the very Olivieresque slaughter of Polonius, kisses him with an unseemly passion after what approximates a rape scene. Paul Scofield's ecclesiastical cadences, enough to render any poor prince impotent, suggest that he may even be playing Freud's ghost, and the uterine tomb into which Hamlet descends to deliver his soliloquy, pierced by a shaft of light, enables Zeffirelli to juxtapose the prince's living features over those of his father's marble ones. Zeffirelli's command of space and of a camera as fluid as anything in Welles or Kozintsev only emphasize here the confining, circular gloom of the enclosure, a miniature version of the elegant stones of the concentric walls of Elsinore, itself tribute to Olivier's flinty paternity. At the scene's conclusion, Gibson's Hamlet pauses at the passageway, as if to give still more thought to the responsibilities of mortality, but a dissolve to the castle above him allows him to be reborn into the light, whereas Nielsen returns to the crypt insistently only to emerge in the knowledge that death can be her only release.

In one of his sublime ravings, Guillaume Apollinaire once raved about Asta. She was a Japanese print come to life; a chanteuse who transformed silence into song; the inebriate's hallucination; the recluse's dream companion; she was all things to all men.[146] A reviewer for the *New York Times* saw her for the first time at the Lexington Theatre where *Hamlet* was being shown on Monday nights in November of 1921, at a time when the feminine ideal of the coy Gibson Girl had given way to Harrison Fisher's well-heeled and well-fed *Cosmopolitan* socialites. The review contains the perceptive observation that the English titlers had been too free in explaining the obvious and so reminding us of Shakespeare, who was best forgotten. The lighting is not what it would be in the United States. Miss Nielsen possesses a control over her body that lends significance to her movements and postures, and seems to embody a hundred characters at once. "Some undoubtedly will call her beautiful, while others, preferring a different type of wife or sweetheart or sister, will say she is merely striking in appearance. But what does all this matter?...She can act."[147]

★ ★ ★

In the years that followed the success of Nielsen's *Hamlet*, a bevy of German Shakespeare films made their way across Europe and America. Paradoxically, while we associate postwar French Impressionist filmmaking most closely with innovative cinematography, Soviet Formalism with montage, and the Expressionist period with radical mise en scène, the most notable feature of these films proves to be narrative experimentation. The first such experiments might even have spurred Nielsen to action, as in later years she claimed that *Hamlet* was her attempt to infuse fine drama into German film. If it was irritation, the irritants were a pair of knockabout Shakespeare farces by another of her directors, Ernst Lubitsch. *Kohlhielsels Tochter*, a shrewish moment of fun for Lubitsch's regular actors that included a comically effective Jannings, and *Romeo und Julia im Schnee*, were made simultaneously and released within days of each other in March 1920. With sunny Italy recast as rural Bavaria, and with its Capulets and Montagues reduced to litigious, snowball-throwing peasant rivals (in other words rather akin to Lubitsch's caricaturist early comedies that were as yet untouched by his subtle "Lubitsch touch"), the films are trifling amusements for those exhausted by tragic Bardolatry. Kristin Thompson, resisting the view that these were projects hoisted on him, remarks that Lubitsch was already Ufa's biggest moneymaker and was encouraged by Davidson to choose his own projects, and that he opted for familiar fare, transforming a "pastiche of Shakespeare's plays" into two "broad rustic comedies."[148] They are not the work of a journeyman: the aptly titled *Kohlhiesls Töchter* even strives for a bravura performance from one of Lubitsch's regular stable of actors, Henny Porten, who took the roles of both older Kate (Liesl) and younger Bianca (Gretel), a dowdy termagant as one and a pretty dimwit as the other, according to Thomspon.[149] Thompson's complaint about the films is not that they are silly, for they were intended to be and popular in their day, but rather that they illustrate the technical shortcomings that Lubtisch, sooner than any other German director, corrected on viewing the American films that began to arrive in quantity in 1921.[150] As yet unfamiliar with the three-point lighting system that American studios had by now developed to eliminate glare and intrusive shadows, Lubitsch tended to disregard eyeline-matching and continued to rely on "v-pattern" lighting with the consequence that cluster lights are reflected in Jannings's cutlery in *Kohlhiesels Töchter*, while the lack of fill lights and backlighting occasionally causes darkly attired characters to disappear into the shadows in *Romeo und Julia im Schnee*.[151] The final distance Lubitsch traveled when he went to the United States is evident in his 1940 satire of Nazism, *To Be or Not to Be*, a sharp-witted return to the Shakespeare pastiches of old and to his beloved theatrical ambience, a developmental arc that warrants our eventual return to the film as an example of the German presence in Hollywood.

The full-scale German Shakespeare films that followed show instead the tragic intensity of Nielsen; all trace of lightheartedness seemed to depart with Lubitsch who, by mid-1923, had embarked on *Rosita*, a successful Mary Pickford vehicle for United Artists. By the end of the year, Warner Bros. had secured his services, and he stayed contentedly in Hollywood, enjoying the most successful career there of any expatriate director save Hitchcock. The best-known film of the German 1920s Shakespeare cycle, however, was directed by another later Hollywood émigré, the originally Russian Dimitri Buchowetzki. In June 1921 the vast Ufa-Palast Theater premiered his film version of *Danton* based on the protocinematic scene fluctuations of Georg Büchner's doom-laden play, *Danton's Death*, whose timing coincided with Reinhardt's 1920 mass-spectacle version of Romain Rolland's antirevolutionary *Danton*. Werner Krauss, who was Reinhardt's Robespierre and fresh from his performance as Dr. Caligari, took the part of Büchner's relentless persecutor, while Emil Jannings played the doomed Danton. The success of *Sappho* (1921) established Buchowetzki as a Ufa director, although the *Othello* of 1922 was, like *Danton*, made for Hilde Wörner's modest company, possibly with some funding from German American distributor Ben Blumenthal.[152] The film was destined to enter posterity for the brutality of Jannings's deranged murder of Ica von Lenkeffy, a fragile, frightened Desdemona who wrings her hands helplessly as Othello questions her about prayer. Even with (censored?) fragments missing from the English release print, its melodramatic excess assured the scene a place in the prologue to the fiendishly clever Vincent Price vehicle, *Theater of Blood*, where it keeps company with Forbes-Robertson's *Hamlet* and Benson's *Richard III*.

Othello has often irked contemporary critics of Shakespeare on film, partly because it has been one of the few easily accessible features of the period that incorporated the kind of *schrei* acting that nowadays seems acceptable only when serial child murderers resort to it, as Peter Lorre does with an equivalent gestural repertoire in *M* (dir. Fritz Lang, 1931), but also because the film, like the play, has plenty in it to offend. Moreover, in this instance, the temptation to equate actors with their roles is irresistible: Jannings retreated from Hollywood to become a particular favorite of Nazi Minister of Propaganda, Josef Goebbels, while Krauss, ever the second fiddle, seemed to collect all the leftover ribbons. Kenneth Rothwell was initially scandalized by Jannings's "scenery chewing" (at one point Jannings places the purloined handkerchief in his mouth, bites it, and rips it apart with his hands), and Buchanan cannot stomach Jannings's reality TV-style willingness to maul a helpless woman while appropriating a race that is not his own. She reminds us of the Ambrosio *Otello* of 1914, a gorgeous film and by a sad irony one of the last Italian films to be distributed by Kleine. There, when Othello extinguishes Desdemona's mortality, the camera pans away to a portrait of the Virgin Mary beneath which a guttering candle peters out into a trail of smoke, transposing Othello's "put out the light" into an act of moral and cinematic finesse (in contrast to Jannings practically throwing Lenkeffy at the camera).[153] The reticence was certainly not unique to Ambrosio productions, and was to be encountered on occasion in prerevolutionary Russian films (as when the camera pans away from two lovers to show wheat fields swaying in the breeze in Piotr Chardynin's *Korobeiniki* [*Wandering Merchants* 1910], or only the lower half of a woman who had hanged herself after being made pregnant by her rapist father-in-law in Aleksander Ivanov-Gai's *Snokhatch* [*The Daughter-in-Law's Lover* 1912]).[154] And even much later, in a film that won the Grand Prize at the Venice film festival, Kenji Mizoguchi refrained from depicting the violation of the Potter's wife in *Ugetsu Monogatari* (1953), showing only the tears of its aftermath. Buchanan applauds Ambrosio for a rare instance in which the cinema can refuse to do what remains unavoidable on stage.

She is similarly sensitive to the possible reception of Buchowetzki's *Othello*. In rapid succession Krauss had played two psychotic characters, Caligari and Robespierre, and as early as 1918 had played alongside Jannings in the fratricidal film version of *The Brothers Karamazov* (codirected by Buchowetzki). By the time *Othello* came along, audiences were, according to her, anticipating Krauss's malevolent designs on Jannings.[155] Perhaps running out of plot devices, Buchowetzki transforms the elderly, shuffling mendicant of *Caligari* into the prancing, capering, closeted Iago whose head is often turned slightly away from the camera, presenting a left profile that grants full effect to his stringy upturned moustache, slicked-down hair, and prominent earring. Iago behaves with a brutal affection toward Emilia, and coyly toward the easily duped men, pinching Roderigo's last ducat and depriving Cassio of the last vestiges of dignity. His seduction scene with the increasingly helpless Othello retains its brutal intensity. It begins with Othello, fitfully asleep on a cot in his striped robe, its black and white symbolic of the cultures he can no longer reconcile. Tossing and turning restlessly, he imagines Desdemona making love to Cassio, projected as a dream balloon in the upper left of the screen, a technique of mitigating the hero's decline that seems to have gained favor with those now wrestling with the play's difficulties: Parker attributes it to Othello's imagination; a 2001 BBC version directed by Geoffrey Sax, scripted by Andrew Davies, has its Iago (a disgruntled policeman who wanted John Othello's job as department chief) exploiting Desdemona's unimagined flirtatiousness. As Jannings writhes in agony, his face contorts into a replica of Edvard Munch's paintings of *The Scream*, his cries audible to Iago who, when we cut to him, is still toying with the handkerchief and ignoring Emilia's entreaties for its return. Pushing her aside, Iago scampers into the chamber. The overwrought Othello tumbles out of bed, kisses the hand Iago proffers, and allows the Ancient to cradle his head in the other. Upon feeling the perspiration on Othello's brow, Iago wipes it off his hand contemptuously with the handkerchief, then gingerly dabs the rest of Othello's sodden face with it before using it to fan him back into consciousness. He then lets it fall into Othello's lap. {"I found it at Cassio's"}, he tells the bewildered Othello nonchalantly.

At this moment Buchanan, perhaps to her credit, reacts scornfully. The scene, like the borrowing from Verdi that has Iago place a foot on the fallen Othello, intends to convey the depths to which the protagonist has descended. She reminds us of Anson Dyer's vicious (British) cartoon of the previous year in which he—in the fashion of early cartoonists like Emile Cohl and J. Stuart Blackton (cofounder of Vitagraph)—leaves a pot of paint for a character to finish a drawing, in this instance supplying ink for a sea-bathing "Othello" to daub blacking on his face: perhaps the beach was Brighton, as Hepworth appears to have produced the film. But it is difficult to share her confidence that the same audience for Dyer's 1920 cartoon short, intended as filler to a longer program, would have paid extra to see an expensive foreign feature. This is not to suggest that the cultural syncretism of much of Modernist art, such as the pervasive influence of African art on Expressionism, ameliorated casual public racism: in fact, in 1912 a certain Dr. Sellman left a revealing account—clearly not pertaining to the unrediscovered sound experiment of Oskar Messter's 1907 scene from Verdi or to Blom's recent film, but perhaps to one yet missing, quite possibly an Italian film, or even the Vitagraph *Othello*—in which he was outraged at the corruption of Shakespeare in Berlin's movie theatres.[156] Rather it is to point out that what remains of the film in its most widely available print probably did not intend to duplicate the cartoon's particular take on race. At any rate, the intertitles conspicuously disregard the play's innumerable derogations, and the early scenes displaying Othello's affection for his wife outnumber even Boito's and Verdi's. Iago's motive emerges as inborn heterophobic psychosis (it is Krauss, after all), triggered by an intense desire for vengeance when, in the ceremonial opening, Othello chooses the "wrong man." (As in Cinzio, it appears to be the ill-fated Desdemona's mention of Cassio that provokes Othello's fury.) At a time when Josephine Baker was constrained to wear a mask of solubilized burnt cork and whitening as she entertained her way out of the slums of St. Louis, when Al Jolson could use it to neutralize one ethnicity through the parody of another when he put talkies on the map in *The Jazz Singer* (dir. Alan Crosland, 1927), when as late as 1934 the application of it could become part of a prologue to one of the more celebrated numbers from a 1930s Musical, *Swingtime*, in which Fred Astaire borrows not only part of a routine from Bill "Bojangles" Robinson but also his performer's mask, the makeup applied to the increasingly white-haired Othello seems comparatively restrained.

In 1920 Krauss was an opportunistic psychopath; Jannings's success made him a nemesis. A tall, burly actor who seems more like the Renaissance portraitist Hans Holbein's Henry VIII (whom he did play in Lubitsch's 1920 *Ann Boleyn*) than the romantic leading man he played so often in his early career, Jannings proved a marketable commodity whose name figures more prominently than Shakespeare's on *Othello*'s introductory title. Before 1922 was out, he held a virtual monopoly on Ufa's fallen heroes: a man of virtue, dignity, talent, or even greatness at the outset, by the film's conclusion he was either a gibbering wreck brought down by the weight circumstance or the resigned, expiring victim of Krauss's slings and arrows. One can understand the admiration the type excited in contemporaries: since by then films were no longer shot in sequence, the calibration of progressive degeneration or moral decay must have imposed tremendous demands on actors. Balázs's admiration for him was largely due to the plasticity of his features and the range that he could command in an essentially restricted Sophoclean oeuvre: he was the only thing worth watching in *Alles für Geld* (*All for Gold*, 1923), where his cruelty and meanness are offset by a tragic childlike quality that is the product of great art (the close-ups, the theorist ventures, prove that a single expression of his could accomplish what pages of literature could not).[157] René Clair, who in *Sous les Toits de Paris* (*Under the Roofs of Paris* 1929) showed himself as one of the first European filmmakers to appreciate the possibilities of amplified synchronized sound, described *Othello* in similar terms: Jannings was essentially childlike, with trembling hands and anxious eyes; Krauss is the evil clown who destroys with movement as Shakespeare's Iago destroys with words; and the film was a pictorial symphony based on a

Shakespearean theme and not a parasitic ingestion of a great work of art.[158] There are moments in the film that might explain the esteem in which contemporaries held it, as when the murderous Othello enters Desdemona's bedchamber and stands in shadow while the dawn light shining through a window seems to envelope her white-clad figure in radiance.

Of course, what we have is not the film that Clair saw. According to Robert Hamilton Ball, the film was drastically reedited for its British and American releases, for the latter by Don Bartlett, and this might explain the progressive messiness of the editing and the appalling, invented Renaissance argot interspersed with smatterings of Shakespeare. A bravura role of cumulative pathos is the least likely to survive the hatchet and the greeting-card dialogue, and Jannings did much better without intertitles as in his famously restrained performance as the Porter in Murnau's *Der Letzte Mann* (*The Last Laugh*, 1924). His Emilia, Lya de Putti, subsequently vamped him with such success in E.A. Dupont's *Variety* (1925) that Hollywood insisted on his services, and his most famous roles are probably in American films. Josef von Sternberg's *The Last Command* (1928), in which he was permitted a final redemption, and Victor Fleming's *The Way of All Flesh* (1927), in which he was not, won him the first "Best Actor" Academy Award, while Marlene Dietrich's unsurpassed imitation of Krauss in Sternberg's *The Blue Angel* (1930) allowed him to plumb depths unimaginable until the arrival of Goebbels. History owes him no reprieve. The case to be made for waiting for a complete print of *Othello* with original titles before dismissing it is really on behalf of Buchowetzki, who was only one of a sizeable number of talented Eastern Europeans whose careers foundered in the post-ParaUfaMet atmosphere of inflated Hollywood expectations: having fled the Russian Revolution, he did not live long enough to witness the fall of the Weimar Republic or to be tainted by the omnipotence of evil.

As for the rival *Othello* released in October of 1923, there is a remarkable critical consensus. Despite surpassing the narrative complexity of *The Last Laugh*, whose eschewal of intertitles it anticipates, American-born Arthur Robison's *Schatten, eine nächtliche Halluzination* (*Warning Shadows*) has long been acknowledged a masterpiece. The best surviving print, restored by the Cineteca di Bologna's *L'immagine Ritrovata*, appears to be in a near complete state, and has been released on DVD. Even so, there is no discussion of it at all in the critical literature on Shakespeare films. How, then, might one account for this strange anomaly? The answer might be the obvious one that, on its own, and given the distance of time, it has ceased be one; it is a Shakespeare film only in relation to the reception accorded it by its contemporaries, their knowledge of the principal actor's theatrical activities, and of Buchowetzki's then recently released film, without which it makes about as much sense as *Casino Royale* (dir. John Huston, 1967) does to someone unfamiliar with the early James Bond films.

Both Kracauer and Eisner commend its extraordinary use of the play of objects and their shadows, and both regard it as quintessentially Expressionist (one explaining why it found little favor in such a cultural climate since the happy ending suggested the triumph of democracy and the other why it expressed the visual style so well).[159] The basic story is that of an Alma Mahler-like wife of a count hosting a quartet of suitors who, by "playing" with her shadow, provoke her husband's jealousy. Since one, "The Lover," is on the point of living up to his appellation, the husband's mental state continues to deteriorate. A master of Chinese shadow puppeteering (and obviously a reader of E.T.A. Hoffmann) arrives and begins a performance in which he succeeds in disengaging their shadows from them, at which point—with the aid of candles, mirrors, shadows, reflections, and even theatrical curtains—the film turns into a visual essay on dimensionality and the cinema's illusionistic properties. The count instigates the wife's murder and, once his deception is umasked, the vengeful suitors murder him. Sanity returns only when the illusionist ends his "game," upon which the film's successive shedding of its visual artifices concludes with scenes of ordinary life. Retelling this story, Kracauer and Eisner provide fascinatingly different accounts to support their views. Noting that (despite Freud's disavowals) his collaborators helped script a tale with a similar theme, Pabst's *Geheimnisser Eine Seele* (*Secrets of a Soul* 1926), in which a "mentally unbalanced" protagonist achieves a cure through "quasi-psychonalaytic" means, Kracauer finds Pabst's appeals to Realism less satisfying than the "cure" effected by Robison's film.[160] Eisner treats Robison's "little illusionist," who steals the characters' shadows and reanimates them in a tale of "repressed unconscious desires," as a figure of Freud.[161] Neither notes a possible Shakespeare connection. However, those who wrote soon after the film's release did. Iris Barry, curator of the film collection at the Museum of Modern Art, mentioned it as such in passing, and in a perceptive 1927 article on Shakespeare's stagecraft J. Isaacs made a case for it as the best of Shakespeare films. As a piece of media criticism that predates the Orson Welles *War of the Worlds* radio broadcast, Isaac's theory of adaptation is well worth recounting:

> It is not uninstructive to take advantage of the bifurcation of the drama in its extremest modern forms for a technical analysis of the Shakespearian theatre. We have...the completely visual element separated out in the cinema, the completely auditory in the wireless play. Both aspects teach us something. The purely visual cinema play is one without explanatory subtitles. Perhaps the greatest film of this kind, *Warning Shadows*, with Fritz Kortner, the great Shakespearian actor, as its chief player, achieved some of its success by taking the Shakespearian Othello theme as its motive, the bodies of the actors and their groupings were the sole material of the play, and our actors visited it to get a rare opportunity of learning their craft. At the other end of the scale it has been found that of all the plays tested on the wireless Shakespeare's have been the most successful, since there is not only verbal scene painting, but verbal time-indications and lighting-effects. The progress of these two attempts at art show remarkable parallels with the development of Elizabethan drama.[162]

Isaacs's analysis may permit us to restore the film to the canon, for its relation to Shakespeare is that of thematic borrowing of the kind once studied by comparatists as *stoffgeschichte*. For students of this textual "matter," it makes sense that a Kurosawa may borrow large amounts of plot and even visual imagery from Shakespeare, that an American filmmaker of the 1950s may colloquialize the dialogue or invent his own, and that a fictional biography may conflate Shakespeare's life with that of his characters and so translate what otherwise might masquerade as literal quotation. As a field of inquiry it has been the province of philologists and historians, but has also given rise to nebulous, highly speculative arguments. Far from being vague, however, Isaacs makes the case for the inclusion of the film in the canon by fashioning an argument comparable in its rigor to Anderegg's, albeit based on medium rather than genre: an ideal Shakespeare film contains no dialogue, either as auditory track or as the intertitles of a visual track, and succeeds purely on the strength of its moving images, a media Puritanism that we might recall gains added force as a result of the disgraceful effusions in the anglicized Buchowetzki film.

The other noteworthy extant contribution to this cluster of films was Peter Paul Felner's *Der Kaufmann von Venerdig*, so riddled with borrowings from Shakespeare's sources (and elsewhere!) that it was released in the United States as *The Jew of Mestri*. The film, in fact, serves as an extreme case that well illustrates the fanciful Germanic Ur-Shakespeare approach of these years. Unlike Marlowe's play *The Jew of Malta*, which dipped into contemporary currents of anti-Semitism to ridicule the hypocrisies of Christians (it was revived on the execution of the queen's converso physician Roderigo Lopez on trumped-up charges), Shakespeare's oblique commentary on Catholic recusancy transformed the sacramental "body and blood" of Christ into the imagery of Lopez's death, his physician's knife now the executioner's blade, his extracted heart the pound of flesh, and his confiscated jewels Portia's and Nerissa's rings.[163] Ball, who dislikes *Othello* but does not regard it as anything more than clumsy filmmaking, finds *The Jew of Mestri* at times so intractable—with even characters identified in the trade papers being indistinguishable—that he suspects some editorial foul play in its anglicization.[164] Released in the United States almost three years after the German censors had passed the film in August 1923, the characters had either at the outset or in the interim been subjected to rebaptism. The opening titles proclaim that the film derives from Shakespeare's principal source, one of a Boccaccioesque series of tales told by two lovers to each other in Ser Giovanni Fiorentino's *Il pecorone*, this being the one Saturnina relates to Frate Auretto on the fourth day. The story is particularly well told and, unusually for a Shakespeare source, contains better motivation and far fewer loose ends than its revision. Giannetto, for instance, accepts the wager that he cannot successfully bed the rich and cunning widow of Belmonte, with the consequence that twice he loses the laden ships provided by his guardian Ansaldo. Only when informed by a maid (perhaps at her mistress's instigation) that his wine was drugged does he, through his own ruse, perform "the duties of marriage." Having thus assumed his matrimonial obligations and the governorship of Belmonte, he one day observes some celebrants of the feast of St. John's and recalls with a pang that it is the day of forfeiture of the pound of flesh specified by Ansaldo's contract with a Jew of Mestri (whose ten thousand ducats outfitted his last ship). The Mistress of Belmonte, posing as a magistrate from the University of Bologna, duly arrives in court to save Ansaldo's bacon, and then beguiles Giannetto of the ring. In contrast, Shakespeare's Bassanio must either frequent Venice's famed fleshpots or be a spendthrift at the start of the play. Antonio's wild risk taking has attracted the attention of numerous scholars, although none among them, as far as I know, has proposed that Shylock, rejecting Freud altogether, intends to use his cleaver to cure the merchant of his habit of uncontrollable spitting or his more dangerous amatory proclivities. Filmmaker Michael Radford does so, of course, in the most exquisite of recent (2005) Shakespeare films, a lovely and lively (if rather casket-heavy) *Merchant*, whose culminating trial scene deftly translates Shakespeare's involved criticism of legal processes into contemporary terms (Jeremy Irons, the Antonio, looks more baleful than ever when strapped into an electric chair; Al Pacino's unforgiving Shylock, forced to plead for undeserved forgiveness, does not sound like coreligionist Tubal but a strangely accented Venetian Corleone). The consequences of being neither quite here nor there are evident at the outset of Radford's film when self-explanatory images alternate with a superfluous and misleading written "documentary" discourse on Venetian anti-Semitism.[165] Similar in its treatment of the trial scene, Felner's film cannot match the visual opulence Radford draws from Titian and the Bellinis, contenting itself with an incorporation of the big public spaces: the Doge's palace, the Rialto, San Marco, and the jostling pigeons. The German Shakespeare films of the 1920s locate exoticism in its Renaissance Mecca, Venice, and worry about the uneasy mix of cultures at a moment when hordes of Scandinavians and Eastern Europeans seemed to be gravitating to Berlin.

Noting its claim that {"[t]he original Florentine tale has been slightly modified to not offend the modern standard of good taste"}, Ball surmises that good taste has nothing to do with the representation of anti-Semitism but rather with the nature of the wager (Freud's beloved caskets take the place of deflowering, as per WS). Surely, though, Shakespeare is not just a fig leaf, opines Ball. Only Giannetto is from "John of Florence," so why is Antonio/Ansaldo now Benito, Shylock Mordecai, Portia Beatrice, Jessica Rachela and Lancelot Marco, even though Lorenzo, Aragon, and Tubal have retained the names the playwright gave them?[166] Despite some plot embellishments that appear to have no textual precedents such as Rachela's betrothal to Tubal's suicidal son Elias, Bassanio's public bankruptcy, and roistering Gentiles whose refusal to honor debts precipitates the death of Mordecai's wife, the major themes remain resolutely Shakespeare's. The only debt to Ser Giovanni (whose work first appeared in English only in 1897) appears to be Henny Porten's carnality as the lady of Belmont, a greyhound-loving (if now portly) *Dame aux camellias* with an unconcealed attraction to Giannetto whose confession of penury proves aphrodisiac enough. What we may observe in the renaming and retitling of the film may be a moderating tension that imbues the mismatches of word and image with local significance. While I cannot suggest sources for the names of all the characters, one stands out. On December 24, 1920 tenor Enrico Caruso gave his final performance at the Metropolitan Opera. Having put the gramophone on the map with the first recordings to sell over a million copies, and having transformed the repertoire of a house dominated by French and German grand opera before his arrival, Caruso set aside Othello to study the part of Eléazar in Jacques Fromental Halévy's 1835 *La Juive*, revived by manager Giulio Gatti-Cassazza at his request. Despite Eugene Scribe's Marlovian libretto, Caruso intended a sympathetic portrayal of a wronged, vengeful goldsmith, and he spent time in synagogues (as Pacino was to do in preparation for Shylock) perfecting his role. Before plunging into a boiling cauldron, Eléazar's adopted daughter Rachel, *la juive* of the title, exonerates her Christian betrayer.

In the film the principal beneficiary of antiquarianism is not Ser Giovanni but the Catholic hunter, Italian-hater, and antitheatrical polemicist, Anthony Munday. Munday had started out at as a onetime seminary student in Rome, turned into (or turned out to be) an informant, and back in England stood at the scaffolds of those he betrayed to jeer at them on their way to disembowelment. He styled himself Antonius Auleus ("the Courtier"), and, as Richard Wilson reports, Francis Meres's famous reference to him as "our best plotter" was probably scornful: all the more reason, one may think, for letting Benito stay Antonio. *Der Kaufmann* follows Shakespeare in jettisoning the prologue of Saturnina's tale, which explains Giannetto's principled poverty, but commences instead with the Jessica/Rachela plot that almost certainly originated in Munday's 1580 *Zelauto, the Fountaine of Fortune*, in which the usurer (Truculento) prefers the right eyes to the suggested right arms of Strabiano and Rodolfo, and forfeits his contract when outmaneuvered in court by two attorneys, one of them, his own daughter Brisana: the plot, concluding with a homage to Euphues and the arrival of his style in England, might even have invited Marlowe's mirth.[167] The plot overtakes the film. Rachela's betrothal to Elias, ordered by Mordecai, sets it in motion: Mordecai's wife attempts to console Rachela but soon expires in the midst of derisive Christian laughter, which sets Mordecai on the path to revenge, the final straw being his daughter's willingness to convert temporarily and purloin her dowry as a means of escaping his designs. At trial he braves the hostile crowd in the grand chamber of the ducal palace, sharpening his knife in ill-concealed delight as a weak-legged Benito bears his chest and refuses Giannetto's offer to take his place. Krauss's vigorous attempt to finish him off at a single stroke fully merits its inclusion in the *Theater of Blood* prologue. He is stopped in his tracks by anomaly, for without warning the intertitles have intimated the unnamed Nerissa's presence as a law clerk, and both she and the doctor play to the assembled patriciate and to the crowd in securing Giannetto's freedom and the rings. One can only wonder whether Max Schreck, impersonating the Doge of Venice fast on the heels of his 1921 Nosferatu for Murnau, could make sense of this textual hecatomb. There is no sense of grudging mutual respect as the glances of the protagonists suggest in Radford's closing montage, for the film concludes with a double wedding that leads to noisy revelry, as a solitary Mordecai stops his ears. Neil Taylor reports that Krauss was incensed by Reinhardt's insistence that Shylock could be played empathetically only by a Jewish actor; but if Krauss had greater latitude outside the orbit of the Deutsches Theater, then the principal effect of this scene of solitary anguish would be to remind us of the inherent pathos of a character who, as Michael Anderegg reminds us, suffers a greater accumulation of causes for revenge than Shakespeare's.[168]

Again, a complete original print would be an invaluable cultural document. In Felner's film Rachela, by the mere expedient of stealing her father's money and swapping religions, gains acceptance in the larger Christian world. It was not an option available to the daughters of any Jewish spectator who may have seen the film on its release when, less than a generation later, its Mordecai played the villainous Rabbi in *Jud Süss*.

★ ★ ★

The brief efflorescence of German Shakespeare films coincided with the rise and illusory fall of the National Socialist German Workers Party whose constitution was 1920's worst April Fools' joke. By 1921 Adolf Hitler was at its helm, but after the failure of the attempted coup of November 1923, Bavarian taverns, at least, seemed safe from the imprisoned Führer. Meanwhile Ufa, as if to serve as a metaphor for the Weimar government, found itself entangled in insurmountable debt, and was compelled to enter the highly disadvantageous ParaUfaMet agreement with the major American studios in 1925. When the Nazis finally seized power in 1933, the exodus of film personnel to Hollywood, a process already under way before the 1925 agreement, accelerated.

The duplicities and subterfuges of the entire period reflect interestingly in the annals of film history. There are two versions of the significance of the German presence in Hollywood. Both Jan-Christopher Horak and Kristin Thompson agree that Hollywood would have maintained its preeminence without them, but offer somewhat different assessments of their immediate impact.[169] Moreover, Thomas Elsaesser documents two antagonistic narratives of German assimilation, the one of the 1920s in which hi-falutin' Ufa personnel arrived not merely to claim American jobs and resources, but also the plum assignments, and the later one of the 1930s of desperate refugees finding a secure second home.[170] Horak points out that, in fact, until 1927 directors were highly dispensable and that any real expatriate power in Hollywood resided with the actors: almost single-handedly Greta Garbo scrapped Buchowetzki's Hollywood career; Academy Awards to Jannings and, previously, to Murnau and his cinematographer Karl Freund for the 1927 *Sunrise*, he implies, sounded the swansong of an age of filmmaking in which language barriers were of marginal consequence. Thompson, assessing the overall impact of their presence, concludes that except for the Horror film and film noir, the long-term stylistic influence was negligible, and both she and Horak note that even at its most sizeable, the Central European presence in Hollywood never exceeded 3 percent.[171] On the other hand, as we have observed, American film distributors both influenced and made use of European production without any exchange of personnel taking place. Both Douglas Fairbanks and Luis Buñuel claimed Lang's *Der Müde Tod* (*Destiny* 1921) as an influence on their filmmaking, and Hitchcock's early training as a director took place in Ufa, whose influence persisted in his films. In Hollywood actors Pola Negri, Rudolph Valentino, Greta Garbo, Hedy Lamarr, Marlene Dietrich, Maurice Chevalier, Adolphe Menjou, and Cary Grant traded on European charm, and bequeathed a certain type of role later filled by homemade stars. Correspondingly, Hollywood's aesthetic influence on such film industries as those of Canada and Australia has been profound even though the proportion of Hollywood-trained personnel working in those industries has been even smaller.

The dichotomous perspectives on the European "invasion" seem to be encapsulated in three films of Shakespearean inspiration by expatriate directors, two of whom had by the 1930s embarked on durable Hollywood careers, Ernst (now Ernest) Lubitsch and Wilhelm (now William) Dieterle. Dieterle was a Reinhardt acting protégé, and was initially assigned to making the German versions of Warner Bros. films. Unlike Hungarian Michael Curtiz (Mihály Kertézs), who having studied his craft as an assistant to Blom at Nordisk entered the Warners' stable in 1926 and cultivated a legendary efficiency that after the coming of synch-sound won him many of the studio's big-budget projects of the 1930s and 1940s, Dieterle transferred to Hollywood only in 1934 as the Nazis consolidated their power. As admired for his ability to nurture performers as Curtiz was notorious for his brusque treatment of them, from 1936 onward he teamed up with another émigré actor, Paul Muni, to make the most famous Biopics of the period. As I have argued elsewhere, the initial surprise that Warners entrusted him with the studio's prestige project of 1935 dissipates on a closer examination of the circumstances and the studio's intent.[172] In the face of relentless Nazi harassment, Max Reinhardt revived the play with which he was most closely associated, *A Midsummer Night's Dream*, and brought it via Florence and London to the Hollywood Bowl in 1934.[173] He had himself directed a few films before the onset of World War I and must have known of the scandalous modern-dress film version of 1913 directed by the Danish writer-director team of Hanns Heinz Ewers and Stellan Rye—the latter also made the first German avant-garde film, *Der Student von Prague* (*The Student of Prague*), together with Reinhardt protégé Paul Wegener, in the same year.[174] Reinhardt might also have been familiar with the Expressionist 1925 film version directed by Hans Neumann that, if rediscovered, might even occasion a revision of the dour associations of German Expressionist films, judging by the absurdist costume designs of Erno Metzner and reports of mirthful intertitles by Alfred Henschke.[175] Its cast included ballet dancers as the fairy folk, including a "Tamara" as Oberon, alluding to the prima ballerina of the Ballets Russes, Tamara Karsavina. The film, a supposed transposition to celluloid of Reinhardt's Hollywood Bowl production (but richly supplied with the studio's emerging and established stars), made use of the most intricate designs ever created by Art Director Anton Grot, an influential reworking of Felix Mendelssohn's incidental music by Erich Wolfgang Korngold, and a troupe of fairy dancers given an ethereal presence by the then principal choreographer of the Ballets Russes, Bronislava Nijinskaya. Despite certain vicissitudes, the film remains among the most beautiful of Shakespeare films and, tellingly, all the moments of beauty are free of dialogue. The only later film to so exemplify the Hollywood studio system at work comes at a moment when that system was itself collapsing and, paradoxically, as the culmination of the post–World War II trend of rewriting and updating Shakespeare's texts. *West Side Story* (dir. Robert Wise and Jerome Robbins, 1961) set new standards for film Musicals in terms of cinematography and subject matter, just as its predecessor had done for musical scoring and set design. It uses the plot as inspiration, unabashedly bending it to refer to New York's contemporary gangland troubles and ethnic tensions, and even sparing its Juliet (Maria) in the end to create a Michelangeloesque Pietà. The jazz- and opera-inspired score, originally written for Broadway by Leonard Bernstein, is the composer's most acclaimed work of composition and the only music associated with a Shakespeare film that receives regular independent performances. The choreography integrated contemporary dance into the musical form, and dancers leaping on one of New York's streets would at times land on another. Yet just as Anton Grot's forest was decimated to make room for overhead lighting, Jerome Robbins's relentless striving to create camera movements that captured the angularity of his choreographic style led to budget overruns and his summary dismissal. The high-style-that-speaks-to-the-masses approach in which a popular genre was repackaged as Shakespeare (rather than Shakespeare's repackaging as juvenile fantasy) was nevertheless vindicated at the box office: the only film to take in more that year was Disney's *101 Dalmations*.

While some Expressionist elements may survive in *A Midsummer Night's Dream*, particularly in the production design and in the unusually vehement performances given by Mickey Rooney (Puck) and James Cagney (Bottom), Reinhardt contented himself with top billing and left much of the physical work of direction to his acolyte who understood sound (and Warner Bros.) much better. The most famous German film Dieterle directed was *Geschlecht in Fesseln: Die Sexualnot der Gefangen* (*Sex in Chains*, 1928), in which he plays a wrongly convicted man who falls in love with, and is later blackmailed by, a fellow convict. Although there is nothing even remotely as sensational in *A Midsummer Night's Dream*, there is evidence that he shot part of a prologue including Theseus's defeat of the Amazons, Hippolyta's enslavement, and intrusions by Bottom's domineering wife.[176] Hollywood, however, was in the process of implementing its most restrictive form of self-censorship up to that point, the Production Code of 1934 drafted under the authority of Will Hays and enforced by the Breen Office. It is tempting to imagine that what followed was intended by the studio from the start, for the modest box-office success of the film did not impede Dieterle's career. Warners jettisoned any material with the potential to offend even the most discriminating of viewers. Of the two authorized tie-in books, Helen

Davidson's appeared in a format designed for younger readers. The president of the Shakespeare Association of America wrote a commendatory letter and received an enthusiastic reply from Will Hays himself. Who was to know that the sweet Changeling Prince (Kenneth Anger), scampering from the arms of one jealous guardian to another, would grow up to be the enfant terrible of American independent cinema? As far as Warners was concerned, Shakespeare's play was now suitable for children of all ages.

By 1942, with war raging in Europe and Poland overrun, some of the youngsters who saw *A Midsummer Night's Dream* and who might have seen Chaplin's devastating satire of Adenoid Hynkel (a.k.a. Adolf Hitler) in *The Great Dictator* (1940) were ready for more resolutely mature fare. In a rather curious way Lubitsch, already the master of adult innuendo, seems to have been transported back to his own youth when he offered his own, equally corrosive jibe with *To Be or Not to Be* (1942). Unlike the Reinhardt-Dieterle film, Lubitsch's belongs to the small, rather distinguished group of films about theatrical companies trying to perform Shakespeare—in this case very unsuccessfully (the Nazi Colonel in charge of Warsaw, prompted by a disguised Joseph Tura into recollection of a performance by the "great actor" Joseph Tura, reveals that "we are doing to Poland what he did to Shakespeare"). Lubitsch's touch is evident from the outset when Adolf Hitler is found wandering the streets on what is clearly a studio back-lot Warsaw, hands clasped defensively in front of him. So when a narrator promises to tell us how he came to be there and invites us to Nazi headquarters, we imagine temporal continuity. It is not until Hitler, entering during the interrogation of a boy, responds to the salutes by saying "Heil Me," that a reverse-angle shot reveals a small, Reinhardt look-alike seated at a desk on the end of a theatre stage. The protests of a lanky, beak-nosed actor, Mr. Greenberg, that a "laugh is nothing to be sneezed at," prevents neither the director's tirade about Mr. Bronsky's improvisation of a line, nor his criticism of the resplendent dress sported by lead actress Maria Tura, who sweeps in and declares that she intends to wear it after her deportation to a concentration camp. Only Joseph's intervention on behalf of his wife turns Director Dobasch's attention to Hitler's makeup. Incensed, Bronsky leaves the theatre to prove his credibility on Warsaw's streets, and we discover that we are in the midst of a flashback explaining Hitler's interest in Warsaw delicatessens. Another sly joke ends the conceit once we return to the present, in which the gaping, silent assembly outside the establishment only recognizes the deception when a small girl, who obviously frequents the theatre, asks Bronsky for his autograph.

The key elements of the running gags typical of Lubitsch's mature comedies have been set up almost at the outset. Joseph Tura keeps reappearing on stage as Hamlet, trying to finish his "To be, or not to be" soliloquy without interruption. On each of the three occasions when he saunters up to the prompter's box, hears the lines, and begins reading out of a little black book, a uniformed man in the audience stands and wends his way through the audience. With each repetition he gets to read less and less of the soliloquy, and on each occasion the preceding line announcing the departure of the conferring Claudius and Polonius ("O heavy burthen"), takes on a new meaning. We soon discover that the rivalrous Maria, who finds young uniformed airmen irresistible, has instructed a fan, an aviator, to visit her dressing room on cue. Before it climaxes, the affair ends with Hitler's Luftwaffe destroying the back lot. In England, as a member of a Polish RAF squadron, the aviator attempts to send Maria the coded phrase, "To be, or not to be," but the resistance leader to whom he divulges it happens to be a traitor, whose interception turns out to be the motivation for the latter half of the film. Meanwhile, the aspiring Greenberg's principal preoccupations seem to be getting a laugh and attempting to prove to Bronsky that he has what it takes to be a lead actor by delivering a suitably modified version ("Have I not eyes?") of Shylock's protest at the Rialto, with each recitation encompassing more lines (and getting more laughs). His great moment comes when the "real" Hitler goes to the theatre in occupied Warsaw and it falls to Greenberg to distract the German troops on guard by playing a crazed saboteur, at which point he gets to deliver most of Shylock's "Rialto scene" speech to the bewildered Nazis. After many a plot twist, things appear to end happily, and Joseph Tura gets his wish to play Hamlet in London. "To be, or not to be," he begins encouragingly. He pauses. No one stirs. He relaxes slightly. A moment passes. Another young uniformed man stands in the audience and threads his way through the crowd. So ends a capsule summary, not only of Lubitsch's need for "a laugh" in his early Shakespeare films but also his riposte to purists and to the Nazis who undertook their own appropriation of Shakespeare.[177]

While Lubitsch had every reason to poke fun at his past, one in which he was typecast in stereotypical acting roles, other directors did not look back in annoyance. As late as 1945 traces of the Expressionist period are still evident in Edgar G. Ulmer's Shakespeare film *Strange Illusion* which, as was not uncommon in Ufa films, depicts psychological extremes embedded into an uncanny framing tale. No one could accuse the peripatetic, studio-hopping Moravian of consistency of style or subject matter, but his pedigree was impeccable. A set designer for Reinhardt at the Deutsches Theater, he helped import the monumental aspect of Reinhardt's style to Ufa, working on the set designs for Lang's Nibelungen films and, subsequently, on Lubitsch's *The Student Prince* (1927), Muranu's *Sunrise* (1927), and even Lang's 1931 *M*. As a director he never seemed to master some of basic principles of the Hollywood continuity style and never really transcended the more evident limitations of "B" movie budgets. The small, elite cult following he presently enjoys—numbering, one suspects, even such noted film scholars as Peter Bogdanovich, Tag Gallagher, and John Belton—is primarily due to his unique Bauhaus-like designs for a low-budget Universal Horror film, *The Black Cat* (1934), an extraordinary assortment of Yiddish films in the 1930s and, thereafter, an oeuvre of surpassing weirdness that includes an early example of the Nudie-cutie, *The Naked Venus* (under the very Danish pseudonym of Ove H. Sehested, 1958), a genre that Russ Meyer was soon to elevate into an instrument of ridicule leveled at a number of film establishments.

Ulmer's Shakespeare film is available on DVD and thus I need concentrate only on those aspects of the plot indicative of a self-parodying association of European "high culture" with unbridled depravity (as contrasted to the wholesomeness of down-home, middle-class morality). And, of course, Welles's strangers and Hitchcock's saboteurs have yet to arrive. In *Strange Illusion* the frame-tale happens to be a hallucinatory nightmare of the Caligari type which, instead of being a distillation of the past as Freud might imagine, contains lots of déjà vu moments pertaining to the future. The Hamlet figure, Paul, whose dream it is, has a rather solicitous college professor of psychology (Vincent) who, like Hamlet's Horatio, has a great deal of time and trust to devote to him, to go fishing, to rationalize dreams, and even to undertake investigations. In Paul's dream the Claudius figure, Brett Curtis, strides through a dry-ice-induced fog in silhouette, and tells his mother, Virginia, former wife of Lieutenant Governor

Cartwright, that Paul should not "waste his breath," stepping out of character to declare as ominously as Darth Vader, "I am your father [now]." As the tale proceeds we encounter a pretty blonde (Hamlet's sister, Dorothy) and a pretty brunette, his eminently sane Ophelia (Lydia), and discover that the less than sane Claudius is under the control of the insane evil doctor and, naturally, eminent psychoanalyst Dr. Mühlbach. University student Paul takes an instant dislike to the Basil Rathbone-suave Brett, but his mother's "Romeo" has little difficulty in persuading her to marry him despite her son's objections. Brett claims not to be able to drive; worse, he is so hobbled by this Achilles' heel that he is fortunate to be able to walk at all. Resentful of Paul's relentless "criminological" investigation of him, he visits the doctor at his private sanatorium, where his lip-smacking description of Dorothy as a "little beauty" provokes Mühlbach into threatening to make him a patient once more. Even so, according to Lydia, he cannot resist following her into the swimming pool where he attempts a (soon overlooked) "stranglehold." Paul manages to persuade the Butler to filch a fingerprint-laden glass Brett has handled and then goes on the offensive, becoming a "guest" at Mühlbach's facility.

It is at this point, when Paul is trapped in a Benthamite panopticon of relentless observation, that he gets to show his paces, and Ulmer—who has so far restricted himself to occasional outbreaks of noir-ish lighting and to a few of his trademark high-speed dolly shots—gets to show his. Two-way mirrors, listening devices, and a profusion of decorative objects all contribute to a riot of shadows, grids, and ominous camera angles, but undaunted Paul uses the doctor's own binoculars to discover the hiding place of crucial stashed evidence and gets to go there by secreting a note to his visiting mentor in a copy of Plato. Curtis (whose name is shared with a famed music institute and a man he murdered) is obviously something of an Aristotelian who tolerates the arts and tries to play a passage of Robert Schumann's Piano Concerto in A Minor, a clear sign of derangement since the music for the film consists almost entirely of a few threateningly rearranged snatches of the concerto. It is twice mentioned in the film, and the composer, Leo Erdody, seems aware that Schumann not only struggled with orchestration but also his sanity (the child murderer in Lang's *M*, one recalls, gives himself away by his habit of whistling a snippet of Edvard Grieg). In truly Schumannesque indecision, Curtis, now revealed to be the known killer Barrington, decides that Dorothy's offer of a car ride takes precedence over the meeting insisted on by a frantic Mühlbach. Hot on their trail the police arrest Mühlbach, however, just as Barrington brings out the romantic in Dorothy, who is coerced into a boat ride with moonlight, stars, and the mere mention of Omar Khayyam. He is about to declaim all the quatrains of the *Rubaiyat*, or worse, when Paul, Lydia, and Dorothy's beau George arrive and burst through the door of the boathouse. Barrington throws Paul to the ground and scavenges a convenient weapon from the wall beside him, but the police arrive just in time to shoot him. The supine Paul, however, is back in his dream. As the dry ice begins to run out, his father arrives, reclaims his mother, and escorts her offscreen, while Lydia suddenly appears from screen right to take Paul's arm.

It is not the last time that Shakespearean filmmakers and Freudian psychoanalysis are to have an occultation, for Oliver's *Hamlet* and *Forbidden Planet* are still to come. Had Freud lived to see *Strange Illusion* though, it might have yielded a chuckle: forget the superego's Miltonic combat with the id, forget repression, it insists—*Hamlet* was Shakespeare's nightmare. He had become Caligari, and the Caligarians had become American.

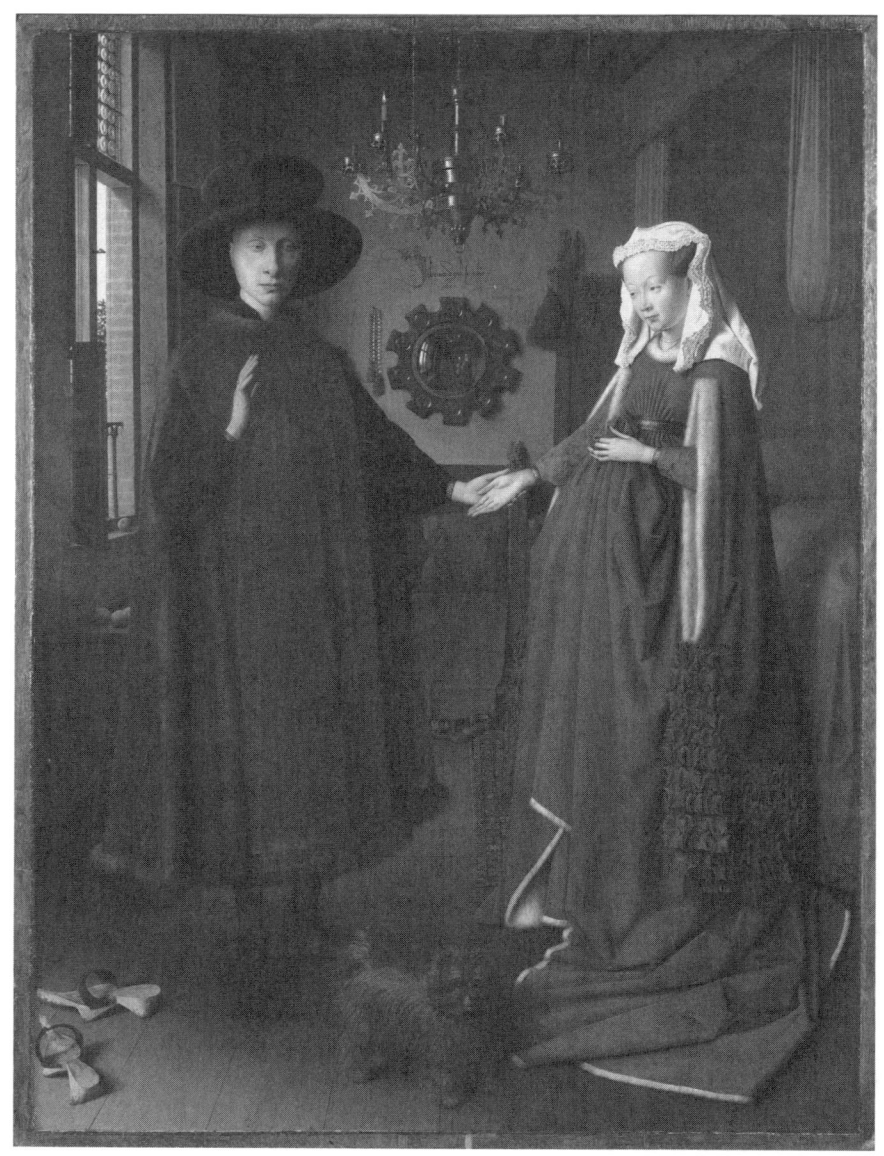

The Arnolfini Portrait. Oil on panel by Jan van Eyck, used as iconographic inspiration by Orson Welles in *Othello* (1952–1954).

Courtesy of the National Gallery, London.

CHAPTER FOUR

Genre, Style, and the Politique des Auteurs: Orson Welles versus "William Shakespeare"

In which an Irish Shakespeare creates a transnational auteur ★ A New Deal for Shakespeare ★ Perhaps not all is true ★ Macbeth and the fear of fear itself ★ Three ghosts and two chairs ★ Montage as homage ★ Sound and fury ★ A Tricontinental Othello ★ Stylish allegory, or becoming film noir ★ Reflecting on race ★ A well-placed Henriad, or the reign in Spain ★ Harridan histories in Ruiz and Welles ★ Charming Chabrol and trifling with Truffaut

When Orson Welles's Shakespeare films were first released, English-speaking critics took upon themselves roles anticipatory of Peter Greenaway's harpie Ariels, gleefully punishing a revolting Caliban on behalf of Shakespeare's Prospero. Time has modified critical sensibilities and practically overturned those judgments in favor of a consensus that would no doubt have alarmed Welles even more. Welles, curiously, has replaced the once Royal Shakespearean Olivier as the quintessential *auteur* among the persistent makers of Shakespeare films.[1] Yet those same films that have endured the slings and arrows of critical fashion defy any such easy categorization. Each of them challenged the then prevailing norms of film adaptations of literary classics, questioning notions of film genre and film style as well as the conception of *auteurism* advanced by Truffaut and the early French New Wave critics. (Welles, it should be noted, was the only American filmmaker to whom both Bazin and Truffaut devoted monographs.) Much later one of the most prominent of the nouvelle vague filmmakers, Godard, was to return to the question of Welles as Shakespearean *auteur* in his own meditation on the movement's gradual erosion, and Godard's posthumous tribute provides a fitting conclusion and point of entry into the subject of the next chapter.

Yet that tribute was hard won. The stories surrounding Welles's struggles to make these films are themselves the stuff of legend, and perhaps more than any other filmmaker, Welles demands the kind of biographical insight once described by New Critics as "intentional fallacy" and revived by New Historicists as a mechanism of cultural contextualization. Working in a host of countries in a barely voluntary exile, and thematizing his enforced internationalism to an even greater extent than many of the diasporic or transnational filmmakers Hamid

Naficy characterizes as "accented,"[2] Welles has more in common with a director such as Raoul Ruiz—a fellow devotee of Shakespeare and Cervantes—than with the individual geniuses who transcended the uniformity of the studio system and first achieved canonization in the pages of the *Cahiers du Cinéma*, the journal inspired and cofounded by Bazin and the cradle of both *auteur* criticism and a new wave of self-conscious *auteur* filmmakers. In distinction to Ruiz, transformed from a practitioner of Chile's brief experiment of Third Cinema (who fell afoul of the Pinochet regime in Chile) into a Parisian *auteur* enjoying a relatively congenial and amazingly productive exile, Welles found no stable second home. Nevertheless, the last of his completed adaptations of Shakespeare, *Chimes at Midnight*, made in a Spain still under the dictatorship of Generalissimo Franco, is in some respects the capstone of his career, his Welles-Falstaff character being a whimsical (rather than despairing) commentary on his own abandonment by the newly enthroned Hals of the still-powerful, if declining, American studios. His Icaran trajectory even encompasses a *Merchant of Venice*—again shrouded in legend, fragmentary test shots, and missing reels of celluloid—that, together with an unrealized *King Lear*, he was still struggling to finance when he died in 1985. But the story of these Shakespeare films began far more optimistically in Ireland, and it is with this "Irish connection" that we should begin if we are to appreciate the full extent of his contribution, profane and profound, to the idea of film adaptation.

National Allegory and Shakespearean History

Surely one of the most remarkable of filmed versions of a written text, not least because it translates a story barely two pages long into an intricately structured historical allegory of Italy's Fascist period, is Bernardo Bertolucci's *The Spider's Stratagem* (*La strategia del ragno*, 1970). In Jorge-Luis Borges's original sketch, which he offers as a "Theme of the Traitor and the Hero," the action could take place anywhere. So the narrator makes the arbitrary choice of early nineteenth-century Ireland: the head of a group of revolutionaries, Fergus Kilpatrick, assigns the task of discovering the informant in their midst to Alexander Nolan. At the appointed hour the leaders assemble, and Nolan offers irrefutable proof that the traitor is none other than their chief, a figure revered by those looking forward to the day of liberation. To redeem himself, Kilpatrick agrees to an elaborate charade devised by Nolan, one that would precipitate the rebellion. By incorporating premonitory scenes in *Macbeth* and *Julius Caesar*, plays Nolan was engaged in translating into Gaelic, Kilpatrick's exemplary punishment would create a double myth: he would be a martyr to the cause and the "enemy," Shakespeare, would be redeemed for Ireland by turning him into part of its own folklore. In a tragic theatrical finale, "prefiguring Lincoln's," an assassin's bullet fells Kilpatrick.

Bertolucci's traitor-hero is Athos Magnani, whose name makes reference to Roberto Rossellini's *Rome, Open City* (1945), the film that heralded Italian Neorealist filmmaking.[3] Although Rossellini had begun his career making propaganda films for Benito Mussolini's Fascist regime, *Open City*, shot even as Rome was being captured by the Allies, celebrated the heroic Partisan resistance to Fascism and made his wife, Anna Magnani, a star. In Bertolucci's film Athos leads a cell of Italian *partigiani* who plot against the local Fascist functionaries, and for the most part the narrative runs parallel to Borges's story. Where the film aspires to an added level of felicity in fashioning its governing conceit is in its substitution of Giuseppe Verdi for Shakespeare, the former occupying an equivalent place in Italian national consciousness to Shakespeare's in England. Verdi, the great adapter of Shakespeare for the lyric stage, further serves Bertolucci in drawing a more substantial historical parallel, for the composer was also an active supporter of the revolutionaries who during the Risorgimento of the 1850s and 1860s sought to unify the peninsula. Just as *Julius Caesar* and *Macbeth* provide the fodder for Ireland's historical myths in Borges's account–an act of patriotic forgery evocative of James MacPherson's (re)invention of Ossian's verses– Verdi's *Rigoletto*, an opera based on one of Victor Hugo's tales of betrayal and self-sacrifice, provides the climax of the Partisans' automythologization. Thus, in addition to furnishing the appropriate historical parallel, Verdi's opera also contributes the narrative occasion for the assassination: at the moment the tragic Fool Rigoletto recognizes the fulfillment of the curse that a betrayed father, Monterone, places on him at the start of the drama, the longed-for bullet finds its mark.

Bertolucci is by no means the only filmmaker to make a connection between the oeuvres of Verdi and Shakespeare. Indeed, I have already had occasion to dwell on Verdi's centrality to Franco Zeffirelli's Shakespeare films. Yet it was Welles who most explicitly drew attention to the connection, even mentioning the librettist's contribution to the rearrangement of Shakespeare's texts. In a 1954 talk given to an assembly of students at Oxford University, Welles defended his most recent Shakespeare adaptation with an appeal to medium specificity: "*Othello*, whether successful or not, is about as close to Shakespeare's play as was Verdi's opera. I think Verdi and Boito were perfectly entitled to change Shakespeare in adapting him to another art form; and assuming that film is an art form, I took the line that you can adapt a classic as freely and vigorously for the cinema." Cinema, adds Welles, is a visual medium, and affirms, somewhat diffidently, that he remains a master of the camera.[4] This Oxford talk is evoked and incorporated, together with a longer, filmed address given in Cambridge, Massachusetts, into a documentary that Welles made for German television, *Filming Othello* (1978), one of his last completed projects and a supplement to his earlier burlesque of the notion of documentary authenticity, *F for Fake* (1974). Yet Welles's "competition" with Verdi was no less intense than his contestation of the highbrow Shakespeare who dominated, and perhaps still dominates, the stage.

Just as *The Spider's Stratagem* carries the notion of adaptive felicity to its limit when it substitutes a polyvalent musical track for spoken "theatrical" dialogue, *Filming Othello* experiments with the retrospective genre of the film-about-the-making-of-a-film. Far from clarifying what the filmmaker and his collaborators intended, the documentary adds yet another layer of uncertainty to an already complicated textual tangle, an issue to which we will return in short order. It will suffice to note for the present that in its original version Welles's *Othello* begins with a narration derived from Shakespeare's principal source, Giraldi Cinzio, drawing attention to Shakespeare's own vigorous refashioning of his sources to the evolving needs of Elizabethan and Jacobean theatre. Welles subsequently reedited versions of the film for its European and American releases, and recycled his own negative for *Filming Othello* (as Michael Anderegg observes, the most recent restoration of the film constitutes yet another *Othello* text).[5]

The original, and in some ways most successful, *Othello*, was the version that in 1952 became the first African film (Morocco's entry) to win the Palm d'Or at Cannes. Even before the film's American release, Welles's costar, Micheál MacLiammóir, appended yet another *Othello* text, a scintillating day-by-day account of the shooting of the film under a title inspired by Iago's repeated injunction, *Put Money in Thy Purse*. In his preface Welles accepts the merciless ribbing he receives at MacLiammóir's hands with characteristically good cheer, except in a single instance when MacLiammóir's suggests that he stooped to an ethnic slur. This, Welles points out, is not among his many deficiencies.[6] That he reads with care and takes the time to refute this solitary calumny with great dignity without holding it against his Iago is also characteristic of this "wannabee" Othello who at times treated the roles he played as intensely self-critical extensions of his own personality.

Despite the impromptu nature of the question and answer session at Oxford, Welles's reference to Verdi could not have been casual: the Verdian progression from *Macbeth* to *Othello* and then to a condensation of the Falstaff plays was no mere coincidence. Indeed, it might well be supposed that, in drawing a premonitory parallel between his Shakespeare adaptations and those of Verdi, Welles must have already been toying with the idea of translating his Falstaff-centric *Five Kings* theatrical reworking of the Henriad into film. The reference also carries more than a hint that as with Shakespeare's historical cycles and Verdi's musical dramas, autobiography and national allegory inform, and in some instances even determine, the textual liberties Welles took with his source material. Considering Welles's own politics he may also have remembered that Verdi's political activism could only have taken place in an art form that popularized an already thriving medium, one whose audience had changed significantly even during the career of its first great exponent, Claudio Monteverdi, who having initially composed for the Mantuan court (where *Rigoletto* is set), concluded his long career writing music drama for a paying Venetian public. It is not, then, the international Verdi of *Aïda* and *Don Carlo* that Welles recalls, but the youthful, idealistic nationalist whose "Va pensiero" chorus of Hebrew slaves from *Nabucco* became the unofficial "hymn" of the Risorgimento, helping to unite the political aspirations of Italy's founding elite and the social aspirations of the common folk who fought the battles for liberation and unification.

Verdi's music spoke the language of national unity, as had the Tuscan Italian forged into the peninsula's literary tongue by his hero and model Giuseppe Manzoni. Welles was not a nationalist in quite the same sense, having been born a good three score and ten years too late to participate in America's (re)-unification, but from the start he seems to have been aware of the potentialities of Shakespeare as shared cultural territory. Even in amateur productions at Todd High School he tried his hand at "putting together" Shakespeare's plays and "taking them apart as best suited his purposes," but his knowledge of contemporary experimental theatre deepened immeasurably when at the end of a painting tour of Ireland the teenager managed to persuade the two affable actor-directors of the Gate Theatre (Yeats's house, and a crucible of Irish literary nationalism) to take him on as an actor.[7] Hilton Edwards, notes Anderegg, had been a member of Charles Doran's Shakespeare Company and later played at the Old Vic, while MacLiammóir had in his youth acted in Herbert Beerbohm Tree's company at His Majesty's. They introduced Welles to the two emerging strains of European avant-garde theatre, the "highly-decorative" and "concept-oriented" work of a wide assortment of Continental dramaturges, as well as the school of historical authenticity epitomized by William Poel and dramatist-producer Harley Granville-Barker who sought to recapture what they believed to be the "simplicity, speed, and intimacy of Elizabethan staging."[8] It is only in the context of Welles's apprenticeship that his remarkably modest inclusion of the conversation between the reunited trio in *Filming Othello* makes sense: with Welles taking on by turns the roles of dinner host, television reporter, and movie critic, Edwards and MacLiammóir, the former his Brabantio, contrive to persuade Welles of the deficiencies of his *Othello* and suggest ways in which it could have been improved, just as they might have to the escapee from Todd whose pretenses of adulthood they had cheerfully indulged nearly half a century earlier.

It is at Todd, also, that Welles and his athletics coach and drama teacher, Roger Hill, collaborated on an edition of some of Shakespeare's plays intended primarily as performing editions for schools and enlivened, to varying degrees, by his fluent drawings of settings and costumes. It initially bore the resonant title *Everybody's Shakespeare*, and it reveals Welles's populism as a natural reflex to the Great Depression to which he returned in the United States after his Irish sojourn, no less than an exaggerated anxiety to wrest Shakespeare from the hands of an officialdom that at times resembled a collection of Don Quixote's giants. Like much else in his later career, Welles's social conscience was immanent in his youthful enthusiasms. Commenting on his raucous return to the United States as a touring player with Katharine Cornell's company, in which he seemed to revel in Mercutio's bombast and Claudius's "swinishness," Anderegg makes the intriguing case that for Welles "Shakespeare was never far removed from Grand Guignol and melodrama...his access to Shakespeare [being] through the low forms of popular theatre...a practice consonant with a particularly American approach."[9] Certainly, Welles throughout displayed a marked propensity to throw "high" and "low" together in a manner that to the likes of Edwards and MacLiammóir would no doubt have suggested a revivification of a mummified Shakespeare, but which was just as surely a nose-thumbing calculated to raise the hackles of his stateside critics whose high class Shakespearean associations—as I have documented in previous chapters—had ample historical precedent.

If taking the classics to the masses began as something of a vocation, it turned out under Roosevelt's administration and the latter's Federal Theatre Project to be a mission with important consequences for media theory, on the one hand, and for his own political future on the other. In fact, by the end of the 1930s, after his widely heralded theatrical production of a Haitian "Voodoo *Macbeth*" with an all-black cast of over a hundred actors, a *Julius Caesar* (subtitled, in a grand American tradition, *The Fall of a Dictator*) that borrowed from the lighting at the Nazi Nuremberg Rally and costumes from Italian Fascists (the sadistic killing of Cinna the Poet by Mussolini's Blackshirts provoked a minor furor), and his eventual radio production of a notorious 1938 *War of the Worlds* adaptation that led to the first mass panic of the golden age of network radio, Welles attained the perihelion of his public visibility. But even as he soared sunward, his well-meaning but unavoidably dilettantish involvement in politics soon softened the wax of his wings. Welles supported Roosevelt, campaigned for his policies, and, as papers preserved at Indiana University's Lilly Library attest, crafted speeches in support of the ill-fated Dewey when an underdog, post-Hiroshima Truman faced his first election. While J. Edgar Hoover's FBI took almost as active an interest in Welles as it did in such openly pro-Soviet associates as Paul Robeson, it is only after the Truman administration ended that an investigation begun in 1941 was curtailed. Even as this investigation was under way, Welles was a frequent visitor to the White House, and might have regarded himself as enjoying presidential favor when he was dispatched as something of a cultural ambassador to make a Pan-American film, the unfinished *It's All True*, promoted by Nelson Rockefeller, FDR's interventionist head of the bureau that acted as coordinator of Inter-American Affairs (CIAA). At first tolerant of the emerging leftist artistic avant-garde of the late 1920s, by 1934 Rockefeller's attitudes had hardened sufficiently for him to halt and later demolish Diego Rivera's mural for New York's Rockefeller Center when the artist refused to suppress Lenin's prominently displayed head. It was as a trustee of the MoMA, to which his family had contributed lavishly, that he transformed the museum's Film Division into an instrument of film propaganda, of which Luis Buñuel (most prominently) proved beneficiary and, when Rockefeller's campaign against Communism intensified, victim.[10] In the interim, Welles proved to be another casualty of the CIAA's efforts to monitor American film production.

Perhaps it was his close association with Roosevelt that had won Welles a unique contract at RKO, of which the Rockefellers were major shareholders. Soon after he finished shooting *The Magnificent Ambersons* (1942), Welles attempted to fulfill the terms of his three-film contract with a "quickie" thriller, *Journey into Fear* (1943), whose direction he delegated to Norman Foster (who was also to assist on Welles's other projects). His haste was the result of a CIAA undertaking that had originated with Brazil's minister of propaganda, who had approached Rockefeller with the idea that a Pan-American propaganda film be produced as a fillip to Roosevelt's Good Neighbor policy; such a film would no doubt have also legitimated Getulio Vargas's dictatorship that was intent on presenting an "advanced," Europeanized Brazil to the world.[11] Welles needed little prompting, agreed to forego a salary, and drastically modified his proposed four-part *It's All True* to accommodate the exigencies of the moment, arriving in Brazil just in time to witness extraordinary popular demonstrations in support of a band of illiterate, dark-skinned fishermen.[12] To his chagrin, Vargas had to join in the acclaim and promise to redress the inequities brought to light by these *jangadeiros* who had voyaged from the impoverished Northeast across a thousand miles of treacherous seas on flimsy rafts to voice the collective grievances of Brazil's fishermen. Welles's efforts to commemorate their heroic voyage and to film a quasi-anthropological study of the annual carnival in Rio de Janeiro soon drew the frantic protests of the Brazilian government, as reported by informants to the studio, which, failing to curb Welles, halted the film and ejected the remnant of his Mercury Players from the RKO lot.

In later television interviews included as supplements to the 1993 laser-disc restoration of the surviving footage, Welles suggested that the studio's retaliation resulted from his portrayal of African American heroes (even in episodes filmed in different countries, he was clearly interested in the African heritage of the Americas and in indigenous cultural practices). Despite his notorious unreliability as a subject of interviews, and the tragedy of one of the *jangadeiros* drowning during Welles's attempt to reenact the triumphant conclusion of their exploit for the camera, he may have been close to the mark in this instance. As Peter Decherny explains it, "[T]he notion of Welles filming in the slums of Rio and the development of story lines about *mestizos* or mixed-race Brazilians worried both Rockefeller officials at CIAA and studio heads at RKO. With the acquiescence of the Motion Picture Association of the Americas, Rockefeller pulled out of the project."[13] The film was confiscated and thought destroyed in its entirety; decades later mislabeled cans of films were found to contain some of the Brazilian and Mexican footage.

Hollywood's fêted wunderkind was now its ill-fated bad boy, and Welles retreated into various radio activities and political speechmaking (on behalf of Roosevelt) after a futile attempt to save *Ambersons* from drastic abridgement and a maudlin ending reshot by a studio hack. It was only after the war ended that he returned to filmmaking with a topical tribute to Hitchcock, *The Stranger* (1945), which costarred Edward G. Robinson (relentlessly hunting a naturalized Nazi, played by Welles, in the film, but soon destined to fall prey to the House Un-American Activities Committee and the studio practice of blacklisting politically vulnerable personnel).[14] The modest success of this low-budget detective thriller did not presage a return to studio consistency. After the consecutive failures of his mammoth theatre Musical based on Jules Verne's *Around the World in Eighty Days* and his Baroque film noir *The Lady from Shanghai* (both 1946), Welles found himself ostracized not for his politics but because he was now perceived as a financial liability. In 1947 he staged a revised version of the *Voodoo Macbeth*, returning it to Darkest Scotland, at the Utah Shakespeare Festival, and managed to secure an agreement with one of Hollywood's B-film studios, Republic, to shoot a $700,000 version of his Utah production.

Much has been made of the supposed clumsiness of the film, its hasty shooting schedule, the occasional incomprehensibility of its Highland Shakespeare dialect (rendered neither credible nor authentic by Welles's experiment in prerecording and redubbing after shooting), and the outlandishness of the characters' costumes that seem more Modernist in the tradition of Continental theatre than primitive à la Holinshed.[15] Arthur Lindley points out perceptively that the film invites ahistorical readings precisely by orchestrating stylistic elements that work against cinema's powers of illusion: "[A] castle of dripping, subterranean rocks whose layout persistently refuses to make literal sense; the self-reflexivity that regularly calls our attention to the soundstage and the diorama against which Banquo's murderers are posed; the use of simultaneous or abstract staging which allows Macbeth, for example, to change scenes by crossing from one part of the set to another."[16] Lindley adds that André Bazin did not fail to note that Jean Cocteau was immediately entranced by its hallucinatory mix of genres;[17] but contemporary English-speaking critics preferred to attribute the Surrealism of its visual incongruities to incompetence. More charitably Robert Willson calls his chapter on *Macbeth* in *Shakespeare in Hollywood* "Shakespeare on Poverty Row," suggesting that it was "a low budget experiment by Hollywood's only budding auteur."[18] In one of the early histories of Shakespeare on film, Roger Manvell had also commented on the restricted budget, but for him Welles's principal deficiencies were the intrusion of lines from other plays, "weak playing" despite the protagonist's larger-than-life presence, and Welles's prefatory voice-over invention of a battle between paganism and Christianity having "no parallel in the text."[19] Naremore observes that Welles's occult fashioning of a clay "voodoo doll" of Macbeth had some precedent in Holinshed, but still finds *Macbeth* "a decidedly minor film in Welles's canon," one whose augmentation of "melodramatic intensity" through a return to "the heart of darkness" comes at the price of losing Shakespeare's incisive commentary on the intrigues of the Jacobean court.[20]

It is Welles's apparent literalism, his persistent penchant for the primitive, and his seeming disregard for Shakespeare's own slippery sense of historical parallax that I suspect contain one of the keys to understanding his approach to a Shakespeare text with which he had been associated for much of his theatrical career. Sensitive as he was to Shakespeare's theatrical dispositions (as was evident as early as *Everybody's Shakespeare*), and alert enough to Shakespeare's sources to render Naremore's suggestion worthy of sustained consideration, Welles's infusion of Shakespeare's language into Republic's "B" Westerns and Universal's aestheticized "B" Horror films caught critics of the What-can-Hollywood-do-for-Shakespeare? School unawares. At the same time, it set a precedent for Modernist archaism in Shakespearean adaptation that would later resurface in the mise en scène of directors as dissimilar as Peter Brook and Raoul Ruiz. It did so, moreover, by providing an alternative Modernism to the aggressive, antiestablishment assault on Shakespeare's text that had once made Jarry's *Ubu roi* such a succès de scandale. A third "unsettling" Wellesian innovation in adapting Shakespeare was to return to a question that had preoccupied critics from A.C. Bradley onward, although in doing so it revolted against *Macbeth*'s sleek, formfitting "Great Tragedy" associations. Bradley's psychological reading of characterization stemmed from a desire to apprehend the dramatic potentialities of Shakespeare's verse and to approach the plays as if one were learning to act all the parts (Welles almost did, furnishing alternative readings of both Othello's and Iago's lines in *Filming Othello*, and dubbing various characters' lines in *Macbeth* and *Chimes at Midnight*). Whereas Bradley argues that "there is no sign whatever in the play that Shakespeare meant the actions of Macbeth to be forced on him by an external power, whether that of the Witches, or of their 'masters,' or of Hecate...[their] prophecies...are presented simply as dangerous circumstances with which Macbeth has to deal," Welles permits them to intercede—no fewer than seven times—in a manner that clearly has a determinative function on his actions and those of his willingly seduced spouse.[21] In fact, Shakespeare criticism has taken a determined turn away from Bradley's psychologism, and the film remarkably anticipates Richard Marienstras, Alvin Kernan, and a number of New Historicists who have seen in *Macbeth* the playwright's most explicit engagement with the preoccupations of his patron, James, who before declaring the Lord Chamberlain's Men his own in 1603, had published diverse tracts on demonology as well as kingship.[22] (Eschewing the overcomplexity of lengthy history lessons, Welles, like Polanski and Kurosawa, omits the concluding pageantry tribute to James as the last in the line of kings descended from Banquo, but in an earlier sequence he does recycle the scene's most prominent prop, a reflecting glass, so enabling him to multiply his authorial address to the spectator, a matter to which we will return in discussing *Othello*.)[23]

In drawing attention to the element of the supernatural, and in emphasizing power as a form of thuggery fought over by equally ruthless forces of good and evil, Welles also drew out interlinked and antithetical themes that later directors have conveniently disengaged in search of apt conceits: ever afterward *Macbeth* seemed to have conformed bimodally to the conventions of either the Horror film per se or to the most current version of the Gangster epic, disregarding the conflict between the action of human will and agency in a rational, if illegitimate and self-damning pursuit of power, and the irresistible intervention of supernatural, irrational, or instinctive forces.[24] Characteristically, Welles attempts to preserve both strands by paring the text down to its essence and by invoking a multiplicity of visual styles and genres that approximate (for modern, cinema-literate audiences) the theatrical shock-effects that occasioned comment even among the play's early spectators. So, for instance, Anthony Davies has been struck by Welles's conflation of elements of the Horror film with the style of film noir under the dominant trope of a nightmarish visual hallucination.[25] Michael Anderegg, on the other hand, has pointed out that, in addition to Welles's gratuitous equestrianism (horses are integral to Kurosawa's *jidai-geki* as weathervanes of evil), the mists and dew-drenched crags of Welles's set are borrowed, quite literally, from Republic's "B" Westerns.[26]

Naremore and Anderegg are among the most influential writers to devote prolonged attention to Welles's Shakespeare, so the sense they convey of an *auteur* arbitrarily fitting the playwright's words to his own purposes perhaps deserves some qualification. There is ample evidence, of course, that Shakespeare and his company emended their playtexts to fit certain occasions: the second, "corrected" quarto of *Hamlet* is twice as long as could have been played on the stage, the lines that contributed the half used in any performance being tailored to the occasion; and it is seems very likely that *Richard II*, suitably modified, served as political propaganda on the eve of the Essex rebellion, a defiance of authority that almost had the players cashiered.[27] In the case of Welles, one could just as easily argue that the filmmaker shared with the audience-minded Lord Chamberlain's (and subsequently king's) Men the desire to appeal to patrons high or low, updated by Welles into a populist impulse to diminish the distancing effect of Shakespeare's heightened (and now temporally far removed) idiom and to bring to light occluded dimensions of his principal themes, thereby reinvigorating those features of the plays that would have struck their original audiences. Adaptation, thus, is for Welles an imperative for renovation of the plays, not a self-serving aesthetic betrayal.

Welles's film, it should also be noted, suffered the misfortune of appearing just before Olivier's knighthood (at the tender age of forty) and his youthful, conventionally Freudian *Hamlet*.[28] *Life* magazine, whose editors seemed to have borne an unusually malevolent animus toward Welles, put Olivier on their cover and heaped praises on his film while seizing every opportunity to ridicule Welles's pretensions.[29] In *Filming Othello*, Welles even makes the claim that he withdrew *Macbeth* from competition at the Venice Film Festival (won that year by *Hamlet*) at the request of the U.S. State Department. In the wake of the turbulence that Welles's vociferous disgruntlement added to the troubled Venetian waters, *Macbeth* and the reputation of its author capsized, obscuring the fact that the film is a richly textured collage of visual and musical influences extending far beyond Welles's competitive emulation of Verdi and Boito. An essay on the possibilities of rendering filmed theatre as visual narrative, a midcentury evocation of a number of currents of European theatrical Modernism, and a challenging precursor of the cycle of pop-Shakespeare genre films soon to take hold in Hollywood (which, in so doing, virtually banished Shakespeare's dialogue from mainstream American cinema), *Macbeth* is a far more cinematically adept and technically informed work than its critics have allowed, and arguably the most underappreciated of Welles's Shakespeare films.

There was perhaps a further irony in the damning comparisons of Welles's with Olivier's films. Olivier's propensity for deep focus compositions owes a readily discernible debt to Welles's popularization of the effect with *Citizen Kane*, and in many respects *Hamlet* observes the rules of screen Realism—such as the use of normal lenses, naturalistic lighting, and "real" locations—prescribed by the selfsame André Bazin who had extolled Welles's use of depth of field compositions in *Kane* as the summit of American film Realism. In contrast, with the possible exception of the illusion of an amalgam of professional and nonprofessional actors giving unstudied performances, *Macbeth* is far less observant of the dicta of a critic who remained a supporter of Welles's later films and whose (not uniformly favorable) remarks about Welles's next Shakespearean opus he quotes at some length in *Filming Othello*. By the same token, *Macbeth* anticipates even Olivier's better-known formal innovations, such as the latter's representation of inner thought by switching from spoken lines to voice-over in Hamlet's "To be or not to be" soliloquy. Welles dubbed the voices of a number of the characters, a technique stemming less from necessity than conscious intent (much later Peter Greenaway, another director similarly obsessed with issues of authorship, also has his Prospero voice other character's lines from *The Tempest*). Yet it is not the implications of authorial intervention alone that dictate Welles's treatment of dialogue, as is evident with his doubling of voices at the point Lady Macbeth takes over as the dominant partner in Macbeth's ascent to the throne. The technique effectively underlines Welles's contention that those predisposed to evil can effect its triumph only through collaborative action. This scene is introduced by the immediate fulfillment of the Weird Sisters' initial prophecy when the chain of office is torn from the captive Cawdor's neck and bestowed on Macbeth who barely has time to digest news of his elevation before night falls.[30] As we see a firelit medium close-up of him seated in profile, we hear his secret thoughts expressed in voice-over: "If chance will have me king, why chance may crown me." He then begins to speak aloud to a scribe, dictating a letter to his "dearest partner of greatness," but at the line "that thou mightst not lose the dues of rejoicing, being ignorant of," Lady Macbeth's voice is conjoined to his: "what greatness is promised thee." As his voice fades, hers augments. "Near to thy heart," we hear her say, and the shot rapidly dissolves from his face to a more distant framing of her on her bed, reading the letter, and speaking the last words of the line "and farewell." The soliloquy that follows, "Come, you spirits that tend on mortal thoughts," begins in a voice-over as she lies in reverie. When she arrives at the lines generally read as a disavowal of maternal instinct, we can associate the earlier imagery of gender perversion: slightly rearranged, the forked staves of the Weird Sisters and the cross-and-circle surmounted staff of the Holy Father could form the traditional symbols for "male" and "female."[31] During the course of the speech she rises and approaches a casement. Her invocation ends in a way unthinkable for the dignified Olivier as the threatening clouds dissolve into high-angled shots of Macbeth riding frantically to his domain to the accompaniment of the scurrying B-Western music obligingly supplied by one of the great composers of Modernist film scores, Jacques Ibert.

This unusual affinity for contrasting visual styles and genres can perhaps best be explained by Welles's unorthodox cinematic background. In his introduction to Jean-Luc Godard's early critical writing, Richard Roud points out that Welles is the first canonical American filmmaker not to have acquired his skills through a studio apprenticeship.[32] He prepared himself for *Citizen Kane* by repeatedly screening the then accepted classics of cinema; he unhesitatingly described himself as a cineaste and often professed his admiration for John Ford, Robert Flaherty and, more surprisingly, the filmmaker-theorist whose Formalism in large part occasioned Bazin's defense of screen Realism, Sergei Eisenstein. But the list of influences Welles digested does not end there. Despite a rather hasty self-schooling in cinema, he was a polymath, a restless and relentless innovator in theatre and radio, and erudite to a degree that few of the "film school" directors who have followed him have been. In addition to bearing traces of Verdi, Boito, Prokofiev, and Eisenstein, Welles's films proved international from outset, drawing from a wide assortment of sources but especially from the visual styles carried to Hollywood by the expatriates from Ufa. *Macbeth*'s visual style, no less than those of the rather different *Mr. Arkadin* (1955) and *The Trial* (1962), evokes various phases of German Expressionism. His next Shakespearean opus *Othello*, like the other middle-period films such as *Lady from Shanghai* and *Touch of Evil*, hews closer to the kinds of films noir beloved of Fritz Lang, another *Cahiers* cause célèbre among underappreciated Hollywood *auteurs*. *Chimes* not only shares a discursive terrain with the *nouvelle vague* filmmakers Truffaut and Chabrol, but also from the sharply etched naturalism of Dürer's engravings and the unflinching immediacy and humanist sentimentality of such Italian Neorealist films as Vittorio De Sica's 1952 *Umberto D*, a film greatly beloved of Bazin.

It seems astonishing that such a mélange of borrowings could, like his elaborate lighting effects, illuminate and contextualize a text as old as the First Folio; yet any simple refutation of Welles's approach crumbles on more considered reflection. Perhaps a comparative approach to the filming of one scene might serve to underline Welles's instinctive feel for theatrical history. In his description of some performances he saw early in 1611 at the Globe, Simon Forman seemed struck by the plot twists and moralizing of *The Winter's Tale* ("beware of trusting feigned beggars or fawninge fellous" he writes of Autolycus), and found the intricacies of *Cymbeline* heavy going, breaking off the summary abruptly after the climatic moment of rediscovery. But the staging of *Macbeth* impressed him. The "3 women feiries or Nimphes" actually stand before the mounted "Mackbeth and Bancko" to voice their prophecies. He almost forgets Lady Macbeth's sleepwalking scene, including it and the physician's reaction as an afterthought, and he omits to mention the dagger (which we must thus presume was purely "of the mind," unlike the conspicuous dagger and the wire on which it is suspended in the Vitagraph *Macbeth* of 1908, or Polanski's levitating pre-Jedi dagger). However, the scene to which Forman devotes the greatest attention is that in which Banquo's ghost responds to Macbeth's toast by joining his feast. "The next night, beinge at supper with his noble men whom he had bid to a feaste to the which also Banco should have com, he began to speak of Noble Banco, and to wish that he wer ther. And as he thus did, standing up to drink a Carouse to him, the ghoste of Banco came and sate down in his cheier behind him. And he turninge About to sit down Again sawe the ghost of Banco, which fronted him, so that he fell into a great passion of fear and fury, Utterynge many wordes about his murder, by which, when they hard that Banco was Murdered they Suspected Mackbet."[33]

Predictably, it is this very scene that reveals the most about the dramatic impulses that inform the best-known screen interpretations of the play. Just as the meticulous planner Hitchcock is in some respects Welles's antithesis as a filmmaker in his rejection of chance and the inspiration of the moment, Akira Kurosawa is Welles's opposite in other respects. Kurosawa was as addicted to telephoto lenses as Welles was to the wide-angle lenses that facilitated deep focus compositions; for large-scale exterior scenes Kurosawa preferred the use of multiple cameras so that even in crowds he could cut-in to details of the action without any visual ambiguity, whereas Welles resolutely shot with one and was unafraid of overlapping dialogue and having characters face away from the camera when speaking. Their versions of *Macbeth*, although released only a few years apart are, intensely dissimilar, despite their shared concern with attaining a nuanced ambience by creating the appropriate historical parallax. Kurosawa's choice was to abandon Shakespeare's dialogue and to set the action in the late fourteenth or early fifteenth century, making reference to a theatrical form that had already achieved its high point by that time. If any Japanese viewer misses the references to Noh drama of the Mugen style (i.e., incorporating fantasy or supernatural elements), then the scene of the apparition of the assassinated Banquo character, Miki, should leave few doubts about Kurosawa's points of reference.[34] The most obvious emphasizes a parallel between scenes in Shakespeare when Kurosawa actually incorporates a version of Hamlet's Mouse Trap into *Komonosujo* (this may also illustrate one of the dangers of Shakespearean overimmersion: in his *Macbeth,* Welles has a tendency to drift into *King Lear* even in the dialogue). On declaring his intention to announce Miki as his heir at an impending banquet, Washizu is startled by his consort's revelation that she is pregnant.[35] There is an abrupt cut to Washizu's old horse running wild in the courtyard of the North Castle that Washizu granted to Miki, whose son warns him to heed the ill portent. Later, after Miki's assassination, his horse gallops into the courtyard during a veteran Noh performer's Kyogen dance chant whose words, rendered in the archaic language traditional to Mugen, refer to treachery and the downfall of murderers just as the courtiers begin to speculate about Miki's absence. An incensed Washizu halts the performance, but as he kneels on his mat in contemplation, the camera tracks in toward his face that suddenly assumes an anxious expression. At this point the camera tracks back rapidly and Washizu drops his sake cup just as Miki's white, immobile ghost (again presented in the form of a Noh mask, in a spectral superimposition) comes into view on the right of the frame. The terrified Washizu scurries across the floor directly in front of the shocked courtiers, but Asaji explains that he has imbibed too freely. Still troubled, he wanders back to his original seated position. The reframing pan no longer includes the immobile ghost in the expected spot, and Washizu appears to regain his composure. But as often happens in Kurosawa's films, at the very moment an active character achieves complete stillness, the camera begins to move, in this instance tracking in toward Washizu so that it can register his stark expression on seeing the ghost, now standing in a different spot, once more. He loses self-control and pulls out his sword to challenge it, and Lady Asaji has to dismiss the courtiers hurriedly before reproving him.

In transforming the play into the formal patterns of Noh drama, Kurosawa combines and eliminates characters as Welles had done; even Macduff proves dispensable. In contrast, Roman Polanski seems to switch attention to Macduff at the point of Duncan's murder, his defection being a strategy of giving added prominence to the shocking rape and murder of his household (commentators, noting the screams and pleadings of Lady Macduff, have often drawn parallels between this scene and the brutal real-life murder of Polanski's own wife by the Manson gang not long previously).[36] In addition to the extreme violence, both seen and suggested by the soundtrack, all the special effects and plot devices conventional to the post-Hammer Horror film, even those only hinted at by Shakespeare's imagery (dreams, hallucinations, grimly authentic bearbaitings, and still-seeing severed heads) are present to an even more oppressive degree than in Welles's film. Banquo's death results from expending his only arrow on the horse of Fleance's pursuer, as a result of which he allows a murderer to sever his spine with an axe. A jarring cut return us to the banquet in progress in Macbeth's castle, where the murderers presently arrive with their mixed news. A more composed Macbeth than Welles's rejoins the company at this point, but when he is invited to sit down there is a point-of-view shot to the table where a silver-haired, brown-robed figure sits in the place indicated. There is a rapid zoom in on Macbeth's startled expression, and a cut to the reverse shot in which the camera zooms in slowly on the seated figure, at which point we begin to hear a low musical rumble. When the figure is near enough to be framed in close-up it spins around, revealing Banquo's livid features. Macbeth, like Washizu before him, drops his cup and stammers in obvious disbelief. The quick cut back to his point-of-view shot then reveals a Banquo smeared with blood. Even as Lady Macbeth admonishes him, the gory figure rises, and Macbeth begins to back away from the ghost who appears to be borne on a gust of wind. Macbeth crumples onto the stone floor, and the advancing ghost, now bare-chested as Cawdor had been at his death, has a hunting falcon perched on his left arm, its wings aflutter. When Lady Macbeth finally makes the cowering Macbeth sit up, the reverse-angle shot (from their perspective) reveals a gallery of standing and now silent celebrants, frozen in disbelief, with no sign of Banquo's ghost.

While Polanski's is more self-evidently the scene described by Forman than Kurosawa's, it is Welles's interpretation that most accurately re-creates the texture of the original through cinematic means. This is not to say that Welles does not take broad interpretive liberties. Unlike Polanski's antiheroic Macbeth who, in a world governed by occult forces, gains stature in defying all the powers ranged against him, Welles plays him as a coward incapable of resisting the temptations of evil, one who begins to sweat (i.e., decompose) even before his murder of Duncan, and who is reduced to a state of abject terror shortly thereafter. In the scene in question, Polanski remains true to the Horror film convention of presenting the action from the monster's or aggressor's eyes: it is in motion that the ghost horrifies. Welles's virtuoso use of point-of-view shots to transform a seated ghost into an object of spectral terror thus remains technically instructive. Banquo is himself dispatched quickly, a silhouette into which daggers are plunged as his out-of-frame voice urges his son to flee. Welles, playing a Macbeth given to violent contrasts of mood, explodes into rage when informed of Fleance's escape. As he then stumbles through a system of caverns toward the banquet hall we hear a voice-over dialogue between him and Banquo, a sonic flashback interspersed with Macbeth's heavy, echoing tread. As the stricken Macbeth pauses by a streaming cataract, Banquo has the last word in the imagined exchange: "I will not fail your feast." It is thus a fear-exhausted Macbeth who bids the guests, who stand on his arrival, be seated: "You know your own degrees." As he sits at the head of the table, offers a perfunctory toast, and drains his cup, Lady Macbeth looks at him anxiously. At her instigation he offers a more formal toast and raises his cup once more with his left hand, casting a heavy shadow on his face as his words trail off: "I drink to our good friend Banquo, whom we miss. Would he were here." At this point Ibert's ominous music underlines his sudden change of expression, one clearly resulting from seeing further than the camera (a point-of-view shot shows the courtiers, arranged in the bilateral symmetry to which Eisenstein was addicted, lower their cups). Lady Macbeth looks at him anxiously as the left side of his face is masked by shadow. As he raises his left hand to indicate the source of his alarm, the silhouette of his index finger advances in an effect eerily reminiscent of the vampire's advancing shadow in Murnau's *Nosferatu*. When we now cut to Macbeth's point of view, however, the courtiers have vanished from their seats, and it is the seated Banquo who faces us. The ghost nods his head, Lady Macbeth looks to the right (where her husband sits), and then follows his line of sight where, once more, we see an empty chair. The music returns in jagged spurts even as she tries to reassure the stone-faced assembly. On reaching his side she upbraids him, but he continues to stare at the empty chair. When she exclaims "this is the air-borne dagger that you said led you to Duncan," he turns his head and, in a reprise of the "dagger of the mind" effect, a racking focus shot brings a hoary image of Duncan into view. Transmuting fear into rage, the usurper staggers toward Banquo's seat and overturns the table so that it seems to fall toward the spot where Banquo would have been seated, now occupied by the camera. By the time Macbeth regains his seat, the cuts back and forth from various individuals reveal their growing realization of his guilt.

In Single Combat: Eisenstein, Welles, and Shakespeare

If Welles's "rediscovery" of Shakespeare's dramaturgy might actually be the accidental result of his sensitivity to the implications of the dialogue (and many of his own line readings, such as "make the green one red," show a consummate command of the verse), then his allusions to Eisenstein in his editing and in such details of mise en scène as symmetrical compositions, the overlapping of profiles of speaking characters, and geometrical phalanxes of seated guests and lance-bearing soldiers, seem far more deliberate. As late as 1958, Welles opined that, after Ford, Eisenstein had been the greatest influence on his filmmaking, although when reminded of his remarks by Peter Bogdanovich, one of the Hollywood *auteurs* to emerge in the 1970s, he was quick to add Hawks, Walsh, Lang, Lubitsch, Murnau, Clair, and ("most of all") Renoir—in effect, the approved *Cahiers* list of *auteurs* who had made films in Hollywood.[37] Moreover, in the case of Eisenstein, his allusions seem more like conscious attempts to outdo the original than to indulge in the extended quotation typical of the *homage*-obsessed *auteurs*. For instance, early in the film, Macbeth's reunion with his wife following her invocation of the spirits takes place in a succession of misty shots showing him riding through a wild landscape. The shots are joined by dissolves rather than the simpler straight cuts favored by Eisenstein. The sequence culminates in a fog-shrouded shot in which a drumbeat fades in, after which there is an abrupt cut to two drummers who, apart from their archaic Scottish costuming, could have been enlisted from the *Voodoo Macbeth*. This is followed by an establishing shot of pigs dispersing upon the arrival of the mounted retinue escorting the old Thane of Cawdor (who remains suspended between two horses). A low angle shot then shows a grim Holy Father, hands clasped, looming above as he strides past the camera. Still adhering to the rhythms of the drumbeats, a high-angle shot in deep focus (with the executioner's blade in the foreground) reveals the old Thane being led up a hillock to his execution. A group of shots taken at steep angles alternating between high and low then show the Holy Father approach and stand beside the executioner's block, his cross-surmounted staff bisecting the frame. It is at this point that we cut to Macbeth riding in and leaping from his horse and throwing the reins into the hands of a waiting groom.

Another cut on the beat reveals the Thane being readied, after which we return to Macbeth striding into a courtyard at the rear of which a corpse dangles on a gibbet. The camera pans quickly to reveal Lady Macbeth in the right foreground, and on reaching her he kisses her forcefully as the groom leads away the horse in the middle ground between the amorous couple and the burdened gallows. A cut to a characteristically Eisensteinian diagonal of poised soldiers reveals the positions of the drummers and the Holy Father whose shadows fall ominously on the walls. In a visual strategy that was already evident in *Citizen Kane*, but here used more portentously (as it is once again at the point Lady Macbeth questions her husband's manhood when he hesitates to assassinate Duncan), the fast-paced montage that follows uses the camera's position to indicate the characters' power relations. The regal Holy Father offers a perfunctory blessing, the Thane's head is mounted on the stone block, and the former moves his staff back to make way for the executioner's descending blade, at which point there is a shock cut to a drummer striking his last beat. Another cut then returns us to Lady Macbeth and her husband, to whom she says in sultry tones and chronometric precision: "Great Glamis; worthy Cawdor." The extreme mise en scène disguises the precise orchestration of the elements, including the use of the soundtrack, and conforms precisely to the principles of that development of metric montage Eisenstein described as "rhythmic montage."[38] Kenneth Rothwell notes the violent contrasts in critical appreciation of the film, but Cocteau's declaration that "no shot is left to chance" today seems much closer to the mark than the bewilderment of then influential critic of the *New York Times*, Bosley Crowther, who only saw "half-mad zealots in a Black Mass."[39]

That in attempting to conjure Shakespeare's own lightly sketched historical periods Welles would turn to Eisenstein can no longer seem arbitrary: recent translations help confirm that the Latvian Soviet director regarded the playwright as an historical turning point.[40] In a late (1940) article on "The Problems of the Soviet Historical Film," Eisenstein contends that, unlike history textbooks, films teach history not through generalization but through vivid particularity and by conveying a sense of place and time, a connection to an epoch through which there must exist meaning for the present.[41] Between the few years in which *Twelfth Night, Hamlet, Lear,* and *Macbeth* appeared, Giordano Bruno was burned at the stake and Boris Godunov's reign came to an end, he observes. In this same essay he also outlines how Shakespeare condensed battle scenes into a succession of single combats, the best example being the last act of *Macbeth*: this narrative strategy is clearly the model for both the Odessa Steps massacre from *The Battleship Potemkin* (where we are introduced to the victims of the Cossacks individually before they are slaughtered one by one), and the Battle on Ice in *Alexander Nevsky* (1938), in which alternating vignettes contrast the dauntless commanders' motives for heroism and those of the ordinary soldiers. Nevsky's ability to communicate with all the strata of his disparate army presages that of Olivier's Henry V, also the protagonist of an anti-Nazi propaganda film, and therefore it is not altogether surprising that the Stalin-commissioned historical epic that transforms the medieval mercenary prince into a national hero—a film much admired by influential critics like James Agee[42]—seems to find echoes in Welles's Shakespeare films from first to last. If anything, Welles's long dialogue with Eisenstein culminates in the lengthy set-piece battle scene at the center of *Chimes*. In it the triangulation between Hotspur, Hal, and Falstaff that provides interludes in the midst of the ferocious montage and the grimly realistic mire of battle, precisely follows the pattern established in the Battle on Ice.

Eisenstein's canonical position in film schools has only amplified his influence on later filmmakers, and Welles's are not the only allusions to him from a filmmaker engaged in adapting Shakespeare. Derek Jarman peoples his version of *The Tempest* (1979) with a somber, sadistic Prospero who cannot decide whether to bestow his attentions on his earthy daughter, an androgynous wild child Miranda, or his ethereal slave, a cogitative, middle-aged Ariel. The Gollum-like Caliban, given to serpentine snacks on raw eggs, is possessed of spectacularly rotten teeth and an even more decidedly lower-class accent than those of other base characters:[43] it all seems heading for a dialectical arm-wrestling match between Wagner and Marx, but at the last minute Brecht pops out and the Göttedämmerung is averted with Jarman's equivalent of the masque, a pared-down Busby-Berkeley musical number in which the chorines are sailors recruited from *The Battleship Potemkin* and hoisted onto the HMS *Pinafore*, where they are obliged to forget revolution and to disport themselves in languorous Eisensteinian symmetries. The goddess they flank, diva Elizabeth Welch, is a serene combination of Iris, Ceres, and Juno, who emerges in a cloud of orange frills to grace the nuptials of Miranda and Ferdinand with a deliciously ripe, if unorthodox, musical epithalamion, Harold Arlen's song "Stormy Weather." What could possibly follow but the Puckish pilfering of choice phrases from *A Midsummer Night's Dream* and the arbitrary transposition of those same lines later kidnapped by Pacino for the opening of *Looking for Richard*? The film that starts as a fairly conventional nightmare progresses through various possibilities of montage and ends as a surreal hyperdream.

Welles, of course, has no intention of subjecting Eisenstein to burlesque (granting that dubious honor, instead, to Truffaut, as an *auteur* in-joke). Indeed, there is no certain evidence that he even had a firsthand acquaintance with Jay Leyda's translations of Eisenstein's writings. Yet his extremely self-conscious use of certain formal techniques, particularly those associated with sound, suggests that by 1948 he might well have encountered the latter's ideas through their widespread discussion in film circles or, as is more likely, through an observant analysis of the singular way sound and image function in *Nevsky*. *Nevsky's* distinctiveness arose in part because Eisenstein worked very closely with Prokofiev, screening the rushes for the composer and discussing the aural effects he required (the cantata Prokofiev extracted from the film score remains, together with his extraordinary ballet score for *Romeo and Juliet*, among his most performed works). The result was an interaction of the image and the music track unprecedented in the era of synchronized dialogue film. Eisenstein theorized this use of sound in great detail, and it furnishes what remains his only concrete example of "overtonal montage," a concept he had introduced in 1929 to describe the mechanism by which the various tracks of cinema might be used to supplement the dominant mood, or "tone" created by the organization of the shots.[44] In a page of his later writing, translated comparatively early into English by Leyda in *Film Sense*, Eisenstein places some bars of the piano score beneath the corresponding images and demonstrates a "vertical" graphic and aural relation between the tracks.[45] The effect is by no means an easy one to sustain in a narrative feature film, and may have been picked up from one of Eisenstein's Hollywood heroes, Mickey Mouse ("mickey-mousing" still refers to the soundtrack's exact mimicry of actions). One of Eisenstein's examples of overtones comes from an episode in Disney's *Birds of a Feather* (1931) in which music denoting love (Jacques Offenbach's "Barcarolle" from *The Tales of Hoffmann*) can be represented by the reflection of a shimmering peacock's tail, the intensity of the glow corresponding to the pulses of the music, creating the overtone of love's "opalescent" waxing and waning.[46]

Eisenstein was especially attuned to Prokofiev's facility for producing certain musical effects. While there have been other composers who have been able to convey sarcasm and irony in music—Ibert was noted for his musical jests—none has done so as vividly, and across as broad a range of instruments and musical genres, as Prokofiev. The composer's music evidently continued to resonate in Welles's ears and influenced the music for *Othello*, whose composition he supervised as closely as Eisenstein did that of *Nevsky*. When we first see the chained Iago being dragged toward the cage he will occupy, the music changes from the solemn bell-like tolling that accompanies the opening funeral procession of Othello and Desdemona into the dyspeptic snorting of a kind that those who have seen *Nevsky* would recognize as the music associated with the barbarous Teutonic Knights. An earlier and even more elaborate example of Welles's use of such an effect follows the scene in which Macbeth's sleeplessness reveals itself to be part of the Weird Sisters' grand plan. Immediately after the Macbeths ruminate over their post-Duncan insomnia, the agents of pagan witchcraft reappear to pronounce maledictions while holding aloft his melting effigy.[47] When they surmount it with a mock crown, a fierce, brassy orchestral chord accompanies the dissolve to a murky image of Macbeth's face in a reflecting glass as he tries on a full-scale crown of the same design. So far the music has served to underline the general mood, often accompanying the spoken words, but when the new monarch turns from self-contemplation to walk toward the throne room, the dissonant, Horror-film-like chords give way to a jaunty tuba figure, ridiculing his regal pretensions while his new subjects bow dutifully when he passes. As he proceeds past a row of soldiers on the ramparts and begins to descend a stairway, other instruments join in the mockery, and on the last steps the tuba emits a razzing descending arpeggio following the arc of descent of the newly elevated assassin. The musical commentary ceases, in fact, only when a distraught, abandoned Lady Macduff turns to confide in Lady Macbeth, so ending a sequence in which Welles achieves the vertical matching of visual and musical tracks, but succeeds in doing so even as the music undermines the solemn visuals. Not coincidentally, Eisenstein, Vsevolod Pudovkin, and Grigori Alexandrov had published a statement soon after the establishment of synchronized dialogue films (1927–1928) arguing for "counterpoint," whereby the deliberate mismatch of sound and image would allow the tracks to comment on each other rather than merely working toward a compliant verisimilitude.[48] Macbeth is only crowned in irony, the overtone of preposterous self-deception predictive of his descent into slurring alcoholism and the meltdown of impending damnation.

If Macbeth's first coronation leads to a virtuoso display of film technique, then a later one might easily be taken as an example of supreme clumsiness. Following Banquo's murder, we see him crownless, and he continues to be so until his confrontation with Lady Macbeth during the sleepwalking scene. Once she has plunged to her death (again in the shock-effect style of a Universal classic, complete with Ibert's angular "Horror music"), we have an instantaneous cut to him wearing chain mail and crowned once more; only, this happens to be entirely the wrong crown. Welles later confessed to Bogdanovich (in the process of making light of his own efforts) that he should have sent the outfit back to the rental agency, Western Costume, as it made him look like the "Statue of Liberty."[49] Yet in blatant disregard for the dictates of continuity (or narrative justification), he dons Liberty's coronet rather late in the film, and the remark seems to indicate that even in the 1970s, Welles was still circumspect about probing the deeper structures of his film. As a careful study of the succeeding shots makes clear, the Liberty crown is fully integrated into the rest of the mise en scène, so that, when he remarks, "She should have died hereafter," the camera moves in to frame him in medium close-up, the jagged spike forming the fish-bone grating of a window neatly placed between the spikes of his crown as it points to his head. As it edges closer, the shot dissolves into a billowing fog beginning with the bottom of the frame, a mindscape seeming to froth in synchrony with the words of the celebrated "Tomorrow" soliloquy. By the time a suicidal Seyton has announced the arrival of Birnham Wood, Macbeth has also mysteriously acquired a staff, a flamboyantly Expressionist and spiky version of Liberty's flame. It seems hardly adequate against the hordes led by Fleance and Macduff, crusaders who march bearing duplicates of the Holy Father's staff. When the latter, urging the troops forward like one of the malevolent bishops in the entourage of Eisenstein's Teutonic Knights, advances too near the ramparts, Macbeth issues his challenge and hurls his staff with deadly accuracy. It fells the Holy Father with a thud so sickening as to anticipate the slick visual and auditory excess of the Horror film cycle inaugurated in the mid-1950s by Hammer Films, arguably the most influential British films of the period and the model for Polanski's grimly witty contributions to the genre (including *Macbeth*).[50] The missiles Welles directed at the forces of the right (the Holy Father being a compound not only of Shakespeare's Ross and Old Man, but also of J. Edgar Hoover and the Hollywood minions of the Breen Office) now seem innocuous, although the outraged howls that attended the premier of Arthur Miller's more transparently referential play *The Crucible*, first staged in 1953 (after the battle was lost and won), suggest that his cautious retreat behind the veil of allegory may not have been unduly precautionary.

Othello's Displacement

There is no evidence to show that Welles was officially exiled from the United States after *Macbeth*, let alone to prove the State Department's role in sabotaging his career. Nor did he share Romeo's belief that life itself would not be worth the price of exile, for being gregarious and an inveterate traveler, he attempted to extract the best from the many places he inhabited. Yet few films bear such eloquent witness to the marks of exile, most particularly an acute sense of displacement and unbelonging refracted through the helpless, even hysterical, need to "belong," as Welles's *Othello*.[51] That he could not make such a film in the United States because of the objections of the Breen Office to the depiction of a black man making love to a white woman, even if played by a white actor in makeup, has been amply documented, and so to lament the loss of a Paul Robeson Othello directed by Welles is futile.[52] Besides, unable to obtain American financing, Welles had to turn to the flamboyant Italian producer of operatic films Montatori Scalera, who from the start envisioned Welles as Verdi's hero back-translated by celluloid into Shakespeare's. Unlike the Othellos of Ira Aldridge and Robeson,

Otello has never received a definitive interpretation by a black protagonist, and in Europe, where social fractures along lines of perceived ethnicity have been more calamitous than those of perceived race, and where the baggage of Jim Crow does not weigh as heavily as in the United States, race-blind casting is common, and Tamagnos, Martinellis, del Monacos, and Domingos have not been looked at askance for their transracial performances.[53] It is Scalera's cavalier attitude to financing the project (culminating in bankruptcy) that led to many a debacle, including a shooting schedule that extended in fits and starts over three years, during which a cast of British, Irish, American, Italian, and North African actors had to be periodically reassembled in Italy, France, and Morocco by a director who had to keep taking acting jobs to finance the film. It is no small irony that this most nomadic of films, one of the supreme struggles of independent filmmaking and Welles's most visually compelling contribution to cinema, proved to be his last sustained intervention in the American public sphere.

In some respects, however, *Othello* does not take the aesthetic risks that *Macbeth* did. The Breen Office was already fighting a rearguard action against the nascent civil rights movement, and Robeson's contempt for the House Un-American Activities Committee resulted in him being stripped of his passport in 1950 while the film was in production. Welles's support of Dewey cost him the regular visits to the White House that he had enjoyed during FDR's presidency, and his objections to the triumphs of the Red Scare artists in Washington or the studio blacklist specialists of Hollywood could now find a voice only in his films. And if, like Jarman, who defied the critical tide and rescued *The Tempest* from Caliban's albuminous clutches, Welles denied Iago the ownership of *Othello* that he had long enjoyed, then he did so in the wake of Robeson whose 1942 reprise of the role in New York's Schubert Theater (with Uta Hagen as his very blonde Desdemona; a dozen years earlier in London it had been a dark-haired Peggy Ashcroft) provoked critical accolades and popular racism. Monumental ebony to Hagen's monumental alabaster, Robeson's proved an assumption of a Shakespeare role so definitive for its time that it virtually cast into oblivion the nineteenth-century diminution of the play that reflected its own imperialist anxieties in portraying Othello as an easily depatinated savage, offering as an alternative a larger-than-life hero whose tragedy it is to succumb to a society governed by those ranged against him.[54]

Even so, in terms of cinematic subtlety, *Othello* is *Macbeth*'s polar opposite. If the latter's extended allegory required Welles to play the protagonist as if in the grip of Lear's *hysterica passio*, then, in deference to Robeson's embodiment of the hero-victim of his race, Welles tones down Othello,[55] domesticating his demons into those that lurked in the psyche of many a Renaissance courtier (the sexual escapades of Elizabeth's entourage led to at least one newsworthy homicide, and the literature of jealous husbands stretched back to the opening pages of Herodotus: Shakespeare's source, Giraldi Cinzio, who provides Welles with his spoken prologue, even alludes to Dante's Paolo and Francesca). While *Macbeth* proved to be an incendiary admixture of plebian genres and patrician filmmaking techniques, *Othello* seemed to repudiate its own virtuosity in endowing film noir, a visual style that underwrote a number of "lowbrow" genres, with transcendent meaning.[56] *Othello* is a parable not only about light and dark, but also about the creatures whose existence depends upon the diurnal cycles that in the course of an ever-darker film go tragically awry. The gradual transformation is of labyrinthine complexity, and it requires a conscious effort of vision, something beyond the trivial recognition that the film employs a basic element of cinematography (high-contrast black-and-white film stock) to comment on race relations, to identify the constituent elements of the governing conceit. Only toward the end do we recognize that the narrative pattern it establishes practically deconstructs the storytelling strategy that typifies the film noir that often begins at the end merely to set the stage for the doomed hero's explanatory intercessions and to illustrate the consequences of the *femme fatale*'s treacheries. In *Othello* the narrator function does not fall to the lot of the doomed hero, and the femme fatale is but the unwitting agent of his downfall. Instead, Iago's lines are regularly reordered and conflated into a commentary on the action, and Desdemona becomes an unknowing accomplice whose glowing presence limns the shadows of Othello's otherness.

The inner allegory is disarmingly fable-like (perhaps Welles's tribute to Shakespeare's borrowings from the Morality Play). Just as the mysterious protagonist of *Mr. Arkadin* at one point gives a Zolaesque account of human nature by relating the entirety of Aesop's "Scorpion and Frog" parable, Iago's metaphorical menagerie provides still earlier proof that Welles could embed allegory within allegory. Like Buñuel, whose entomological background persuaded him to give his protagonists the elemental psychologies of insects, Welles contrives to give moral meaning to his human geography: his is an Iago with a spider's predatory sexuality and sinuous gait, an Othello with the indecisiveness of a moth, evershrouded by mesh-like shadows and darkness, but always fluttering toward the light, a Cassio with the trivial self-absorption of the bright-winged fly whose wanton flights fatally distract the moth, and a Desdemona whose candle-flame flicker baits the web. Stephen Greenblatt has made the case that Iago's opportunistic genius thrives on being able to read the other characters as they are unable to read him: a consummate tactician with an arrow for every Achilles' heel, he can dictate and refashion the play's metaphors, mixing and twisting them into the strands of his web.[57] The fly wriggles free as flies will, but not so the self-deceiving moth for whom the web is truly intended: Othello has been tricked by the Ottoman-besieged Venetian senators (who exchange knowing glances) into believing that military prowess is his passport into their society, their "gift" of Desdemona being the ocular proof of his assimilation.

True to this interpretation, and as if in anticipation of Frantz Fanon's *Black Skin, White Masks*, Welles plays an Othello whose psyche has been colonized. It is the task of the ravening spider to strip him of this mask of whiteness, which he does with fatal finesse. And there, as with Cinzio's concluding caution (that women should marry according to their station), the matter might have ended. But Welles, who in his radio addresses derided the complacent beneficiaries of social inequity as those trapped in a system of their own devising, has other masks in mind as well, and so places a much greater emphasis on Shakespeare's insistence on the Machiavel's ultimate failure. Hardly has the film begun before we see Iago hoisted on his own triumphant metaphor of entrapment, the same, empty cage to which the camera, on returning to the start of the action, pans ominously when from the battlements a herald proclaims Othello's naval victory and the revelries associated with his nuptials. It is the same cage in which, as Welles tells us in *Filming Othello*, "the sun will scorch him and the gulls will peck at his flesh," and that hangs high above Iago in a later shot as he informs Roderigo: "[S]o will I weave the net that will enmesh them all." The futility of this spider's stratagem redefines the nature of the tragedy at its outset.

Mirror, Mirror

Save for the overtly Eisensteinian montage of its opening and two later sequences that have won the admiration of film aficionados—a consummately timed reverse tracking shot in the course of which Iago, now set loose in his Cypriot lair, "seduces" the hapless Othello with shifting, mobile metaphors and innuendo, and the equally celebrated Turkish bath sequence in which Iago knows the terrain so well that his blade unerringly plunges toward a Roderigo concealed beneath a platform of wooden slats—*Othello* departs from Welles's early films in integrating virtuoso camerawork and technical finesse into a taut narrative.[58] Iago's "unmasking" of Othello, a moment of particular semantic density and the turning point of the film, requires only the simplest and most characteristic of means: Welles's trusty mirror. Mirrors and copulations are abominable according to a heresiarch in Borges's short story "Tlön, Uqbar, Orbis Tertius," because they multiply the numbers of man; but here as elsewhere, mirrors are themselves multiplied. They are so prevalent in Welles's films, in fact, that Deleuze begins his argument about "time-crystals" with them, and Donaldson, noting that there are at least four mirrors and numerous reflected images in *Othello*, discusses it in terms of a rereading of Jean-Louis Baudry's infamous ur-text of apparatus theory (that made the case that the witness of classical cinema identified not with the narrative images themselves but with the machine—i.e., projecting device—that arranged them for the spectatorial gaze).[59] Welles, argues Donaldson, constantly implicates the spectator by using optical tricks to place her in the space of the illusion, "to disturb the mirror function of the screen as Baudry understands it, and to deflate the omnipotent position of the film spectator."[60] Analogously, but extending Bergson's observation that a mirror image must at once be virtual (an inverted reflection of the real) and real (the image in the mirror)—part of a lengthy exploration in terms of cinematic space and time of how the human mind accounts for extension beyond the here and now—Gilles Deleuze pays particular attention to Welles's use of mirrors, mentioning Max Ophüls and Joseph Losey in this regard, but inexplicably bypassing the conclusive cinematic example of Bergson's insight, Jean Cocteau. Welles is the principal exhibit in Deleuze's hall of mirrors not because of the pyrotechnics of the well-known scene from *The Lady From Shanghai* whose climax has the antagonist pursue his quarry into a "Chinese box" room and spray bullets into rows of mirrors bearing identical images of his intended victim (played, naturally, by Welles), shattering one reflection after another to uncover the reality behind the illusion. Rather, observes Deleuze, Welles's critique of the overfacile distinction between the real and the illusory begins with *Citizen Kane*, when the protagonist walks between two facing mirrors.[61]

So perhaps we would do well to pause before one such mirror in *Othello*. When it was pointed out to Welles (by a self-important academic) that two iconographic elements appear to derive from Jan van Eyck's wedding portrait of Giovanni Arnolfini and Giovanna Cenami, he, with the pretense of unreflective jesting, asserted that all the visuals derive from the elaborate frescoes of Vittore Carpaccio where the dog is a Tenerife and not a terrier: the footage of the exchange is included in *Filming Othello*. And true enough, most of the mise en scène, including the dog that led to this bone of contention, serves a pleasantly decorative function in one of Carpaccio's frescoes; that dog has even continued to exert a creative influence on novelists such as Vikram Seth. As simple metaphor the lap dog, associated throughout with Roderigo, serves to indicate his relation to Iago. But Welles fails to explain the other iconographic link, the mirror, which is unmistakably of Eyckian provenance (the dog, in the painting, being the symbol of marital fidelity). It also seems an interesting coincidence that van Eyck's painting receives detailed consideration in Eisenstein's essay on "the synchronization of the senses."[62] This essay, one of his most wide-ranging philosophical meditations, treats the overarching question of realistic representation, and is one of the earliest examples of a filmmaker and pedagogue demonstrating the productive interface between the aesthetic principles of different art forms. In a diary passage of the Goncourts, for instance, Eisenstein finds an example of the synchronization of all sensory experience, as a result of which he envisions what Leyda translates as "vertical montage" (i.e., a special case, as I pointed out in discussing *Macbeth*, of overtonal montage).[63] Dealing with such questions as the expressive matching of sound, movement, and color, until he arrives at the idea that the synchronization of formal properties can represent a world view (an idea he ascribes to Nietzsche, Heinrich Wölfflin and, subsequently, René Guilleré), Eisenstein points out that Roman squares or villas, or the parks at Versailles, could be the "prototypes" of the structures of classical music. He even proceeds to an assessment of jazz diametrically opposed to the later contentions of Theodor Adorno: for Eisenstein the flash and color of neon signs in urban settings correspond to the rhythmic emphasis of modern music and the fragmentation or abandonment of linear perspective in painting.[64] Although something of a footnote to a paean to El Greco's discovery of the montage of simultaneous perspectives in painting, Eisenstein's discussion of perspective also includes an illustration of van Eyck's earlier painting (complete with lines of perspective). In the wedding portrait the three vanishing points may have been "an unconscious method, but what a wonderful *intensity of depth* this painting gains thereby!"[65] (emphasis in the original).

The positioning of the Arnolfini mirror in Welles's film is not the result of coincidence. It is, from the start, indicative of Othello's alienation and self-doubt. We first encounter it after Desdemona has pleaded Cassio's cause victoriously, and the tracking shot along the ramparts of the fortress terminates in what appears to be a cul-de-sac. Iago, who seems unfailingly to guide Othello to gratings, goat pens, or cage-like enclosures, now shepherds him into the belly of the fortress, where he poisons his ears while peeling off his captain's armor. A few insinuations later, Othello wanders into an adjacent cell where the mirror hangs. Jack Jorgens, no doubt responding to such features as the canted framings of characters as seen through Iago's eyes, noted that in the film two distinct visual systems govern the representation of space. Cutting, pasting, and at times leaving Jorgens's prose with his own (including a clever précis that overstates Jorgens's criticism of Olivier), the narrator of *Filming Othello* informs us: "In Olivier's *Othello*, which was a cinematic record of a stage production, its core was the shocking spectacle of a man reverting to savagery, eaten up by jealousy, until he murders the woman he loves. My film, by contrast, tried to depict a whole world in collapse, a world that is a metaphor not just for Othello's mind but for an epic, pre-modern age. And here I am quoting, or mis-quoting, to not very good effect, a critic Jack J. Jorgens...and I am going to leave out the good things he said and the bad ones...the visual style of the film mirrors the marriage at the center of the play, which is not that of Othello and Desdemona, but the perverse marriage of Othello and Iago."[66] Despite the disclaimer, he recognizes immediately that Jorgens captures the essence of the film's structures of seeing: "[T]he longer we are in Cyprus," states Jorgens-Welles, "the more the involuted Iago style triumphs over the lyric [and] heroic Othello style,"[67] and nowhere else is that perverse marriage so clearly depicted as in the distorted perspectives of the Arnolfini mirror.

Having sown doubts about Cassio, Iago strips Othello of his metallic "shell," concluding with the recollection that Desdemona seemed to look on him with love while betraying her father. Othello, clearly in a state of shock, can barely murmur a profane vow, "I am bound to thee for ever," whose double meaning is accentuated visually rather than verbally. As he and Iago walk into the adjacent chamber, Othello turns to the mirror suspended on the wall and Iago, sidling up to the camera, says, "I see this has a little dashed your spirits." Othello's dark reflection appears to start to speak, but the response, "Not a jot," is transferred to the deceived and dissembling "real" image as he turns toward Iago and the camera. By the time Iago reasons with him about "nature erring from itself," they have wandered into another chamber in which Iago seems to stand behind a second such mirror, now detached from the wall and resting on a ledge, reflecting Othello who occupies the right of the frame. As Iago builds to a crescendo with "thought unnatural," Othello's face seems to dissolve in this mirror of self-contemplation before he tears himself away and stalks out, with Iago in pursuit. If van Eyck represented himself as a diminutive reflected figure, artist-witness to the marriage vows, then the architect of Jorgens's "perverse marriage," initially a momentary and shadowy reflection, displaces the mirror itself and dominates the frame. Yet a third version of such a mirror hangs in the bedchamber, from which Iago takes his leave when Desdemona enters. Having brushed her aside and trampled the fateful handkerchief with which she attempts to bind his forehead, Othello approaches within inches of it, disfigured by self-doubt and self-loathing. In what is clearly a mental projection (for it is spatially impossible), he imagines the reflection of the approaching Desdemona. When he turns to face her, the camera retreats, showing the back of his head in the mirror and her white-robed reflection bisecting its surface. Momentarily Othello seems to hesitate, resisting his conjectures, and a muted French horn solo accompanies his tender framing of her face in his hands; but a cut to Emilia picking up the handkerchief again marks a change of register, and an ominous drumbeat gives way to frantic chords (the more common character of a score that is more relentlessly doom-laden than Ibert's for *Macbeth*, despite its superlative rerecording for the restoration). The soundtrack anticipates the violent change in Othello's temperament as he brusquely turns away and throws open the curtains that enclose their bedchamber.[68]

Whereas the mirrors of *Othello* witness the distorted perspectives of the characters' psyches, another visual motif, the vertiginous spiral popularly associated with Hitchcock's style, punctuates the film's conflict between light and darkness. In the scenes following Iago's suggestion of Desdemona's infidelity, Othello wears a flowing white robe, and from this point onward the camera and the lighting contrive to make his entire being appear increasingly dark as he is engulfed by Iago's inner blackness. Its stark hue accords with Welles's triumphant response ("we are dealing with a Puritan") to one of MacLiammóir's observations about *Othello* in the documentary, and it flutters in the gusts that sweep the fortress as Iago reveals Cassio's "dream" and Desdemona's gift of the handkerchief to him. It is at this point that he starts seeing in the same off-kilter perspective as Iago. A few shots later he wears a hooded white cloak when Iago, looming over him in ever-more sharply tilted framings, promises to tease the truth out of Cassio. Having provoked Cassio's overheard laughter, Iago returns and leads Othello past a goat pen, where he reports, "Lie with her, on her, what you will," while the camera seems to slither on stone as it tilts upward. The shot dissolves into gulls shrieking and circling in the sky—Othello's point of view, as he regains consciousness—and the camera describes a contracting spiral until the Cypriots standing on the towering battlements appear to be upside down. When he recovers enough to voice the "Farewell" soliloquy, the lines end with the back of his head, in black silhouette, dipping precipitously into the frame.

The encircling and enveloping blackness of the film is nowhere better illustrated than in the sequence in which Othello pays his final visit to Desdemona's bedchamber. As he steels himself, his shadow grows, falling first against a wall, and, after we see her preparing for the night, engulfing the camera. In total blackness he exclaims: "It is the cause, it is the cause, [O] my soul."[69] On the words "chaste stars," the camera pans to reveal his face in film noir side-lit profile, the lines delivered in voice-over as he edges toward the camera. The soliloquy concluded, he strides through a porticoed antechamber, pausing at an altar to extinguish the light. As he resumes his progress he strides past the camera, smothering it with his cloak, thereby placing the spectator in Desdemona's impending subject position. When Othello pulls the curtains open for the last time, he is a black silhouette, Iago's calumny now translated into menacing physical presence. Eventually, stripped of his command and convinced of Desdemona's innocence, he stabs himself. The camera, carried low to the ground, spins vertiginously around the vaulting above his head. The visual motif of circling repeats in the narrative when we now return to the silhouettes of the opening funerary procession. Again the camera again dips down beneath a light-denying parapet, from which we cut to the closing credits. After a moment of silence, the graceful, highly structured Renaissance lute music heard at the start of the film plays over a "submerged" black tower whose reflection is dappled with the light. *Othello* concludes by reminding us of the cost of maintaining the social order and the contrivance behind the calm facades of the Serenissima, even as it offers its ill-fated protagonists a wordless echo of distant benediction.

A Choice of Exile

A melancholy, twilight character also suffuses *Chimes at Midnight*, arguably the most consistently well-acted and self-revelatory of Welles's Shakespeare films. Visually influenced by the sharply etched outlines and hard contrasts of Albrecht Dürer's engravings, the film was shot entirely in a Spain still in the throes of Generalissimo Francisco Franco's dictatorship, and, in keeping with the by-now-established pattern of debacles with distribution and exhibition, failed to attract major audiences on its initial release.[70] Yet it is the only Welles Shakespeare film to have a critical anthology (by Bridget Lyons) devoted to it and is without question the most influential. Enough has been written about it to obviate any need to detail its extraordinary evocation of atmosphere and mood, but a few salient features might well be worth noting in the context of its prolonged engagement with questions of historical representation and authorship, as well as its influence on later Shakespearean *auteurs*.[71]

It may be best to begin by considering *Chimes* in the context of remarks Welles made about transnationalism in *Filming Othello*, for in them Welles anticipates both New Historicist anecdotalism and Naficy's argument for the interstitiality of the modes of production in most accented cinemas. One way of perceiving *Chimes* is as a typically arch anecdote about his own cinematic biography and his situation vis-à-vis the French New Wave *auteurs*; another is to see it as a meditation on the nature of history's winners and losers. Neither kind of reading, if the Welles of *Filming Othello* is correct, is mutually exclusive: "*Othello* began as a French-Italian co-production, but after months of working on the sets in the south of France with Alexander Trauner, Scalera announced that the French portion of the deal had fallen through...Time and chance and many, many a vicissitude had taken us over half of Italy to England...and we were all over Morocco...At the end we had no nationality at all. *Othello* was a movie without a country, which meant, of course, that there was no legal way to export it from anywhere to anywhere." And having related the amusing way in which he discovered that it was the first African film to win the Grand Prize at Cannes (in 1952), Welles admits: "[T]hat's an anecdote, but not I think a digression, because it illustrates the sort of quandary which changed just not the lives of those of us who made the picture but changed the style, the character of the picture itself. Maybe that has something to do with what we were praised for, in other words mere chance, losing as we did more than one nationality, and forced as it were to adapt ourselves to a whole series of sudden alterations and violent retreats."

As we have had ample opportunity to observe, Welles consistently adopted the "Hollywood interview" mode of downplaying the intricate constructedness of his films by emphasizing the role of the aleatory and accidental, in part because of his conjuror's delight in prestidigitation, and in part to avoid falling prey to pigeonholing (the proscription of intellectual filmmaking in post-1940s Hollywood went hand in hand with punitive anti-Communism). He succeeded so well that confused critics often interpreted their lack of cinematic sophistication as his incoherence (or worse). There is, of course, no element of chance involved in matching an action begun in a shot taken in Mogador to its conclusion in another shot taken months apart in Florence; rather, it is the inner world of the film into which Welles invited improvisation. This aspect of his filmmaking, more than any other, might reflect the nature of nomadism in cinema, the incorporation of the sudden alterations into the rhythm of the film's march. Roderigo's violent retreat into the bowels of a Turkish bath might have taken place in the absence of costumes in a Moroccan fish market, but without that fish market (or with the promised costumes) there would have been no Turkish bath and perhaps a less effective visualization of the impotent Iago's frantic thrusts. Movement and stillness (Othello always pauses when in doubt), vastness and enclosure, serve as part of a dialectical conflict that leaves darkness victorious. For despite its cloud-capped towers, its gorgeous palaces, its cavernous cisterns, and its spacious chambers, *Othello* creates the feeling of a world that hems in its wanderers, a world that shrinks inexorably. The most extreme contraction of space comes at the close, in the gauzelike mask that frames Desdemona's face as Othello suffocates her (again, with a kiss), a double metaphor of the loss of his mask and the closing in of the trap in which Iago, true to his word and to his own undoing, can "enmesh them all."

If by his own account Welles's sensitivity to space and movement in *Othello* stemmed from an enforced nomadism, then a corresponding sense of nostalgic regret, a heightened awareness of the passage of time and of history's malleability, permeates *Chimes*.[72] This may, in part, be attributable to his decision to pin his tent pegs for extended periods in various locales in Europe, a way of escaping as much from his tarnished Hollywood myth as from public scrutiny. The result was that the Welles of the 1960s had time for retrospection. In *An Accented Cinema,* Naficy is careful to distinguish between internal exile (politically exiled filmmakers sent from one location to another within a national polity) and the external exile suffered by those evicted from their countries; Welles might be thought of as an exile in yet another sense, as one parted from the mythic domain of Hollywood, locus classicus of a dominant and exclusionary film industry that defined its "nation's" filmmaking. Yet it is no coincidence that the Icarus who had once soared over the labyrinth of Iago's Cypriot lair crash-landed in the heartland of a Spain governed by a Minotaur (to borrow the exiled Picasso's image). This is not to argue that the origins of *Chimes* did not long predate his Spanish sojourn, as it could well be argued that it began even before *Citizen Kane.* Originally conceived by Welles as *The Five Kings,* a theatrical adaptation of "the whole sweep of the English history plays," the first part premiered in Boston's Colonial Theatre in February of 1939 under the auspices of the Mercury Theatre and Theatre Guild. It consisted, as does the film, of a condensation of the two parts of *Henry IV* and of *Henry V* (with additional lines from *Richard II* and *The Merry Wives of Windsor*). Its run was short-lived, and it did not make it as far as Broadway. Welles never left the past behind him, least of all his own, and he made periodic revisions over decades, the penultimate version renewing the Irish connection. He goes so far as to describe his 1960 production of *Chimes at Midnight* at the Gate in Dublin, with Hilton Edwards serving as director, as "a sort of tryout for the movie."[73]

Its protagonist's penchant for yarns, notwithstanding, it is not an Irish film in a Spanish setting hoisted on his local producers. Welles's Spanish connection also had roots, if not quite as deep. In 1937 he read the narration for *This Spanish Earth,* a film shot on the Republican front lines by Socialist documentarian Joris Ivens (in the event, in a curiously Wellesian way, Ernest Hemingway rerecorded his own commentary, and it was released with his voice).[74] At the time he made *Chimes,* later released in the United States as *Falstaff (Chimes at Midnight),* Welles was periodically a guest of one of Hemingway's heroes, Spain's most famous living bullfighter, Antonio Ordoñez, and his wife Pilar Lezcano, in the mountainous Ronda also beloved of Rilke. Historians and biographers of today may well elucidate the manner in which the literary intelligentsia of the 1930s, Dos Passos and Orwell no less than Hemingway, might have misunderstood both the politics and military acumen of Spain's Left, which had veered toward hard-line Stalinism even before the clouds of civil war gathered.[75] But at the time the eyes of the democratic world viewed the conflict in another light, and the failure of their cause seemed to signal the triumph of European Fascism. Welles could admit defeat, as they eventually did, but habituated to the situational politics of the Roosevelt years, he proved constitutionally incapable of accepting that defeat was total. He was, however, no longer fired with the same manic energy or part of the same social configuration that gave rise to the contumacious spectacles of his youth. So there is nothing on the surface of *Chimes* that would mark it as propaganda or a "political film," and the variety of critical readings it has produced readily attests to a textual richness quite beyond its "Spanishness." Yet Welles could not have been unaware that under Franco Spain was something of a pariah nation, and that unlike most exiles he could choose the location of his exile. In our present world of boycotts and unabating military intervention, when the very notion that star presence may have an ameliorative effect and may contribute to the cause of the softening of a dictatorship (and Franco's dictatorship did presently soften into a *dictablanda*) seems outmoded, Welles might appear to have been contributing to the most damning myth that pursued him—that he was Charlie Kane, seeking to be news when he could no longer make news. But Welles, who also shot parts of a film based on Cervantes, was genuinely quixotic, and prepared to uphold a knightly ideal in the face of decay and defeat. And, of course, Franco was one of those dictators susceptible to the role of artists in society.

Still another connection readily suggests itself. Welles's rebellious Worcester, Fernando Rey, also played the perennial protagonist of Luis Buñuel's films. Not long previously Buñuel had returned to Spain at Franco's invitation and then proved an inspiration to later local directors by ridiculing aspects of the dictator's policies in his film *Viridiana* (1962), in which Rey reveled in a particularly repugnant portrayal of an incestuous uncle. For his part Welles appears to have contrived a work even more consonant with those of later Spanish directors who, with the backing of producer Elias Querejeta, were soon to create an oppositional cinema at once subtle (in its undermining of official discourse) and richly nuanced.[76] There was, for instance, an official interdiction of representations of the Spanish civil war at the time of Welles's film, and Shakespeare's entire cycle revolves around noble factions vying for national ascendancy, leading to the recurrent patterns of violence and retribution of Kott's Grand Mechanism. In *Chimes* Welles makes the Battle of Shrewsbury, the culmination of civil war, as long in duration and as complex in terms of montage (even to the extent of incorporating comic interludes) as the Battle on Ice in *Alexander Nevsky*.[77] The aftermath of victory too is salutary punishment and a continuing struggle for the crown—hardly the vision of power consonant with the ideals of Fascist order.

Had he been more alert, Franco might well have noted the parallels between his situation and that of Gielgud's Henry IV, the latter as overburdened by what is within his head as that which sits atop it, as the invisible narrator informs us almost at the beginning. The film opens to a snowy scene in which a ruined, wintry Falstaff totters into a deserted structure (later revealed to be the site of revelries), led by a shriveled Justice Shallow. Shallow's ruminations bring forth Falstaff's own recollections of the good times shared beyond the hours of the midnight chimes, a shattered three-quarter profile of Welles superimposed pitilessly over that of Shallow, whose banter fails to provide the intended comfort. As the credits appear over a structure of Tudor design, brassy, modal fanfares confirm the film's period. This is followed by what later proves to be a flash-forward to the aftermath of Shrewsbury, a brief insert shot of soldiers standing beside captives suspended from gibbets over which appears the caption, "NARRATION BASED ON HOLINSHED'S CHRONICLES SPOKEN BY RALPH RICHARDSON." As if on cue Richardson begins to speak as the image fades to white and the camera tilts down to reveal a castle sitting atop a mountain. "King Richard the Second was murdered [a church-bell chimes], some say at the command of the Duke Henry Bolingbroke, in Pomfret castle on February 14, 1400. [Another chime, after which the music incorporates periodic chiming sounds]. Before this the Duke Henry had been crowned King [there is a rapid dissolve to John Gielgud's enthroned figure, illuminated by shafts of light falling through high windows], though the true heir to the realm was Edmund Mortimer, who was held prisoner by the Welsh rebels. [With veiled sarcasm] The new king was not hasty to purchase his deliverance, and to prove this Mortimer's cousins, the Percys, came to the King unto Windsor. [The nobles begin to file past the camera.] There came Northumberland, his son Henry Percy called Hotspur, and Worcester, whose purpose was ever to procure malice and set things in a broil."[78] At this point the diegetic dialogue cuts in, as the camera looks down on the seated nobility of the realm from behind the usurper's ornate crown. If Holinshed's voice seemed but a dispiriting recapitulation of recent history to those who had heard it in its original Spanish release, as *Las Campañadas a la Medianoche*, then at least there were those who benefited directly from Welles's presence, among them numerous Spanish actors as well as his assistant director, Juan Cobos, who as filmmaker and scholar was to become a prominent figure in Spain's cultural life.

History's Invisibility

Despite offering two distinctive takes on the same slice of English history, there is a curious but essential parallel between *Chimes* and the "partial" adaptation of *Richard III* by Raoul Ruiz. In describing Ruiz, Naficy argues that he is among a select group of filmmakers who, having undergone the "crises and tensions of exilic migrancy," have transformed their "liminality and interstitiality" into "passionate sources of creativity and dynamism."[79] As noted with Welles, Naficy uses interstitiality to designate filmmaking strategies other than the mainstream ones of host countries, ones that permit transnational directors to address a double audience from the "home" left behind and the present one. Such directors are liminal by virtue of being neither quite "here" nor "there" but somewhere in between (Ruiz is exemplary in this regard, sometimes crediting himself Raúl, its original Chilean form, and at others the French Raoul.) Naficy also finds Ruiz's fondness for playing with language and with the soundtrack of his films characteristic of these directors: "[I]f the dominant cinema is driven by the hegemony of synchronous sound and a strict alignment of speaker and voice, accented films are counter-hegemonic insofar as many of them de-emphasize synchronous sound and insist on first person and other voice-over narrations... [thereby creating] a slippage between voice and speaker."[80] The same words, of course, could well describe the soundtracks of Welles's post-Hollywood films. *Chimes*, in particular, was initially condemned even by sympathetic critics for its inadvertently poor delivery of dialogue, criticism subsequently contested in detail by Dudley Andrew and Michael Anderegg.[81]

Superficially, Ruiz is loyal to Shakespeare's lines, which he prunes but does not regraft. Yet while appearing to respect the one track that according to Anderegg endorses the Shakespeareanness of a film, he undoes the play's murderously insistent narrative trajectory. The words give rise to a host of visual conceits that have no parallel in Shakespeare's imagery: at the start of the film, for instance, Richard's upraised sword is an inversion of the cross, and later in the film the mailed hand that held it aloft finds a visual equivalent in the gnarled claws of a black chicken, a symbol associated with witchcraft. The alternating naturalism and stylization of the mise en scène and the pairing of lines subtly transform Shakespeare's emphases. The drawn-out, self-justifying casuistry of Clarence's assassins takes place before livid background colors. The biggest surprise is reserved for the end, for where classical narrative structure demands a resolution after the climax, Ruiz chooses to forego both the climax and the resolution Shakespeare provides.

In fact, Ruiz subtly undermines the apparent dominance of the dialogue track. One of Ruiz's more remarkable uses of sound is that of a chisel carving out patterns in blocks of wood. The conceit is of an artist who inscribes a slab of wood for the purpose of striking prints, a form of mechanical reproduction that achieved its high point in the Renaissance and that facilitated, amongst other things, the wide dissemination of devotional images and propagandistic ones celebrating the achievements of rulers. Ruiz juxtaposes this form of visual culture designed for popular appeal with the more elevated forms of Dutch still life painting and group portraiture, which inspire many of his visual compositions, even to details of the courtiers' attire. Just before Hastings arrives to inform him that Clarence has borne his imprisonment patiently, Richard contemplates his brother's murder in a bunker-like cavern, a sequence of shots redolent of the Renaissance *natura morta* (the flowers of a cyclamen, a widely used contraceptive, sprout from a bottle, splashing red onto the frame).[82] This is further emphasized by a still life hanging on a wall, its iconography an allegory of transience: a lute, a glass of wine, a vase of flowers, and a checkered board. As Hastings concludes his declaration, a figure on the left of the frame, patiently tapping away, reveals himself to be recording the scene graphically, giving permanence to the moment at which Richard finalizes plans to dispose of his brother and thus begin his ascent. Invisible and inaudible to the other characters, he is not part of the diegesis but the figure of official History, alerting the spectators to the partiality and selectivity of his presence. In *Chimes* Richardson remains invisible: like the voice-of-God narrator of documentary, he is History made audible, translating the words of Shakespeare's principal historical source into sounds for the spectator's ear. As does Richardson's Holinshed, Ruiz's carver of history reappears at the watershed moments of the film: he is there, for instance, when the ailing king gives his last address to his jockeying courtiers, when Gloucester literally leaps into the scene. But these frozen moments are the chronicler's fabrication: by making change and motion History's enemy, Ruiz disallows the notion that the unitary voice of officialdom can record the truth of the real.

Ruiz goes even further in his contestation of what is, in Bakhtin's phrase, "monological" history, one intolerant of the competing histories it strives to silence; hence Ruiz's metaphor of blindness for the inability to see things as they are. Characters who succumb to Gloucester's methods lack eyes or wear dark glasses, and when the funeral cortege Anne accompanies is brought to a halt by her family's executioner, she is veiled. In the shot/reverse shot compositions in which he accomplishes his triumphant seduction of her, the viewer is as deceived as she is: she sees Gloucester mistily through her veil, and the camera moves with both of them so that they stand in an eye-pleasing, orchid-festooned bower, as she succumbs to his wiles. As in Shakespeare, the senses deceive, and it is the ear that is pleased by eloquence most of all. Ruiz devotes an entire reel to Clarence's murderers convincing themselves to reject his arguments and the voices of conscience pleading for his life. And the world in which power dictates such choices is as sterile as cyclamen, as old as stone, stylized in gaudy colors or, like the throne room filled with stalactites and stalagmites, in danger of the ossification that literally overtakes some characters.

Yet the voice that opposes this world's false lyricism is unremittingly harsh. Loncraine can dispense with Margaret altogether. Not Ruiz, who elevates her into a screaming, male-voiced harridan, foaming at the mouth and (in the deliberately androgynous performance of the director of the stage version Ruiz adapted into film, Philippe Morier-Genoud) uttering the maledictions of an alternative history that accuses those who have commandeered the official version of things. That accusatory history is replete with absences: empty landscapes and silences in which perambulator-like carts, sometimes processions of them that, like the rickety contraption that transports Falstaff's remains, carry the dead to their anonymous graves. While there is finality to Welles's film (the old Hollywood that could accommodate him having given way to one that has, in effect, consigned him to the grave; the triumph of the official voices over those of the tavern), there can be none for Ruiz. In fact, the film ends abruptly at the apogee of Gloucester's triumph. This is not just an expression of Ruiz's revulsion for the narrative structure of Hollywood films, a reaction so visceral that it led to extraordinary experiments with alternative forms of narration.[83] The abridgement (of a film evidently not shot in sequence) stands for more than a shortage of funds or time, or even experiment alone, in that it acknowledges that in a world in which Pinochet was still in power and much of Latin America, including neighboring Argentina, in the grip of dictatorship, Shakespeare's moralizing ending would have been too complacent, too false to present reality. The world of Ruiz's film is anything but that of the Warde-Keane *Richard III* and its providential symmetries. "Mildendo, 203 avant GULLIVER," a caption warns us at the start of Ruiz's film, setting the clock ticking just before the camera tilts down the length of the victorious Gloucester's raised sword to the black armor encasing his hand. The history the film offers as an alternative is that of the now against the then, the ongoing and unfinished against what is set down, and a rebuke to the teleologies of Hegel, his descendent Marx, and their progeny. And, of course, Margaret's curse did descend on Pinochet, and Gulliver did trample the junta that ruled Argentina.

If for Welles and Ruiz official history wears the cloak of invisibility, then their conceptions of a countervailing history could not be more different. For Ruiz, as we have observed, history's oppositional voice, compounded of tragic memory, grates on the ears and seems to flesh out Fredric Jameson's formulation of history as "what hurts." Welles instead offers a merry popular history that exists separately from the staid official one of the court, a separation of styles that seems remarkably akin to Bakhtin's contrast of official and popular discourse. High culture and popular culture, for Bakhtin, are in a constant state of interaction, the latter often being a carnivalesque parody of the former; and for much of the film there is a suggestive alternation of scenes between the high characters contemplating usurpation and rebellion in their palaces, and those of lesser station engaged as strenuously in petty theft and misdemeanor in taverns and rustic settings.[84] Thus when Welles, having drawn a portrait of Falstaff that emphasizes his warts by lingering over his cowardice, his corrupt recruitment of soldiers, and his deception concerning the slaying of Hotspur, still asserts that the braggart who consciously makes himself a laughingstock is a truly "good man," he underlines the difference (felt so keenly by Shakespeare) between naive opportunism and ruthless manipulation, between the uncalculating betrayal of trust and murderous treachery, and between bending the truth and turning its shattered edges into executioners' blades.

If the dual visual patterns of *Othello* define the contrast between the protagonist and his nemesis, then the opposed visual styles of *Chimes* delineate two versions of history. The tavern scenes are shot with a freewheeling camera that weaves through beams and rafters, and dips knee-high like Yasujiro Ozu's, a frenetic visual rhythm reinforced by scampering characters and juxtaposed shots of uneven length. To the realm of official history belongs the majestic mise en scène of the court, the nobles' hieratic posturings, the struggle for a crown less often dropped but even more symbolically charged than Olivier's in his *Richard III*. Indeed, the contrast between town and crown, and the motive-filled liminality of the prince who slips between them, finds its most felicitous expression in a sequence that parallels one from *Ivan the Terrible*. At one point in Eisenstein's film, the noble boyars, thinking the fevered Ivan to be dead, plot an abortive coup, thereby inviting a terrible vengeance. When Henry IV believes himself to be ailing, he requests that his crown be set on a pillow by his head as he lies down, while the nobles, their bearded profiles boyar-like in their solemnity, whisper in consternation. Recovering enough to stand at a casement, Gielgud delivers an anguished, richly sculpted soliloquy on the burdens of kingship in which Welles, synecdochically substituting the crown for Kott's Grand Mechanism, requires Gielgud to reprise his most universally admired stage assumption, Shakespeare's Richard II, and inform us with stolen lines that his stolen crown lies uneasily (but firmly) upon his head. Hardly has he finished before we dissolve to a close-up of the prince in the flower of youth, as apparent in the blossoming branch behind his head. An interlude of revelries follows at the Boar's Head. When Hal returns to court, it is to find the nobles gathered round the sick bed. He kneels, his face framed vertically against the prone form of his father, just as Othello's was to Desdemona's on her last night (initially, in fact, it is not the king's profile but the cushioned crown that occupies the right of the frame). As the chanting begins outside the chamber, the prince makes the sign of the cross, voicing a token repentance and the formulae of filial piety before seizing the crown, rising, exiting the chamber, and kneeling in prayer. Another town scene follows and this one is a continuation of the sequence from the start of the film when Falstaff and Shallow walked through the snow, a shot we now recognize as the opening flash-forward. The barely comprehensible musings of the old reprobates are followed by a cut to the vigorous (offscreen) cries of the king, making us aware that the prince's power lust has caused him to so "wish" his father dead as to mistake appearance for fact. The revived monarch rushes out to recover his ill-gotten trinket, and when the father does finally find a seat, his son, now wearing the crown, improvises as skillfully as Iago, convincing his father of the grand strategy behind his dissipation while slipping the purloined crown back into his hands. "How I came by the crown, O God forgive," says the monarch, who expires pronouncing benedictions on his son. Hal rises and in an Olivieresque crescendo delivers a resonant address to the kneeling courtiers.

The film's structure, then, hinges on its parallels and antitheses. Life-affirming sexual congress precedes the grotesque realism of bloody conflict, even as two false fathers vie for the affections of sons who are neither their own, nor what they seem.[85] If real fathers precipitate war, then the false sons, each as profligate in their opposed ways, determine the outcome. In urging his kinsmen to battle, Hotspur leads them to their doom, while Hal appears to hasten his acquisition of the crown by breaking his father's heart. From very early on, in fact, we discover the extent to which the sons determine their fathers' destinies. When dismissed by King Henry in the opening scene at court, the conspirators (Hotspur, his father, and his uncle) are decided in their course of action by Hotspur's tirade. Hal's ascendancy over Falstaff is shown more subtly, at the termination of the sequence depicting the tavern ménage. Having baited the old scoundrel and planned a caper with him, the prince's trusted accomplice, Poins, exits, and we see horsemen (from an otherwise concealed retinue) ride away. Hal follows and Falstaff ambles after him and detains him at the stockade-like doorway. In an unusual ninety-degree cut, the camera places Hal in the foreground and Falstaff behind him, framed centrally. On hearing Falstaff's justification of thievery, the prince, now occupying the left of the frame, turns away from Falstaff to deliver the famous soliloquy in *1 Henry IV* in which he compares himself to a crafty sun [son] deliberately concealing his radiance behind clouds until the time for revelation is ripe [i.e., at the death of the father]. While the prince makes his address to the left, beyond the frame, Falstaff looks at the camera as if frozen in theatrical convention, his face appearing to register emotions not entirely connected with the prince's words. Welles, who seldom eschewed deep focus in such compositions, emphasizes Falstaff's obliviousness to the prince's instrumental use of him, chortling at the very moment Hal is about to reveal to the spectators that the slightly out-of-focus figure behind him would eventually be cast off. Hal's ability to "freeze" his roguish father in place, and that father's immobility and incomprehension, seem in retrospect the certain indices of the subservient role whose very acceptance necessitates a show of public bravado.

Nowhere is such involved role-playing better illustrated than in the scene of the "play extempore" in which Hal and Falstaff take turns impersonating the formers' father before an audience of bawds and drunkards on a Truffautesque stagelike set in the Boar's Head. The anthropologist Claude Lévi-Strauss associated improvisation and the use of found objects with pretechnological cultures, and in a classic act of such bricolage, Falstaff transforms a saucepan into the king's crown and saucily imitates Gielgud's verbal mannerisms and fruity delivery.[86] When Hal takes on the same role, he can only play himself as king, and a humorless one at that. Wounded by the all-too-serious threat of banishment, Falstaff-as-Falstaff first suggests that very punishment for his rival and Hal's sidekick Poins, and then volunteers his own henchman Bardolph, before running his hands over his globular contours to declare, "Banish Jack Falstaff, and banish all the world."

The quadrangular relationship between fathers and sons culminates in a scene as distinctive for its repeated, and again uncharacteristic, close-ups as the earlier one that placed Falstaff out of focus. It is presaged by a duel fought before the eyes of one of the fathers—and his alone—to regain the attentions, if not the affections, of the other. Having witnessed Hal's victory, and having almost tricked him by playing dead, Falstaff soon revives once his false son departs, only to then play false and abdicate all title to fatherhood for the sake of property (by his reckoning at least an earldom or dukedom). The battle done, he carries the lifeless Harry Percy right past the prince and then pauses to drop him as if he were a sack of potatoes. Rendered even more globose by his armor, Falstaff resumes his metaphor of the world and observes in dismay: "How the world is given to lying." When Hal insists that he saw them both dead, Falstaff improvises yet again with a tale of mutual revival and combat. The camera cuts to Hal's glare, whereupon the king, as if he has been an unseen presence all along, turns suspiciously from one to the other. Hal lowers his head and then shoots a glance at his father, whose expression registers annoyance. Falstaff summons a suitably shocked expression. Having surveyed the corpse and then glanced up at his son, the king strides past, his cloak billowing. For all his "goodness," Falstaff has declined in our estimation to the extent that the prince's subsequent behavior seems amply motivated, if hardly justified. Nor does the king stand redeemed: he must for his part pretend that he is confident of success in a conflict largely of his making. Engaged in his ruse, he fails to see through Falstaff's. The stentorian tones in which he proclaims an end to civil strife are undercut by his slumping slightly on his horse as his sickness grips him. We discover, presently, that instead of rewarding Falstaff he has ordered his separation from the prince. When Falstaff tries to win Hal back, the prince, having no more use for him, turns and walks away, tossing aside his cup and leaving Falstaff to toast his receding figure.

French Connections, or the *Auteur* Paradox

The deluded clown-rogue who in defying the march of History treats laughter as its antidote and a cure-all even for his own misdeeds was transparently engrafted onto Welles's larger-than-life public persona. Naremore, for one, perceives that as director, Welles used the camera to accentuate his dissipated features and a ballooning girth supplemented with padding.[87] Like Falstaff, Welles profits most at his own expense. The sphere of the world to which Falstaff refers ironically,[88] inviting carnivalesque laughter by subsuming the future king's territorial ambitions into a bodily metaphor, refers not only to the external world of Elizabethan realpolitik, but also to the diminished and hitherto largely self-contained world of independent filmmaking. The "world" is also the world of the film and filmmaker, then, and not just the world represented and allegorically refracted by the film. Unlike Shakespeare's Falstaff whose self-deceptions must take in the audience for the better part of three plays, the film predicts its outcome rather early. From the outset there is no doubt that the narrator conspires with Hal, that the prince has official history on his side. So it is that a secret confidence to the spectator in an early scene grows into a mirthless, calculated jest before the cronies at the Boar's Head, and finally into the new king's first proclamation before the assembled nobility: he does banish Jack Falstaff in the end, as promised, but having done so still claims a fair chunk of the more substantial world.

Anderegg too has noted the centrality of history as a theme in *Chimes*, and further that the film confronts the viewer with an uneasy juxtaposition of premodern, modern, and postmodern.[89] The premodern consists of a world that antedates the emergent one governed by political calculation, in a sense the world of Bakhtin's perennial and never fully suppressed folk culture that Welles, unlike him (but like Shakespeare), sees defeated at the hands of its inexorable successor, the world we call "early modern." The postmodern, which Anderegg sees in the aesthetic terms of a Linda Hutcheon rather than that of the political diffidence of a Fredric Jameson, resides in the radical disruption of a series of texts in the process of constituting another vastly different in tone and genre, if faithful to its surface features (and, indeed, Welles was still attached to a Modernist conception of art as socially relevant and potentially transformative). It is Welles's modernity, then, that is most in question, for it is not only Shakespeare's sense of change in Tudor England that he evokes but also late modernity in the form of theatrical modernism and both the major phases of cinematic modernism. Theatrical modernism is present not only stylistically, but in a sense corporeally, in that among male actors the disembodied Ralph Richardson and the doomed, if omnipresent John Gielgud, represented the best-known alternatives to Olivier's heroic Shakespearean style. Welles's citations of cinematic modernism are more esoteric, evident not only in the presence of iconic actors such as Fernando Rey and Jeanne Moreau, but also in stylistic references to the European avant-gardes of the 1920s (incorporating elements of German Expressionism in the mise en scène and, most explicitly, what remained of Soviet Formalism in Eisenstein's late films), and rather more poignantly the second, late phase of cinematic modernity that began in the 1950s with the New American Cinema and culminated with the European avant-garde cinemas of the late 1950s and early 1960s.

Of the European avant-garde cinemas of the 1960s, the closest to Welles in every respect was the French New Wave. If André Bazin was the adopted intellectual father figure to the critics of the journal he founded, the *Cahiers du Cinéma*, then Welles's equivalent surrogacy was as their cinematic father, a quasi-incestuous relationship echoed in those of *Chimes*. In articulating a *politique des auteurs*, a policy (or politics) of authorship, the *Cahiers* critics caught the wind of popular sentiment, a boredom with Hollywood's post–World War II dominance of France's box office. In turn they influenced American filmmaking in the 1970s: for them Welles belonged at the summit of a pantheon that Ford and Hawks (and later Hitchcock) occupied for the very reason that his style transcended Hollywood's industrial uniformity, and he was an inspirational icon because that style was discernible as much outside the system as within its gilded confines.[90]

My passing mention of Truffaut as a possible model for the theatre-within-film scenes at the Boar's Head was not casual, although a zealous critic might point out that I might just as plausibly have selected Jean Renoir or Marcel Carné. Such a critic, though, would have to account for the wistful Jeanne Moreau who, but for her presence in Welles's previous completed feature *The Trial* (1962), seems a most unlikely choice for a Doll Tearsheet given to dropping rather more than her "H"s when repeatedly rendering "whoreson" "Orson." The extended sequence that reveals the extent of Welles's engagement with the *nouvelle vague* begins with Falstaff sending a letter through a page (played charmingly by young Beatrice Welles), warning him of Poins's ill intentions. When we return to Sir John at the Boar's head, he at first seems overcome with melancholy, but presently revives by defending Doll's honor against Pistol's lascivious advances. The punishment complete, she calls him an "Orson chop," before tumbling to the floor beside him, whispering endearments, just as Poins and Hal arrive to spy on them from the rafters. In short order the "bastard son" of the king and "his brother" leap down and roll the fat knight over, with Doll on top of him, Hal pinning his right side, and Poins taking up the left with an arm girding Doll's waist. It is Hal, however, who draws Doll to him in a proprietary embrace while they strive to keep Falstaff pinned down. By the time Falstaff has extricated himself it is Hal who is exchanging kisses with Doll, and by the time the deflated amorist departs, even Poins has been displaced to a corner of the frame and the acquiescent Doll has her head buried in the prince's chest. Hal's musings about the nature of man provoke Poins to a trenchant ascription of his moralizing to hypocrisy. Framed by Poins's remarks, the merry ending to the sequence, in which Falstaff fills the frame once more in a raucous jig with the revelers in the inner courtyard, strikes a deliberately false note, the communal laughter ringing hollow.

Throughout these scenes, whether in terms of the themes of a lust triangle, or of shot composition, or even the mercurial shifts of mood, the prolonged allusions to the then recent *Jules et Jim* (1961) are unmistakable. Truffaut's masterpiece, described by Robert Stam as "perhaps one of the most poignantly memorable films ever made,"[91] concerns the title characters' love for the impulsive Catherine, played by Moreau. The spirit of the jazz age as embodied in the liberated woman whose polymorphous sexuality resembles one of Brazilian modernist novelist Jorge Amado's characters (in that for her choices, especially of sexual partners, are intolerably burdensome) is transformed into the halfpenny Renaissance harlot shared by false father and feigning son, but available equally to any but the most impecunious of men. The citation is a just one of many, because along with a cavalcade of cinematic techniques (including the freeze frames and stills beloved of Godard, Alain Resnais, and Chris Marker), "Shakespeare" serves as the tagline to a running gag in *Jules et Jim*. Catherine's instability results in the death of one of the protagonists and her own, while Welles is far more literal than Shakespeare in treating Falstaff's death as a direct result of his rejection by Hal. Moreover, at the time Truffaut made *Jules et Jim*, there appears to have been something of a quarrel between him and Godard who, according to Stam, were not "sharing their women amicably." Godard, he points out, associated the imminent dissipation of the New Wave with the divisive consequences of female intimacies: "Each of us has gone to our own separate planet...Every day the women we sleep with separate us more than they bring us together. It is not normal."[92] Forces other than women (and sexual competition) were actually at work to bring independent cinema with popular appeal to an end, and Godard simultaneously impugned and courted sources of funding rather more assiduously than he did Truffaut's amorous conquests. By the mid-1960s, even as state-sponsored cinemas were springing up throughout Europe and producing a new crop of *auteurs* who dominated the prize-givings at film festivals, independent cinema of the kind deemed necessary by the 1950s makers of the New American Cinema and desirable by the New Wave filmmakers (who, after initial box-office favor became rather dependent on state support and studio facilities) began to decline. Some filmmakers, Truffaut and Godard among them, proved successful enough early on to attract producers who furnished them with adequate budgets in the expectation of prestige or profit. If *Chimes* is to be read as autobiographical, then, it is also a diary of the travails of the independent filmmaker and the end of the old, less budget-dominated approach to filmmaking.

One of the New Wave *auteurs* who gained just such an early celebrity was Claude Chabrol, and his connection to Welles might also be worth considering. Chabrol's take on *Hamlet* is, for instance, a send-up of Olivier's gendered madness (in that Olivier portrays Hamlet's as artful and contrived, while Ophelia's is not only real but verging on that of nineteenth-century French clinical descriptions of female hysteria). It also parodies Olivier's imagery of quasi-cultish and entirely religious self-celebration (images of crucifixion, for example, develop the theme of Hamlet's willing martyrdom).[93] Both the plot and imagery of *Ophélia* (1962) satirize the repeated image of Hamlet in the borrowed French release poster: indeed, Yvan, the protagonist, does not even have to see the film to decide that his destiny parallels that of the Danish prince. Standing outside a provincial movie theatre, his point-of-view close-ups of the poster result in a montage of the key scenes as envisioned by his illustrious predecessor. In an offhanded compliment to Shakespeare's discussion of genre in the play, passersby seeing the poster speculate on the kind of the film it happens to be, ranging from a love story to a history (as with Shakespeare's parody of classicism, here a parody of the Tradition of Quality). Visiting his favorite bar, Yvan sees the hostess, Ginette, carrying away a mouse dangling from a trap, from which he takes his inspiration for a plan of action. This he describes to the Horatio character, François, in a high-angle shot in which the empty mousetrap can be seen to lie on a table beside their wine glasses. Ginette, François, and a comical gravedigger star in his silent film version of "The Mousetrap," which his unsuspecting uncle Adrien (husband to his recently bereaved mother, Claudia, played by Alida Valli, the famously mysterious woman of Carol Reed's 1949 film *The Third Man*) screens for invited guests. Adrien follows precedent and borrows a pistol to put an end to Yvan, but loses his resolve when the latter awakens; instead, he swallows poison, and in a parodic death scene that rivals that of Madame Bovary in duration, ensures that the film ends on a note of "profoundly Oedipal" anagnoresis when he reveals that he is Yvan's real father. Only Lucy, Yvan's girlfriend and the daughter of André, the blustering Polonius character, consistently refuses to accept the role accorded her by Yvan (the film, therefore, notably lacks Ophelia). Even after her father's accidental death in a tree, she remains remarkably calm and steadfastly declares her love for Yvan, even as he lies babbling in her arms.[94] So it turns out that, while the fathers and sons are deranged, the women (whether chaste or carnal) are eminently sane. The treetop "crucifixion" of the Polonius character and an overly literal dead mouse lying on a table ridicule the conflicting drives behind Hamlet's revenge-necessitating theology. It stands to reason, then, that it is the commercially successful, philo-American Chabrol who completes the cinematic circle by giving Welles a role in *Ten Days' Wonder* (*La Décade Prodigieuse*, 1971), one that permitted the aging actor, at least in the realm of memory, to return to the United States.

Ten Days' Wonder is a portmanteau of Wellesian themes, its fable-like structure drawing on the Magic Realism that Welles incorporated into *The Immortal Story* (1968). It is no small coincidence that Chabrol's film reunited Welles the actor with his onetime star, Anthony Perkins. Perkins, meanwhile, was embroiled in a futile struggle to escape the clutches of the woman who proved to be his immortal mother, Mrs. Bates, from Hitchcock's *Psycho* (1960), no less than the pinions of jurisprudence in *The Trial*, the Welles feature that preceded *Chimes* and his most transparent commentary on his condemnation without proper trial or reprieve. Welles's rewriting of Kafka is, of course, more than a political screed: Josef K is trapped in a psychosexual nightmare in which only he seems to be punished for wanton concupiscence, a hopeless attraction to a fetching bevy of loose women who either abandon or betray him. If this invented catalogue of film noir femmes fatales was not enough, K is granted a degree of agency in resisting his captors and executioners that Kafka's character never is. At the conclusion, Welles's K even attempts to discard the dynamite his executioners throw toward his feet, and whether he succeeds or not is left ambiguous by a Hiroshima-evoking conclusion that is in its own way as ironic as the tenebrous Adagio (a musical forgery once attributed to Tomaso Albinoni) that punctuates the key moments of the film. Perkins's performance for Chabrol and the director's use of vertiginous canted frames at the start of the film intimate Welles's presence (the latter effect has even been ascribed to his influence even as an actor on films such as *The Third Man* [dir. Carol Reed, 1949], but probably derives from a sequence in *The Trial* in which the unremitting disorientation that afflicts the protagonist manifests itself as vertigo). Moreover, the central plot device of the film is purloined (presumably with Welles's approval) from *Mr. Arkadin*: "Watch me, follow me... I am afraid of killing someone," exclaims the sculptor Charles, as he enlists his friend Paul (played by another regular New Wave actor, Michel Piccoli) to undertake the quest of unraveling a myth of origins. The dominant theme of *Chimes*, patricide by false sons in the quest for temporal power, reappears in the Oedipalism of Charles, adopted son of a war profiteer and business magnate who, Gatsby-like, has created an artificial world for himself, enclosing it in a shell that resists change. Welles plays a "German" who claims to be "American," a role reminiscent of the one he gave himself in *The Stranger*. And in Charles's inferior and bombastic assemblage of unfinished and unsold works, there is even a reference to the decrepit Charles Foster Kane's gallery of statues in his decaying pleasure palace, Xanadu. Welles even gets to play with the idea of biography in lines whose ripe resonance suggests yet another test of his improvisatory powers (he had the incurable habit of rewriting his lines to suit his interpretations): "After all, what is a man to do with his money? Of course one helps to keep the world in good repair. And for one's pleasure. Well, with money you can make choices. You can choose the place in the world where you are happiest to live. I chose not only the place but the time: 1925. The Fall of 1925." Once again, then, we have an embodiment of Welles's battle against the tides of history, indeed against the very passage of time, in a film that remains a commentary on, if no longer part of, the cinematic movement that rescued Welles from critical obloquy and enshrined his posthumous reputation. Here, too, is the best evidence that by 1971 Welles's situation as much as his oeuvre was being treated as the touchstone of independent cinema.

It is this idea of Welles as the embodiment of an ethos that reappears in Godard's *King Lear*. The adulatory, even reverential homage to a pantheon of directors in his prologue invests the Barthes-Foucault declaration of the "death of the author" with an entirely new meaning. Godard's Brechtian pleasure-pain tactic of drawing spectators in by offering and then disrupting certain visual pleasures had by now become a trademark widely associated with the increasing rigor of his style. Citing his stylistically distinctive predecessors was thus an assertion of his status as *auteur* and a confirmation and reiteration of his belief in the political value of individual intervention in aesthetic discourse. That he interleaves a substantial part of Welles's oeuvre with his own Shakespeare film and cites Welles's allegorical self-representation (i.e., form rather than content) in the case of *Chimes*, redefines and refines canonicity in a way that addresses the shifting fortunes of the author in French critical theory as much as it disputes the particular political economy of the sign already found in Pasolini's conception of *contenutismo*. Pasolini's inclusion in the *King Lear* pantheon of directors and the spectator's "inclusion" in the text—the well-meaning if ineffectual spirits attempting to forestall tragedy in direct contradiction of Pasolini's willful proletarian participants capable of intervention at a number of levels—positions her as the subject who must be shocked in Brechtian fashion into an awareness of her idiocy and complacency, is also characteristic of Godard's later style.

The choice is neither convenient nor casual. Welles's experiment with filming Shakespeare's textual traces, transmuting them into a world entirely his own, remains a singular achievement. Lubitsch, Cukor, Olivier, Kurosawa, Kozintsev, Zeffirelli, and Branagh also alluded to the visual and musical cultures that informed or grew out of the Shakespearean corpus, and they too drew from the wide range of performance traditions that have accrued to the plays. Yet even in their most spirited attempts to escape the fetters of theatricality forced on them by their idiom, their films, for better or worse, seem to retain the trapdoors beneath the actors' feet. Welles alone treated Shakespeare as an authentic screenwriter, and an inventive and socially relevant one to boot. No wonder Godard's resurrection of him in *King Lear* gives notice of the rebirth of the author. That the last of Welles's Shakespeare films continued to inspire later *auteurs* even after *King Lear*'s hard-won obscurity demands the more extended treatment of intertextuality that I accord it in the chapter that follows.

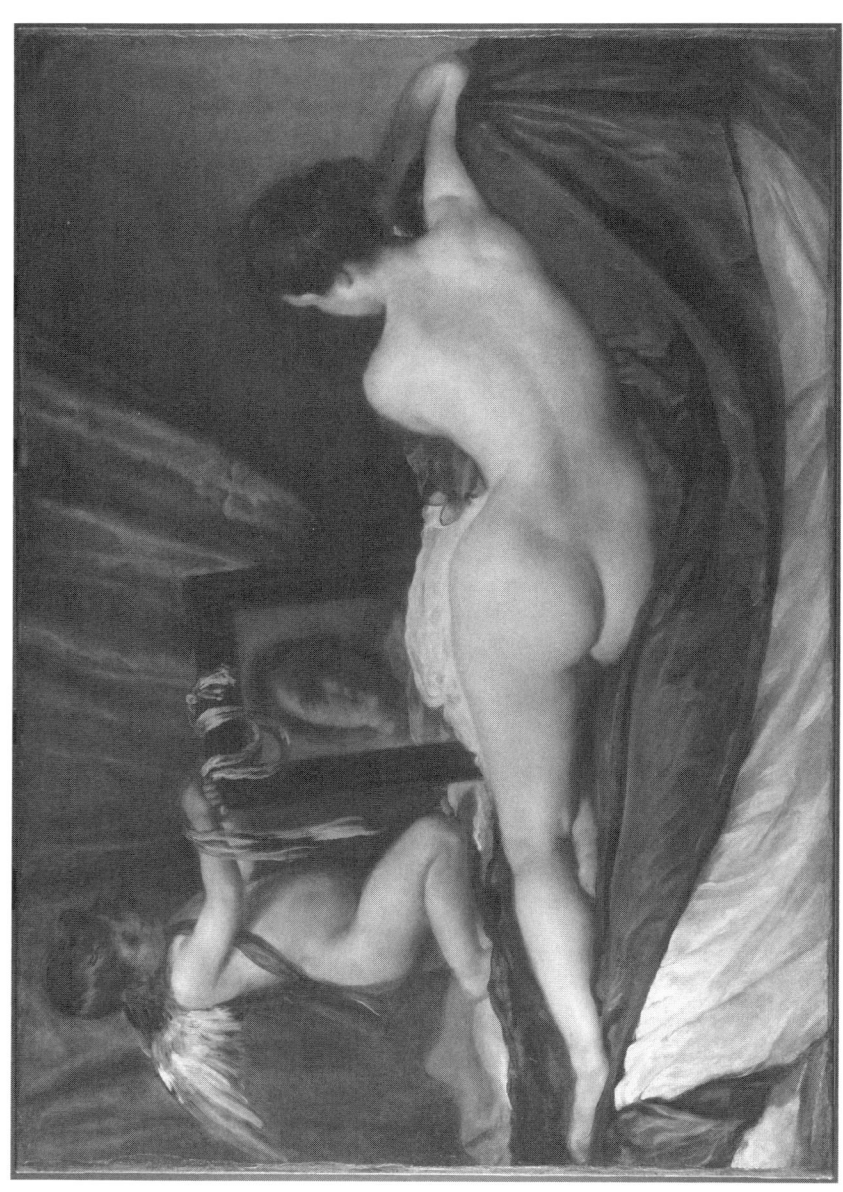

The Rokeby Venus. Oil on canvas by Diego Velázquez, pictured in Pier Paolo Pasolini's *Che cosa sono le nuvole?* (1968). Courtesy of the National Gallery, London.

CHAPTER FIVE

Six Authors in Search of a Text: The Shakespeares of Van Sant, Branagh, Godard, Pasolini, Greenaway, and Luhrmann

In which a semblance of order can be found in a riot of texts ★ *Miola's method* ★ *Slumming with the Bard in the Midwest* ★ *Hal as Henry, or righteous ruthlessness* ★ *Godard's book of revelations* ★ *W.S., puppetmaster and cad* ★ *Caliban's book, or the artist as the author of his own age* ★ *Will Shakespeare raise the Red Curtain?*

Each of the foregoing chapters encapsulates a different dimension of the idea that adaptation consists not of single process of translation but, instead, of a multitude of simultaneous interpretive acts. True, any particular Shakespeare adaptation enjoys a unique relation to groups of words attributed with varying degrees of confidence to a late Renaissance author whose very biography remains a matter of conjecture. Even so, the veneration accorded Shakespeare in his native land, further augmented by the mystique of the Great Shakespeare of other national traditions, grants his works a self-evident cultural and historical particularity. Needless to say, the films discussed in these pages bear witness to layers of prior textualization involving images, words, sounds, and perhaps even other sensory stimuli. Shakespeare films are innately hybrid texts: the smell of greasepaint and the taste of popcorn, no less than the residues of printers' ink, can be felt in them.

This may explain the tendency among students of such films to substitute the seemingly more precise term "intertextuality" for the all-too-general "adaptation." After all, "adaptation" may even insinuate a deliberate departure from the original, not just an interpretation. Yet, as Robert Miola discerns, "intertextuality" is one of the foremost examples of terminological imprecision to have attained a certain critical celebrity. Its best-intentioned adherents (no less than its least) appear to be unaware that, if it was confined to early modern literature alone, the term would still denote at least seven different types of textual relationship, and this even when the idea of "text" is defined strictly as an interpretable work of human creation.[1] Used loosely and in conjunction with such other indefinite terms as "postmodern" and "popular culture," intertextuality, far from rescuing Shakespeare from adaptation, can ensnare him in obfuscation.

Alternatively, if we treat intertextuality as representative of a range of related processes distinct from the catchall of "adaptation" (i.e., the attempt to recreate an earlier text or group of texts), then we may turn once more to Orson Welles in seeking a point of entry into the more challenging issues pertaining to the field Miola defines, broadly, as "intertextual transactions."[2] Precisely because Welles and some of his fellow filmmakers have been sensitive to Shakespeare's use of his own sources, Miola's clarification of "intertextuality" proves surprisingly applicable to the context of cinema. Miola argues that for the sake of convenience the seven types of intertextuality might be grouped by function into three categories: the division between types and categories is neither absolute nor exclusive, but "appear[s] on a continuum with various shadings and overlappings." While concurring with Heinrich Plett that the interpretation of the term by Julia Kristeva, Roland Barthes, and Jacques Derrida proves inadmissibly narrow in treating textual histories, he endorses one that preoccupied reception theorists: namely, the intertextual connections made by readers of other texts, a process Cesare Segre describes as "interdiscursivity."[3] Hence, to his first category, texts mediated directly through the author, belong revision, translation, quotation, and direct response to source material; to the second, invocations of textual traditions, belong literary conventions and configurations; to the third, "paralogues" resulting from audience association, belong alternative texts that illuminate the intellectual, social, theological, or political meanings inherent to the original.[4]

In addition to Miola's categories, I have also suggested that history and autobiography serve as the submerged but insistent subtexts in such films as *Chimes at Midnight* and Ruiz's *Richard III*. I cannot, therefore, claim a perfect correspondence between his description of Renaissance intertextuality and the patterns of intertextual transactions that the following pages document: after all, my observations pertain to a broader terrain that involves different media and the parallel histories of a variety of artistic traditions. Nevertheless, once we recognize that the interpretations offered by Pasolini, Godard, and Greenaway—to take only the most strikingly divergent examples—each corresponds to a different type within a separate category specified by Miola (i.e., primarily but by no means exclusively revision, configuration, and paralogism), then his insights do appear to extend to, and even be amplified by, films of Shakespearean derivation. When, for instance, Miola discovers that Chapman, despite his claim to direct inspiration from Homer, portrays a more contemporary drama than the *Iliad* (Patroclus and Hector acquire biblical "souls" at a historical moment when the rendering of sacred scripture in common tongues was fraught with political overtones), the process of translation he describes was rediscovered, in an arguably even more ideologically perilous context, by Pasternak, Shostakovich, and Kozintsev.[5]

The Echoes of *Chimes*

In terms of the date of its release, *Chimes at Midnight* is not the first of the films in the discussion that follows; indeed, as has been my practice so far, I resist purely chronological arrangement in the interest of grouping films (or sequences of films) that illustrate facets of each other. Nevertheless, since I have already dwelt on the historical and autobiographical subtext in Welles, I would be remiss not to mention the compelling afterlife of a film whose concluding images are a poignant reminder of history's impersonality in the face of human mortality.

We last left the living Welles with Chabrol, trying desperately to stay the hand of time in a remote château. Stateside, the rise of the new crop of Hollywood *auteurs* in the 1970s coincided with the increasing availability of "classic" studio-era films through the video rental market, with the predictable transformation of the New Wave *auteur*'s cinephile *homage*-by-citation into an irresistible compulsion to allude to the chestnuts of film history. Not surprisingly, as films began to reference the medium of cinema with increasing regularity, acts of filial impiety such as those of Chabrol turned into a veritable necrophiliac celebration of Welles as the archetype of the American filmmaker who, while continuing to seek a box office and engage with a popular audience, still chose to go his own way.

It is the nation's heartland, in fact, in which Welles's Falstaff achieved his most explicit reincarnation. In his book on Welles, Anderegg begins his commentary on *Chimes* with an expression of surprise: "[A]bout a third of the way through Gus Van Sant's exploration of street hustling in the urban underworlds of the Pacific Northwest" [in] *My Own Private Idaho* (1991), [we encounter] "an extended borrowing of Shakespeare's Falstaff/Hal plays, which is at the same time stylistically indebted to Welles's *Chimes at Midnight*."[6] Unannounced, a man the boys call the Fat Guy (the cocaine supplier, Bob Pigeon) appears on the scene with one of the hustlers at his side, his first words being "The things that we have seen." Miola might discern quotation in this, but it actually turns out not to be quotation of Shakespeare. A minute later, Pigeon offers the non sequitur that he could never see a thing as lovely as a tree (quotation apparently being of itself risible). On entering a building with a pillared interior evocative of Welles's beamed set for the Boar's Head, however, the hustler (Budd) assumes the part of Justice Shallow and repeats the very lines that Welles did previously: "Jesus, the things that we've seen." To which the Fat Guy responds, in dialogue entirely inappropriate to the situation, "We have heard the chimes at midnight." This draws the response, "That we have. That we have. Jesus, the things that we have seen." At this point, the Welles-inspired scenes, while remaining within Miola's initial category of intertextuality, move from near quotation to a pattern of modernizing revision. The "time of day" speech the prince tosses off early on in *Chimes* now reemerges from the mouth of Scott Favor, the Hal character played by Keanu Reeves as the slumming son of a wheelchair-bound real estate baron turned politician. "Why you don't even look at a clock unless hours were lines of coke ... or time itself is a fair hustler in black leather," he chides the Fat Guy. So much for "flame-coloured taffeta." The unfair hustlers soon plan the brigandage that will embarrass Bob. "I will change when people expect it least," concludes the updated soliloquy, confided to the camera in anticipation of coming into a fortune when Scott turns twenty-one.

Anderegg categorizes Van Sant's debt as being primarily owed to Welles's cinematography and mise en scène.[7] Yet his scenes follow those of *Chimes*—sometimes even their order—in all the "Falstaff" episodes. Even the conclusion provides the occasion for a Wellesian joke. When Scott returns from Italy with the girl who proves to be his true love and his access to a restorative heterosexual intimacy, he is readily accepted into his father's privileged circles and invited to their festivities. As tuxedoed partygoers shower him with strategic compliments, a disheveled Bob bursts in and falls to his knees, demanding recognition. "I don't know you old man," says the aspiring politician-tycoon, and although Scott leavens his renunciation with the admission that he had loved his own father less, the young magnate categorically charges the derelict not to come near him.

Bob's cocaine-induced decline is as precipitous as his predecessor's in *Chimes*, but the mise en scène of a shot depicting him feet first on his deathbed is actually arranged to resemble that of the dead Cardinal Wolsey—itself a composition based on Andrea Mantegna's dramatically foreshortened tempera painting of the *Lamentation over the Dead Christ*—whom Welles played in Fred Zinnemann's *A Man For All Seasons* (1966). Nor is the pattern of intertextuality governed solely by the dictates of narrative compression and paraphrase. Some themes are actually expanded or rendered more explicit. The search for "true" fathers becomes rather more literal (and even gives way to a search for true mothers), and Poins's intimacy with Hal is recast as a grand, if painfully unrequited passion suffered by a narcoleptic River Phoenix, a role marginally amplified by Welles but here given sufficient prominence to serve as the short-lived actor's most admired screen performance. Moreover, Van Sant translates long passages of the dialogue into an unstable and deliberately disconcerting amalgam of Welles's abridgement, lines drawn directly from the plays, and a patently invented contemporary street hustler argot. The thematic connections, in fact, are entirely consistent with Van Sant's reading of *Chimes* as an expression of homosocial intimacy manqué, with Welles's battle between the court and tavern recast as the battle between a lower-class boy hustler underworld and an elite, normative, and adult heterosexuality.

Intentionally attenuated though it may be, this is by no means a preposterous reading: Welles's male characters seem to stage elaborate presentations to impress each other, and they handle each other in a manner that, however authentic to the Renaissance, to the contemporary eye suggests heightened intimacy or exaggerated masculine bravado. When, for instance, Welles wishes to undercut Hotspur's rhetorical posturing, he places him in a bathtub in which he stands to make a grand statement about his horse being his throne, as a result of which he drops his towel revealingly. In other words, Van Sant's is a medium-centered intertextuality, demanding of its ideal spectator a better memory of a rather obscure film than of a sequence of well-known plays. The film repays close study, and benefits greatly from the Criterion DVD reissue that boasts extensive (tongue-in-cheek) scholarly commentaries, together with an innovative "distressed" cover design.

Less evidently of Wellesian inspiration, Branagh's *Henry V* proved more directly influential in heralding the revival of filmed Shakespeare in the last decade of the twentieth century. Like Chabrol's *Ophélia*, this film succeeds as an autonomous text while simultaneously being an extension of Welles's interpretation of Hal and an obvious reaction against Olivier's earlier adaptation of *Henry V*. Branagh even begins with a negative tribute to Olivier's giant shadow by drawing on the self-referential device of depicting the process of the film's creation (one found not only in his immediate predecessors, Welles, Truffaut, and Carlos Saura, but even much earlier and with equal felicity in Wladislaw Starewicz and Dziga Vertov).[8] It is not altogether surprising, therefore, that in playing against Olivier's film Branagh amplifies Welles's insertions of the visceral Realism characteristic of the early Italian Neorealist films into the battle scenes of *Chimes*. Although interspersed with the grim comedy also found in such early Neorealist films as Roberto Rossellini's *Paisà* (1946) and Vittorio De Sica's *Miracle in Milan* (*Miracolo à Milano*, 1948), Welles's civil war is as muddy as it is bloody, and the abundant sounds of hacked flesh and sights of oozing blood in *Henry V* suggest that Branagh is not to be outdone in the extent of the carnage he visits on the vasty fields of France. The sumptuous reds and blues of Olivier's film are reduced to drab browns and grays, and the actors' faces are as coarse and grimy as in any recent Hollywood war movie. Save for the occasional extra being shot twice by the same arrow, Branagh's version of battle is even more immediate in its sensory impact than Welles's, inviting a reflex of empathy rather than prolonged meditation about the nature of nationalist bloodletting or the political dissembling that is its cause.

Branagh, in fact, seems to follow the pattern of post–World War II British theatre directors in concerning himself with his characters' inner psychology rather than with the overtly propagandistic message of national unity in Shakespeare's play (as Olivier did) or the relation of the artist to the social and political currents of his time (as Welles did). He is partial to driven and devious protagonists, although they have grown less dangerously manipulative as evidenced in his own films: Henry's successor, Hamlet-the-Machiavel, gives way to a hyperactive Benedick and he, in turn, to a boisterous Berowne (it also explains his supreme performance to date on film, an overpowering, genuinely vengeful Iago for Oliver Parker who, in his *Othello*, also summons Laurence Fishburne's action hero parts and the seductive innocence of Irène Jacob from her celebrated roles for Krzystof Kieslowski). The Vincent Price effect can be cumulative.

Predictably, Branagh's first such assumption, a Harry both wrathful and warlike, can hardly repress a subterranean, volcanic rage: mounted and in a hot sweat, he threatens the citizens of Harfleur with murder, rape, and pillage, seeming much more himself in his public ferocity than when upon their capitulation he privately sanctions mercy. This is a Henry who resembles Olivier's Henry much less than he does Welles's Macbeth, being like him in imminent danger of liquefaction. Throughout the film he is so bespattered with blood, sweat, toil, and tears that the Chorus's elliptical intercessions (at once commentaries on unfolding events and "fast-forwards" to later points in the action) seem increasingly to be explanations of the warrior-king's deeper need both to inflict and receive physical punishment. Although eventually the loudest of Choruses on film, Derek Jacobi—who many might argue, is the Gielgud among the veteran Shakespearean actors still in their heyday, a Claudius who willingly yielded his crown to Hamlet—begins his interpretation with a meditative quietness that is in marked contrast to Olivier's consciously "stagey" presentation of his Chorus. Recall that the latter delivers his imaginative challenge to the audience having planted himself on the sweetest spot of the Globe's projecting stage. Branagh's solitary Chorus walks through a sound stage festooned with the apparatus of filmmaking. The camera keeps him centered in the frame as it tracks laterally, until it pauses with him to spin around and display the mess of an unfinished film as he utters the words: "[D]ared on this unworthy scaffold to bring forth so great an object." As the music that begins in mid-sentence grows more urgent, Jacobi keeps pace with it in a verbal crescendo and accelerando, shouting the last lines as he throws open a vast door to reveal a coven of scheming prelates rendered in warty close-ups worthy of *The Passion of Joan of Arc*. When shortly thereafter we meet the new king demanding an "interpretation" of the Law Salique, he again does so in the heightened whisper brought into fashion by today's close-up-prone stars and made feasible by ever-more-sensitive unidirectional boom microphones. His voice augments in volume only when he rises to answer the Dauphin's mock, again a display of managed anger whose controlled release masquerades for restraint. It seems perverse, therefore, that Branagh shouts to his troops on the battlefield, eschewing Olivier's use of selective sound enhancement when he amplified his delivery as the camera drew back in the set speeches, until we recall that the conventions of recent war film blockbusters demand the Direct Cinema approach of handheld cameras and the closely observed rants of military commanders.

In this sense, one might argue that among the persistent Shakespeareans, Branagh is the quintessence of that generation of filmmakers who positively requires their audience's intimate familiarity with cinema, even to the extent of demanding a specialized knowledge of the Golden Age Musical from the audiences of *Love's Labour's Lost*. His films and the individuality of his interpretations define themselves against those of his contemporaries and predecessors. At the same time, he abides by Hollywood's traditions of mobilizing star appeal and contrasting newer (and implicitly more advanced) technologies to the ones available to the filmmakers of yesteryear. With the unabashed complicity of today's machinery of production he contrives to be even more his own star than Olivier: he reserves the lion's share of the music for his own Henry, for example—as he later does for Hamlet and Benedick—blending it with the dialogue so that both increase in volume and tempo simultaneously, a technique that has gained popularity as the digital attenuation and compression of audio tracks have become a matter of routine. The music energizes the delivery: when calm, the young king's words and their accompaniment are measured; faster music and a torrent of words presage frenzied action. Both in terms of the apparatus of filmmaking and his interpretation of the character, then, Branagh imparts a sense of intense calculation.

So, for instance, he reserves the flashback, one of the oldest and most familiar editing techniques that came to be regarded as characteristic of film narration, exclusively for the new king's cold-blooded days of counterfeited profligacy (particularly noteworthy here for being in marked contrast with his later use of the device to clarify textual intricacies in *Hamlet*, and so on). On hearing that Falstaff has taken ill, Mistress Quickly exclaims, "[T]he king has killed his heart." As in the overlapping narrations of *Citizen Kane*, the point of view now shifts to that of Hal's former cronies who delight in a repartee that owes more to Welles's condensations than to Shakespeare. It is they who envision the hoary reprobate approach the prince, an as-yet-unmotivated fear of punishment writ large on his quivering, fleshy maw. "Banish plump Jack and banish all the world," he mumbles, and when the prince's features harden (revealing the thoughts given to us in voice-over, "I do. I will"), Falstaff descends to wheedling, making a character substitution worthy of Welles's more libertine exploits with the green pencil: "But we have heard the chimes at midnight, Master Harry." Then, after a further moment of silence, we have a broken whisper: "Jesus, the days that we have seen." Again, what he sees on Hal's face makes Falstaff back away, as the prince's voice-over leaps hundreds of lines into the future: "I know thee not old man."

If this is not enough to convince us that the dense Wellesian alternations of scenes have given way to a compression that foregrounds realpolitik as public demonstrations of ruthlessness, then the interlude of Bardolph's hanging leaves little room for doubt. The noose is held a head's length away in deference to the watching king, who acquiesces with a nod. Once more a flashback recounts yet another ominous silence, this time in response to the drunken but less pathetic Bardolph's inquiry as to whether as king the prince would spare thieves from hanging. At this we return abruptly to a present that demands yet another nod to signal Bardolph's toppling from a cart and his wild thrashings before he asphyxiates. Tears now stream down Henry's face, just as blood and the primordial ooze of the battle-churned earth dripped down his face in earlier scenes. They are the molten proof that the prince has blossomed into a statesman-monarch well versed in the arts of doling out Machiavelli's prescribed measures of cruelty and kindness, one who regrets the necessity of war but who regards war as necessary, one who is held in thrall by his power over human lives and so must make his abbreviations of them exemplary.

Branagh's Henry reverses the pattern of domination conceived by Welles's Hal: indeed, his entire film treats *Chimes* as a "source coincident" (to use Miola's Latinate description) with which it exists in a dynamic tension, using Welles's characterizations as a point of departure and as matter for revision.[9] While Hal's triumph over his manipulative fathers proves to be the culmination of a deeply conceived, unfolding strategy, Branagh's prince (like Van Sant's) uses the power inherent to his position to vanquish his fathers at the outset as a means of manipulating them subsequently. His situation is, of course, different from that of Welles's Hal, in that he no longer has to contend with a natural father who clings unto death to the trappings of power. Yet Branagh's sequel goes to some lengths to rehash Hal's rejection of one adopted father, Falstaff, who is recognizably a much-diminished version of Welles's, one evidently habituated to sadistic silences and their ominous portent. Likewise, in the French monarch Charles VII (played memorably by a tremulous Paul Scofield, who on film has specialized in Shakespeare's failing kings on one side of the grave or another), Henry adopts another father preemptively reduced to subservience. The courtship of Charles's daughter is a perfunctory affair devoid of Olivier's gallantry, and when Henry demands his father-in-law's blessing for their union, it comes as an addendum to unconditional surrender. Critics have tried to resolve the contradictions of the character by one extrapolation or another, or given up in the attempt: does Branagh, who often asserts his working-class Irish origins and, like Patrick Stewart, admits to the enforced deprovincialization of his accent, gloss over the lines in the play that seem to valorize Essex's nomination to the command of his Irish misadventure? Does the ascending actor-manager invite the Prince of Wales to his film set as a ratification of his own translation into Royal Shakespeareanness? Does his glamorization of Terminator-style violence foreclose upon the possibility of disengaging brutalizing necessity from necessary brutality? Does Branagh posture for the camera with as much contrivance as Henry does for his courtly audiences, since even in such moments of intimacy as a profile shot of him facing Catherine, he contrives to show not his "good" side but the one with two parallel abrasions behind his right cheek that are suspiciously like marks left by what she, with a relish more in keeping with her shrewish namesake or with Cleopatra, has pronounced "Niles"? Yet such contradictions are in many ways what makes Henry convincing as the contemporary CEO who happens to inherit Great Britain, Inc., and who rapidly effects a hostile takeover of France Ltd. Welles's *Chimes* lacks the glossy Realism available to our contemporaries, but in retrospect, his complicated politics seem less ambiguous and more consistent, marked inevitably by shifts in the world and in the world of filmmaking, but not by the stylistic dictates of the triumphant model of filmmaking so despised by Ruiz. It is the father, in this instance, who may have outshone the son.

Old Hats and New Waves

The little we know of Shakespeare, including a scattering of lines from *King Lear*, suggests that his relations with his daughters, particularly Judith, were sometimes strained. In Godard's per-version of the play, it is not sons (Edgar and Edmund are but minor presences), but daughters who are at issue, and invented progeny serve as a derisive metaphor for pure textual lineages. It is the unlikely fifth-generation descendant (of an unknown descendant) of a line long believed extinct who finds himself entrusted with the retrieval of his ancestor's lost works. From the start the comic plays out against the tragic: the idea of the sacrifice of the son (Isaac and Jesus) finds itself repeated in the iconography of Cordelia's ritualized death and in the repeated references to a Christian eschatology drawing on St. Paul and *The Book of Revelations*, that grows out of the historical conceit that the film begins where Grigori Kozintsev's *King Lear* ends, requiring a baffled lineal descendent of Shakespeare (!) to go in search of his ancestors' lost oeuvre in a postapocalyptic world that is in the process of recovering from the Chernobyl catastrophe. When the grizzled, scarcely comprehensible Professor Pluggy, played by Godard, succeeds in reinventing the lost art of cinema and stages a trial screening, he attempts futilely to explain its workings to a self-important reporter from the *New York Times*; another guest who converses only in French arrives, one Professor Kozintsev from Leningrad, who ignores her. As the film progresses, the voice of the actor who took the part of Kozintsev's Lear begins his quiet monologue with the word "Cordelia," the line from the early scene of division in Kozintsev's film. As the film is about to play, {NO THING}, an intertitle repeated no fewer than seven times in the course of Godard's film (and uttered even more often as dialogue), appears on the screen. It comments amongst other things on the representational nature of cinema, the fact that projected images are insubstantial, cinema itself being what Christian Metz called the "imaginary signifier"; and it remains the key to one of the textual layers of the film. It will suffice for the present to note that the pretense of Shakespeare's authorial disappearance—the character playing Edgar even burns the crumpled pages of a Shakespeare edition when he first discovers a mechanical technology for lighting fires—further comments on the then ebbing tide of New Wave dogma. If any notion of *fidelity* runs through Godard's film, then it resides in an emphasis on essence rather than the verbal substance of a play dominated by the parallels drawn between forms of sin, atonement, martyrdom, and redemptive suffering.

Lineal descendant William Shakespeare Jr. V's investigative methods seem to follow the Platonic logic that knowledge must be remembered rather than acquired through experience, but they also have an ironically Jungian dimension in that his capacity to recall the Bard's lines transforms him into a genetic conduit for a collective Shakespeare-consciousness embedded in a postapocalyptic tribal memory. We see evidence of this just as the *Lear* narrative begins: a dining-room encounter in a hotel with an attractive young woman and her much older escort appears to stimulate recollection, even if it diverts Will Jr. from his "to be or not to be" project. "As you which, As you what" he mumbles, and then a triumphant "As you like it." He thanks her for this sudden access of memory, and she, in turn, having assured the old man that unlike her espoused sisters (reduced to effusive telegrams) she cannot love her father at all, turns to young Will to thank him for having just saved her life by lighting her cigarette. "Are you making a play for my daughter?" asks the punningly possessive old man. The unstated answer, we know, must be "yes." Yet as one of the authors of film authorship, and an ardent adherent throughout his career of the idea of aesthetic individuality, Godard regards adaptation as a necessary violation of

Shakespeare's original "daughter play": when chanced upon, surviving folio pages are burned for fuel, the art of kindling fires being a more significant human rediscovery than the "text." In fact, quite unlike Greenaway's reading of *The Tempest* which posits adaptation as a literal act of multiple authorship and textual preservation, each of his scenes being an explanatory—paralogic—footnote to a narrative of the written text,[10] Godard's *King Lear* selectively reconstitutes an inert textual residue, alluding not to the sources of Shakespeare's thought as Greenaway does, but to the author Jean-Luc Godard's own tropes and devices for reading a work irrevocably contaminated by such later textual accretions as Welles's and Kozintsev's.

Such an oblique adaptation may appear to have only a remote connection to the more verisimilar and narratively cohesive *Chimes*, but Godard goes to some pains to elaborate on his debt to Welles under the pretext of remaking the aborted *Lear*. Indeed, Godard's film appears to imply that, like the New Testament in relation to the Old, it brings to fruition what has been promised, albeit in a world of withered fruit and lost faith. So he flaunts his indebtedness. He creates a gallery of the cinematic elect, calling directors by their first names as if they were departed saints. Welles is granted a subgallery of his own, his most famous roles being incorporated as reproduced production stills in a book through whose leaves Godard's own hand keeps flipping. The photographs alternate with reproductions of famous works of art. Godard never finishes turning all the pages since the last page has to be Welles's absence (a blank leaf?) juxtaposed with a frame of Godard's completion of his film.

For his part, Welles never fully relinquished the dream of returning to filmmaking: the lingering image of his unquenchable ambition to make *King Lear* (which he had scripted in detail and was on the point of shooting in 1985 when, allegedly, the money promised by French government agencies evaporated) is a photograph of himself in his Lear costume—not the earlier attire in which he played the role for Peter Brook, but one in the spirit of a film conceived as yet another experiment in genre, a Shakespeare film that like Dreyer's *Passion of Joan of Arc* was to be shot almost entirely in close-ups.[11] If Godard's extensive allusions to Dreyer recuperate Welles's ambition, then adaptation for him is akin to Hamlet acting in apparent conformity with the Orestean directives of his betrayed father, feigning a maddening textual digressiveness only to place himself in an auterist line of succession. The searing analysis of Hamlet's rhetorical skullduggery—literally a language game—in Stoppard's *Rosenkrantz and Guildenstern Are Dead*, which won the Grand Prize at the Venice Film Festival in the year of its release (1990), parallels the treatment to which Godard subjects the language of cinema.

We may even surmise that Godard exploits the imprecision of natural language to emphasize the rhetoric of image juxtaposition. One rhetorical figure to which Shakespeare was addicted (and which irritated his later editor Samuel Johnson) was the quibble, now better known as the pun. Its recrudescence in Godard seems at first an irritating affliction. "Mr. Alien," the dying Sparky calls out, "Mr. Alien"—who when he appears to edit the film proves to be the nearest thing to a Welles descendant, the Hollywoodphobic Mr. Allen. Yet the puns can be more complex, extending from one sign system (such as natural language) to another: in Godard's invented Welles book, for example, we encounter a reproduction of Jan Vermeer's *The Girl with the Pearl Earring*, with an emphasis on the pearl (we see it twice, the second being a closer view). Although juxtaposed with an image of Welles as Macbeth, the repeated image probably alludes to one of Othello's last lines about the base Indian throwing away a pearl worth more than all his tribe, the tribe being the artisans in charge of film production, the discarded pearl Welles himself.

So we may justly conclude that Welles's presence in Godard, both as individual and as oeuvre, signifies more than an attractive conceit, and that indeed it makes for a remarkable allegory by analogy: if Welles-Falstaff is a viable alternative cinema independent of studio financing or obligatory state support, then Godard-Cordelia is the French New Wave that did so much to rehabilitate him, their fates parallel even to the bitter end. In and of itself this is a striking instance of what Miola describes as the process of drawing on textual conventions and configurations, but Godard additionally contrives to equate his own evolution as critic-filmmaker, and his status of guardian of true cinema and therefore of Welles's legacy, to the central drama of the Lear story. However, this only becomes apparent only in piecing together what remains of Shakespeare's characters and his plot.

Godard begins with disobedience. In the absence of Welles, he claims, the producers insisted that he stick with a name-brand Lear, with the consequence that in the film's prologue they find themselves targets of auteurist ire directed against "Jewish gangster" Hollywood studio bosses. It is clear, however, that Godard's attempts to cast superstar novelist Norman Mailer as Don Learo are doomed to failure: {*A Picture Shot in the Back*} announces a title card, and then {*King Lear, Fear and Loathing*} or {*King Lear, a Study*} or {*An Approach*}, or {*King Lear, a Clearing*}. Not once {*King Lear, an Adaptation*}. Mailer was unnerved by Godard's eccentricities to the point of demanding that the director say "action" when he wanted the actors to act. And he was obviously queasy about his role as an overfamiliar paterfamilias who must kiss his own daughter on screen, slipping into Freudianism at one point. "Why does she take my hand instead of me taking her?" Mailer (as Mailer) demands of Godard.[12] Fast abandoned, the director settles on Burgess Meredith, one of Hollywood's most familiar midlevel actors if a rather unlikely Learo, and the most apt of Cordelias in Molly Ringwald, Mazursky's rebellious Miranda and thus Godard's most immediate connection to the improvisatory performance style characteristic of Cassavetes and the Manhattan incarnation of the New American Cinema. The insistent repetition of Cordelia's "nothing" (rendered even more explicit by the intertitle signifying her initial resistance to yielding her maidenhood, {"No-thing"}), makes Godard's gangster boss all the more repellent when a hotel chambermaid reacts in shock to what she sees on the bed sheets. Although this Cordelia succumbs to her father and must perish to conceal a grim secret, unlike Shakespeare's who returns dutifully to die fighting over the territory she could not win with words, we begin to understand Godard's absent sisters rather better. The spunky fragility that carries over from her Miranda (at one moment also courted by her father following an appropriately ritualized Greco-Egyptian dance) suits her ideally to the role of the headstrong Shakespearean daughter. If Van Sant, *pace* Tarantino, was aware of Godard's film, his reading of Welles's "the things that we have seen" seems rather less attenuated. Neither the choice of play, nor Godard's self-appointed role as Lear's voice of conscience (Professor Pluggy, the Fool) distracts from the film's essential point that the death of *auteur* cinema as it was initially conceived was more than a little connected to the ultracapitalist business model that Hollywood had exported with such success. Nor, when Pluggy expires, does Godard's recourse to the ministrations of another *auteur* who had a close association with the New York art scene and who experiences intense alienation in Los Angeles in his mock autobiography, the 1973 film *Annie Hall*, come as a surprise.

Interestingly enough, *King Lear* was not Godard's first, or even his best-known, assault on the arrogant, self-serving studio producer. It is, in fact, a recondite, even gnomic pendant to the 1963 *Le Mépris* (*Contempt*), in which Godard's contempt for Hollywood's contemporary power brokers and their willing minions (here personified by the acquiescent scriptwriter) turns into an essay on the limits of artistic freedom. The hero of *Le Mépris* is a multilingual film director who attempts to resist the dumbing-down of *The Odyssey* insisted on by the aggressive, philandering, pseudo-intellectual producer, Jerry Prokosch. That in contrast the true filmmaker, the director, is a visionary capable of great compassion becomes evident when he pauses to explain the consequences of authorial changes to Hölderlin's verse to the poetically inclined secretary-translator who is subjected to the married scriptwriter's competitive courtship and used in various capacities (including that of a foldable desk) by Prokosch. The director is none other than Fritz Lang, played by a Lang so uncharacteristically benign as to offer the tiresome producer patient explanations of the difference between words and images. He is permitted only one moment of sarcasm when he points out that Prokosch has made a chance discovery of Greek culture when, in attempting to hurl a can of film across the projection room, he assumes the posture of Myron's famed statue of a discus thrower, the *Diskobolos*. In the pantheon of film greats, an unstable but long-standing Godardian preoccupation, Lang, once maker of the grandest epics of Europe's biggest studio, Ufa, and by now making genre films in post-1948 Hollywood, still loomed large. As he is on his way to meet Lang, the awestruck scriptwriter reminds us that in 1933, Göebbels offered to place the director in charge of all of Germany's centralized film production, but that Lang immediately fled the country. Godard's contempt, then, extends over a considerable historical period, and already by 1963, he despaired of the rescue of the New Wave from the encroachments of commercialization. Hence, the "silence" of the film's conclusion. Lang points his camera over an expanse of still water (i.e., water with barely a wave, old or new), and signals the start of filming at the moment when Odysseus first sees his home in Ithaca after his many years of wandering. "Silenzio," announces a production assistant, and the camera begins a slow track past the back of a man in a Greek tunic with sword upraised. Godard's camera keeps tracking past the scene until we lose the figures and there is silence over a blue expanse of calm water. "Silence," "Silenzio," the offscreen voices announce again, in French and Italian.

Yet another way of looking at *King Lear*, whose narrative trajectory ends similarly (albeit with a shotgun-wielding Lear seated on a rocky outcrop contemplating the still waters), is that it is an extended inquiry into the relationship of still and moving images, the deeper question addressed being one fundamental to the processes that inhere to adaptation: the nature of visual cultures displaced in time such as reproductions of Renaissance or Baroque paintings in modern books, and temporal disjunctions between media and what they represent such as still photographs shot on moving 35 mm film. At the time Godard conceived the project that was to become his variously subtitled *King Lear*, Roland Barthes's *Camera Lucida*, which remains one of the most influential critical treatises on still photography, appeared shortly after its author succumbed to his injuries.

A tribute to his recently deceased mother, Barthes's book-length essay is a meditation on and metaphor for memory and mortality. In it he seemed to foresee his own tragic end, as when he dilates on the silence betokened by his decision to "say nothing of the death of one whom I love most," a first death in which his own death is "inscribed."[13] One of Barthes's points of departure in *Camera Lucida* is that, in contrast to the moving image, the still image allowed its spectator time for contemplation and retrospection, thus modifying the *studium*—the intended substance of a photograph—by the play of memory and by some sign of the chance intrusion of reality, a visual discrepancy or *punctum* that pierces through the discourse of the photographer and provides the image with an unintended life of its own.[14] Of a photograph of Lewis Payne, would-be assassin of Secretary of State W.H. Seward, he writes: "The photograph is handsome, as is the boy: that is the *studium*. But the *punctum* is *he is going to die... This will be* and *this has been*. I observe with horror an anterior future of which death is the stake."[15] The photograph, then, is the closest thing Barthes found to a moment of time, a crystallization of the present that a hundred years into the future would represent a long-dead now, a transience that demanded the respect of silence.[16] It seems hardly a coincidence that in the same year that *Camera Lucida* saw print the Pulitzer Prize happened to be awarded to *The Executioner's Song*, penned by none other than Godard's substitute star and the very man who made of murder and impending death something of a populist-academic industry (in addition to writing a best seller about the execution of Gary Gilmore, he also helped secure the release of murderer, Jack Abbott, who committed another murder shortly thereafter). Its vicissitudes condemned Godard's film to a belated and very limited release, but it is very much of the same cultural moment, the 1980s rediscovery, as it were, of that current of diffident Modernism (exemplified by Proust, Kafka, Musil, Svevo, and the Expressionists) in the context of the persistence of colonialisms, the failure of the popular movements of the 1960s and its new waves, and the retrenchment of oligarchic government in the 1970s.[17] "O Death," intones the personifying and personified voice of Virginia Woolf, commenting on a film in which a father consumes the life he has given. The tactic enables Godard's text to flaunt instances of paralogism, reproducing the critical syntax of Barthes and other contemporary cultural critics, but with such authors as Shakespeare, Woolf, Welles, and Kozintsev taking his side against them.

In making a case that moving images can render stillness with all the pathos Barthes grants to the fixed image, Godard incorporates images of numerous photographs, paintings, and drawings into *King Lear*, among them images of paternal monstrousness and contrasting ones of paternal benevolence (such as Francisco de Goya's allegory of Time, *Saturn Devouring His Children*, or Rembrandt van Rijn's intensely moving idealization of forgiveness, *The Return of the Prodigal Son*). Chris Marker had previously made a film composed entirely of still photographs, the influential *La Jetée* (1963), whose medium-specificity revealed itself only in two barely noticeable camera movements. The author of those photographs, however, happened to be Marker, who made them for the purpose of the film. By 1968, when Godard made *Le Gai Savoir* (*The Joy of Learning*), he was juxtaposing found photographs and experimenting with the notion of assembling meaningful filmic sequences of them (just as Esfir Schub and Dziga Vertov had done with filmed news footage in the 1920s).[18] The postapocalyptic parable of twenty years later, in which Godard seems willfully to bite all hands that approach close enough to feed him, is also in part a reaction to the critical fallout from *Le Gai Savoir*. The criticism Godard clearly found most toxic had come from the Situationists, a philosophically inclined collective of artists, writers, and musicians who accused Godard of having becoming the arch priest of the establishment (in scathing terms reminiscent of Soyinka's later attack on the Leftocracy, or sociologist Pierre Bourdieu's on the Homo academicus). Moreover, while they advocated plagiarism and misappropriation as potent forms of resistance to the pervasiveness of proprietary capitalism, they rather illogically charged Godard with stealing techniques used by their leader, Guy Debord, who had then recently achieved cult status with the publication of *The Society of Spectacle*.[19] Godard's use of intertextuality as a mechanism of complex citation goes beyond the Situationist concept of *detournement*, the kidnapping or hijacking of an existing aesthetic object and its radical recontextualization.[20] Nowhere is this more evident than in his appropriation of Welles's unrealized *King Lear*, marking his own text not as an addition to Shakespeare's Shakespeare (or the critics' perception of Shakespeare's Shakespeare) but to Welles's Shakespeare: the textual "game" thus illustrates not only the extent of his continuing dispute with the Situationists, but also his preoccupation with contemporary semiologists and other contributors to the debate over the *politique des auteurs*.

Godard thus recasts the process of "remaking" a preexisting text as a cross-referential layering involving each of Miola's three categories in various admixtures, even as he continues to address the issues of individuality, authorship, and adaptation that had so exercised Truffaut. Additionally, in *King Lear* the preponderance of intertexts associated with "high culture" (Modernist literature and film, a drawing by Rubens, paintings by Titian and Renoir, the same fresco of *The Annunciation* that once inspired Norma Shearer's coiffeur as Juliet, and so on) has as its aesthetic excuse an unwilling conformity to the dictates of the "Jewish gangster" representatives of the demands of a commercial medium, his producers. It is a pretense that disguises another extended rejoinder to the Situationist assaults on the canonical, since far from desecrating the cited texts, the citations draw on their expressive force to underline the conflicting themes that pervade Shakespeare's play. Moreover, Godard frequently organizes such references into sets or clusters of citations, including those alluding to his own filmography and critical commentaries.

The directors' pantheon with Welles presiding in Jovian eminence provides a conspicuous instance of this tendency. The sequence is reminiscent in its list-like character of Andrew Sarris's ranking of important *auteurs*, but this was itself the result of a certain tendency acquired from the early writings of Godard and the *Cahiers* critics. Once upon a time, when Godard was a professional critic and before he had begun making films, those gods had been a few of the B-movie directors such as Nicholas Ray who had gained belated critical respect (at least in France), together with the handful of names that still resound in college Film Studies courses. For the Godard of 1958, Kenji Mizoguchi, darling of the Venice Film Festival, proved superior to the more consciously "exotic" Kurosawa: with his 1953 *Ugetsu Monogatari* Mizoguchi "ranked on equal terms with Griffith, Eisenstein and Renoir."[21] By the same token, Ingmar Bergman, for whom aesthetic rigor was not an end in itself, represented the *politique des auteurs*, while Luchino Visconti led the tribe subscribing to the *politique des metteurs en scène*, a contrast Godard also extended to Rossellini and Welles on the one hand (makers of "roomy," chance-filled films) and the masters of planned precision, Hitchcock and Lang, on the other. Of these, it was Bergman whom Godard considered especially noteworthy because his films are his alone. "Unlike Bresson or Visconti, who transfigure a starting point into something entirely personal, Bergman creates his adventures and his characters out of nothing."[22] Godard's critical evolution commenced early: by 1963, for instance, Lang had been reclassified.

Godard's renewed and mildly ironic (even self-parodic) revision of the pantheon in *King Lear* represents still another attempt to rewrite the histories of cinema, a project to which he returned in the 1990s with renewed vigor and systematicity (notably in his made-for-television series released in 1998, *Les Histoires du Cinéma*). He introduces the *Lear* pantheon of still images immediately after a narrator (representing one of his voices) wonders why Canon Films did not have "some goblin shoot this twisted fairytale." The intertitle {KING LEAR, A STUDY} then gives way to a portrait photograph of a character referred to by his first name, upon which the narrator muses: "a picture. Sometimes you could put it in film. It will not transform itself in contact with other images." This is no doubt meant ironically in light of Chris Marker's film, but the allusion to Barthes—here using words to suggest their opposite—now seems more an expression of suspicion toward an overrigorous semiology than a belated denunciation: the narrator's assertions more generally call into question the 1960s Structuralist notion of the "shot" as the basic unit of film, an argument proposed and later abandoned by Christian Metz and other film semiologists writing in the wake of Barthes's early analyses of narrative structure.[23] Yet by functioning as what Barthes termed "anchorage," the words themselves help pin down the meanings of the still photographs Godard translates into cinematic shots. Two images drawn from opposite ends of the "high" and "low" cultural spectrum, a reproduction of *Judith with the Head of Holofernes* and a pornographic still of a woman revealing the secrets of her sex, occur in succession, bridged only by the narrator's comment about visual analogy, "It is a resemblance of connection." With this self-reflexive preamble to his Ravennian gallery of a cinematic elect, Godard contrasts the hagiography of the image (a succession of images of image makers) to the hagiography of the word (Shakespeare's pristine, preapocalyptic text sought by a philologist-lackey enslaved to a heritage of words, necessarily played by stage director Peter Sellars).

Another form of Godardian reflexivity might extend Miola's typology still further to include autoparaphrase. In one register, Dreyer's presence summons Welles to witness one of his own films in the making. In another, it recapitulates Godard's darkly Zolaesque film, *Vivre Sa Vie* (*My Life to Live*, 1962), in which the heroine Nana (played affectingly by Anna Karina) witnessed the foreshadowed spectacle of her own degradation. Early in the film, Nana tells a friend that rather than sharing dinner she wants to see a film, and that film turns out to be *The Passion of Joan of Arc*. Godard simply quotes a chunk of the film, cutting from a close-up of Joan's tears on being told that she should prepare herself for death, to a close-up of Nana with tears welling in her eyes. The quoted sequence is a famous one, for Dreyer had so brutalized his Joan, Renée Falconetti, subjecting her to physical and emotional ordeals parallel to the saint's, that he could reputedly command her tears at will. There is no such sense of premonition in Ringwald's reenactments of Falconetti's gestures or of her increasing resemblance to Joan even in details of attire, but Godard's double citation (of himself and of Dreyer) once again brings up the Christian theme of redemptive suffering; and

Shakespeare's play, as the vast critical literature devoted to it attests, is all about such suffering. This is not to argue that Godard is alone in finding incest lurking in the backstories of Shakespeare's plays—just think of the predatory sexuality of Zeffirelli's Gertrude, Glenn Close, or of the true morbidity in Walter Pidgeon's revelation of the "monsters of the Id"—but rather to illustrate the insistence of Godard's thematic cross-referencing. Adaptation is, of course, always a political gesture toward a textual residue, but Godard transforms the process into one of intense interrogation of a "sacred" original. If Ruiz and other directors have been his successors, then possibly only Pasolini could be thought of as a predecessor: who but Godard, in seeming to desecrate a text by interleaving it with others, would turn to the figure of Joan, citing his own earlier citation in the process of invoking a figure Shakespeare treats as both saint and witch, passing both off as the making of the very film that the similarly mystical and messianic Welles could not make? The film's governing conceit, then, is that it is postmodernism's homage to Modernism, allegory masquerading as quasi-documentary pastiche.

In her martyr's death Cordelia becomes a figure of an art movement defiled, born from the *cinéphile*'s addiction to the classical period of Hollywood's studio filmmaking, and violated by the money-mania of that very system depicted by Godard as having fallen into incestuous decline. If Godard's purpose in *King Lear* is to weave together documentary images extracted from cinematic performances and reproductions of other images, then he is transforming genres that claim to record reality, *pace* Plato, into a catalogue of metafictions of the film's status as a fictional retelling of a play. For such a conceit to work, Welles must become integral to the new document to avoid any pretense of the latter being either a documentary about Shakespeare's play or a fictional version of that play (Welles's film roles were roles after all, projections of artists' imaginations.) *King Lear* is thus rescued from any impulse merely to reproduce Shakespeare, and is instead reconfigured as part of an account of the unmaking of Welles's putative *King Lear* and of Godard's "postapocalyptic" revivification of the project. Unlike Cordelia's virgin knot, Godard's rules of allegory-by-citation remain unbroken: in the face of relentless pressure by commercial cinema, the French New Wave must lose her innocence en route to a death transfigured as a promise of resurrection into a new kind of cinema.

Perverse Authorship and Shakespearean Sadomasochism

Godard's self-presentation as the end point of cinema, its *omega*, has gained widespread critical acceptance that is at least in part due to his longevity as a filmmaker; one who with each film he makes provides a fresh answer to Bazin's famous interrogative: "What is cinema?" By the mid-1980s, Robert Stam would compose the work that became *Reflexivity in Film and Literature: From Don Quixote to Jean-Luc Godard*. Five years later, in the course of chastising New Historicists for their improper refusal to adhere to the productive theories that contribute to their insights, Fredric Jameson, who would later revise his attitude toward their "nominalism," manages to situate Godard in their midst as a filmmaking fellow traveler with equally "undecidable" conceptions.[24] Godard even achieved an unsought immortality on the Star Trek TV series that sent him up (both literally and figuratively) into space in the form of the extremely articulate Shakespearean Jean-Luc Picard, Captain of the Starship Enterprise and fellow sufferer of ambiguous citizenship.

Godard's late celebrity notwithstanding, it was his frequent disputant Pasolini who, having been incarcerated for blasphemy and having won early notoriety as literary critic, writer of fictions, poet, and filmmaking provocateur, first achieved celebrity in theoretical circles.[25] Indeed, even today it is widely recognized that alone among Italy's public intellectuals of the time Pasolini was regarded a worthy disputant of Umberto Eco, and that he and A.J. Greimas were the first semioticians since Ferdinand de Saussure to propose major modifications of the science of signs initially proposed by the American pragmatist Charles Sanders Peirce (Pasolini's insistence that symbolic signs were "contaminated" by other related signs even anticipated Jacques Derrida's critique of Saussure.) Pasolini's connection with Godard began almost by accident, one nostalgically signaled by his presence in the *King Lear* pantheon: in the episode Pasolini contributed to the omnibus film, *RoGoPaG* (1963), Welles plays a film director entrusted—as was Pasolini at the time—with making a film about Christ's passion. The aptly titled *La ricotta*, quite possibly an inspiration to the Monty Python collective when they conceived of one of the most popular of "parallel lives" comedies, *The Life of Brian* (1979), focused on a desperately impoverished film extra who, having lost even a stolen meal, gorges on ill-gotten cheese and expires on a cross while trying to play the Good Thief.[26] If this were not provocation enough, Welles-the-Director makes scathing remarks about the backwardness of Italian culture to an obtuse reporter. It was this film that occasioned Pasolini's imprisonment under an anachronistic law enacted by the Fascists proscribing attacks on the state religion. As if to compound the irony, Welles had just completed his adaptation of Kafka's *The Trial*, and Godard had enlisted Lang to play his director-surrogate in *Le Mépris*, a project that obviously occupied more of his attention than his comparatively slight contribution to *RoGoPaG*.

Despite the proximity of their thought, when Pasolini turned his hand to adapting a Shakespeare play, he engaged less with Godard's thought than with historian Michel Foucault's notion of pervasive power, to which he contrasted a vision of proletarian agency that bears a striking resemblance to the theories of Mikhail Bakhtin (whose then largely untranslated body of work he is unlikely to have known) and to those of Antonio Gramsci (to which he devoted both critical insights and poetry, and which remained an influence throughout his career).[27] Gramsci, in fact, takes on the form of a Marxist intellectual (what else but a talking raven?) in Pasolini's feature-length *Uccellacci e uccellini* (1966), a double fable with parallel stories and as remarkable a meditation on the Marxist impulses of Christianity as the more celebrated, if less theoretically elaborate, *Gospel According to Matthew* (1964). Pasolini's contribution to adaptations of Shakespeare consists of a 1968 miniature scarcely twenty minutes in duration, *Che cosa sono le nuvole?* (*So What Are Clouds?*), but in it he contrives to bring a performance of *Othello* to a more definitive standstill than the Bollywood-besotted audience in *Shakespeare Wallah* did to the more orthodox version of the play. That very interruption, in fact, seems rooted in the most fundamental impulses that inform Gramsci and Bakhtin, supporting the idea that revolution is the collective non-acquiescence in the operation of hegemony (the former's term for the dominance of an elite minority through the tacit acquiescence or approval of a majority), and that elite or "high" culture depends upon the license granted to it by proletarian or, as Bakhtin would have it, "folk" culture. It is hardly a coincidence that Italy's most celebrated comic actor Totò, best known for his "folksy" Neopolitan-inflected verbal humor, and the inarticulate, insouciant street-boy lout who was Pasolini's perennial star, Ninetto Davoli, reprise their performances in *Uccellacci e uccellini* as the sinister, would-be plutocrat and the suggestible naïf in the still more archetypal form of puppets in *Clouds*.

Having alerted us to Pasolini's view of adaptation as "a reflective and self-conscious art, which would promote a constructive resistance to the values of a bourgeois, post-capitalist, consumerist society," Sonia Massai identifies four Velázquez paintings that serve as posters for the intended sequence of short films within which *Clouds* belongs.[28] The poster for *La terra vista dalla luna* reproduces *The Portrait of Don Diego de Acedo*, while *Le avventure del re magio randagio* (*The Adventures of the Lost Wise King*), a film Pasolini never made but that might have inspired a film on the lost Magi by Ermanno Olmi and *Mandolini* (*Mandolins*) make use of royal portraits of Felipe IV and Baltasar Carlos. The most famous royal group portrait of all, *Las Meninas*, provides *Clouds* with its poster. Observing that Foucault had treated *Las Meninas* in the opening chapter of his freshly published *The Order of Things* (1966), Massai contends that "through this visual citation, Pasolini acknowledges Velázquez and Foucault as further sources of inspiration besides Shakespeare and gives his audience a powerful interpretive key for the film as a whole."[29] In the present context I concentrate on a Velázquez painting that Massai does not discuss—one actually brought to my attention almost twenty years ago by Guido Fink—in an attempt to illustrate that for Pasolini Velázquez becomes an artist's way of "talking back" to two authors, Foucault and Shakespeare.[30] Rather than being a film whose citations expand the field of authorship, Pasolini's work may be unique among Shakespeare films in its proximity to the Third Cinema position that invests adaptation with the power of cultural critique, indeed with the obligation to interrogate the original source as a means of contrasting the initial author's cultural situation with that of the author of the adaptation.[31]

Since *Clouds* is not widely available, it may prove helpful to summarize some of the narrative components of the film to place this painting, *The Rokeby Venus*, in its proper context. The film begins with a Caretaker filling a dumpster with the outtakes from an edited film, although the building behind him is not devoted to showing films as such but covertly houses a Sicilian Marionette theatre in which life-size puppets, stacked vertically in rows, begin to wonder what is in store for them (a fate perhaps intimated by the Velázquez-based posters found nearby). Pasolini explores multiple dimensions of the interchangeability of living actors and puppets, the question of characters' independence of their author being only the most obvious. But the tactic is not unprecedented: as with Kurosawa, he often transforms his actors into essences or types, stylizing their actions (in his case drawing explicitly on classical Greek theatrical traditions rather than Noh, as when an African standing before a grave in the 1970 *Notes for an African Oresteia*, acts unaware that he is Orestes, or when Maria Callas's Medea borrows from her savage interpretation of the role in Luigi Cherubini's opera).

A chocolate-colored Marionette turns out to be Otello, a flirtatious blonde one who presently tempts him with cherries dangling from her ears (he has to learn to nibble), Desdemona, and an older, hatchet-faced one painted a bright, jealous green, Jago. From the outset, Jago casts suspicion on Cassio, whose affair with Bianca is developed as his teasing refusal to place the bird he holds in the nest she proffers, an incident that incites Cypriot alarm about foreigners seizing their women and that leads to Otello's demotion of him. Jago's antiquated phraseology as filtered through a Neopolitan dialect permits him puns (such as Cassio and "cazzo," or "prick") unavailable to untranslated Shakespeare, and it is he who, as in the play, gets to share his thoughts with the audience in soliloquy and to peep around corners when monitoring the effects of the advice and insinuations he showers on the childlike Otello. The brown puppet, however, seems far less certain of his role than his theatrical counterpart and finds his green mentor's explanations inadequately convincing.[32] Moreover, having witnessed Jago's handkerchief deception, the audience in the theatre—whose reactions Pasolini registers by taking his camera onto the stage, as it were, behind the puppets—begins to hoot in derision. Jago's insistence that the easily deceived Otello choke Desdemona draws forth catcalls, and at this point even the callow Otello begins to resist authority. "Why am I so stupid?" he wants to know, "why do I always have to believe Jago?" The camera turns upward, and the puppet master tries to convince him that he does so of his own volition and that he wants to kill Desdemona. "But why? Does killing please me?" Otello perseveres. "Perhaps because Desdemona wants to be killed," offers the puppeteer. Otello is in a quandary. "What counsel should I follow? What the spectators say, what's in me, or what he says up there?" As the spectators continue to protest, Jago warns Otello not to name what is within him: "[W]hen you name it you lose it." Calm returns when the camera cuts to two mandolin players strumming in the pit. Desdemona emerges in a white dress. Otello runs to her and slaps her. Delighted, she inquires whether he would like to give her another. He tries to throttle her. Jago guffaws with glee, but the incensed spectators storm the stage as the mandolins, now abandoning the pretense of Renaissance verisimilitude, launch into a frenzied cancan. Jago and Otello are beaten to the ground, Cassio is raised aloft in triumph, and female spectators try to revive Desdemona. A cut now takes us outside the theatre to the dumpster containing the two battered male miscreants. When we return briefly to the interior, we hear the puppets—once again stacked upright with a restored Desdemona in their midst—lament the tragic outcome. Outside, the Caretaker's street song can be heard once more and, in short order, the discarded Otello and Jago are bouncing amidst the refuse on the back of his truck, wondering what fate has in store for them. It is now, when we cut to the Caretaker at the wheel that we notice that the image behind and partly concealed by his head is the languid, shapely back of Velázquez's reclining Venus. Indeed, although he is far from sitting still, we never see the entire image. Already debased as publicity posters, Velázquez's classical figure (who in the original has a winged Cupid holding up a mirror in which she contemplates her face) is now a pin-up. Velázquez's mirror has become Pasolini's movie screen, just as the artist's steady gaze in the poster for *Clouds* is no longer the gaze authorized by royal patron-sitters but Pasolini's, directed at the film's spectator.[33] The framing device now confirms the distinction between the inner world of art, the puppet theatre, and the external world of everyday reality: the caretaker empties his load down a slope, and the tumbling puppets come to rest on a midden of refuse. An awestruck Otello, his gaze fixed on a blue expanse of sky, inquires, "[W]hat are those things?" and on being told that they are clouds, extols their beauty, upon which even Iago's hitherto bookish explanations yield to wonderment at the "marvelous and piercing beauty of creation."

Before contemplating the constituent parts of Pasolini's fantasy, it may be worth considering the point of origin of his disagreement with Foucault about the nature of artistic self-consciousness.[34] That *Clouds* is, in a sense, a response to Foucault follows from his seminal 1966 essay on the role of artistic works in society, "The End of the Avant-Garde," that he composed as he prepared to make the film. In it he suggests that social reality expresses itself in a language of its own, alluding to Foucault's formulation of "discourse" in mentioning "a new book by Foucault which I have not yet read."[35] The essay begins as a response to Lucien Goldmann and Roland Barthes who, like Foucault, had begun to acknowledge that classical Marxism had entered a state of crisis. Pasolini reserves his more scathing remarks for the fashionably inclined but politically moribund aesthetic avant-garde, and he takes issue with Goldmann and Barthes over the terms in which they framed the crisis rather than with their more general conclusions.[36] Indeed, he emphasizes the convergences of their thought. "What intrigues me—and intrigues me because I am mature about it—is that the two most advanced and most extraordinary representatives of European essay writing that I know, Goldmann and Barthes, are both what we in Italy would call '*contenutisti*,' that is, they focus on the content of a work." Tellingly, when Pasolini goes on to describe his own "tortuous" discovery of *contenutismo*, the idea that the content of a stylistically coherent work determines its form, a discovery that prompted him to transfer his attention from natural language (primarily the novel) to moving pictures, his illustration purports to derive from a film he is planning in which Totò teaches the apathetic Ninetto about the language of cinema. "Cinema does not evoke reality, as literature does," cries Totò, "it does not copy reality, as painting does; it does not mime reality as drama does. Cinema *reproduces* reality, image and sound." Cinema, therefore, is the "written language" of reality, furnishing us with a "semiology of reality in its natural state."[37]

Clouds, the closest Pasolini came to realizing such a film, is an astonishing translation of style (according to him the key missing component of Goldmann's and Barthes's *contenutismo*) into just such a semiology of reality.[38] Moreover, the camera shapes this reality into a depiction of social structure that gives a decidedly Gramscian twist to Marx's agonistic depiction of class interests.[39] For Gramsci, social divisions that ensure the hegemony of a ruling elite can be sustained only through the consent and formal acquiescence of individuals within differing social strata, and in *Clouds* Pasolini contrives to group his shots into a rigorous series of compositions in which each actor represents a particular Gramscian social agent. If the complacent proletarian finds representatives in the singing Caretaker and the opportunistic mandolin players, then effective collective action falls to the lot of the subproletarian spectators who storm the stage. Ninetto-Otello, still too naïve to have been interpellated into a bourgeois value system, is poised on the verge of individual consciousness, and in denying his instinct seals his fate. Desdemona and the majority of other puppets are manifestations of the complacency of the bourgeoisie for whom even sex is nothing more than a ritualized game. It is the author of the spectacle, Shakespeare the perverse puppeteer, who is the hegemon who pulls the strings and determines the extent of Desdemona's masochism, Cassio's complicity, and even the reluctant Otello's violence. In this scheme, Jago is not the play's presiding genius but the interpreter of the puppet master's directives, and thus representative of that category of organic intellectual who facilitates the dominance of the "author's" representational regime.[40]

It is in Pasolini's reframing of Velázquez, first as mass-manufactured poster and then, in the world beyond art and theatre, as frameless kitsch—a term whose precise meaning we reencounter—that his disagreement with Foucault (whom he had obviously read by this time) becomes most evident. Foucault's famous and minute analysis begins with Velázquez's apparent resistance to his royal patrons by making himself the central figure of *Las Meninas*, standing at his "full height," transforming his spectator into an element within the text and the royal entourage into his props. As the analysis proceeds, however, the syntax of the painting, that is, the orchestration of its elements, reveals itself as a manifestation of the power of the two indistinct faces in the mirror that occupies its central axis, those of King Philip IV and Queen Mariana. Thus placed, the patrons become the true spectators, and the observer of the painting merely the witness to this. Representation itself is part of an organized system in which even aesthetic innovation can only reflect and magnify an act of royal permission.[41]

Within the aesthetic confines of the puppet theatre, the world of imagination and artifice, Pasolini appears initially to share Foucault's diffidence. The original spectator of the Velázquez posters is in fact puppet-like, granted the illusion of active spectatorship only to be incorporated into the hermetic, officially sanctioned message ("we permit our artist to occupy the most prominent position in a spectacle we ordain and in which you serve as witness"). Such an artist thus mediates between the First Estate and the Third more effectively, even, than the ordained members of the Second Estate. No less a stranger to perversions than Foucault, Pasolini even suggests that Velázquez's creation of an intrinsic spectator, even an invisible one, is an act of authorial sadism; appointed as representative, not merely a go-between, the artist must ensure the spectator's passive acceptance of a prescribed role, and in this regard the author of the play is no less complicit than the painter.[42] Does it not stand to reason then that Desdemona, seemingly so anxious first to provoke her father by choosing so ill-favored a partner, and subsequently her husband with her persistent intercessions on behalf of Cassio/Cazzo, enjoys being slapped and might very well want to get killed? Come to think of it, Pasolini's insight actually explains the dynamic of a number of plays, for is not the unjustly neglected spectator-participant Christopher Sly in *The Taming of the Shrew* rather a good approximation of the spectator in Pasolini's puppet theatre? The verbal sparring of Katherine and Petruchio (no less than that of Beatrice and Benedick in *Much Ado*) can readily be configured as the play of patriarchy, but Shakespeare quite possibly also understands it as foreplay, as do some of the play's interpreters. Even in the (superficially) anodyne form of the movie Musical, Kate has to earn her licking no less than her kissing in *Kiss Me Kate*. Nor did it take Jan Kott to remind us of the sexual undercurrent of *A Midsummer Night's Dream*, for as theatre directors from Max Reinhardt onward have recognized, it is not Titania alone whose plenilunar fantasies border on perversion. (Helena, for instance, has to prompt Demetrius to lavish on her some of the satisfactions he otherwise reserves for his spaniel.)[43]

Art, however, is not merely the sublimation of desire for Pasolini as it is for Foucault (or Debord), but integral to culture as a whole, as Velázquez's eventual fate as truck decorator, no less than the discarded puppets' jettisoning from that truck, attests. Nor is Pasolini satisfied by a distinction between "high" and "low" founded on Foucault's power principle. The revolution staged by spectators amidst the Sicilian Marionettes, reminiscent though it may be of Don Quixote's earlier comical attack on Saracen Marionettes in defense of Christianity, does have an impact on the world beyond the theatre. In attempting to shield (and thus draw attention) to the better parts of Venus's venery, Pasolini's "folksy" twist to *The Rokeby Venus* derives from the same source as Rabelais's (according to Bakhtin), namely the satirical "material bodily lower stratum" celebrated perennially in folk culture.[44] Once intended as an aphrodisiac for noble delectation, the expanse of Venus's supine back now frustrates the film spectator's voyeuristic impulses in the manner of a Barthesian striptease in which surplus value is placed on that which is concealed. Thus, even the seemingly complacent singing proletarian who mediates the transition between the world of art and the detritus of the real world, the endpoint of Bakhtin's lower stratum, can appropriate, desecrate, and even delimit access to an object most readily associated with the highest of high culture. This is a Pasolini-Velázquez who can wink at the film's spectator: high culture is paying for its own degradation.

In making Pasolini's Caretaker representative of a force greater than himself, Pasolini also extends Miola's conception of revision to an interrogation of authorial prerogative that converges with Bakhtin's perspective that authorship is not a purely individual but a collective act, a concurrence of contending social forces. In the presence of folk culture, Shakespeare ceases to enjoy the prerogatives that a complacent, well-trained bourgeois audience would grant the author of a well-oiled Tragedy. He is, in fact, the rural migrant representative of a culture that even found ways of mocking the increasingly continental theatrical demands that in the final efflorescence of his London career produced the Magical non-Realism of that concluding cycle to which some editors grant the distinction of "Romances." It is this culture that brought Stratford and its midsummer and midwinter festivities to London. The undercurrent of the carnivalesque contributes to the richness of the dramatist's language: ever prescient, in *Twelfth Night* Shakespeare even nods in Bakhtin's direction when he makes fun of his own coat of arms and apparent social climbing in the figure of Malvolio, who undone by writing is cast into a wintry darkness from which he pleads to be permitted to write. Malvolio is, after all, the spirit of Lenten Puritanism, whose far from pleasant antagonists are permitted their bitter jests precisely because the spirit of festivity, found at its purest in Feste, prescribes the deregulation of social roles.

It is hardly surprising that Verdi's anarchic figure of Shakespearean carnival, Falstaff, invisibly pays a backstage visit to Pasolini's *Othello*, for this film came early in a series of cinematic efforts to remind a popular audience of the perennial power of the submerged classes to enact carnival's revolutionary potential (expressed most fully in medieval story cycles in Boccaccio, Chaucer, and *The Thousand and One Nights*). *Clouds* is an act of faith in human resistance to the tyranny of foregone conclusions, to the authority vested in authorship. It was Pasolini's tragedy that that the gruesome death that left him a broken puppet, one close to that of many of his characters, came at a moment in which he had lost this sustaining faith.

The Texts in the Author, or Peter Gielgud's Word-Image Plays

If any canonical, much-studied film director could claim to have a diametrical opposite, then Pasolini the *contenutista* has been so favored with Peter Greenaway the ultra-Formalist. Just as Pasolini found content pressing against the boundaries of form, that tension necessitating an appropriate style, Greenaway's fanatical adherence to structural conceits unfailingly tests the limits of cinema's representational capacities. His films, like such favorite devices as books or suitcases, serve as containers that enforce order on panoplies of things contained.

In striving to situate his early work within the orbit of 1970s experimental cinema, the primary advocates of Neoformalist film criticism, Kristin Thompson and David Bordwell, offer the acerbic commentary that he "gleefully disclosed obscure, exfoliating narratives lurking within nearly every structural principal—numbers, colors, alphabets." "His films," they continue, "though based on categorical structures are far from minimal; they are jammed with whimsical anecdotes and arcane references." Having thus compelled the spectator to engage in a game of active reconstruction, Greenaway seizes the opportunity to "parody the clichés of experimental film through negative footage, tinted shots, looping and rephotographed shots of rippling water."[45]

Structural obsessions carried to the point of parody may certainly be attributed to such early works as *A Walk through H: The Reincarnation of an Ornithologist* (1978), a send-up of the investigative documentary, and may be discerned even as late as *Drowning by Numbers* (1988). Yet, while being recondite, even arcane as Thompson and Bordwell suggest, Greenaway's teasing and at times insoluble puzzles propose a compelling alternative to the idea of well-constructed narratives as the natural and inevitable consequence of integrated beginnings, middles, and ends. His early films may, indeed, mock experimentalists as diverse as Hollis Frampton and Peter Kubelka, and there is, no doubt, a certain ingenious ingenuousness to the tripartite division of *Prospero's Books* into Past, Present, and Future based on Prospero's narration of his history, his present "machinations for revenge," and the eventual subsumation of his future, dynastic ambitions in acceptance and universal forgiveness. But at least two of the film's more evident structural principles—the four classical elements and the Aristotelian encyclopedia that reemerged in the Middle Ages, took a theoretical and classicizing turn in the Renaissance, and achieved its apogee in Enlightenment France—offer serious augmentations of the potentialities both of scholarly approaches to Shakespeare and of theories of adaptation.

Even a cursory consideration of the latter reminds us of Greenaway's "negative" connection to Pasolini with whom he shares an affinity for major medieval literary works, in his case as wide-ranging of those of fellow list-makers Sei Shonagon and Dante. Pasolini interprets the written text as a signifying practice in which a preliminary cultural transaction between author and reader that, through the process of adaptation, instigates a second between the adaptor and his or her audience. Greenaway, on the other hand, interprets a work of literature as a New Historicist would, with the author standing at a point of intersection between a particular culture and the histories that gave rise to the world in which such a text could have come into being. If Pasolini translates words into hieroglyphic visual metaphors, Greenaway extends writing into a metonymic cinematic calligraphy.

Aptly, for a work obsessed with reenvisioning a historically particular culture of writing (that marked the transition from the handcrafted manuscript to a printed age of mechanical reproduction) as an equally particular visual culture (the advent of a transition from celluloid into televisual and digital media), *Prospero's Books* introduces the idea of the fluidity of a text at the outset. Greenaway describes *The Book of Water,* the first seen representative of Prospero's literary dukedom, as having a thick cover "impervious to the world's water getting in and the book's water getting out."[46] Indeed, the light captured by the camera's lens dissolves Shakespeare's play as cerebral fluid might a soluble ink, distilling and fractionating separate historical essences from its constituent parts. The systematicity of the process may seem daunting even to a historicist: instead of one Spirit of Air, for instance, we have a quartet of visual references, a minor tribe of Ariels drawn from late Renaissance visual personifications of the element. The Seasons are similarly pluripersonified, but arrive at a time when the masque within the larger masque is indeed something of a conjuring trick, for they are a motley bunch summoned by a magus whose powers are waning and whose characters are steadily acquiring lives of their own. The resulting film thus reconstitutes Shakespeare's drama as a work in the process of being authored, and whose narrative components are imaginative extensions of the contents found within the volumes of Shakespeare's library. So it is that Prospero's study, derived from an illustration of St. Jerome, to whom Shakespeare parallels the exiled bibliophile, comes from Antonello da Messina's elaborately architectural rendering of the seated, contemplative saint and is anything but a "poor cell"; in contrast, the figure of Prospero himself seems to be drawn from the other extreme of the genre, modeled on Georges de la Tour's later painting of a penitent St. Jerome "stripped and humbled before a book."[47] Knowledge is reimagined as story, and cinema becomes a technology that reverses the traditional practice of the annotated edition of a Shakespeare play through a process that in *Hyper/Text/Theory* George Landow describes as "hyperlinking": the author of *Prospero's Books* is a playful New Historicist who uses the available technologies of visual narration to create a second textual stratum consisting of scholarly, quasi-documentary annotations, from which dramatic elements, existing on a separate register, evolve.[48] Greenaway even imagines a seventeenth-century encyclopedist as the likely author (and, in the case of autobiographies and Vesalian anatomies, forger) of these books that furnish the film with its visual and linguistic referents, Shakespeare's younger contemporary Athanaseus Kircher: it is not the old school BBC voice, used to good (and sometimes ironic) effect in earlier films, that narrates *Prospero's Books*, in fact, but an older fruity instrument that suggests the garrulous Jesuit polymath.[49] The corollary question that Greenaway addresses in creating a separate register of textual annotations is whether we are the products of what we in one way or another read, the natural consequence of imagining that the rigors of Prospero's exile were mitigated by his being permitted to roam an expanse of imagination in the form of a library that he claims to hold more dear than his lost "dukedom." His answer turns out to be an exemplary paralogism, the articulation of Shakespeare's (frequently visualized) printed and written text as a layering of a series of other texts including those Prospero uses to effect his magic. As Greenaway takes pains to note, the intertext that is hyperlinked to the twenty-four-volume library, the manuscript of *The Tempest*, has an "ironic" existence, since Prospero is seen writing it "with a truncated quill, precursor of the electric stylus, producing a longhand manuscript that—like all other Shakespeare manuscripts [sic]—has never been seen. The film's ending interferes with chronology and history and plays a game with this loss that is lamented by every Shakespearean enthusiast."[50] This is a New Historicist who might have chanced upon Derrida, transforming the idea of writing's anteriority to the spoken word into cheeky insouciance.[51]

If Greenaway's vision of what constitutes text differs from Pasolini's, then his attitude to authorship varies to an even greater degree. Like Barthes and Foucault, Pasolini attempts to redeem a text from the author even as he acknowledges her contaminating presence as a shadow that at once shapes and obscures. Greenaway treats authorship as a textual immanence and Shakespeare's authorship of *The Tempest* as nesting within his own: witness the title of his book "treatment" of the film and the nineteen blank pages at the start of the twenty-fourth and last encountered volume among Prospero's books, a 1623 collected edition of Shakespeare's plays. Such a conception of text is reminiscent of that of Seymour Chatman who, in one of the high watermarks of American Structuralism, proposed that narrative consists of a conjoined structure with a content plane ("story") and an expression plane ("discourse"), and that narration presupposes an implicit author who is in turn an extension of the real author. Within this scheme, adaptation literally brackets the world of the original author within that of another, whether invented, as Cervantes's Sidi Hamete Benengeli was, or "real," as Greenaway's Shakespeare was.[52] But, of course, Greenaway's Structuralism is not without irony and an astonishing twist at the end, and at various stages in the film we must work hard to distinguish between the authorial voices of Greenaway, Shakespeare, and Prospero. Matters are rendered even more complex by his explanatory book about the film (a complementary text that does much more than outline the screenplay), for at its beginning he credits John Gielgud, his principal actor and the "authorial" voice of many of the characters, with the idea for the adaptation.[53] Both Gielgud's later disavowal of the film as a record of his theatrical performance or of his view of the play, as well as his status as a metonymy for Shakespeare himself for much of the latter half of his long life (impersonated in Indian cinema, Shakespeare personified in Castellani, a compound of the dramatist's kings in Welles, parodied in spoof Shakespeares), add unexpected layers to Chatman's "story." If Greenaway remains the master of discourse who can at any moment halt the action (and intervene with explanatory interruptions), then Barthes's "author-function" appears—at least initially—to come to life in Gielgud, sullying any easy distinction between Shakespeare's authorship, the narrator in the text, the title character, and even the other personages who are projections of Shakespeare-Prospero's imagination.

One aspect of Greenaway's assertion of authorial presence that has occasioned considerable critical comment is his use of technology to achieve unprecedented visual textures. As Yvonne Spielman observes, in *Prospero's Books* Greenaway resumes the aesthetic experimentation in relating word, image, and sound that characterized early twentieth-century avant-garde art.[54] Not only does he produce "a new type of image through the simulation of movement when he electronically animates single frames of phase photography," but also, through his use of the Quantal Paintbox's capacity to superimpose computer-manipulated images over those produced through standard cinematography, effects contrasting types of animation and movement in frame-within-frame compositions, so instituting an entirely new relation between fixed images and moving ones that contributes significantly to the theory of cinema.[55] Greenaway has himself expressed the same concerns that Maya Deren, Stan Brakhage, Jonas Mekas, and other proponents of the New American Cinema of the 1950s seemed to share: that film become a medium worthy of the aesthetic advances in the other arts (Greenaway's specific examples of achievement in this regard being Joyce, Cubism, and the Senecan strain inherited from Jacobean drama still found not only in Ionesco and Peter Brook, but also in filmmakers Buñuel and Pasolini).[56] Michael Anderegg, perplexed by the film's spoofily bardolatrous "post-Shakespeareanness," observes that many more texts are present in *Prospero's Books* than the twenty-four conjured up by Greenway,[57] but even that number is not the casual consequence of an arbitrary impulse. Rather, it evidences a particular textual-visual relation that Greenaway explores repeatedly in the film, and is based on factors of 12: once Caliban has done his duty and adapted the slim volume of *The Tempest* that he inherits, so composing the text that takes up blank pages at the start, there would be thirty-six plays in the First Folio; that Folio is the last of twenty-four books in Prospero's dukedom. Moreover, while the least number of time-sequenced still images that can create the illusion of continuous motion is twelve per second, as Greenaway illustrates by "slowing down" a figure in motion à la pioneer filmmaker Eadweard Muybridge, the number that became the worldwide cinematic standard soon after the permanent introduction of sound-synchronization happens to be twenty-four.[58]

Anderegg, even though intensely aware of Greenaway's use of technology as a means of re-creating earlier effects available to other media (note, for instance, how his camera tracks backward or laterally through illusionistic layers of mise en scène), maintains that the director's technological sleights of hand are redolent of the very early filmmaking experiments of Muybridge and Georges Méliès, just as his visual references—notably Piranesi, Michelangelo, Rubens, Titian, Tintoretto, and the sixteenth-century English manuscript illustrator who depicted nearly naked Native Americans, John White—are "anachronistic" in both pre- and postdating Shakespeare.[59] But, of course, Shakespeare's reading was also a bit behind the times by Italian standards, and Anderegg is quick to note that many of Greenaway's effects are precisely those used by Inigo Jones at Whitehall where, indeed, Shakespeare's play received its earliest recorded performance on November 1, 1611.[60] Indeed, if Anderegg's subsequent comparison of Greenaway's adaptation to Jarman's seems relevant to the issue of the visual cultures inhering both to drama and cinema, then it is because these two directors appear to have revived Shakespeare's wicked parody of the feuding Ben Jonson and Inigo Jones in *Timon of Athens*.[61] If Jarman adopts an ascetic mise en scène, siding with the Poet and poking fun at the play's intrusive masque through (camp?) overproduction, then Greenaway's sympathies are decidedly with the Painter. It was a Renaissance theorist of the visual, Leon Battista Alberti, after all, who systematized architect Filippo Brunelleschi's rediscovery of vanishing points and the lost Roman art of perspectival illusion, and for Greenaway Prospero's capacity to be an "eclectic architectural scholar, perfectly capable of prophetic borrowing" (thereby allowing a Piranesi etching to furnish him with a mental picture that can be collaged onto the image, and so on), epitomizes the governing premise of the film, namely "the role of deception implied by Prospero's magic and by the illusion and deception practiced by a playwright."[62] If the Renaissance *paragone* took as its starting point Aristotle's defense of mimesis against Plato's condemnation of fictional representation, then Greenaway's invention of anthologies of facts to explain Shakespeare's powers of deception confront us with a Baudrillardian dilemma in which simulacra are real and the triumph of virtue and truth guaranteed only by the success of illusions.[63]

Another critic fascinated both by Greenaway's prestidigitalism and his apparent debt to Jarman, Douglas Lanier, notes that rather than discarding a reified Shakespearean text the shared conceit (that both films are emanations of Prospero's psyche) contributes to refocusing attention on those very folio pages in which *The Tempest* occupies pride of place.[64] Like Godard, Greenaway is partial to visual puns, and Prospero-Shakespeare's doodles at times slip into the medieval illuminator's habits such as elaborating the "l" of "sail" into a ship's sail. By reframing the text in this decorative manner, argues Lanier, "Greenaway acknowledges his desire to be faithful to it while dismantling its received monumentality and authority" in favor of the visualized and the performative, signaled at the start by Prospero's testing of various readings of "Boatswain."[65] Indeed, at every opportunity Greenaway makes the contents of books mutate and the books themselves move. Pointing out the resemblance of Greenaway's project to those of such critics as Harry Berger, Jr. and Samuel Crowl (who according to him have sought to divert Shakespeare studies from text-based to performance-based criticism), Lanier claims an "immanent theory" for *Prospero's Books* in that it meditates "on the theoretical ground of its own existence."[66]

Such a meditation is only possible, of course, because Greenaway succeeds in "alchemically" transmuting technological innovation into an evocation of style in which he parallels the ultramodern to late Renaissance and early Baroque illusionism, thus eliciting a heightened awareness of the very transformations that Shakespeare's theatre was undergoing at the time he completed *The Tempest*. No wonder Mariacristina Cavecchi contends that Greenaway's amplification of those elements of Shakespeare's play that most clearly betray a sense of aesthetic crisis—the metatheatrical foregrounding of the relationship of artist and spectator and the disruption of spatial and temporal unities—reveal a Mannerist reading of the play.[67] Likewise, in the film's insistent emphasis on written text as graphic sign, James Tweedie discerns an incipient calligraphism (revealed more fully in *The Pillow Book*) that, according to him, is an attempt to include the codex (and presumably formal calligraphy) into a 2000-year-old "tradition of visuality." Such a mobilization of "the archive of archaic knowledge," he notes, provides a cogent cinematic example of what Omar Calabrese has termed a contemporary Neo-Baroque revival, a tendency that Tweedie also attributes to Jarman, Godard, and Ruiz.[68]

The critical urge to periodize may, in fact, result from an attempt to reconcile Greenaway's historical precision with a fundamental structural dissonance between the play and the film. In the original *Tempest,* the masque substitutes for a formal epithalamion, and as with song-and-dance sequences in the integrated film Musicals of later times, Shakespeare attempts to find a dramatic logic for its insertion into the play (as he does in *Macbeth* and various interludes in the later plays). *Prospero's Books*, on the other hand, is masque-like from the outset, each of Prospero's imaginings replete with the vivified marginalia of sexualized dancing automata, hermaphrodites, chimerical half-human hybrids, and other Renaissance signifiers of fecundation. Even as it superimposes an elaborate meditation on authorial individuality over the traditional identification of the magic-abjuring magus with the playwright's farewell to the magic of the stage, the film subordinates its tirelessly proliferating imagery to a recognizably Jacobean dramatic impulse. None of Greenaway's simulated protests against the two-dimensionality of the printed page, the trompe l'oeil effects, the choreographed allegorical dance sequences, the profusions of classical allusions, the pop-up models of Palladian architectural symmetries, the books with tipped-in floral specimens that conflate the signs of things and the things themselves, or even a magus with the reputed power to transform the latter into the former (such as John Dee or Robert Fludd), would have occasioned especial surprise in the Stuart court, but their collocation attests to the transformation of Gurr's imaginative auditor into Debord's demanding spectator: Inigo Jones, it seems, has declared Jonson's prefatory praises unnecessary for Prospero's twenty-fourth book.

It is, in fact, an attempt to account for the fate of this last encyclopedic folio that brings me to two commonly encountered critical oversights. One, the confident assertion that the characters begin to speak their lines only toward the end of the play when Prospero's desire for revenge gives way to his recognition of his characters' agency (exemplified by Ferdinand's spontaneous love for Miranda), might be the result of auditory insufficiency; the other, an inadequate consideration of the role of the four elements in the film, stems from those deficiencies of spectatorship that have trivialized Caliban and diminished his role as the Spirit of the Earth. H.R. Coursen, for instance, denounces *Prospero's Books* as an "interminable Home Shopping Network sequence" in which out-of-work actors have pawned their clothing, and maintains that their defeated director "can do nothing with Caliban, giving us instead a standard new critical version of the play."[69] Even Anderegg contributes to Caliban's diminution by reducing him to an unsavory physical presence, a "bald, grotesquely obscene figure."[70]

In fact, save for some perfunctory, stylized body makeup and sinuously serpentine dance movements designed to draw attention to *Genesis* and the Eve-Miranda connection, Caliban seems much closer to the Greek ideal of physical grace (or of Michelangelo's *ignudi*) than the deformed hybrid imagined by Shakespeare-Prospero. His first appearance, indeed, is one of the moments in which Greenaway most revealingly shows an authorial hand independent of Shakespeare's, albeit as irony embedded in the books contained in a library that serves as a metaphor for power, one modeled on the Florentine library Michelangelo designed for the omnipotent Medici. Other than Prospero's wife Susannah, connected to Adam by means of *An Alphabetical Inventory of the Dead* and summoned as a physical presence to illustrate the manner of her death in strict accordance with the illustrative principles of Vesalius's lost *Anatomy of Birth*, Caliban is the only character granted a "formal" introduction in *Prospero's Books*.[71] In addition to *The Book of Earth*, of which he is the somatic correlative and whose contents are explained to us as Prospero leads Miranda toward him, two other books pertain to him. *The Ninety-Two Conceits of the Minotaur*, a parody of Ovid's satirical poem *The Metamorphoses*, could have contained a hundred such conceits, had not the puritanical Theseus slain the storyteller: the narrator claims that it should be of especial interest to Caliban because he is the offspring of a bestial union. Prospero, who like any Puritan is obsessed by sex and sin, would surely side with the censorious Theseus, just as he could not but disapprove of the film's textual and technological hybridity. Nor would he approve of the twenty-first book, a compendious pornography called *The Autobiographies of Pasiphae and Semiramis* that must surely be its sequel. An alert critic might well recognize in this obsession with hybridity a central tenet of postcolonial theory, that the resistance to the notion of cultural plurality (and hence the presupposition of a pure and potentially superior culture) is part of nationalist and imperialist discourse.[72] Caliban must await Prospero's renunciation of his powers to discover the incipient postcoloniality that before his induction into the world of writing exists exclusively as the politics of a disobedient corporeality.

It seems hardly a coincidence that the Spirit of the Earth seems to have an existence independent of that of the other characters, for in his interpretation of Caliban Michael Clark, the Scottish dancer-choreographer notorious for his flashy lifestyle and dissident anti-classicalism, deftly evokes his own predecessor, Vaslav Nijinsky, and one of the central events of modern art. It was Nijinsky who, under the Prospero-like gaze of impresario Sergei Diaghilev, inaugurated the decisive (if never complete) break with the classical tradition of ballet when on May 29, 1912, the *Ballets Russes* premiered *L'après midi d'un faune*. Based on Stéphane Mallarmé's Symbolist poem, "Le Faun," the work was, as Thomas Munro points out, the first definitively twentieth-century exploration of the interrelation of the arts.[73] Guided by the seemingly lateral motions of dancers depicted on Greek ceramics, garbed in diaphanous costumes and frieze-like sets of the same derivation by Léon Bakst and Odilon Redon, and accompanied by an exotic pan flutelike score by Claude Debussy, *L'après midi* depicts a young faun's frustrated pursuit of three nubile nymphs. The audience at the Théâtre du Châtelet, habituated to astonishments, demanded an encore; it was the press (primarily in the form of the owner-editor of *Le Figaro*, Gaston Calmette, who the following day declared it to be pornography) that created the succès de scandale and set the stage for the shocker of the following season, the Igor Stravinsky–Nijinsky–Nikolai Roerich *Le Sacre du printemps* whose wild dissonances and virgin sacrifice engulfed the theatre in frenzied rioting and, according to Modris Eksteins, epitomized a prewar *weltanschauung* of apocalyptic hysteria. Clark's updating of Nijinsky's piquant high Modernist *vulgarité* to in-your-face Postmodern high kitsch–dispensing altogether with his predecessor's dappled faun-suit, modifying the recognizably angular, planar movements with acrobatic squatting and tumbling motions, and concluding with an even more literal image of sexual release, topped off with much lewd wiggling of the tongue–no doubt owes as much to the dancer's inspiration as to Greenaway's encouragement.[74]

Caliban's six sewers are what may have been seen beyond the bone heaps by the retreating angel in Paul Klee's painting *Angelus Novus*, whose gaping mouth the painting's owner Walter Benjamin described as an expression of horror at the hecatomb of the past (i.e., history) as he is blown backward into the future by the winds of progress.[75] That these are Caliban's native waters is not of his choosing: when Prospero permits, he readily emerges into the wider world. It is his immersion in the spoor of History that relates his tiny island to those of Aimé Césaire, George Lamming, and Derek Walcott. As Donaldson observes, Gielgud-Prospero's patriarchy extends to an appropriation of the maternal, the womb of culture (or as Lamming notes the exile's "womb of space"), in that he prescribes the manner of Miranda's delivery, appears to preside over Caliban's shocking emergence into the world, and, in Greenaway-Shakespeare's recurring vision of Caesarian birth, facilitates Ariel's extraction into existence.[76] So, too, Miranda's ideal partner, Ferdinand, must be reborn as Venus was born from the pure waters of the ocean, which is to say washed clean by civilization, a colorless (if tempestuous) excretion of the Spirit of Air. When Prospero's books burst into flames on contact with the subterranean waters of Caliban's lair, the destructive elements yield to the creative ones that Nietzsche might have regarded as Apollonian in Ariel and Dionysiac in Caliban.

If the horned and tailed Caliban owes something to Nijinsky's faun, then it stands to reason that the sound tracks, not just the image tracks, must conspire in his colonial subjugation. Prospero, presiding over Miranda's dream of shipwreck, voices her lines in girlish wonderment, and she responds in the same tempo and intonation as if coached by him (we hear her distinctly because the electronic blending of the voices renders them slightly out of phase). When she awakens and Prospero guides her to Caliban, Michael Nyman's shimmering, pulsating serial clusters of synthesized arpeggios turn instead into stark, ominously deep timbres, preparing us for Caliban's growling responses to Prospero (it is Prospero-Shakespeare speaking for him, but Gielgud's voice has been digitally lowered in pitch and made more reverberant). When Prospero, calling out "Slave, Caliban," sets him a-swimming toward the rock to which he has ostensibly been banished, the narrator halts the action to elucidate the mineral-rich contents of *The Book of the Earth*. Yet in Prospero's imagination, Caliban is not merely incapable of proper human speech, but also a destroyer of knowledge and civilization (a montage warns us that he is liable to mock Prospero's maternity on a purloined codex by splattering it with eggs, slash pages with a dagger gripped by hideous furry claws, spew a yellow film of vomit over the writing, drench the leaves with beer-colored urine, or even soak them in watery excrement). How is it then that on his island he harbors a book he has stolen from Prospero, a book we cannot even identify until Greenaway's publication of Prospero's twenty-fifth book, wherein it is revealed to be *The Ninety-Two Conceits of the Minotaur*? The answer, of course, resides in the much-misunderstood conclusion of the film. It is Ariel who commands the magic of flames, and so it is he who surreptitiously spares the twenty-fourth of Prospero's volumes and his *Tempest* manuscript as they break the surface of the water, from which Caliban rises to seize them. The film ends with the release of Caliban and Ariel for they are responsible for the images we see, these images being encoded into those nineteen bound pages.

Critics have generally concurred that *Prospero's Books* takes scant account of postcolonial readings and adaptations of *The Tempest*, which is perhaps because Greenaway's film is of itself a figure of postcoloniality. Like Montaigne (present in the play through his admiring translator John Florio as the utopian Gonzalo), Shakespeare refuses to silence the populations subject to conquest; he even returns Caliban's island to him. As Ngugi wa thiong'O points out, Caliban embodies all the stereotypes that later came to be justifications of the machinery of colonialism, and so Ngugi is struck by the energy with which Shakespeare invests him, his capacity to say "No," a capacity that by the time J.M. Coetzee rewrites Daniel Defoe's *Robinson Crusoe* the islander Friday, who has had his tongue torn out, no longer possesses.[77] For Houston Baker it is this ability to deform language, and so to reappropriate a subaltern subjectivity through an inversion of language as a tool of subjugation that transforms plight into resistance.[78] Richard Halpern makes the interesting observation that, for the New Historicists, Shakespeare's characters act as surrogates for the author's own role as native informant to the historical ethnologist reading the Renaissance; Shakespeare is at once Prospero and Caliban.[79] But both Greenblatt and Ngugi are intrigued by Caliban's "scamels," and Greenaway seems to endorse their puzzlement by making us, at the very end, rethink and reconfigure our assumptions. Those earlier images of Caliban despoiling the pages of Prospero's own book turn out to be Caliban imagining Prospero imagining Caliban; the deformed voice we hear is Caliban's idea of Prospero's idea of his voice, casting him therefore as an informing native rather than a native informant. When Caliban seizes the book of *Thirty-Six Plays*, all of Western literature, and a cultural inheritance of millennia embodied in and hyperlinked to those works, passes into the hands of those who once were taught to curse in a distant tongue. *Prospero's Books* is the paralogical antecedent, the prequel, if you will, to Shakespeare's play *The Tempest*. The film that we see and hear emerge from the blank canvas of the screen represents Greenaway's eye and voice alchemically blended with those of Césaire, Lamming, Walcott, and Ngugi in the great collective "No" uttered by Caliban and copied faithfully by his scribe Ariel.

A Dis-Barding from Down Under, or Post-Glob[e]al Shakespeare

Throughout his long, eventful life, mathematician, cartographer, geomancer, and fanatical book collector John Dee claimed to be on the side of the angels. Tried on various charges, including conducting unauthorized celestial conversations and "calculating" his way through the star charts of successive Tudor monarchs, this first great promoter of the "British Empire" (he himself was Welsh), who advocated naval supremacy in his 1577 *General and Rare Memorials pertayning to the Perfecte Arte of Navigation,* won over his antagonists, retired reluctantly to his country home in 1605, and died some months before the first recorded production of *The Tempest*. The work of empire continued.

Greenaway's Prospero, conversing with his airy spirits and poring over his lively books, seems even more Dee-like than Shakespeare's, but in the end the filmmaker's digital alchemy elicits sympathy for the devil by investing his native islander with the invisible mantle of resistant subalternity. Like Frantz Fanon, Caliban sows the fertile seeds of rebellion throughout the Caribbean and beyond. Another islander, fully attuned to the implications of his own colonized past and to the location of his island on the periphery of imperial culture, continues to prefer the company of angels and surreptitiously gives his adaptation of Shakespeare to the brightest of them, Juliet. At the Capulet Ball, an ecstatic Romeo, perhaps a little susceptible to literalism (having ingested mind-enhancing substances), seems entranced by the wings that sprout from her shoulders, and perhaps by her exceptional ability to speak with unadorned sincerity. Whether the cruciform "+" in Baz Luhrmann's enigmatically titled *William Shakespeare's Romeo + Juliet* signifies the crossing of stars or serves as an acknowledgment of Shakespeare's allegory of Christian sectarianism remains unresolved, but set in Verona Beach (Miami), populated with Hollywood's teen idol glitterati, and shot in Mexico with the aid of personnel from four continents, the film for most critics constitutes the quintessence of "global Shakespeare."

Despite eliciting a critical nomenclature resembling that accorded to *Prospero's Books,* inviting liberal doses of "popular culture," and provoking such derogations as "Kitsch" (in addition to such usual signifiers of ambivalence as "global" and "Postmodern"), *Romeo + Juliet* is as resolutely technophobic as its illusionistic predecessor is technophilic. Its computer desktop editing style is all the more surprising because the freedom of camera movement and shock cutting that one associates with such television fare as MTV might appear to provide just the occasion for extremes of image manipulation. Nevertheless, a certain ironic self-awareness (not unlike Shakespeare's) allows the film a certain distance from, even ambivalence toward, the genres it cites insistently: reality TV, the teen pic, MTV, the Bollywood extravaganza and, of course, the previous film adaptations of Robbins and Wise (from which it borrows and modifies the interethnic conflict while playfully burlesquing its artsy inclinations as when

Paul Sorvino, playing the voluble, bottom-pinching arriviste Fulgencio Capulet, unleashes an operatic bellow) and Zeffirelli (from whom, much to the earlier director's chagrin, it shamelessly unwraps and repackages the baby boom, anti-Vietnam teen-generation-against-the-self-interested-older-world theme on behalf of casually disaffected Generation Xers). In contrast to the material it commandeers, its teenagers are even less proficient in matters of judgment than their elders; instances of subordination of the action to the soundtrack are neither celebratory nor heroic but invariably presage calamitous confrontation; and the products of technology and pharmacology prove to be unengagingly cool, if depressingly effective media.

This pervasive skepticism is evident from the outset. While his predecessors did away with the Chorus's inconvenient "spoilers," Luhrmann multiplies the effect by repetition. In the first instance, the opening lines are pared down to a brief newscast that emanates from a primitive, 1970s-style TV set lodged in the center of the frame: even a slow zoom-in does not permit the newscaster to occupy more than a marginal amount of screen space, the cartoonish inset icon of a fractured ring being, symbolically and symptomatically, larger than her head. Only when she has uttered her final phrase, "two-hours' traffic of our stage," is there a sudden zoom into the center of the screen, revealing the constitutive lines of a low-resolution televisual image. It may then seem that there occurs a sudden advance in technology when helicopter-borne skycams zoom in with alarming rapidity on a massive statue of Christ that towers over Verona Beach. Yet those zooms are clearly accomplished in the editing room, as is the freezing of the frame on the out-of-focus head of the statue. Another such close-up of the city's emblem appears as a black-and-white dot matrix pattern that a zoom-out reveals as a photocollaged backdrop to the inset photographs of the feuding Montagues and Capulets dominating the front page of the *Verona Beach Herald*. Buildings bearing tacky outsize posters flank the remarkably medieval Montague and Capulet towers, two lofty skyscrapers surmounted by the family emblems; one poster declares "Retail'd to posterity by Montague," while another uses the white-on-red curves of the all-pervasive Coca-Cola logo to advertise the product known as L'amour. As a second montage of images of violent confrontation begins, a baritone voice repeats the first six lines of the Chorus's introductory speech adopting the tones of shocked rapture characteristic of narrators of television crime drama series. His words are picked out in the close-up titles of such overtly populist newspapers as the *People's Eye* and *Verona Today*, or by the red-bordered newsmagazine *Timely*, whose images blur into those of *Prophecy*, which in turn overlap with those of the hobby magazine *Bullet*. His phrases even turn into the intertitles of silent films, with his recitation of "a pair of star-cross'd lovers" concluding with a black screen filled with a line of boldface letters {TAKE THEIR LIFE} the first "T" being ornamented into a Gothic cross, one of Luhrmann's talismans, being the same "+" that is picked out in neon lights in the title credit *Romeo + Juliet* and that is later given an ornate, Celtic cast in the imposing black tattoo emblazoned on the back of progressive, drug swilling, and possibly pedophilic Friar Laurence. The montage (concluding with a sequence of flash-forward vignettes) that follows the narration parodies the credit sequences of docudramas, each character's name being associated with his or her dramatic function (e.g., CAPTAIN PRINCE Chief of Police, DAVE PARIS The Governor's Son or, just before a shootout, the explanatory TYBALT CAPULET Prince of Cats Juliet's Cousin).

The process of translation thus reveals itself as precisely the reverse of Greenaway's use of images to annotate the written word in that Luhrmann's focus of interest is not the poetry but the dramatic content of the play, the printed text underlined or highlighted to explain the profusion of images associated with the action. As the media forms mutate from surveillance footage to documentary to docudrama during the course of the film's evolution from newscast into fiction film, the successive remediations seem to dwell on the overt commercialism of the various messages. We may lose the Bard's lines, but we get to see Rosaline, a tarty redhead who anchors the nightly "Lifestyles of the Filthy Rich" slot on TV. Surely this is more akin to an Adornoesque critique of parasitic consumerism than to a valorization of the signs of a global migration of image repertoires, the latter attitude by now verging on critical consensus in Luhrmann's case. The two-hours' traffic of this stage resists any facile dismissal as pandering to a self-celebratory teen culture, just as it challenges that lively school of authenticity that has sprung up around the resurrected Globe, in that it simultaneously redeems and ridicules Shakespeare's language: it is almost all Shakespeare, but nearly three-quarters of the lines have been jettisoned so that the others can be repeated or embroidered with images in the style of one of the more playful illuminated medieval manuscripts. Within this structural model that privileges actions over words, Luhrmann's imagery remains consistent: just as Juliet is associated with light, whether as candle flame or as elaborate systems of backlighting, Romeo is associated with fluidity (he clears his head by splashing his face with water; true love comes when he first espies Juliet through an aquarium; he tumbles with Juliet into a swimming pool where they declare and demonstrate their love; he shoots Tybalt who falls into a fountain; and he is not quite dead, and so can shed a final tear, when Juliet shoots herself with his gun). The consistency extends over each of the five tracks of cinema: the still images derive from commercial photography, the moving images pay homage to popular film genres, the written word resembles the lettering of advertisements and logos, the spoken accents (urban American, Latino, Italianate) pay homage to earlier Shakespeare films, and the music is dominated by the voices of black soloists and choristers. Nor is the appeal to stylized genres in any way incidental to the film. Having given the guns treasured by the rival clans names drawn from Shakespeare's more modest arsenal, Luhrmann sets the incendiary opening shootout at a gas station (evoking Hitchcock), quoting shot compositions including the camera-behind-the-trigger-hand trademark of Sergio Leone's Spaghetti Westerns, and the slow-motion aerial acrobatics and gun-in-either-hand frenzy of John Woo's Hong Kong action movies. The scaredy-cat Montague boys are forced into confrontation by the "Prince of Cats," who stops grinding his teeth long enough to whip open his jacket to reveal a garish Sacred-Heart T-shirt and the fancy gangland paraphernalia he puts to deadly use. Ritualized tragedy, no less than culturally hybrid genre transposition, inheres to the citations themselves. It is not Luhrmann's lack of method, surely, but his unmitigated tongue-in-cheekiness in seizing on generic clichés and attempting to erase historical distance by sacrificing swordplay for wordplay—both procedures indicative of his irreverence for such major cultural institutions as academic Shakespeare and popular film genres —that continues to provoke umbrage.

It is instructive, therefore, to survey the kinds of criticism that this perplexing film invites, in part because film criticism is no less indicative of the tenor of the times than as any text it might address. We could well begin with a bracingly pithy example that coincided with the film's release. In her review for the *New York Times,* Janet Maslin observes what seems to be an overpowering tension between a "sacrosanct" attitude to the language of the play and the "radical revisionism" of all else, with the overall result being a "witty and sometimes successful experiment, an attempt to reinvent 'Romeo and Juliet' in the hyperkinetic vocabulary of post-modern kitsch."[80] It is rather difficult to think of a "postmodernism" dissociated from the decay of Modernism, and hence with "kitsch": the terms reinforce each other.

Subsequent commentary evidences a proliferation of such descriptions, which is not to associate all such criticism with profligacy, but rather to observe that, depending on the critic (and here I seize on three exceptionally able ones), the same terms could be laudatory or condemnatory, or even, on occasion, both. Having conceded that among recent Shakespeare films "Luhrmann's not only more stridently advertises itself as a product of global capitalism but also knowingly flaunts how that culture consumes 'Shakespeare'," Barbara Hodgdon still finds such heterogeneities as Des'ree's ballad "Kissing you" (during which the protagonists first make eye contact from opposite sides of an aquarium), Prince's "When Doves Cry," and Leontyne Price's recording of the *liebestod* from *Tristan und Isolde* rising to a crescendo over the dying lovers, indicative of a self-conscious postmodernity that serves as a preexisting answer to those very critics who find fault with his anachronisms and impossible juxtapositions. "Coming from the right or the left, such queries suggest critics who imagine they reside somewhere other than an America where such blurrings and crossings of ethnic, racial, gender, and class boundaries occur daily," she argues, having reminded us of Peter Matthew's claim that the film constitutes "the most radical reinvention of a classic text since *Throne of Blood*." "If this be postmodernism," she declares enticingly, "give me excess of it."[81] For Courtney Lehmann, who cites Fredric Jameson to the effect that postmodern aesthetics require aspiring authors dwelling in "a world in which stylistic innovation is no longer possible" to engage in "the random cannibalization of all the styles of the past," Luhrmann's "postmodern tour de force" has as its most striking formal feature a "barrage of boldly incongruous images."[82] Amplifying Zeffirelli's more suggestive textual elaborations, Luhrmann uses the camera lens, in her description, as the "magnifying glass of a consuming intertextuality."[83] In recognizing that Shakespeare suffered a similar Oedipal anxiety in relation to his principal source for the play, Arthur Brooke, Lehmann goes on to argue that "rife with images of fish, water, and baited hooks, Brooke's *Tragicall Historye* contains a lure that not even Luhrmann can resist—so strong is the pull of this 'ghostly father' reluctantly entombed in Shakespeare's play."[84] Thus, Luhrmann's elaborate water symbolism turns out to be the prolongation, in a postmodern register, of Shakespeare's early modern battle with textual authority.

If Hodgdon celebrates Luhrmann's postmodernism and Lehmann finds mitigation enough to forgive it, then Chris Palmer, writing for the *Australian Humanities Review*, finds sufficient variety to condone and condemn it simultaneously. For him the most vivid images are those associated with what he terms "catholic kitsch," namely statues of the Virgin Mary, crosses, "holy cards," and churches containing outsize "artistically sterile" devotional statues. He notes this having observed that "if camp is a matter of putting emotional investment, and artistic investment, into something that you know you can't seriously believe in, something that is artificial, an image and no more, then this film's campness says interesting things about the connection between our moment and that of Shakespeare's *Romeo and Juliet*." With a décor and imagery that is "popular and populist in a certain way," the film's eschewal of "serious, WASP modern life" permits it a "kind of Deleuzian holiday from order and authority."[85] Its preference for the "wet" over the "dry" suggests (but apparently only to those "led too far by a kind of postmodernist zeal") "libidinal liquidity" that again has a connection to Deleuze. Noting the affective power of the final scene in the Capulet chapel and the lovers' tender isolation, Palmer inquires, "Given that this film is so thorough-going in its inventive embrace of the postmodern, what business has it celebrating natural and innocent bodies and deploying unstinted emotional attentiveness?" To which he replies, by way of conclusion, "[I]f this is a problem for Postmodernist theorists and critics working away at it by rethinking the body, we can only wish them a touch of Luhrmann's verve and wit."[86] In other words, if Palmer's *peripateia* at the end is intentional as the pervasive tone of irony might imply, if after the cultural degradations Luhrmann has supposedly inflicted on Shakespeare's work, and if after worrying openly about Postmodern zealots exaggerating libidinal liquidity, he still would have critics adopt Luhrmann's wit in their own Postmodernist contemplations of the body, then this body surely belongs to the shaggiest of dogs.

Curiously, in the context of such fluid libidinalities, an overview of Luhrmann's excisions reveals his Shakespeare to be a bit of a prude. True, he amplifies some risqué elements of previous film interpretations: Stephen Buhler, for instance, discerns that Luhrmann's Mercutio, John Perrineau, even exaggerates John Barrymore's scene-chewing theatricality (in Cukor) and John McEnery's low-key longing for Romeo (in Zeffirelli) by transforming himself into the pill-wielding, tripping Queen Mab of his own hallucinatory soliloquy while decked out in "full drag queen regalia."[87] And Luhrmann may well borrow from theatrical antecedents when he ensures that Romeo, and not just the audience, lingers long enough to appreciate the extent of Juliet's love for him, the Apothecary having previously been rendered a little less true by Cibber and Garrick, showmen both who would no doubt have envied the ability to fill the equivalent of a stage proscenium with an actor's face to reveal his last tear.[88] Even so, the majority of the cut lines, including some from Juliet's most impassioned soliloquies, most from comic exchanges between minor characters, and those resulting in Paris's salvation through disappearance and Friar Laurence's eventual redundancy, all have in common a reduction of any perception of rhetorical excess or violation of stage decorum. Anderegg, who makes this observation, goes on to point out that these "pressure points" in the play, whose failure to observe the rules of classical and neoclassical drama were once thought scandalous, are also those deemed indigestible for a contemporary audience: "[B]oth *Shakespeare in Love*, which pretends to take us back to the origins of *Romeo and Juliet*, and Luhrmann's film, which projects Shakespeare's play into the twenty-first century, elide or gloss over the very same elements, the elements that run counter to the idea of Shakespeare as a screenwriter, an entertainer, 'one of us.'"[89]

It is perhaps our determination to readmit a Renaissance pop icon into our ranks (by which we do not mean the moldering ranks of academics, but a presumptively younger, hipper, and much more popular crowd) that requires his varied avatars to be retrofitted within critical discourse—rather than in cinema per se—with Saturnian haloes consisting of the solar debris of postmodernist kitsch, global pop cultural camp, or their various equivalents and permutations.

For while "pop culture" may be a useful generalization in certain circumstances, it is anything but helpful in describing Luhrmann's methodical use of related repertoires of signs and his obvious familiarity with and respect for what celebrants of pop culture would decry as high culture. In the death scene, when the mortally wounded Juliet curls up beside the expiring Romeo, a vertiginously suspended camera makes them appear to float above a sea of candles, the composition creating a trompe l'oeil that reverses the effect of a late Renaissance or Baroque ceiling fresco. The effect is both magical and disturbing, in the way Edith Wharton, contemplating a ceiling fresco by Andrea Mantegna, described the "obstructive" effect of such a perspectival reversal: "Any trompe-l'oeil is permissible in decorative art if it gives the impression of pleasure; but the inherent sense of fitness is shocked by the act of walking upon upturned faces."[90] To appreciate art is to recognize that the lovers have been defiled.

The novelist may also provide an interesting commentary to Luhrmann's music for the scene. Grand opera, the most lavishly produced of repeated public spectacles, for instance, had a well-worn association with Europeanate high culture even before Wharton, something of a fin-de-siècle arbiter of taste, came to describe its then provincial embrace by Manhattan's upper crust with a mixture of reverence and ridicule. So we might do well to reflect on why a director who is equally at home directing productions of Giaccomo Puccini and Benjamin Britten as with making music videos, who is unafraid to justify his approach with appeals to Shakespeare's sources, who ascribes his condensation of the plot of *Romeo and Juliet* to its essentials as stemming from his own "mythomania" and to the residual influence of Joseph Campbell, the scholar of mythic archetypes, who persuades Leontyne Price to sing Isolde's *libestod* over the dying lovers, and who makes numerous visual and auditory references to prior film adaptations (even such a use of Price's rendition of Wagner's paean to dying for love, already to be found in Franc Roddam's sequence in the 1998 omnibus film, *Aria*), would go to such pains to address the purportedly callow teen audience to whom the majority of these references would be unintelligible.[91] Or is Luhrmann setting us the challenge of considering whether such an imagined popular culture that either belongs to or encapsulates youth (as opposed to the perennial Bakhtinian one of the dispossessed) is saturated with the arcane, the redundant, the superstitious? If Luhrmann's attempts as stage director to reimagine the settings of canonical operas to broaden their appeal—an oft-confessed project that has a Wellesian Modernist ring to it—then must "Postmodern" in his case simply stand for "indecipherably heterogenous"? And how does Luhrmann mobilize the cult of Shakespeare that is hardly a popular cult outside the narrow claims of national or cultural property of the sort revealed by Pacino's provocations?

Any adequate response to these interrogatives would also have to account for the auxiliary term "globalization," that in so much of critical discourse has become a high-flown euphemism for "cultural mishmash." Film historian Tom O'Regan, writing before the film's release, pointed out that a midsize, English-language cinema such as that of Australia typically operated in Hollywood's shadow (Luhrmann's previous feature, *Strictly Ballroom* [1992], being a "retro-homage to the Hollywood Musical") and relied on transnational appeal, and that in the 1990s Australian cinema took a decidedly multiculturalist turn.[92] Some Shakespeare scholars too have been alert to the film's subterranean Australianness: Donaldson, for example, has observed that Luhrmann's version of carnival owes as much to the fetishistic zeal of Sydney's cosmopolitan Gay and Lesbian Mardi Gras as to that of "nearby" New Orleans.[93] It is Donaldson also, who observes that through Romeo Luhrmann stages another Situationist strategy of resistance to the encroachments of consumer culture, "*la dérive*," or spontaneous and purposeless wandering.[94] Following the initial affray, Ted and Caroline Montague, riding in a limousine adorned with an imposing wooden cross bearing Christ's lifeless body, anguish over Romeo's addiction to darkness and to "Sycamore Grove," the ruined theatre whose proscenium resembles a shattered Roman archway surmounting a stage. Neil Taylor remarks that this "redundant piece of architecture stranded on the beach" is a figure of the Globe itself. Its positioning, facing away from the direction of the waves, seems to have a symbolic value even beyond its significance for Taylor as "multi-ethnic and supra-national."[95] Whether treated as a matter of textual strategy or as a matter of audience reception, the film's pluri(cult)ural embrace of otherness seems a characteristically marsupial incorporation of otherwise unassimilable temporal, geographical, and ethnic diversities into the safe and yet challenging confines of art. The film transforms what has already been appropriated by consumer culture into a reappropriation, in which can be discerned an inner truth in a cross cleansed of its garish, commodified surface, and in which the author responsible for the renascence of the Globe continues to survive the tides of time on the very beaches where once the paramount representatives of the high culture of his native land deposited the lowest of its outcasts.

Romeo + Juliet begins and ends with the same news anchor and the same antiquated TV set receding to the screen's epicentric vanishing point, and the most often remarked of Luhrmann's alleged concessions to American popular culture has been his devotion to American television, especially to MTV. Kenneth Anger may have reason to resent the attribution of the cutting of image tracks to the sound tracks, just as he might recognize Luhrmann's incessant visual punning as being of his own stamp. There is, perhaps, an Oedipal element in Luhrmann's Benjamin Britten-inspired music video, "Now until the Break of Day" (2001), in which he reuses a considerable amount of footage from the Reinhardt-Dieterle *Midsummer Night's Dream*, but substitutes a rather more explicit Indian Changeling Prince for the affectionate child once played by Anger. The clearest instance of MTV visual technique in *Romeo + Juliet* occurs to the strains of "Kissing You," which begins with the placid waters of the fish tank through which the soon-to-be-lovers first see each other. It is a reminder of our first glimpse of Juliet *à dérive* (and perhaps through her of Dustin Hoffman's Graduate), submerged mermaid-like in a swimming pool from which her mother's piercing shrieks extract her. In contrast to the disinterest she shows in "The Year's Most Eligible Bachelor," Dave Paris, whose face occupies the cover of a copy of *Timely* brandished by her mother, she responds with instant engagement upon accidentally catching sight of Romeo's face through the tank as an Emperor Fish and a Yellow Tang (marine life indigenous to warm Pacific waters) flit over his earnest features, a synecdoche of the Great Barrier Reef separating them. As Gloria Capulet, in all her leering Ptolemaic decadence, attempts to make her daughter dance the New Year in with cheesy Mr. All-American Paris (the Stars and Stripes evident on the sleeve of his astronaut suit), the lovers' furtive expressions and actions synchronize with the rhythms of "Kissing You." It is hardly surprising that the balcony scene rapidly turns into a swimming pool scene, and that Desiree has correctly foreseen some rather wet kissing.

The moment of encounter, which shortly leads into an appropriation of Zeffirelli's staging of the moment Romeo grasps Juliet's hand, is part of a larger Capulet Ball sequence notable for its startling juxtapositions. Lady Capulet's outfitting as Cleopatra is speeded up to a comic opera accompaniment; in what may be another involved pun, Mercutio gets an entire disco number to himself, its parodic theatricalization of gender reminiscent of *Paris Is Burning* (dir. Jennie Livingston, 1991); with a Hitchcockian precision the camera isolates the lovers against emblematic statues as they flee controlling gazes. Quilted into a larger configuration in which the musical interludes punctuate violent juxtapositions of contrary emotions, this is MTV as Bollywood envisions MTV, yet another spice to add to a manic masala mix of heightened sensations.

The primordial influence of Indian cinema as felt in *Romeo + Juliet* might be worth dwelling on because of its increasing relevance to what Luhrmann would eventually dub his "Red Curtain Trilogy," whose tenets (despite his protestations to the contrary) read like a rejoinder to the asceticism of the Dogme manifesto. Recall that the later 1995 manifesto proved programmatic, its tenfold Vow of Chastity underwriting a style of filmmaking that had yet to come into being. In his send-up of Dogme, Luhrmann only recognizes that *Strictly Ballroom*, *Romeo + Juliet*, and the 2001 *Moulin Rouge* constitute an equivalent aesthetic program just before their release as a DVD box set. Where Dogme objects to film's increasing technological dependency, the Red Curtain films hark back to the Musicals made at the height of the studio system, initially triumphs of sound technology and then of color. Where Dogme rejects the artifice of genre, Red Curtain filmmakers insist on a recognizable story shape that eschews suspense or surprise conclusions. Whereas Dogme films rely on plausibility, Red Curtain films evoke a heightened world of fantasy; whereas Dogme films operate under the conceit of effacing stardom and star turns, Red Curtain films flaunt the attributes and talents of their personnel and strive to provoke a participatory response from an audience that can thus respond to wrenching transitions from comedy to tragedy to musical number.

Although Luhrmann slyly claims to have recognized his own emerging filmmaking dogma with its most developed expression in *Moulin Rouge*, his flamboyant departure from the nighted colors of the abstemious Danes, his predilection for narrative transparency, and perhaps even his distillation of the plot to its "mythic" essentials—itself a staple of a number of India's popular cinemas where it signals social allegory—suggest a subcontinental inception to the style. In a pubic interview published in Britain's *Guardian* newspaper (in September 2001), he parallels Shakespeare's attitude to genre ("low comedy and then you die in five minutes") to his experience of seeing a Hindi film when researching *A Midsummer Night's Dream* in India in 1993. "We went to this huge, ice-cream picture palace to see a Bollywood movie," he explains. "Here we were, with 2,000 Indians watching a film in Hindi, and there was the lowest possible comedy and then incredible drama and tragedy and then they break out in songs... We thought we had suddenly learnt Hindi because we understood everything. We thought it was incredible how involved the audience were. How uncool they were—how their coolness had been ripped aside... The thrill of thinking 'could we ever do that in the west? Could we ever get past the "cerebral cool" and the "perceived cool." It required this idea of comic-tragedy. Could you make those switches?"[96]

The structural influence of Indian popular cinema appears in fully digested form in *Moulin Rouge* with its flickering shifts of emotional register and spontaneous eruptions into song. In one of the film's set-piece numbers, composer

Sameer's "Chamma chamma," borrowed from a popular Hindi film, pairs Nicole Kidman (singing a version of a hit film song associated with Marilyn Monroe, "Diamonds Are a Girl's Best Friend") with noted playback singer Alka Yagnik. By the start of shooting, Ganesh, the elephant-headed Hindu god of good fortune, appears to have replaced the Gothic cross as Luhrmann's talisman, and the film itself received its premiere in India. Australian audiences, however, would have not have been susceptible to the illusion that this represented a progressive Indianization of Luhrmann's sensibility. In fact, the most distinctly subcontinental of any Luhrmann production was the version of Benjamin Britten's opera *A Midsummer Night's Dream* for the Sydney Opera in 1993. It might have also resurrected (if by chance) one of the great unfulfilled visions of Modernist music, that of composer Alexander Scriabin who before his unexpected death envisaged staging his newest composition in a purpose-built Indian temple scented with perfumes and incense and his musicians and dancers bedecked in sacred vestments and rainbow-colored apparel. In setting the action in an Indian hill station resort in 1923, the waning days of the British Raj, Luhrmann gives Britten's mocking opera a seriously Sciabinesque twist. (Britten transformed his Thisbe, the tenor Peter Pears, into an Australian icon, coloratura soprano Dame Joan Sutherland, parodying her mad scene from *Lucia di Lammermoor*; Scriabin, on the other hand, rather earnestly planned his trip to India and even purchased a pith helmet as protection from the sun.) In the Sydney production, Luhrmann puts the musicians into military uniforms and has them occupy a large bandstand on stage, a structure inundated by moist Deleuzian deluges and festooned with rampant vines as the opera progresses. The fairy-folk are painted and attired as Hindu deities and among them a Kama Sutran polymorphous sexuality runs riot, threatening to engulf the prissy colonists in their midst: Tytania, quite unlike Kott's anxious upper-class matron, seems delighted that Bottom acquires more than just the head of an ass, Helena offers Demetrius a riding crop for her chastisement, and the Lion has his way with Thisbe. A rampant Union Jack gradually begins to droop, and by the end, all the insignias of imperialism have been torn down or overtaken by undergrowth. "Among the showers of petals and a fizzy firework display, Oberon and Tytania assume control of their liberated country," writes Peter Conrad of the conclusion of the 2003 revival in Sydney's renowned opera house (infused, for the occasion, with the scent of sandalwood oil, incense, and curry powder).[97]

To suggest that Luhrmann has merely Indi[a]genized Britten's opera would be as facetious as to insist that the lineaments of *Romeo + Juliet* merely conform to Bollywood's conventions. Rather, his makeovers of Britten and Shakespeare attest to a preference for a more up-to-date set of clichés than those of Edwardian pastoralism and pre-Raphaelite pictorialism that have dominated recent theatrical and cinematic interpretations of the two plays. The elements of *Romeo + Juliet* that most test the reflexes of critics happen to be the ones most characteristic of Indian popular films: those familiar with their stylistic conventions would instantly recognize the hodgepodgery of generic mixing, of hyperkinetic camera movements, of the incessant borrowings and incongruous juxtapositions of elements of canonical texts both "high" and "low," of the cult of stardom elevated to the level of quasi-religious veneration, and of musical numbers themselves derived from the chorus-rich Busby Berkeleyesque model that Hollywood once offered as universal eye candy. If this be postmodernism, Indian audiences need be given no further excess of it, for they have been postmodern spectators for half a century and more.

Even if we can thus explain the predominant style of *Romeo + Juliet*, there remains the question of whether that style is kitsch. In a recent, fiercely insightful essay in which at a certain point he alights on the two great insults of literary criticism, *vulgarité* and kitsch, Milan Kundera points out that the latter term had a precise meaning at its birth in Munich, when it signified the decadence of Romanticism. Unlike the *vulgarité* of Rabelais or Flaubert, which is self-ironic, kitsch demands to be taken seriously. Thus, even before the Nazis had transformed Wagner into *überkitsch*, modeling their own cult on his, the Viennese novelist Hermann Broch described his operas as exemplary kitsch (an effect perhaps even heightened when the greatest of Verdi sopranos sings them).[98] Luhrmann's film fails as kitsch precisely because his duplication of a Wagnerian *liebestod* and a host of other such devices parade themselves as kitsch, whereas many an epic film and a preponderant amount of what we call "theory" succeed by remaining oblivious to their Wagnerian character.

But does Luhrmann's self-awareness imply that he regards contemporary Shakespeare as kitsch? What makes a film Shakespearean in character, according to Anderegg, is its use of language, and Luhrmann's irreverent modernizations have the effect both of reversing the traditional subordination of action to words and of heightening the archaic sonorities of individual words and phrases. Nor is the archaism merely a dissonance between Renaissance diction and a contemporary setting, but a consequence of what we may think of as the Pierre Menard effect. Menard, you may recall, attempted to translate the *Quijote* perfectly, but after decades of labor succeeded in leaving only a few completed passages in his notebooks. The words in the translated passages happened to be identical to those of Cervantes. Yet, as Jorge Luis Borges points out, Menard's fragmentary *Quijote* is subtler than Cervantes's. Avoiding the stock-in-trade of the historical novel, the gypsies, the conquistadors, the mystics, the inquisitors, and the Hapsburgs, Menard abjures the temptations of local color just as he abstains from infusing the work with his individual psychology. Uttered by Cervantes, a group of words could be a mere rhetorical conceit, but the passage of time gives them an entirely new meaning.[99] Just so Luhrmann's translation of Shakespeare into images or into the miasma of Miamian argot, as natural to the old-time mobsters as cowboy talk is to the heroes of a Western, provides a translation more rigorous than *Cardenio*. And in this strange felicity resides the root cause of critics' unhappiness, for as Greenblatt—eliciting the aid of J.L. Austin's speech act theory—observes in his Norton Anthology notes to *Romeo and Juliet*, the language of the play is already rich in multiple meanings and filled with the potentiality of action.[100] Conscientious objectors resent Shakespeare's apparent relegation to the status of supernumerary, Luhrmann's curtain raiser, as it were. As in the aptly Italian adage, *traditore traduttore*, Luhrmann and Menard are good translators only to the extent that they are good traducers, a dimension of intertextuality that could not fail to amuse Miola.

Shocked amusement might also have been John Dee's reaction had one of his better angels made him aware that his dreams of empire would come to this. Surely, the courtly Welsh bookworm could never have imagined that it was less the perfection of the art of seafaring than the poetry of the son of a disgraced Warwickshire recusant that would be his passport through the shoals of history to new worlds and new media. If stepping into the role of Benjamin's angel he could contemplate the present, it might be to observe that Luhrmann's old-fashioned, newfangled film is not only a testament to the four-century circumnavigation of *The Dragon*—to the triumph of what we now call and miscall "globalization"—but also to its cost.

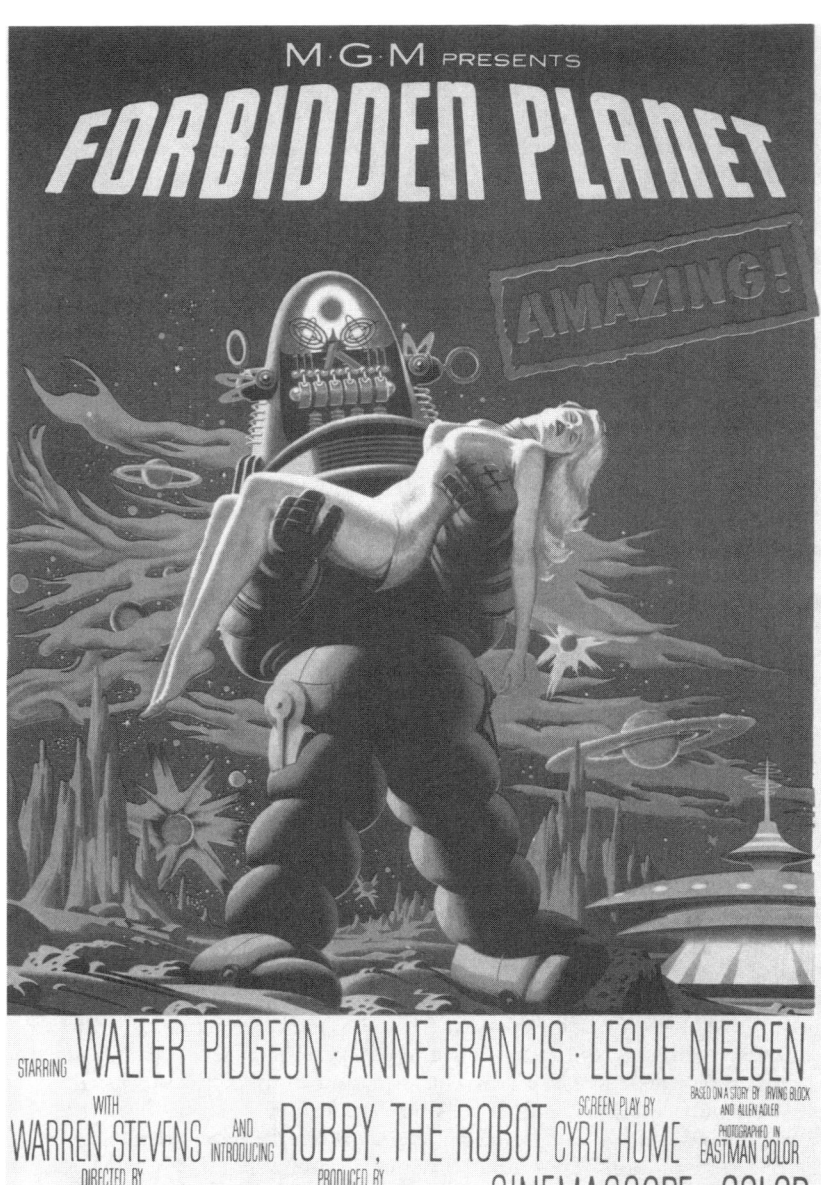

Poster to Fred McLeod Wilcox's *Forbidden Planet* (1956).
Courtesy of www.moviegoods.com

NOTES

What's in a Name? Or, Something like an Introduction

1. See *Will in the World* 203–220. The Shakebag of *Arden of Faversham*, sometimes attributed to Thomas Kyd, might be the same character.
2. See Kermode 40–412. In June 2006 a veritable cottage industry achieved a new level of academic respectability with the opening of the "Searching for Shakespeare" exhibition at the Yale Center for British Art, about which Grace Glueck concludes in a newspaper review that it richly documents how little we actually know (see B30).
3. Méliès scholar Paolo Cherchi-Usai informs me that neither it nor the *Hamlet* of the same year appears to have emerged from the vaults.
4. Zecca's own *Cléopatre* (1910), which does survive (I have examined the copy at the British Film Institute with German subtitles), makes the play hinge not only on imperial rivalry but also on the battle between the women vying for Marc Antony's attentions, but is otherwise an uncharacteristically stolid affair of grand gestures loosely based on episodes from the eponymous play by Victorien Sardou and Émile Moreau, for whom Shakespeare was a source, and hence Eddie Sammons's claim (see 3) that "Shakespeare's influence is clearly evident." Its best moment is probably an example of what passed at the time for Oriental cruelty, when a female dancer, Stacia Napierkowska, dressed as one of the queen's male entourage, brings bad tidings and must poison himself, thus expiring with acrobatic flair. Méliès's own *Cléopatre* (1899) was made early in his career and did not even have Sardou for legitimation: it showed a sorcerer chopping up the queen's mummy and then reanimating Cleopatra from the bits. Two *Cleopatra*s being actively sought by the American Film Institute, one starring Helen Gardner (1912) and the other Theda Bara (1912), both specialists in the role of "vamp," received lavish praise in the trade literature, but are based primarily on Sardou and Moreau.
5. See Hamilton Ball 34, in which he describes three previous films that are suggestive in title but remote in their relation to the plays, the first having no identifiable theatrical precedent. In her account of the 1907–1915 period of American cinema, Eileen Bowser describes Gaston quite aptly as a "rascal" who betrayed both his brother and his equally unscrupulous business partners (see 30). As the sum of his innovations becomes increasingly apparent, assessments of Méliès's achievements have become correspondingly more generous. Paul Virilio, for instance, credits him in his 1991 essay "The Aesthetics of Disappearance" with having first simulated in moving images the process of temporal contraction through the loss of fragments of time, the "picnolepsis" that occurs naturally in human perception, thus (paradoxically) introducing a new element of realism to cinematic narrative in producing his illusions (see 62–63).
6. See *Shakespeare on Silent Film* 35–36.
7. See 174.
8. Thomas Cartelli cites an astute observation by Jonathan Bate that "the history of appropriation may suggest that 'Shakespeare' is not a man who lived from 1564 to 1616 but a body of work that is refashioned by each subsequent age in the image of itself." Cartelli adds, "[T]his tendency becomes even more pronounced when 'Shakespeare' is 'refashioned' outside the national boundaries of British culture and society 'in the image' of cultures and societies seeking either to establish their independence from imperial influence or to identify, assert, and define their own national values or priorities" (2).

9. It is hardly necessary for me to elaborate on the details of the film since it has generated a considerable volume of critical commentary, but the reasonable view Anderegg takes in "James Dean Meets Ethel the Pirate's Daughter," comparing the modes of audience address in Baz Luhrmann's *Romeo + Juliet* to those of Madden's film, is instructive in this context and is reprieved in the final chapter.
10. See "Racial Memory and Literary History," *PMLA* 116.1 (Jan. 2001: 48–63): 49–52.
11. See *Shakespeare for All Time* 37.
12. See Ackroyd 19–20.
13. See Kermode 35–48.
14. See *Will in the World* 111.
15. I have omitted James Shapiro's brilliantly researched and documented microhistory, *A Year in the Life of William Shakespeare: 1599*, from this abridged catalogue of recent commentaries merely because Shapiro, while acknowledging the Catholicism of Shakespeare's paternal and (especially) maternal relatives, makes the sensible argument that, at a moment of intense doctrinal uncertainty, even Shakespeare might have shared the situation of the majority of his countrymen in not having quite known what he was (see especially 142,145–148).
16. Gurr 133–134.
17. I will treat this episode at more length presently.
18. Vittachi 68–69.
19. Ibid. 76–100.
20. Two of the essays collected by M.E. Moss in *Benedetto Croce: Essays on Literature and Literary Criticism* treat Shakespeare, and of all of them these are the most encompassing in seeking the art and the poetic sensibility of a writer. Moss also argues that for Croce, Shakespeare was a model of the organic unity between form and content. He was the supreme representative of his age only because of the essential and transcendental uniqueness of his inspiration (see 2–3, 107–116, 117–126).
21. Borges "Shakespeare's Memory" 514.
22. Ungar 42.
23. Rothwell, *A History* 123–135.
24. For reasons that I hope will be apparent in what follows, I have concentrated on these films, which I think are exemplars of linguistic translation as cultural translation. I have not treated such films as *Twelfth Night* of 1955 (dir. Yakov Fried), and even some silent versions of the Romanov period that have yet to come to light.
25. An additional motive for my contrast of American studio-based filmmaking with the state-regulated filmmaking of the Soviet period might be Robert F. Willson's *Shakespeare in Hollywood, 1929–1956*, an engaging survey of the major studio films up to 1956 that omits this crucial dimension of Hollywood's reliance on upscaled genres and technological innovation in the films of the late 1950s and 1960s. His concluding discussion is limited to a few, select examples of poststudio filmmaking until the advent of the Branagh era.
26. Yury Levin 78.
27. Ibid. 79.
28. Ibid. 91.
29. See Morgan 13–14.
30. Levin 89. The term "Hamletisme" was coined by Jules Laforgue in 1886 who wrote a direct response addressed to Shakespeare and visited Elsinore "in order to converse with Hamlet's ghost" (see Taranow, *The Bernhardt Hamlet* 9).
31. Ibid. 88–90. Oblomov, thus, is surely Hamlet's first cousin. Note that, as with his Hamlet, the vengeful protagonist of Turgenev's "King Lear of the Steppes" (1870) is again overturned in the twentieth century in favor of a Lear who gains social enlightenment at the heaviest price of all.
32. See Nina Diakonova's useful comparison of a story more loosely structured on its source than those of Turgenev, and with echoes in *Madame Bovary* (107–109).
33. See *Testimony* 18–19.
34. Ibid. 83–91. Particularly noteworthy is the account of how the director Nikolai Akimov decided to do away with the hesitant Hamlet and show a blatant power struggle for the crown; Ophelia, a pregnant spy, drowns herself; Boris Shchukin, who first had trouble playing Polonius, scored a triumph when, unknown to audiences, he decided to imitate the mannerisms of Stanislavsky (see 88–90).

35. Ibid. 113–115.
36. See *Testimony* 256–264.
37. Howard 177. For a description of the preparatory version of *Hamlet* given by Raikh—domineering, dangerously contemptuous of Stalin's apparatchiks and physically a most unlikely Hamlet—see also 167, 174–179.
38. Anna France suggests that Pasternak's translations served him as a means of personal creative expression, through the very choice of subject and through changes introduced into the wording of the original text, at a time when other avenues of artistic self-expression were closed to him, when he could not express himself freely or hope to have his work published in the Soviet Union (see 6).
39. Buhler, *Shakespeare in the Cinema* 19.
40. Kozintsev, *King Lear* 174.
41. Ibid. 31.
42. Ibid. No one who has seen the 1963 *Lord of the Flies* could be under the misimpression that Brook simply does not understand the camera (fewer still underestimate the Bressonian precision of his editing). It is Kozintsev, incidentally, who reports on how Brook discovered a new cinematic form in the seventeen sequences of *Marat/Sade* (1967), which Brook described accurately as "half way between theatre and cinema" (22). Kozintsev also points out the influence of Carl Theodor Dreyer's *La Passion de Jeanne d'Arc* (1928) on Brook's use of close-ups as an expressive device, albeit in his case a means of removing extraneous details of mise en scène from Shakespeare's dialogue.
43. Ibid. 32, 108.
44. Ibid. 252. Note also to the pages devoted to their dialogue about the appropriateness of themes for characters, an idea Kozintsev rejected, and the various "voices" in the music (see 242–248).
45. Ibid. 174. Tolstoy had, of course, famously attacked Shakespeare's poor characterization in *Shakespeare and the Drama,* although as John Gross implies in his gloss (74) Tolstoy's principal objection was to the separation of styles (in particular to what he felt to be the debased language of characters of lesser station). But Tolstoy, tolerant only of Falstaff, was decidedly in a minority.
46. See 14.
47. Stam observes in his *Subversive Pleasures: Bakhtin, Cultural Criticism, and Film* that Bakhtin has relatively little to say about Shakespeare and even less about film. It is possibly because his ideas were controversial enough without wandering deeper into the minefield (see 17).
48. Quoted in Gross 80–81.
49. See *King Lear* 252–255.
50. See 112.
51. See *Filming Shakespeare's Plays* 169–170.
52. In *King Lear: The Space of Tragedy,* Kozintsev makes an important observation about one of the cinematic technologies of translation: to find words of the right length to permit adequate dubbing into Russian, Yarvet was given a rather crude Estonian translation of Pasternak. Despite his obvious difficulties with Russian, it was Yarvet who, with affecting humility, promised to master Pasternak's poetic lines (see 76–77).
53. See, especially, Kozintsev's reminiscences of accompanying Eisenstein to see Kabuki performances in August 1928 that imparted the "structure of cinematography" to the latter and his own later experience of Noh theater in Japan (see 5–8). See, also, his notes on Eisenstein's *Ivan the Terrible* (27–31), as well as the recollections of Meyerhold (in particular, 103–110), who was shot after months of torture.
54. James Welsh notes that even in this instance Kozintsev was wary of overstatement, rejecting footage of a tiny Lear being buffeted by gusts of wind (see "To See It Feelingly" 155).
55. See Yutkevich, "The Conscience of the King" 192–196.
56. See Lipkov 138–139.
57. Ibid. 140.
58. See *Shakespeare in the Cinema* 20–21.
59. France, "Iago and Othello" 76.
60. Similarities with other, earlier adaptations of *Othello* may be incidental. For instance, Yutkevich makes elaborate use of a famous Shakespearean prop, the fatal handkerchief. Iago returns it to Desdemona with elaborate courtesy when she accidentally drops it, Emilia plays a sexual game with Iago in giving it to him (a goat that inexplicably preceded Desdemona's arrival in the preceding scene now stands in the distance behind the prize fluttering in Emilia's hand), and

the spying Othello turns his head away in dismay when Bianca practically hurls it at Cassio. Similarly, in the 1922 *Othello* of Russian émigré director Dmitri Buchowetzki, Iago turns it into a multipurpose prop. Buchowetzki's Othello is also reduced to a Freudian state of infantile orality—to the delight of present-day critics—when he chews on the fatal fabric.
61. It was "restored" for the subsequent LP recording and had been attempted in the film, as explained to me by the Desdemona, Katia Ricciarelli, after a 1988 recital in the city of Carpi.
62. See *King Lear* 39.
63. Roger Manvell's early book *Shakespeare and the Film* (1971) is invaluable for its inclusion of such secondary documentation as interviews and reviews, including Yutkevich's comments to Derek Prouse as detailed in the film journal *Sight and Sound* (see Yutkevich 76–77).
64. In *Repositioning Shakespeare,* Cartelli addresses some of the issues on which scholars of postcoloniality have focused, arguing controversially (but intriguingly) that the United States, often associated with Neocolonialism, also experienced postcoloniality and achieved it at greater cost of life than many other fledgling nations (see 1–14). Many would argue that the colonized population was, in fact, the Native American one and that postcoloniality, in this sense, has yet to arrive (Ireland's case is analogous and even more complex), or that it arrived in the nineteenth century with the loss of the vernacular languages and cultural autonomy of the survivors.
65. See Turney, "The Astor Place Riot."
66. See *Storytelling in the New Hollywood* 1.
67. The comments on the film are cited in Lillich (249) and in Rothwell's preface to *Shakespeare into Film* edited by James Welsh, Richard Vela, and John C. Tibbets (see xi). I treat the issue of intermediate texts in the chapter pertaining to the first Shakespeare feature film, the 1912 *Richard III*, but this edition is of particular interest because Winter felt that, in abandoning the Sly and Bianca-Lucentio subplots, Garrick attained a purer version of Shakespeare's play (those additions being attributed to Robert Greene) (see 5).
68. Hitchock's sound films were soon obtaining successful releases in the United States, as Donald Crafton observes in the case of the 1930 *Murder!* (see 435).
69. Bristol 3.
70. Ibid. 76.
71. See Marx 27. Useful information about *West Side Story* can be found on the Website http://home.graffiti.net/classicfilms:graffiti.net/WSS.htm, which suggests that the libretto and lines of dialogue were crafted by Jerome Robbins's collaborator, Arthur Laurents, in consultation with the composer. Apparently, when Robbins and Bernstein first conceived of an adaptation of *Romeo and Juliet*, they thought of the rival New York gangs as Italian and Jewish, but rejected the idea as insufficiently contemporary.
72. In his *Shakespeare in the Cinema*, Buhler discusses the juxtaposition of documentary footage, fanciful reenactment, and various other devices in this film in some detail (37–39).
73. See 80.
74. See McGilligan for the relevant extract (from *Time*) 378.
75. Thalberg's comments precede the play text and the shooting script in *Romeo and Juliet: A Motion Picture Edition* (see 15).
76. In arguing that Bazin is a more consistent humanist than a Realist, Thompson demonstrates that many of the film's seemingly realist effects are the result of extreme contrivance (see 197–217). The impact of Bazin's thought, however, had an incalculable effect on the French New Wave and beyond.
77. See *Cinematic Shakespeare* 63.
78. Ibid. 62.
79. See Rothwell, *A History* 119. For pictorial influences on Castellani, see Welsh et al. 80, Anderegg's *Cinematic Shakespeare* 63, Rothwell 128, and Tatspaugh 156.
80. This conceit—the basis of one of the most popular and widely performed of all Italian *verismo* operas, Ruggiero Leoncavallo's 1892 *I Pagliacci*—is, as I note elsewhere, also to be found in one of the more notable silent Shakespeare films, August Blom's 1912 *Desdemona*.
81. Kauffman 100, 103, 106, 110.
82. Albert Furtwangler points out that tragic tyrannicide was a consciously treated concept in Shakespeare and that the rival brothers assumed the roles of two of the best known, Brutus and Hamlet (see viii–ix, 9–11, 31–47, 95–141).
83. Although there are much earlier accounts of Shakespeare's influence (he was, for instance, frequently quoted by a number of the Founding Fathers and held up as a beacon of liberty), Lincoln's attachment to Shakespeare appears to have had a decisive influence on him, one

evident in the form of substantial recitations to his bewildered secretaries, and in the heartbroken obsequies attending the death of his son in 1862.

84. Joyce Vining Morgan suggests that visits to Venice and Paris in 1895 introduced Stanislavsky to the mise en scène (and even a young North African Arab willing to pose for him) that inspired his visualization of his 1896 production of *Othello* (see 19–25). Still more apposite might be the ill-fated production of 1930 that was withdrawn after ten performances following the sudden death of the actor playing Iago. The performance was already gathering notoriety because of the mental instability of Leonid Leonidov, the actor playing Othello, who had apparently started holding on to props and even actors during longer speeches (see 130–134).

85. Further evidence that Kanin could hardly have been unaware that the Actors Studio was in the offing might be the presence of Warren Stevens, a charter member, in Kanin's mirthful comedy *Smile at the World*, where he played alongside Gordon, the playwright's wife and collaborator. Stevens had just acted in Kazan's production of *Sundown Beach*.

86. Much of my brief history of the Method is corroborated by Steve Vineberg's *Method Actors* (see especially 5–16, 19–84, 92–113).

87. See Brode 52. Perhaps it is this normative character that has also led to the use of genre to parody film interpretations of the play. *The Secret Sex Lives of Romeo and Juliet* (dir. Bethel Buckalew), a 1969 Russ Meyer-inspired "nudie-cutie" send-up of Castellani's and Zeffirelli's versions of *Romeo and Juliet*, borrows its bosomy redheads (including Juliet's amorous nurse) from him, but also draws on the humor inherent to its subgarlic bargain-basement production values: its actors put on "Italian" accents and employ the Homeric tactic of attaching an epithet to a beloved city whenever it is mentioned, although, of course, we never get to visit "fair, downtown Verona." The subsequent development of the underground "cult" film, as pioneered by Dusan Makavejev, and the "gross-out" film essayed by John Waters, finds expression in Lloyd Kaufman's *Tromeo and Juliet* (1997). Indeed, Kaufman, wearing a Big Bill T-shirt derived from Droeshout's engraving for the First Folio, argues in one of the outtake segments included in a special feature section of the 2002 "interactive" DVD release of his film that his decision to exclude that sequence rested on its formal features ("this scene you are going to see had plenty of the blood and gore and vomit and things like that that Troma Films is famous for, but unfortunately it had, er...it had characterization and substance and stuff that I certainly don't want anything to have to do with; er, so we cut it out"). Affecting conversational polysyndetons much as a Shakespeare character might have, Kaufman satirizes the model of filmmaking codified as normative through a negative invocation of the conventions perfected by that very studio system. The iconoclasm achieves its climax with the pummeling to death of the incestuous Capulet with a massive copy of the Yale Shakespeare. Hard-core *auteur* Ren Savant limited himself to *West Side* in 2000, with a clear allusion to the film being parodied (via Luhrmann), although he has also dipped more explicitly into back-stage biography with *Shakespeare Revealed* (2000) where we see nothing of Shakespeare but a great deal of Romeo and Juliet. In "Out Damned Scot" Courtney Lehmann (see 239–242) describes Stuart Canterbury's use of Shakespeare as hard-core *Macbeth* scenarist for *In the Flesh* (1998); Canterbury's use of him as occasional scriptwriter for *A Midsummer Night's Cream* (2000) gives Jan Kott's reading of the play some alarming twists.

88. Ibid. 48–49.
89. See *The American Film Musical* 116.
90. Ibid. 136–139.
91. Ibid. 141–161.
92. Ibid. 111. Note that in addition to being forms of social commentary genre translations can also be a form of cultural negotiation, as witnessed, for instance, in the Kathakali-inspired *Othellos* of South India, or in such recent films as Vishal Bhardwaj's 2006 *Omkara* (*Othello* as an admixture of popular melodrama and Indian art film), Feng Xiogang's 2006 *Ye yan* (*The Banquet*, a *Macbeth* set in Imperial China and rendered as a high-production value Martial Arts epic in the manner of Zhang Yimou and Ang Lee), and Ivan Lipkies's 2004 *Huapango* (a loose Mexican version of *Othello* that resembles Carlos Saura's flamenco films in its blending of the character's lives with the dance routines they attempt to perform).
93. See, for example, the Turner Classic Movies Web site regarding the genesis of the film (http://www.turnerclassicmovies.com/ThisMonth/Article/0,18579%7C18681%7C18630,00.html).
94. See 96–103, 152–157.
95. See Zabus 181–194. The conceit that this was Shakespeare without "Shakespeare" extended to the personnel working on the film, as it perhaps did for the other genre Shakespeares of the

period. I had the opportunity to discuss *Forbidden Planet* with its star, Leslie Nielsen, in 2004, and he assured me that none of the actors had any idea of the Shakespearean provenance of the plot.
96. Ibid. 183.
97. Ibid.
98. See Packard 85–86.
99. Bristol 3.
100. Of course Jean-Luc Picard is not the only starship captain to encounter Shakespeare, although as Douglas Lanier notes, one of the most famous (among many) of the playwright's "cameos" occurs in the feature *Star Trek IV* (dir. Nicholas Meyer, 1991). It proves his "universality," but is the source of a multiplicity of embarrassments to the captain of the spaceship Enterprise, James T. Kirk. We discover that Kirk, played by William Shatner (an actor associated largely with television celebrity), turns out not to know his Shakespeare as well as the duplicitous Klingon envoy Chancellor Gorkon, played by Shakespearean actor David Warner, whose remark that "You've not experienced Shakespeare until you've read him in the original Klingon" provokes his bloodthirsty, Mongol-warrior-like compatriot, General Chang, to launch into the "To be, or not be" soliloquy in the original (see Lanier, *Shakespeare and Modern Popular Culture* 1–20). The actor portraying Chang, Christopher Plummer, was not only a renowned stage Shakespearean, but he also gained a certain notoriety for his Atahualpa in Irving Lerner's *The Royal Hunt of the Sun* (1969), where he rendered the Inca god-king in accents so authentic that the entire part had to be dubbed, just as Shakespeare has had to be translated from the original Klingon into a comprehensible Renaissance English for modern academics and their charges.
101. See Magro and Douglas 48.
102. See Isherwood 1.
103. The actual symbioses between emerging media such as cinema and established ones such as poetry are still being discovered, as revealed, for instance, by Christophe Wall-Romana's article on "Mallarmé's Cinepoetics."
104. For instance, in the inaugural issue of the *Literature/Film Association News*, Thomas Leitch defends the humanistic and belletristic approaches that arise from what James Naremore ascribes to "submerged common sense," as well as the multifarious, carnivalesque appropriations that Robert Stam associates with Mikhail Bakhtin (see 2–8). In that same issue, Walter Metz also calls for a return to Dudley Andrew's proposed sociology of adaptation (see 3, 10), both he and Leitch no doubt responding to the challenge offered by Robert Ray in the opening essay of Naremore's anthology, *Film Adaptation,* in which he argues that since the pioneering works of George Bluestone and Robert Ray the study of film adaptation had fallen into "disrepute," thus forfeiting the opportunity to address fundamental issues regarding the nature of the medium (38). In *A Theory of Adaptation,* Linda Hutcheon proposes yet another reason for the subject's neglect: what was once a fairly discreet cultural exchange between one textual stratum and another has now become so ubiquitous as to generally pass without notice, adaptations now encompassing all the media beloved of Victorians as well as present-day electronic media, theme parks, historical reenactments, and even virtual reality experiments (see xi–xiv).
105. In his chapter on "Modernism, Adaptation, and the French New Wave," in *Literature through Film*, Stam points out that "the *Cahiers* critics…were profoundly ambivalent about literature, which they saw as both a model to be emulated and an enemy to be abjured" (254). He goes on to outline André Bazin's position on adaptation, which was according to his "Defense of Mixed Cinema" and "Adaptation, or the Cinema as Digest," a perennial and essential process in the arts. In contrast, Truffaut's 1954 attack on the indefatigable adapters of French classics among screenwriters, Jean Aurenche and Pierre Bost, treated adaptation as a form of failed and inflationary imitation that actually violated the original text (see 255–257), although Stam also notes that with the passage of time his views on the matter of adaptation gained in sophistication (a topic to which I return in "Film Studies" section of this introduction). It will suffice here to say that in *Literature through Film* Stam goes on to detail the various strategies that the New Wave and Left Bank filmmakers subsequently adopted, especially those of the Left Bank filmmaker Alain Resnais, whose *cine-romans* used scripts by such celebrated luminaries of the *nouveau roman* as Marguerite Duras and Alain Robbe-Grillet (see 258–278). Note, also, that Hutcheon's use of "intertextuality" stemming from a carefully elaborated argument concerning postmodernity shows much greater restraint than those definitions I have taken to task in the concluding chapter. The phrases I cite can be found in Hutcheon 16–22.

106. Among the works that emphasize this register are Lorne Buchman's *Still in Movement*, Sarah Cardwell's *Adaptation Revisited* and Sarah Hatchuel's *Shakespeare, From Stage to Screen*.
107. See, in particular, John Collick's *Shakespeare, Cinema and Society*, Robert Stam's *Literature through Film*, and Cartelli's and Rowe's *New Wave Shakespeares on Screen*.
108. Cardwell 27.
109. See Thompson and Bordwell 444–451.
110. See Richard Wilson 247–270. The play, in particular the scene in it that Rohmer partly reproduces, forms the centerpiece of the chapter devoted to "The Statue of Our Queen" in *Secret Shakespeare*, in which Wilson argues that the religious allegory addressed King James himself. Although even the borrowed themes are heavily reworked (Thomas Cartelli and Katherine Rowe refer to it as a "consummate work of surrogated artistry" 39), Rohmer succeeds in incorporating strange substitutions and coincidences, epiphanal moments, a mother's quasi-spiritual longing for her daughter's father, and the benevolence of providence: Felicie, who falls in love with Charles while on vacation, loses touch with him through an accident, and soon has a child. She goes to the theatre with her bookish friend Loic, where we see them witness Hermione's reanimation, a sequence that serves a narrative purpose in propelling Felicie toward the happily-ever-after conclusion, but that also refers to one of the most elaborate pieces of stagecraft Shakespeare inserted into a play, his own version of Giulio Romano's trompe l'oeil effects and the Italian Mannerist illusionism imported into the Jacobean theatre by the most famous production designer of the age, Inigo Jones. It is her disagreement about the play's conclusion that results in her rejection of him: Loic believes that the notion of a woman remaining inanimate but alive for sixteen years or a statue coming to life as a particular person is equally improbable; she recognizes it as an allegory of faith wherein belief in ideals prevails. She takes up with the owner of the beauty parlor where she works, Maxence, and goes to Nevers (Marguerite Duras's city of memory) where he opens a new store, but feels so out of place that she returns to Paris, where chance brings Charles to her. The *Four Seasons* cycle (1989–1998), inspired by Antonio Vivaldi's 4-movement sinfonia and associated poetry, are, to use a Rohmer-like metaphor, speckled with thematic references and plot parallels to Shakespeare, Hugo von Hofmanstaahl, Jane Austen, Greek myth, and a number of other writers, painters, and musicians (one of Rohmer's mottoes is "artists of the world unite!").
111. For some recent examples of the latter, see Douglas Lanier's "Will of the People."
112. Jorgens 161, 167–168.
113. For the centrality of the voices of narrators in documentary see, for instance, Bill Nichols's "The Voice of Documentary."
114. Neil Sinyard appears to share this view in "Shakespeare Meets *The Godfather*" in which he also points out the degree to which Pacino, who actually made the film over four years, appears to respond directly to the assertions of the subjects of his interviews (actually a sign of good editing in conserving what he wanted of the interview footage). Thus, when Peter Brook points out that film has the advantage of the "close-up" over theatre, Pacino appears to respond immediately by whispering his "self-communing" lines in close-up while adopting a more declamatory style for his public delivery (see 64). Unlike, for example, his deeply motivated Shylock in Michael Radford's 2005 *The Merchant of Venice*, much admired by Samuel Crowl, who argues that "not since Marlon Brando's Mark Antony fifty years ago has an American actor given such an intelligent, subtle and accomplished performance of a major Shakespearean role in the movies" (see "Looking for Shylock" 118), I find his knowing, raw, probing Richard more persuasive.
115. The comic effect of dis(s)quotation can survive both paraphrase and translation as evident in two adaptations of *Romeo and Juliet*, Cheah Chee Kong's *Chicken Rice War* (2000) and Miguel Delgado's *Romeo y Julieta* (1943), the latter featuring Mexico's only internationally popular star (other than the exported Dolores Del Rio and Luis Buñuel's art house favorites, Fernando Rey and Silvia Pinal), Cantinflas (a.k.a. comic Mario Moreno). Richard Vela, who kindly sent me a copy of the film, describes *Romeo y Julieta* as "balancing formal diction with street slang and comic rhymes" wherewith Cantinflas "deflates the pretensions of official high culture through verbal and visual twists on the play" (see 233). Vela also notes (see 232–233, 235) that in Mexico Shakespearean dis(s)quotation mocked official culture and "high" Spanish (which acquired a name, "Chicaspeare," through Moreno's joke in this film), and that, as with many Cantinflas films of the period, this one is a parody of a Hollywood film, in this instance Cukor's opulent 1936 *Romeo and Juliet* that I discuss in greater detail in short order.

116. See Allen and Gomery 115–124.
117. Ibid. 117.
118. Cf. Thomas Pendleton's "What [?] Price [?] Shakespeare [?]."
119. Roger Manvell gives a laudably complete account of Heston's imposing assumption of Antony—to Gielgud's insistent Caesar—as his Player King was to be for Branagh (see *Shakespeare and the Film* 91–96).
120. See Eggert "Sure Can Sing and Dance."
121. See Donaldson, *Shakespearean Films* 127–143 and Taylor 261–273.
122. For an interesting discussion of Nunn's elaborate use of cross-cutting, see Laurie Osborne's "Cutting up Characters."
123. See, for instance, 192–193, where Richard Wilson argues that, in one instance, Feste makes fun of the racking of Thomas Campion, while the play as a whole mocks Puritan antitheatricality and the recusant hunting practiced by such militant Anglicans as Thomas Hoby and William Cecil (271–282).
124. See Buchanan 3–5.
125. See, for instance, the March 12 issue of *The Motion Picture Story Magazine* for an account of the 1912 *Cardinal Wolsey* (73–80), the October 1912 issue (page 33–47, which confirms Charles Kent as the director of *As You Like It*), and the January 1913 issue (where on page 116 a reader, Henry Kiefer, takes issue with the film's anachronisms).
126. Sklar 154.
127. See 45–50.
128. Murch discusses a number of these techniques, including the use of digital editing of 35 mm film, in *In the Blink of an Eye*.
129. For a summary of some of the processes used, see, for instance, Leo Enticknap's book on *Moving Image Technology* 187–210.
130. See especially 8 where Canby recognizes only "superficial plot lines and some character names" and Sarris discerns "a disaster of sufficient magnitude to require the services less of a critic than of a coroner."
131. See xi–xxviii.
132. See 1–20.
133. See *An Introduction to Visual Culture* 1–31. In a recent article, "On Visuality," *Journal of Visual Culture* 5, no. 1 (2006): 53–79, Mirzoeff restates his position that it is a field of inquiry.
134. See 10–31.
135. See 1–44.
136. See "Murdering Peasants."
137. See Moelwyn Merchant 57–76.
138. Ibid. 1.
139. Ibid. 76–78.
140. See, for example, Kalman Burnim and Philip Highfill 5–6, 10–14.
141. Friedman 3–4, 81–85.
142. As Stephen Orgel points out, the mistake may well have been deliberate, a kind of code that signals instead Romano's widely circulated pornographic illustrations of Pietro Aretino's *I modi* (see *Imagining Shakespeare* 112–143). A painting mentioned in a Shakespeare play that has attracted some commentary is a supposed reference to a copy of *Jupiter and Io*, an oil painting by Correggio (Antonio Allegri) now in the Kunsthistorisches Museum in Vienna. It is mentioned in the Induction to *The Taming of the Shrew*, and serves as yet another means of persuading the inebriated tinker, Christopher Sly, that he is in fact the lord of a mansion. A copy of Coreggio's work adorned the ceiling of Belvoir Castle, seat of the noble Rutland family, whose library contained many of the books that served as Shakespeare's sources. Célestin Demblon adduces it as evidence that the works attributed to Shakespeare were, in fact, largely penned by Roger Manners, the Fifth Earl of Rutland, who also knew Rosencrantz and Guildenstern (Guyldenstern) when they were students at the University of Padua (see Michell 215). However, as Jean Howard points out in the Norton Shakespeare edition (see 133–141), there is general acceptance that both *The Shrew* and another play called *The Taming of a Shrew* (1594) were of an early date, perhaps as early as 1592, and Manners would have been sixteen years of age when the one we know was performed. Correggio completed a series of four paintings of *Loves of Jupiter* for Duke Federigo Gonzaga of Mantua in 1531, but the other paintings mentioned in the second part of the play's Induction (see lines 47–58 in the Norton edition), a *Venus and Adonis* and *Apollo and Daphne*, were not part of

this cycle, although frequently encountered subjects among the erotic paintings that adorned noble households.
143. For a more solemn reading than mine, see John Dixon Hunt's "Shakespeare and the *Paragone*," in which he points out that Anthony Blunt (of all people) first noted Shakespeare's use of the Italian *topos* (initiated by Leonardo, touched upon in Castiglione's *The Courtier*, and beloved of Neoplatonists) in a 1939 issue of the *Journal of the Warburg Institute*.
144. Warburg 89–156. Georges Didi-Huberman has devoted a number of works to Warburg's reading of Botticelli, and his article "The Imaginary Breeze" (Warburg rendered the phrase in his German manuscript in French as *brise imaginaire*) makes the point that Warburg leaves unsaid the idea that the fluidity of air animated all it touched, that the representation of motion itself became the subject of painting rather than the rendering of the physical object. The air, he writes, also "sends a quiver through souls" (278). Philippe-Alain Michaud also suggests that Warburg's sensitivity to motion paralleled developments in photography (which he used extensively) and motion studies in early cinema (see 41–91, 277–291).
145. Cf. Stephen Buhler's "Antic Dispositions."
146. See *Cinematic Shakespeare* 62, 64.
147. See Lillich 258–259. Lillich also gives Filippo and Filippino Lippi as influences, which I have not been able to verify, and a portrait by Veneziano as a model for a shot of Juliet, which is possible although the resemblance is not compelling.
148. See 29.
149. See, for example, Ace Pilkington 100–102. One of the brutalities commonly ascribed to Henry is the roasting alive in chains of militant Lollard Sir John Oldcastle (the original name Shakespeare gave to Falstaff), but Pilkington goes to some lengths to show that Henry was in France at the time and had earlier done what he could to appease Sir John (150–151).
150. Silviria 23.
151. Ibid. 23–24.
152. See Geduld, *Filmguide to* Henry V 27–29.
153. See 26.
154. *Filmguide to* Henry V 18. In *Shakespeare and Film* Roger Manvell reports Olivier as saying that his use of the camera reacted against the convention of the star close-up that he perceived as a weakness on seeing Cukor's *Romeo and Juliet* (see 378).
155. Davies 29. The time-space functions Davies adduces are perhaps best described by Mikhail Bakhtin's concept of the "chronotope" (which I have treated in more depth, for instance, in the article "The Birth of a New Realism"), a measure of space-time representation in the arts against the reader's or spectator's experience of space and time.
156. See *Filmguide to* Henry V 18–19.
157. See 109.
158. Cited in Geduld, *Filmguide to* Henry V 69.
159. Mitsuhiro Yoshimoto does not discuss the film in terms of a relationship to Shakespeare, but makes the interesting case that it is less explicit than other socially critical films of the period, serving as a metaphor for the wave of antigovernment and antibureaucratic protests on the eve of its making.
160. See Manvell 102–105.
161. Ibid. 104. James Goodwin suggests that the chant that begins and ends *Kumonosu-jô* reiterates a Buddhist teaching on *mujokan*, "the impermanence and brevity of worldly aims," further emphasized by his reference to *mu* (nothingness) through its secondary attribute *ku* (empty space) as found in Noh, haiku, the Zen garden, and the tea ceremony (see 177).
162. See "*Throne of Blood*."
163. Brian Parker observes that Kurosawa may have also had the Noh play *Tsuchigomo* (which contains a demon spider) in mind and that the eighth episode of *Dreams*, "Crows," not only puts Martin Scorsese in Van Gogh's role but pays homage to the artist's last work, *Crows Flying over a Cornfield*.
164. Although they do not mention Peter Brook's approval of Kurosawa's approach, Anthony Davies and Stanley Wells do recount the debate between Ben Blumenthal who in 1965 argued the former case and John Gerlach (see 7) who published the rejoinder eight years later.
165. For Kurosawa's use of animal imagery in the film, see Julie Kane's "From the Baroque to Wabi." Zvika Serper also notes that Kaede bears the characteristics of both the fox and the serpent and that it is only in her final scene that her kimono combines both characters (see the summary in 156).
166. See, for instance, Penelope Mason (196) and Miyajima Shin'chi and Sato Yasuhiro (12, 46).

167. See Sadao Hibi and Kumio Fukuda 3, 28, 99. Note that by turning to the Japanese aesthetics of color I amplify and modify James Goodwin's interpretations of them (see 213–214).
168. The dominance of Buddhist painting in the Japanese tradition is evident, for instance, in Ernest Fenellosa's two-volume *Epochs of Chinese and Japanese Art* and in the works of such present-day art historians as Ichimatsu Tanaka and Penelope Mason.
169. An anthology of the best-known literature by Malcolm Bradbury and James McFarlane bears the title *Modernism, 1890–1930*, while Modris Eksteins attributes the dawning crisis of Modernism (culminating in World War I) to the 1913 Ballets Russes production of *The Rite of Spring*. In discussing the economic determinism of Karl Marx and Max Weber, Hugh Grady distinguishes between Modernism (aesthetic) and "modernization" (social, economic, and technological), arguing that the former was, in fact, a response to the latter, and pointing out that, when Frederick James Furnivall announced the program of The New Shakespeare Society in 1873, he consciously rejected the accretions of Romanticism with his "modernizing" quasi-mathematical approach. Grady adds that it is only in the twentieth century that G. Wilson Knight, T.S. Eliot, and the New Critics established a "Modernist" paradigm. Viewed from the position of critical paradigms, this one gives way to a "postmodern" Shakespeare paradigm under the influence of late structuralist and post-structuralist criticism in the 1960s and 1970s (see 45–112; 190–246).
170. This is the use to which Nestor García Canclini, for example, puts the term, and that is implicit in John Thompson's rejection of the idea of the postmodern as significant social transformation, since he relates modernity to a long historical process that begins with the rise of print culture in the "early modern period" (see 1–9).
171. See Habermas, who views the discourse of modernity as coalescing around the central figure of Hegel (23–44) and that of postmodernity as originating with Nietzsche (see 83–105).
172. See especially 41, 69–71, 223–226.
173. See Naremore and Brantlinger 1–23, as well as Jameson's *A Singular Modernity* (in particular 29, 40, 55, and 94, although one senses that there is a slight element of jesting, well known though the definitions are, in the creation of a category that is essentially impossible to define other than negatively).
174. Halpern's most sustained (and sometimes rather caustic) treatment of this problematic can be found in *Shakespeare among the Moderns*. Jameson believes the Lyotard of *The Postmodern Condition* to resemble Gilles Deleuze in being a "quintessential modernist" (see *A Singular Modernity* 4–5), and regards Anthony Giddens's "flirtation" with the idea of postmodernity to be an evasion (11–13), although it seems to me that Giddens in this instance attempts to frame a sociological reply to Lyotard (see Giddens, *The Consequences of Modernity* 2–54). See, also, Jameson's own definition of the postmodern in *Postmodernism, or the Cultural Logic of Late Capitalism* (6). David Harvey takes a view similar to Jameson's (see especially 113–120, 327–342), in distinction to other theorists such as Ihab Hassan and Linda Hutcheon who treat it with less unease.
175. See Wollen 155–157.
176. See, in this context, Guha's *History at the Limit of World History*, Chakrabarty's *Habitations of Modernity*, *At Home in Diaspora* (edited by Assayag and Bénéï), and *Post-colonial Shakespeares* edited by Loomba and Orkin.
177. See Appadurai's *Modernity at Large*, Giddens's *Runaway World*, Lechner's and Boli's *The Globalization Reader*, and Tomlinson's *Globalization and Culture*.
178. See *Global Modernities*.
179. See Mignolo's *The Darker Side of the Renaissance* and *Local Histories/Global Designs*, as well as García Canclini's *Hybrid Cultures* and *Consumers and Citizens*.
180. Extracts of the journals are given by P.E.H. Hair (see 34). On the previous day Keeling referred to Fernandez, the king's interpreter (for the Portuguese had traded there for over a century and had good relations with the then monarch Buré) as a man of "marvailous redie witt" who "speakes in eloquent Portugues," an observation that might have come from the Dragon's own Portuguese interpreter, John Rogers (see 33). Two merchants aboard the *Hector*, John Hearne and William Finch, record only that "after dinner" four huntsmen, one of them Keeling, shot an elephant at close range, but that it was too late to follow the wounded beast as he fled (33).
181. See Gary Taylor's "Travel to Africa" (220) subsection of "*Hamlet* in Africa 1607", and his account of the implications of the performance (223–248).
182. See "Shakespeare in the Bush."
183. See Soyinka 5, 103–105.
184. See *Culture and Imperialism* 212.

185. For a discussion of Bergman's status as the quintessential *auteur*, his international influence, and his part in the rapid move to globalization in the cinemas of Scandinavian countries, see Linda Rugg's "Globalization and the Auteur."
186. In "Aki Kaurismäki's Crossroads," Andrew Nestingen notes Kaurismäki's ironic use of genre in the case of the road movie, and notes also that his next (1988) film belongs to this genre (despite its title, *Ariel* owes little else to Shakespeare and is resolutely, perhaps even Calibanesquely, terrestrial).
187. For a discussion of precursors see especially Jack Stevenson 25–36.
188. See Hjort, "A Small Nation's Response to Globalisation" and "The Globalisation of Dogma: The Dynamics of Metaculture and Counter-publicity" (133–134, 147).
189. J.G. Saunders notes that in the Brook *King Lear* (staged with Charles Marowitz as his assistant) the director struggled with a central character in his interpretation, Edgar, and his "switch" to being Poor Tom, a dynamic not present in *The King Is Alive*. However, there are other larger coincidences. In Kozintsev's book on his *King Lear*, for instance, he reproduces a letter (of October 1969) from Brook in which he talks about filming in the frigid condition of Jutland, achieving a "simple picture, not by period, which is impossible, but by basing everything on shapes and objects that are dictated by climatic conditions...a sort of Lapland Eskimo world...we are both trying to tell the same story, [but] with very different means within very different cultures" (240–241).
190. See, for instance, Paisely Livingston 107.
191. See Paul Varley 238.
192. At a time when Japan's relations with the West were developing in unpredictable directions, the great novelist Natsume Soseki perhaps summed up some of the rationale among intellectuals for adapting Shakespeare through the accepted forms of Japanese theatre in his anticipatory 1908 work *A Theory of Literature*: "When I appeal to my own experience, I learn that the realm of poetry created by Shakespeare does not possess that universality that European critics ascribe to it. For us Japanese it requires years of training to develop a proper appreciation of Shakespeare, and even then this is only a dim appreciation based on a deliberate adaptation of our sensibilities" (quoted in Karatani Kojin 12–13).
193. I owe the details of the foregoing account to Varley (see 265–295) and Tetsuo Anzai (see 3–12). For an account of the importance of Kurosawa's brother to his filmmaking (drawn from Kurosawa's own extraordinary autobiography), see James Goodwin 33–37.
194. So much so that Donald Richie suggests that Kurosawa is the master of the *shakai-mono* film (or social concern film), and that this overarching generic concern absorbs even the *jidai-geki* in which realism and artifice achieve a delicate balance (see 166–176).
195. See Collick 161.
196. See Yoshimoto 250–269.
197. In this context see both the interview with Takemitsu printed on the sleeve notes to the Criterion DVD and Saviour Catania's "Wailing Woodwind Wild."
198. See Jyostsna Singh 120–152.
199. See Trivedi and Bartholomeusz (15–17), who note Garrick's participation in the creation of the first Western theatrical space in India and the eventual emergence of multicultural Shakespeare (13–43).
200. See Verma, "Shakespeare in Hindi Cinema."
201. See Esha Nayogi De 20 and Verma 278.
202. Homi Bhabha, *The Location of Culture* 85–92.
203. Verma 280–281.
204. See Ismail Merchant 56–64.
205. Parmita Kapadia also gives other instances where such techniques of montage and cinematography indicate a growing separation between contemporary audiences in a decolonized India and the "lost" players (see 45, 49–50), although the extracts of filming Bollywood movies seem to me less an indication of a "moribund British theater, carrying the cultural marks of colonialism" being "symbolically preempted by the energy, sensuality, and sheer volume of the Hindi film," than an affectionate parody of both cultural forms in depicting the failure of the stage actors to transcend Bollywood's looming presence (as evident in the split-screen, simultaneous action device in the *Othello* sequence to show Manjula's actions and reactions), and the failure of the Bollywood director to get Manjula to perform her seductive dance routine, which in the end he has to perform for her by way of coaching.

One   Reconstituting *King John*: Victorian Theatrical Photorealism and the Protocinema of Adaptation

1. Raymond Williams's early observation, no less than the preceding ones of Mikhail Bakhtin and his associate V.N. Voloshinov regarding the mutability of natural languages, led to my initial recognition- later supplemented by my work on postcards-that media of communication must, of necessity, work in symbiotic relationships with one another beyond any superficial antagonism. For the foregoing argument in Williams see, in particular, 119–120 of *Television: Technology and Cultural Form*.
2. Schoch 11.
3. Ibid. 73–74.
4. Ibid. 78.
5. Ibid. 75.
6. Ibid. 26.
7. Ibid. 37.
8. There are scholars who believe that some of the surviving plays performed by the company and attributed to Shakespeare when published by those who also printed his later work are, in fact, his own hastily written early plays whose plots and language he retained in later revisions since they were his own. Peter Ackroyd, for instance, summarizes the most optimistic reading in this regard as it would significantly increase Shakespeare's extant oeuvre to include preliminary versions of *Hamlet, Pericles,* and *The Taming of the Shrew*, unrevised plays such as *Edmund Ironside* and *Edward the Third*, and, of course, *The Troublesome Reigne of King John*, all completed before 1588 (see 149–169). Conversely, the deletions of scenes and drastic changes in characterization in Shakespeare's revisions (as with the *King Lear* acted by the company) suggest the work of more than one hand, as Ackroyd himself concedes (see 164–165).
9. See Wood 105.
10. See *Will in the World* 28–29.
11. See *The Norton Shakespeare* 1017. G.B. Harrison gives the play the early date of June 1596 and suggests numerous topical references to crises in France and the queen's declining health (see especially 217–281).
12. Ibid. 1015. Acknowledging the shift in critical writing about the play from the 1940s onward, but opposed to Sigurd Burckhardt's assertion that *King John* documented the maturing of the poet's own modernity, Steve Longstaffe maintains that Shakespeare's historical omissions and amplifications would not have significantly challenged what he insists were the prevailing antipapist, anti-Catholic, and anti-Spanish sentiments of his audiences. However, the more common recent consensus, as voiced by the Norton editors, would be that the play is "modern" in its skepticism about its own historical sources.
13. See Schoch 37.
14. See *The Age of Shakespeare* 39.
15. See *Shakespeare on Silent Film* 22.
16. Ibid. 21–23.
17. That Shaw did regard the notion of putting well-wrought plays on silent film an absurdity can be discerned in the comments Vachel Lindsay cites in his 1916 defense of the cinema as an art form, *The Art of the Moving Picture*. He quotes Shaw as saying, "Strike the dialogue from Molière's *Tartuffe*, and what audience would bear its mere stage-business? Imagine the scene in which Iago poisons Othello's mind against Desdemona conveyed in dumb show" (see 68). Shaw's illustrative examples are particularly interesting as they were destined to become notable examples of the Expressionist period of filmmaking in Germany, Emil Jannings playing the protagonists in Dmitri Buchowetzki's *Othello* (1922) as well as those of W.F. Murnau's *Herr Tartüff* and *Faust* (both 1926). For Shaw the especial province of early cinema was in conveying epic spectacle and fast-paced narrative, not the business of the stage (see 69). In his newsreel Shaw again mocks the image (and Mussolini no less) with grotesque mummery.
18. See 240–241 of *Herbert Beerbohm Tree* for Shaw's remarks in the chapter entitled "The Point of View of a Playwright."
19. Ibid. 248.
20. See 5.

21. See Hall 225–226. It is certainly noteworthy that Wilde wrote enthusiastically about Shakespeare. Of the best-known commentaries, "The Portrait of Mr. W.H." brings up the idea (in the form of dialogue) that Shakespeare's sonnets were principally addressed to a boy actor, William Hughes, who defected from Shakespeare's company (a theory finally revealed to be a fabrication). "The Truth of Masks: A Note on Illusion" is a more straightforward defense of Shakespeare's reliance on props and costumes against Lord Lytton and his fellows who rejected the archaeological approach to Shakespeare: in other words, in contesting the tacit assumption by critics that Shakespeare was indifferent to costume, Wilde defended Tree's type of revival that emphasized "the splendour of mounting" (see Wilde 899–914 and 937–957).
22. I have taken the quote from Max Beerbohm's contribution to the *Saturday Review*, in which he observes that, as the poisoned king is to be carried out on a chair, monks hurry noiselessly "through apple-trees" to the chapel of Swinstead Abbey (see the reprint in Wells, *Shakespeare in the Theatre* 160–163).
23. The reproductions are interleaved after page 108 on unnumbered pages, but are themselves indicated as plates 20 and 21 on the captions, from which I quote.
24. See her contribution to Max Beerbohm's *Herbert Beerbohm Tree* (149).
25. Winter's comments are also reproduced in Wells's *Shakespeare in the Theatre* (see especially 119, 126).
26. See "Some Interesting Fallacies of the Modern Stage" 3. It is interesting that in the talk he confesses that, asked to contemplate his politics, he had to declare himself an "anti-Gladstonian Socialist" (see 4).
27. For a more detailed elaboration of the impact of photography on the visual arts and the development of cinema as a medium see, for example, my article "The Birth of a New Realism."
28. Vardac 234–235.
29. Ibid. 98.
30. I have drawn this account of D'Annunzio's dissemination of Pre-Raphaelitism during the 1880s from Giuliana Pieri's "D'Annunzio and Alma-Tadema." Holman Hunt and J.E. Millais also favored illustrating scenes taken directly from their readings of the plays.
31. See Spiers 5–6.
32. See page 7 of Chapter Nine (as indexed on the Art Renewal Center Web site) of Vern Grosvener Swanson's biography of Alma-Tadema.
33. I again draw on reminiscences in Max Beerbohm's commemorative volume (see 148).
34. Ibid. 132.
35. Ibid. 111.
36. Ibid.
37. This was, for instance, Ball's conjecture (see "The Shakespeare Film" 228–229).
38. McKernan and Terris 82.
39. See the uncredited interview of Smedley, 4.
40. See McKernan, "Shakespeare on Film" 50.
41. Note that in his most recent invocation of the phrase the Cinema of Attractions (see "Early Film, Its Spectator, and the Avant-Garde") Gunning observes that he has modified Eisenstein's quasi-physiological conception that relied initially on its emotional effect on the theatre spectator, and that in the case of film was defined as "any demonstrable fact (an action, an object, a phenomenon, a conscious combination, and so on) that is known and proven to exercise a definite effect on the attention and emotions of the audience and that, combined with others, possesses the characteristic of concentrating the audience's emotions in any direction dictated by the production's purpose" (Eisenstein, "The Montage of Film Attractions" 35–36).
42. See Kachur, "The First Shakespeare Film" 48–49. The costume designs for both *King John* (authentically sumptuous) and *A Midsummer Night's Dream* (imaginatively resplendent) survive in the theatre collection archives of the University of Bristol.
43. For a recent view of Tree's historicism in this regard, see Orgel, *The Authentic Shakespeare* 56.
44. See Villars (20), whose comment might be rendered: "Between the second and third acts Mr. Tree has interpolated a scene not found in Shakespeare. A sacrilege, one might say—but not so. The scene he has added is silent, a tableau vivant, that represents King John granting the English barons the great charter that is to this day the foundation of the liberties of the English people."
45. See Petric 32. Vertov's emphatic rejection of acted footage led to a heated debate on the nature of cinema's "truth-telling" with the eminent Formalist critic Viktor Shklovsky serving

as advocate of Eisenstein's enactments of historical events (see Taylor and Christie 153–154, 161–162).
46. See *Shakespeare on Silent Film* 30–32.
47. For an account of the rediscovery of this film, see Christie and Elliot 165. Apparently, Dziga Vertov had been assigned to help the young Proletkult filmmakers, but he soon left the production and might have been parodied in the film for his insistence on "non-acting"; it was all the more surprising, therefore, that Eisenstein's miniature was found edited into one of his newsreel compilations. For the reciprocal influence of Meyerhold and the circus see, for instance, http://www.marxists.org/subject/art/literature/children/texts/circus/meyerhold.html. See, also, the acclaimed recent translations by Richard Taylor and William Powell of Eisenstein's early essays "The Montage of Attractions" (29–34) and "The Montage of Film Attractions" (35–52).
48. See Kachur, "*Othello*" 189–190.
49. Ibid. 192.
50. Ball discusses the filmed scenes in the main narrative of *Shakespeare on Silent Film* (see 78–82) and "The Shakespeare Film as Record," but he also supplements this work with a valuable appendix concerning his sources (320–322) that details his reasons for being unable to decide on the length of the film (which could have been three reels or more). I have not been able to discover more about Ball's claim that the film was excluded from the United States by the Trust companies (it seems very much like the fare George Kleine might have wished to promote, as he had done *The Tempest* in 1905).
51. Ibid. 230.
52. Ibid. 235.
53. Ibid. See, also, King's "Made for the Masses with an Appeal to the Classes."
54. See "Shrieking from below the Gratings" 252–258, 271.
55. Ibid. 259–266. In "The Shakespeare Film as Record" Ball notes that Emerson found Tree's tendency to wander out of the frame exasperating, even resorting to the use of cameras that had not been loaded with film to indulge Tree's insistence on speaking the lines (see 234). Obviously the close-ups would have required greater cooperation from the star, an aspect of filming that would not have troubled Johnston Forbes-Robertson whose valedictory Hamlet for Hay Plumb's film (for the Hepworth Company) also had its star drifting off the frame but with the cameras loaded for many of his speeches.
56. Ball, *Shakespeare in Silent Cinema* 235.
57. It was Dickson's assistant cameraman on the early Edison films, William Heise, who shot the medium-long-shot composition of a comical kiss between May Irwin and John Rice, actors who re-created their stage roles in the concurrent *The Widow Jones* (1896). It was the first known restaging of a theatrical scene for the camera, but consisted of one shot—as was the practice for most of the films taken in the Edison studio, the Black Maria—with the background suppressed.
58. Ball, "Tree's *King John*" 455.
59. Kachur, "The First Shakespearean Film" 55.
60. Kachur, "Shakespeare Politicized" 28.
61. The comment appears in the unnumbered pages in the souvenir program available to the patrons of Tree's theatrical production, the same one so richly supplied with photographs of the actors credited to Biograph.
62. Indeed, Gary Williams notes the assimilation of the play into various British Imperialist tropes even with the Henry Bishop and Frederick Rowley operatic adaptation of 1816, the first to be influenced by Romanticism (see 76–92). Williams calls Beerbohm Tree's production of the play "almost a patriotic occasion," a restorative kept on the stages from January to May by a public shocked by the reverses suffered in the Transvaal during Black Week in December 1898 (see 132).
63. See Schoenbaum 44, 49.
64. These ideas are in some ways the culmination of the debates between Walter Benjamin and Theodor Adorno, left unresolved after the former's death, as to the role media play in social processes. Mikhail Bakhtin anticipates the notion that it is popular culture that determines the nature of social transformation in his work on the phenomenon of carnival during the 1920s and 1930s, as is reflected in his subsequent writings (see, in particular, *Rabelais and His World*). It should be noted that Bakhtin extends his postulation temporally, making the even broader claim that "folk culture" is perennial and that it exercised just such a determinative function even before the advent of industrial modernity.

65. See Kachur, "Shakespeare Politicized" 30.
66. Ibid.
67. See "Beerbohm Tree's *King John* Rediscovered" 35.
68. Ibid. 36.
69. See "Shakespeare on Film" 49.
70. Ibid. 50.
71. See *Walking Shadows* 2–3.
72. Ibid. 82.
73. See Wells, *Shakespeare in the Theatre* 162. In his "AT HER MAJESTY'S" column in *The Saturday Review* of January 20, 1900, Max declares *A Midsummer Night's Dream* the most perfect of Shakespeare's plays and *Julius Caesar* easier to stage than the rather "dull" *King John*, whose many voids had to be "filled up with spectacular effects" 77–78.
74. For Ginzburg's work on the relationship of literature and history, see "Proofs and Possibilities"; for a general consideration of scientific empiricism and other evidentiary techniques, see the essays of *Clues, Myths and the Historical Method*, and for his study of the relationship of folklore and anthropology to formal history, see his *Ecstasies*.
75. See 118.
76. See the September 20, 1899 issue of *Sketch*, 3.
77. See the September 21, 1899 issue of *The Westminster Gazette*, 4.
78. See the fourth page of the *Times* of London of September 21, 1899.
79. See page 412 of the September 27, 1899 issue of *Sketch*. As Britain mustered forces to attack the revolting Boers, the local press adopted a tone of supreme condescension toward the cross-channel judicial illegitimacies. An editorial of June 3, 1899 in the *Saturday Review* heaped praise on Zola and ridiculed the fickle mob that fast turned from attacking him to hero worship (see 677–678).
80. See Émile-Zola and Massin 4. In 1997 a collection of Zola's photographs of Norwood that passed to his grandson, Jean-Claude Le Blond-Zola, was exhibited by the Norwood Society and reproduced in a catalogue.
81. Ibid. 4.

Two Featuring the Bard: Frederick Warde's Shakespeare and the Transformation of American Cinema

1. I am summarizing a memorable passage of Jasper Fforde's playful 2001 novel *The Eyre Affair* (see 182–185). In Fforde's subsequent novel, *Something Rotten*, Hamlet finds himself transported to another such "pre-futuristic" England by the Chestertonian detective hero of both novels, Thursday Next, to assess the issue of whether he is a "ditherer."
2. Indeed, it is such anticipation, the translation of lines of dialogue into clichés by a process of overfamiliarization (marked by cheers of recognition), that Eco finds most cultish about such cult movies, with a secondary characteristic being an agglomeration of intensely familiar intertextual references (see *Casablaca*). Like Susan Sontag, Eco regards "cult" movies as something of an assertive celebration of deliberately clumsy filmmaking, which though it may well add to the cult value of films such as those of Ed Wood for instance, may not be an essential prerequisite of films with an appeal to the "cultists" in the audience, as I endeavor to illustrate in the case of Baz Luhrmann in my concluding chapter.
3. Recall that in his argument about the effects of mechanical reproduction Walter Benjamin contends that the aura dissipates as a result of the loss of oneness between image and that which is represented, an issue I treat at greater length in chapter 3.
4. See Bowser, *The Transformation of Cinema*, in which she quotes an exhibitor writing to the popular trade journal the *Moving Picture World* imploring fellow exhibitors of *Queen Elizabeth* not to show her concluding "death flop into the pile of cushions placed before the throne for no other reason than to save the Bernhardt bones" (92). According to Eve Golden, Bernhardt acted in her 1912 feature *Camille* for $30,000 and obtained 10 percent of the gross as well as the appearance fee of $35,000 when Adolph Zukor bought the American rights to her next film.

5. The boast for *Cleopatra* is emblazoned on the inside back cover of the *New York Dramatic Mirror* of December 4, 1912 (issue 58.1772).
6. See Ramsaye 516. While it is relatively clear that by the end of 1912 the trade papers reserved the term "feature" for a film of four 900-foot reels or more, the actual origins of feature filmmaking are as elusive and almost as protracted as any of the other assumed singularities of cinema such as synchronized soundtracks (*ca.* 1894–1926) and the adoption of naturalistic color processes (*ca.* 1896–1940s). While multireel boxing films and cinematic Passion Plays had been screened on occasion in Europe and the United States, and while Australian Charles Tait made *The Story of the Kelly Gang* in 1906 and Michel Carre made the first French feature, *L'enfant prodigue*, the following year, the most powerful sector of the U.S. film industry vacillated about the adoption of the longer formats increasingly evident in European filmmaking from 1910 onward. The twelve-minute, 900-foot format standardized by the Motion Picture Patents Company had habituated both producers and patrons to normative conventions that emphasized speed of shooting, increasingly naturalistic acting, quick editing, and rapid scene transitions. Yet the mood of change was already in the air when in 1911 a feature made the previous year in Italy, Milano Film's fifty-six-minute version of *L'Inferno* (believed to have been directed by Giuseppe de Liguoro), became the first feature-length film shown in the United States: it was praised by W. Stephen Bush of the trade periodical the *Moving Picture World* as transforming the cinema into an art form. By then, Bush and his fellow critics had already been agitating for "better" pictures and higher prices for more than a year.
7. Ibid. 597–598.
8. See Ramsaye 601 and Jacobs 91. This is not to argue that Bernhardt's film did anything more than legitimize an industrial inevitability. Even at the beginning of 1911, W. Stephen Bush of the *Moving Picture World* could predict the great transformation that now came apace: "Within the last six months the production of subjects, consisting of two or more reels, has shown a marked increase. The most notable of them, Dante's 'Inferno' and Torquato Tasso's 'Jerusalem Delivered,' the former in five and the latter in four reels, have been produced in Europe and marketed in this country independently of any organization of film makers. The success of these two features has greatly stimulated a trend toward releases of greater length among American manufacturers, who have begun to give the possibility of longer films their earnest attention. There is every reason to believe that this tendency toward feature films of greater length will continue and that the growing number of such films will bring about some important changes in the business of exhibiting moving pictures" (see the *Moving Picture World* 10.4 [Nov. 4, 1911]: 275).
9. See Gomery, "What Was Adolph Zukor Doing?" 205.
10. See, for instance, Bordwell, Staiger, and Thompson 130. Bowser notes that *The Life of Moses* ran as a feature with the reels shown in sequence at the Schubert Theater in New Orleans for eight days in April 1910 (see 196–197). Uricchio and Pearson emphasize the centrality of the figure of Moses to contemporary religious discussions and on Vitagraph's canny marketing strategy that included planting stories in the trade papers and the distribution of a full-color poster for the last reel with the aim of promoting the exhibition of all five reels (see 160–194).
11. See the *Moving Picture World* 12.9 (Jun. 1, 1912): 838.
12. *Moving Picture World* 10.5 (4 Nov. 1911): 275.
13. *Moving Picture World* 10.6 (11 Nov. 1911): 489.
14. See Staiger's "Combination and Litigation" 60–61, 71. Note that a steady supply of features proved difficult for American companies, just as they were to be the undoing of the Italian feature filmmakers in 1914: after initial experiments with longer features, the Patents companies Kalem and Selig soon returned to two- and three-reelers. The failure of the MPPC to compete in this market was probably industrial in origin (standardization rendering adaptation to new modes of production difficult), for General Film did its best to claim a spot in the new market niche, producing and distributing the first American fiction feature *Oliver Twist* (1912), and advertising in detail its plans for feature distribution: a two-page spread in the trade journal *Motography*, for instance, claimed that "beginning Nov. 11, 1912, the General Film Company will place at the disposition of its customers two feature Multiple Reel Subjects each week; these will be released Mondays and Fridays" (*Motography* 8.10 [Nov. 9, 1912]: 6–7). An even earlier back-page advertisement in the *New York Dramatic Mirror* sported a list of twenty-six films of two to four reels in length with release dates ranging from May 6 to November 18, 1912 (see issue 58.1769 [Oct. 15, 1912]: back cover).

15. *Moving Picture World* 14.10 (Dec. 7, 1912): 1058.
16. *New York Dramatic Mirror* 57.1746 (Jun. 5, 1912), back cover.
17. These arguments are presented in rather more detail in Allen's "Motion Picture Exhibition" and "Manhattan Myopia" and in Singer's "Manhattan's Nickelodeons."
18. See "Early Cinema" 22–230. In a more extensive treatment of these issues in her book *Babel and Babylon,* Hansen goes on to argue that "rather than disassociate the cinema from its working-class clientele, as the industry's initial courting of the *'better classes'* might have implied, the long-range strategy was to submerge all class distinctions in an ostensibly homogenous culture of consumption" (see *Babel and Babylon* 65).
19. I refer to Rabinovitz's *For the Love of Pleasure.*
20. Much of this information can be found in the bound AFI press release for its Los Angeles premier (Richard III, October 29, 1996), sent to me by Ken Wlaschin.
21. For an indication of the prominence that the Roxy and its founder Samuel Lionel "Roxy" Rothafel attained, see Ross Melnick's "Station R-O-X-Y."
22. See Brode, 30–31. Note that I have cited Brode's engaging book elsewhere in more favorable contexts.
23. In "Early Shakespeare Movies," Rothwell follows Janet Staiger and other historians of the period in suggesting that features produced by independents—most often transient companies set up to exploit single films as in the case of *Richard III,* whose financiers metamorphosed in stages from the Sterling Camera Company to the Shakespeare Film Company—contributed to the disintegration of the monopoly on standardized film production and distribution claimed by the Motion Picture Production Company cartel led by Thomas Edison (see 15).
24. In *Shakespeare on Silent Film,* Ball lists not only such major reviewers as the *New York Times* but also the local newspapers from Charleston, Jacksonville, Savannah, and Augusta, most of which extol the merits of the film (see 156–159).
25. Ibid. 162.
26. See *A History of Shakespeare on Screen* 19–20. With regard to the Benson *Richard,* John Collick quite correctly takes British economic historian Rachel Low to task for succumbing to an anachronistic notion of progressive filmmaking, albeit for the equally dubious notion that the British film's rejection of North American techniques of filming and spatial organization was not, as Low claimed, a cinematically illiterate retrogression but the result of a "frantic" struggle to assert a "uniquely English, high-class culture" (in the shape of filmed National Theatre) to withstand the "gradual encroachment of American melodramatic narrative into the country's cinemas" (see 42–46). Yet it is self-evident that the Warde-Keane *Richard* shares similar non-Griffithian elements while being designed not as a bulwark against American success but as an enticement for the country bumpkins and urban immigrants to translate their leisure capital into the cultural capital associated with a WASP urban elite.
27. See Ball, *Shakespeare on Silent Film* 158–159.
28. See "Representing *King Lear* on Screen" 213.
29. This information and the observations that follow are mostly drawn from *Fifty Years of Make-Believe.* Booth and Irving also played opposite each other.
30. Warde is cited in the *New York Dramatic Mirror* (58.1769, Nov. 13, 1912: 35) as revealing these feelings to a reporter for the *Brooklyn Eagle.*
31. Again, the most substantial recollections are to be found in *Fifty Years of Make-Believe* (see especially 64–65, 109).
32. See *Shakespeare on Silent Film* 46.
33. Noting that Norman Holland made a strong case for Shakespeare having been able to read Machiavelli through Innocent Gentillet's [French Protestant] argument against him, Steven Mullaney suggests that in a play such as *Measure for Measure* the Italian political theorist served less as "a literary source than a cultural locus" pointing to a nexus of historical precedents and theatrical conventions (see 90–92).
34. In her contribution to *Shakespeare et le Cinéma,* Laetitia Coussement has noted that, in addition to the textual deformity resulting from the amputation of the latter part of the play, Ruiz introduces other deformations, by having the dialogue anticipated by visual metaphors and having the music provide a grandiose, ironic commentary on characters shown in a debased or diminished form in the visuals. This technique, Coussement suggests, is Ruiz's forceful reply to André Bazin's idea of the ontological veracity of the cinematic image. I would add

that the author of the *Poetics of Cinema* emphasizes disjunction by making cinema's tracks work against each other, emphasizing the irreality and hypertheatricality of mise en scène and performance.
35. I am here indebted to Stephen Greenblatt's treatment of the manifestation of the cult in Austen's novel in his essay on "Racial Memory and Literary History" (see 49–52).
36. See *The Henry Irving Shakespeare, Vol. III* 10.
37. See Winter's unnumbered preface to the edition by Edwin Booth and William Winter of *Edwin Booth's Prompt-Book of Richard III*.
38. Note that in the Benson version, which owes much less to Cibber, the sword is raised but twice.
39. Erin Blake of the Folger Shakespeare Library has pointed out to me that Edmund Keane's assumption of the role was definitive to the degree that later statuettes commemorating the famous impersonators of Gloster maintain every detail of his costuming, merely grafting different heads onto Keane's body!
40. See *Early Shakespeare Movies* 15–16.
41. This was published in New York by Henry L. Hinton in preparation for the performance of May 1, 1872, and is prefaced by advertisements for jewelers, carpet merchants, clothiers and purveyors of various instruments, articles of furniture, and restorative nostrums.
42. See *Fifty Years of Make-Believe*, 64–65, 109.
43. See Buchanan 39–42.
44. Ibid. 38.
45. In "Early Shakespeare Movies," Rothwell has suggested that the 1916 *King Lear*, which with its "richly textured" opening montages to its freedom of camera movement addressed some of the misgivings that Warde himself had about *Richard III*, confirmed that Edwin and Gertrude Thanhouser were the "heroic martyrs unsung" of silent Shakespeare movies (see 16–18).
46. A well-received one-reel version of *The Tempest* (1911) and a longer one of *The Merchant of Venice* (1911) are yet to be rediscovered.
47. Buchanan also notes that Edmund's conspiratorial looks to the camera foreshadow those of a host of later cinematic Machiavels in the form of Richards and Iagos (see 44–45).
48. Buchanan observes that Ernest wears the same hat and Fool's scepter as those of his predecessor and makes the intriguing argument that Ernest's allusion to the earlier film, as well as to his status as son and director of the star, has textual significance (see 45–46).

Three   The Exfoliating Folio, or Transnational and International Avant-Gardes from Bernhardt's *Hamlets* to Hollywood's Europeans

1. See *Will in the World* 298–325.
2. I am here indebted to Marianna De Sanctis whose admirable thesis, "Amleto nel cinema muto europeo," not only established the locations of the silent Hamlet adaptations presently known to survive, but also pointed out that this play remains the most adapted of all single texts in any medium (see 5).
3. See De Sanctis 66–74 and Kliman, although note that Kliman's insistence that two of the fragments in the Museum of Modern Art (MoMA) archives are from the same Lux film (see Kliman 236–245) seems intriguing in that the film bore at least two titles. The Italian release was, according to De Sanctis, called *Cuor di padre*, which would make its highly ambulatory Ghost the hero (see 80), one of them obviously in English as well since the MoMA print Kliman describes bears English intertitles. Moreover, De Sanctis mentions obvious departures from Shakespeare such as the second appearance of the ghost to Amleto and Ofelia, while Kliman's untitled print has a very young Hamlet (De Sanctis's appears to be the great French stage Hamlet, Bernhardt's onetime lover Jean Mounet-Sully) and a rather more predictable Ghost (the fragment does not contain his reappearance). Paul Mounet was also playing significant roles by this time at Films d'Art under the direction of André Calmettes, and in *Shakespeare on Silent Film* Robert Hamilton Ball mentions another possible *Hamlet* film with Mounet-Sully (259). To further add to the confusion, De Sanctis notes that Ball included reviews in two respected

trade journals, the British *Bioscope* and the American *Moving Picture World*, that disagreed as to the quality of the film (see De Sanctis 79). I have not had the time to devote to the painstaking task of getting to the heart of this Hamlet mystery. However, I have studied the British Film Institute version of Caserini's film that follows the order given in De Sanctis's reconstruction of the Associazione Italiana per le Richerche di Storia del Cinema print housed in the Cineteca Nazionale, although even with the inclusion of the same three (German) intertitles as given by Kliman, the British Film Institute version appears to consist of seventeen shots (with scene changes effected with pans) with a Ghost that is sometimes translucent and at others an opaque white depending on the background used for the superimposition (cf. De Sanctis 159–164). De Sanctis's argument that intertitles were lost during the conflation of fragmentary material seems persuasive (see 73), as is Kliman's contention that the film would have included at least one further scene showing Hamlet's killing of Claudius (230).
4. See De Sanctis 64.
5. Ibid. 97–98.
6. See Jorgens 7–35 and the section Davies devotes to "The Film Actor" (167–183) in *Filming Shakespeare's Plays*.
7. In the context of one of the versions of *Hamlet* that I discuss in due course, that of Asta Nielsen, elements of the story borrowed by Shakespeare have to be suppressed to maintain the film's governing conceit. Thus, there is no indication that the backstory alluded to at the start of the film, once it veers into the supposed thesis advanced by Vining, has much more to do with the original that is in some ways closer to Shakespeare than the intermediate Renaissance reworking by Belleforest. For instance, Amleth's feigned madness, also manifesting itself in riddles and verbal play, seems so methodical that his uncle even tests it with the lure of a comely wench, a foster sister whom Amleth actually ravishes but enjoins to silence (Belleforest makes her Hamlet's mistress). Saxo's Amleth suffers no gender confusions: the forged letter that proves the undoing of Rosencrantz and Amleth in Shakespeare garners Amleth a second wife, the English king's daughter, which does not prevent him from killing his father-in-law; and he murders his antagonists with Viking ferocity, eventually meeting his own end as a result of further dynastic battles.
8. See Shapiro 285–286, 293–297. Perhaps a residual memory from childhood also made its way into the play, for Judith Cook recounts an inquest held in Stratford on February 11, 1580 concerning the body of a woman, Katherine Hamlet, who had been found drowned in the Avon. The wording of the jurors' findings, according to Cook, implies that there might have been some debate as to whether the death had been accidental and whether the body could be buried in consecrated ground (see 102–103).
9. Various elements of Belleforest, such as the queen's adultery, were preserved in the often-performed Neoclassical stage version (rendered fittingly in Alexandrines) by Jean-François Ducis, against which the Schwob-Morand version attempted its more "authentic" scene restoration and Villonization (see, for instance, Taranow *The Bernhardt Hamlet* 3).
10. This is all the more notable since, as Irene Dash points out, it is Gertrude whose lines, whether at the hands of Gielgud, John Houseman, or Burton, are most likely to suffer the unkindest cuts (see 123).
11. The fine film *The Madness of King George* (dir. Nicholas Hytner, 1994) omits to acknowledge that the King's return to sanity (proved when he insists on a happy ending for *King Lear*) is not a Georgian innovation but a restoration of the kinder original.
12. Quoted in Gidel 262–263.
13. Cited in Howard 111.
14. Although I see no compelling evidence of the influence of the tradition of the *onnegata* (or stage female impersonator) on Bernhardt's *Hamlet* who, like Sarah Siddons's before her, displayed a mastery of fencing skills, it might be worth noting that Japanese graphic art had a profound impact both on Symbolism and on the French incarnation of Art Nouveau, its most important impresario being Siegfried Bing who—following the early lead of James McNeill Whistler and Edmond de Goncourt—transformed *japonisme* into the serious study and appreciation of Japanese art (see, for instance, Weisberg et al.).
15. Binstock 11, 19–25.
16. Arwas 7, 10–11.
17. See Mucha et al. 14–37 and Arwas 8.
18. See Mucha et al. 14–22 and Arwas 10–12.

19. Ulmer 7–8.
20. Ibid.
21. Arwas 11.
22. Mucha et al. 37.
23. Notably Bernhardt later described Lorenzo as her "Florentine Hamlet," Rostand's Aiglon as her "White Hamlet," and Shakespeare's as her "Black Hamlet" (all three male roles).
24. For details about Bernhardt's appeal to the tradition of *travesti,* see Taranow, *Sarah Bernhardt* 210–227.
25. Russell Jackson recounts this incident in some detail (see *The Cambridge Companion* 326–327), although some versions of the proximate cause suggest that it was Bernhardt's use of a blonde wig that provoked journalist Georges Vanour's sarcasm, which compelled the playwright Catulle Mendés to defend her honor. In *The Bernhardt Hamlet,* Gerda Taranow points out that the omission of the descriptive "fat" derived from an accepted textual emendation, and that Eugène Morand was a seasoned man of the theatre, while his collaborator on the translation, Marcel Schwob, was not only a scholar of English, German, and such classical languages as Sanskrit, but also a researcher of Renaissance revenge drama and such source material as Snorri Starlason, Saxo, and Belleforest (see 27–28). She also mentions that the wounded Catulle Mendés was twice Vanour's age (33–35). No one appears to have volunteered to defend Olivier's honor in similarly reckless ways when his blonde wig was also ridiculed more than half a century later.
26. See Taranow, *The Bernhardt Hamlet* 178.
27. Howard notes its general influence on French Modernism (see especially 12–16), and says that Baudelaire hung the prints in his apartment, while in *The Bernhardt Hamlet* Taranow (8–9) observes that Mallarmé kept a Manet pastel depicting Hamlet in the graveyard scene.
28. See, for instance, Dash 127. Robert Young mentions that Garrick's omission of the gravediggers and rewriting of the fifth act in 1772 occurred after a visit to France (64).
29. Taranow, *The Bernhardt Hamlet* 171–175.
30. See Howard 14.
31. See Mannoni 423, 459 and De Sanctis 45.
32. See Sadoul 111 and Geduld, who in *The Birth of the Talkies* also notes the role of Henri Lioret in the invention of the Phono-Cinéma-Théâtre (50–52).
33. See Geduld, *The Birth of the Talkies* 53–54.
34. Geduld 55–56 and Taranow, *The Bernhardt Hamlet* 172–173.
35. See Toulet 104–106 and Gunning, "Vienna Avant-Garde and Early Cinema."
36. See Marín and Martínez Sierra 15, something of the flavor of which might be caught by the following:
    > Most gracious lady: may these sundry lines capture a remembrance of your beauteous gestures, of the nobly romantic attitude with which you so generously yielded your flesh to the heart of Prince Hamlet. I, with but paltry words, have striven also to seize the memory of your spirit, the crystal clarity of your voice, the sorcery of femininity triumphant, thanks to which you have managed to instill so refined a sentiment in the depths of that tormented heart.
37. See *The Bernhardt Hamlet* 178.
38. Ibid. 176–186.
39. Ibid. 180.
40. For the emergence of avant-garde realism as the result of the discovery of efficient photographic processes, see my essay "The Birth of a New Realism."
41. See, for example, that of a model posed, *ca.* 1900, for *Aiglon,* as reproduced in Ovenden, 75, plate 70.
42. See the uncredited "The Art and Design of Alphons Mucha" in http://www.ragnarokpress.com/scriptorium/mucha.html.
43. Arwas 13.
44. Taranow comments in *The Bernhardt Hamlet* that this scene may even have influenced Gielgud (see 170–172), who similarly shows the prince die standing.
45. See *The Bernhardt Hamlet* regarding Sardou's practice of entrusting the stage improvisations to Bernhardt (12).
46. I refer to the chapter on "Accessories" in *Acting in the Cinema* (83–98).
47. I add the seemingly salacious (and perhaps invented) detail about Tellegen because it was part of the publicity behind the American release of the films—as Heather McPherson points out,

Benrhardt, no less than Siddons, skillfully blended the public with the private in the image culture that she promoted (see 76–116).
48. For the cultural influence Shakespeare's character exerted over Baudelaire, Mallarmé, and even Joyce, see Alexander Welsh 140–173.
49. See Max's well-known commentary in the *Saturday Review* (Jun. 17, 1899): 747–748.
50. See, for instance, Neuringer 143 and Chertok 515.
51. See Gay, who also notes Freud's correspondence with Arthur Schnitzler (317–323). Nabokov, for his part, gives "repression" a possibly intentional double entendre by repeatedly attacking psychoanalysis. Lisa Starks devotes considerable attention to the development of psychoanalysis (see "Remember Me"), but in terms of Freud's general influence and the relevance of his theories to Shakespeare films, I emphasize the concurrence of his thought with developments in the cinema (psychoanalysis itself being a manifestation of Freud's repressed desire for cinema).
52. See *The Interpretation of Dreams* 298.
53. See Taranow, *The Bernhardt Hamlet* 162–163. Freud would no doubt maintain that Hamlet could only be capable of striking Claudius if he could not see him.
54. Ibid. 143.
55. See *The Interpretation of Dreams* 299. In fact, it was probably Freud's conviction that Hamlet represented the inner reaches of his author's psychology that led him much later (in 1923) to adopt the view that, since the more traumatic events of Edward de Vere's life seem to have a historical connection with those of the character, the seventeenth Earl of Oxford was the more likely author of the plays (see Michell 161–189).
56. See Eliot 25–26.
57. See *Five Lectures on Psycho-analysis* 47.
58. Ibid.
59. See, in particular, the section he devotes to "Hysterical Phantasies."
60. See, for instance, the reasons given by Roberta Pearson for the subtitle of *Eloquent Gestures* (10–16).
61. Although the reasons for claiming copyright are not entirely clear, it is generally assumed that, as with the sudden appearance of company logos on the films' décor, it was a mechanism of preventing outright piracy. As a method it was far from systematic, and we cannot even be certain how many films there actually were (it appears that not all were submitted for copyright). What was copyrighted, too, varied widely from film to film: the fragments I have examined at the Library of Congress could not be more different from each other, some shot with a high degree of technical competence, others with patchy lighting and tacky props; some with apt costuming or impressive use of locations, others with prefabricated painted backdrops that limit the plane of action to within a few feet of the camera. Just as interesting is the variety of what was sent to the Library of Congress from the *Macbeth* accorded paper-print copyright on April 2, 1908 to an existing full-reel *Twelfth Night* completed two years later. The 17 scene fragments of *Macbeth* are the second most ample at 44–55 frames each; the *Othello* that achieved copyright on May 26, 1908 does not appear to have survived; *Romeo and Juliet* exists integrally, but its 15 copyright fragments are only 42 to 51 frames in length; the 17 scene fragments of *Richard III* are, at 49 to 55 frames, as long as those of *Macbeth*, although their copyright came on September 19, 1908, after those of the more abbreviated *Romeo and Juliet*; the *Merchant of Venice* copyrighted on December 9, 1908 contributes 19 scenes (I was unable to count the frames numbers for this or for the 1908 *Antony and Cleopatra*). The 1909 *King Lear* is represented by 16 fragments of only 21 to 29 frames (although it fortunately survives), as is the *Midsummer Night's Dream* believed to be of the same year, but which appears not to have had paper prints submitted for copyright at all. The longest and least innovative of the films are the *Twelfth Night* of 1910 and the 1912 *As You Like It* (starring stage celebrity Rose Caughlin), although they are interesting films. By then the cycle had run its course, and the 1912 Florence Turner vehicle *An Indian Romeo and Juliet* transforms Shakespeare to a metaphor. The 1908 *Comedy of Errors* is not Shakespeare.
62. The films might, in fact, have had added interest for the Americanness of their Shakespeare whose condensations might well have been influenced by stage versions. Meanwhile, the American branch of Star run by Gaston Méliès and Pathé's American concern were busy producing Westerns intended to feed the European taste for American frontier adventures.
63. Judith Buchanan's observation about the senator who sleeps though most of *Julius Caesar* suggests that the actors selectively resorted to the grand manner.

64. Naremore also observes that even the naturalism of actors such as Spencer Tracy involves a degree of ostensiveness that "marks it off from quotidian behavior," and that an actor such as Chaplin could use virtuoso displays of theatrical movement to draw attention to his performance precisely by being "more stylized and poetically unnatural than the people he plays alongside" (*Acting in the Cinema* 17). The converse might be argued of Griffith's stars, most notably Lillian Gish, whose gestural language, favored with close-ups, is markedly more naturalistic than that of those who share her scenes when she plays "heroic" roles, although she is more ostensive when she plays the role of victim.
65. See my article "The Birth of a New Realism" for a more detailed consideration of the types of cinema and performance to be found in the formative years of the medium.
66. See De Cordova 55–61. He goes on to mention that by the end of 1910 all the major studios save Biograph were disseminating the names of stars in their publicity materials.
67. Ibid. 36–46.
68. Oksiloff 123.
69. This is the Lukács of 1913 (see Oksiloff 124–125).
70. Ibid. 128–129.
71. Ibid. 135–137.
72. Ibid. 136.
73. For a further consideration of these issues see my article "The Birth of a New Realism."
74. For Benjamin's acute reading of Riegl, see Karen Lang 147–157.
75. See Hansen, "Of Mice and Ducks" 29–31.
76. See "The Work of Art" in Benjamin's *Illuminations* (I have persisted in using this version of the essay since the essential problem of "aura" with which my chapter concerns itself would be most familiar to readers as stated in this form).
77. Hansen, "Benjamin's Ghosts" 44.
78. Ibid. 45.
79. Ibid. 56.
80. Ibid. 59.
81. See O'Pray "Eisenstein and Stokes on Disney."
82. See Hansen, "Of Mice and Ducks" 31–32.
83. Ibid. 32.
84. Bakhtin articulates these views in their most elaborate form in the work translated into English as *Rabelais and His World*.
85. See "Nur Stars" in *Béla Balázs: Essay, Kritik 1922–1932*, 83–86.
86. Dyer, *Heavenly Bodies* 2–3.
87. Benjamin, *Illuminations* 228–229.
88. Ibid. 231.
89. She was not the first female Hamlet, as is often supposed, but was certainly the first woman to take herself seriously as Hamlet: Colly Cibber's daughter, Charlotte Clarke, made light of her assumption of the role two generations earlier (see Howard 36–38).
90. Some seven years after this performance, her fencing master's wife published an extended pamphlet under the title *Mrs. Galindo's Letter to Mrs. Siddons*, the kind of publication that capitalizes on public voyeurism that stretches in an unbroken line from the Duke of Wellington to the present, achieving its apogee (or is it nadir?) with displays of Princess Di, Paris Hilton, and the like. In his biography of Siddons, Roger Manvell notes in passing that she added Hamlet to her repertoire during her six-year exile to the provinces (see *Sarah Siddons* 47). The observations about her embodying Melpomene in the minds of the public are those of Shearer West, who also notes her skill at blending the roles of actor as muse and the public figure as mother (see 1–3).
91. Thomas Campbell, one of Siddons's biographers, suggests that at least one of the reasons why Garrick acquiesced in her dismissal was her failure to allow him to hog the limelight (see 41–42).
92. In fact Joshua Reynolds, himself a devotee of Renaissance artists and classical antiquity, facilitated such role-playing by keeping a store of props and costumes for his sitters' use, all the while cultivating his skills in persuading both noble ladies and courtesans to affect them (see Bennett and Leonard 101–107).
93. Asleson 53.
94. Ibid. 52.
95. See "The 'Incomparable' Siddons as Reynolds's Muse" 120–123.
96. Cf. Asleson, "Crafting the Siddons Legend" 46–47.

97. James Barry called it the "finest picture of the kind, perhaps in the world" and Thomas Lawrence, a close friend of the actress, declared it to be "indisputably the finest female portrait in the world" (see Michael Wilson 120).
98. See Bennett and Leonard 113–115.
99. Ibid. 128.
100. Ibid.
101. Asleson, "Crafting the Siddons Legend" 47.
102. Ibid. 73.
103. Ibid. 47.
104. Indeed, the first fiction feature to attain widespread distribution was the hour-long *L'Inferno di Dante*, directed by Giuseppe de Liguoro and released by Milano Films in March of 1911.
105. Note that Maxim Gorky's 1896 critique of some of the Lumière films, and Frank Norris's comments about the wonders of moving pictures in *McTeague* (see Geduld *Authors on Film* 8–9) initiated a long tradition in which motion has been treated as the most fundamental capacity of the medium. And yet, cognitive scientists from Münsterberg onward have been puzzled by the series of deceptions involved in tricking the eye and the mind. Other writers have looked back to Effraim G. Lessing's distinction between spatial and temporal arts: citing him, Vachel Lindsay made a case in 1915 for moving pictures as "sculpture in motion," an idea revisited by the director Andrei Tarkovsky, much later, in insisting that cinema is sculpting in time. Movement underwrites the French concept of *photogénie*, which emphasized capturing motion in aesthetically pleasing visual compositions. In an essay written in 1934 and included in his *Film as Art*, Rudolf Arnheim argues persuasively that this most artificial of the arts attains eloquence when "the actors and the director emphasize the expressive qualities of motion" (see 182); while for the arch Realist Siegfried Kracauer certain types of motion (such as chase scenes, Fred Astaire's dancing, and the contrast of moving and inanimate objects) lend themselves particularly to film's destiny to represent the truth of history and of the everyday (see *Film as Art* 41–46). In the structuralist movement of the 1960s, Christian Metz begins his work on *Film Language* with a brief consideration of the "impression of reality" experienced by the spectator, arguing that motion (by virtue of its contrast with the still image) heightens the perception of realism and of the corporeality of objects by virtue of their extension in time (see 7–12). Among more recent theorists, Noël Carroll argues against medium specificity in treating movement as a cinematic phenomenon (see especially 3–74), while Gilles Deleuze moves both forward and backward to ponder the cinematic implications of the phenomenon Robert Stam calls Henri Bergson's "movementism", by which he means the psychology of extension in time and in the space within and beyond the frame, the central themes of Deleuze's contributions to the study of film. Yet another philosopher, Stanley Cavell, ponders the possibilities of slow motion and freeze frames in *The World Viewed* (see 133–146). Considering the importance motion has held for theorists, the lack of attention to motion as integrated into the gestural language of cinema before the adoption of synchronized soundtracks is rather surprising, and I have tried to redress this in my discussions of Bernhardt, Bertini, and Nielsen.
106. See *A History of Shakespeare on Screen* 15. The film seems influenced by a more condensed Cines *Giulietta e Romeo* (1908) that was possibly directed by Mario Caserini. The print preserved by the Cineteca di Bologna begins in a garden in which Romeo hides in the background (presumably after the Capulet Ball), and omits a number of characters in its compressed sixteen shots. The six not-quite-explanatory intertitles here seem necessary because of the rather amplified parental intrigues that precipitate calamity in the midst of screen-filling verdure and imposing architectural features. See, also, Buchanan's *Shakespeare on Film* 53.
107. See *Streetwalking on a Ruined Map* 14.
108. Interestingly, Richard Abel suggests that *Dante's Inferno* and an Ambrosio film dubbed *Satan* (1912) that seems an intriguing forerunner to Griffith's *Intolerance* (1916) served as models for Kleine's strategy of elaborate advertising campaigns developed during the course of exploiting *Quo Vadis?* (see 34–35).
109. Vachel Lindsay, a celebrant of Griffith and an ardent advocate of the American style of making sculpture move, was among a handful of dissenters who, while admiring *Cabiria*'s "vital patriotic splendor," found its inclusion of material suited to "twenty great productions" distracting (85). Grau, incidentally, observes that "When 'Quo Vadis' broke records throughout the country, attention was naturally directed to the manner in which the colossal Kleine-Cines production was exploited" (114).

110. *Moving Picture World* feels compelled to comment that Baur plays a Shylock "somewhat different from those we have seen in America, inasmuch as he portrays a less dignified Jew" (see Ball, *Shakespeare on Silent Film*, 178).
111. Ball thinks the other principals who were film actors took to the medium more naturally (see *Shakespeare on Silent Film* 261–262).
112. See *Shakespeare on Film* 55–57.
113. Hepworth 117–119.
114. Ibid. 119.
115. Apparently, he later complained that they had hurt his feet (see Emma Smith 120).
116. See Clement Scott 149–153.
117. While Mitsuhiro Yoshimoto does not grant *The Bad Sleep Well* (1960) the distinction of being a Shakespeare film—until recently only a minority of Kurosawa scholars did—he treats the issue of corporate and governmental immorality and the "personal sacrifices imposed on those who are less powerful," Kurosawa's commentary on the political crises of 1959 and 1960, as evident in the film's acceptance of "corruption as an established fact," emphasizing the parallels between Denmark's rottenness and that of 1960s Japan.
118. World War I led to the consolidation of domestic film markets, especially those with the largest audience bases in Europe (Germany) and North America (the United States). Nordisk was fully capable of supplying such markets—production peaked from 1914 to 1916—but, as Thomas Christensen points out, the precipitous decline thereafter cannot be explained by the industrial consequences of war or by artistic stagnation (see 12–18).
119. See Kristin Thompson's *Herr Lubitsch Goes to Hollywood* (13). In proposing a revisionist account of the German film industry of the 1920s, Thompson corrects the commonly held historical view that, until the disastrous ParaUfaMet agreement of 1925, little trace of the influence of American cinema could be found in Germany (14–16).
120. See Prust 79–84, 86–89. Note that I have amended some of Prust's information (and that given by other sources) in conformity with release dates of the films provided by the Danish Film Institute.
121. See Nemeskurty 80.
122. See Torben Skodt Jensen's recent documentary *Asta Nielsen: The Talking Muse* (2003) that also features an interview of her biographer, Marguerite Engberg.
123. See Kreimeier 7–9, 16–17, 40–42.
124. Thomas Koebner (123) mentions the German authorities' refusal to allow Nielsen to return to Denmark.
125. Tony Howard outlines Gade's role in the film and Ibsen's influence on her choice of career (143) and Lawrence Guntner suggests the possibility of the influence of Bernhardt's staging (92). Heinz Schall, Nielsen's old acquaintance in Denmark, may have assisted Gade with the direction, but this is not acknowledged in the original film credits.
126. David Kuhns notes that while Expressionist stagings had been undertaken before Reinhardt's preeminence, his rapid assimilation of new technologies of lighting and stage machinery (and especially his 1911 season of August Strindberg's plays) spearheaded a "transition from Naturalist to Expressionist staging" (see 96).
127. See Howard 145. In "'Remember Me'" Starks suggests that the experience of technology-induced trauma during World War I led to the acceptance and expansion of psychoanalysis, and astutely observes that the film's "expressionistic mode of melodrama" explored the irreconcilable aspects of Vining's thesis, contemporary history, German cinema, and psychoanalysis (see especially 185–192).
128. See Starks's "'Remember Me'" and Buchanan's *Shakespeare on Film* 62–64.
129. Although he entitles his article "Expressionist Shakespeare," Lawrence Guntner does note that Gade, often treated as a marginal figure, might have drawn on a range of influences including Reinhardt and Lubitsch, Expressionist cinema, and "Scandinavian" techniques for outdoor shooting (see 90). Although he was not associated with Swedish pictorialism (which was very outdoorsy before and during World War I), Gade, notes Howard, was known principally as a set designer and director of experimental theatre before this point, adding that after a sojourn in Hollywood he returned to Danish theatre (see 140–143). Nielsen hired both him and writer-researcher Erwin Gepard for the project.
130. See Thompson, *Herr Lubitsch* 21.

131. Although Guntner gives the film a Kracauerian reading (the younger generation destroys itself in resisting the corrupt older one), and even finds Nielsen's lean figure in black tights reminiscent of Cesare, the bare bodkin-wielding Somnambulist in *Caligari*, he records the accolades the film received from contemporaries in Europe and the United States (see 92–98), as does Howard (see 139–140, 142–143).
132. Kracauer, *From Caligari to Hitler* 94.
133. Arnheim 9.
134. Eisner also remarks that the actress she regarded as Nielsen's successor, Elisabeth Bergner, who came to the fore as one of Max Reinhardt's stars in his Shakespeare productions, also demonstrated similar abilities in such roles as Rosalind (see 197–199, 260). This has regrettably not survived in Czinner's static film.
135. Eisner 63–64.
136. Ibid. 260–262.
137. Ibid. 82.
138. Howard 144.
139. See *The Theory of the Film* 64–66.
140. Another confirmation that the film is not really an example of Expressionist filmmaking might be found in Patrice Petro's discussion of female spectatorship and the fashion for passive male characters in the Kammerspielfilm and the Street Film (see especially 153–219).
141. See Seidl's "Room for Asta."
142. Guntner 93.
143. See *The Mystery of Hamlet* 46–61.
144. See Howard 23.
145. Tony Howard offers an interesting commentary on the film. When the award-winning director Metin Erksan (a close associate of the dissident Yilmaz Güney) cast Turkey's leading activist-actress, Fatma Girik, as his Hamlet in *Intikam Malegi Kadin Hamlet* (1976), he departed from most conventions of filming Shakespeare. Borrowing from American genres and even spaghetti Westerns and soft-core films such as Russ Meyer's, Erksan even anticipated the later American Shakespeare exploitation films. Lady Hamlet conforms to the traditional "family" imperative of revenge but—having received a "modern" schooling—not to rural gender norms that emphasized female submissiveness. Yet unlike Nielsen, who plays up the gender anomalies, Girik's Ophelia counterpart is a weak male suitor, while Rosenkrantz and Guildenstern have become fashion-conscious playgirls (see 210–221).
146. See Guntner 92 and Howard 143–144.
147. See "The Screen" review of November 9, 1921.
148. See *Herr Lubitsch Goes to Hollywood* 12–16.
149. Ibid. 94.
150. Ibid. 21–22. Thompson observes that Lubitsch's assimilation of American studio lighting practice, in particular, was hastened first by his association with affiliates of American producers in Berlin and then by a 1921 visit to the United States with Davidson (see 22–24).
151. Ibid. 42, 45.
152. See Kreimeier 91–92.
153. See Buchanan 55.
154. See Usai 6–8.
155. Buchanan 65–66.
156. Dr. Sellmann's verbatim account in Berlin slang is reproduced in Lippmann (see 19–21), and it provides a vivid picture of Berlin's moviegoing in 1912: "'Othello, a Moor, comes home from great conquests. There he finds that his mistress—please sir, in the second row, get up and let the pretty lady pass—so he finds that one Mr. Rodrigo is chasing after her, which provokes the black fellow to go berserk with jealousy.—You, Madam, please quieten your child a bit—Now there is Mr. Jago, who stirs Othello up'...and on it goes, in fluently authentic street dialect...and for the Moor's shattering passion the good man employs the following words: 'Now look at the way the black chap eyes his pretty wife. You can detect that—the gentleman up front to the right, you sir, smoking is prohibited here—the Moor's jealousy has reached boiling point...Look at how she declares her innocence. But what does the black monster do?—I have to ask for silence at this gripping moment. Go to Luna Park if you want to laugh—so what does he do? He strangles the most beautiful image of femininity the earth has beheld. Look how she twitches one last time. And now she's dead.'"

157. See *Essay, Kritik* 275–277.
158. Clair is cited, with some liberty, by Ian Johnson 11–12.
159. See Kracauer 113–114 and Eisner 133–137.
160. Kracauer 170–172.
161. Eisner 136.
162. Isaacs 316–317.
163. Richard Wilson shows with a convincing wealth of example that *The Merchant of Venice* dealt specifically with the issue of Catholic recusancy, whereas in *Romeo and Juliet* Shakespeare commented on the consequences of religious extremism (his patrons, scions of the Montague family, educated their more promising sons in Rome; "Jewliet" was popular slang for Protestant, and so on). Shakespeare's transformation of Giovanni Fiorentino's Belmonte to Belmont might even have been a teasing pun on the lavish, upriver Sussex Palace of the Montagues, one well stocked with musicians, where the play might even have been performed (see 254–257).
164. Ball, *Shakespeare on Silent Film* 287. I should note that Rothwell holds it in higher regard (see 26).
165. Monique Pittman argues that the film's return to a "period" setting after a decade of "radicalized adaptive strategies" implicates an ideology of verisimilitude, a "correctness" of locale, language, and politics that requires considerable manipulations of both adapted text and "adapted" history (see "Locating the Bard").
166. See Ball, *Shakespeare on Silent Film* 287.
167. See Munday 113–180. Richard Wilson documents the extreme unlikelihood that Shakespeare had any sympathy for Munday's views, especially since Munday's testimony sent a number of Stratford residents to the torture chambers and gallows (see 71–73, 79–99). He adds that Shakespeare was in the habit of reading "hostile" sources carefully and of using them, perhaps even as a way of dissociating himself from the extreme actions of his Catholic kinsmen. For instance, Samuel Harsnett's *Declaration of Egregious Popish Impostures* supposedly revealed the satanic inspiration of the rituals practiced by followers of Thomas Campion (a Jesuit for some time concealed in the environs of Stratford) and by Shakespeare's executed neighbor Robert Debdale. Harsnett's phrases make their way into *Macbeth* and, especially, *King Lear*, and Wilson suggests that Shakespeare and his eager (sometimes recusant) readers used ridicule of the executed Jesuits and exorcists as a "smoke screen" for their own, more moderate, sympathies (see 186–205).
168. See Neil Taylor 268 and Anderegg, *Cinematic Shakespeare* 9.
169. See Horak's "Sauerkraut and Sausages" and Thompsson's *Herr Lubitsch* 15–16.
170. See Elsaesser, "Ethnicity, Authenticity, and Exile."
171. See especially Horak 243, 249, and Thompson's *Herr Lubitsch* 16.
172. See "Thou Dost Usurp Authority" 41–45.
173. For a more ample survey of the various stylistic permutations of Reinhardt's innumerable restagings, see Gary Williams 164–186.
174. See Kreimeier 17.
175. See See Lippmann 22 and Ball, *Shakespeare on Silent Film* 297.
176. See Russell Jackson's "Surprising Find" and Michael Jensen's "Fragments of *A Dream*."
177. The leading German Mefisto in Goethe's *Faust*, for example, Gustaf Gründgens, eagerly accepted the Nazis' appointment to head the Prussian State Theater in Berlin in 1934, where he transformed Hamlet into a ruthless and decisive revenger who would cleanse Denmark at any cost (see Symington 182–202); it is his ruthless prince who may be burlesqued by Lubitsch, and he became the subject of an extraordinary portrayal by Klaus Maria Brandauer in Istvan Szabo's *Mephisto* (1985).

Four Genre, Style, and the *Politique des Auteurs*: Orson Welles versus "William Shakespeare"

1. For example, Gherardo Casale devotes an important book to the argument that while Italian critical conceptions of Welles pictures him primarily as screen actor and filmmaker, Welles's multifarious career revolved around Shakespeare rather than cinema (he lists thirty-five distinct performances and adaptations between 1928 and 1985, and these do not even include some of the adaptations of adaptations for different media). The rise in Welles's

fortunes as Shakespearean is evident in Anderegg's admired monograph, and even Shakespeare scholars seem to concur in relocating Welles's films from the doghouse to what Kenneth Rothwell terms (in a chapter heading) the "art house."
2. Naficy's formulation revolves principally around filmmakers whose works bear the trace of traumatic movement from one system of industrial production to another, largely through involuntary departures from their homelands. Frequently, such filmmakers have addressed both the "new" audiences and those "left behind," so negotiating between systems of production (i.e., "interstitial" filmmaking as defined in *Home, Exile, Homeland* 125–150). Welles provides an interesting instance of an interstitial filmmaker who negotiated the intersections of Hollywood's model of production, the aesthetics of European art cinema, and the political consciousness of the movement characterized broadly by Teshome Gabriel and others as Third Cinema, as I have discussed in some detail in my introduction to *Rethinking Third Cinema* (see 1–28).
3. Many commentators have observed that Mario Camerini's and Fernando Poggioli's contemporary realist melodramas, and, of course, Luchino Visconti's *Ossessione* (1943), predate Rossellini's film in terms of the thematic matter and visual style associated with Neorealism. However, most writers on Italian cinema (such as Peter Bondanella, Millicent Marcus, Gianpiero Brunetta, and Pierre Sorlin) readily acknowledge the crucial impetus the film gave to the movement's emergence as the major European filmmaking practice of its time, its historical position underscored by its "documentary" references to the events of 1945.
4. See Welles 121.
5. Anderegg might also have included the Criterion laserdisc that preceded the drastic Castle Hill "restoration" of 1992. He does observe that according to Anthony Davies and Stanley Wells even the European releases differed substantially from each other, the BBC archives being in possession of a series of differing recensions. As he notes, Welles's conscious dispute with his own "text," as well as his conflation of Shakespeare and his source Giraldi Cinzio, might be taken to represent a "Postmodernist" sense of metatextuality.
6. See vii.
7. See Anderegg's *Orson Welles* 20–21.
8. Ibid. 21. Anderegg gives further examples of these influences: the austerities and monumentalism of Poel and Craig, for instance, in Welles's drawn set designs for *Twelfth Night* and *The Merchant of Venice* in *Everybody's Shakespeare*, not to mention the innovations of Henry Irving and David Belasco. Although Welles's audio edition of *Macbeth* for Columbia Records came after the famous Harlem *Voodoo Macbeth* of 1936, the recording and notes seem less adventurous, perhaps the result of having been rushed by the June 1940 start of scheduled shooting for *Citizen Kane*. Holinshed is pressed into service to fill in missing gaps in the text, while Beerbohm Tree's 1911 "archeological" production seems to have had a greater influence on the sketched sets than the experimental *Voodoo Macbeth* (see 44, 53). Casale also makes a case for the formative influence of Edward's theory of "Theatrical Theater," emphasizing the presence of the spectator and a self-referential anti-Naturalism indebted to Craig's conceptions (see especially 46–72).
9. Ibid. 23–24.
10. Decherny 141–143.
11. Ibid. 144.
12. His agreement to contribute his services gratis to Rockefeller's project was detailed in a later interview with Peter Bogdanovich (published as *This Is Orson Welles*), and this part rings true even if Welles improvises some of the other details (see 156–164).
13. Decherny 144–145.
14. On its connection to *Shadow of a Doubt* (1942), see Naremore (123–124). The film may also be a surprisingly direct criticism of the State Department's lax treatment of Nazi war criminals: the subject matter could not have been congenial to Washington.
15. In his admirable study of the role of the dialogue track in cinema (in which he argues convincingly that the human voice is privileged over music and sound effects), Michel Chion makes a rare mistake in describing what appears to be this film: "Elsewhere I have suggested the parallel between Orson Welles's work and the primary experience of the puppet theater, where the child projects his own voice. Remember that among Welles's projects was a film to be shot entirely in playback over prerecorded voices. The fact that he never realized this project may well be due to the technical problems posed by synching to the unstable flow of speech (while the flow of song is, in western music at least, metronomic and thus easier to follow)" (161). Welles's intent in *Macbeth* was to establish the rhythms of the film based on the dialogue track, inverting the traditional priority granted

the visual tracks (hence in strict accordance with the argument Anderegg makes for elevating Shakespeare films to the status of a genre). Despite critical condemnation, Welles's Scottish accents are rather less distracting than those adopted inconsistently by the actors in the minimalist Royal Shakespeare Company version of *Macbeth* (1979) as filmed by television director Philip Casson. For instance, one of the Weird Sisters seems all the weirder for sounding decidedly English. An actor in Branagh's parody of auditions in *A Midwinter's Tale*, permitted to try out an accent, hunches his back, dangles an arm, and affects broad MacWelles as he mangles Richard's first line.

16. Lindley 142–143.
17. Ibid. 143.
18. See 130–142. Willson does note, however, that for Columbia the budget was quite handsome and perhaps even a means of enhancing the studio's reputation by borrowing from Welles's high-cultural theatrical associations (see 131–132).
19. See Manvell, *Shakespeare and the Film* 58–59.
20. See Naremore, *The Magic World of Orson Welles* 136–139.
21. Bradley set these arguments out in a series of lectures on the four "Great Tragedies," *Hamlet*, *Othello*, *Lear*, and *Macbeth*, in which he tried to argue for the rationalism of Shakespeare's characters (see xxv, 286–287).
22. Kernan devotes his most convincing chapter on the previous effects of James's patronage of Shakespeare's company to "The Politics of Madness and Demonism," a discussion of the August 7, 1606 staging of *Macbeth* at Hampton Court (see 71–88). This is not to say that the play does not contain its author's customary explorations of ambiguity and epistemological paradox. Marienstras observes that L.C. Knights, writing in 1933, was among the first commentators to react against Bradley and his "school," and accepts his reading of the play as developing a series of insupportable antitheses: for Marienstras, Welles's "astonishingly real" witches go beyond either Bradley's dismissal of them or E.M.W. Tillyard's view of them as representatives of "an all-powerful providence...against which Macbeth struggles in vain" (see 80–81). Marienstras points out that the Weird Sisters' predictive ability, while appearing to exonerate Macbeth, defies the pure causality associated with a natural order whose representatives employ methods no different from theirs (86). But we would be mistaken in thinking that such a Shakespearean dialectic was a newfound Jacobean predilection. James Shapiro notes that Essex's Irish adventure runs through the Henriad, and the Chorus of *Henry V* not only mentions Essex but undermines some of the Tudor claims to martial glory. Essex's presence can also be felt in *Julius Caesar* composed later in 1599, and Shapiro's words seem to confirm Welles's intuitive sense of Shakespeare: "In *Julius Caesar* Shakespeare is not so much interested in drawing a one-to-one comparison—that was never his style—but in steeping classical history in contemporary political concerns" (129). Moreover, Shakespeare seldom failed to explore representational ambiguities in his late plays, and as Marjorie Garber argues (see especially 87–123), *Macbeth* could also have played to Jacobean gender anxieties, an element of the play Polanski and his Shakespeare-seasoned cowriter, Kenneth Tynan, emphasized by borrowing the castration-decapitation anxiety suffered by protagonists of Horror films.
23. As I note at greater length, both Donaldson and Deleuze have noted the centrality of self-multiplication to Welles's filmmaking in the device of the mirror.
24. Welles might have been the first stage and film director to render Macbeth the weak-willed and hapless victim of forces far greater than himself, but certainly not the last. Klaus Knoesel's *Rave Macbeth* (2003) boasts a psychedelic credit-sequence that hints at the psychotropic ingredients of its elixir of evil, but it actually demotes its "main" character to relative insignificance, turning the real antihero into a bearded, all-powerful Hecate, whose distant (though unlikely) inspiration could have been the Sorcerer character who leads the chorus of witches in Welles's *Voodoo Macbeth,* although it seems more likely that he may have spent some time in Eastwick studying Jack Nicholson's mannerisms. A Nietzschean projection of transcendent amorality, he keeps reappearing in a control room throughout the course of the action to command the three luscious witches charged with turning the film's Macbeth into an effective soul-stealing drug lord. Taking place entirely within the confines of a rave club, the film seems to exonerate the "accidental" human participants in the spread of evil by confining Macbeth's putsch to the Beer Hall (a lightly German-accented narrator acting as surrogate for the director informs us that Shakespeare might himself have resided in Darkest Scotland or, at the very least, been unaware of the Darkest Reginald Scot: "At a time when people didn't dare to doubt the magic power of wizards and witches, Shakespeare immortalized the story of Macbeth: a man who let himself be seduced by such [sic] forces into a dangerous game of power, madness, greed, and love"). Hecate's

all-but-unexplained rise to the top, on the other hand, seems incongruous in the light of recent textual analyses that suggest that he alone among the play's characters may not be Shakespeare's but a later Jacobean performative interpolation who crept into the only authoritative text we have, that of the (late) First Folio (see Greenblatt's notes in *The Norton Shakespeare* 2560).

25. Davies 87–90.
26. See Anderegg, *Orson Welles* 74–97. Anderegg has also noted perceptively, with a nod to the Frankfurt-based cultural critic Theodor Adorno, that most of Welles's post–*Citizen Kane* films were "attempts on his part to drive his gypsy wagon outside the great hall of the culture industry." As my reading of the film indicates, however, there are occult dimensions to the film that render its status as cultural object fairly complex despite the obvious traces of its genesis at Republic, and I would not agree that "*Macbeth*...was the last project he worked on that still remained within the hall, however much it strained to get out" (56). In Kurosawa's case, horses have premonitory instincts, imagery borrowed from Shakespeare's metaphors (as is, for instance, Polanski's bearbaiting). So too have the birds of ill omen, although Kurosawa metaphorically anticipates Hitchcock by transforming his feathered aggressors into the quills of arrows that eventually riddle the trapped Washizu.
27. I have treated the latter incident in more detail at the start of "Reconstituting *King John*," in which I also offer a contextualization of Welles and *auteur* filmmaking. Note that critics have tended to downplay the company's role in dramatizing rebellion, thus complacently accepting the "we did it for the money" explanation. In fact, prosecutor Francis Bacon used the statement made by Augustine Phillips, the players' spokesman (who emphasized the players' reluctance to restage an old play), to secure the capital conviction of one of the ringleaders of the rebellion, Gilley Meyrick (see, for instance, *The Norton Shakespeare* 3333).
28. The most comprehensive analysis of Olivier's visual metaphors of Hamlet's Oedipalism can be found in Donaldson's discussion of the film (see the chapter on "Olivier, Hamlet, and Freud" 31–67 in his *Shakespearean Films*).
29. See Anderegg's discussion in his book on Welles of *Life*'s exceptional vehemence (74).
30. Even this confusion of night and day has ample textual justification, as Nicholas Brooke points out, since staging night scenes through various means formed part of the elaborate Baroque stagecraft just being introduced into Jacobean theatrical practice (see 1–20).
31. As Carol Clover notes in *Men, Women and Chainsaws*, symbolic excess and the ungendering of the body have long remained integral to the Horror film.
32. See Roud 9.
33. See the entry in *The Norton Shakespeare* (3336–3337) which reproduces Forman's diary account.
34. There are other distinct references. As Michael Jeck observes in his commentary to the Criterion DVD edition of the film, the Forest Witch derives explicitly from the Yamauba (Woman of the Mountains) mask from the Mugen play *The Black Mound* (it is spelled Yamanba, the flesh-eating hag of the play *Kurozuka* in the English translation of Tadao Sato's interview with Kurosawa [see Manvell 103]).
35. Jeck also mentions that Olivier also had a hand in this *Macbeth*, although again his was a negative contribution: he probably did not realize that the great Kanto earthquake and the atomic explosions of Hiroshima and Nagasaki had left searing impressions on Kurosawa when he recommended that Asaji actually give birth to a deformed fetus, a suggestion that so incensed Kurosawa that he broke off the correspondence as I have mentioned earlier.
36. At its start Polanski's film appears to pay tribute to both Welles and Kurosawa. After the three physically differing Weird Sisters (characteristic of the woodcuts of such infernal triumvirates by Northern Renaissance artists of the order of Hans Baldung-Grien) utter their incantation and plot their meeting with Macbeth, a dense fog seems to roll in and obliterate a gruesomely audible battle, only to clear away magically to reveal the felling of the wounded. It is a vigorous, mounted Duncan who promises to reward the victorious Macbeth as he wrests the chain of office from the bound and prostrate Cawdor's neck with the tip of his drawn sword. Only now do we see Macbeth on a different field, overseeing the hanging of struggling captives. He rides off with Banquo, and presently they encounter the Weird Sisters and have their futures foretold, predictions to which they initially react with mirth. As in Welles's film, no sooner do Macbeth and Banquo rest than the former begins to soliloquize in voice-over (a technique used to an extraordinary degree in the early part of the film). By the time Macbeth places Cawdor's chain of office—given to him by Ross—on his neck, he too mixes spoken thoughts and voice-over. But these are not the only evident borrowings. Fleance's mellifluous minstrelsy at the banquet celebrating Macbeth's ascension reprises the set-piece

song that had brought the Capulet Ball to a halt in Zeffirrelli's recent blockbuster *Romeo and Juliet.* A point of characterization in which Polanski deviates markedly from his predecessors is the obvious affection that Macbeth and Lady Macbeth initially share (not unlike that of Welles's Othello and Desdemona), and Polanski's rich palette of colors not only serves to create a textured sense of a world contemporary to Shakespeare's but also the world of the contemporary historical Horror film. Rumor has it that Polanski's vivacious Lady Macbeth was not an innovation, and that Olivier objected to Vivien Leigh playing Welles's Lady Macbeth; despite a keen and initially comical rivalry, their relationship was founded on immense mutual respect, and Olivier later went out of his way to salvage Welles's theatrical fortunes by commissioning him to direct Ionesco's *Rhinoceros* (in which he starred in the 1960 English Stage Company production). There exists, also, a smiling photograph of Olivier backstage greeting Welles during the 1960 Irish run of the theatrical *Chimes at Midnight.*

37. See Welles and Bogdanovich 143. In his biography of Welles, Frank Brady tantalizingly mentions a "correspondence" between Welles and Eisenstein, but reproduces only one telegram in which the latter informs the producer Alexander Korda that Welles would be an ideal Bezhukov in *War and Peace,* but that Eisenstein is too busy working on *Ivan the Terrible* to participate (vii, 357–358).
38. See Eisenstein's 1929 essay "The Fourth Dimension in Cinema" (116–117) for his definitions of metric and rhythmic montage. Welles is one of Deleuze's chief exhibits in defense of his idea of multiple time frames and time crystals in films (see 68–97).
39. See *A History of Shakespeare on Screen* 71.
40. In his *History,* Rothwell suggests that the editing structure (or découpage) of *Othello* as exemplified by the funeral procession is "cliché Eisenstein" (see 77), but, in fact, no completed Eisenstein film before *Alexander Nevsky* uses such an editing system: even here Welles engages with Eisenstein rather than merely borrowing from him, dynamic montage being interspersed with extended deep-focus compositions. With regard to Eisenstein's view of Shakespeare, it is more than coincidental that his contemporary, Bakhtin, took a parallel position, in that he avoided the commonplace endorsement of Shakespeare as universal genius and strove, instead, to point out that his literary impulse (like that of Rabelais) grew out of Renaissance folk culture. Pasolini's cinematic treatment of this argument is dealt with in the context of intertextuality in the final chapter.
41. See *The Eisenstein Reader* 146–149.
42. Reviewing the first part of *Ivan the Terrible,* Agee remained singularly undeceived about Eisenstein's situation in Soviet Russia: "For years, as everyone knows, Eisenstein has been working as if in prison, under the supervision of jailers who are not only peculiarly dangerous and merciless but also as sudden to change their minds as minnows their direction... I hardly know which seems the more tragic: the possibility that he is still essentially a free man, his own master, doing the best he can under annihilating difficulties, or the possibility that he accepts the crucifixion and has helped drive in such nails as, in that predicament, he could manage" (250).
43. Noting that later readings of *The Tempest* have tended to treat the Prospero-Caliban relationship as the axial one of the play, Steven Dillon points out that Jarman foregrounds the homosocial undertones of the relationship between Prospero and Ariel. He hints that the alchemy of desire (Prospero's magic as exercised on the other characters and the audience) drew Jarman to the play, the director already having been a student of the celebrated Renaissance scholar of the occult, Frances Yates (see 90–93).
44. Note his observations in "On the Fourth Dimension of Cinema" (111–123).
45. See Eisenstein, *Film Sense* 157–216, and especially the illustration appended between pages 175 and 176.
46. Ibid. 161–162.
47. The convergence between Macbeth's thoughts and the Weird Sisters' prophetic utterances becomes apparent as the film progresses: when, for instance, in a Lear-like moment he rushes out into a storm amidst flashes of lightning and demands an audience with the "black and midnight hags," his subsequent dialogue takes place with their disembodied voices, a spotlight illuminating him as the light around him fades to black. While Lear's exposure to the elements augments his awareness of the condition of the wretched, the witches' warnings only deceive Macbeth further.
48. Despite its brevity the "Statement on Sound" remains one of Eisenstein's best-known theoretical arguments and one that he revisited often (see 80–81).
49. See *This Is Orson Welles* 207.
50. Welles's hastily acquired prop might have yet another explanation. At the time of the film's release, a number of those against whom *Macbeth* takes aim, particularly Hoover, were enjoying a halcyon period. The latter, in particular, took intense delight in pursuing those who, like Welles, openly

acknowledged being "Liberal" (Welles had himself aroused intense suspicion by speaking on behalf of opening a second front during the German army's siege of Leningrad, although Welles's liberality was more well intentioned than consistent). In Welles's films of the period (such as the 1946 *The Stranger*), Welles seems to take simultaneous aim at the slack postwar treatment of Nazis and at the gathering forces soon to march under the banner of Senator Joseph McCarthy and his minions, such as Hoover's informant (and McCarthy's right-hand man) in the anti-Communist witch hunts, Roy Cohn. In the aptly titled *Citizen Cohn*, Nicholas von Hoffman provides a detailed account of Cohn's methods, including his proud boasts about suborning the perjury of David Greenglass that assured the 1953 death sentence for his sister, Ethel Rosenberg (a cause célèbre for the Left).

51. Of course the concept of exile in its multitude of forms has been the subject of intense study of late, and Welles's own singular aesthetic expressions of the manifestation of exile he experienced conform well to what Hamid Naficy describes as the multifariousness of exilic discourse ("All displaced people do not experience exile equally or uniformly. Exile discourse thrives on detail, specificity, and locality. There is a there *there* in exile" [*Home, Exile, Homeland* 4]). Later in the same anthology John Peters adds: "Nothing is more dispersed in intellectual life today than the concept of diaspora, nothing more nomadic than the concept of nomadism." While for him "exile" suggests "painful banishment" and "pining for home," the collective condition of "diaspora" suggests simultaneous migration with resultant "networks among compatriots" living outside their points of origin. "Nomadism" dispenses altogether with the "idea of a fixed home or center" (see 18–20). Although it is beyond the scope of the present work to analyze Welles's most elaborate meditations on the subject, *Mr. Arkadin* (1955, a film much admired by Godard) and *The Immortal Story* (1968, also featuring Jeanne Moreau), it will suffice to say that *Othello* and *Chimes* exemplify the gradual shift in his relations to the idea of "home" (i.e., Hollywood), a reversal of the normal course of such distancing: what seems to begin as voluntary nomadism gradually turns into something akin to self-imposed exile, and eventually to capitulation and a return to television commercials and an inner exile in his "homeland." In trying to generalize his mercurial progress, I use "exile" as a general term describing Welles's situation at any given time.

52. Biographers such as Simon Callow have been placed in an awkward position by emphasizing Welles's apparent pigment envy, compounded by his evident partiality to women with dark complexions (see Callow 226–228, 244–245). But the criticisms tend to be anachronistic projections of (quite justifiable) present-day objections to derogatory racial impersonations. Interestingly, despite the Holocaust of the Nazi period, similar objections have not been made about Gentile actors impersonating Shylock, a matter well worth considering and which I have touched on in the first chapter.

53. The most legitimate objection to race-based casting is, I think, made rather eloquently by Liz White by the very example of her *Othello* of 1980 that boasts a versatile all-black cast (see Donaldson, *Shakespearean Films* 127–143): if the principle of racial typing is adhered to in the interests of an artificial verisimilitude, then it debars most nonwhite actors from the majority of the classical and newly scripted roles, as has demonstrably been the case in such centers of industrial film production as Hollywood.

54. That Welles's public concerns had not deserted him even as late as the mid-1970s is apparent in an aside in *Filming Othello*, which uses a number of Moroccan extras (most prominently two blind singers). "While we were sitting there in Mogador the idea came to us that we could make our costumes—which had never been made in Rome, or if they had were being held by the Sheriff—by using the local Jewish tailors, of which there were several. There was a big Jewish quarter in Mogador and they lived, incidentally, very happily with the Arabs [pausing and turning to face the camera]; in those happy bygone days. And so the Jewish tailors were hired and pictures of Carpaccio gentlemen and ladies were shown them and pretty soon the costumes slowly began to be made; but they would not be ready for ten days, and what could we shoot?"

55. As Richard Dyer, for one, notes (see 64–136), Robeson's star image and his access to "white cultural spaces" were intimately associated with his physical characteristics. His outsize personality and diversity of talents were so prodigious as to be almost beyond belief, but it was also significant that these talents were framed in a visual ideal celebrated by artists ranging from the sculptor Jacob Epstein, who sought in a portrait bust to capture the tragic dignity of his race, to the photographer Nickolas Muray, whose prints transformed him into a "black-is-beautiful" poster boy. As such he posed the supreme threat to the segregationist social order that Hoover, in particular, upheld to his own advantage.

56. It seems almost superfluous to note that Welles's most characteristic films noir, *The Stranger*, *The Lady from Shanghai*, *Othello*, and *Touch of Evil*, all test the limits of their respective generic configurations.

57. See, in particular, the chapter on "the Improvisation of Power" in *Renaissance Self-fashioning* (222–254). On his Web page "Curiosities of Biological Nomenclature: Etymologies" (http://home.earthlink.net/~misaak/taxonomy/taxEtym.html), Mark Isaak claims that a quartet of recently named giant Hawaiian spiders bear the names Orsonwelles othello, O. macbeth, O. falstaffius, and O. ambersonorum, which if true, seems to lend my hypotheses an exceptional degree of scientific validity.
58. Just as Kurosawa, in a moment of inspiration, borrows from *Hamlet*, Welles, in desperation (Scalera's promised costumes were still in Italy), reflexively turned to the same play, albeit representing Polonius's end from his point of view.
59. See *The Time-Image* 68–70 and Peter Donaldson, *Shakespearean Films* 93–126.
60. Peter Donaldson, *Shakespearean Films* 122.
61. For Deleuze's examples see 70, but the entire section on time crystals might serve better for context (see 68–97). Welles, incidentally, borrows and elaborates on the multiple mirror trick played by his friend, the even more hapless victim of Hoover's FBI, Charlie Chaplin, who places it in its most natural milieu in *The Circus* (1928).
62. See *Film Sense* 68–109.
63. Ibid. 72–74.
64. Ibid. 81–83, 86–93.
65. Ibid. 101–102.
66. By way of comparison, see Jorgens 175–176.
67. Ibid. 180. Welles owes quite a bit to Boito's cutting of lines and making Cypress the epicenter of the action, and to Verdi's sharply differing musical styles for Iago and Othello (deceptive trills and growled cadences for Iago; lush, if increasingly despairing melodies for Othello and Desdemona). The music was originally to be taken from Verdi's opera, but Welles persuaded Francesco Lavagnino (also the principal composer of the Walton-like score for *Chimes at Midnight*) and Alberto Barberis to provide a freshly minted score. It demands a chorus that sings on vowels, at times producing the fearsome dissonances characteristic of Modernist compositions (outdoing even Maurice Ravel's *Daphnis et Chlöe* in this regard). Notable, for instance, are the polytonal bursts of sound announcing Othello's rending of the curtain of Desdemona's bedchamber with the intent of smothering her. Although his reputation was for ever tarnished by Pushkin as Mozart's jealous poisoner, Antonio Salieri created a large number of comic operas, among them a *Falstaff* (1799) based on *The Merry Wives of Windsor* pared down to three ruses, with occasional lines taken from other plays. The measure of its influence on Boito's more ample libretto, which still presents Falstaff in a major key, is difficult to ascertain. Welles proceeds in the opposite direction in *Chimes*, concentrating on the Henriad and except for the scenes of merriment diminishing the presence of the ill-fitting occasional comedy.
68. The exigencies of filming led to a number of changes of Desdemona, and Suzanne Cloutier gives a cloyingly sweet performance that, if the comments in *Filming Othello* are to be believed, Welles could not have found entirely satisfactory. Much has been made by critics of the film's "masculine" perspectives, and it is a common error to regard the characters Welles's portrayed as autobiographical extensions. Among the most common misconceptions is that Welles's sympathetic portrayal of Othello implies subscription to his character's masculine aggression. In *Filming Othello* a discussion of jealousy as the play's central motivating force leads to an extended rejoinder to Edwards's observation that in literature female jealousy is always comical: "I would say that the reason for that is that all dramatic literature that we know about has been written under patriarchal, male-dominated societies, for males, in which the final decision in all matters belongs to the male. What can be the problem of a woman if she is jealous or not since she is owned?" Edwards: "Therefore, I should be sympathetic with the public's attitude at laughing at the cuckold. I am not so." Welles [raising his voice]: "Because the public is partly female, and the public sees the essential comedy in the situation." They then go on to discuss the different manifestations of jealousy in men and women, Welles contending that women translate jealousy into hate, while Othello remains "a perfect male type," in that he will "kill Desdemona adoring her. Now isn't that male? Isn't that enormously masculine: to murder this girl adoring her? No woman would do that." To MacLiammóir he adds: "Desdemona is no cringing blonde. She is not a born loser. If she dies a loser, it's no fault of her own." In discussing Iago's strategies he later declares: "[T]here really isn't any reason to speak of Othello, as some critics do, as childishly simple…Small wonder that the doubt falls where it usually does in life, not on the slanderer but on the innocent object of the slander."
69. This interpolated "O" of wounded and betrayed sexuality reappears as the story of a different "O," an *Othello* that translates out-of-placeness into competitive teenage jealousy and sexual angst

in Tim Blake Nelson's 2001 film *O*. A high school dean, standing in for the Venetian patriciate and not just Brabantio, reluctantly permits his daughter, Desi, to consort with the school's (black) star basketball player, Odin James. The oval "O" of the title provides a number of images, but it is a mirror of that shape that causes an abrupt change in Odin. Having succumbed easily to the insinuations of the jealous son of the team coach, Hugo, an anxious Odin takes Desi up on her offer to let him have her "any way" he wants; but on seeing his own reflection change to that of the Cassio figure, Michael, he reacts with such violence that Desi pleads futilely for him to stop. A cut to roosting white doves seems a metaphor of un-Wellesian obviousness, but the preceding sequence makes the provenance of the imagery clearer, for Hugo "thanks" Emily for having stolen Desi's scarf for him by spreading it over her face and kissing her through it as he makes love, a reference to the culmination of Welles's film. Moreover, the secondary theme of rivalry between an underachieving real son and an unlikely, but glittering "false" son (the Iago, "Hugo,") finds his coach father's preference for Odin intolerable) resembles the father-son mirrorings of *Chimes*.

70. In a conversation with Juan Cobos and Miguel Rubio, Welles admitted occasional lapses into "demagoguery," as when he would on occasion attempt to win over skeptical audiences by "admitting" that Shakespeare could not be filmed adequately. He also makes revealing comments about realism and stylization in terms of decor, the pictorial expression of an inner rhythm in the film, about his interpretation of Falstaff as "the greatest conception of a good man" in all drama, and about the scenes deleted in the cutting room (see 255–266).

71. Bosley Crowther proved characteristically hostile, and the film failed when it opened in New York, but French critics appreciated its merits immediately. Dudley Andrew, making note of the use of sound, was not alone in arguing (in 1984) that it is "perhaps the greatest adaptation of Shakespeare that the cinema has yet produced" (see 321).

72. Although much of the substance of the plot derives from *I Henry IV*, the prevailing mood of *Chimes* is that of *2 Henry IV*, which emphasizes the warts of Falstaff's portrait and lends the film its "pervasive concern with the passing of time" (a comment made by Jean Howard in the prefatory remarks to the play in *The Norton Shakespeare* 1295).

73. See Welles and Bogdanovich 259–261.

74. Ibid. 337. Frank Brady suggests that Welles and Hemingway even planned a joint homage to the matador Antonio Ordóñez, with Welles as director-narrator and Hemingway as writer, but that plans did not proceed beyond a contentious dinner (424).

75. In this context see Stanley Payne's *The Spanish Civil War, the Soviet Union, and Communism,* and Stephen Koch's *Hemingway, Dos Passos and the Murder of José Robles*.

76. Carlos Saura, one of the architects of the New Spanish Cinema of the 1970s and 1980s commented that "[t]he peculiar conditions of our country, the difficulties in telling things directly, on a 'first level' as the French say, have obliged us to search for other systems of narrating—more indirect systems. Naturally, as a result of having to go around in circles to tell what I want to tell, my head has been pushed into a mental exercise that has proved very useful" (cited in Bartholomew 28).

77. Bridget Lyons suggests that the cumulative effect of the extraordinarily high number of shots Welles juxtaposes is to diminish whatever glory might be associated with battle, a theme taken up by Kenneth Branagh (see Lyons 14).

78. The narrator next speaks at the conclusion of the Battle of Shrewsbury, when a shot of armored knights riding forth dissolves into a low-angle shot showing eight corpses hanging from gibbets. His confident words are: "[F]rom the first, King Henry's reign was troubled with rebellion. But in the Year of Our Lord, 1408, the last of his enemies had been vanquished. The King held his Christmas this year in London, being sore vexed with sickness."

79. See *An Accented Cinema* 13.

80. Ibid. 24.

81. See Andrew's "Echoes of Art" and Anderegg's "Every Third Word a Lie."

82. Ruiz's choice may not be for color alone, and it appears to symbolize Richard's mental preparation to "sterilize" the royal line that stands in the way of his crown, the cyclamen and its medicinal properties no doubt being part of Shakespeare's extensive herbal knowledge. A beautiful illustration of the plant exists in a copy of Leonart Fuchs's *De Historia Stirpium* once owned by a contemporary of Shakespeare's, the assiduous plantsman Henry Dineley. Dineley lived a little downstream on the Avon in the parish of Cropthorne, and even visited Stratford when Shakespeare was a boy. His sustained search for English examples of Fuchs's herbs and his tests of their medicinal properties survive in his annotated copy, now housed at the Folger Shakespeare library. See, also, Anna Pavord's discussion of cyclamen in *The Naming of Names* 33–34.

83. Early in his important collection of essays, *The Poetics of Cinema*, Ruiz observes that, even when he was eighteen, he could not accept a dogma later pounded into him in film schools—that the ideal of cinema was distraction and that distraction was best accomplished by central conflict. Among the deficiencies of central conflict theory are the insistence on a direct relationship between the will, which, he writes, "is to me some thing dark and oceanic," and the "petty play around strategies and tactics around a goal which, if not in itself banal, is certainly rendered so" (11). Gloucester's goal-directedness is thus not an overarching plot conceit, but simply an extreme version of the self-interest that governs the actions of the other characters who oppose or cooperate with him to further their own competing motivations.
84. Bahktin argues that the forms of popular or, more precisely, folk culture play a more determinative role on high culture than the reverse, and that the process of "novelization" occurs as cultures (high, low, and other) interact. Thus, the carnivalesque send-up of the norms of high culture very often insinuate themselves into high culture as in the case of the literary production of Rabelais and Shakespeare (in this context, see especially *Rabelais and His World* and Bakhtin's response to an interviewer of the journal *Novy Mir* found in *Speech Genres* 4–5).
85. In an interview included in an issue of *Positif* devoted to Welles, Keith Baxter notes Welles's own emphasis of the father-son theme in the film (see 29). Both David Bordwell and Ace Pilkington have argued against "seeing Falstaff as Hal's victim" (Pilkington 154) on the grounds that Welles's portrayal of Falstaff is ironic, an argument I do not dispute but instead recontextualize (see especially Pilkington 130–155).
86. Lévi-Strauss introduced the idea of bricolage in *The Savage Mind* (1962), one of the foundational works of Structuralism. Often misused, the term specifically allows for technical competence stemming from improvisation and intuition (i.e., knowledge that precedes the scientific know-how of the craftsman), a function he also grants to mythic narrative. Georges Méliès furnishes him with a modern example of bricolage (see 16–22).
87. As Naremore remarks of Hank Quinlan in *Touch of Evil*, Welles uses "the puffy, big-nosed plainness of a lower class W.C. Fields" to very good effect, his disintegrating face and bulging contours often filling the frame (see *The Magic World of Orson Welles* 151).
88. John Donne uses the sphere as a "classical" metaphor both for divine perfection and all that the world encompasses ("Let mans Soule be a Spheare" he implores in his poem "Good Friday, 1613. Riding Westward" 246–247). The symbolism was well recognized by Karl Jung and others interested in archetypes. Gaston Bachelard thus corrects Karl Jaspers's statement that "every being seems in itself round," avoiding the tautology of "being" and "seeming" with "being is round" (see 232–234). Welles's roundness contains two worlds—the obvious metaphor of microcosm as macrocosm—but also self-reference as a synecdoche for the world of independent filmmaking. Bakhtin's corresponding idea is that essential human culture, for which his term is "folk culture," is also circular, governed by the passage of the seasons and the cycles of life—the premodern England to which Welles's Falstaff belongs.
89. See *Orson Welles* 126.
90. I provide a more comprehensive treatment of the various issues pertaining to adaptations of Shakespeare and of notions of authorship in "Thou dost usurp authority."
91. See *François Truffaut and Friends* vii.
92. Ibid. 102. The portrayal of Catherine as the promiscuous individual in a love triangle occasions from Stam the comment that this exchange between Truffaut and Godard constitutes "a rather extreme case of *mauvaise foi*" (see 103). Godard's idiosyncratic vision of normality, his rewriting of film history on the basis of stylistic distinction (a theme he has subsequently explored in greater detail), and his tribute to Welles coalesce in *King Lear*.
93. Chabrol's radicalism notwithstanding, Greenblatt attempts a reading of Shakespeare's play in *Hamlet in Purgatory* that retrospectively grants a critical validity to Olivier's interpretation of a protagonist who suffers equally from Freud's sexual neuroses and Marx's Messiah complex. Olivier might not have studied Freud, but he later spoke of his debt to the British Freudian Ernest Jones. Jones's book *Hamlet and Oedipus* (1949) appeared after the film did, and may be an attempt to capitalize on the film's success. Yet as early as 1910, Jones attempted to build on Freud's innovations in applying psychoanalysis to the study of "genius and artistic creativity" (72), and, in fact, he claims to expand Freud's footnote about Hamlet in the 1900 edition of *The Interpretation of Dreams* in furnishing his comprehensive account in which he also concedes an awareness of Vining's "extravagance" (see 74). Jones dismisses the possibility that Hamlet is by nature hesitant (again following Freud) or that he felt qualms about avenging his murdered father, and that his false excuses for his hesitancy to kill

his uncle (about which he agonizes) are the result of "*specific aboulia*" (86–87)—in the 1948 book revised as manic depression or hysteria on a cyclothymic basis—because his uncle has seized the opportunity to take his father's place (99). He relates this to Shakespeare's biography about which he provides a more complete account in the later book (in which he emphasizes Shakespeare's identification with his character). In time Olivier became aware of his Hamlet's narcissism, and much of the wit of *Richard III* derives from the parodic degradation of his own heroic image.

94. Chabrol's is by no means the only approach to a "New Wave" Shakespeare in the 1960s. The New Wave's sweep was immediate and it broke on British shores almost immediately (evoked splendidly, for instance, by Richard Lester in his films showcasing the Beatles). In addition to a highly sexualized fairy kingdom whose Puck (played by Ian Holm) seems to restore Reinhardt's original animal conception of the role, Peter Hall's *A Midsummer Night's Dream* (1968), made at the height of the *auteur* movement, seems to borrow a highly fragmented editing style, coupled with continuous narrative and elaborate camera movements that seem to pay tribute to Godard and Truffaut without departing from Shakespeare's lines. The film is particularly fortunate in splendid performances by its actresses, each associated with a particular use of the camera: Diana Rigg's Helena is shot with a handheld moving camera, a technique beloved of Godard; Judi Dench's longer speeches appear to be divided almost line by line with jump cuts, another Godardian tactic; and Helen Mirren's Hermia seems to be pictured almost entirely in close-up almost until the muddied lovers interact. The mud and the opening images of rain suggest the wet summers that critics have used to attribute a date to the play, but the anachronisms of dress (or in the case of Dench undress) certainly pay tribute to avant-garde cinema and no doubt influenced the still more sexually aware television production by Celestino Coronado (the extraordinary Mirren, incidentally, plays both Ophelia and Gertrude in Coronado's 1976 *Hamlet*).

Five Six Authors in Search of a Text: The Shakespeares of Van Sant, Branagh, Godard, Pasolini, Greenaway, and Luhrmann

1. See Miola 23.
2. Ibid.
3. Ibid. 23–24. At the margin of this argument lies the thorny issue of responsible and irresponsible critical conjecture, especially because the reader of a Shakespeare film reads another's reading of a play. For example, would I, knowing of Branagh's competitive familiarity with the films of his predecessors, venture too far in suggesting that, while the images of crucifixion that keep appearing in Olivier's *Hamlet* suggest a Catholic reading of the play, the bare crosses that keep reappearing behind the heads of Beatrice and Benedick in *Much Ado* imply a post-Reformation interpretation? Is the suspicion I harbor, that Taymor's *homage* in *Titus* (2000) to Greenaway has the grotesque comedy of the Vincent Price effect in its background, a false one? (Recall that one of murders committed by rejected-thespian-turned-revenger Lionheart models itself on Titus's cannibal feast, and that Price's disguise is the same cook's costume.)

Taymor's consciously millennial film, in which she felt ethically constrained not only to address the Fascist violence of the twentieth century but also to change Shakespeare's ending (whose spirit informed her earlier theatrical adaptation) for a redemptive one suggesting hope for future generations, has, precisely because of its overt allusiveness, attracted intense critical scrutiny. The chef's attire sported by Anthony Hopkins, for instance, is even more reminiscent of that Peter Greenaway's Cook preparing a similar cannibal feast in the 1989 *The Cook, The Thief, His Wife and Her Lover* than of Price's. She playfully invokes Kurosawa's *Komonosu-djo* when showers of anachronistic longbow arrows dispatched by Goth troops fall ineffectually on the orgiasts in Saturninus's imperial palace, a scene that starts out in imitation of Federico Fellini's 1969 *Satyricon*, the latter indebted both to the presence of set designer Dante Ferretti who had worked on that film and to her use of a studio in the vast Roman Cinecittà complex initially set up in the cause of Mussolini's Fascist regime but soon overtaken by the likes of the left-leaning Italian Neorealists. Yet another scene, perhaps the most profoundly referential and paralogically complex, has continued to perplex critics. Titus, tricked by Aaron into sacrificing his left hand as an offering for the lives of his two sons, is again deceived when transformed into a seated spectator as the remains of both hand and sons are delivered to him. David McCandless describes it this way: "In the fourth [of Taymor's penny arcade nightmare sequences], a derelict biker-clown pulls a wagon functioning as a mobile arcade, framed by the ubiquitous red velvet curtains, and, after grotesquely dancing about and manically promoting his 'show' like a demented carny barker, he unveils the severed heads of Titus's two sons and the hand Titus severed to ransom them" (495, 500), and Lucian Ghita compares it to "a cinematic mock ritual that parodies the street puppet shows of fin de siècle France and Italy" (see the opening of "Reality and Metaphor"). It is, in fact, an overt allusion to a scene in Fellini's film *La Strada* (1954), even to the extent of mimicking the jaunty musical track provided by his longtime collaborator, Nino Rota, a reference also to the film's position in the history of cinema. *La Strada* also happened to be an early and unusual example of the international casting that Taymor associates with the age of globalization (hence the presence of Hollywood star Jessica Lang, in addition to mixed European cast): at Fellini's insistence Hollywood star Anthony Quinn took the role of Zampanò, although it is Giulietta Masina, as Gelsomina, who stole the show— quite literally, in this scene, since the comical duck-shooting routine Zampanò has trained her to perform as a prelude to his own feats of chain-snapping delights the spectators gathered near the rickety, motorized contraption in which they travel from one village to another. Fellini emphasizes Gelsomina's comic pathos by making her at times resemble Charlie Chaplin's Tramp, but Taymor need not have looked further for a cinematic model of tragicomedy. In the scenes that precede the circus clown and strongman routine, we see Zampanò first buy and then rape Gelsomina, eventually training her to perform comic routines by insulting and even beating her.

Taymor may even have had the furor the film caused in mind when she decided to allude to the overdone theatricality of this scene, in that she consciously rejected realism as an adequate way to present Titus the heads of his sons. Italy's most eminent critic of the period, the Marxist Guido Aristarco, accused *La Strada* of lacking the reality of everyday life and of betraying the Neorealist project of presenting collective struggles in favor of "the poetry of the solitary man," while Bazin wrote to praise the film's stylistic command. Critics such as Peter Bondanella see *La Strada* as the definitive break with Neorealism, heralding the emergence of a group of important Italian *auteurs* who enjoyed a similar prominence to those of the concurrent French New Wave (see *Italian Cinema* 134–137). Fully aware that the most viable alternative to megabudget Hollywood Shakespeare is no longer poverty-row Neorealism, but one that involves such concessions to popular taste as the use of star actors and at least the pretense of high production values, Taymor's simulated theatre-within-film that harks back to Olivier's evocation of the Globe and to Kurosawa's use of Noh drama, while looking forward to the digital age in which the skilled artisanry of Fellini's set designers in re-creating the decadence of the Roman imperium achieves the high classicism of a medium millennially self-conscious of its own barbarization.

4. Ibid. 24–37.
5. Ibid. 28.
6. See *Orson Welles* 123.
7. Ibid.
8. This is not a chance observation: Vertov, after whom Godard named a period of his oeuvre as part of a filmmaking collective, was according to David Sterritt one of the three fundamental influences on him together with the obvious one of Brecht and the much less obvious Mao Zhe Dong, one that has (if present at all) surely been in abeyance.
9. Miola 31. Note also the paralogism of of Branagh's homage-parody of Castellaniesque sartorial opulence and Kurosawan *shakai-mono* seriousness in *As You Like It* (2007).
10. Drowning acquires a metaphysical context in Greenaway' films, but here his water cosmology is quasi-Vedic, the element being at once a vivifying force that invigorates the instinctual and a destructive one that threatens to engulf civilization and knowledge.
11. See Rosenbaum 170.
12. In his brief, sympathetic account of the film's production and (non)reception, Wheeler Winston Dixon notes that Godard had a penchant for squabbling with his lead actors (even those as accomplished as Gérard Depardieu) and for recycling the spent footage once the star stormed off (see 5, 172–176).
13. Barthes, *Camera Lucida* 92–93.
14. Ibid 25–27. I have treated Barthes's work in relation to Benjamin and the emergence of early documentary filmmaking in the article "The Birth of a New Realism." In contrast to the normal practice of his famously elliptical style, Barthes defines *studium* and *punctum* as they apply to each of his distinctions, and while I have summed up his general intent in "Birth," I would point

out that his most encompassing definition comes as a revelation near the end of his essay: "At [the beginning of this book] I thought that I could distinguish between a field of cultural interest (the *studium*) from that unexpected flash that sometimes crosses this field and that I called the *punctum*. I now know there exists another *punctum*...no longer of form but of intensity...Time, the lacerating emphasis of the *noeme* ("*that-has-been*"), its pure representation" (93–94).
15. Ibid. 95–96.
16. I should mention in passing the respect that Godard accords to silence. Kaja Silverman and Haroun Farocki have noted Godard's experiment in *Vivre Sa Vie* (*My Life to Live* 1962), of reversing the normal emphases of sound cinema—where the moving image and dialogue tracks dominate—so that "every sound and image is equal" (2). In *King Lear* Godard grants just such an importance to silences and, at times, to the lack of the "expected" images.
17. It is beyond the scope of the present work to pronounce on the heated scholarly debate as to whether Godard is a late Modernist keeping alive a faith (stigmatized by some critics as elitist) in the socially redemptive potentials of cinema, or a postmodernist because of his use of such techniques as intertextual collage or pastiche, his valorization of media widely associated with "pop culture," and his apparent acceptance of what Jean Baudrillard would later term simulation (signs referring only to other signs and emptied of fixed or real referents). Marcia Landy argues that, "Godard's radical investigation of the cinema introduces 'reflection into the image itself.'" But that this is not mere reference to the formal features of artistic production but a "larger essay into the conditions of possibility, if any, for a cinema of thought, belief, and action" (29): in other words, Godard thematizes the crisis of cinema's late Modernism. Analyses by Peter Wollen (see especially 155–175), Yosefa Loshitsky, Susan Bennett, and Nicholas Paige confirm that a recurrent conundrum addressed early in his career remains unresolved, as might be deduced from Godard's extensive, disjointed, and evolving oeuvre.
18. Brian Price, for instance, notes that early in the film Godard binds together a seemingly paratactic series of found stills with a syntactically coherent string of words "The Lords of Imperialism have Transformed Technological Progress and Sexuality into Instruments of Repression" (see 68).
19. Ibid. 66, 68.
20. Price has observed that Godard's practice of taking familiar images out of context and using them repeatedly in differing associations in *Le Gai Savoir* consciously mimics the Situationist strategy of "detournement," but that the plagiarism of the plagiarists while adhering to his established stylistic repertoire actually functions as a critique of their rejection of authorship.
21. See Godard 71.
22. Ibid. 79–80.
23. During the late 1960s and early 1970s he and Pier Paolo Pasolini, collaborators in *RoGoPaG* (1963), developed opposed notions about the nature of signs in the cinema. However, Godard's commentary on the semiotics of word and image in *King Lear* treats even symbolic signs as part of a language system, in that signs are modified by the signs adjacent to them (icons in paintings, shot relations in film, and so on), a concept Pasolini termed "contamination." Observe that here the narrator's words function analogously to the opening sentences of Jacques Derrida's "The Law of Genre," when he states, "Genres should not be mixed. I will not mix genres." Here, too, Godard "plays" with the idea of the postmodern.
24. See especially Jameson's discussion in *Postmodernism* 190–192.
25. Metz, for instance, cites him to the effect that "cinematic codifications are related to a kind of grammar and a kind of rhetoric and it makes no difference which it is; because the very possibility of distinguishing between them arises only when the language exists as an autonomous organization (French, English, etc.)." (See *The Imaginary Signifier* 221–222.)
26. In *The Life of Brian* (1979) one of the distant spectators who overhears the Sermon on the Mount reports that the speaker might have said "Blessed are the cheesemakers," to which a pompous Greek merchant adds that he obviously did not mean that literally but referred to "all manufacturers of dairy products."
27. In an interview (of 1968) that occurred not long after Pasolini completed the film, Oswald Stack attempted to have Pasolini respond to the "accusation" that he was a Gramscian, to which he responded: "When I spoke earlier about reading marxist texts, the most important, even more important than Marx himself, was Gramsci...Gramsci's ideas coincided with mine; they won me over immediately, and he had a fundamental role in my formation" (23).
28. See Massai 96.
29. Ibid. 98.

30. Sam Rohdie makes a useful catalogue of Pasolini's variations of the theme of authorship. He observes his penchant for citing well-known medieval and Renaissance painters (Duccio, Masaccio, Michelangelo, Pontormo, and Rosso Fiorentino), noting further that, in Giotto's case, citation takes the form of mockery, stylistic imitation, and even biographical impersonation (see 20–21), yet another form of intertextuality that would intrigue Miola.
31. I have touched upon this briefly in the introduction to *Rethinking Third Cinema* (see 5–6).
32. It might also be noted that Verdi referred to *Otello* as his "chocolate project" and that "Green" puns on the composer's name (partly because of his extensive quotations from Chaplin's films, particularly *Modern Times* [1936] and *Monsieur Verdoux* [1945], Pasolini made *Uccellacci e uccellini* in black and white, but he obviously had reason to make this film in color). Pasolini's substitution of an Offenbach cancan as the spectators rewrite the conclusion suggests that the filmmaker, attuned as he was to third world issues, could not forgive either Verdi or Shakespeare for their ending and burlesqued it in his translation of the incipient colonialism in the racial dynamics of the play into Gramsci's reconfiguration of Marx's notion of class struggle.
33. It is Shakespeare's Iago, of course, who shares confidences with the audience, but by creating an unlearned subproletarian audience, unwilling to permit the conventions of bourgeois propriety to dictate a tragic outcome, Pasolini recasts Iago's self-evident duplicity as an ill-advised attempt to win spectatorial complicity with authorial (i.e., the puppetmaster's) hegemony. In what proved to be a rare moment of Pasolinian optimism, the spectators rebel.
34. Massai believes the film to concur broadly with Foucault's notion of power and points out that by the time Pasolini came to write his 1973 play *Calderon*, in which Velázquez is a character and *Las Meninas* part of the setting, Pasolini's thought approached Foucault's more closely (a situation for which I would use the metaphor of a loss of faith in the project of modernity under the weight of postmodernism's conviction in the inescapable grasp of power).
35. See Pasolini 135.
36. Here, too, the Gramscian foundation of his idea of crisis can readily be appreciated (see Boothman's introduction to Gramsci's *Prison Notebooks*, xlvii, and Gramsci 219–229).
37. See Pasolini 132–135.
38. As Maurizio Viano points out, his previous short film, also starring the father-son team of Totò and Ninetto (here staging a *trucco* in which they try to collect money to forestall the attempted suicide of Totò's deaf-mute wife), similarly extends the languages of cinema by incorporating the acting techniques of silent cinemas with avant-garde techniques, a way of contrasting realism and naturalism in film (see 164–165).
39. Rather early on Giuliana Bruno foresaw the change in the critical tide when she wrote that Pasolini's semiology was "not understood insofar as it was much ahead of its time" (91). Viano even suggests that Pasolini's epistemology of realism, founded on the premise that cinema modifies and structures our perception of reality (quite unlike Bazin's ontological argument), anticipated Eco's and Baudrillard's visions of "heperreality" and "simulacra," and even elements of Gianni Vattimo's conclusions about the dissolution of reality into competing regimes of images (see viii–ix). See, also, the interview with Oswald Stack in which Pasolini underlines his preference for dubbing voices because it "raises a character out of the zone of naturalism. I believe deeply in reality, in realism, but I can't stand naturalism" (39).
40. In this Massai even discerns an anticipatory reply to Greenblatt's apparent valorization of Iago's Machiavellian *virtù* (see 103), although the price of Iago's displacement is, of course, the interruption of the play.
41. See Foucault 3–16.
42. Because of his concern with realism and his rejection of naturalism (verisimilitude), Pasolini is perhaps the filmmaker par excellence who takes up the theme of the *paragone* (the debate between the representational fidelity of the painter and poet) inherited from classical Greek aesthetic philosophy and revived in the Renaissance by Leonardo da Vinci, Philip Sidney, Nicholas Hilliard, and a host of other writers and artists. We will have occasion to return to Shakespeare's contribution to the *paragone* in *Timon of Athens* in our discussion of Peter Greenaway.
43. In a related vein I might add that, even setting aside the disputed authorship of George Wilkins, who was by no means alone among the theatrical fraternity in his involvement in the associated bordello business, *Pericles*, though popular enough to be repeatedly printed in quarto and possibly treated with high seriousness by some of its early readers, seems best read as *Shamela* delivered in the tone of *Pamela* (Samuel Richardson's novel parodied by Henry Fielding).
44. See especially Bakhtin *Rabelais* 21–26.

45. See Thompson and Bordwell 597–598.
46. See Greenaway 42.
47. Ibid. 40, 50.
48. In his introduction Landow makes careful note of the convergences between influential recent theories and the formal properties of hypertext: the linked anterior texts that reconceive the relationship of author and reader (Barthes and Derrida), intertextuality (Kristeva), plurivocality (Bakhtin), networks of power (Foucault), rhizomatic thought (Eco, Deleuze, and Félix Guattari), not to mention the even more recent work of theorists of postcoloniality, globalization, and the dispersal of hegemonies (Arjun Appadurai). He also makes the distinction between axial hypertext structure (links that act as footnotes to a given text) and network-structured hypertext (in which one web of information connects to others creating chains of information); *Prospero's Books* being an adaptation of a canonical text retains axial tendencies, but in being linked to Greenaway's larger oeuvre and those of others remains suggestive of a network structure (see 1–2, 23–31). It is no coincidence that of all adaptations this one would invite the largest number of references to theory. Commenting that *Prospero's Books* is at once a book, a film, a video, a product of computer art, a nexus of competing languages, a history of art and postmodern pastiche, a homage to an actor, and a film that seems at times empty of human presence, Michael Anderegg suggests that the film constantly circles back to its origins, recapitulating the history of theatre and film in the process of "incorporating" an early seventeenth-century text into "a late-twentieth-century hypertext," a term he uses with the same specificity as Landow (see *Cinematic Shakespeare* 191, 196). He also notes that Peter Donaldson has embarked on the process of hyperlinking sequences of the film to their myriad referents as part of the Shakespeare Web (see *Cinematic Shakespeare* 196 and 205).
49. See Greenaway 50–51.
50. Ibid 32.
51. Jests aside, Greenaway chances upon a notion central to Derrida's early work "Of Grammatology," in which the latter argues (using a multiplicity of examples, including Descartes) that the constitution of the individual subject occurs in language (logocentrism) and generally expresses itself as speech (phonocentrism). For speech to work as a system of signs, however, he reasons that there must be a code that determines the arrangement of phonemes (i.e., writing or arche-writing) and that guarantees the separateness of one phoneme or linguistic sign from another (*différance*); thus to speak is to signal an absence (or "trace"), and that absence is writing: as Gayatri Spivak explains it, "'[W]riting' is the name of the structure always already inhabited by the trace" (Derrida, *Of Grammatology* xxxix). The imagined manuscript of *The Tempest* is a wonderful figuration of the arche-writing that is the trace signaled by Gielgud-Shakespeare's voice.
52. See especially 22–31, 146–151. There is also an element of Greenaway's characteristic arch humor in that the Botticellian breezes that traverse many a filmscape early on blow sand away from Roman ruins (Prospero's flight of fancy begins in something akin to the Baths of Caracalla), revealing imperial profiles on medallions, an overt reference to one of Gielgud's less savory toga-roles as a senator who commits suicide in a gory bathtub sequence.
53. Note that Greenaway's book is an orderly iconographic tour of the film, an alternative text of *Prospero's Books* that is self-consciously adapted to the culture of print.
54. See Spielman 56.
55. Ibid. 55–56. Note that she suggests that Greenaway accomplishes something new in relating older, established media, and newer media, although her use of the term "intermedia" to describe "certain forms of image" in which "elements of the static and the moving image are interrelated to create a third form of the image," a concept possibly borrowed from André Gaudreault's idea of "intermediality" as occupying an indeterminate realm between established media (see Tweedie 124), differs from my use of intermediation to describe symbiotic interactions between media in the optimal processing of message content. As I have already noted, motion has interested a host of the classical and recent theorists of cinema, but in most of these considerations, images are taken either to be fixed or contributing to one illusion of motion or another.
56. See his comments in Rodgers 12–13.
57. See *Cinematic Shakespeare* 191–192.
58. The numbers 3 and 4 reappear regularly in such configurations as the film's three consecutive time frames and the four classical elements, as do 2 and 6, the other factors of 12.
59. See *Cinematic Shakespeare* 193.
60. Ibid. 196–197.

61. The Jonson-Jones squabble did not become public until 1611, three years or so after the presumed date of *Timon*'s composition, but of course Jonson was famously disputatious, his incendiary caricatures leading to the short-lived Poets' War with Marston and Dekker at the start of the century. His collaboration with Jones began in 1605 (presumably enough time for their rivalry to be an open secret). Intriguingly, Greenaway claimed that a "long time" before undertaking *Prospero's Books*, he composed a script he entitled "Jonson and Jones." Although they were "very antagonistic and jealous of one another," in their masques they had to "fashion their two opposed interests [which he identifies as "word" and "spectacle"] into a coherent whole...And in a way that is also the quandary of cinema" (see the interview in Rodgers 11). Jarman's attachment to the poetic word may be sensed in *The Angelic Conversations* (1985), in which Judi Dench reads some of Shakespeare's sonnets over an image track depicting various phases of a gay relationship.
62. Greenaway 32–33.
63. I am not suggesting here, or in my discussion of Derrida, that Greenaway is an avid reader of theory as Pasolini was, but rather that Prospero's island playground bears more than a passing resemblance to Baudrillard's description of Disneyland, the "perfect model of all the entangled orders of simulation" where the hyperreal and imaginary serve as an analogue of the world outside, an architectural embodiment of narrative in which plots, restorative matrimonies, revenge dramas, and forgiving benedictions serve as an allegorical idealization that synecdochically signifies the whole of America-as-it-should-be (see 12–15). It seems an interesting coincidence that in the preceding discussion Baudrillard discusses the ethnological fiction of not destroying its object of study as another strategy of colonization. There were two possible responses to the discovery of the New World, according to Baudrillard: "[E]ither admit that this Law [of the Gospel] was not universal, or exterminate the Indians to efface the evidence" (see 10). Shakespeare, in granting Caliban language and the ability to recognize its colonizing force, refuses to efface him: Caliban's curses save him.
64. See *"Prospero's Books* and the Textual Shakespeare" 182. In Greenaway's case, at least, this is unambiguous: the white text that scrolls over a black background at the start of *Prospero's Books* assures us that, "one evening, Prospero imagines creating a storm powerful enough to bring his old enemies to his island. He begins to write a play about this tempest, speaking aloud the lines of each of his characters. It is the story of Prospero's past, and his revenge." Lia Hotchkiss makes a similar point about the film's "incorporation of word as image," although I would stress that what she calls "cinematic introjection" of theatrical conventions and his "reduction" of books to the "objects they represent" (see 9–10), actually historicize and juxtapose two particular emanations of visual culture (the illustrated Renaissance encyclopedia and digital cinema) as a form of restitution for the many losses endured by Shakespeare, Prospero, Caliban, Miranda, and Gielgud.
65. Ibid. 183. Note also that the first words of the film, lines about his prized books that are later spoken in character, happen to be written on parchment in the elegant italic hand that reveals itself as Prospero's own and that, when Prospero stands in a Roman bath and utters the freshly discovered opening word of the play, his trials of it are echoed with varying inflections by Ariel who in this putto manifestation stands behind him with the word superimposed (by means of a dissolve) over both of them.
66. Ibid. 192–194. James Tweedie reveals the strategy Greenaway adopts to effect such a metatheoretical reading in pointing out that, by creating a "reconfigured cinematic space" in which he situates the viewer in a "liminal position somewhere at the crossroads of the arts, Greenaway extends adaptation into a formally radical interpretation of Shakespeare that has broader cultural implications" (see 105).
67. See Cavecchi's "Peter Greenaway's *Prospero's Books*."
68. Tweedie 114. Although Tweedie makes the curious (incorrect) point that the *Book of Motion* remains unopened because it trembles in a way that threatens to break the fetters that encase its binding, thus bursting into a flutter of pages, spiraling into the dances of which the human body is capable, and suggesting the motions inherent to cinema itself, thereby revealing Greenaway's alternative genealogy of the book as part of a two thousand-year-old "tradition of visuality" (see 106, 110).
69. For good measure he adds: "[T]hat this film has become the favorite of the theorists argues that it was not made to bring a new interpretation of a complicated script before audiences but to attract the avant-garde to its gimmicks. Not much time will go by before the film is seen for the travesty that it is" (Coursen 17).

70. See *Cinematic Shakespeare* 199.
71. Donaldson's observation in "Sexual and Electronic Magic" that Prospero appropriates the powers of maternity, I think, extends beyond patriarchy to the parthenogenic Creator God of Genesis, in that through him mind (the nous in the first line of John's Gospel) becomes matter.
72. It is probably Homi Bhabha who turned "hybridity" into one of the key (hotly debated) terms among theorists of postcoloniality and subaltern studies. See, for instance, "DissemiNation" 314 and *The Location of Culture* 111–116.
73. Significantly, Clark based his most famous later ballet, *Mmm* (1992), on Nijinsky's choreography of Stravinsky's score for *Le Sacre du printemps* (1913). As Joan Acocella observes, of the four ballets Nijinsky choreographed for the Ballets Russes, only that of *The Afternoon of a Faun* survives (and even then probably in dilute form), and thus any reworking of *Le Sacre* is perforce conjectural (see 168–190). For the crucial distinction between the dynamics of *vulgarité* and kitsch, I continue to rely on Kundera, of course (see 34–35).
74. See, in this context, Munro 95–96.
75. See Benjamin, *Illuminations* 392–393 for the reference. As happened with other artists and musicians who worked for Diaghilev and the Ballets Russes, Klee attained a Nazi classification as a "degenerate" artist.
76. I refer to "Sexual and Electronic Magic" in which Peter Donaldson extends Kay Stockholder's and Janet Adelman's readings of *The Tempest* to Greenaway's film (see 111–112). Lamming, who devotes two chapters of *The Pleasures of Exile* to *The Tempest* (one indirectly in imagining Toussaint Louverture as staging Caliban's successful revolt against Napoleon), contrasts Ariel's servitude with Caliban's slavery, contrasting indenture to bondage, observing of the slave that despite a terrifying predicament "the spirit of freedom never deserts him" (101). It is not Prospero, who has merely given him words, but Miranda who has been his teacher, and it is Prospero's psychoses that create a monster capable of anything and of imagining everything—and filmmakers appear to concur (see 95–117).
77. See Ngugi 15–17.
78. See especially 389–395.
79. See Halpern 44–50.
80. Maslin C1.
81. See Hodgdon 89–95.
82. Lehmann 191–194.
83. Ibid. 193.
84. Ibid. 198–201.
85. One would hope that this is a Deleuze who would recognize that Brian Dennehy's Ted Montague bears more than a passing resemblance to Ted Kennedy, and that Luhrmann's religious conversion of the "myth" translates the antagonists into liberal Irish Catholics and conservative Cuban ones.
86. I have migrated from key term to key term as the article does, preserving the sequence of the terms.
87. Buhler 91. Mercutio's application of Shakespeare's gnat metaphor in the Queen Mab speech to an ecstasy pill is surprisingly felicitous.
88. Ibid. 92–93.
89. See *Cinematic Shakespeare* 78–79.
90. The phrase comes from *The Decoration of Houses* (1897), and can be found in Eleanor Dwight's biography (see 54).
91. See Geoff Andrew's extensive 2001 interview of Luhrmann for *The Guardian*.
92. O'Regan 20–25, 82–83, 103.
93. Donaldson, "In Fair Verona" 72.
94. Ibid. 69–70.
95. See "National and Racial Stereotypes" 271.
96. See Andrew's interview of Luhrmann.
97. See Conrad's review "Indian Summer."
98. See Kundera 34–35.
99. See "Pierre Menard, Author of the *Quixote*" 88–95.
100. See 865–870.

WORKS CITED

Abel, Richard. *Americanizing the Movies and "Movie-Mad" Audiences: 1910–1914*. Berkeley: University of California Press, 2006.
Ackroyd, Peter. *Shakespeare: The Biography*. New York: Doubleday, 2006.
Acocella, Joan. *Twenty-eight Artists and Two Saints*. New York: Pantheon Books, 2007.
Agee, James. *Agee on Film*. Vol. 1. New York: Grosset and Dunlap, 1969.
Allen, Robert C. "Manhattan Myopia; Or, Oh! Iowa! Robert C. Allen on Ben Singer's 'Manhattan Nickelodeons: New Data on Audiences and Exhibitors.'" *Cinema Journal* 35.3 (Spring 1996): 75–103.
———. "Motion Picture Exhibition in Manhattan 1906–1912: Beyond the Nickelodeon." *Cinema Journal* 28.2 (Spring 1979): 2–15.
Allen, Robert, and Douglas Gomery. *Film History: Theory and Practice*. New York: Alfred A. Knopf, 1985.
Altick, Richard D. *Paintings from Books: Art and Literature in Britain, 1760–1900*. Columbus: Ohio State University Press, 1985.
Altman, Rick. *The American Film Musical*. Bloomington: Indiana University Press, 1987.
Anderegg, Michael. *Cinematic Shakespeare*. Lanham, MD: Rowman and Littlefield, 2004.
———. "Every Third Word a Lie": Rhetoric and History in Orson Welles's *Chimes at Midnight*." In Lyons, Bridget Gellert. *Chimes at Midnight*. New Brunswick, NJ: Rutgers University Press, 1988. 326–334.
———. "James Dean Meets the Pirate's Daughter: Passion and Parody in *William Shakespeare's Romeo + Juliet* and *Shakespeare in Love*." In Burt, Richard and Lynda E. Boose. Eds. *Shakespeare, the Movie, II: Popularizing the Plays on Film, TV, Video, and DVD*. London: Routledge, 2003.
———. *Orson Welles, Shakespeare, and Popular Culture*. New York: Columbia University Press, 1999.
Andrew, Dudley. "Echoes of Art." In Lyons, Bridget Gellert. *Chimes at Midnight*. New Brunswick, NJ: Rutgers University Press, 1988. 320–325.
Andrew, Geoff. "Baz Luhrmann (1), *The Guardian* / NFT Interview." http://film.guardian.co.uk.interview/interviewpages/0,548458,00.html
Anzai, Tetsuo. "A Century of Shakespeare in Japan: A Brief Historical Survey." In Anzai, Tetsuo, Soji Iwasaki, Holger Klein, and Peter Milward S.J. Eds. *Shakespeare in Japan*. Lewiston, NY: Edwin Mellen Press, 1999. 3–12.
Appadurai, Arjun. *Modernity at Large: Cultural Dimensions of Globalization*. Minneapolis: University of Minnesota Press, 1996.
Arnheim, Rudolf. *Film as Art*. Berkeley: University of California Press, 1957.
The Art of Shakespeare. Uncredited Catalogue of the Korein Shakespeare Collection. New York: Corkey, 1989.
Arwas, Victor. *Alphonse Mucha: Master of Art Nouveau*. London: Academy Editions, 1985.
Asleson, Robyn. "'She Was Tragedy Personified': Crafting the Siddons Legend in Art and Life." In Asleson, Robyn. Ed. *A Passion for Performance: Sarah Siddons and Her Portraitists*. Los Angeles: J. Paul Getty Museum, 1999. 41–96.
Assayag, Jackie, and Véronique Bénéï. Eds. *At Home in Diaspora: South Asian Scholars and the West*. New Delhi: Permanent Black, 2003.

Auden, W.H. *Lectures on Shakespeare*. Reconstructed and edited by Arthur Kirsch. Princeton: Princeton University Press, 2000.
Bachelard, Gaston. *The Poetics of Space*. Boston: Beacon Press, 1994 (orig. 1958).
Baker, Houston, Jr. "Caliban's Triple Play." In Gates, Henry Lewis. Ed. *Race, Writing and Difference*. Chicago: University of Chicago Press, 1985. 381–395.
Bakhtin, Mikhail. *Rabelais and His World*. Trans. Hélène Iswolsky. Bloomington: Indiana University Press, 1984.
———. "A Response to the *Novy Mir* Editorial Staff." Trans. and ed. Vern McGee. Ed. Caryl Emerson and Michael Holquist. *Speech Genres and Other Late Essays*. Austin: University of Texas Press, 1986.
Balázs, Béla. *Béla Balázs: Essay, Kritik 1922–1932*. Eds. Gertraude Kühn, Manfred Lichtenstein, and Eckart Jahnke. Berlin: Staatliches Filmarchiv der DDR, 1973.
———. *Theory of the Film: Character and Growth of a New Art*. Trans. Edith Bone. New York: Dover Publications, 1970 (orig. 1945 in Russian, trans. from Hungarian in 1952).
Ball, Robert Hamilton. "The Shakespeare Film as Record: Sir Herbert Beerbohm Tree." *Shakespeare Quarterly* 3.3 (Jul. 1952): 227–236.
———. *Shakespeare on Silent Film*. London: George Allen and Unwin, 1968.
———. "Tree's King John Film: An Addendum." *Shakespeare Quarterly* 24.4 (Fall 1973): 455–459.
Barnard, Malcolm. *Art, Design and Visual Culture: An Introduction*. New York: St. Martin's Press, 1998.
Barthes, Roland. *Camera Lucida*. Trans. Richard Howard. New York: Hill and Wang, 1982 (orig. 1980).
Bartholomew, Gail. "The Development of Carlos Saura." *Journal of the University Film and Video Association* 35.3 (Summer 1983): 15–34.
Basler, Roy P. *A Touchstone for Greatness: Essays, Addresses, and Occasional Pieces about Abraham Lincoln*. Westport, CT: Greenwood Press, 1973.
Baudrillard, Jean. *Simulacra and Simulation*. Trans. Sheila Faria Glaser. Ann Arbor: University of Michigan Press, 1994.
Baudry, Jean-Louis. "Ideological Effects of the Basic Cinematographic Apparatus." *Film Quarterly* 28.2 (Winter 1974–75): 39–47.
Baxter, Keith. "Filming Falstaff." Redacted by François Thomas. *Positif* 378 (Jul.–Aug. 1992): 29–35.
Beerbohm, Max. *Herbert Beerbohm Tree: Some Memories of Him and of His Art Collected by Max Beerbohm*. New York: E.P. Dutton, 1920.
———. Review of Herbert Beerbohm Tree's Production of *King John*. In Wells, Stanley. Ed. *Shakespeare in the Theatre. An Anthology of Criticism*: Oxford: Clarendon Press, 1997. 160–163.
Benjamin, Walter. *Illuminations*. Trans. Harry Zohn. Ed. Hannah Arendt. New York: Schocken Books, 1968.
———. *Selected Writings*. Vol. 4. Trans. Harry Zohn. Cambridge: Harvard University Press, 2003 (orig. 1940).
Bennett, Shelley, and Mark Leonard. "'A Sublime and Masterly Performance': The Making of Joshua Reynolds's *Sarah Siddons as the Tragic Muse*." In Asleson, Robyn. Ed. *A Passion for Performance: Sarah Siddons and Her Portraitists*. Los Angeles: The J. Paul Getty Museum, 1999. 97–140.
Bennett, Susan. "Godard and *Lear*: Trashing the Can(n)on. *Theatre Survey* 39.1 (May 1998): 7–19.
Bhabha, Homi. "DissemiNation: Time, Narrative, and the Margins of the Modern Nation." In Homi Bhabha. Ed. *Nation and Narration*. London: Routledge, 1990. 291–322.
———. *The Location of Culture*. London: Routledge, 1994.
Binstock, Benjamin. "Aloïs Riegl, Monumental Ruin: Why We Still Need to Read *Historical Grammar of the Visual Arts*. In Riegl, Aloïs. *Historical Grammar of the Visual Arts*. Trans. Jacqueline E. Jung. New York: Zone Books, 2004. 11–36.
Bloom, Harold. *Shakespeare: The Invention of the Human*. New York: Riverhead Books, 1998.
Bluestone, George. *Novels into Film*. Berkeley: University of California Press, 1973 (orig. 1957).
Bohanan, Laura. "Shakespeare in the Bush." *PEN* 1.2 (Fall 2001): 66–76.
Bolter, Jay David, and Richard Grusin. *Remediation: Understanding New Media*. Cambridge, MA: Massachusetts Institute of Technology Press, 1999.

Bondanella, Peter. *Hollywood Italians: Dagos, Palookas, Romeos, Wise Guys, and Sopranos*. New York: Continuum, 2004.

———. *Italian Cinema: From Neorealism to the Present*. 3rd ed. New York: Continuum, 2001 (orig. 1993).

Booth, Edwin, and William Winter, eds. *Edwin Booth's Prompt-Book of Richard III*. Philadelphia: Penn Publishing, 1912.

Bordwell, David, Janet Staiger, and Kristin Thompson. *The Classical Hollywood Cinema: Film Style and Mode of Production to 1960*. New York: Columbia University Press, 1985.

Borges, Jorge Luis. "Pierre Menard, Author of the *Quixote*." In *Collected Fictions*. Trans. Andrew Hurley. New York: Penguin, 1998. 88–95.

———. "Shakespeare's Memory." In *Collected Fictions*. Trans. and ed. Andrew Hurley. New York: Penguin, 1998. 508–515.

———. "The Theme of the Traitor and the Hero." In *Collected Fictions*. Trans. and ed. Andrew Hurley. New York: Penguin Books, 1998. 143–146.

Bowser, Eileen. *The Transformation of Cinema, 1907–1915. History of the American Cinema*. Vol. 2. Berkeley: University of California Press, 1994.

Bradbury, Malcolm, and James McFarlane. Eds. *Modernism, 1890–1930*. London: Penguin, 1991 (orig. 1976).

Bradley, A.C. *Shakespearean Tragedy: Lectures on* Hamlet, Othello, King Lear *and* Macbeth. New York: St. Martin's Press, 1985 (orig. 1909).

Brady, Frank. *Citizen Welles: A Biography of Orson Welles*. New York: Charles Scribner's, 1989.

Brewster, Ben, and Lea Jacobs. *Theatre to Cinema: Stage Pictorialism and the Early Feature Film*. Oxford: Oxford University Press, 1997.

Bristol, Michael. *Shakespeare's America, America's Shakespeare*. London: Routledge, 1990.

Brode, Douglas. *Shakespeare in the Movies: From the Silent Era to* Shakespeare in Love. Oxford: Oxford University Press, 2000.

Brooke, Nicholas. "Introduction." *Macbeth*. Oxford: Oxford University Press, 1990. 1–20.

Bruno, Giuliana. "The Body of Pasolini's Semiotics: A Sequel Twenty Years Later." In Patrick Rumble and Bart Testa. Eds. *Pier Paolo Pasolini: Contemporary Perspectives*. Toronto: University of Toronto Press, 1994. 88–105.

———. *Streetwalking on a Ruined Map: Cultural Theory and the City Films of Elvira Notari*. Princeton: Princeton University Press, 1992.

Buchanan, Judith. *Shakespeare on Film*. Harlow, UK: Pearson Longman, 2005.

Buchman, Lorne M. *Still in Movement: Shakespeare on Screen*. New York: Oxford University Press, 1991.

Buhler, Stephen. "Antic Dispositions: Shakespeare and Steve Martin's L.A. Story." In Klein, Holger, and Dimiter Daphinoff. Eds. Hamlet *on Screen*. Lewiston, NY: Edwin Mellen Press, 1997. 212–229.

———. *Shakespeare in the Cinema: Ocular Proof*. Albany, NY: State University of New York Press, 2001.

Burnim, Kalman, and Philip H. Highfill Jr. *John Bell, Patron of British Theatrical Portraiture*. Carbondale: Southern Illinois University Press, 1998.

Calinescu, Matei. *Five Faces of Modernity*. Durham, NC: Duke University Press, 2006 (orig. 1987).

Callow, Simon. *Orson Welles: The Road to Xanadu*. New York: Penguin, 1995.

Campbell, Thomas. *Life of Mrs. Siddons*. New York: Benjamin Blom, 1972.

Canclini, Néstor García. *Consumers and Citizens: Globalization and Multicultural Conflicts*. Trans. George Yúdice. Minneapolis: University of Minnesota Press, 2001.

———. *Hybrid Cultures: Strategies for Entering and Leaving Modernity*. Trans. Christopher Chiappani and Silvia López. Minneapolis: University of Minnesota Press, 1995.

Cardwell, Sarah. *Adaptation Revisited: Television and the Classic Novel*. Manchester: Manchester University Press, 2002.

Carroll, Noël. *Theorizing the Moving Image*. Cambridge: Cambridge University Press, 1996.

Cartelli, Thomas. *Repositioning Shakespeare: National Formations, Postcolonial Appropriations*. London: Routledge, 1999.

Cartelli, Thomas, and Katherine Rowe. *New Wave Shakespeares on Screen*. London: Polity Press, 2007.

Casale, Gherardo. *L'incantesimo è compiuto: Shakespeare secondo Orson Welles*. Turin: Lindau, 2001.

Catania, Saviour. "Wailing Woodwind Wild: The Noh Transcription of Shakespeare's Silent Sounds in Kurosawa's *Ran*." *Literature/Film Quarterly* 34.2 (2006): 85–92.

Cavecchi, Mariacristina. "Peter Greenaway's *Prospero's Books*: A Tempest between Word and Image." *Literature/Film Quarterly* 25.2 (Apr. 1997): 83–90.

Cavell, Stanley. *The World Viewed: Reflections on the Ontology of Film*. New York: Viking Press, 1971.

Chakrabarty, Dipesh. *Habitations of Modernity: Essays in the Wake of Subaltern Studies*. Chicago: University of Chicago Press, 2002.

Chatman, Seymour. *Story and Discourse: Narrative Structure in Fiction and Film*. Ithaca: Cornell University Press, 1978.

Chertok, Léon. "Freud in Paris: A Crucial Stage." *International Journal of Psychoanalysis* 51 (1970): 511–520.

Chion, Michel. *The Voice in the Cinema*. Ed. and trans. Claudia Gorbman. New York: Columbia University Press, 1999.

Christensen, Thomas C. "Nordisk Films Kompagni and the First World War." In Fullerton, John, and Jan Olsson. Eds. *Nordic Explorations: Film before 1930*. Sydney: John Libby, 1999. 12–18.

Christie, Ian, and David Elliot. Eds. *Eisenstein at Ninety*. London: British Film Institute and the Museum of Modern Art, 1988.

Clover, Carol. *Men, Women, and Chainsaws*. Princeton: Princeton University Press, 1992.

Cobos, Juan, and Miguel Rubio. "Welles and Falstaff." In Lyons, Bridget Gellert. *Chimes at Midnight*. New Brunswick, NJ: Rutgers University Press, 1988. 259–266.

Collick, John. *Shakespeare, Cinema and Society*. Manchester: Manchester University Press, 1989.

Conrad, Peter. "Indian Summer." *New Statesman* (Oct. 27, 2003). http://www.newstatesman.com/200310270038.

Cook, Judith. *Shakespeare's Players: A Look at Some of the Major Roles in Shakespeare and Those Who Have Played Them*. London: Harrap, 1983.

Coppedge, Walter. "Mazursky's Tempest: Something Rich and Strange." *Literature/Film Quarterly* 21.1 (1993): 18–25.

Coursen, H.R. *Shakespeare in Space: Recent Shakespeare Productions on Screen*. New York: Peter Lang, 2002.

Coussemier, Laetitia. "*Richard III* de Raoul Ruiz: entre difformités et deformations." In Patricia Dorval. Ed. *Shakespeare et le Cinéma: Société Française Shakespeare, Actes du Congrès de 1998*. Paris: Jean-Marie Maguin, 1998. 77–90.

Crafton, Donald. *The Talkies: American Cinema's Transition to Sound, 1921–1931*. Berkeley: University of California Press, 1997.

Croce, Benedetto. *Benedetto Croce: Essays on Literature and Literary Criticism*. Trans. and ed. M.E. Moss. Albany: State University of New York Press, 1990.

Crowl, Samuel. "Looking for Shylock: Stephen Greenblatt, Michael Radford and Al Pacino." In Burnett, Mark Thornton, and Ramona Wray. Eds. *Screening Shakespeare in the Twenty-First Century*. Edinburgh: University of Edinburgh Press, 2006. 113–126.

———. *Shakespeare at the Cineplex: The Kenneth Branagh Era*. Athens: Ohio University Press, 2003.

Dash, Irene. *Women's Worlds in Shakespeare's Plays*. Newark: University of Delaware Press, 1997.

Davies, Anthony. *Filming Shakespeare's Plays: The Adaptations of Laurence Olivier, Orson Welles, Peter Brook and Akira Kurosawa*. Cambridge: Cambridge University Press, 1994 (orig. 1988).

Davies, Anthony, and Stanley Welles. Eds. *Shakespeare and the Moving Image: The Plays on Film and Television*. Cambridge: Cambridge University Press, 1997 (orig. 1994).

Decherny, Peter. *Hollywood and the Cultural Elite: How the Movies Became American*. New York: Columbia University Press, 2005.

De, Esha Niyogi. "Modern Shakespeares in Popular Bombay Cinema: Translation, Subjectivity, and Community." *Screen* 43.1 (Spring 2002): 19–40.

De Cordova, Richard. *Picture Personalities: The Emergence of the Star System in America*. Urbana: University of Chicago Press, 1990.

Deleuze, Gilles. *Cinema 2. The Time-Image*. Trans. Hugh Tomlinson and Robert Galeta. Minneapolis: University of Minnesota Press, 2003 (orig. 1985).

De Luca, Maria, and Mary Lindroth. "Mayhem, Madness, Method: An Interview with Julie Taymor." *Cineaste* 25.3 (2000): 28–31.

Derrida, Jacques. "The Law of Genre." *Glyph* 7 (1980): 202–232.

———. *Of Grammatology. Corrected Edition*. Trans. Gayatri Chakravorty Spivak. Baltimore: Johns Hopkins University Press, 1997 (orig. 1967).

De Sanctis, Marianna. *Amleto nel cinema muto europeo*. Thesis for the laurea of the Facoltà di Lettere e Filosofia. Università di Bologna, 2003.

Diakonova, Nina. "Three Shakespearean Stories in Nineteenth-Century Russia." In Parfenov, Alexandr and Joseph G. Price. Eds. *Russian Essays on Shakespeare and His Contemporaries*. Newark, DE: University of Delaware Press, 1997. 97–111.

Didi-Huberman, Georges. "The Imaginary Breeze: Remarks on the Air of the Quattrocento." *Journal of Visual Culture* 2.3 (2003): 275–289.

Dillon, Steven. *Derek Jarman and Lyric Film: The Mirror and the Sea*. Austin: University of Texas Press, 2004.

Dixon, Wheeler Winston. *The Films of Jean-Luc Godard*. New York: State University of New York Press, 1997.

Donaldson, Frances. *The Actor-Managers*. Chicago: Henry Regnery, 1970.

Donaldson, Peter. *Shakespearean Films/Shakespearean Directors*. Boston: Unwin Hyman, 1990.

———. "'In Fair Verona': Media, Spectacle and Performance in *Romeo+Juliet*." *Shakespeare after Mass Media*. In Richard Burt. Ed. New York: Palgrave, 2002. 59–82.

———. "Shakespeare in the Age of Post-mechanical Reproduction: Sexual and Electronic Magic in Prospero's Books." In Burt, Richard and Lynda Boose. Eds. *Shakespeare, the Movie, II: Popularizing the Plays on Film, TV, Video and DVD*. London: Routledge, 2003. 105–119.

Donne, John. *The Complete Poetry and Selected Prose of John Donne*. Ed. Charles M. Coffin. New York: Modern Library, 1952.

Dunant, Caroline. "Olympian Dreamscapes: The Photographic Canvas. The Wide-Screen Paintings of Leighton, Poynter and Alma-Tadema." In Bratton, Jacky, Jim Cook, and Christine Gledhill. Eds. *Melodrama: Stage, Picture, Screen*. London: British Film Institute, 1994. 82–93.

Durgnat, Raymond. *A Mirror for England: British Movies from Austerity to Affluence*. London: Faber and Faber, 1970.

Dwight, Eleanor. *Edith Wharton: An Extraordinary Life*. New York: Harry N. Abrams, 1994.

Dyer, Richard. *Heavenly Bodies: Film Stars and Society*. 2nd ed. London: Routledge, 2004.

Eco, Umberto. "*Casablanca*: Cult Movies and Intertextual Collage." In *Travels in Hyperreality*. New York: Harvest Books, 1986. 197–212.

Eggert, Katherine. "Sure Can Sing and Dance: Minstrelsy, the Star System, and the Post-postcoloniality of Kenneth Branagh's *Love's Labour's Lost* and Trevor Nunn's *Twelfth Night*." In Burt, Richard, and Lynda E. Boose. Eds. *Shakespeare, The Movie, II: Popularizing the Plays on Film, TV, Video, and DVD*. London: Routledge: 2003. 72–88.

Eisenstein, Sergei. "Form and Content: Practice." In *The Film Sense*. Trans. and ed. Jay Leyda. New York: A Harvest Book, 1975: 157–216 (orig. 1942).

———. "The Fourth Dimension in Cinema." In *The Eisenstein Reader*. Ed. Richard Taylor. Trans. Richard Taylor and William Powell. London: BFI Publishing. 1998. 111–123.

———. "The Montage of Attractions." In Richard Taylor. Ed. *The Eisenstein Reader*. Trans. Richard Taylor and William Powell. London: BFI Publishing, 1991. 29–34.

———. "The Montage of Film Attractions." In Richard Taylor. Ed. *The Eisenstein Reader*. Trans. Richard Taylor and William Powell. London: BFI Publishing, 1991. 35–52.

———. "The Synchronization of Senses." In *The Film Sense*. Trans. and ed. Jay Leyda. New York: A Harvest Book, 1975 (orig. 1942). 69–112.

Eisenstein, Sergei, Vsevolod Pudovkin, and Grigori Alexandrov. "Statement on Sound." In *The Eisenstein Reader*. Ed. Richard Taylor. Trans. Richard Taylor and William Powell. London: BFI Publishing. 1998. 80–81.

Eisner, Lotte. *The Haunted Screen: Expressionism in the German Cinema and the Influence of Max Reinhardt*. Berkeley: University of California Press, 1973 (orig. 1952).

Eksteins, Modris. *Rites of Spring: The Great War and the Birth of the Modern Age*. New York: Houghton Mifflin, 1998.

Eliot, T.S. "Hamlet and His Problems." In Bevington, David. Ed. *Twentieth Century Interpretations of Hamlet: A Collection of Critical Essays*. Englewood Cliffs, NJ: Prentice-Hall, 1968. 22–26.

Elliott, Michael A. *The Culture Concept: Writing and Difference in the Age of Realism*. Minneapolis: University of Minnesota Press, 2002.

Elsaesser, Thomas. "Ethnicity, Authenticity, and Exile: A Counterfeit Trade? German Filmmakers and Hollywood." In Naficy, Hamid. Ed. *Home, Exile, Homeland: Film, Media, and the Politics of Place*. New York: Routledge, 1999. 97–123.

Émile-Zola, François, and Massin. *Zola Photographer*. Tr. Liliane Emery Tuck. New York: Seaver Books, 1988.

Enticknap, Leo. *Moving Image Technology: From Zoetrope to Digital*. London: Wallflower Press, 2005.

Evans, Jessica, and Stuart Hall. *Visual Culture: The Reader*. London: Sage, 2000.

Fanon, Frantz. *Black Skin, White Masks*. Trans. Charles Markmann. New York: Grove Press, 1967.

Featherstone, Mike, Scott Lash, and Roland Robertson. Eds. *Global Modernities*. London: Sage, 1997 (orig. 1995).

Fenellosa, Ernest. *Epochs of Chinese and Japanese Art: An Outline History of East Asiatic Design*. Vols. 1 and 2. New York: Dover Publications, 1912.

Fforde, Jasper. *The Eyre Affair*. New York: Viking Press, 2001.

———. *Something Rotten*. London: Hodder & Stoughton, 2004.

Fiorentino, Ser Giovanni. *The Pecorone of Ser Giovanni, now first translated into English*. Trans. W.G. Waters. London: Lawrence and Bullen, 1897.

Foucault, Michel. *The Order of Things: An Archaeology of the Human Sciences* (orig. *Les Mots et les choses*). Trans. New York: Vintage Books, 1994 (orig. 1966).

France, Anna Kay. *Boris Pasternak's Translations of Shakespeare*. Berkeley: University of California Press, 1978.

———. "Iago and Othello in Boris Pasternak's Translation." *Shakespeare Quarterly* 28.1 (Winter 1977): 73–84.

Freedland, Michael. *The Warner Brothers*. New York: St. Martin's Press, 1983.

Freud, Sigmund. *Five Lectures on Psycho-analysis*. Trans. and ed. James Strachey. New York: W.W. Norton, 1977 (orig. 1909).

———. "Hysterical Phantasies and Their Relation to Bisexuality." In *Dora: An Analysis of a Case of Hysteria*. Ed. Philip Rieff. New York: Collier Books, 1963 (orig. 1908). 145–152.

———. *The Interpretation of Dreams*. Trans. and ed. James Strachey. New York: Avon Books, 1965 (orig. 1900).

Friedman, Winifred. *Boydell's Shakespeare Gallery*. New York: Garland Publishing, 1976.

Furtwangler, Albert. *Assassin on Stage: Brutus, Hamlet, and the Death of Lincoln*. Urbana: University of Illinois Press, 1991.

Galindo, Catherine Gough. *Mrs. Galindo's Letter to Mrs. Siddons: Being a Circumstantial Detail of Mrs. Siddons's Life for the Last Seven Years; With Several of Her Letters*. London: Self published, 1809.

Garber, Marjorie. *Shakespeare's Ghost Writers: Literature as Uncanny Causality*. New York: Routledge, 1997 (orig. 1987).

Gay, Peter. *Freud: A Life for Our Time*. New York: W.W. Norton and Co., 1998.

Geduld, Harry M. Ed. *Authors on Film*. Bloomington, IN: Indiana University Press, 1972.

———. *The Birth of the Talkies: From Edison to Jolson*. Bloomington: Indiana University Press, 1975.

———. *Filmguide to* Henry V. Bloomington: Indiana University Press, 1973.

Ghita, Lucian. "Reality and Metaphor in Jane Howell's and Julie Taymor's Productions of Shakespeare's *Titus Andronicus*." In *Comparative Literature and Culture: A WWWeb Journal* 6.1 *(Mar. 2004)*: http://clcwebjournal.lib.purdue.edu/clcweb04–1/ghita04.html.

Giddens, Anthony. *The Consequences of Modernity*. Stanford, CA: Stanford University Press, 1990.

———. *Runaway World: How Globalisation Is Reshaping Our Lives*. New York: Routledge, 2003.

Gidel, Henry. *Sarah Bernhardt*. Paris: Flammarion, 2006.

Ginzburg, Carlo. *Clues, Myths and the Historical Method*. Trans. John and Anne Tedeschi. Baltimore: Johns Hopkins University Press, 1989.

———. *Ecstasies: Deciphering the Witches' Sabbath*. Trans. Raymond Rosenthal. Chicago: University of Chicago Press, 2004 (orig. 1991).

———. "Proofs and Possibilities: In the Margins of Natalie Zemon Davis' *The Return of Martin Guerre*." Translated with an introduction by Anthony R. Guneratne. *YCGL* 37 (1988): 113–127.

Glueck, Grace. "How Shall We Know Thee? By Severe, Bohemian or Courtly Mien?" *New York Times,* Jun. 23, 2006, B30.

Godard, Jean-Luc. *Godard on Godard. Critical Writings by Jean-Luc Godard*. New foreword by Annette Michelson. Edited by Jean Narboni and Tom Milne, with an introduction by Richard Roude. Trans. and ed. Tom Milne. New York: Da Capo Press, 1972.

Golden, Eve. "From Stage to Screen: The Film Career of Sarah Bernhardt." www.classicimages.com/1997/june/bernhard.html.

Gomery, Douglas. "What Was Adolph Zukor Doing in 1927?" *Film History* 17.2/3 (2005): 205–216.

Goodwin, James. *Akira Kurosawa and Intertextual Cinema*. Baltimore: Johns Hopkins University Press, 1994.

Grady, Hugh. *The Modernist Shakespeare*. Oxford: Clarendon Press, 1995 (orig. 1991).

Gramsci, Antonio. *Further Selections from the Prison Notebooks*. Trans. and ed. Derek Boothman. Minneapolis: University of Minnesota Press, 1995.

Grau, Robert. *The Theatre of Science: A Volume of Progress and Achievement in the Motion Picture Industry*. New York: Benjamin Bloom, 1969 (orig. 1914).

Greenaway, Peter. *Prospero's Books: A Film of Shakespeare's* The Tempest. London: Chatto and Windus, 1991.

Greenblatt, Stephen. *Learning to Curse: Essays in Early Modern Culture*. New York: Routledge, 1998.

———. "Murdering Peasants: Status, Genre, and the Representation of Rebellion." *Representations* 1 (Feb. 1983): 1–29.

———. "Racial Memory and Literary History." *PMLA* 116.1 (Jan. 2001): 48–63.

———. *Renaissance Self-fashioning: From More to Shakespeare*. Chicago: University of Chicago Press, 1984 (orig. 1980).

———. *Will in the World: How Shakespeare Became Shakespeare*. New York: W.W. Norton, 2004.

Gross, John. *After Shakespeare: An Anthology*. Oxford: Oxford University Press, 2002.

Guha, Ranajit. *History at the Limit of World-History*. New York: Columbia University Press, 2002.

Guneratne, Anthony. "The Birth of a New Realism: Painting, Photography and the Advent of Documentary Cinema." *Film History* 10.2 (1998): 165–187.

———. "'Thou Dost Usurp Authority': Beerbohm Tree, Reinhardt, Olivier, Welles, and the Politics of Adapting Shakespeare." In Diana Henderson. Ed. *A Concise Companion to Shakespeare on Screen*. Malden, MA: Blackwell Publishing, 2005. 31–53.

Guneratne, Anthony, and Wimal Dissanayake. Eds. *Rethinking Third Cinema*. London: Routledge, 2003.

Gunning, Tom. "The Cinema of Attraction: Early Film, Its Spectator, and the Avant-Garde." In Stam, Robert and Toby Miller. Eds. *Film and Theory: An Anthology*. Malden, MA: Blackwell Publishers, 2000. 229–235.

———. "Vienna Avant-Garde and Early Cinema." Reproduced as part of the Symposion Das fruuhe kino und die Avantgarde. http://www.sixpackfilm.com/archive/veranstaltung/festivals/earlycinema/symposion/symposion_gunning.html.

Guntner, J. Lawrence. "Expressionist Shakespeare: The Gade/Nielsen *Hamlet* (1920) and the History of Shakespeare on Film." *Post Script* 17.2 (Winter–Spring 1998): 90–102.

Gurr, Andrew. *Playgoing in Shakespeare's London*. 3rd ed. Cambridge: Cambridge University Press, 2004.

Habermas, Jürgen. *The Philosophical Discourse of Modernity: Twelve Lectures*. Trans. Frederick G. Lawrence. Boston: Massachusetts University Press, 2000 (orig. 1985).

Habicht, Werner, D.J. Palmer, and Roger Pringle. Eds. *Images of Shakespeare: Proceedings of the Third Congress of the International Shakespeare Association, 1986*. Newark, DE: University of Delaware Press, 1988.

Hair, P.E.H. *Sierra Leone and the English in 1607: Extracts from the Unpublished Journals of the Keeling Voyage to the East Indies.*

Hall, N. John. *Max Beerbohm: A Kind of Life.* New Haven, CT: Yale University Press, 2002.

Halpern, Richard. *Shakespeare among the Moderns.* Ithaca: Cornell University Press, 1997.

Hansen, Miriam. *Babel and Babylon: Spectatorship and the American Silent Film.* Cambridge: Harvard University Press, 1991.

———. "Benjamin and Cinema: Not a One-way Street." In Richter, Gerhard. Ed. *Benjamin's Ghosts: Interventions in Contemporary Literary and Cultural Theory.* Stanford: Stanford University Press, 2002.

———. "Early Cinema: Whose Public Sphere?" In *Early Cinema: Space, Frame, Narrative.* Ed. Thomas Elsaesser. London: BFI Publishing, 1990. 228–246.

———. "Of Mice and Ducks: Benjamin and Adorno on Disney." *South Atlantic Quarterly* 92.1 (Winter 1993): 27–61.

Harrison, G.B. "Shakespeare's Topical Significances." In Bradby, Anne. Ed. *Shakespeare Criticism, 1919–35.* London: Humphrey Milford, 1936. 271–291.

Harvey, David. *The Condition of Postmodernity: An Enquiry into the Origins of Cultural Change.* Cambridge, MA: Blackwell, 1990.

Hatchuel, Sarah. *Shakespeare, from Stage to Screen.* Cambridge: Cambridge University Press, 2004.

Hedrick, Donald. "War is Mud: Branagh's *Dirty Harry V* and the Types of Political Ambiguity." In Burt, Richard and Lynda Boose. Eds. *Shakespeare, the Movie, II: Popularizing the Plays on Film, TV, Video and DVD.* London: Routledge, 2003. 213–230.

Hepworth, Cecil. *Came the Dawn.* London: Phoenix House, 1951.

Hibi, Sadao, and Kunio Fukuda. *The Colors of Japan.* Trans. John Baxter. Tokyo: Kodansha International, 2000.

Hjort, Mette. "The Globalisation of Dogma: The Dynamics of Meta-Culture and Counter-Publicity." In Hjort, Mette, and Scott MacKenzie. Eds. *Purity and Provocation: Dogma 95.* London: British Film Institute, 2003. 133–157.

———. "A Small Nation's Response to Globalisation." In Hjort, Mette, and Scott MacKenzie. Eds. *Purity and Provocation: Dogma 95.* London: British Film Institute, 2003. 31–47.

Hodgdon, Barbara. "*William Shakespeare's Romeo + Juliet*: Everything's Nice in America." *Shakespeare Survey* 52 (1999): 88–99.

Holderness, Graham. Ed. *The Shakespeare Myth.* Manchester: Manchester University Press, 1988.

Horak, Jan-Christopher. "Sauerkraut and Sausages with a Little Goulash: Germans in Hollywood, 1927." *Film History* 17.2/3 (2005): 241–260.

Hotchkiss, Lia. "The Incorporation of Word as Image in *Prospero's Books*." *Postscript* 17.2 (Winter–Spring 1998): 8–25.

Howard, Tony. *Women as Hamlet: Performance and Interpretation in Theatre, Film and Television.* Cambridge: Cambridge University Press, 2007.

Howlett, Kathy. *Framing Shakespeare on Film.* Athens: Ohio University Press, 2000.

Humm, Maggie. *Modernist Women and Visual Cultures: Virginia Woolf, Vanessa Bell, Photography and Cinema.* New Brunswick, NJ: Rutgers University Press, 2003.

Hunt, John Dixon. "Shakespeare and the *Paragone*: A Reading of *Timon of Athens*." In Habicht et al. Eds. 47–63.

Hutcheon, Linda. *A Theory of Adaptation.* New York: Routledge, 2006.

Irving, Henry, and F.A. Marshall. Eds. *The Henry Irving Shakespeare.* Vol. 3. London: Blackie and Son, 1888.

Isaacs, J. "Shakespeare as Man of the Theatre." In Bradby, Ann. Ed. *Shakespeare Criticism, 1919–1935.* London: Humphrey Milford, 1936. 292–326.

Isherwood, Charles. "The New British Invasion: Why America's Classics Are in the Hands of London's Directors." *New York Times*, Feb. 27, 2005, Section 2, pp. 1, 8.

Jackson, Russell. "Surprising Find in British Archive: A Shooting Script for the Reinhardt-Dieterle *Dream*: The War with the Amazons, Bottom's Wife, and Other 'Missing' Scenes." *Shakespeare Bulletin* 16.4 (Fall 1998): 39–41.

———. Ed. *The Cambridge Companion to Shakespeare on Film.* Cambridge: Cambridge University Press, 2000.

Jacobs, Lewis. *The Rise of the American Film: A Critical History with an Essay, Experimental Cinema in America 1921–1947.* New York: Teachers College Press, 1968 (orig. 1939).
Jameson, Fredric. *Postmodernism, or the Cultural Logic of Late Capitalism.* Durham, NC: Duke University Press, 1994 (orig. 1991).
———. *A Singular Modernity: Essay on the Ontology of the Present.* London: Verso, 2002.
Jensen, Michael P. "Fragments of a *Dream*: Photos of Three Scenes Missing from the Reinhardt-Dieterle Dream." *Shakespeare Bulletin* 18.4 (Fall 2000): 37–38.
Johnson, Ian. "Merely Players." In Eckert, Charles. Ed. *Focus on Shakespeare Films.* Englewood Cliffs, NJ: Prentice-Hall Inc., 1972. 7–26.
Jones, Ernest. "The Oedipus Complex as an Explanation of Hamlet's Mystery: A Study in Motive." *American Journal of Psychology* 21.1 (Jan. 1910): 72–113.
Jorgens, Jack J. *Shakespeare on Film.* Bloomington: Indiana University Press, 1977.
Kachur, B.A. "The First Shakespeare Film: A Reconsideration and Reconstruction of Tree's *King John.*" *Theatre Survey* 32 (May 1991): 43–63.
———. "*Othello* on the Edwardian Stage: Beerbohm Tree's Revival, 1912." In Vaughan, Virginia Mason, and Kent Cartwright. Eds. *Othello: New Perspectives.* Cranbury, NJ: Associated University Presses, 1991.
———. "Shakespeare Politicized: Beerbohm Tree's *King John* and the Boer War." *Theatre History Studies* XII (1992): 25–44.
Kane, Julie. "From the Baroque to the Wabi: Translating Animal Imagery from Shakespeare's *King Lear* to Kurosawa's *Ran.*" *Literature/Film Quarterly* 25.2 (Apr. 1997): 146–151.
Kapadia, Parmita. "Shakespeare Transposed: The British Stage on the Post-colonial Screen." In Keller, James, and Leslie Stratyner. Eds. *Almost Shakespeare: Reinventing His Works for Cinema and Television.* Jefferson, NC: McFarland, 2004. 42–56.
Kauffman, Michael W. *American Brutus: John Wilkes Booth and the Lincoln Conspiracies.* New York: Random House, 2004.
Kennedy, Dennis. *Looking at Shakespeare: A Visual History of Twentieth-Century Performance.* 2nd ed. Cambridge: Cambridge University Press, 2001.
Kermode, Frank. *The Age of Shakespeare.* New York: Modern Library, 2003.
Kernan, Alvin. *Shakespeare, the King's Playwright: Theater in the Stuart Court, 1603–1613.* New Haven: Yale University Press, 1995.
King, Rob. "Made for the Masses with an Appeal to the Classes: The Triangle Film Corporation and the Failure of Highbrow Film Culture." *Cinema Journal* 44.2 (Winter 2004): 3–33.
Klein, Holger, and James L. Harner. Eds. *Shakespeare and the Visual Arts.* Lewiston, NY: Edwin Mellen Press, 2001.
Kliman, Bernice. *Hamlet: Film, Television, and Audio Performance.* London and Toronto: Associated University Presses, 1988.
Koch, Stephen. *Hemingway, Dos Passos and the Murder of José Robles.* New York: Counterpoint, 2005.
Koebner, Thomas. "Hamlet as a Woman: Asta Nielsen's Shakespeare Film of 1921." In Klein, Holger, and Dimiter Daphinoff. Eds. *Hamlet on Screen.* Lewiston, New York: Edwin Mellon Press, 1997. 125–132.
Kojin, Karatani. *Origins of Modern Japanese Literature.* Trans. and ed. Brett de Bary. Durham, NC: Duke University Press, 1993.
Kott, Jan. *Shakespeare Our Contemporary.* Trans. Boleslaw Taborski. New York: W.W. Norton, 1974 (orig. 1964).
Kozintsev, Grigori. *King Lear: The Space of Tragedy: The Diary of a Director.* Trans. Mary Mackintosh. London: Heinemann, 1977.
———. *Shakespeare: Time and Conscience.* Trans. Joyce Vining. New York: Hill and Wang, 1966.
Kracauer, Siegfried. *From Caligari to Hitler: A Psychological History of the German Film.* Princeton: Princeton University Press, 1974 (orig. 1947).
———. *Theory of Film: The Redemption of Physical Reality.* Princeton: Princeton University Press, 1997 (orig. 1960).
Kreimeier, Klaus. *The Ufa Story: A History of Germany's Greatest Film Company, 1918–1945.* Trans. Robert and Rita Kimber. Berkeley: University of California Press, 1999 (orig. 1992).

Kuhns, David F. *German Expressionist Theatre: The Actor and the Stage*. Cambridge: Cambridge University Press, 2000.
Kundera, Milan. "*Die Weltliteratur*: How We Read One Another." Trans. Linda Asher. *New Yorker* (Jan. 8, 2007): 28–35.
Lamming, George. *The Pleasures of Exile*. Ann Arbor: University of Michigan Press, 1960.
Landow, George. *Hyper/Text/Theory*. Baltimore: Johns Hopkins University Press, 1994.
Landy, Marcia. "Just an Image: Godard, Cinema, and Philosophy." *Critical Quarterly* 43.3 (Oct. 2001): 9–31.
Lane, Anthony. "The Current Cinema Unmasked: *The Phantom of the Opera*, *The Merchant of Venice*." *New Yorker* (Jan. 3, 2005): 78–81.
Lang, Karen. *Chaos and Cosmos: On the Image in Aesthetics and Art History*. Ithaca: Cornell University Press, 2006.
Lanier, Douglas. "Prospero's Books and the Textual Shakespeare." In Robert Shaughnessy. Ed. New Casebooks: *Shakespeare on Film*. New York: St. Martin's Press, 1998.
———. *Shakespeare and Modern Popular Culture*. Oxford: Oxford University Press, 2002.
———. "Will of the People: Recent Shakespeare Film Parody and the Politics of Popularization." In Henderson, Diana. Ed. *A Concise Companion to Shakespeare on Film*. Malden, MA: Basil Blackwell, 2006. 176–196.
Lechner, Frank, and John Boli. Eds. *The Globalization Reader*. Malden, MA: Blackwell, 2000.
Lehmann, Courtney. "Strictly Shakespeare? Dead Letters, Ghostly Fathers, and the Cultural Pathology of Authorship in Baz Luhrmann's *William Shakespeare's Romeo + Juliet*." Shakespeare Quarterly 52.2 (Summer 2001): 189–221.
———. "Out Damned Scot: Dislocating Macbeth in Transnational Film and Media Culture." In Richard Burt and Lynda E. Boose, eds. *Shakespeare the Movie II: Popularizing the Films on Film, TV, Video, and DVD*. 231–251.
Leitch, Thomas. "Where Are We Going, Where Have We Been?" *LFA News* 1.1 (Sept. 2003): 2, 6, 8.
Levin, Yury. "Shakespeare and Russian Literature: Nineteenth-Century Attitudes." In Parfenov, Alexandr, and Joseph G. Price. Eds. *Russian Essays on Shakespeare and His Contemporaries*. Newark, DE: University of Delaware Press, 1997. 78–96.
Lévi-Strauss, Claude. *The Savage Mind*. Chicago: University of Chicago Press, 1968 (orig. 1962).
Lillich, Meredith. "Shakespeare on the Screen: A Survey of How His Plays Have Been Made into Movies." *Films in Review* 7.6 (Jun./Jul. 1956): 247–260.
Lindley, Arthur. "Scotland Saved from History: Welles's *Macbeth* and the Ahistoricism of Medieval Film." In Welsh, James, Richard Vela, and John C. Tibbets. Eds. *Shakespeare into Film*. New York: Checkmark Books, 2002. 141–145.
Lindsay, Vachel. *The Art of the Moving Picture*. New York: Liveright, 1970 (orig. 1915).
Lipkov, A. *Shakespeare's Screen*. Moscow: Art Press, 1975.
Lippmann, Max. Ed. *Shakespeare in Film*. Wiesbaden: Deutsches Institut für Filmkunde, 1964.
Livingston, Paisley. "Artistic Self-reflexivity in *The King Is Alive* and *Strass*." In Hjort, Mette, and Scott MacKenzie. Eds. *Purity and Provocation: Dogma 95*. London: British Film Institute, 2003. 102–110.
Longstaffe, Steve. "The Limits of Modernity in Shakespeare's King John." In Klein, Holger and Rowland Wymer. Eds. *Shakespeare and History*. Lewiston, ME: Edward Mellen Press, 1996. 91–118.
Loomba, Ania, and Martin Orkin. Eds. *Post-colonial Shakespeares*. London: Routledge, 2005.
Loshitsky, Yosefa. "More than Style: Bertolucci's Postmodernism versus Godard's Modernism." *Criticism* 34.1 (Winter 1992): 119–142.
Lyons, Bridget Gellert. *Chimes at Midnight*. New Brunswick, NJ: Rutgers University Press, 1988.
Lyotard, Jean-François. *The Postmodern Condition: A Report on Knowledge*. Trans. Geoff Bennington and Brian Masumi. Minneapolis: University of Minnesota Press, 1997 (orig. 1979).
MacLaimmóir, Micheál. *Put Money in Thy Purse: The Diary of the Film of Othello*. London: Methuen, 1952.
Magro, Maria F., and Mark Douglas. "Reflections on Sex, Shakespeare and Nostalgia in Trevor Nunn's *Twelfth Night*." In Deborah Cartmell, I.Q. Hunter, and Imelda Whelehan. Eds. *Retrovisions: Reinventing the Past in Film and Fiction*. London: Pluto Press, 2001. 41–58.

Mannoni, Laurent. *The Great Art of Light and Shadow: Archaeology of the Cinema.* Trans. and ed. Richard Crangle. Exeter, UK: University of Exeter Press, 2000 (orig. 1995).
Manvell, Roger. *Sarah Siddons: Portrait of an Actress.* London: Heinemann, 1970.
Manvell, Roger. *Shakespeare and the Film.* New York: Praeger Publishers, 1971.
Marcus, Millicent. *Filmmaking by the Book: Italian Cinema and Literary Adaptation.* Baltimore: Johns Hopkins University Press, 1993.
Marienstras, Richard. *New Perspectives on the Shakespearean World.* Trans. Janet Lloyd. Cambridge: Cambridge University Press, 1985.
Marín, Ricardo, and G. Martínez Sierra. *Hamlet y el Cuerpo de Sarah Bernhardt.* Madrid: L. Williams, 1905.
Martineau, Jane, and Desmond Shawe-Taylor. *Shakespeare in Art.* London: Merrel, 2003.
Marx, Samuel. "A Mythical Kingdom: The Hollywood Film Industry of the 1930s and 1940s." In Wendell Aycock and Michael Schoendecke. Eds. *Film and Literature: A Comparative Approach to Adaptation.* Lubbock: Texas Tech University Press, 1988. 21–32.
Maslin, Janet. "Soft, What Light? It's Flash, Romeo." *New York Times,* Nov. 1, 1996, C1, C12.
Mason, Penelope. *History of Japanese Art.* New York: Harry N. Abrams, 1993.
Massai, Sonia. "Subjection and Redemption in Pasolini's *Othello*." In Sonia Massai. Ed. *World-Wide Shakespeares: Local Appropriations in Film and Performance.* London: Routledge, 2005. 95–103.
McCandless, David. "A Tale of Two *Titus*es: Julie Taymor's Vision on Stage and Screen." *Shakespeare Quarterly* 53.5 (2001): 487–511.
McFarlane, Brian. *Novel to Film: An Introduction to the Theory of Adaptation.* Oxford: Clarendon Press, 1996.
McGilligan, Patrick. *George Cukor: A Double Life.* New York: St. Martin's Press, 1991.
McKernan, Luke. "Beerbohm Tree's *King John* Rediscovered: The First Shakespeare Film, September 1899." *Shakespeare Bulletin* (Winter 1993): 35–36.
———. "Shakespeare on Film: Further Notes on Beerbohm Tree's *King John*." *Shakespeare Bulletin* (Spring 1993): 49–50.
McKernan, Luke, and Olwen Terris. *Walking Shadows: Shakespeare in the National Film and Television Archive.* London: BFI Publishing, 1994.
McLuhan, Marshall. *Understanding Media: The Extensions of Man.* Cambridge: MIT Press, 1994 (orig. 1964).
McPherson, Heather. *The Modern Portrait in Nineteenth-Century France.* Cambridge: Cambridge University Press, 2001.
Melnick, Ross. "Station R-O-X-Y: Roxy and the Radio." *Film History* 17.2/3 (2005): 217–233.
Merchant, Ismail. *My Passage to India: A Filmmaker's Journey from Bombay to Hollywood and Beyond.* New York: Viking Studio, 2002.
Merchant, W. Moelwyn. *Shakespeare and the Artist.* London: Oxford University Press, 1959.
Messel, Oliver. *Romeo and Juliet, with Designs by Oliver Messel.* London: Batsford, 1936.
Metz, Christian. *Film Language: A Semiotics of the Cinema.* Trans. Michael Taylor. Chicago: The Univerity of Chicago Press. 1991 (orig. 1971).
———. *The Imaginary Signifier: Psychoanalysis and Cinema.* Trans. Celia Britton, Anwyl Williams, Ben Brewster, and Alfred Guzzetti. London: Macmillan, 1982.
Metz, Walter. "The Future of Adaptation Studies." *LFA News* 1.1 (Sept. 2003): 10.
Michaud, Philippe-Alain. *Aby Warburg and the Image in Motion.* Trans. Sophie Hawkes. New York: Zone Books, 2004.
———. "On Visuality." *Journal of Visual Culture* 5.1 (Apr. 2006): 53–79.
Michell, John. *Who Wrote Shakespeare?* London: Thames and Hudson, 1999 (orig. 1996).
Mignolo, Walter. *The Darker Side of the Renaissance: Literacy, Territoriality, and Colonization.* Ann Arbor: University of Michigan Press, 1995.
———. *Local Histories/Global Designs: Coloniality, Subaltern Knowledges, and Border Thinking.* Princeton: Princeton University Press, 2000.
Miola, Robert S. "Seven Types of Intertextuality." In Michele Marripodi. Ed. *Shakespeare and Intertextuality: The Transition of Cultures between Italy and England in the Early Modern Period.* Rome: Bulzoni Editore, 2000. 23–38.
Mirzoeff, Nicholas. *An Introduction to Visual Culture.* London: Routledge, 1999.

Miyajima Shin'chi, and Yasuhiro Sato. *Japanese Ink Painting.* Los Angeles: Los Angeles County Museum of Art, 1985.
Morgan, Joyce Vining. *Stanislavski's Encounter with Shakespeare: The Evolution of a Method.* Ann Arbor: UMI Research Press, 1984.
Mucha, Jiri, Marina Henderson, and Aaron Scharf. *Alphonse Mucha: Posters and Photographs.* London: Academy Editions, 1971.
Mullaney, Steven. *The Place of the Stage: License, Play, and Power in Renaissance England.* Ann Arbor: University of Michigan Press, 1998 (orig. 1988).
Munday, Anthony. *Anthony Munday's Zelauto: The Fountain of Fame.* Ed. Jack Stillinger. Carbondale: Southern Illinois University Press, 1963.
Munro, Thomas. "*The Afternoon of a Faun* and the Interrelation of the Arts." *Journal of Aesthetics and Art Criticism* X.2 (Dec. 1951): 95–111.
Murch, Walter. *In the Blink of an Eye.* 2nd ed. New York: Silman-James Press, 2001.
Naficy, Hamid. Ed. *An Accented Cinema: Exilic and Diasporic Filmmaking.* Princeton: Princeton University Press, 2001.
———. *Home, Exile, Homeland: Film, Media, and the Politics of Place.* New York: Routledge, 1999.
Naremore, James. *Acting in the Cinema.* Berkeley: University of California Press, 1988.
———. *The Magic World of Orson Welles.* Rev. Ed. Dallas: Southern Methodist UP, 1989.
———. Ed. *Film Adaptation.* New Bruswick, NJ: Rutgers University Press, 2000.
Naremore, James, and Patrick Brantlinger. *Modernity and Mass Culture.* Bloomington: Indiana University Press, 1991.
Negt, Oskar, and Alexander Kluge. *Public Sphere and Experience: Toward an Analysis of the Bourgeois and Proletarian Public Sphere.* Foreword by Miriam Hansen. Trans. Peter Labanyi, Jamie Owen Daniel, and Assenka Oksiloff. Minneapolis: University of Minnesota Press, 1993.
Nemeskurty, Istvan. "In the Beginning, 1896–1911." In Fell, John. Ed. *Film before Griffith.* Berkeley: University of California Press, 1983. 75–80.
Nestingen, Andrew. "Aki Kaurismäki's Crossroads: National Cinema and the Road Movie." In Nestingen, Andrew, and Trevor Elkington. Eds. *Transnational Cinema in a Global North: Nordic Cinema in Transition.* Detroit: Wayne State University Press, 2005. 279–305.
Neuringer, Charles. "Freud and the Theatre." *Journal of the American Academy of Psychoanalysis and Dynamic Psychiatry* 20 (1992): 142–148.
Ngugi wa Thiong'o. *Moving the Center: The Struggle for Cultural Freedoms.* Portsmouth, NH: Heinemann, 1993.
Nichols, Bill. "The Voice of Documentary." In Nichols, Bill. Ed. *Movies and Methods.* Vol. 3. Berkeley: University of California Press, 1985. 258–273.
Nipe, Christine. "Mrs. Siddons' Currency." *Theatre Survey* 40.2 (Nov. 1999): 70–77.
Norwood Society. *Emile Zola, Photographer in Norwood, South London, 1898–1899.* London: Norwood Society, 1997.
Oksiloff, Assenka. *Visual Culture, Ethnography, and Early German Cinema.* New York: Palgrave, 2001.
O'Pray, Michael. "Eisenstein and Stokes on Disney: Film Animation and Omnipotence." In Pilling, Jayne. Ed. *A Reader in Animation Studies.* Sydney: John Libbey, 1997. 195–202.
O'Regan, Tom. *Australian National Cinema.* London: Routledge, 1996.
Orgel, Stephen. *The Authentic Shakespeare, and Other Problems of the Early Modern Stage.* New York: Routledge, 2002.
———. *Imagining Shakespeare: A History of Texts and Visions.* Houndsmills, UK: Palgrave Macmillan, 2003.
Osborne, Laurie. "Cutting up Characters: The Erotic Politics of Trevor Nunn's *Twelfth Night*." In Lehman, Courtney, and Lisa Starks. Eds. *Spectacular Shakespeare: Critical Theory and Popular Culture.* Madison: Fairleigh Dickinson Press, 2002. 89–109.
Ovenden, Graham. *Alphonse Mucha Photographs.* London: Academy Editions; New York: St. Martin's Press, 1974.
Packard, Vance. *The Hidden Persuaders.* New York: David McCay, 1957.
Paige, Nicholas. "Bardot and Godard in 1963 (Historicizing the Postmodern Image)." *Representations* 88 (Fall 2004): 1–25.

Palmer, Chris. Baz Luhrmann's *Romeo & Juliet*: Kitsch and Tears." http://www.lib.latrobe.edu.au/AHR/archive/Issue-November-1997/palmer.html.

Parker, Brian. "Nature and Society in Akira Kurosawa's *Throne of Blood*." *University of Toronto Quarterly* 66.3 (Summer 1997): 508–526.

Pasolini, Pier-Paolo. "The End of the Avant-Garde." In *Heretical Empiricism*. Trans. Ben Lawton and Louise K. Barnett. Washington, DC: New Academia Publishing, 2005 (orig. 1972).

Pavis, Patrice. *Analyzing Performance: Theater, Dance and Film*. Trans. David Williams. Ann Arbor: University of Michigan Press, 2003.

Pavord, Anna. *The Naming of Names: The Search for Order in the World of Plants*. London: Bloomsbury, 2005.

Payne, Stanley. *The Spanish Civil War, the Soviet Union, and Communism*. New Haven: Yale University Press, 2004.

Pearson, Hesketh. *Beerbohm Tree: His Life and Laughter*. London: Methuen, 1956.

Pearson, Roberta. *Eloquent Gestures: The Transformation of Performance Style in the Griffith Biograph Films*. Berkeley: University of California Press, 1992.

Pendleton, Thomas. "What [?] Price [?] Shakespeare [?]." *Literature/Film Quarterly* 29.2 (2001): 135–147.

Peters, John Durham. "Exile, Nomadism, Diaspora: The Stakes of Mobility in the Western Canon." In Naficy, Hamid. Ed. *Home, Exile, Homeland: Film, Media, and the Politics of Place*. New York: Routledge, 1999. 17–44.

Petric, Vlada. "Dziga Vertov as Theorist." *Cinema Journal* 28.1 (Fall 1978): 28–44.

Petro, Patrice. *Joyless Streets: Women and Melodramatic Representation in Weimar Germany*. Princeton: Princeton University Press, 1989.

Pieri, Giuliana. "D'Annunzio and Alma-Tadema: Between Pre-Raphaelitism and Aestheticism." *Modern Language Review* 96.2 (Apr. 2001): 361–368.

Pilkington, Ace G. *Screening Shakespeare from Richard II to Henry V*. Newark, DE: University of Delaware Press, 1991.

Pittman, L. Monique. "Locating the Bard: Adaptation and Authority in Michael Radford's *The Merchant of Venice*." *Shakespeare Bulletin* 25.2 (Summer 2007): 13–33.

Price, Brian. "Plagiarizing the Plagiarist: Godard Meets the Situationsists." *Film Comment* 33.6 (Nov./Dec. 1997): 66–69.

Prust, Maren. "That's Why the Lady Is a Vamp: The Danish Origins of the Screen's First Dangerous Lady." In Stevenson, Jack. Ed. *Fleshpot: Cinema's Sexual Myth Makers and Taboo Breakers*. Manchester: Head Press, 2002. 77–89.

Quarenghi, Paola. *Shakespeare e gli inganni del cinema*. Rome: Bulzoni Editore, 2002.

Rabinovtiz, Lauren. *For the Love of Pleasure: Women, Movies and Culture in Turn-of-the-Century Chicago*. New Brunswick, NJ: Rutgers University Press, 1998.

Ramsaye, Terry. *A Million and One Nights: A History of the Motion Picture through 1925*. New York: Simon and Schuster, 1986 (orig. 1926).

Ray, Robert. "The Field of 'Literature and Film.'" In Naremore, James. Ed. *Film Adaptation*. New Bruswick, NJ: Rutgers University Press, 2000. 38–53.

Richie, Donald. *A Hundred Years of Japanese Film: A Concise Guide, with a Selective Guide to Videos and DVDs*. Tokyo: Kodansha International, 2001.

Roddick, Nick. *A New Deal in Entertainment: Warner Brothers in the 1930s*. London: British Film Institute, 1983.

Rodgers, Marlene. "*Prospero's Books*—Word and Spectacle: An Interview with Peter Greenaway." *Film Quarterly* 45.2 (Winter 1991–92): 11–19.

Rohdie, Sam. *The Passion of Pier Paolo Pasolini*. Bloomington: Indiana University Press and the British Film Institute, 1995.

Rosenbaum, Jonathan. "The Invisible Orson Welles: A First Inventory." *Sight and Sound* 55 (1986): 164–71.

Rothwell, Kenneth. "Early Shakespeare Movies: How the Spurned Spawned Art." Published separately as *International Shakespeare Association Occasional Paper No. 8*, 2000.

———. *A History of Shakespeare on Screen: A Century of Film and Television*. 2nd ed. Cambridge: Cambridge University Press, 2004.

Rothwell, Kenneth. "Representing *King Lear* on Screen: From 'Meta-Theater' to 'Meta-Cinema.'" In Davies, Anthony, and Stanley Wells. Eds. *Shakespeare and the Moving Image: The Plays on Film and Television*. Cambridge: Cambridge University Press, 1994. 211–233.

Roud, Richard. "Introduction." In *Godard on Godard*. Trans. and ed. Tom Milne. New York: Da Capo Press, 1986.

Rugg, Linda Haverty. "Globalization and the Auteur: Ingmar Bergman Projected Internationally." In Nestingen, Andrew, and Trevor Elkington. Eds. *Transnational Cinema in a Global North: Nordic Cinema in Transition*. Detroit: Wayne State University Press, 2005. 221–242.

Ruiz, Raúl. *Poetics of Cinema 1. Miscellanies*. Trans. Brian Holmes. Paris: Éditions Dis Voir, 2005.

Rushdie, Salman. "Outside the Whale." In *Imaginary Homelands: Essays and Criticism, 1981–1991*. London: Granta Books, 1992. 87–101.

Sadoul, Georges. *Histoire Générale du Cinéma II: Les Pionniers du cinéma, 1897–1909*. Paris: Les Éditions Denoël, 1947.

Said, Edward. *Culture and Imperialism*. New York: Alfred A. Knopf, 1993.

Sammons, Eddie. *Shakespeare: A Hundred Years on Film*. Oxford: Scarecrow Press, 2004.

Saunders, J. G. "'Apparent Perversities': Text and Subtext in the Construction of the Role of Edgar in Brook's Film of *King Lear*." *The Review of English Studies* 47.187 (Aug. 1996): 317–330.

Schatz, Thomas. *The Genius of the System*. New York: Pantheon, 1990.

Schoch, Richard. *Shakespeare's Victorian Stage: Performing History in the Theatre of Charles Kean*. Cambridge: Cambridge University Press, 1998.

Schoenbaum, Samuel. "*Richard II* and the Realities of Power." In Farrell, Kirby. Ed. *Critical Essays on Shakespeare's* Richard II. New York: G.K. Hall, 1999. 41–57.

Scott, Clement. *Some Notable Hamlets of the Present Time (Sarah Bernhardt, Henry Irving, Wilson Barrett, Beerbohm Tree and Forbes Robertson)*. London: Greening, 1900.

Scott, A.O. "Putting a Still-Vexed Play in a Historical Context." *New York Times*, Dec. 29, 2004, B1, B7.

Scott-Douglas, Amy. "Dogme Shakespeare 95: European Cinema, Anti-Hollywood Sentiment, and the Bard." In Burt, Richard and Lynda Boose. Eds. *Shakespeare, the Movie II: Popularizing the Plays on Film, TV, Video, and DVD*. London: Routledge, 2003. 252–264.

"The Screen." Review of *Hamlet*. *New York Times*, Nov. 9, 1921). http://movies2.nytimes.com/mem/movies/review.html?title=Hamlet&title2=&review=&update=19211109&v_id=.

Seidl, Monika. "Room for Asta: Gender Roles and Melodrama in Asta Nielsen's Filmic Version of *Hamlet* (1920)." *Literature/Film Quarterly* 30.3 (2002): 208–216.

Serper, Zvika. "Lady Kaede in Kurosawa's *Ran*: Verbal and Visual Characterization through Animal Traditions." *Japan Forum* 13.2 (2001): 145–158.

Shakespeare, William. *Romeo and Juliet: A Motion Picture Edition Illustrated with Photographs*. New York: Random House, 1936.

———. *The Riverside Shakespeare*. General ed. G. Blakemore Evans. Boston: Houghton Mifflin Company, 1974.

———. *The Norton Shakespeare, Based on the Oxford Edition*. General ed. Stephen Greenblatt. New York: W.W. Norton and Company, 1997.

Shapiro, James. *A Year in the Life of William Shakespeare: 1599*. New York: Harper Collins, 2005.

Shklovsky, Viktor. "The Cine-Eyes and Intertitles." In Taylor, Richard, and Ian Christie. Eds. *The Film Factory: Russian and Soviet Cinema in Documents*. Cambridge, MA: Harvard University Press, 1988. 153–154.

———. "Sergei Eisenstein and the 'Non-Played' Film." Taylor, Richard, and Ian Christie. Eds. *The Film Factory: Russian and Soviet Cinema in Documents*. Cambridge, Massachusetts: Harvard University Press, 1988. 161–162.

Shostakovich, Dmitri. *Testimony; The Memoirs of Dmitri Shostakovich*. Ed. Solomon Volkov. Trans. Antonina W. Bouis. New York: Limelight Editions, 2004 (orig. 1979).

Silverman, Kaja, and Harun Farocki. *Speaking about Godard*. New York: New York University Press, 1998.

Silviria, Dale. *Laurence Olivier and the Art of Film Making*. London: Associated University Presses, 1985.

Singer, Ben. "Manhattan's Nickelodeons: New Data on Audiences and Exhibitors." *Cinema Journal* 34.3 (Spring 1995): 5–35.

Singh, Jyotsna G. *Colonial Narratives/Cultural Dialogues: Discoveries of India in the Language of Colonialism.* London: Routledge, 1996.
Sinyard, Neil. "Shakespeare Meets *The Godfather*: The Postmodern Populism of Al Pacino's *Looking for Richard*." In Burnett, Mark Thornton, and Ramona Wray. Eds. *Shakespeare, Film, Fin de Siécle.* London: Palgrave Macmillan, 2000. 58–72.
Sklar, Robert. *A World History of Film.* New York: Harry N. Abrams, 2002.
Smedley, G.W. Interview. "'*King John*' in the Mutoscope. A Glimpse at Mr. Tree for a Penny." *Westminster Gazette* (Sept. 21, 1899): 4.
Smith, Emma. "'Either for Tragedy or Comedy': Attitudes to *Hamlet* in Kenneth Branagh's *In the Bleak Midwinter* and *Hamlet*." In Burnett, Mark Thornton, and Ramona Ray. Eds. *Shakespeare, Film, Fin de Siècle.* Houndsmills, UK: Macmillan, 2000. 137–146.
———. "'Remember Me': The Gaumont-Hepworth *Hamlet* (1913). In Klein, Holger, and Dimiter Daphinoff. Eds. *Hamlet on Screen.* Lewiston, New York: Edwin Mellon Press, 1997. 110, 124.
Soyinka, Wole. *King Baabu.* London: Methuen, 2002.
Spevack, Marvin. *The Harvard Concordance to Shakespeare.* Cambridge, MA: Harvard University Press, 1973.
Spielman, Yvonne. "Intermedia in Electronic Images." *Leonardo* 34.1 (2001): 55–61.
Spiers, R. Phené. *The Architecture of "Coriolanus" at the Lyceum Theatre. Illustrated by the Original Designs of Sir Laurence Alma-Tadema, R.A.* London: Offices of the Architectural Review, 1901.
Stack, Oswald. *Pasolini on Pasolini. Interviews with Oswald Stack.* Bloomington: Indiana University Press, 1969.
Staiger, Janet. "Combination and Litigation: Structures of U.S. Film Distribution, 1896–1917." *Cinema Journal* 23.2 (Winter 1984): 41–72. Revised version in *Early Cinema: Space, Frame, Narrative.* Ed. Thomas Elsaesser. London: BFI Publishing, 1990. 189–210.
Stam, Robert. *Film Theory: An Introduction.* New York: Basil Blackwell, 2000.
———. *François Truffaut and Friends: Modernism, Sexuality, and Film Adaptation.* New Brunswick, NJ: Rutgers University Press, 2006.
———. *Literature through Film: Realism, Magic, and the Art of Adaptation.* New York: Basil Blackwell, 2004.
———. *Reflexivity in Film and Literature: From Don Quixote to Jean-Luc Godard.* New York: Columbia University Press, 1992.
———. *Subversive Pleasures: Bakhtin, Cultural Criticism, and Film.* Baltimore: Johns Hopkins University Press, 1992.
Starks, Lisa. "'Remember Me': Psychoanalysis, Cinema, and the Crisis of Modernity." *Shakespeare Quarterly* 53.2 (Summer 2002): 181–200.
Sterritt, David. *The Films of Jean-Luc Godard: Seeing the Invisible.* Cambridge: Cambridge University Press, 1999.
Swanson, Vern Grosvenor. *The Biography of Sir Lawrence Alma-Tadema* (1994). Reproduced in full by the Art Renewal Center. http://www.artrenewal.org/articles/2001/Alma-Tadema/tadema9.asp.
Symington, Rodney. *The Nazi Appropriation of Shakespeare: Cultural Politics in the Third Reich.* Lewiston, NY: Edwin Mellen Press, 2005.
Tanaka, Ichimasu. *Japanese Ink Painting: Shubun to Sesshu.* New York and Tokyo: Weatherhill/Heaibonsha, 1972.
Taranow, Gerda. *The Bernhardt Hamlet: Culture and Context.* New York: Peter Lang, 1996.
———. *Sarah Bernhardt: The Art within the Legend.* Princeton: Princeton University Press, 1972.
Tatspaugh, Patricia. "The Tragedies of Love on Film." In Russell Jackson. Ed. *The Cambridge Companion to Shakespeare.* Cambridge: Cambridge University Press, 2000. 135–162.
Taylor, Gary. "*Hamlet* in Africa 1607." In Kamps, Ivo, and Jyotsna Singh. Eds. *Travel Knowledge: European "Discoveries" in the Early Modern Period.* New York: Palgrave, 2001. 211–248.
———. *Reinventing Shakespeare: A Cultural History, from the Restoration to the Present.* New York: Weidenfeld and Nicolson, 1989.
Taylor, Neil. "National and Racial Stereotypes in Shakespeare Films." In Jackson, Russell. Ed. *The Cambridge Companion to Shakespeare on Film.* Cambridge: Cambridge University Press, 2000. 261–273.
Thomas, Bob. *Thalberg: Life and Legend.* Beverly Hills: New Millennium Press, 2000 (orig. 1969).

Thompson, John. *The Media and Modernity: A Social Theory of the Media.* Palo Alto: Stanford University Press, 1995.
Thompson, Kristin. *Breaking the Glass Armor: Neoformalist Film Analysis.* Princeton: Princeton University Press, 1988.
———. *Herr Lubitsch Goes to Hollywood: German and American Film after World War I.* Amsterdam: Amsterdam University Press, 2005.
———. *Storytelling in the New Hollywood: Understanding Classical Narrative Technique.* Cambridge, MA: Harvard University Press, 1999.
Thompson, Kristin, and David Bordwell. *Film History: An Introduction.* 2nd ed. New York: McGraw-Hill, 2003.
Tomlinson, John. *Globalization and Culture.* Chicago: University of Chicago Press, 1999.
Toulet, Emmanuelle. *Birth of the Motion Picture.* Trans. Susan Emanuel. New York: Harry N. Abrams, 1995. (First French edition in 1988).
Tree, Herbert Beerbohm. *Henry VIII and His Court.* New York: Funk and Wagnalls, 1910.
———. *Shakespeare's Historical Drama* King John *Produced at Her Majesty's Theatre by Herbert Beerbohm Tree on the 20th of September,* MDCCCXCIX. London: British Mutoscope and Biograph Company, 1899.
———. "Some Interesting Fallacies of the Modern Stage." Private printing of an address given to the Playgoer's Club on December 6, 1891 (bound presentation copy at the Folger Shakespeare Library).
Trivedi, Poonam, and Dennis Bartolomeusz. Eds. *India's Shakespeare: Translation, Interpretation, and Performance.* Newark, DE: University of Delaware Press, 2005.
Truffaut, François. "A Certain Tendency of the French Cinema." In Nichols, Bill. Ed. *Movies and Methods.* Berkeley: University of California Press, 1976. 224–236.
Turney, Wayne. "The Astor Place Riot." http://www.wayneturney.20m.com/astorplaceriot.htm.
Tweedie, James. "Caliban's Books: The Hybrid Text in Peter Greenaway's *Prospero's Books.*" Cinema Journal 40.1 (Fall 2001): 104–126.
Ulmer, Renate. *Alfons Mucha, 1860–1939: Master of Art Nouveau.* Cologne: Taschen, 2002.
Ungar, Frederick. "An Account of Schiller's Life and Work." In Ungar, Friedrich. Ed. *Friedrich Schiller: An Anthology for Our Time.* New York: Frederick Ungar, 1959.
Uricchio, William, and Roberta Pearson. *Reframing Culture: The Case of the Vitagraph Quality Films.* Princeton: Princeton University Press, 1993.
Usai, Paolo Cherchi. "Frame Enlargements and the Study of Early Cinema: The Case of Russian Films (1908–1917) at Gosfilmofond, Moscow." Cinefocus 2.1 (Fall 1991): 3–12.
Vardac, A. Nicholas. *Stage to Screen: Theatrical Origins of Early Film, from Garrick to Griffith.* Cambridge, MA: Harvard University Press, 1949.
Varley, Paul. *Japanese Culture.* 4th ed. Honolulu: University of Hawai'i Press, 2000.
Vela, Richard. "Shakespeare, Hollywood, and Mexico: The Cantinflas *Romeo y Julieta.*" Literature/Film Quarterly 30.3 (2002): 231–238.
Verma, Rajiva. "Shakespeare in Hindi Cinema." In Trivedi, Poonam, and Dennis Bartolomeusz. Eds. 269–290.
Viano, Maurizio. *A Certain Realism: Making Use of Pasolini's Film Theory and Practice.* Berkeley: University of California Press, 1993.
Villars, P. "Le Théâtre a Londres: King John, de Shakespeare, au Her Majesty's Theatre." Le Théâtre I (Mar. 1999): 18–21.
Vineberg, Steve. *Method Actors: Three Generations of an American Acting Style.* New York: Schirmer Books, 1991.
Vining, Edward P. *The Mystery of Hamlet: An Attempt to Solve an Old Problem.* Philadelphia: J.B. Lippincott, 1881.
Virilio, Paul. "The Aesthetics of Disappearance." Trans. Philip Beitchman. In *The Paul Virilio Reader.* Ed. Steve Redhead. New York: Columbia University Press, 2004. 58–81.
Vittachi, Tarzie. *Trials of Transition in the Island in the Sun.* Colombo: Associated Newspapers of Ceylon, 1961.
Wall-Romana, Christophe. "Mallarmé's Cinepoetics: The Poem Uncoiled by the Cinématographe, 1893–98." PMLA 120.1 (Winter 2005): 128–147.

Warburg, Aby. *The Renewal of Pagan Antiquity: Contributions to the Cultural History of the European Renaissance.* Trans. David Britt. Los Angeles: Getty Research Institute for the History of Art and the Humanities, 1999.
Warde, Frederick. *Fifty Years of Make-Believe.* New York: International Press Syndicate, 1920.
Weisberg, Gabriel, Edwin Becker, and Évelyne Possémé. Eds. *The Origins of L'Art Nouveau: The Bing Empire.* Amsterdam: Van Gogh Museum, 2004.
Welles, Orson. Interview. "The Third Audience." *Sight and Sound* 23 (Jan.–Mar. 1954): 120–122.
Welles, Orson, and Peter Bogdanovich. *This Is Orson Welles.* Ed. Jonathan Rosenbaum. New York: HarperPerennial, 1992.
Wells, Stanley. Ed. *Shakespeare for All Time.* Oxford: Oxford University Press, 2003.
———. *Shakespeare in the Theatre: An Anthology of Criticism.* Oxford: Clarendon Press, 1997.
Welsh, Alexander. *Hamlet in His Modern Guises.* Princeton: Princeton University Press, 2001.
Welsh, James. "To See It Feelingly: *King Lear* Through Russian Eyes." *Literature/Film Quarterly* 4.2 (Spring 1976): 153–158.
Welsh, James, Richard Vela, and John Tibbets. *Shakespeare into Film.* New York: Checkmark Books, 2002.
West, Shearer. "The Public and Private Roles of Sarah Siddons." In Asleson, Robyn. Ed. *A Passion for Performance: Sarah Siddons and Her Portraitists.* Los Angeles: The J. Paul Getty Museum, 1999. 1–40.
Wilde, Oscar. *The Complete Works of Oscar Wilde.* New York: Dorset Press, 1988.
Williams, Gary. *Our Midnight Revels:* A Midsummer Night's Dream *in the Theatre.* Iowa City: University of Iowa Press, 1997.
Williams, Raymond. *Television: Technology and Cultural Form.* New York: Schocken Books, 1974.
Wills, Garry. *Lincoln at Gettysburg: The Words That Remade America.* New York: Simon and Schuster, 1992.
Willson, Robert F. *Shakespeare in Hollywood, 1929–1956.* Madison, WI: Associated University Presses, 2000.
Wilson, Michael S. "The 'Incomparable' Siddons as Reynolds's Muse: Art and Ideology on the British Stage." In Hurley, Ann and Kate Greenspan. Eds. *So Rich a Tapestry: The Sister Arts and Cultural Studies.* Lewisburg: Bucknell University Press, 1995. 116–150.
Wilson, Richard. *Secret Shakespeare: Studies in Theatre, Religion and Resistance.* Manchester: Manchester University Press, 2004.
Winter, William. Ed. *Edwin Booth's Promptbook of Katharine and Petruchio.* Philadelphia: Pen Publishing, 1924 (from the 1878 edition).
Wollen, Peter. *Signs and Meaning in the Cinema.* Bloomington: Indiana University Press, 1977.
Wood, Michael. *Shakespeare.* New York: Basic Books, 2003.
Yoshimoto, Mitsuhiro. *Kurosawa: Film Studies and Japanese Cinema.* Durham, North Carolina: Duke University Press, 2000.
Young, Robert. Hamlet *and the Visual Arts.* Newark: University of Delaware Press, 2002.
Yutkevich, Sergei. "The Conscience of the King: Kozitsev's *King Lear.*" *Sight and Sound* 40.4 (Aug. 1971): 192–196.
Zabus, Chantal. *Tempests after Shakespeare.* New York: Palgrave, 2002.
Zambrano, Ana Laura. "*Throne of Blood*: Kurosawa's *Macbeth.*" *Literature/Film Quarterly* 2 (1974): 262–274.
Zierold, Norman. *The Moguls.* New York: Coward-McCann, 1969.
Žižek, Slavoj. *Looking Awry: An Introduction to Jacques Lacan through Popular Culture.* Cambridge, MA: MIT Press, 1992.

INDEX

10 Things I Hate about You (Junger, 1999), 28
101 Dalmations (prod. Disney, 1961), 168
3-D film technology in Shakespeare films, 25

Abel, Richard, 273
Abrams, Leon, 142. See also *La Voyante* (Abrams, 1923)
Academy Award: 7 won by *Shakespeare in Love*, 4, 28; 10 won by *West Side Story*, 25; nominations (9) for Olivier, 29; to Jannings, 167; to Karl Freund, 167; to Philip Yordan, 26
Ackroyd, Peter, 5, 252, 262
Acocella, Joan, 291
acting: as parodied in *A Double Life*, 22–23; as ridiculed in *Theater of Blood*, 39–40; as subject in *Looking for Richard*, 35–37; Bernhardt's style, 121–125; Bertini's style, 138–140; contrast of Forbes-Robertson and Ruggeri, 143–146; Gielgud as Shakespeare, 53; Gish's style, 272; in theatrical style for the camera, 64–65; Jannings's style, 158–162; Jannings's use of *schrei* acting, 159; modes of performance, 116; Nielsen's style, 152–158; *schrei* acting, 151; stardom, 131–137, 138–140; theories, 152–153; Vertov's challenge to its legitimacy, 132
actors: and stardom, 131–137; of Vitagraph actors' appreciation of film as a medium, 131; disparities of American and British styles, 29–30, 36. See also acting
the Actors Studio, 23, 255
adaptation: its five tendencies, 31; its three registers, 31; recent theories of, 256; Welles's *Five Kings* and its residual influence on *Chimes at Midnight*, 198
Adelman, Janet, 291
Adler, Allen, 26
Adler, Stella, 23
Adorno, Theodor, 279; critique of consumerism, 242; dispute with Walter Benjamin, 134, 264; distrust of popular culture, 134; divergence from Eisenstein about Jazz music, 194
The Adventures of Robin Hood (Curtiz, 1938), 77
Aesop, 192
L'Affaire Dreyfus (Méliès, 1899), 90
Afgrunden (Gad, 1910), 150–151; creation of an international star system, 150–151
Agate, James, 18
Agee, James, 58, 187, 280
Aguirre, der Zorn Gottes (Herzog, 1972), 107
Aïda (Verdi), 176
Aitken, Harry, 87
Aitken, Roy, 87
Akimov, Nikolai, 252
Akroyd, Peter, 5
Alberti, Leon Battista, 52, 235
Aldridge, Ira, 190
Alexander Nevsky (Eisenstein, 1938), 187–189, 199, 280
Alexandrov, Alexander, 11
Alexandrov, Grigori, 189

allegory: in Godard, 225; in Levring, 64–66; in Ruiz, 200–202; in Warde-Keane, 108–109; in Welles, 189–190, 205
Allen, Robert, 38, 99, 267
Allen, Woody, 48, 81; as American *auteur*, 219; as media theorist, 75; association with Manhattan's art scene, 220–221; cameo in Mazursky, 46; performance in Godard's *King Lear*, 219–221. See also *Annie Hall* (Allen, 1977); *A Midsummer Night's Sex Comedy* (Allen, 1982)
Alles für Geld (Schünzel, 1923), 161
Alma-Tadema, Laurence, 263; use of photography in set design, 82–83, 86
Almereyda, Michael, 28, 34, 44, 116, 146–147. See also *Hamlet* (Almereyda, 2000)
Altman, Rick, 24
Amado, Jorge, 207
America (Griffith, 1924), 16
American Chautauqua Association, 104–105
American Laboratory Theatre, 23
Amleto (Rodolfi, 1917), 143, 145–146; as response to Forbes-Robertson's performance, 143
An Indian Romeo and Juliet (prod. Vitagraph, 1912), 271
Anderegg, Michael, 39, 166, 175–177, 181, 200, 205, 213, 235–237, 244, 252–254, 276–279, 283, 289; history as the theme of *Chimes at Midnight*, 205; on Shakespeare films as genre, 34, 38–39, 163–164, 249
Anderson, Percy: costume designs for Tree, 85. See also costume design
Andrew, Dudley, 43, 200, 256, 283
Andrews, Harry, 41
Angelus Novus (Klee): impact on Benjamin, 238
Anger, Kenneth, 169, 246
Ann Boleyn (Lubitsch, 1920), 161
Annie Hall (Allen, 1977), 75, 221
anti-Nazi films, 167–170; Lubitsch's satire, 169–170; Reinhardt's pluralism, 167–168
Antoine, André, 82
Antonello da Messina, 53, 233

Antony and Cleopatra (prod. Vitagraph, 1908), 271
Antony and Cleopatra (Guazzoni, 1913): see *Marcantonio e Cleopatra*
Antony and Cleopatra (Heston, 1971), 42
Anzai, Tetsuo, 261
Apollinaire, Guillaume, 157–158
Appadurai, Arjun, 62, 260, 289
apparatus theory: as described by Baudry, 193; Welles's use of mirrors in *Othello* (1952), 193–195
L'après midi d'un faune (Debussy, Nijinsky): influence on twentieth century dance, 238; influence on Michael Clark in *Prospero's Books*, 238–239
Aravindan, Govindan, 68. See also *Marattam* (Aravindan, 1988)
Arden of Faversham (Kyd), 251
Aretino, Pietro, 258; pornographic influence on Shakespeare, 258
Aria (omnibus film), 245
Aristotle, 235
Arlen, Harold, 188
Armin, Robert, 43
Arnheim, Rudolf, 152, 273
Arnolfini mirror: in Welles' *Othello* (1952), 193–195
Around the World in Eighty Days (adaptation of Jules Verne by Welles), 179
Art Directors (in Hollywood's Golden Age), 20–21. See also Gibbons; Grot; Menzies
The Art of Limning (1624), 39, 51
Art Nouveau, 119; as Bernhardt's adopted style, 120–123; in Marín's drawings of Bernhardt, 123–125; in Mucha's posters, 125–127
As You Like It (Kent, prod. Vitagraph, 1910), 258, 271
As You Like It (Czinner, 1936), 56
As You Like It (Branagh, 2007), 286
Ashcroft, Peggy, 191
Asleson, Robyn, 136–137
Assunta spina (Bertini, 1914), 138
Asta Nielsen: The Talking Muse (Jensen, 2003), 274
Astaire, Fred, 161, 273
At Freddie's: reference to *King John*, 84

AT & T, sound synchronization technology, 38
Atlantis (Blom, 1913), 116
Attenborough, Richard 42. See also *Gandhi* (Attenborough, 1982)
Audion Tube, 38
aura: attempt to capture Forbes-Robertson's, 146; difficulties in Benjamin's concept, 133–134; the aura associated with star narrators in early cinema, 96
Aurenche, Jean, 256
L'Aurore, 90
Austin, J.L., 249; on doing things with words, 249
Azzuri, Paolo, 140. See also *A Midsummer Night's Dream* (Azzuri, 1913)

Bachelard, Gaston, 284
Baclanova, Olga, 23
The Bad Sleep Well (Kurosawa, 1960), 32, 58, 274; as social commentary, 58
Baker, Houston, 239
Baker, Josephine, 161
Bakhtin, Mikhail, 13, 52, 99, 134, 201–202, 205, 226–227, 245, 253, 256, 259, 262, 264, 280, 284; and Rabelaisian carnival, 230–231, 264, 272, 288
Bakst, Léon, 238
Balázs, Béla, 122; and physignomy, 133–134, 161; and the issue of stardom, 132; defense of cinema, 132; on Nielsen, 152–153
Ball, Robert Hamilton, 87–88, 101, 143, 145, 150, 162, 268–269, 276; and Méliès, 3; and *The Jew of Mestri*, 164–165, 274; and Tree's *King John*, 78–79; and Warde as narrator, 103–104
ballet: *see* dance
Balletdanserinden (Blom, 1911), 150
Ballets Russes, 132, 238, 260, 291; influence on the 1935 *A Midsummer Night's Dream*, 168
Balzac, Honoré de: use of castrato in *Massimilla Doni*, 112; *Sarrasine*, 112
Bansali, Sanjay, 72
Bara, Theda (ps. Theodosia Goodman), 88, 96, 148, 251

Barberis, Alberto, 282
Barker, William, 87, 116. See also *Hamlet* (Barker, 1910 or 1912); *Henry VIII* (Barker, 1911)
Barnard, Malcolm, 49
Barrie, J.M., 88; author of *The Real Thing at Last* (1916), a filmed parody of the *Macbeth* starring Tree
Barry, Iris, 163
Barry, James, 273
Barrymore, Drew, 28
Barrymore, John, 20, 244; as Gloucester in the first released sound film to present Shakespeare, 39
Barthes, Roland, 212, 221–222, 229, 231, 234; anchorage, 224; *studium* and *punctum*, 286–287
Bartlett, Don, 162
Bartók, Béla, 132
Bate, Jonathan, 92
The Battleship Potemkin (Eisenstein, 1925), 44, 187–188
Battistini, Mattia, 8
Baudelaire, Charles, 121–122, 270, 271
Baudrillard, Jean, 133, 235, 287, 288, 290, 294; comparison of Prospero's playground to Disneyland, 290; comparison with Benjamin's "phantasmagoria," 133
Baudry, Jean Louis, 193
Baur, Harry, 142, 274
Baxter, Keith, 284
Bazin, André, 14, 173–174, 179, 225, 254, 267; *Cahiers du Cinéma*, 32–33, 206; and Neorealism, 21–22, 183, 286; and the genius of Hollywood's system, 20; and theories of adaptation, 256; and Welles, 173, 179, 182; in contrast to Pasolini, 288; on Realism and theatre, 56
Beach, Sylvia, 155
Beach, Thomas, 135–136
Béatrice et Bénédict (Berlioz), 8
Beaumarchais, Pierre, 121
Beerbohm, Max, 263; commentary on Bernhadt's *Hamlet*, 127; commentary on *King John*, 79–80
Belasco, David, 82, 104–105, 277
Belinksy, Vissarion, 10
Bell, John, 50

Bell, Vanessa, 49
Belleforest, François de, 117
Belton, John, 170
Bender, Jack, 28. See also *The Tempest* (Bender, 1998)
Benjamin, Walter, 133, 249, 264, 265, 272, 286–287; aura, 134–135, 137; chromolithography and mechanical reproducibility, 125; innervation, 134–135; synthetic aura, 135, 137; view of history, 238, 291
Bennett, Susan, 287
benshi, 66, 102. See also narrators of silent film
Benson, F.R., 102, 159, 267, 268. See also *Richard III* (Benson, 1911); *The Taming of a Shrew* (Benson, 1911)
Berger, Jr., Harry, 236
Bergman, Ingmar, 45, 47–48, 63, 223; as *auteur*, 43, 223–224, 261; as echoed in Nunn, 43; as influence on Allen, 48, 75; as influence on Levring, 65. See also *Fanny and Alexander* (Bergman, 1982); *The Seventh Seal* (Bergman, 1957); *Smiles of a Summer Night* (Bergman, 1955); *The Virgin Spring* (1960); *Wild Strawberries* (Bergman, 1957)
Bergner, Elisabeth, 275
Bergson, Henri, 193; as influence on Deleuze's notions of space, time, and movement, 273
Berkely, Busby, 25, 188, 248
Berlioz, Hector, 8
Bernhardt, Sarah, 38, 115, 117–120, 122–127, 135, 265, 270; adaptation of *Hamlet*, 117–118; adoption of Art Nouveau, 119–123; and Freud, 127–129; and the alternation of rhythms of movement, 122–123; as Sardou's Tosca, 126; as vocal phenomenon, 38, 122, 128; role in the emergence of the feature film in the U.S., 96. See also *Hamlet* (Maurice, 1900)
Bernstein, Leonard, 168, 264
Berthon, L.A., 122
Bertini, Francesca, 150, 153; and the emergence of the film diva, 138–140; and the use of motion in her style, 138, 273. See also *Assunta spina* (Bertini, 1914)
Bertolucci, Bernardo, 8, 174–175; and the Italian equation of Verdi and Shakespeare, 175. See also *The Spider's Stratagem* (Bertolucci, 1970)
Bhabha, Homi, 261; and the bivalence of mimicry, 68–69; and hybridity, 291
Bhardwaj, Vishal, 70–72, 255; as composer, 70–71; attachment to thug-based plots, 71, 72. See also *Maqbool* (Bhardwaj, 2004); *Omkara* (Bhardwaj, 2006)
Bhaskar, Sanjeev, 29
The Bicycle Thieves (De Sica, 1948), 21
Bing, Siegfried, 119, 269
Binstock, Benjamin, 119, 294
Birds of a Feather (prod. Disney, 1931), 189–190
The Birth of a Nation (Griffith, 1915), 87, 96, 112
The Birth of Venus (Botticelli), 52; as commented on by Aby Warburg, 51–52; citation in Castellani's *Romeo and Juliet*; citation in *L.A. Story*, 53; citation in *Prospero's Books*, 52
The Birth of the Virgin (Ghirlandaio), 53
Bishop, Henry, 264
Bitzer, Billy, 84, 140
Björnstrand, Gunnar, 43, 47
Blackmail (1929), 18
Blackton, J. Stuart, 160
Blake, Erin, 268
Blitzer, Billy, 84
Block, Irvin, 26
Blom, August, 116, 148–150, 161, 167, 254; rivalry with Viggo Larsen, 149. See also *Atlantis* (Blom, 1913); *Balletdanserinden* (Blom, 1911); *Desdemona* (Blom, 1912); *Hamlet* (Blom, 1910); *Vampyrdanserinden* (Blom, 1912)
Bloom, Claire, 55
Bloom, Harold, 7
The Blue Angel (von Sternberg, 1930), 162
Bluestone, George, 31, 256
Blumenthal, Ben, 159, 259
Blunt, Anthony, 259

Boas, Franz, 154; and the "culture" concept, 48; and the rejection of phrenology, 156
Boccaccio, Giovanni, 54, 231
Boer War, 90, 265
Bogdanovich, Peter, 170; and Welles, 186, 189–190, 277, 280
Boito, Arrigo, 8, 9, 161, 183; as influence on Welles, 175, 181, 282
Boleslavsky, Richard, 23
Boli, John, 62
Bolter, Jay David, 44
Bonahan, Laura, 63
Bondanella, Peter, 277, 286
Bondarchuk, Sergei, 15
Bonham-Carter, Helena, 43
Booth, Edwin, 18, 22, 80, 82, 104, 107, 137, 267, 268; and Vining, 155; as an influence on Warde's Gloster, 108
Booth, John Wilkes, 22–23, 108
Booth's Theatre, 104
Bordwell, David, 232, 257, 266, 284
Borelli, Lyda, 138
Borges, Jorge Luis, 8, 174–175, 249, 252
Boris Godunov (Pushkin and Mussorgsky), 9, 187
Bost, Pierre, 256
Botticelli, Sandro, 125, 259, 289; influence on Castellani's *Romeo and Juliet* (1954), 53–54; influence on *L.A Story* (1991), 52–53; influence on *Prospero's Books*, 52
Boucicault, Dion, 78, 82; as mentor to Frederick Warde, 104–105
Bourdieu, Pierre, 98, 223
Bourgeois, Gérard, 116. See also *Hamlet* (Bourgeois, 1910)
Bowser, Eileen, 97, 251, 265, 266
Boydell, Josiah, 50
Bradbury, Malcolm, 260
Bradley, A.C., 278; and psychologism in Shakespeare criticism, 180. See also L.C. Knights
Brady, Frank, 280, 283
Brahms, Johannes, 147
Brakhage, Stan, 234
Branagh, Kenneth, 29, 32, 37, 42, 116, 118, 283, 286; as a war-like Harry 214–217; as influenced by Welles, 214–217; use of music underlaying dialogue, 216. See also *As You Like It* (2007); *Hamlet* (Branagh, 1996); *Henry V* (Branagh, 1989); *Love's Labours Lost* (Branagh, 2000); *A Midwinter's Tale* (Branagh, 1995); *Much Ado About Nothing* (Branagh, 1993)
Brandauer, Klaus Maria, 276
Brandes, Georg, 128, 150, 155
Brando, Marlon, 22–23, 25, 72, 257
Brantlinger, Patrick, 260
Brecht, Berthold, 286; in Godard, 209; in Jarman, 188
Bresson, Robert, 64, 224, 253
Brighton School, 91, 143
Bristol, Michael, 16, 19, 29
British Free Cinema movement, 24
Britten, Benjamin, 245, 246 248; in Luhrmann's Sydney Opera production of *A Midsummer Night's Dream*, 248
Broch, Hermann, 249
Brode, Douglas, 24
Broken Lance (Dmytryk, 1954), 26
Brook, Peter, 64–65, 71, 180, 219, 235, 253, 259; as actor-commentator for Pacino, 36, 257; Kozintsev's comments on use of stylization, 12; use of location in 1971 *King Lear*, 261; use of Scofield as an actor, 112; use of Welles as an actor, 261. See also *King Lear* (Brook-McCullough, 1953); *King Lear* (Brook, 1971); *Lord of the Flies* (Brook, 1963)
Brooke, Arthur, 243
Brooke, Nicholas, 279
The Brothers Karamazov (Dostoyevsky), 9–10
The Brothers Karamazov (Buchowetzki, 1918), 160
Brown, John, 22
Browne, Coral, 41
Browne, Tom, 80
Brueghel, Pieter, the Elder, as visual inspiration for Olivier's *Richard III*, 55
Brunel, Adrian, 18
Brunelleschi, Filippo, 235
Bruno, Giordano, 187
Bruno, Giuliana, 140, 288

Bruto (prod. Cines, 1910), 142
Buchanan, Judith, 26, 43–44, 110, 111, 139, 143, 151, 159, 160–161, 268, 271
Buchman, Lorne, 257
Büchner, Georg, 159
Buchowetzki, Dimitri, 159–162, 164, 167, 254, 262. See also *The Brothers Karamazov* (Buchowetzki, 1918); *Othello* (Buchowetzki, 1922); *Sappho* (Buchowetzki, 1921)
Buckalew, Bethel, 255. See also *The Secret Sex Lives of Romeo and Juliet* (Buckalew, 1969)
Buffam, William, 100
Buhler, Stephen, 3, 11, 14, 244, 253, 254
Buñuel, Luis, 167, 178, 192, 199, 257; influence on Greenaway, 235; influence on Rushdie, 72–73. See also *Viridiana* (Buñuel, 1952)
Burbage, Richard, 121
Burckhardt, Sigurd, 262
Buré, Farim, 63, 260
Burge, Stuart, 42. See also *Julius Caesar* (Burge, 1970)
Burton, Richard, 20, 118, 269
Bush, Stephen, 97, 98–99, 266
Bushman, Francis X., 88

Cabaret (Fosse, 1972), 34
The Cabinet of Dr. Caligari (Wiene, 1920), 151
Cabiria (Pastrone, 1913), 82, 105, 141, 273
Cagney, James, 168
Cahiers du Cinéma, 21, 33, 174, 183, 186, 206, 223–224, 256
Calabrese, Omar, 236, 290
Calderon (Pasolini, 1973), 288
Calinescu, Matei: on conflicting aesthetic modernities, 61
Callas, Maria, 227
Callow, Simon, 281
Calmette, Gaston: accuser of Nijinsky and Diaghilev of pornography, 238
Calmettes, André, 96, 141, 268. See also *Camille* (Calmettes, 1911); *La Dame aux Camélias* (Calmettes, 1912); *Macbeth* (Calmettes, 1908); *Richard III* (Calmettes, 1912)
Camerini, Mario, 277
Campbell, Joseph, 245

Campbell, Thomas, 272
Campion, Thomas, 258, 276
Canby, Vincent, 46, 258
Canclini, Néstor García, 62, 260
Cannes Film Festival: award of Palm d'Or to Morocco's entry, Welles's *Othello* (1952), 176; award of Palm d'Or to Yutkevich (1956), 14
Canon Films, 224
Canterbury, Stuart, 255. See also *In the Flesh* (Canterbury, 2000); *A Midsummer Night's Cream* (Canterbury, 2000)
Cantinflas (ps. Mario Moreno), 257
Cardinal Wolsey (prod. Vitagraph, 1912), adaptation of *All Is True*, 44, 258, 271
Cardwell, Sarah, 32, 257
Carjat, Étienne, 93
Carné, Marcel, 206
Carnival (Knoles, 1921), 149
Carnival (Wilcox, 1931), 149
carnivalesque: see Bakhtin
Carpaccio, Vittore, 53, 54, 193, 281
Carr, J. Comyns, 80
Carre, Michel, 266
Carroll, Noël, 273
Cartelli, Thomas, 15–16, 251, 254, 257
Cartwright, Lisa, 49
Caruso, Enrico, 165
Casale, Gherardo, 276–277
Caserini, Mario, 116, 138, 141, 269, 273. See also *Giulietta e Romeo* (Caserini, 1908); *Hamlet* (Caserini, 1908); *Macbeth* (Caserini, 1909); *Gli ultimi giorni di Pompeii* (Caserini, 1913)
Casino Royale (Huston, 1967), 162
Cassavetes, John, 45–46, 64, 220; influence on Dogme 95, 64
Casson, Phillip, 278
Castellani, Renato, 20–22, 53–54, 234, 254, 255; aesthetic experiments in period Realism, 53–54; over-reliance on Hollywood box-office, 24. See also *Romeo and Juliet* (Castellani, 1954)
Castiglione, Baldassare, 7
Catherine and Petruchio (Garrick), 18
Caughlin, Rose, 271
Cavalleria Rusticana (Mascagni), 9
Cavecchi, Mariacristina, 236

Cavell, Stanley, 273
Cecil, William, Lord Burghley, 258
Ceddo (Sembène, 1976), 65
Cervantes, Miguel de, 174, 199, 234, 249; influence on Shakespeare, 51; Titian's Charles V as the physical portrait of Don Quijote, 51
Césaire, Aimé, 63, 238–240
Cézanne, Paul, 93
Chabrol, Claude, 147, 183, 213; as parodist of Olivier's *Hamlet*, 206–208; work with Welles, 207–208. See also *Ophélia* (Chabrol, 1962); *Ten Days' Wonder* (Chabrol, 1971)
Chakrabarty, Dipesh, 61, 260
Chamberlain, Joseph, 90
Chaplin, Charlie, 18, 169, 272, 282, 286; and theories of film performance, 127, 132, 134, 272; as parodist of *Hamlet*, 33; as read by Pasolini, 288. See also *The Circus* (1928); *The Great Dictator* (Chaplin, 1940); *A King in New York* (Chaplin, 1954)
Charcot, Jean-Martin, 127
Chardynin, Piotr, 160. See also *Korobeiniki* (Chardynin, 1910)
Chaucer, Geoffrey, 231
Che cosa sono le nuvole? (Pasolini, 1968), 225–231; use of a theatre of life-size marionettes, 227–228; use of Velázquez to dispute Foucault, 227, 229–231
Cheah Chee Kong, Philip, 286. See also *Chicken Rice War* (Cheah, 2000)
The Cheat (DeMille, 1915), 19
Chekhov, Anton, 66
Chekhov, Mikhail, 10, 23
Chéret, Jules: technique of designing chromolithographic posters, 120, 125
Cherubini, Luigi, 227
Chevalier, Maurice, 25, 167
Chicken Rice Wars (Kong, 2000), 257
Chimes at Midnight (Welles, 1965), 196–200, 202–207; as poised between Hollywood and the French New Wave, 206–208; as dialogue with the avant-garde, 205–209; exilic autobigraphy in, 196–200; parallels to *Richard III* (Ruiz, 1965), 200–205

Chion, Michel: criticism of Welles's *Macbeth*, 277–278
Chitty Chitty Bang Bang (Hughes, 1968), 48
Chorley, Henry, 126
Chrétien de Troyes, 33
Christensen, Benjamin: assessment of Nielsen, 150
Christensen, Thomas, 274
CIAA (Coordinator of Inter-American Affairs), 178
Cibber, Colley, 55, 78, 102–103, 105, 244, 272; *Richard III* (1700) as model for cinematic adaptations, 105–108
Cimino, Michael, 34
Cinema of Attractions, 263
Cinématogaphe géant, 123
Cinéorama, 123
Cinzio, Giraldi, 8, 161, 175, 191, 192, 277
Citizen Kane (Welles, 1941), 14, 181–182, 193, 187, 216, 277, 279; influence on *The King Is Alive*, 65
Clair, René, 161–162, 186, 276. See also *Sous les Toits de Paris* (Clair, 1929)
Clark, Michael, 238; and Nijinsky, 291; as Caliban, 235; as staging postcoloniality, 237–240
Clarke, Charlotte, 272
Cleopatra (Zecca, 1910), 251
Cléopâtre (Méliès, 1899), 251
Clifford, Jim, 48
Close, Glenn, 29, 118, 137, 225
Cloutier, Suzanne, 282
Clover, Carol, 279
Clueless (Heckerling, 1995), 116
Cobos, Juan, 200, 238
Cocteau, Jean, 179, 187, 193
Coetzee, J.M., 239
Cohl, Émile, 160
Cohn, Alfred, 148. See also *Den Svide Slavinde* (Cohn, 1907)
Collick, John, 67, 257, 267
Colman, Ronald, 23
Comedy of Errors (prod. Vitagraph, 1908), 271
Comerio, Luca, 116. See also *Hamlet* (Comerio, 1908)
Commedia dell'arte, 149
communication theory, 75–76
Connery, Sean, 42

Conrad, Peter, 248
Conte d'hiver (Rohmer, 1972), 33, 257
contemporary localism, 10. See also domestication
contenutismo, 209, 229, 231. See also Pasolini
Cook, Judith, 269
The Cook, The Thief, His Wife, and Her Lover (Greenaway, 1989), 285
Coote, Robert, 41
Coppedge, Walter, 46
Coppola, Francis Ford: influence on *Looking for Richard*, 36–37; influence on *Maqbool*, 72; influence on *Men of Respect*, 26. See also *Godfather III* (Coppola, 1990)
Coquelin, 123
Corbould, E.H., 77
Coriolanus (Alma-Tadema, set design), 83
Corman, Roger, 40. See also *The Tower of London* (Corman, 1962)
Cornell, Katherine, 177
Coronado, Celestino, 285
Correggio (Antonio Allegri), 258–259
The Corsican Brothers (Dumas), 78
Cosmopolitan, 158
costume design as art form: excess in Jarman, 188; excessive costumelessness in Greenaway, 238; historical accuracy in *King John*, 77; opulent historicity in Castellani, 22; parody in Branagh, 286. See also Anderson; Messel
Coursen, H.R., 237, 290
Coussement, Laetitia, 267
Coward, Noël, 23
Crafton, Donald, 254
Craig, Gordan, 88, 277
Crane, Walter, 119
Crawford, Cheryl, 23
Criterion DVD issue: Bergman's *Hamlet*s, 47; cover design for Van Sant, 214; Olivier's *Richard III*, 44
Croce, Benedetto, 8, 252
Crosland, Alan, 161. See also *The Jazz Singer* (Crosland, 1927)
Crowl, Samuel, 236, 257
Crows Flying over a Cornfield (Van Gogh), 259

Crowther, Bosley: hostility to Welles's *Macbeth*, 187; hostility to Welles's *Chimes*, 283
The Crucible (Miller, 1953), 190
Cukor, George, 20, 22–23, 53, 209, 244, 257, 259; preemptive parody of Method Acting, 22. See also *A Double Life* (Cukor, 1947); *Romeo and Juliet* (Cukor, 1936)
cult audiences, 96
cultural geography: Folger Shakespeare Library, 19
Curtiz, Michael, 77, 167. See also *The Adventures of Robin Hood* (Curtiz, 1938)
Cushing, Peter, 35
Cushman, Charlotte, 137
Cymbeline (Alma-Tadema, set design), 83
Cymbeline (prod. Thanhouser, 1913), 111
Czinner, Paul, 56, 275. See also *As You Like It* (Czinner, 1936)
Czolgosz, Leon, 131

Daly, Augustin, 82
Daguerre, Louis, 82
La Dame aux Camélias (Calmettes, 1912), 96
dance: ballet in *A Midsummer Night's Dream* (Neumann, 1925), 167–168; ballet in *A Midsummer Night's Dream* (Reinhardt-Dieterle, 1935), 168; ballets choreographed by Nijinskaya, 168; ballets choreographed by Nijinsky, 238–239; choreography for Musicals by Hermes Pan, 25; Clark's performance in *Prospero's Books*, 237–238; Eifman's choregraphy for the ballet *Russian Hamlet*, 10; kodiyettam in *Kaliyattam*, 68; kodiyettam in *Marattam*, 68; Robbins's choreography for *West Side Story*, 25; *Romeo and Juliet* (Prokofiev), 11
Daniels, Joseph, 103
D'Annunzio, Gabriele, 82, 141, 263
Dante, 23, 191, 232
Danton (Rolland), 159
Danton's Death (Büchner, 1920), 159
Darío, Rubén: originator of the term "modernismo," 61
Das Liebes-ABC (Stifter, 1916), 156

Das Lied von der Erde (Mahler), 67
David, Jacques-Louis, 3
Davidson, Helen, 169
Davidson, Paul, 150–151, 158
Davies, Anthony, 56, 116, 181, 259, 277
Davies, Delmer, 26. See also *Jubal* (Davies, 1956)
Davoli, Ninetto, 227
de Chavanne, Puvis, 120
De Cordova, Richard, 272
De Forest, Lee, 38–39. See also *The Merchant of Venice* (De Forest, 1926[?])
de Liguoro, Giuseppe, 141, 266, 273. See also *L'Inferno di Dante* (de Liguoro, 1911)
de Maupassant, Guy, 65
de Montfort, Simon, 77
de Musset, Alfred, 120
De Niro, Robert, 72
de Putti, Lya, 162
De Sanctis, Marianna, 116, 268–269
De Sica, Vittorio, 183, 214; as exemplar of Realism, 21. See also *The Bicycle Thieves* (De Sica, 1948); *Miracle in Milan* (De Sica, 1948); *Umberto D* (De Sica, 1952)
de Vere, Edward, Earl of Oxford, 5, 271
Dead Poets Society (Weir, 1989), 33
Dean, James, 24
Debdale, Robert, 276
Debord, Guy, 223, 230, 237
Debussy, Claude, 238. See also *L'après midi d'un faun*
Decherney, Peter, 178
The Decoration of Houses (1897): Wharton's views on frescoes, 291
Dee, John, 236, 240, 249
Defoe, Daniel, 239
Del Giudice, Filippo, 56
Del Rio, Dolores, 257
Delacroix, iconography in engravings of *Hamlet*, 121, 122
de la Tour, Georges, 233
Deleuze, Gilles, 149, 260, 278; and Welles's use of mirrors, 193–196; debt to Bergson, 193
Delgado, Miguel, 257. See also *Romeo y Julieta* (Delgado, 1943)
Demblon, Célestin, 258

DeMille, Cecil B., 19, 33. See also *The Cheat* (DeMille, 1915), *Triumph* (DeMille, 1924)
Den Hvide Slavehandel (Larsen, 1910), 148
Den Svide Slavinde (Cohn, 1907), 148
Dench, Judi, 285, 290
Deni, Victor, 15
Dennehy, Brian, 291
Dent, Alan, 32, 55, 106
Depardieu, Gérard, 286
Déprats, Jean-Marie, 106
Deren, Maya, 234
Derrida, Jacques, 93, 212, 226, 233, 290; on archewriting, 289; on the instability of genre, 287
Desdemona (Blom, 1912): *see For Abend Taeppe*
Desfontaines, Henri, 96, 116, 141. See also *Hamlet* (1910): *Le Marchand de Venise* (Desfontaines, 1912); *La Mergere approvisée* (Desfontaines, 1911)
Des'ree, 243
DeVito, Danny, 33
Dewey, Thomas, 177, 191
Diaghilev, Sergei, 238, 291
Diakonova, Nina, 252
Dickens, Charles, 31, 80, 100
Dickson, William Kennedy Laurie, 84–85, 91, 264
Didi-Huberman, Georges: on the qualities of air in Botticelli and Warburg, 259
Die Sexualnot der Gefangen (Dieterle, 1928), 168
Dieterle, Wilhelm, 167–169, 246. See also *Die Sexualnot der Gefangen* (Dieterle, 1928); *Geschlecht in Fesseln* (Dieterle, 1928); *A Midsummer Night's Dream* (Reinhardt-Dieterle, 1935)
Dietrich, Marlene, 167; and her imitation of Werner Krauss, 162
digital film techniques: audio tracks, 44, 216; restoration, 44–45; Vitagraph reanimations, 45
Dillon, Steven, 280
Dineley, Henry, 283
Direct Cinema, 216
dis(s)quotation, 257; as genre, 37; by Cantinflas, 257; by Stoppard, 37–38; in *Theater of Blood*, 41–42

The Diskobolos (Myron), 221
Disraeli, Benjamin, 81
Dixon, Wheeler Winston, 286
Dmytryk, Edward, 26. See also *Broken Lance* (Dmytryk, 1954)
Doctor Zhivago (Pasternak), 11
Dodeskaden (Kurosawa, 1970), 67
Dogme 95 movement, 64–66, 118; as a response to globalization, 64; indebtedness to Cassavetes, 64
domestication: of Shakespeare plots and characters, 10
Don Carlo (Verdi), 72
Domingo, Plácido, 9; as Verdi's Alfredo for Zeffirelli, 9; as Verdi's Otello for Zeffirelli, 9
Don Quijote (Cervantes), 51–52; Renaissance theories of motion, 51; and Titian, 51
Donaldson, Frances, 80
Donaldson, Peter, 43, 193, 238, 245–246, 258, 278, 282, 289, 290, 291; hyperlinking film and text, 289; Shakespeare text and web intermediation, 45
Donne, John, 284
Doran, Charles, 176
Dos Passos, John, 198, 283
Dostoevsky, Feodor, 9–10, 128
A Double Life (Cukor, 1947), 22–24; as parody of Method acting, 22–23
Douglas, Mark, 29–30
Dreyer, Carl Theodor, 150, 219, 224–225, 253; influence on Brook, 253; influence on Welles, 219; influence on Godard, 224–225. See also *La Passion d Jeanne d'Arc* (Dreyer, 1928)
Dreyfus, Alfred, 90; political activism in Tree's *King John*, 93
Dreyfuss, Richard, 38
Drowning by Numbers (Greenaway, 1988), 232
Dryden, John, 43–44
du Maurier, George, 80
Duccio, Agostino di, 52, 288
Ducis, Jean-François, 269
Dulac, Germaine, 132
Dunant, Caroline, 82
Dupont, E.A., 162. See also *Variety* (Dupont, 1925)

Duras, Marguerite, 256, 257
Dürer, Albrecht, 49; influence on *Chimes at Midnight*, 183, 196
Duse, Eleanora, 8, 138
Dussaud, C.F., 122
DVD: as example of intermediation, 44; completeness of *Fanny and Alexander* (Bergman), 47; cover design innovation in Van Sant, 214; excellence of commentaries on Kurosawa, 44; excellence of restored *Shakespeare Wallah* (Ivory), 69–70; Olivier as the medium's particular beneficiary, 44. See also Criterion DVD issue
Dwight, Eleanor, 291
Dyer, Anson, 160
Dyer, Richard, 134, 135, 281

East-West Stories (Rushdie), 73
Eclipse Shakespeare cycle, 97–98, 116, 141–142. See also *Falstaff* (Desfontaines, 1911, unrediscovered); *Hamlet* (Desfontaines, 1910, unrediscovered); *La Mergere approvisée* (Desfontaines, 1911); *Shylock, ou le More de Venice* (Desfontaines, 1912)
Eco, Umberto, 96–97, 226, 265; definition of cult films, 96, 265; dispute with Pasolini over semiotics, 226
Eder, Bruce, 56
Edison, Thomas, 84, 100; as MPPC monopolist, 267; film exploitation in Kinetoscope parlors, 17; invention of films as accompaniment to sound recordings, 16; Kinetophone, 38; patent disputes, 140. See also *Rip Van Winkle* (prod. Edison, 1896)
Edwards, Hilton, 176–177, 198, 282
Eggert, Catherine, 42–43
Eifman, Boris, 10
Eisenstein, Sergei, 44, 182, 203, 206, 280; and Kabuki, 253; and Mickey Mouse, 134; and Robeson, 15; and the montage of attractions, 86, 263; as Stalin's victim, 11; commentary on perspective, 194; defense of legitimacy of acting in films, 132, 263–264; influence

on Welles, 186–190; influence on Yutkevich, 12; Meyerhold as mentor, 13; on contributions to film from other arts, 31; overtonal montage, 188–190; tonal montage, 12; vertical montage, 194. See also *Alexander Nevsky* (Eisenstein, 1938); *The Battleship Potemkin* (Eisenstein, 1925); *Ivan the Terrible* trilogy (Eistenstein, 1945–1946)
Eisner, Lotte, 152–153, 162–163, 275
Eksteins, Modris, 238, 260
El Greco, 31, 194
Electra, My Love (Jancsó, 1974), 80
Eliot, T.S., 129, 260
Elliott, Michael, 48
Elsaesser, Thomas, 31, 167
Elstree Calling (Hitchcock-Brunel, 1930), 18–19, 28
Emerson, John, 87–88; collaboration with Griffith to film Tree, 87. See also *Henry VIII* (Emerson, 1916)
Emerson, Ralph Waldo, 19, 29
L'Enfant prodigue (Carre, 1907), 266
Engberg, Marguerite, 274
Engel, Joseph, 96
engravings: of Delacroix, 121–122; of Dürer, 183, 196
Enough Simplicity in Every Wise Man (Ostrovsky), 86
Enticknap, Leo, 258
Epistle on Poetry (Sumarokov), 9
Epstein, Jacob, 281
Epstein, Jean, 132
Erdody, Leo, 171
Erksan, Metin, 275
Esaki, Kohei, 59
Eugene O'Neill effect 37–42; in *Rosenkrantz and Guildenstern Are Dead*, 37–38; in *Theater of Blood*, 39–42. See also dis(s)quotation
Evans, Jessica, 49
Everybody's Shakespeare, 177
Ewers, Hanns Heinz, 167–168. See also *A Midsummer Night's Dream* (Ewers-Rye, 1913)
exile, 281; as theme in Welles' *Chimes at Midnight* (1965), 196–198; of Raoul Ruiz, 200–202

Expressionism, 151–152, 161–164; in Ulmer's *Strange Illusion* (1945), 170–171; in Welles's *Macbeth*, 183
The Eyre Affair (Fforde), 95, 112, 265

F for Fake (Welles, 1974), 175
Fairbanks, Douglas, 18, 21, 167
Falconetti, Renée, 224–225
Falstaff (Verdi), 8, 176, 231
Fame (Parker, 1980), 33
Famous Players in Famous Plays Company, 96
Fanon, Frantz, 192, 240, 298
Fanny and Alexander (Bergman, 1982), 43, 47–48
Farocki, Haroun, 287
Faure, Félix, 119
Faust (Murnau, 1926), 262
Featherstone, Mike, 62
Fédora (Sardou), 126
Fellini, Federico, 105, 285–286. See also *La Strada* (Fellini, 1954); *Satyricon* (Fellini, 1969)
Felner, Peter Paul, 164–166. See also *Der Kaufmann von Venerdig*, or *The Jew of Mestri* (Felner, 1923)
Fenellosa, Ernest, 66, 67, 260
Feng Xiaogang, 255. See also *Ye yan* (Feng, 2006)
Ferretti, Dante, 285
Feuillade, Louis, 142. See also *A Village King Lear* (Feuillade, 1911)
Fforde, Jasper, 95–97, 265
Field, Richard, 6
Fielding, Henry: author of *Shamela*, 288
Film d'Arte Italiana Shakespeare cycle, 138–140. See also *Giulietta e Romeo* (Lo Savio, 1911); *King Lear* (Lo Savio, 1910); *The Merchant of Venice* (Lo Savio, 1910); *Otello* (Lo Savio, 1909)
filmed theater and its dissimilarity to actual theatrical performance: Bernhardt's, 123–124; Forbes-Robertson's, 143–145; Tree's, 84–85
Filming Othello (Welles, 1978), 175, 192, 196–197, 281
Finch, Jon, 34
Finch, William, 260
Fink, Guido, 227
Fiorentino, Giovanni, 164, 276

Firenzuola, Agnolo, 7
Fishburne, Laurence, 215
Fisher, Harrison, 158
Fitzgerald, Penelope, 84
Flaherty, Robert, 182
Flaubert, Gustave, 249
Fleming, Victor, 162. See also *The Way of All Flesh* (Fleming, 1927)
Fliess, Wilhelm, 128
Florio, John, 117, 239
Fludd, Robert, 236–237
Flynn, Errol, 77
Folger Shakespeare Library, 19, 83, 131, 137, 268, 283
Fonda, Peter, 28
Fontanesi, Antonio, 66
For Abent Taeppe (Blom, 1908) 149, 254
Forbes-Robertson, Johnston, 122, 159, 264; as Hamlet, 143–145; comparison with Ruggeri's Hamlet, 143, 145; contrast to Nielsen, 156
Forbidden Planet (Wilcox, 1956), 26–28, 171, 256; and Cold War critiques of science, 27; and mass-market advertising, 27
Ford, Harrison, 137
Ford, John, 182, 186. See also *Stagecoach* (Ford, 1939); *My Darling Clementine* (Ford, 1948)
Forman, Simon, 6, 183, 185
Fosse, Bob, *Cabaret* (Fosse, 1972), 34
Foster, Norman, 178. See also *Journey Into Fear* (Foster-Welles, 1943)
Foucault, Michel, 97, 234, 288, 289; as disputed by Pasolini, 226–227, 229–230; commentary on Velázquez, 230; declaration of the death of the author, 209
Foulon, Otto, 132
Fra Angelico (Guido di Pietro), 53
Frampton, Hollis, 232
France, Anna Kay, 13, 14, 253
Franco, Francisco, 174, 196, 198–199
Frankfurt School, 99
Franklin, Chester M., *The Toll of the Sea*, (Franklin, 1922), 18
Freed, Arthur, 25
French New Wave, 21, 31, 33, 116, 197, 208, 213, 286; affinity for Welles, 206–207; and adaptation, 256; and Bazin, 206, 254; as critics, 173–174; disputes over women, 207; influence on Peter Hall, 285
Freud, Sigmund, 4, 271, 284; development of the Oedipus theory, 127–129, 279; influence on Asta Nielsen, 156–157; *The Interpretation of Dreams*, 128–129; interpreting Bernhardt's performance of Hamlet, 127–129; the logic of dreams, 157; parodies of, 170–171; use of pop psychology in *Forbidden Planet*, 26–27; visit to America, 130
Freund, Karl, 167
Fried, Yakov, 252
Friedman, Winifred, 50
Frusta, Arrigo, 116
Fuchs, Leonart, 283
Fukuda, Kumio, 260
Funeral of St. Ursula (Carpaccio), 54
Furnivall, James, 260
Furse, Roger, 56–58
Furtwangler, Albert, 254

Gabriel, Teshome, 277
Gad, Urban, 150, 155. See also *Afgrunden* (Gad, 1910); *Jugend und Tollheit* (Gad, 1913)
Gaddi, Taddeo, 57
Gade, Svend, 150, 269, 274. See also *Hamlet, Ein Rachedrama* (Gade, 1921)
Le Gai Savoir (Godard, 1968), 287; use of photography, 222–223
Gainsborough, Thomas, 136
Galerie de l'Art Nouveau, 119
Gallagher, Tag, 170
Gance, Abel, 123
Gandhi (Attenborough, 1982), 42
Garber, Marjorie, 278
Garbo, Greta, 152, 167
Gardner, Helen, 96, 99, 149, 251
Garrick Theater, 97
Garrick, David, 3, 121, 136, 244, 254, 270; and the Shakespeare cult, 50; establishment of European theatre in India, 261; use of *Catherine and Petruchio* in the Pickford-Fairbanks *Taming of the Shrew*, 18; use of Colley Cibber, 105
Gassman, Vittorio, 45

Gate Theatre (Dublin), 176–177, 198
Gaudreault, André, 289
Gaugin, Paul, 120
Gay, Peter, 128, 271
Geheimnisser Eine Seele (Pabst, 1926), 163
Geldud, Harry, 57, 122–123, 270, 273
General and Rare Memorials pertayning to the Perfecte Arte of Navigation (Dee, 1577), 240
General Film Company, 98, 100, 141–142, 266
Generation X, 28, 147, 241
genre: Biopic 3, 167; Documentary, 35–37, 257; experiments in, 34–35, 219; Gangster film, 26, 180; *gendai-geki*, 35; Gross out film, 255; Hard-core pornography, 255; historical costume drama, 151; Horror film, 34–35; *jidai-geki*, 32, 58–59, 67, 181, 261; Kammerspiel, 151; Musical, 19–20, 24–25, 45–47, 68, 168, 247–248; Nudie Cutie, 170; Road Movie, 64; Western, 25–26; Sci-fi Film, 26–28; serial melodrama, 109; *shakai-mono*, 261; Spaghetti Western, 242; Street Film, 151; Teen Pic, 28; risqué and macabre genres in Denmark, 148, 150
Gentillet, Innocent, 267
Gepard, Erwin, 155–156, 274
Gere, Richard, 137
Gerlach, Arthur von, 152. See also *Vanina* (von Gerlach, 1923)
Gerlach, John, 259
Gérôme, Jean-Léon, 83
Geschlecht in Fesseln (Dieterle, 1928), 168
Ghirlandaio, Domenico, 53
Ghita, Lucian, 286
Gibbons, Cedric, 21
Gibson, Mel, 9, 42, 116, 137, 157
Giddens, Anthony, 62, 260
Gide, André, 11
Gidel, Henry, 269
Gielgud, John, 25, 35–36, 42, 53, 55, 56, 118, 199, 203–205, 215, 234, 258, 269, 270, 289, 290; as Shakespeare and his characters in *Prospero's Books*, 234, 289; as Shakespeare in Castellani's *Romeo and Juliet*, 53
Gifford, Henry, 13

Gilray, James, 50
Ginzburg, Carlo, 92, 265
Giotto di Bondone, 288
Girik, Fatma, 275
The Girl with The Pearl Earring (Vermeer), 219–220
Gish, Lillian, 132, 150, 153, 272
Gismonda (Sardou), 120, 125–126
Giulietta e Romeo, (Lo Savio, 1911), 139, 273
Gli ultimi giorni di Pompeii (Caserini, 1913), 141. See also under *ultimi*
globalization, 245, 249, 260; discussions of, 61–62
Glück, C.W., 39
Godard, Jean-Luc, 33, 53, 65, 110, 182, 212, 236, 284, 285, 286, 287; adaptation and authorship, 218–220; and Barthes, 221–222; and Debord, 222–223; and Dreyer, 224–225; and Truffaut, 219, 284; and Vertov, 286; and Welles, 173, 209, 219–221, 223–224, 281; contempt for studio practices, 221; in Rushdie, 73; use of Allen as *auteur*, 219–221; use of still images, 207. See also *King Lear* (Godard, 1980); *Le Mépris* (Godard, 1963); *Vivre Sa Vie* (Godard, 1962)
Godfather III (Coppola, 1990): as parodied by Reilly, 26; Pacino's allusion to the Godfather trilogy's parallels with *Hamlet* and *King Lear* in *Looking for Richard*, 37
Göebbels, Josef, 159, 162, 221
Goethe, Johann Wilhelm von, 128, 155, 276; as German national symbol, 8
Golden, Eva, 265
Goldman Sachs, 38
Goldmann, Lucien, 229
Gombrich, Ernst, 119
Gomery, Douglas, 38, 96
Goncourt, Edmond de, 120, 194, 269
Goodfellas (Scorsese, 1990): as parodied by Reilly, 26
Good Neighbor Policy, 178
Goodwin, James, 259, 260
Goodwin, Nat, 100
Gorky, Maxim, 66, 273
Gosnell, Raja, 28. See also *Never Been Kissed* (Gosnell, 1999)

The Gospel According to Matthew (Pasolini, 1964), 226
Gounod, Charles, 8
Goya, Francisco de, 222
Gozzoli, Benozzo, 53
Gradiva (Jensen), 128
The Graduate (Nichols, 1967), 147, 246
Grady, Hugh, 260
Gramsci, Antonio, 98; as an influence on Pasolini, 226–227, 229, 287, 288
Grant, Cary, 167
Granville-Barker, Harley, 88, 177
Grasset, Eugène, 120
Grau, Robert, 132, 133, 273
The Great Dictator (Chaplin, 1940), 169
Greed (Stroheim, 1923), 47
Green, Valentine, 136
Greenaway, Peter, 44, 173, 182, 212, 285, 286, 289, 290, 291; and authorship, 182, 219, 234–235; and Baudrillard, 289; and Derrida, 289; and Pasolini, 231–234; attitudes to the *paragone*, 51, 235, 288; Formalist approach, 232–242, 290; structural conceits, 234. See also *Drowning by Numbers* (Greenaway, 1988); *Prospero's Books* (Greenaway, 1991); *A Walk through H: The Reincarnation of an Ornithologist* (Greenaway, 1978)
Greenberg, Clement, 61
Greenblatt, Stephen, 2, 10, 115, 117, 192, 239, 249, 268, 279, 284, 288; on Albrecht Dürer and visual cultures, 49; on Hamlet, 115; on Iago, 192; on Shakespeare's religious relativism, 5–6
Greene, Robert, 2, 51, 254
Greimas, A.J., 226
Greville-Smith, Anthony, 41
Grieg, Edvard, 171
Griffith, D.W., [David Wark], 3, 16, 18, 84, 87, 88, 96, 101, 105, 111, 112, 130, 149, 223, 272, 273. See also *America* (Griffith, 1924); *The Birth of a Nation* (D.W. Griffith, 1915); *Intolerance* (Griffith, 1916); *The Taming of the Shrew* (Griffith, 1908)
Grimm, Jakob, 155
Grimoin-Sanson, R., 123
Gross, John, 253

Grot, Anton, 21; as Art Director for Warners Bros.' *A Midsummer Night's Dream*, 168
The Ground Beneath Her Feet (Rushdie), 73
Group Theatre, 23
Gründgens, Gustaf, 276
Grusin, Richard, 44
Guazzoni, Enrico, 141. See also *Marcantonio e Cleopatra* (Guazzoni, 1913); *Quo Vadis?* (Guazzoni, 1911)
Guha, Ranajit, 61, 260
Gunning, Tom, 85, 123; on the "Cinema of Attractions," 263
Gurr, Andrew, 237; on Renaissance spectatorship, 6

Habermas, Jurgen, 260
Hackett, Charles, 101
Hagen, Uta, 15, 191
Hair, P.E.H., 260
Hall, N. John, 79
Hall, Peter, 40, 285
Hall, Stuart, 49
Hallam, Henry, 92
Halpern, Richard, 61, 239, 260
Hamilton, William, 135–136
Hamlet (Thomas), 8
Hamlet (Turgenev), 252
"Hamlet and Don Quixote" (Turgenev), 10
Hamlet (Maurice-Bernhardt, 1900), 119–129; as rearranged for the camera, 122–124
Hamlet (Méliès, 1907), as first multi-scene Shakespeare film, 121
Hamlet (Caserini, 1908), 116
Hamlet (Comerio, 1908), 116
Hamlet (Bourgeois, 1910), 116
Hamlet (Desfontaines, 1910), 116
Hamlet (Blom, 1910), 116, 148
Hamlet (Barker, 1910 or 1912), 116
Hamlet (Hepworth-Plumb, 1914), 116, 143–145; use by Almereyda, 147; use in *Theater of Blood*, 159
Hamlet (Olivier, 1948): as the bane of Welles's *Macbeth*, 181; Ernest Jones's version of Freud in, 284–285
Hamlet (Kozintsev, 1964), 11, 13
Hamlet (Coronado, 1976), 285

Hamlet (Zeffirelli, 1990), 9, 29, 157; incest in, 157; Ophelia's pregnancy in, 50
Hamlet (Branagh, 1996), 32; interpolated annotations in, 32, 144; treatment of Ophelia as pregnant spy, 118
Hamlet (Almereyda, 2000), 146–147; parodied in the dialogue track of *Scotland, PA*, 34, 37 ; postmodern pastiche in, 146–147
Hamlet (Scott, 2000), 146
Hamlet, Ein Rachedrama (Gade, 1921), 150–158; as a reversion to Shakespeare's sources, 118, 154–157
Hamlet Goes Business (Kaurismaki, 1987), 64; parody of Kurosawa, 64; parody of Kozintsev, 146
The Hamlet of Shchigiri District (Leskov), 10
Hamm, Walter, 78
Handley, Tommy, 18, 28
Hansen, Miriam, 267; on Benjamin, 133–134, 272; on the cultivation of consumerism, 99
Hardy, Thomas, 111. See also *Tess of the Durbevilles*
Harlan, Veidt, 142. See also *Jud Süss* (Harlan, 1943)
Harms, Rudolf, 132
Harrison, G.B., 262
Harsnett, Samuel, 276
Hartlaub, Gustav, 151
Harvey, David, 61, 260
Harvey, Laurence, 24
Hassan, Ihab, 260
Hassan, Kamal, 72
Hatchuel, Sarah, 257
Hawkins, Jack, 41
Hawks, Howard, 186, 206
Hawthorne, Nigel, 42
Hayakawa, Sessue, 18–19
Hays Convention, 20
Hays, Will, 20, 168–169
Hayworth, Rita, 21
Hearne, John, 260
Heckerling, Amy, 116
Hegel, G.W.F., 202, 260
Heise, William, 264
Hemingway, Ernest, as rival to Welles, 198, 283
Hendry, Ian, 41

Henry V (Olivier, 1944), 32, 33, 54, 56–58, 187, 259; as essay on cinematic space and time, 56–57; as propaganda, 56, 58
Henry V (Branagh, 1989), 214–217; as related to Olivier's *Henry V*, 214–215; as related to Welles *Chimes at Midnight*, 215–217
Henry VIII (Barker, 1911), 87
Henry VIII (Emerson, 1916), 87–88
Henry VIII and His Court (Tree), 87
The Henry Irving Shakespeare 107
Henschke, Alfred, 168
Hepworth, Cecil, 115, 143–145, 146, 160, 264. See also *Hamlet* (Plumb-Hepworth, 1914)
heraldry, Shakespeare's coat of arms, 2
Herodotus, 191
Herr Tartüffe (Lubitsch, 1926), 262
Herzog, Werner, 107. See also *Aguirre* (Herzog, 1972)
Heston, Charlton, 42, 71, 258
Hibi, Sadao, 260
Hickox, Douglas, 159. See also *Theater of Blood* (Hickox, 1973)
Hill, Roger, 177
Hilliard, Nicholas, 39, 40, 57, 288
Hilton, Paris, 272
Les Histoires du Cinéma (Godard, 1998), 224
Hitchcock, Alfred, 29, 159, 183, 206–208, 224; experiments in synchronized sound technology, 18–19. See also *Blackmail* (Hitchcock, 1929); *Elstree Calling* (Hitchcock-Brunel, 1930); *Psycho* (Hitchcock, 1960); *Vertigo* (Hitchcock, 1958)
Hitler, Adolf, 166, 169–170
Hjort, Mette, 64, 261
Hoby, Thomas, 258
Hodgdon, Barbara, 243
Hoffman, Dustin, 147, 246
Hoffman, Michael, 9. See also *A Midsummer Night's Dream* (Hoffman, 1999)
Hoffmann, E.T.A., 162–163, 189
Hofmannsthal, Hugo von, 132
hogaku, 67
Holbein, Hans, 161; use in Olivier's *Richard III*, 55

Holinshed, Raphael, 179, 199–200, 201, 277, 280–281
Holinshed's Chronicles (Raphael Holinshed), 199–200
Holland, Norman, 267
Holm, Ian, 285
Hoover, J. Edgar, 177, 190, 280–281, 282
Hopkins, Anthony, 285–286
Horak, Jan-Christopher, 166–167
Hordern, Michael, 41
Hotchkiss, Lea, 290
House Un-American Activities Committee, 26, 179, 191
Howard, Jean, 258, 283
Howard, Leslie, 20
Howard, Tony, 11, 270, 272, 274, 275
Howells, William Dean, 119
Huapango (Lipkies, 2004), 255
Hughes, Ken, 26, 48. See also *Chitty Chitty Bang Bang* (Hughes, 1968); *Joe MacBeth* (Hughes, 1955)
Hugo, Victor, 121, 175
Huillet, Danielle, 64
Humm, Maggie, 49
Hunt, Holman, 263
Hunt, John Dixon, 259
Hunter, Ian, 40
Huston, John, 162. See also *Casino Royale* (Huston, 1967)
Hutcheon, Linda, 31, 205, 256, 260
Hytner, Nicholas, 42, 269. See also *The Madness of King George* (Hytner, 1994)

Ibert, Jacques, 182, 185–186, 189, 195; as Modernist, 182, 189
Ibsen, Henryk, 66, 138, 149, 151, 274
iconography: in Botticelli, 51–52; in Mucha, 125; in Carpaccio, 193–194; in Ruiz, 201; in van Eyck, 194–196; in Velázquez, 227–231
The Immortal Story (Welles, 1968), 208, 281
In the Flesh (Canterbury, 2000), 255
Indian Education Act of 1835, 67
L'Inferno di Dante (de Liguoro, 1911), 141, 266, 273
intermediation, as a theory of media symbiosis, 43–46, 75–76, 92, 289; television as freeing Bergman to make multiple texts of *Fanny and Alexander*, 43, 47–48. See also digital film techniques, DVD, television
Intikam Malegi Kadin Hamlet (Erksan, 1976), 275
Intolerance (Griffith, 1916), 105, 273
Ionesco, Eugene, 235
Irons, Jeremy, 164
Irving, Henry, 79, 80–83, 102, 104, 107, 267, 277
Irving, Washington, 85, 91
Isaacs, J., and theory of adaptation of Shakespeare, 163
Isherwood, Charles, 30
Isherwood, Christopher, 34
It's All True (Welles, 1941), 178–179
Italian-Amerian secret organizations, 109
Ivan the Terrible (Eistenstein, 1945–1948), 11, 12, 203, 253
Ivanov-Gai, Aleksander, 160. See also *Snokhatch* (Ivanov-Gai, 1912)
Ivens, Joris, 198

Jackson, Mick, 52–53, 121. See also *L.A. Story* (Jackson, 1991)
Jackson, Russell, 270, 276
Jacob, Irène, 215
Jacobi, Derek, 35–36, 215
Jacobs, Lewis, 96, 99
Jaffrey, Madhur, 69
James I of England: demonology 180, 278; patronage of theatre, 278
Jameson, Fredric, 61, 202, 205, 225, 243, 260, 287
Jancsó, Miklós, 80. See also *Electra, My Love* (Jancsó, 1974)
Jannings, Emil, 132, 152, 158–159, 160–162, 262. See also acting
Jarman, Derek, 106, 188, 236, 280, 290; influence on Greenaway, 235. See also *The Tempest* (Jarman, 1979)
Järvet, Jüri: see Yarvet, Yuri
Jaspers, Karl, 284
Jaubert, G.F., 122
The Jew of Mestri (Felner, 1923): see *Der Kaufmann von Venerdig*
Jayaraaj, 68. See also *Kaliyattam* (Jayaraaj, 1998)
The Jazz Singer (Crosland, 1927), 161
Jean, Duc de Berry 57

Jeck, Michael, 279
Jefferson, Joseph, 84
Jensen, Anders Thomas, 65
Jensen, Torben Skodt, 274. See also *Asta Nielsen: The Talking Muse* (Jensen, 2003)
Jensen, Wilhelm, 128
La Jetée (Marker, 1963), 222
The Jew of Malta (Marlowe), 106, 164
The Jew of Mestri: see Der Kaufmann der Venerdig
Joe MacBeth (Hughes, 1955): British imitations of American "underworld" speech genres, 26
Johnson, Ian, 276
Johnson, Samuel, 111, 219
Jolson, Al, 161
Jones, Ernest: Olivier's source for Freud and Hamlet, 284–285
Jones, Inigo, 235–237, 257: feud with Ben Jonson, 235, 290
Jones, Terry, 226, 287. See also *The Life of Brian* (Jones, 1979)
Jonson, Ben, 5, 117, 235, 237, 290
Jorgens, Jack, 35, 116–117, 194–195
Journey into Fear (Foster-Welles, 1943), 178
Joyce, James, 155, 234, 271
The Joyless Street (Pabst, 1923), 152
Jubal (Davies, 1956), 26
Jud Süss (Harlan, 1943), 142
Jugend und Tollheit (Gad, 1913), 155
La Juive (Halévy), 165
Jules et Jim (Truffaut, 1961), 206–207
Julia, Raul, 45
Julius Caesar (Alma-Tadema, set design), 82
Julius Caesar (prod. Vitagraph, 1908), 110
Julius Caesar (prod. Edison, 1913), with synchronized sound (?), 38
Julius Ceasar (Bradley, 1950), 42
Julius Caesar (Mankiewicz, 1953), 25
Julius Caesar (Burge, 1970), 42
Jung, Karl, 284
Junger, Gil, *10 Things I Hate about You* (Junger, 1999), 28

Kabuki drama, 253; *The Merchant of Venice* (Genzo), 66
Kachur, B.A., 87–92, 263
Kael, Pauline, 46

Kafka, Franz, 208, 222, 226
Kaliyattam (Jayaraaj, 1998), 68
Kamakura scroll painting, Kurasawa's incorporation in film sets, 59
Kane, Julie, 259
Kapadia, Parmita, 261
Kapoor, Shashi, 69
Karina, Anna, 224
Karsavina, Tamara, as creator of roles in Modernist ballet, 168
Katsu, Genzo, 66
Kauffman, Michael, 22
Kaufman, Lloyd, 255. See also *Tromeo and Juliet* (Kaufman, 1997)
Der Kaufmann von Venerdig (Felner, 1923), 164–166
Kaurismäki, Aki, 64, 146, 261. See also *Hamlet Goes Business* (Kaurismäki, 1987)
Kauro, Osanai, 66
Kazan, Elia, 22–23, 255
Kean, Charles, 77
Kean, Edmund, 80, 105, 268
Keane, James, 101–105, 108. See also *Richard III* (Warde-Keane, 1912/1913); *Spreading Evil* (Keane, 1918)
Keats, John, 83
Keeling, William, 62–63, 260
Kemble, Charles, 77, 92
Kemble, John Philip, 77
Kendal, Felicity, 69
Kendal, Geoffrey, 69
Kennedy, Ted, 291
Kent, Charles, 140, 258. See also *As You Like It* (Kent, 1912); *Twelfth Night* (Kent, 1910)
Kermode, Frank, 2, 5, 78, 251, 252
Kernan, Alvin, 180, 278
Khachaturian, Aram, 11–12, 14–15
Kidman, Nicole, 137, 248
Kiefer, Henry, 258
Kieslowski, Krzystof, 215
King Baabu (Soyinka), 63
A King in New York (Chaplin, 1954), 33
The King is Alive (Levring, 2000), 64–65
King John (Tree), 76–93; as first cinematic adapation of a theatrical scene, 84–86; critical conjecture regarding *Kin John*, 78–79, 88–92; relevance to contemporary politics, 89–93

King Lear (prod. Vitagraph 1909), 111, 130–131, 271
King Lear (Lo Savio, 1910), 139–140
King Lear (Warde, prod. Thanhouser, 1916), 111–113
King Lear (Brook-McCullough, 1953), 219
King Lear (Kozintsev, 1971), 13–14, 253
King Lear (Brook, 1971), 71, 112
King Lear (Godard, 1987), 65, 209, 218–225
"King Lear of the Steppes" (Turgenev), 252
King of Texas (Miller, 2002), 26, 29
King, Rob, 87
King's Men, 4
Kingsley, Ben, dis(s)quotation by, 42–43
Kinski, Klaus, 107
Kinugasa, Teinosuke, 44. See also *A Page of Madness* (Kinugasa, 1926)
Kircher, Athanaseus, 233
Kiss Me Kate (Sidney, 1953), 19, 25; and sexual perversity, 230
kitsch, 61, 230, 238, 240, 243–245; Kundera's definition as it pertains to *Romeo + Juliet*, 249, 291
Klee, Paul, 238
Kleinschmidt, Capt. Frank, 97. *See also Alaska-Siberian Expedition* (Kleinschmidt, 1911)
Kliene, George, 86, 137, 159, 264, 273; as a financial force behind French and Italian Shakespeare film production, 118, 137, 140–142
Kliman, Bernice, 13, 116, 268, 269
Knight, G. Wilson, 260
Knights, L.C., 278
Knoesel, Klaus, 278–279. See also *Rave Macbeth* (Knoesel, 2003)
Knoles, Harley, 149. See also *Carnival* (Knoles, 1921)
Koch, Stephen, 283
Koebner, Thomas, 274
Kohlhielsels Töchter (Lubitsch, 1920), 158–159
Kojin, Karatani, 261
Kokan, Shiba, 66
Korda, Alexander, 280
Korngold, Erich Wolfgang, 48, 168
Korobeiniki (Chardynin, 1910), 160

Korol Lir (Kozintsev): see *King Lear* (Kozintsev)
Kott, Jan, 34, 230, 248, 255; on Shakespeare's Grand Mechanism, 67, 199, 203
Kozintsev, Grigori, 11, 12–14, 15, 30, 32, 50, 60, 64, 112, 146–147, 157, 209, 212; and Brook, 253, 261; and Godard, 218–219, 222; commentary on Brook's techniques, 253; use of music, 12; theories of performance, 253. See also *Hamlet* (Kozintsev,1956); *King Lear* (Kozintsev, 1970)
Kracauer, Siegfried, 151–152, 155, 162–163, 273
Krasker, Robert, 54
Krauss, Werner, 159–162, 166
Kriteva, Julia, 212, 289
Krushchev, Nikita, 10, 13
Kubelka, Peter, 232
Kuhns, David, 274
Kumonosu-jô (Kurosawa, 1957), 58–59, 67, 183–184, 269: circularity of construction, 59; disputes over adaptation, 59; visual translation of Shakespeare's imagery, 163, 279
Kundera, Milan: theory of Kitsch, 249, 291
Kurosawa, Akira, 10, 12, 26–28, 32, 58–60, 66, 112, 146, 180, 183, 209, 223, 259, 274, 279; and Buddhism, 60, 259; and cinematography, 60; and modernity, 65–66; cultural dialogism, 66; *jidai-geki*, 67; rupture with Olivier, 58; use of color, 59–60; use of music, 67; use of Noh, 259, 279. See also *The Bad Sleep Well* (Kurosawa, 1960); *Dodeskaden* (Kurosawa, 1970); *Kumonosu-jô* (Kurosawa, 1957); *Ran* (Kurosawa, 1985)
Kustodiev, Boris, 10
Kyd, Thomas, 117, 251

L.A. Story (Jackson, 1991), 52–53 , 121; influence of Botticelli's paintings in, 52–53
LaBadie, Florence, 111
The Lady from Shanghai (Welles, 1946), 179, 183, 193, 281

Lady Macbeth of Mtsensk District
    (Shostakovich), 10
Laemmle, Carl, 132
Laforgue, Jules, 252
Lamarr, Hedy, 167
Lambarde, William, 89
Lamentation over the Dead Christ
    (Mantegna), 214
Lamming, George, 238, 240, 291
Landow, George, 233, 289
Landy, Marcia, 287
Lang, Fritz, 159, 159, 183, 224; as actor
    for Godard, 221. See also *M* (Lang,
    1931); *Der Müde Tod* (Lang, 1921)
Lang, Matheson, 149
Lanier, Douglas, 235–236, 256, 257
Larsen, Viggo, 148–149. See also *Den
    Hvide Slavehandel* (Larsen, 1910);
    Othello (Larsen, 1908)
Lash, Scott, 62
Last Action Hero (McTiernan, 1993), 121,
    147
The Last Command (von Sternberg, 1928),
    162
Laswell, Harold, 76
Laurents, Arthur, 254
Lautrec, Toulouse, 120
Lavagnino, Francesco, 282
Lawrence, Florence, 132
Lawrence, Thomas, 136, 273
Le Blond-Zola, Jean-Claude, 265
Lechner, Frank, 62
Lee, Ang, 255
Lee, Christopher, 35
Lee, Rowland V., 40. See also *Son of
    Frankenstein* (Lee, 1939); *The Tower of
    London* (Lee, 1939)
Left Bank filmmakers, 256
LeGros, James, 34
Lehar, Franz: influence of operetta on the
    development of the Musical, 24–25
Lehmann, Courtney, 243, 255
Leigh, Jennifer Jason, 64
Leigh, Vivien, 23, 280
Lenkeffy, Ica von, 159
Lenin, Nikolai, 178
lenses: normal, 182; wide-angle, 183;
    telephoto, 183
Leoncavallo, Ruggiero, 149, 254
Leone, Sergio, 242

Leonidov, Leonid, 255
Lerner, Irving, 256. See also *The Royal
    Hunt of the Sun,* (Lerner, 1969)
Les Miserables (prod. Vitagraph, 1909), 97
Leskov, Nikolai, 10
Lessing, Effraim G., 273
Lester, Richard, 285
Der Letzte Mann (1924), 162
Levin, Yuri, 9, 10, 252
Lévi-Strauss, Claude, 204; bricolage,
    284
Levring, Kristian, 64–65; the Dogme 95
    transcendence of nationality, 118. See
    also *The King is Alive* (Levring, 2000)
Lewis, Robert, 23
Leyda, Jay, 188, 194
Lezcano, Pilar, 198
Das Lied von der Erde (Mahler), 67
Life, 181
*The Life and Adventures of Lieutenant
    Petrosino* (1912), 100, 109
Life of Brian, The (Monty Python, 1979),
    226, 287
The Life of Moses (Vitagraph, 1910), 96,
    266
Lillich, Meredith, 53, 254, 259
Limbourg, Pol de, 57
L'immagine ritrovata (Bologna), 162
Lincoln, Abraham, 22, 255
Lindley, Arthur, 179
Lindsay, Vachel, 132, 262, 273
Lindt, Otto, 132
Lippi, Filippino, 259
Lippi, Filippo, 259
Lipkies, Ivan, 255. See also *Huapango*
    (Lipkies, 2004)
Lipkov, A., 14
Lippmann, Max, 275
Livingston, Jennie, 247. See also *Paris is
    Burning* (Livingston, 1991)
Lo Savio, Girolamo, 138–140. See
    also *King Lear* (Lo Savio, 1910);
    The Merchant of Venice (Lo Savio,
    1910); *Otello* (Lo Savio, 1910);
    The Taming of the Shrew (Lo Savio,
    1910); *Giulietta e Romeo,* (Lo Savio,
    1939)
localism, 10. See also contemporary
    localism, domestication
Lolita (Nabokov), 128

Loncraine, Richard, 102, 106, 113, 201; Gloucester as Fascist, 102–103. See also *Richard III* (Loncraine, 1995)
A Long Days Journey Into Night (O'Neill), 37
Longstaffe, Steve, 262
Looking for Richard (Pacino, 1996), 35–37, 188; as documentary, 36–37; as experimentation with acting techniques, 36–37; as Gangster film, 37
Loomba, Ania, 62
Lopez, Roderigo, 7, 164
Lord of the Flies (Brook, 1963), 253
Lorre, Peter, 152, 159
Losey, Joseph, 193
Loshitsky, Yosefa, 287
Louverture, Toussaint, 291
Love's Labour's Lost (Branagh, 2000): conventions of Renaissance English theatre, 32; use of the Golden Age Hollywood Musical, 216
Low, Rachel, 267
Lowe, Arthur, 41
Lowe, Marie, 149
Lubitsch, Ernst,152, 158–159, 161, 169–170, 186, 209, 274, 275; and Shakespeare as farce, 158–159; and Viennese operetta, 25; success at Ufa, 151; success in Hollywood, 167. See also *Ann Boleyn* (Lubitsch, 1920); *Herr Tartüffe* (1926); *Kohlhielsels Töchter* (Lubitsch, 1920), *Madame Dubarry* (Lubitsch, 1919); *Romeo und Julia am Schnee* (Lubitsch, 1920); *The Student Prince* (Lubitsch, 1927); *To Be or Not to Be* (Lubitsch, 1942)
Luhrmann, Baz, 16, 44, 146, 240–252, 255, 265, 291; and Indian cinema, 247–248; inter-nationalism; 240–241, 247–248; mixing of high and low cultural forms, 243;. See also *Moulin Rouge* (Luhrmann, 2001); "Now Until the Break of Day" (Luhrmann, 2001); *Romeo + Juliet* (Luhrmann, 1996); *Strictly Ballroom* (Luhrmann, 1992)
Lukács, György, 132
Lyceum Theatre, 79
Lyons, Bridget, 196, 283

Lyotard, Jean-François, 61, 260

M (Lang, 1931), 159
Macbeth (prod. Vitagraph, 1908), 131, 141, 271
Macbeth (Calmettes, 1908), 96
Macbeth (Caserini, 1909), 138
Macbeth (Welles, 1948), 179–183, 185–190; as critique of American politics, 189–190; as spoken in opaque Scots accents, 277–278
Macbeth (Polanski, 1971), 184–185; alluded to in *Maqbool*, 71; as Horror film, 35; as parodied in *Scotland, PA*, 34
Macbeth (Casson, 1979)
MacDonald, Jeannette, 25
MacDonald, Philip, 26
Machiavelli, Niccolò, 89, 217, 267
Macintosh, Rennie, 119
MacLiammóir, Micheal, 176–177, 195, 282
MacNeil, Robert, 146
MacPherson, James, 175
Macready, William Charles, 16
Madame Dubarry (Lubitsh, 1919), 151
Madden, John, 4–5, 28, 252; send-up of contemporary theory, 4. See also *Shakespeare in Love* (Madden, 1998)
The Madness of King George, (Hytner, 1994), 42, 269
Maeterlinck, Maurice, 81
Maggi, Luigi, 116
Magna Carta, 77–78, 85, 86, 92
Magnani, Anna, 174
Magnificent Ambersons, The (Welles, 1942), 178–179
Magro, Maria, 29
Mahler, Gustav, 67
Mailer, Norman, 220; and Gary Gilmore, 222; and Jack Abbott, 222; as actor for Godard, 220
Makart, Hans, 120
Makowska, Elena, 143
Makavejev, Dusan, 255
Malibran, Maria, 8
Mallarmé, Stéphane, 238, 256, 270, 271; and cinema, 256
A Man For All Seasons (Zinnemann, 1966), 214

Mankiewicz, Joseph, 25. See also *Julius Caesar* (Mankiewicz, 1953)
Manners, Roger, Earl of Rutland, 258
Mantegna, Andrea, 214, 245
Manvell, Roger, 58, 179, 254, 258, 259, 272, 278, 279
Manzoni, Giuseppe, 176
Mao Zhe Dong, 286
Maqbool (Bhardwaj, 2004), 70–72
Marattam (Govindan, 1988), 68
Marcantonio e Cleopatra (Guazzoni, 1913), 142
Le Marchand de Venice (Desfontaines, 1912), 97
Mareorama, 123
Marienstras, Richard, 180, 278
Marín, Ricardo, 123–125, 270
Marker, Chris, 207, 222–224. See also *La Jetée* (Marker, 1963)
Marlowe, Christopher: biography 4–5, 6; *Doctor Faustus* 4; *The Jew of Malta* 106, 164
Marowitz, Charles, 261
Marshall, F.A., 107
Marshall, Penny, 33. See also *Renaissance Man* (Marshall, 1994)
Martin, Steve, 121
Martínez Sierra, G., 123–125; florid praises of Bernhardt, 123, 270
Marx, Karl, 188, 202, 260, 288; agonistic class relations, 229
Marx, Samuel, 19
Masina, Giuletta, 286
Maslin, Janet, 243
Mason, James, 25
Mason, Penelope, 259, 260
Masaccio, 288
Massai, Sonia, 227, 288
Massimilla Doni (Balzac), 112
Master Will Shakespeare (Tourneur), 20
Matthews, Peter, 243
Maurel, Victor, 122–123
Maurice, Clément, 124, 129; as cinematic pioneer, 122–123
Mayakovsky, Vladimir, 147
Mazursky, Paul, 45–47, 220; use of Shakespearean themes in his films, 46. See also *The Tempest* (Mazursky, 1982)
McCandless, David, 286

McCarthy, Joseph, 281
McCutcheon, Gaston, 3
McCutcheon, Wallace, 3
McEnery, John, 244
McFarlane, James, 260
McKaye, Steele, 82
McKellen, Ian, 102–103, 106
McKernan, Luke, 85, 90–92
McLuhan, Marshall, 44, 75, 133
McPherson, Heather, 270, 271
McTiernan, John, 121, 147. See also *Last Action Hero* (McTiernan, 1993)
Medici, Lorenzo de: as originator of a *concetto* used by Botticelli, 54
Meiji Restoration, 62
Mekas, Jonas, 234
Méliès, Gaston, 271
Méliès, Georges, 2–4, 83, 90, 121, 130, 235, 251, 284; the first Shakespeare Biopic, 2–3; the first version of an entire Shakespeare drama, 2. See also *L'Affaire Dreyfus* (Méliès, 1899); *Cléopâtre* (Méliès, 1899); *Hamlet* (Méliès, 1907); *Le Mélomane* (Méliès, 1903); *Shakespeare writing Julius Ceasar* (Méliès, 1907)
Melnick, Ross, 267
Le Mélomane (Méliès), 2
Melville, Herman, 29, 65
Men of Respect (Reilly, 1991), 26; use of underwold argot as in *Joe MacBeth*, 26
Mendelssohn, Felix, 48, 168
Mendés, Catulle, 135, 270
Las Meninas (Velázquez), 227
Menjou, Adolphe, 167
Menzies, William Cameron: set design for *Taming of the Shrew* (Taylor, 1929), 21
Mephisto (Szabo, 1985), 276
Le Mépris (Godard, 1963), 221, 226
Mercanton, Louis, 96
Merchant, M. Moelwyn, 50
The Merchant of Venice (Katsu), 66
The Merchant of Venice (prod. Vitagraph, 1908), 271
The Merchant of Venice (Lo Savio, 1910), 138–139
The Merchant of Venice (De Forest, 1926[?]), the first Shakespeare talkie, 38–39

The Merchant of Venice (Radford, 2005), 166, 257; visual opulence based on Venetian painting, 139, 164–165
The Mercury Theater, 198
Meredith, Burgess, 220
Meres, Francis, 165
La Mergere approvisée (Desfontaines, 1911), 97–98, 141
The Merry Widow (Lehar), 24
The Merry Wives of Windsor (prod. Beckfilm, 1917), with synchronized music by Otto Nicolai (?), 38
Messel, Oliver, 20–21
Messter, Oskar, 161
Metz, Christian, 218, 224, 273, 287
Metz, Walter, 256
Metzner, Erno, 168
Meyer, Nicholas, 256. See also *Star Trek IV* (Meyer, 1991)
Meyer, Russ, 170, 255, 275
Meyerhold, Vsevolod, 10, 11, 86, 150, 253, 264; influence on Eisenstein, 13; influence on Kozintsev, 13
Meyrick, Gilley, 279
Michaud, Phillipe-Alain, 259
Michelangelo Buonarroti, 136, 235–237, 235, 288
Mickey Mouse, 188; and innervation, 134
Midnight's Children (Rushdie), 73
A Midsummer Night's Cream (Canterbury, 2000), 255
A Midsummer Night's Dream (Britten), 247–248
A Midsummer Night's Dream (Kent, prod. Vitagraph, 1909), 130, 271
A Midsummer Night's Dream (Azzuri, 1913), 140
A Midsummer Night's Dream (Ewers-Rye, 1913), 167
A Midsummer Night's Dream (Neumann, 1925), 167–168
A Midsummer Night's Dream (Reinhardt-Dieterle, 1935), 167–169
A Midsummer Night's Dream (Hall, 1968), 40; influence of the French New Wave in, 285
A Midsummer Night's Dream (Hoffman, 1999), 9
A Midsummer Night's Sex Comedy (Allen, 1982), 48

A Midwinter's Tale (Branagh, 1995), 118
Mifune, Toshiro, 59
Mignolo, Walter, 62
Mikhoels, Solomon, 12
Millais, John Everett, 50, 87, 144, 145, 263
Miller, Arthur, 190
Miola, Robert, 211–213, 223, 231
Miracle in Milan (De Sica, 1948), 214
Mirren, Helen, 285
Mirzoeff, Nicholas, 49, 258
Mitchell, W.J.T., 49
Mitry, Jean, 56
Mizoguchi, Kenji, 59, 73, 160, 223. See also *Ugetsu Monogatari* (Mizoguchi, 1953)
Modern Times (Chaplin, 1936), 288
Modernism, 260, 282, 287; and visual culture, 49; in Welles's *Chimes at Midnight*, 205–206
modernity (contestatory definitions): aesthetic, 61; historical, 61–62; India's entry into, 67–73; Japan's entry into, 66–67; social, 62
Modi, Sohrab, 68
Molière (ps. Jean-Baptiste Poquelin), 262
Monroe, Marilyn, 248
Monsieur Verdoux (Chaplin, 1945), 288
Montaigne, Michel de, 89, 117, 239
Monteverdi, Claudio, 176
Monty Python, 226
Moor's Last Sigh, The (Rushdie), 72–73
Moorhouse, Jocelyn, 33. See also *A Thousand Acres* (Moorhouse, 1997)
Morand, Eugène, 117–118, 124–125, 127, 270
Moreau, Émile, 251
Moreau, Gustave, 127
Moreau, Jeanne, 206–207, 281
Morgan, Joyce Vining, 10, 255
Morgan, Mae, 26
Morier-Genoud, Phillipe, 202
Morley, Robert, 41
Morricone, Ennio, 106
Morris, William, 119
Morrissette, Billy, 34. See also *Scotland, PA* (Morrissette, 2001)
Moscow Art Theatre, 23, 82
Mosley, Oswald, 103
Moss, M.E., 252

motion: in Renaissance painting 51–52; in silent film acting 138, 152–153
Motion Picture Association of the Americas, 179
Motion Picture Patents Company (MPPC), 3, 98, 140, 266
Motion Picture Story Magazine, 44
Moulin Rouge (Luhrmann, 2001), 247–248
Mounet, Paul, 268
Mounet-Sully, Jean, 268
Moving Picture World, 97, 266
Mr. Arkadin (Welles, 1955), 183
Mucha, Alfons, 119–121; Bernhardt's role in his adoption of Art Nouveau, 125–127
Mucha, Jiri, 120
Der Müde Tod (Lang, 1921), 167
Mugen, 184
Muggeridge, Malcolm, 79
mujokan, 259
Munch, Edvard, 160
Munday, Anthony, 165–166, 276
Muni, Paul, 167
Münsterberg, Hugo, 132, 273
Muradeli, Vano, 11
Muray, Nickolas, 281
Murch, Walter, 44, 258
Murnau, W.F., 55, 162, 166, 167, 170, 186, 262. See also *Faust* (Murnau, 1926); *Der Letzte Mann* (Murnau, 1924), *Sunrise* (W.F. Murnau, 1927)
Murray, Bill, 147
music in Shakespeare films: by Bhardwaj, 70–71; by Bernstein, 168; by Cole Porter, 19; by Ibert, 182, 189; by Khachaturian, 11–12; by Korngold, 48, 168; by Lavagnino, 282; by Morricone, 106; by Nyman, 239; by Rota, 8–9; by Shostakovich, 12; by Takemitsu, 67; by Walton, 54; imitation of Rota in Taymor's *Titus*, 286; in Branagh, 216; in Hoffman, 9; in Luhrmann, 243, 247–248; in Mazursky's *The Tempest*, 45, 46; use of Arlen by Jarman, 188
Mussolini, Benito, 79, 174, 177, 262
Mussorgsky, Modest, 9, 252
Muybridge, Eadweard, 235
My Darling Clementine (Ford, 1948), 25

My Own Private Idaho (Van Sant, 1991), as a rereading of *Chimes at Midnight* (1965), 213–214
Myron, 221
Myaskovsky, Nikolai, 11

Naayakan (Ratnam 1987), 72
Nabokov, Vladimir, 128, 271
Nabucco (Verdi), 176
Nadar (ps. Gaspard Félix de Tournachon), 126
Naficy, Hamid, 174, 197, 198, 200, 277, 281
The Naked Venus (Ulmer, 1958), 170
Napierkowska, Stacia, 251
Naremore, James, 127, 131, 179, 180, 181, 205, 256, 278, 284; ostensiveness in acting, 272
Nargis, 68, 69
narrators of silent film, 102, 103–104, 161, 275. See also *benshi*
national allegory: Australian, 245–246; Borges, 174–175; Verdi, 176; Welles, 176, 189–190
national film industries: Indian Shakespeare films, 68; Finland's marginalization, 64; Danish internationalism, 64–66; Denmark's industrial relation to Germany, 148–150; the influence of Japanese theatre on Japanese cinema, 66
nationalism: Astor Place riot, 16; Risorgimento, 175–176; Russian, 9
Naturalism: in literature, 93
Negri, Pola, 151, 152–153, 167
Negroni, Baldassare, 51. See also *Una tragedia alla corte di Sicilia* (Negroni, 1913)
Nelson, Tim Blake, 28, 34, 283. See also *O* (Nelson, 2001)
neocolonialism, 62
Neorealism: and Bertolucci, 174–175; in Castellani's *Romeo and Juliet*, 21, 53; in Welles, 214
Nestingen, Andrew, 261
Neue Sachlichkeit, 151–152
Neumann, Hans, 167–168. See also *A Midsummer Night's Dream* (Neumann, 1925)
Never Been Kissed (Gosnell, 1999), 28

New Criticism, 173
New Historicism, 4, 173, 180, 197–198, 232–233, 239
New Shakespeare Society, 260
The New York Dramatic Mirror, 99, 266–267
The New York Times, 158, 187, 243
Ngugi wa Thiong'O, 239, 240
Nichols, Bill, 257
Nichols, Mike, 147. See also *The Graduate* (Nichols, 1967)
Nicholson, Jack, 278
nickelodeons, demise of, 98–99
Nielsen, Asta, 150–152, 156, 159, 274, 275; physiognomic resemblance to Hamlet, 122; portrayal of Hamlet, 151–158; use of sources, 118, 269; virtuosity of performance, 132, 150, 152–155, 273
Nielsen, Leslie, 256
Nietzsche, Friedrich, 194, 260; Apollonian and Dionysiac, 238
nihonga, 60, 67
Nijinskaya, Bronislava: choreography in Reinhardt-Dieterle *A Midsummer Night's Dream*, 168
Nijinsky, Vaslav, Modernist dancer and choreographer, 238–239
Noh drama, 12, 227, 253, 259, 286; Kurosawa's use of, 58–60, 67, 184; Mugen 184
Norman, Marc, 4, 5
Norris, Frank, 93, 273
Northcote, James, 50
Nosferatu (Murnau, 1921), 55, 166,186
Notes for an African Oresteia (Pasolini, 1970), 227
Novelli, Ermete, 139
Novello, Ivor, 149
"Now Until the Break of Day" (Luhrmann, music video, 2001), 246
Nunn, Trevor, 29–30, 42–43, 258. See also *Twelfth Night* (Nunn, 1996)
Nyman, Michael, 239

O (Nelson, 2001), 28, 34, 283
O'Mahony, Lt. Col. C.C.S., 88
O'Neill, Eugene, 37, 80
O'Pray, Michael, 134
O'Regan, Tom, 245
Oath of the Horatii (David), 3

Offenbach, Jacques, 189, 288
Oksiloff, Assenka, 132
Old Vic Theatre, 176; earliest synchronized dialogue recording of Shakespeare, 39
Oliver Twist (Dickens, stage adaptation), 80
Oliver Twist (prod. General Film, 1912), 80, 100, 266
Olivier, Laurence, 20, 23, 29, 32, 41, 42, 68, 106, 115, 143, 157, 173, 194, 203, 205, 214–217, 259, 279, 284, 285, 286; as parodied by Chabrol, 207–208; as parodied by McTiernan, 147; in comparison to Welles's Shakespeare, 181–182; influence on Branagh, 214–217; influence on Pacino, 36–37; influence on Yutkevich, 14; portrayal of Shylock, 7; self-parody, 284–285; use of Cibber, 106; use of experimental techniques and technologies in film, 33, 54–55; visual influences on *Henry V*, 55, 57–58; visual influences on *Richard III*, 55. See also *Hamlet* (1948); *Henry V* (Olivier, 1944); *Richard III* (Olivier, 1955)
Olmi, Ermanno, 227
Omkara (Bhardwaj, 2006), 72, 255
opera [*also, musica lirica*]: influence of Pushkin on *Boris Godunov* (Mussorgsky, 9); influence of Shakespeare on, 8; influence on Luhrmann, 245; influence on Welles, 190–191; influence on Zeffirelli through Verdi, 8–9
Ophélia (Chabrol, 1962), 207–208
Ophüls, Max, 193
Ordóñez, Antonio, 198, 283
Orfeo (Glück), 39
Orgel, Stephen, 7, 91–92, 258, 263
Orkin, Martin, 62
Orwell, George, 62
Osborne, Laurie, 258
Ossessione (Visconti, 1943), 277
Ostrovsky, Alexander, 86
Otello (Rossini), 8
Otello (Verdi), 8
Otello (Lo Savio, 1909), 138
Otello (Maggi, 1914), 159
Othello (Stanislavsky), 255

Index

Othello (Zeffirelli, 1986), 9; use of Plácido Domingo and Katia Ricciarelli in, 9
Othello (Messter, 1907), with synchonized music by Verdi (?), 38
Othello (Larsen, 1908), 149
Othello (prod. Vitagraph, 1908), 271
Othello (Buchowetski, 1922), 159–162, 262
Othello (Welles, 1952), 14, 176–177, 190–196; narrative structure, 192; relation to *film noir*, 191–192; use of mirrors, 193–195
Othello (Yutkevich, 1955), 11–12, 14–15; cinematography, 14; Iago as Stalin; 13; Sovcolor process, 15; use of music, 11–12
Othello (Zeffirelli, 1986), 9; use of Plácido Domingo and Katia Riciarelli in, 9
Othello (Parker, 2001), 160; Vincent Price effect in, 215
Othello (Sax, 2001), 26; British contemporary localism in, 160
Ouspenskaya, Maria, 23
Ovid, 52
Ozu, Yasujiro, 68, 202

Pabst, Georg Wilhelm, 152, 163. See also *The Joyless Street* (Pabst, 1923); *Geheimnisser Eine Seele* (Pabst, 1926)
Pacino, Al, 35–37, 42, 95, 106, 164, 165, 188, 245, 257. See also *Looking for Richard* (Pacino, 1996)
Packard, Vance, 27
A Page of Madness (Kinugasa, 1926), 44
I Pagliacci (Leoncavallo), 149, 254
Paige, Nicholas, 287
paintings: influence on filmmakers, 201; influence on Castellani, 53–54; influence on Godard, 221–224; influence on Greenaway, 52, 235; influence on Jackson, 52–53; influence on Kozintsev, 50, 53–54; influence on Kurosawa, 58–60; influence on Olivier, 54–58; influence on Pasolini, 227–231; influence on Welles, 193–195; Siddons's use of it for publicity, 135–137
Paisà (Rossellini, 1946), 214
Palm d'Or: *see* Cannes Film Festival
Palmer, Chris, 243–244

Pan, Hermes, 25
Panofsky, Irwin, 119
paper prints at the Library of Congress (Vitagraph): 45, 130–131
paragone: in the *Quijote*, 51; in Greenaway, 51, 235, 238
ParaUfaMet agreement, 162, 166, 274
Paris is Burning (Livingston, 1991), 247
Parker, Brian, 259
Parker, Alan, 33, 53, 160, 215. See also *Fame* (Parker, 1980); *Othello* (Parker, 2001)
Parker, Sarah Jessica, 53
Pascal's Wager: in Rohmer's films, 33
Pasolini, Pier Paolo, 113, 209, 212, 225, 226–231, 232, 234, 280, 287, 288, 289, 290; and Bakhtin, 231; and Eco, 226; and Gramsci, 229; and Peirce, 226; contamination, 226; *contenutismo*, 229; correspondences with Greenaway, 235; transforming characters into essences in the manner of Kurosawa, 227. See also *Che cosa sono le nuvole?* (Pasolini, 1968); *Porcile* (Pasolini, 1969); *Uccellacci e uccellini* (Pasolini, 1966)
La Passion de Jeanne d'Arc (Dreyer, 1928), 215; quoted in Godard's *King Lear*, 224–225, 253
Pasternak, Boris, 9–11, 12–13, 14, 150, 212, 253; intepretation of Shakespeare, 13
Pastrone, Giovanni, 105, 141. See also *Cabiria* (Pastrone, 1913)
Pathé, Charles, 3; as inaugurator of vertical integration, 17
Pavord, Anna, 283
Payne, Lewis, 222
Payne, Stanley, 283
Pears, Peter, 248
Pearson, Hesketh, 79
Pearson, Roberta, 88, 98, 266
Peirce, Charles Sanders, 226
Pendleton, Thomas, 258
Perceval (Rohmer, 1978), 33
performance: *see* acting
performance traditions: cinematic, 14–28; operatic, 8–12; televisual, 28–29; the Musical, 24–25; theatrical, 9–14; use of Cibber in America, 102–108
Perkins, Anthony, 208

Perrineau, John, 244
Peters, John, 281
Petit, Pierre, 93
Petro, Patrice, 275
Pfeiffer, Michelle, 137, 142
Phenakistoscope, 82
Phillips, Augustine, 279
Phipps, Charles, 85
Phoenix, River, 214
Phono-Cinéma-Théâtre, 122–123, 270
Phonofilms apparatus, 38–39
Phonorama, 122
photography: Alma-Tadema's use of in set design, 82–83; as found in Tree's *King John*, 85; Godard's response to Barthes, 221–222; in Mucha's posters, 125; influence on theatrical design, 81–82
photorealism, 81–83. See also photography
Picard, Jean-Luc, 226
Piccoli, Michel, 208
Pickford, Mary, 18, 159
picnolepsis, 251
Pidgeon, Walter, 225
Pieri, Giuliana, 263
Pierret, Marguerite, 122
Pilkington, Ace, 259, 284
Pinal, Silvia, 257
Pinochet, Augusto, 174, 202
Pinter, Harold, 46
Piranesi, Giovanni Battista, 235
Pisanello (Antonio Pisano), 53
Piscator, Erwin, 23
Pittman, Monique, 276
Planché, J.R., 77–78, 82, 92, 108
Plateau, Joseph, 82
Plato, 171, 225, 235
Plett, Heinrich, 212
Plowright, Joan, 147
Plumb, Hay, 115, 143, 145, 146, 264. See also *Hamlet* (Hepworth-Plumb, 1914)
Plummer, Christopher, 256
Plutarch, 142
Poel, William, 88, 177, 277
Poggioli, Ferdinando, 277
Polanski, Roman, 34–35, 180, 183–185, 190, 278, 279; acknowledgement in *Maqbool*, 71; collaboration with Tynan, 34; use of Hammer Horror Film conventions, 35. See also *Macbeth* (Polanski, 1971)
Poliziano, Agnolo, 52, 125
Pontormo (Jacopo Carucci), 288
Porcile (Pasolini, 1969), 113
Porten, Henry, 154, 158, 165
Porter, Cole, 19
Porter, Edwin S., 96, 100–101, 131. See also *The Prisoner of Zenda* (Porter, 1913)
Portrait of Don Diego Acedo, or *The Dwarf Don Diego Acedo "El Primo"* (Velázquez), 227
Portrait of Felipe IV (Velázquez), 227
Portrait of Prince Balthasar Carlos (Velázquez), 227
Positif, 284
posters: by Mucha, 120, 125–127; historical significance in the Warde-Keane *Richard III*, 102; use of Olivier's for *Hamlet* by Chabrol in *Ophélia*, 207
postmodernism, 61, 260; contrasting definitions, 61, 205, 243–244; in Almereyda, 145–146; in *Romeo + Juliet* (1996), 243–249; in *Theater of Blood*, 39–41
Poussin, Nicolas, 77
Powell, William, 264
Pre-Raphaelite painting, 82–83, 87, 145. See also Laurence Alma Tadema, Holman Hunt, John Everett Millais, Dante Gabrielli Rossetti
Price, Brian, 287
Price, Dennis, 41
Price, Leontyne, 243, 245
Price, Vincent, 39–41, 159; as master of dis(s)quotation, 41–42
Primavera (Botticelli), 52; influence on Cukor's *Romeo and Juliet*, 53; influence on Castellani's *Romeo and Juliet*, 53
Prince, 243
Princess Theatre, 77
La Princesse Lointaine (Rostand), 126
The Prisoner of Zenda (Porter, 1913), 101
Production Code of 1934, 168
Prokofiev, Sergei, 11, 183; use of musical effects in Eisenstein's films, 188–189. See also *Romeo and Juliet* (Prokofiev)

Promio, Alexandre, 105
Prospero's Books (Greenaway, 1991), 51, 231–240, 290; disapproval of Gielgud, 234; relationship of sounds and images to words in, 234–237, 289, 290; use of Botticelli, 289; use of Inigo Jones, 235, 290
Prouse, Derek, 254
Psilander, Valdemar, 149
Psycho (Hitchcock, 1960), 208
Puccini, Giaccomo, 126, 245
Pudovkin, Vsevolod, 189
Puri, Om, 71
Pushkin, Alexander, 9, 12–13, 15, 31, 252, 282
Pygmalion (Shaw), 79

Queen Elizabeth (Desfontaines-Mercanton, 1912), 96, 127
Queen Victoria, 77, 81, 86
Querejeta, Elias, and the New Spanish Cinema, 199
Quinn, Anthony, 286
Quiz Show (Redford, 1994), 37
Quo Vadis? (Guazzoni, 1911), the first blockbuster released in the US, 141

Rabelais, François, 231, 249, 264, 280, 284
Rabinovitz, Lauren, 100
Radford, Michael, 139, 164–166, 257. See also *The Merchant of Venice* (Radford, 2005)
Raikh, Zinaida, 11, 150, 253
Rainey, Paul J., 97. See also *Paul J. Rainey's African Hunt* (Rainey, 1911)
Ramsaye, Terry, 96, 266
Ran (Kurosawa, 1985), 26, 59–60, 67; use of *sumi-e*, 59, 60; use of Takemitsu's music, 67
Raphael (Rafaello Sanzio), 53
Rathbone, Basil, 20, 40
Ratnam, Mani, 72. See also *Naayakan* (Ratnam, 1987)
Rave Macbeth (Knoesel, 2003), 278–279
Ravel, Gaston, 138. See also *Il nodo* (Ravel, 1920)
Ray, Nicholas, 223
Ray, Robert, 256
Ray, Satyajit, 69, 73

Realism in the cinema: borrowings from Neorealism in Branagh, 214–215, 217; grotesque realism in Welles 203; Olivier, 182–183; period Realism in Castellani and Cukor, 21–22; Thalberg on realism, 21
Red Curtain aesthetics, 247
Red Scare, the, 25–26, 191
Redford, Robert, 37. See also *Quiz Show* (Redford, 1994)
Redon, Odilon, 238
Reed, Carol, 208. See also *The Third Man* (Reed, 1949)
Reese, John, 16
Reeves, Keanu, 213
Reilly, William, 26. See also *Men of Respect* (Reilly, 1991)
Reinhardt, Max, 20, 132, 151, 152, 159, 166, 167–168, 170, 230, 246, 274, 275, 276, 285
Reitherman, Wolfgang, 77. See also *101 Dalmations* (Reitherman, Geromini, Luske, 1961); *Robin Hood* (Reitherman, 1973)
Rembrandt van Rijn, 222
remediation, 44, 294; by Almereyda, 146; by Luhrmann, 242
Renaissance Man (Marshall, 1994), 33
Renoir, Jean, 206
Resnais, Alain, 33, 207, 256
The Return of the Prodigal Son (Rembrandt), 222
Rey, Fernando, 199, 205, 257
Reynolds, Joshua, 50, 135–136, 272
Ricciarelli, Katia, 254
Rice, John, 264
Richard III (Cibber, 1700): as model for cinematic adaptations, 102–108
Richard III (prod. Vitagraph, 1908), 271
Richard III (Calmettes, 1912), 254
Richard III (Warde-Keane, 1912/1913), 100–109; double text for use with live narration, 102–104; historical relevance of the movie poster, 102; importance to cultural historians, 101
Richard III (Olivier, 1955), 28, 44, 54–56; use of VistaVision in, 55, 56
Richard III (Ruiz, 1986), 212; parallels to Welles's situation, 200–205

Richard III (Loncraine, 1995), 102
Richardson, Ralph, 199–201, 205
Richardson, Samuel: author of *Pamela*, 288
Richie, Donald, 261
Richter, Hans, 153
Riegl, Aloïs, 119, 129, 133, 272
Rigg, Diana, 39–41, 285
Rigoletto (Verdi), 175
Rilke, Rainer Maria, 198
Ringwald, Molly, 42, 46, 220, 224–225
Rip Van Winkle (Irving), 85, 91
Rivera, Diego, 178
Robards, Jason, 42
Robbe-Grillet, Alain, 256
Robbins, Jerome, 25, 168, 240, 254. See also *West Side Story* (Wise and Robbins, 1961)
Robertson, Roland, 62
Robeson, Paul, 15, 177–178, 190–191
Robin Hood (Reitherman, 1973), 77
Robinson, Bill "Bojangles", 161
Robinson, Edward G., 179
Robinson Crusoe (Defoe), 239
Robison, Arthur, 162, 163, 164. See also *Schatten, eine nächtliche Halluzination* (Robison, 1922)
Rockefeller, Nelson, 179, 277; campaign against Communism, 178
Roddam, Frank, 245. See also *Aria*
Rodolfi, Eleuterio, 115, 118, 143, 145. See also *Amleto* (Rodolfi, 1917)
Roerich, Nikolai, 238
Rogers, John, 260
Roget, P.M., 82
RoGoPaG (omnibus film, 1963), 226
Rohdie, Sam, 288
Rohmer, Eric, 32–33, 257. See also *Perceval* (Rohmer, 1978)
Rohmer, Sax, 33
The Rokeby Venus (Velázquez), 227–231
Romain Rolland, 159
Romano, Giulio, 51, 257
Rome, Open City (Rossellini, 1945), 174
Romeo + Juliet (Luhrmann, 1996), 240–249, 252
Romeo and Juliet (Prokofiev), 11, 188
Romeo and Juliet (Vitagraph 1908), 98, 130–131, 271

Romeo and Juliet (Lo Savio, 1911): see *Giulietta e Romeo*
Romeo and Juliet (prod. Thanhouser 1911), 110–111
Romeo and Juliet (Cukor, 1936), 20–22, 257
Romeo and Juliet (Castellani, 1954), 53–54; influence of Botticelli's paintings in, 54; Neorealism in, 53
Romeo and Juliet (Zeffirelli, 1968), 54, 280
Roméo et Juliette (Berlioz), 88
Romeo und Julia am Schnee (Lubitsch, 1920), 158–159
Romeo y Julieta (Delgado), 1943), 257
Romney, George, 50, 136
Rooney, Mickey, 168
Roosevelt, Franklin Delano, 177–179
Rosenberg, Ethel, 281
Rosenkrantz and Gildenstern Are Dead (Stoppard, 1990), 37–38, 219; as di(s) quotation, 37
Rossellini, Roberto, 174, 214, 223, 277. See also *Paisà* (Rossellini, 1946); *Rome, Open City* (Rossellini, 1945)
Rossini, Giaocchino, 8
Rosso Fiorentino (Giovanni Battista Rosso), 288
Rostand, Edmond, 126, 270
Rota, Nino, 8–9, 286
Rothafel, Samuel Lionel (Roxy), 267
Rothwell, Kenneth, 102, 104, 108, 139, 159, 187, 252, 254, 267, 268, 277, 280; on Jonathan Miller, 22; on Zeffirelli and opera, 8
Roud, Richard, 182
Rowlands, Gena, 45
Rowley, Frederick, 264
Royal Academy of Dramatic Arts, 81
The Royal Hunt of the Sun (Lerner, 1969), 256
Rubens, Peter Paul, 136, 223, 235
Rubio, Miguel, 283
Ruffo, Titta, 8
Rugg, Linda, 261
Ruggeri, Ruggero, 143, 145
Ruiz, Raoul, 106, 174, 180, 200–205, 217, 225, 267, 284; and the poetics of the unfinished, 95. See also *Richard III* (Ruiz, 1986)

Rushdie, Salman, 137: allusions to *Hamlet* 73; allusions to *Othello*, 72–73
Ruskin, John, 119
Russian Hamlet (Eifman), 10
Rye, Stellan, 167

Le Sacre du Printemps (Stravinsky, Nijinsky): Modernism and Pre-WWI hysteria, 238
Sadoul, Georges, 122
Sahu, Kishore, 68–69
Said, Edward, 63
Saint George and the Princess of Trebizond (Pisanello), 53
Salieri, Antonio, 282
Salvini, Tommaso, 8
Sammons, Eddie, 251
Sappho (Buchowetzki, 1921), 159
Sarandon, Susan, 45
Sardou, Victorien, 96, 120, 126, 251
Sarrasine (Balzac), 112
Sarris, Andrew, 46, 223, 258
Satanic Verses (Rushdie), 73
Sato, Tadao, 58–59
Saturday Review, 79
Saturn Devouring His Children (Goya), 222
Satyricon (Fellini, 1969), 285
Saunders, J.G., 261
Saura, Carlos, 214, 255, 283
Saussure, Fernand de, 226
Savant, Ren, 255. See also *In the Flesh* (Canterbury, 2000), 255; *Shakespeare Revealed* (Savant, 2000), 255
Sax, Geoffrey, 160. See also *Othello* (Sax, 2001), 160
Sax-Meiningen Group, 82
Saxo Grammaticus, 117, 118, 154–155, 156, 269, 270
Scalera, Montatori, 190–191
Schatten, eine nächtliche Halluzination (Robison, 1922), 162–163
Schindler's List (Spielberg, 1993), 42
Schlegel, A.W., 8
Schnitzler, Arthur, 271
Schoch, Richard, 77, 92
Schopenhauer, Arthur, 121
Schreck, Max, 166
Schub, Esfir, 222
Schubert Theater, 15, 191

Schulz, David, 81
Schumann, Robert, 171
Schünzel, Reinhold, 161. See also *Alles für Geld* (Schünzel, 1923)
Schwarzenegger, Arnold, 42, 121, 128, 147
Schwob, Marcel, 117–118, 124–125, 127, 270
Scofield, Paul, 12, 112, 157, 217
Scorsese, Martin, 26, 72, 259. See also *Goodfellas* (Scorsese, 1990)
Scotland, PA (Morrissette), 34–35
Scott, Campbell, 146. See also *Hamlet* (Scott, 2000)
Scott, Clement, 144
The Scream (Munch), 160
Scribe, Eugene, 165
The Secret Sex Lives of Romeo and Juliet (Buckalew, 1969), 255
Segre, Cesare, 212
Seidl, Monika, 154
Sellars, Coleman, 82
Sellars, Peter, 224
Sellman, Dr., 161, 275
Sembène, Ousmane, 65. See also *Ceddo* (Sembène, 1976)
semiotics, 43–44; Eco as Pasolini's disputant, 226, 287; Godard's use of cinema's tracks for pluri-signification, 219–220
Serper, Zvika, 259
Seth, Vikram, 193
The Seventh Seal (Bergman, 1857), 65
Seward, W.H., 222
Shah, Naseeruddin, 71–72
Shakespeare, William: and New Historicism, 4; as national property, 5–7; biography, 2, 5–7, 251; characterization on television, 29; identity, 2, 251; parody of the *paragone*, 235; relationship with his daughters, 217–218; religious persuasion, 2, 5–6, 276; satirical reference as Shake-scene, 2; satirical reference as Shake-bag, 251; sources, 8, 77, 117–118, 122, 164–166, 191, 243, 262; translations of 11–14; *All Is True*, 87, *Hamlet*, 47, 66, 71; *1 Henry IV*, 198, 204, 213; *2 Henry IV*, 198; *Henry V*, 89; *Julius Caesar*, 177;

Shakespeare, William—continued
  King John, 71, 76–78; King Lear, 191;
  Macbeth, 71; Measure for Measure, 9;
  The Merchant of Venice, 66; The Merry
  Wives of Windsor, 198; A Midsummer
  Night's Dream, 230; Much Ado About
  Nothing, 230; Othello, 9, 191; Richard
  II, 89, 181, 198; Richard III, 108;
  The Taming of the Shrew, 230; The
  Tempest, 4; Timon of Athens, 235;
  Twelfth Night, 231; Two Gentlemen of
  Verona, 4
Shakespeare in Love (Madden, 1998),
  4–5, 28
Shakespeare Revealed (Savant, 2000), 255
Shakespeare Wallah (Ivory, 1965), 69–70
The Shakespeare Web, 45
Shakespeare Writing Julius Ceasar (Méliès,
  1907), the first Shakespeare Biopic,
  2–4
Shakespeareana, 69
Shapiro, James, 117, 252, 278
Shatner, William, 256
Shaw, George Bernard, 78–79, 83, 96,
  111, 138; on silent film and theatre,
  262
Shchukin, Boris, 252
Shearer, Norma, 20, 69, 223
Shepherd, Sam, 147
Sheriff, Paul, 56–58
shimpa, 66
Shin'chi, Miyajima, 259
Shklovsky, Viktor, 263
Shonagon, Sei, 232
Shostakovich, Dmitri, 10–12, 147, 212;
  "Muddle instead of Music," 11–12
The Show of Shows (prod. Warner Bros.,
  1930), 39
Shoyo, Tsubouchi, 66
Shylock, ou le Marchand de Venise: see le
  Marchand de Venise
Sibirska Ledi Magbet (Wajda, 1961), 10
Siddons, Sarah, 135–136, 269; star power
  of, 137
Sidney, George, 19, 25, 230. See also Kiss
  Me Kate (Sidney)
Sidney, Philip, 41, 51
Sierra, G. Martínez: see Martínez
Signorelli, Luca, 52
Silverman, Kaja, 287
Silverstone, Alicia, 116
Silviria, Dale, 54, 56
Simmel, Georg, 133
Simon, John, 46
Singer, Ben, 99, 267
Sinyard, Neil, 257
Situationism: and Godard, 223, 246, 287
Sklar, Robert, 44
Skobtseva, Irina, 9
Smedley, G.W., 85
Smiles of a Summer Night (Bergman,
  1955), 48
Smith, George Albert, 91
Smithson, Harriet, 8
Snokhatch (Ivanon-Gai, 1912), 160
Society for Cinema and (Media) Studies
  (SCMS), 31
Son of Frankenstein (Lee, 1939), 40
sonnets (Shakespeare): Number 56, 28;
  Number 74, 13, Number 141, 28;
  Wilde's hypothesis, 263; narration
  in The Angelic Conversations (Jarman,
  1985), 290
Sontag, Susan, 265
Sorvino, Paul, 241
Soseki, Natsume, 261
sound synchronization: as redefining
  Shakespeare films 34, 38–39; in
  De Forest's The Merchant of Venice,
  38–39; in Theater of Blood, 39; in
  Warner Bros. Vitaphone review The
  Show of Shows, 39
Sous les Toits de Paris (Clair, 1929), 161
Soyinka, Wole, 63, 223
Spacey, Kevin, 36–37
Speech Act Theory: see Austin
Spewack, Bella, 19–20
Spewack, Sam, 19–20
The Spider's Strategem (Bertolucci, 1970),
  174–175
Spielberg, Steven, 42. See also Schindler's
  List (Spielberg, 1993)
Spielman, Yvonne, 234
Spiers, Phené, 83
the spiral motif, 195–196
Spivak, Gayatri, 289
Spreading Evil (Keane, 1918), 103
Stack, Oswald, 287, 288
Stagecoach (Ford, 1939), 25
Staiger, Janet, 266, 267

Stalin, Joseph, 253; as music critic, 10–11; subject of allegory, 13–14, 15, 22, 150, 187, 198
Stam, Robert, 206–207, 225, 253, 256, 273, 284; on adaptation, 31, 256, 257
Stanislavsky, Konstantin, 8, 15, 23, 252, 255
Star Trek IV (Meyer, 1991), 256. translation of Hamlet's lines from the original Klingon, 256
Star Trek series, 225–226
stardom, 132–134; art as vehicle for, 135–137
Starewicz, Wladislaw, 214
Starks, Lisa, 151, 271, 274
Starlason, Snorri, 270
La Strada (Fellini, 1954), 286
Stravinsky, Igor, 238, 291
Sterling Camera Company, 267
Sternberg, Josef von, 162. See also *The Blue Angel* (von Sternberg, 1930); *The Last Command* (von Sternberg, 1928)
Sterritt, David, 286
Stevens, Warren, 255
Stevens, George, 161. See also *Swingtime* (Stevens, 1936)
Stewart, Patrick, 29, 52, 217
Stiles, Julia, 28
Stockholder, Kay, 291
stoffgeschichte, 163
Stofter, Magnus, 156. See also *Das Liebes-ABC* (Stofter, 1916)
Stoppard, Tom, 4, 37–38, 157, 219. See also *Rosenkrantz and Gildenstern Are Dead* (Stoppard, 1990)
The Story of the Kelly Gang (Tait, 1906), 266
Strachey, James, 27, 129
Strange Illusion (Ulmer, 1945), 170–171
The Stranger (Welles, 1945), 179
Strasberg, Lee, 23
Straub, Jean-Marie, 64
Strauss, Richard, 132
A Streetcar Named Desire Williams), 23, 30
Strictly Ballroom (Luhrmann, 1992), 245, 247
Strindberg, August, 274
Stroheim, Erich von, 33, 47. See also *Greed* (Stroheim, 1923)
Strunk, William, 20–21

Stubbs, Imogen, 43
The Student Prince (Lubitsch, 1927), 170
Der Student von Prague (Wegener, 1925), 167
studios: Ambrosio, 138, 140–141, 159; Biograph, 3, 84–85, 130, 140, 149; Cines, 138, 141, 142; Decla-Bioscop, 151; Deutsche-Bioscop, 150; Film d'Arte Italiana (Pathé subsidiary), 138–139; Great Northern Company, 148; Hammer Films, 35, 40, 184, 190; Imp. 132; Itala 138; MGM 20–21; Milano Films, 116, 141, 266; Nordisk, 148; Pathé, 141; Paramount, 96; Projektions Union, 150; Republic, 179; RKO, 178; Star Films 2–4; Thanhouser, 109–113, 183, 221; Triangle, 87–88; Ufa, 148, 150, 166–167, 170; United Artists, 17–18, 159; Universal, 22, 189; Urban-Eclipse, 141–142; Vitagraph, 17, 97–98, 110, 111, 130, 140, 183, 271; Warner Bros., 20, 38, 48, 159, 167–169
Sturken, Marita, 49
Sumarokov, Alexander, 9
sumi-e painting in *Ran* (Kurosawa, 1985), 59–60
Sundown Beach (Kazan), 255
Sunrise (W.F. Murnau, 1927), 167, 170
Sutherland, Joan, 248
Swanson, Vern Grosvener, 263
Swingtime (George Stevens, 1936), 161
Symbolism: in painting, 127; in the theatre, 81
Symphonie Fantastique (Berlioz), 8
synthetic aura, 135, 137. *See also* Benjamin
Szabo, Istvan, 276. See also *Mephisto* (Szabo, 1985)

Tabu, 70
Tait, Charles, 266. See also *The Story of the Kelly Gang* (Tait, 1906)
Takemitsu, Toru, 67, 261
Tales of Hoffmann (Hoffmann), 189
Tales of Hoffmann (Offenbach), 189
The Taming of the Shrew (Desfontaines, 1911): *see La Mergere approvisée*
The Taming of the Shrew (Lo Savio, 1910), 138–139

The Taming of the Shrew (Desfontaines, 1911), 97
The Taming of the Shrew (prod. British and Colonial, 1915), with synchronized sound (?), 38
The Taming of the Shrew (Taylor, 1929), 18
The Taming of the Shrew (Zeffirelli, 1966), 20, 24
Tanaka, Ichimatsu, 260
Taranow, Gerda, 121, 123–124, 125, 269, 270
Tarantino, Quentin, 220
Tarkovsky, Andrei, 273
Tartuffe (Molière), 262
Taylor, Elizabeth, 20, 24
Taylor, Gary, 5, 62, 260
Taylor, Neil, 43, 166, 246, 276
Taylor, Richard, 264
Taylor, Samuel, 21. See also *The Taming of the Shrew* (Taylor, 1929)
Taymor, Julie, 285–286
Tchaikovsky, Pyotr Ilyich, 8, 64
Technicolor process, 25, 54, 73; in *Forbidden Planet*, 26; in *Kiss Me Kate*, 25
technological determinism, 75
technological history of film, 38; development of wide-screen technology, 54–55; dialogue, recording, 39; film restoration, 44–45
television, 19, 28–29; as both technology and cultural form for Williams, 262; as liberation for Bergman as *auteur* filmmaker, 43; as instant news event in Luhrmann, 146; as political analysis in Almereyda, 145; as seductive opiate in Mazursky, 45; symbiosis with contemporary cinema, 44
Tellegen, Lou, 96, 127, 270
Telluride Film Festival, 29–30
Temne [people of Sierra Leone], 62–63
The Tempest (Bender, 1998), 28
The Tempest (Jarman, 1979), 106, 188, 235; as Prospero's nightmare, 188
Tempest (Mazursky, 1982), 45–47; Manhattan as Milan, 45; Broadway versus television, 45–46

Ten Days' Wonder (Chabrol, 1971), 208–209
Tenshin, Okakura, 66
La terra vista dalla luna (Pasolini, 1967), 227
Tess of the Durbevilles (Hardy), 5
Thalberg, Irving, 20, 21, 254
Thanhouser, Edwin, 109
Thanhouser Shakespeare cycle, 109–113. See also *All's Well That Ends Wells* (1914, unrediscovered); *Cymbeline* (1913); *King Lear* (1916); *The Merchant of Venice* (1912, unrediscovered); *Romeo and Juliet* (1911); *The Tempest* (1911, unrediscovered); *Winter Tale* (1910)
Theater of Blood (Hickox, 1973), 39–42, 159; as exemplar of dis(s)quotation, 41–42
Théâtre Sarah Bernhardt, 121
Théodora (Sardou), 126
Thief of Bagdad (Walsh, 1924), 18, 21
Thomas, Ambroise, 8
theoretical imprecision, 211–212
Theron, Charlize, 137, 142
The Thief of Bagdad, (Walsh, 1924), 18
Third Cinema, 65, 174
The Third Man (Reed, 1949), 208
Thompson, John, 260
Thompson, Kristin, 17, 21, 158–159, 166–167, 232, 254, 260, 274, 275
A Thousand Acres (Moorhouse, 1997), 33
Throne of Blood: see *Kumonosu-jô*
Tibbets, John, 21, 254
Tiffany, Louis Comfort, 119
Tillyard, E.M.W., 278
Tintoretto (Jacopo Robusti), 235
Titian (Tiziano Vecelli), 165, 223, 235; and Cervantes, 51
Titus (Taymor, 2000), 285–286; allusion to Fellini's *La Strada*, 285–286; as example of contemporary inter-national filmmaking, 285
Tiv (people of West Africa), 63
To Be or Not to Be (Lubitsch, 1942), 169–170
The Toll of the Sea (Franklin, 1922), 18
Tolstoy, 13, 253
Tomlinson, John, 62, 260
Tosca (Sardou), 126
Touch of Evil (Welles, 1957), 106

Tourneur, Jacques, 20. See also *Master Will Shakespeare* (Tourneur, 1936)
The Tower of London (Corman, 1962), 40
The Tower of London (Lee, 1939), 40
tracks of cinema: use in Morrisette, 34; use in Ruiz, 267–268
Tracy, Spencer, 272
Traffic in Souls (Tucker, 1913), 148
Una tragedia alla corte di Sicilia (Negroni, 1913), 51
translation: and adaptation, 211; Chapman, 212; Florio, 239; German 8; Japanese, 66–67; Pasternak, 11–13; Russian, 10–15
transnational filmmaking: American films made for European audiences, 130–131; Danish filmmakers in Germany 150; Ufa personnel in Hollywood, 166–171; Levring, 64–66; Welles 173–174, 176–177, 196–197; Ruiz 200–202; Taymor, 285–286
Trauner, Alexander, 197
La Traviata (Verdi), 9
La Traviata (Zeffirelli, 1982), 9
Tree, Maud, 80, 81, 83, 86
Tree, Sir Herbert Beerbohm, 78, 83, 119, 123, 130, 138, 176, 262–265; contract with Triangle Film Corporation, 87–88; portrayal of King John, 76–81, 91; portrayal of Shylock, 80
Tretyakov, Sergei, 86
The Trial (Kafka), 226
The Trial (Welles, 1962), 183, 206
Tristan und Isolde (Wagner), 243
Triumph (DeMille, 1924), 33
Tromeo and Juliet (Kaufman, 1997), 255
Truffaut, François, 204, 214, 284, 285; advocacy of *auteur* filmmaking, 21; 173; and Welles, 173, 183; as teased by Welles, 188, 206–207; attack on the Tradition of Quality, 21, 256; theories of adaptation, 31, 33, 214, 223. See also *Jules et Jim* (Truffaut, 1961)
Truman, Harry S., 177–178
Tucker, George Loane, 148. See also *Traffic in Souls* (Tucker, 1914)
Turgenev, Ivan, 10, 252

Turner, Florence, 271
Tweedie, James, 236, 289, 290
Twelfth Night (Kent, prod. Vitagraph, 1910), 140, 271
Twelfth Night (Fried, 1955), 252
Twelfth Night (Nunn, 1996), 42–43
Tynan, Kenneth, 34, 278
typography, as unique to each poster in Mucha's Bernhardt cycle, 125

Ubu Roi (Jarry), 63, 180
Uccellacci e uccellini (Pasolini, 1966), 226
Uchatius, Baron, 82
Ufa-Palast Theater, 159
Ugetsu Monogatari (Mizoguchi, 1953), 223
Ulmer, Edgar G., 170–171. See also *Strange Illusion* (Ulmer, 1945); *The Naked Venus* (Ulmer, 1958)
Ulmer, Renate, 120
Gli ultimi giorni di Pompeii (Caserini, 1913), 141
Ulysses (Joyce), 155
Umberto D (De Sica, 1952), 183
Uncle Tom's Cabin (prod. Vitagraph, 1910), 96
Under Western Skies (Yarborough, 1945), 25
Ungerleider, Mor, 150
Urban, Charles, 86, 140
Uricchio, William, 88, 98, 266
Usai, Paolo Cherchi, 251
Ustinov, Peter, 76–77
Utah Shakespeare Festival, 179

Valentino, Rudolph, 167, 135
Valli, Alida, 208
Vampydanserinden (Blom, 1912), 148
van der Rohe, Miles, 61
Van Dyke, Dick, 48
van Eyck, Jan, 193–195
van Gogh, Vincent, 59, 59
Vanina (von Gerlach, 1922), 152
Van Sant, Gus, 213–214, 217, 220. See also *My Own Private Idaho* (Van Sant, 1991)
Vanour, Georges, 135, 270
Varda, Agnès, 33
Vardac, Nicholas, 82
Vargas, Getulio, 178
Variety (Dupont, 1925), 162

Veblen, Thorstein, 81
Vela, Richard, 21, 42, 254, 257
Velázquez y Silva, Diego, 226–231; as interpreted by Foucault, 227, 230; as interpreted by Pasolini, 227–231
Venice Film Festival, 181; award of the Golden Lion to Castellani, 54; award of the Golden Lion to Olivier, 181; award of the Grand Prize to Stoppard, 219; repeated victories by Mizoguchi, 223
Veneziano, Domenico, 259
Verdi, Giuseppe, 38, 53, 72, 122–123, 149, 249, 288; as Shakespeare substitute in *The Spider's Strategem*, 175; film adaptation by Messter, 38; influence on Buchowetzki, 160–161; influence on Welles, 175–176, 181, 183, 190, 282; influence on Zeffirelli, 175; influence on Yutkevich, 12, 14–15; Pasolini's rejoinder, 288; Shakespearean opera and Italian nationalism, 8–9, 176; use of music by Hoffman, 9; use of music by Zeffirelli, 9
Verma, Rajiva, 68
Vermeer, Jan, 219–220
Verne, Jules, 179
Vertigo (Hitchcock, 1958), 147
Vertov, Dziga, 214, 222, 263–264, 286; rejection of acted cinema, 86, 132
Vesalius, 233, 237
Viano, Maurizio, 288
Vienna Secession, 119
A Village King Lear (Feuillade, 1911), 142
Vincent Price effect, 39–43, 159, 215; Alicia Silverstone in Branagh's *Love's Labours Lost*, 116; Ben Kingsley (unintentionally) in Nunn's *Twelfth Night*, 42–43; Boris Karloff in Lee's *The Tower of London*, 40; Diana Rigg in *Theater of Blood*, 40; Irène Jacob in Parker's *Othello*, 215; Molly Ringwald in Godard's *King Lear*, 220; Pacino in *Looking for Richard*, 36–37, 42; Steve Martin in *L.A. Story*, 52
Vineberg, Steve, 255
Vining, Edward Payson, 118, 150, 154, 155–156, 269, 274, 284

Vinterberg, Thomas, 64
The Virgin Spring (Bergman, 1960), 47
Viridiana (Buñuel, 1952), 199
Virilio, Paul, 251
Visconti, Luchino, 9, 223, 224, 277. See also *Ossessione* (Visconti, 1943)
VistaVision, 54, 55
Vitagraph Shakespeare cycle, including those that are integral, fragmentary, and unrediscovered, 271. See also *Antony and Cleopatra* (1908), *As You Like It* (1912), *Cardinal Wolsey* (1912), *Comedy of Errors* (1908), *Julius Caesar* (1908), *King Lear* (1909), *Macbeth* (1908), *Merchant of Venice* (1908), *A Midsummer Night's Dream* (1909), *Othello* (1908), *Romeo and Juliet* (1908), *Richard III* (1908), *Twelfth Night* (1910)
Vittachi, Tarzie, 6–7, 48, 252
Vivaldi, Antonio, 257; and Rohmer, 257
Vivre Sa Vie (Godard, 1962), 224, 287
Volkov, Solomon, 11
Von Trier, Lars, 64
Voodoo Macbeth, 177–179, 186, 277
La Voyante (Abrams, 1923), 142

Wagner, Richard, 188, 245, 249
Wajda, Andrzej, 10. See also *Sibirska Ledi Magbet* (Wajda, 1961)
Walcott, Derek, 238, 240
A Walk through H: The Reincarnation of an Ornithologist (Greenaway, 1978), 232
Walken, Christopher, 34
Wall-Romana, Christophe, 256
Walsh, Raoul, *The Thief of Bagdad* (Walsh, 1924), 18, 21, 186
Walsingham Francis, 6, 77–78, 147
War of the Worlds (Welles, 1938), 177
Warburg, Aby, 51–52, 259; Botticelli's adaptation of Poliziano, 52; immanent motion in early Renaissance painting, 125
Warde, Ernest, 111–112. See also *King Lear* (Ernest Warde, 1916)
Warde, Frederick, 101–105, 109, 112
Warner, David, 256
Warning Shadows (Robison, 1922): see *Schatten, eine nächtliche Halluzination*
The Way of All Flesh (1927), 162

Wajda, Andrzej, 10. See also *Sibirska Ledi Magbet* (Wajda, 1961); as satire on Communism, 10
Waters, John, 255
Weber, Max, 260
Wedekind, Frank, 61
Wegener, Paul, 152, 167
Weir, Peter, 33
Welch, Elizabeth, 188
Welles, Orson, 9, 32, 37, 106, 163, 173–176, 181, 212–216, 223, 226, 280–285; and autobiographical identification with Falstaff, 174, 199, 205, 207; and Chabrol, 207–209; and Godard, 219; and Modernist theater, 1776–177; and Pasolini, 226; and Truffaut, 188, 206–207; Eisenstein's influence on, 186–190; political involvement, 178–180; stylistic originality of, 183–184; theatrical adaptations, 177–179, 186; treatment of Shakespeare, comparison to Olivier's, 181–182; unfinished *King Lear*, 218; unfinished *Merchant of Venice*, 174. See also *Chimes at Midnight* (Welles, 1965); *Citizen Kane* (Welles, 1941); *F for Fake* (Welles, 1974); *Filming Othello* (Welles, 1978); *The Immortal Story* (Welles, 1968); *It's All True* (Welles, 1941); *Journey into Fear* (Welles, 1943); *The Lady from Shanghai* (Welles, 1946); *Macbeth* (Welles, 1948); *The Magnificent Ambersons* (Welles, 1942); *Mr. Arkadin* (Welles, 1955); *Othello* (Welles, 1952); *The Stranger* (Welles, 1945); *Touch of Evil* (Welles, 1957); *The Trial* (Welles, 1962)
Wells, Stanley, 5, 259, 263, 265, 277
Welsh, Alexander, 271
Welsh, James, 21, 253–254
West Side (Savant, 2000), 255
West Side Story (Wise and Robbins, 1961), 20, 30, 168, 254
Western Electric, 38
Wharton, Edith: appreciation of frescoes, 245
Whistler, James McNeill, 269
White, John, 235
White, Liz, 281

The Widow Jones (prod. Edison, 1896), 264
Wiene, Robert, 151. See also *The Cabinet of Dr. Caligari*. See also *The Cabinet of Dr. Caligari* (Wiene, 1920)
Wieth, Clara, 148
Wilcox, Fred, 26–28. See also *Forbidden Planet* (Wilcox, 1956)
Wilcox, Herbert, 149. See also *Carnival* (Wilcox, 1931)
Wild Strawberries (Bergman, 1957), 48
Wilde, Oscar, 80, 127, 263
Wilkins, George: as co-author of *Pericles*, 288
Williams, Gary, 89, 264, 276
Williams, Raymond, 75–76, 262
Williams, Tennessee, 23
Williamson, James, 91
Willson, Robert, 179, 252, 278
Wilson, Richard, 165, 257, 258; Shakespeare as religious moderate, 6, 276; Shakespeare as secret Catholic, 43, 276
Wilson, Robert F., 252
Winter Tale (prod. Thanhouser, 1910), 110–111
Winter, William, 18, 80–81, 155, 254, 268
Wise, Robert, 168
Wlaschin, Ken, 267
Wollen, Peter, 147, 287
Wong, Anna Mae, 18–19
Woo, John, 242
Wood, Ed, 265
Woods, Alan, 104
Woolf, Virginia, 49, 222
Wörner, Hilde, 159

Yagnik, Alka, 248
Yamada, Isuzu, 59
Yarborough, Jean, 25. See also *Under Western Skies* (Yarborough, 1945)
Yarvet, Yuri, 13, 112, 253
Yasuhiro, Sato, 259
Yates, Fraces, 280
Ye yan (Feng, 2006), 255
A Year in the Life of Shakespeare: 1599 (Shapiro), 252
yoga, 67

yogaku, 67
Yordan, Phillip, as scriptwriter for genre experiments in Shakespeare films, 26
Yoshimoto, Mitsuhiro, 67, 259, 274
Young, Robert, 51, 270
Yutkevich, Sergei, 9, 27, 253, 254; cinematography in *Othello*, 14. See also *Othello* (Yutkevich, 1955); competitive allusion to Welles, 9, 14–15

Zabus, Chantal, 26, 27
Zambrano, Ana Laura, 59
Zecca, Ferdinand, 3, 251. See also *Cleopatra* (Zecca, 1910)
Zeffirelli, Franco, 8–9, 13, 15, 16, 20, 24, 29, 50, 54, 106, 116, 118, 175, 225, 241, 243, 244, 247, 255; popular success with adaptations, 24; use of space in soliloquy, 157. See also *Hamlett* (Zeffirelli, 1990); *Othello* (Zeffirelli, 1961); *Romeo and Juliet* (Zeffirelli, 1968); *The Taming of the Shrew* (Zeffirelli, 1966); *La Traviata* (Zeffirelli, 1982)
Zhang Yimou, 255
Zinnemann, Fred, 214. See also *A Man For All Seasons* (Zinnemann, 1966)
Zola, Émile, 89–90, 93, 119, 128, 192, 224, 265; as influence on the association of the Dreyfus case and Tree's *King John*, 93
Zukor, Adolph, 96, 100, 141, 265

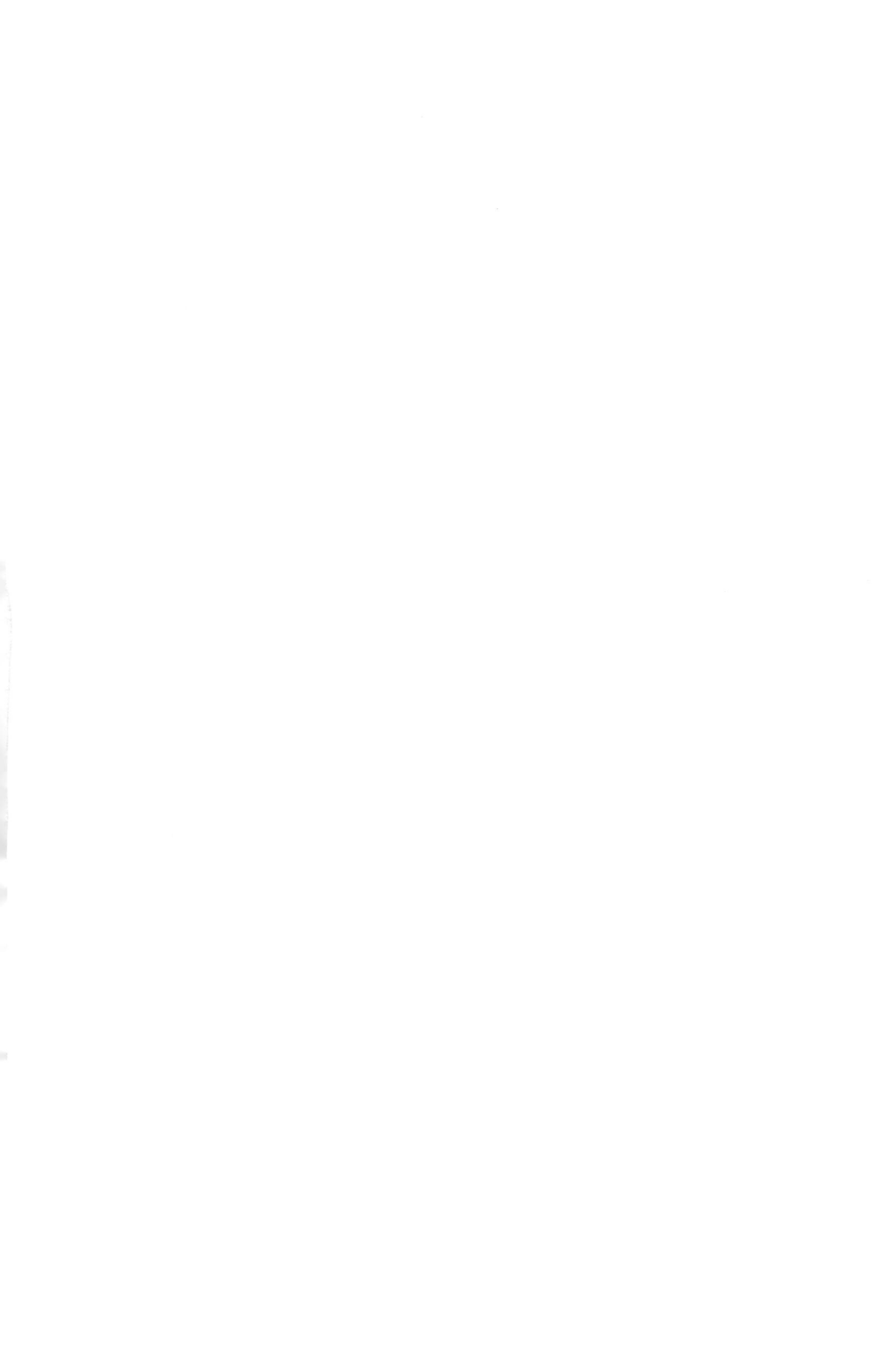